MW00654657

YOUR BIRTHDAY

Unlock the Power of the Day You Were Born with Astrology, Tarot, and More

YOUR BIRTHDAY

Unlock the Power of the Day You Were Born with Astrology, Tarot, and More

JESSICA ADAMS
with RACHEL WELLS

RUNNING PRESS
PHILADELPHIA

Running Press
Hachette Book Group
1290 Avenue of the Americas, New York, NY 10104
www.runningpress.com
@Running_Press

First Edition: October 2024

Published by Running Press, an imprint of Hachette Book Group, Inc. The Running Press name and logo are trademarks of Hachette Book Group, Inc.

Running Press books may be purchased in bulk for business, educational, or promotional use. For more information, please contact your local bookseller or the Hachette Book Group Special Markets Department at Special.Markets@hbgusa.com.

The publisher is not responsible for websites (or their content) that are not owned by the publisher.

Print book cover and interior design by Susan Van Horn

Names: Adams, Jessica, 1964- author. | Wells, Rachel (Children's author), author.
Title: Your birthday : unlock the power of the day you were born with astrology, tarot, and more / Jessica Adams and Rachel Wells.
Description: First edition. | Philadelphia : Running Press, [2024]
Identifiers: LCCN 2024016329 | ISBN 9780762488087 (paperback) | ISBN 9780762488094 (ebook)
Subjects: LCSH: Birthdays--Miscellanea. | Horoscopes. | Astrology. | Tarot.
Classification: LCC BF1729.B45 A33 2024 | DDC 133.5/4042--dc23/eng/20240515
LC record available at https://lccn.loc.gov/2024016329

ISBNs: 978-0-7624-8808-7 (paperback), 978-0-7624-8809-4 (ebook)

Printed in the United States of America

LSC-C

Printing 1, 2024

CONTENTS

INTRODUCTION

Welcome to *Your Birthday* by Jessica Adams with Rachel Wells.

You may know Jessica from her number one worldwide Apple spirituality podcast *The Astrology Show* or Rachel from her *Sunday Times* bestsellers in the Alfie The Doorstep Cat series. Jessica has been a top international astrologer for thirty years after beginning her career at *Elle*. Her horoscopes have appeared in *Vogue Japan* and *Harper's Bazaar UK*, and she's even forecast fashion trends at Bloomingdale's. Jessica's novels include *Tom, Dick and Debbie Harry*, and her travel books include *The Holiday Goddess Guide to New York*.

Rachel has written eight Alfie books which have been translated into several languages. Alfie The Doorstep Cat even has its own merchandising line in Japan. The sixth book, *A Friend Called Alfie*, also features Jessica Adams's astrology for the first time.

Rachel lives in Devon in the UK with her cat Lady Alfie, and Jessica lives in Australia with her dog Tess. They collaborate creatively over Zoom. Jessica and Rachel have been friends since they first worked on the Girls' Night In and Kids' Night In series of anthologies, which have raised three million dollars for the children's charity War Child. Set in London, the series of several best-selling short-story collections featured many famous names including Stella McCartney and J. K. Rowling.

Rachel's keen interest in astrology and Tarot and Jessica's long career as a psychic horoscope writer have led to them working on other projects together since that time, including *The Aries Billionaire*, the debut audiobook in the Leo Moon Astrologer Detective series for Audible. Released at the end of 2023, it's the first in a twelve-part series featuring each of the Western astrology zodiac signs in episodes of cozy astrological crime. Oliver Chris of *The Crown* is the narrator.

The book you are reading now, *Your Birthday*, is Jessica and Rachel's latest look at astrology and Tarot, offering a deeper insight into the meaning of your birth date, along with those of your partners, relatives, and friends. It combines Jessica's knowledge of horoscope history, astrological house systems, and Egyptian, Indian, and Asian signs with Rachel's fresh take on the Tarot. History graduate Rachel has also uncovered the folklore behind your birth month as well as the traditional associations with your sign.

You can use this book in many different ways—either going through section by section or jumping to what calls to you. There is no right or wrong way.

Discover your birthstone, birth flower, emblematic animal, and the Native American Moon you were born under. Find out more about your date's personality at a glance or decode your last relationship in depth. *Your Birthday* is an uncannily accurate guide to the 366 birth dates of the year and all that they reveal—not only about character but also destiny.

You can also use the ancient Egyptian method of astrological decans, which split your sign into three sections, to find out more about the cycles of time deciding your future in the years ahead. If you have ever wondered why you are different to others born under your zodiac sign, your Egyptian decan may just be the answer.

In this book, you can give yourself a three-way reading using your Egyptian, Asian, and Indian sign, together with the detailed explanation of your Western birthday chart. *Your Birthday* is a global guide, because the ancient practice of astrology is also global.

You can also utilize the detailed descriptions of the Waite-Smith Tarot deck, created by Pamela Colman Smith with Arthur E. Waite, in the final section to give yourself a birthday Tarot reading. That way you can check in with yourself on where you are for the year ahead.

The book and its accompanying website—jessicaadams.com/yourbirthday—have been designed as a gift that goes on giving. You will be able to delve deeper into your various astrological signs, send personalized e-cards, and even have your Tarot read for you using the online cards. Special spreads exclusive to the book will make the website an interactive experience, too. *Your Birthday* is not just for your bookshelf; you can take it onto your phone or computer.

Jessica and Rachel would like to thank Eileen Cope, Shannon Fabricant, Alicia Fulton, Amber Morris, Justin Tabari, Belinda Tierney, and James Williams for helping to bring *Your Birthday* to life. It's a book you can give to the people you care about—or just to yourself. And if it's your birthday as you read this? Happy Birthday. Many Happy Solar Returns!

YOUR BIRTHDAY MONTH BY MONTH

History agrees that birthdays were first celebrated in Egyptian times. In fact, the earliest reference to birthdays was dated approximately 3000 BCE and referred to a pharaoh being crowned. So a birthday was in fact to celebrate his "birth" as a king—his coronation. This could still be considered his birthday in the way we think of it because it was believed that when Egyptian pharaohs were crowned they transformed into gods.

The ancient Greeks took up the Egyptian tradition to mark the birthday of their gods as well. However, they also believed that this event could encourage evil spirits, so they adopted traditions that would ward off the evil and keep them safe. This may explain your birthday cake. The Greeks made cakes to honor the moon goddess Artemis, who was known for her association with childbirth. They lit candles and made loud noises to scare the evil spirits away.

The Romans were then the first to celebrate the birthdays of the so-called "common" person, marking the day someone was born. Roman citizens would celebrate the birthdays of their friends and family, and the government created public holidays in honor of more famous citizens. A Roman turning fifty years old would receive a special cake made with flour, olive oil, grated cheese, and honey. At first, only men were treated to this birthday celebration. High-ranking females were only celebrated from the twelfth century onward. And it wasn't until the fourth century CE that Christians began celebrating the birth of Jesus Christ—which is, of course, Christmas. For the Christians, this was the first and greatest birthday celebration.

Moving forward, in medieval times only nobility celebrated birthdays. Commoners of the period often celebrated saint days—the feast day of the saint they were named after—rather than the day on which they were born.

Your Birthday in History

The day and month you were born decides your birth horoscope, but so much more. There is also historic meaning attached to your birthday, no matter if it's the folklore, the birthstone, or the birth flower.

The month you were born was no accident. You were fated to arrive then, and the associated traditions are significant, in terms of your personality and destiny. That may be the creature most associated with your birthday, the story surrounding your own flower, or even the lunar phase.

What is working here is synchronicity: the famous principle of deeply meaningful coincidence. Carl Jung first named this phenomenon, but it is at the heart of astrology and the Tarot, too, which you can explore later on in *Your Birthday*.

If you want to understand your friends, family, and partners, then always begin with the birth month and its layers of meaning. Then go to the birthday itself—as all 366 days of the year have their own unique significance.

Knowing who you are and where you come from means discovering the past as it influences the present—right here.

What symbols do we turn to today for the celebration of our birthdays? Let's look at these month by month to begin connecting to the themes in our lives and our soul's purpose. In the sections that follow, we will look at the zodiac signs that align with the Sun in your birth month and what they convey about you, significant facts about your birth month, as well as your birthstone, birth flower, emblematic animals, and the Native American Moons.

Your Birthstone

Scholars have traced the origin of birthstones back to the Bible and the book of Exodus. Aaron, the brother of Moses, had a breastplate adorned with twelve gemstones which represented the twelve tribes of Israel. On this religious garment, each gemstone had special symbolism related to the tribes.

This again had evolved by the ninth century into people only wearing each stone in a given month, in the belief that this would bring more luck. Birthstones, therefore, have a long history with astrology.

In the Middle Ages, the stones were widely used for medicinal purposes—often crushed into powder and given to the patient that way. This is why many stones still have healing associations. There is a story that healing stones would be tied to criminals once they had been poisoned. If the criminal lived, they would be rewarded for proving the effectiveness of the stone. There is no record of how many survived!

Your Birthday Flower

Birth flowers, usually tied to the month, originated in Roman times when flowers were given as a gift to the Roman gods and used to decorate altars for celebrations. In the early eighteenth century this evolved along with the language of floriography. The idea of flowers having a symbolic meaning was introduced in England by Lady Mary Wortley Montagu and became popular among the Victorians. During that era, flowers could be used to convey hidden messages to a lover without obviously breaking with the strict codes of propriety of the time.

Your Emblematic Animal

Native American astrology emphasizes living in harmony with nature. Some tribes connect with nature through spirit guides in animal form believed to help people throughout their lives. Totem poles are an example of such spirit animals among cultures of the Pacific Northwest.

For this astrological guide, we have sought out emblematic animals for each month with characteristics most closely related to you. You can explore how yours can serve to guide your path and connect you to the natural world.

Native American Moons in Your Birth Month

In order to record time, the early Native American tribes used seasons and lunar months. This was not a uniform system: some tribes had four seasons, others five, and some used twelve or thirteen Moons. Each tribe would give the Full Moons (lunar months) different names, so there are a varying number of names for each Moon. But all were usually grounded in nature and tied to the seasons, so they do have common themes.

Colonial Americans adopted some of the Native American Full Moon names, and they are now applied to the Gregorian calendar system we use today. They still maintain the connection to nature, but also carry special and spiritual meanings.

The Native American Moons have become significant to the wider populace as a way to track lunar time and the specific periods of each season in nature. It has become very popular to mark Full Moons with suggested pagan rituals, so it's interesting to discover why and perhaps use the Native American Moon of your birth month to set your intentions for your year ahead.

HAPPY BIRTHDAY TO YOU

In 1893, Patty Hill and Mildred J. Hill, sisters and schoolteachers from Kentucky, wrote a song called "Good Morning to All." This was to be sung by students every morning to start the school day. In 1924 Robert Coleman published a songbook that featured this song but with added lyrics, and it became what we know as "Happy Birthday to You." In 1933 this was popularized in an Irving Berlin musical and is perhaps the only song nearly every single person sings at some point in the Western world.

Born in January

January always ends the old year. If you were born in January, then your life is like a series of books with first pages and final chapters. You transform your appearance and career on a regular basis—sometimes your relationships, too. You are good at saying goodbye—to jobs, to homes, to people, and even to an old version of yourself.

January is the month when many nations have also implemented a new constitution following independence. Using January 1 as a start date, whole countries have said farewell to the past and made a fresh start for a different future.

The zodiac signs Capricorn and Aquarius belong to January. Capricorn the Goat starts at the bottom and climbs to the top, never looking back or going back. Aquarius is ruled by Uranus, the planet which ends the old and starts the new in astrology. If you were born in January then you do not regret *what was*; you are only ever interested in *what might be*.

Your appearance, your job title, your qualifications, and/or your status (married or single) may not change any more frequently compared to others born in different months, but when you do get rid of the past, it is gone forever. You are very good at walking away. "That was then, this is now" is your motto.

JANUARY FACTS

- January is named after the Roman god Janus, protector of gates and doorways. He has two faces: one looks to the past; the other sees the future. And thus he symbolizes beginnings and endings.

- Numa (c. 715–673 BCE), who was one of seven kings to rule Rome before the republic, changed the Roman calendar replacing March with January as the first month of the year.

- January 15 was Dr. Martin Luther King Jr.'s birthday. In his honor Martin Luther King Day is celebrated on the third Monday of January as a federal holiday in the United States.

- The first Monday after Epiphany (January 6) is Plough Monday. This designation dates back to the fifteenth century and marks the start of the agricultural season. More a celebration than a workday for farmworkers, it is a festival of eating, singing, and dancing, and hope for a good year ahead.

- Perihelion, the point of the Earth's orbit nearest to the Sun, always happens in early January—usually roughly two weeks after the December solstice.

- January has often been seen as the weather forecast for the rest of the year because of its position as the first month. Weather folklore around January includes that fog in January brings a wet spring and a nice January forecasts a good year. However, beware if grass grows in January, for that means it will grow badly for the rest of the year. And, if it's a summerlike January, then spring will be like winter.

BIRTHSTONE
Garnet

The traditional garnet is a deep red, but this stone does come in other colors—notably yellow, orange, and green. The name is derived from the Latin word for "seed," mostly assumed to be the pomegranate seed. It's a sign of protection, love, friendship, trust, and commitment. In Roman times a garnet would be worn by warriors to keep them safe when going to war and as talismans to protect from the plague or ill-health.

The garnet was sometimes referred to as "Gem of Faith" by people who believed wearing one would bring good your way. It was said that garnets would change color to warn of approaching danger.

The garnet was widely believed to protect the wearer from evil thoughts and negativity. It is also a sign of friendship: if given to a friend, it will definitely enhance that friendship.

BIRTH FLOWER
Snowdrop

As the name suggests, the snowdrop is the earliest garden flower to bloom in winter, so named because it can sprout up through the snow. Historically it grew in cold mountainous areas.

It is said that the snowdrop was brought to Europe by monks for medicinal use because the extract was used by ancient Greeks for its mind-altering effects.

As a gift snowdrops are used for both sympathy or celebration. This bloom represents optimism and hope, but also compassion. Its white hue denotes purity and innocence.

According to one biblical story, an angel turned snowflakes into snowdrops and gave them to Adam and Eve as a sign of hope after their banishment from the Garden of Eden. In the Victorian times, the snowdrop also represented hope.

EMBLEMATIC ANIMAL
Mountain Goat

Adapted for the cold, the mountain goat is the perfect animal for January. As an animal guide the mountain goat is all about reaching new heights. They work through difficulties and are unwavering when it comes to reaching goals. They are seen to represent the growth and development of one's skills. Also, the mountain goat is independent and can prove that anything is possible—after all, they make clinging to the mountain edge effortless. If you actually see one of these goats perched on a steep incline, it's impressive how they manage both to get to and stay in their positions.

Symbolically the mountain goat stands for abundance and trust. The behavioral message is to guide yourself through the rocky areas of life with grace and dignity. The mountain goat can show us how to explore the unknown and gives us the courage to access areas that other animals cannot—beyond the ordinary.

FAMOUS ANIMAL
Larry the Downing Street Cat

Larry, who resides at the UK prime minister's home, Number 10 Downing Street in London, was born in January 2007. He has served the very important role of chief mouser to the cabinet office of the United Kingdom since 2011 when he was adopted from Battersea Dogs and Cats Home. He is the first cat to be given the title and has become quite a celebrity—a role he seems to enjoy.

He has his own X account with 834,000 followers and is possibly more popular than the many prime ministers he has let share his home.

NATIVE AMERICAN MOON
Wolf Moon

The Wolf Moon is the name given to the Full Moon of January because it was believed that wolves howled more at this time, possibly from the hunger they felt in the sparse winter month. Today we know wolves use howling to connect to their packs, so perhaps they are just talking to each other more this month, maybe making plans for the future.

On a spiritual level, the Wolf Moon suggests a time for deep self-reflection. You may feel more emotional during this month, and so communication and connection with others is key. Some believe this is the most powerful time for meditation and rituals. Setting intentions for the year ahead is a very "New Year" thing to do in January, but perhaps this Moon encourages you to take things a step further and talk to others about your aims and goals, putting them out into the universe under the light of the Wolf Moon.

Born in February

Aquarius and Pisces are the two zodiac signs associated with February. Aquarius is about friendship; Pisces is about partnership. If you were born in February, then you feel at home in close friendships and all kinds of duets and double acts, romantic or not. You need strong connections in your life.

The symbol for Aquarius the Water Bearer is a figure holding a jug. This comes from ancient Rome as aquarii were the workers who supplied the communal baths with water. Roman baths were a combination swimming pool, library, and club, and friends gathered there. Pisces is the two fish which swim in opposite directions but are always together. They are never separated.

Chaucer's poem "Parlement of the Foules" written in the 1300s reveals how birds choose their mates on St. Valentine's Day. Throughout your life you will experiment with different kinds of relationships with people, just like his birds. You will of course have a range of boyfriends or girlfriends. You may also find work partners or even just tennis partners.

When February 29 appears on the calendar every leap year, all bets are off. Traditionally, women were allowed to propose marriage to men on this date. Although today a woman can of course suggest a commitment at any time, this history explains why February may be the month so associated with love.

If you were born in February, you can never be alone for too long. Even when you are not in a romantic relationship you will find a way to pair off with a friend just to have the company on a work project or with a favorite hobby.

FEBRUARY FACTS

- The name *February* originates from the Latin word *februa* which means "to cleanse." The Romans had a monthlong celebration of atonement and purification which took place in Februalia. The Roman god Februus was named after the month, not the other way round.

- February is the only month to have fewer than thirty days. It was chosen by the Roman Numa to have twenty-eight days, apart from every fourth year when it has twenty-nine to keep the calendar aligned to the seasons.

- The most notable day of the month may be Valentine's Day on February 14—widely celebrated as a day of love. This started being a proper holiday in the fourteenth century, although in the eighth it was already the feast day of St. Valentine. Some legends suggest he was a priest who could heal the sick but was martyred for trying to convert Emperor Claudius to Christianity. It is also said that Valentine went against the emperor's orders and married couples to spare the man going to war, hence the link with romance.

- February is African American History Month.

- The Anglo-Saxons called February cake-month because cakes were offered to gods during that month.

- February 2 is known as Candlemas Day, which in ancient folklore makes it the end of the worst of winter. It is a day for lighting candles and celebrating that it will get warmer and lighter in the coming days.

- American Alan Shepard became the first man to hit a golf ball on the moon in February 1971.

BIRTHSTONE

Amethyst

This is a vibrant purple or violet stone. In ancient times the Greeks believed amethyst could protect them from intoxication or drunkenness. In fact, the name comes from the Greek word *amethystos*, which literally means "not drunk." Greeks would even grind some into their drink to stop inebriation.

Scientists dispute that this stone can actually keep you sober, but many through the years have worn one or even put one into their wineglass to either prevent getting drunk or to ward off hangovers!

In Exodus in the Bible, the amethyst was one of the stones on Aaron's breastplate as the priest of New Jerusalem as mentioned earlier. Some Christians believed the color represents the blood of Christ.

In medieval times, doctors would wear this stone, and it was favored in rosaries. Purple is often associated with royalty, and amethysts were traditionally beloved by the ruling class. Nowadays amethyst represents love and spirituality and is very popular in jewelry for its strong color.

It is also a calming stone and a symbol of healing, spirituality, and clarity.

BIRTH FLOWER
Violet

Not many flowers bloom in February; however, the violet thrives in winter conditions. These woodland flowers come into their own in this wintry month. The color has a strong connection to the amethyst as well.

The gorgeous violet bloom is a symbol of modesty, faithfulness, everlasting love, and innocence. If given as a gift in Victorian times, it was a declaration to be true. Among friends, it shows loyalty and the fact you will always be there. In a romantic sense it indicates that you are fully committed to your relationship.

Christian legend held that violets blossomed when the angel Gabriel announced to Mary that she was pregnant with Jesus. Symbolically violets represent faith, awareness, inspiration, and spirituality.

EMBLEMATIC ANIMAL
Dolphin

The dolphin is intelligent, creative, and progressive. They are often seen as more intelligent than most humans, but they are also playful and fun. They possess a quirky nature and are almost universally loved. Often seeing or swimming with them is on people's bucket lists. They are happiest frolicking free in the sea. Dolphins in captivity have been known to get depressed, and they do not like to be isolated.

Dolphins are innovators and visionaries who can show others the way. They are also highly sociable animals on their own terms. They symbolize luck, new opportunities, and wisdom as well as cooperation and freedom. They also represent peace and harmony.

FAMOUS ANIMAL
Skippy

Skippy the bush kangaroo was born on February 5, 1968, and is one of Australia's most famous animals, if not its most famous. The classic Australian TV series of this name was about ten-year-old Sonny and his very intelligent roo. Skippy was a friend to all. He was also thoughtful, caring, and dutiful, and his main aim was keeping people happy as he and Sonny went on their many adventures together.

Skippy enjoyed three series and even a feature film spin-off. The character was eventually played by several kangaroos. According to the trainer, kangaroos are quite hard to train, and so for the TV show they often would put paws on sticks for close-ups!

NATIVE AMERICAN MOON
Snow Moon

The February Full Moon is known as the Snow Moon because February is the time of the heaviest snowfall. As hunting was traditionally very difficult at this time, it has also been known as the Hunger Moon.

This Moon reminds us that change can be subtle. It illuminates gently but at the same time can create the most meaningful transformations. It is a time to trust yourself and what you know. There is opportunity for significant achievement—so use this time to go after your personal and intellectual goals. Perhaps it is a time for steely ambition to be realized. If it's your birth month, then maybe set your career goals now for the upcoming year.

Born in March

March ushers in spring in the Northern Hemisphere and autumn in the Southern Hemisphere. It was March, not January, which was the first calendar month in Rome.

If you were born in March, then you are a person who always takes the initiative, and you have a pattern of big launches and beginnings. Your life is full of important firsts. You enjoy regularly starting work or business ventures, for example, or writing important new chapters throughout your life with partners, family, or friends. Nothing inspires you like a fresh start.

March produces Aries and Pisces children. As peak lambing time, March calls to mind Aries and its lambs and sheep, as well as the ram. This accompanies the idea that you enjoy giving birth to all that is new. March is also the month when the first IVF shark was born in Australia (on March 3). Pisces is the sign of the fish.

Even if you never have children, you will always be drawn to producing a brainchild, and this may characterize your career or your hobbies. You are destined to lead a life full of births, arrivals, and launches.

MARCH FACTS

- March is named after the Roman god of war Mars. He is often depicted wearing a helmet and carrying a spear.

- In weather folklore if March comes in like a lion, it goes out like a lamb.

- This is the time when animals start to wake from their winter hibernation.
- In the United States, March is Women's History Month, and International Women's Day is March 8.
- St. Joseph's Day, March 19, celebrates the husband of the Virgin Mary and father of Christ.
- March 25 is Tichborne Dole Day—an eccentric British tradition from the thirteenth century. Lady Mabella asked her husband Roger De Tichborne to donate some of their wealth to the poor. He set her an impossible task: She had to make her way around the land holding a blazing torch. For the amount of land she covered before the torch went out, he would donate to the poor. His wife was unwell, so she had to literally crawl around the land in order to do this. But to his surprise and dismay she managed twenty-three acres. So anything grown on that land was donated to the poor. This is known today as "the crawl" and is still celebrated today.
- March 5, 1770, was the Boston Massacre, a deadly riot that broke out between American colonists and British soldiers.
- March 17 is St. Patrick's Day—a huge day marking the death of this patron saint of Ireland and the arrival of Christianity to the island. It also celebrates the Irish culture and heritage, and is often marked by parades and parties.

BIRTHSTONE
Aquamarine

Not only is aquamarine the birthstone for March, but it's also an established gift for the nineteenth wedding anniversary. In Greek mythology, Poseidon, god of the seas, crafted the aquamarine from the waves.

Most aquamarines are light blue in hue, but the darker or more intense the blue, the more valuable the stone. The name comes from the Latin for seawater. Ancient sailors claimed that the stone could keep waves calm and therefore offered protection at sea. Aquamarines are also said to bring marriage happiness and make the wearer smarter!

Physical healing properties including pain relief, quicker recovery from surgery, and helping with hormonal imbalances are attributed to aquamarines.

In 1936 the government of Brazil gave First Lady Eleanor Roosevelt a dark blue rectangular aquamarine that weighed a whopping 1,298 carats.

BIRTH FLOWER
Daffodil

Romans introduced daffodils to Britain from Spain and Portugal, where the largest variety of daffodils can be found. They planted daffodils in memory of loved ones or those who were lost in battle.

The daffodil as a symbol represents rebirth and new beginnings. Their vibrant yellow color means it is a flower of happiness, and as it is one of the first flowers to bloom at the end of winter, it heralds the beginning of spring. They also symbolize creativity, energy, and forgiveness. In Victorian times this was a flower of chivalry.

Shakespeare described the daffodil as the flower that "comes before the swallow dares."

EMBLEMATIC ANIMAL
Koi

Not only beautiful and decorative, koi swim in pairs side by side. *Koi* means "affection or love" in Japanese. These fish are often seen as a symbol of prosperity; they are often kept to bring luck and as a sign of wealth in many cultures. They represent love, romance, and matrimony.

They are also very peaceful fish. Koi are domesticated and adaptable and can live for up to seventy years; thus these carp are associated with longevity. They are linked with strength of character, courage, and good fortune and are very coveted because they are so beautiful and lucky.

FAMOUS ANIMAL
Shergar

Born on March 3, 1978, Shergar was a famous and very successful thoroughbred racehorse. Irish bred and British trained, he won the Epsom Derby in 1981 by ten lengths—the longest winning margin in the race's history. He was worth over $15 million.

Shergar was kidnapped in Ireland in 1983, sparking a huge outcry and search. A £2 million ransom demand was issued, which was not paid. Some claimed he was taken by the IRA. No arrests were ever made for his kidnapping, but films have documented lots of speculation surrounding him. No one knows exactly what happened, but popular opinion was that he was injured during the kidnapping and had to be put out of his misery.

NATIVE AMERICAN MOON
Sap Moon

The Shawnee have traditionally referred to the March Moon as the Sap Moon, because it was when the sap would start to run in the maple trees. It signifies the beginning of spring. The Pueblo Indians of the American Southwest call it "moon when the leaves break forth," as spring is usually a little further along at the same time in their region.

The Sap Moon is a dynamic moon when energy of the Full Moon meets the Earth's energy as it emerges from winter. It is symbolically a time of hope, of new beginnings and abundance. But also March is an in-between month and can be unpredictable, so it's a good time to take stock of where you are and make plans for when spring truly settles in.

Born in April

The zodiac signs Aries and Taurus are associated with April. These are strong signs, and you are a strong person. Aries the Ram is ruled by the element of fire and Mars, the planet of action. Taurus the Bull is a fixed sign and stable as solid earth. You have staying power if you were born in April. Mahatma Gandhi completed his Salt March on April 6 and led India to independence. Queen Elizabeth II was born on April 21.

You are well-known for facing tests of strength and overcoming them if you were born in April. You are a survivor. The *Titanic* sank on April 15, 1912—the most famous survival challenge in cruise ship history.

If you were born in April you are courageous and also firm. You have to be, because life makes you that way. Every obstacle you encounter will make you tougher and more determined. It is quite common for people born in April to have planets in both Aries and Taurus in their natal (birth) charts, and this combination is well-known in astrology for a refusal to give in or give up.

Anybody who thinks you are a pushover had better think again, as whenever you face great odds, it only increases your willpower and sense of purpose. Children born in April reveal this at school when playing sports or just dealing with the ups and downs of life in the classroom. Even into old age, you are a force to be reckoned with.

APRIL FACTS

- The name *April* derives from the Latin *aperire* which means "to open"—like flowers opening in spring.

- On April 6, 1896, the first Olympics of the modern era was held in Athens.
- April is the start of spring in the Northern Hemisphere.
- Easter is usually celebrated in April, although the date differs each year depending on the moon.
- April is National Poetry Month in the United States and Canada.
- The most famous date in April might be April 1 or All Fools' Day. No one really knows where this association originated, but early mentions of it in written records can be traced back to the Renaissance. It is probably older than that, though. There are different ways of celebrating, but today it's all about the pranks. In France the pranked person is called *poisson d'avril* (April fish), because it was common for French schoolchildren to pin paper fish on the backs of their unsuspecting friends.
- The American Revolutionary War began on April 19, 1775.
- The Great 1906 San Francisco Earthquake took place on April 17.

BIRTHSTONE
Diamond

The diamond is April's birthstone. Today we find diamonds traditionally as a sign of luxury and also perhaps most widely used in engagement rings as the representation of eternal love. Symbolically wearing a diamond promotes better relationships and inner strength.

Coming from the Greek word *adamas*, it means "invincible," and in ancient Rome it would be tied to the left arm of the soldier to give them courage.

During the Middle Ages, diamonds were thought to hold healing powers and so became fashionable among the European elite. However, the love for the diamond began in India, where the stone was collected from streams and rivers. Traded as early as the fourth century BCE, they have ever since been a sign of wealth. But it was believed that if a diamond was stolen, then it would curse the thief!

The first diamond engagement ring recorded was given by Archduke Maximilian of Austria to Mary of Burgundy in 1477. Known today as the king of the birthstones, as well as the purest way to declare love, it's a wonderful gift for an April birthday!

BIRTH FLOWER
Sweet Pea

Native to Italy, the sweet pea is a vibrant, beautiful flower which comes in a number of colors and varieties and is well-known for its fragrant smell.

Sweet peas became particularly popular during Victorian times, often appearing at weddings and gatherings of nobles. Meaning blissful pleasure, they also symbolize friendship and gratitude, so were often used as gifts to say thank you and goodbye.

In France, they were traditionally given to brides on their wedding day for good luck. In some cultures they are even thought to have magical properties.

EMBLEMATIC ANIMAL
Ram

In early Egyptian myth, the ram is said to have created the first men out of clay. Fiery and intelligent rams are natural-born leaders. They are social and determined with high energy. Hence the association with a "battering ram"—a military tool used to break down the gates of fortresses originally with a carved ram's head at the end. Solving problems with headbutting sums up how they are warriors with deep strength. However, their high energy levels can cause instability and overenthusiasm.

The ram is a symbol of action, overcoming obstacles, strength, and achievement. They are also associated with honesty. In Hinduism the ram symbolizes doing the right thing. In Native American traditions they were very highly respected, a totem animal whose spirit helped provide for the tribe.

FAMOUS ANIMAL
Cher Ami

Cher Ami, born in 1918, was a homing pigeon donated by Great Britain to American troops in France during World War I. She saved U.S. troops by delivering messages during the war and so became a hero.

She succeeded where many other carrier pigeons failed to save the Lost Battalion in France by safely delivering her message despite being hit by a German bullet. She was brave and determined. Cher Ami's body was preserved, stuffed, and put on display at the Smithsonian Institution in 1921.

NATIVE AMERICAN MOON
Pink Moon

This moon was named after an early blooming wildflower of North America, a pink blossom of April.

Symbolically this moon urges you to take a break and recharge your batteries. If you are feeling burned-out, then it's time to give yourself a moment, reflect, and tune in to your intuition—which is especially strong at this time.

The Pink Moon is known in Christianity as the Paschal Moon—the first Full Moon after the spring equinox used to set the date for Easter. In Judaism it is known as the Passover Moon.

Born in May

May has always been associated with trade, merchants, business, and finance. The Sun always passes from Taurus, the sign of the bull, bull markets, and gold bullion, and into Gemini, ruled by Mercury, the god of commerce, in May. May is also linked to valuables, jewelry, and fine art. May rules taxation, banking, and economics, too. If you were born in May, you enjoy making, spending, or saving money more than most. In astrology, it is common to find May babies born with both Gemini and Taurus planets in the birth chart. If you have this, then you are a good bargainer and also have an instinct for business.

Thanks to your lifestyle, your career, your hobbies, or just your personality everything you own, earn, or owe in your life will always define who you are and what happens to you.

MAY FACTS

- May is named for the Latin *Maius*, from Maia, the goddess of growth and fertility. Her name means "mother," and she was responsible for the growth of plants, animals, and humans.

- The Anglo-Saxons called this month *thrilmilce* because cows could be milked three times a day.

- "Cast not a clout til May is out" is a saying from F. K. Robinson's Whitby Glossary. This means that you should not change your seasonal fashion until after May!

- You may be familiar with the line "Here we go gathering nuts in May" from an Old English children's song. It's derived from the original children's game "here we go gathering knots in May," when they would gather knots of flowers for the annual May Day celebration.

- May 18 in England is when the ceremony of the Newbiggin Freeholders takes place, where tolls were once collected from ships at this important port. Today the freeholders still collect money but also give away peanuts.

- May 19 is St. Dunstan's Day. He is the patron saint of goldsmiths and jewelers, and this is the traditional day to do spring cleaning.

- The Great Exhibition, the world's first trade fair, opened in London on May 1, 1851.

- The eventual end of wartime rationing in 1945 and the return of normal shopping began on May 8 with Victory in Europe Day after World War II.

- Mayfair, one of the richest places in London—and the location of one of the UK's most famous stores, Harrods—is named for the annual May Fair which happened on its West End London site.

- May 14 is "Pag-Rag" Day. In Lincolnshire, fairs were held in market towns, and new clothes were bought. It was also often the day when workers would move on from their current jobs and look for a new master or situation, so hiring fairs were also widely held on this day.

- The last Monday in May is Memorial Day in the United States, a federal holiday honoring the members of the military who lost their lives in service to their country.

BIRTHSTONE
Emerald

May's birthstone is the emerald, a rare transparent green gemstone which holds great beauty and value. *Emerald* translates as "green" in Greek, and the ancient Greeks associated the emerald with Aphrodite, the goddess of love and beauty. The stone was said to protect from unfaithfulness, and in ancient times it was believed that if the wearer were unfaithful, the stone would lose it color. It was also worn in childbirth to minimize the dangers of anything going wrong.

As a birthstone the emerald is believed to represent good fortune, insightfulness, and youth. It is closely associated with the heart chakra and calms emotions. It is said that you should wear an emerald close to your heart for wellness and a long, happy life.

Love is a big theme with emeralds, linking back to Aphrodite. It is said to promote friendship, peace, and harmony, and the giving and receiving of unconditional love. It is also the stone of domestic bliss.

Its physical and medical attributes include strengthening memory and healing any heart problems.

BIRTH FLOWER
Lily of the Valley

On May 1, 1560, King Charles IX of France was presented with lilies of the valley as a lucky charm. As a result, these flowers are given as gifts to loved ones in France on May Day. They also happen to be the national flower of Finland.

In Greek mythology, it was said that the lily of the valley was created by the god Apollo to cover the ground like a scented carpet for his nymphs to walk on.

This flower is a symbol of purity and has religious associations as well. It is believed that the blooms are symbolic of Eve's tears after God expelled her from the Garden of Eden. And lilies of the valley are said to be taken to the gates of heaven to measure one's purity after death.

The lily of the valley has associations with motherhood, sweetness, purity, and humility. It is a happy flower, because it blooms when we are all looking forward to summer.

In Victorian times the lily of the valley was given as a romantic gesture carrying the message, "You have made my life complete."

EMBLEMATIC ANIMAL
Bull

The bull is both adaptable and stubborn at the same time. It is linked to strength and abundance. However, these animals can be aggressive and unpredictable. They are considered a symbol of masculine energy. The bull is levelheaded, goal-oriented, and generous but can be easy to anger and immovable—literally!

In the Bible the bull represents hard work, burdens, and self-sacrifice. In ancient Egypt the bull was a symbol of fertility. In early Greek culture, not only was it a symbol of strength, but it was believed that bulls' blood had magical qualities. In Hinduism the bull is sacred, because Shiva's steed is the bull.

FAMOUS ANIMAL
Eddie

Eddie the dog from the TV show *Frasier* was born on May 15, 1990. For many years Eddie participated in one of the highest-rated, most widely syndicated hits on television. This large Jack Russell terrier belonged to Frasier's father Martin and was Frasier's nemesis. Like all Taurus animals he had the Midas touch—a golden paw for the *Frasier* brand—and lived in a luxury apartment.

NATIVE AMERICAN MOON
Flower Moon

Called the Flower Moon because of the abundant blooming that happens during the month of May, this moon shines when spring is at its fullest. Other names for it include the Hare Moon and the Milk Moon.

There's no surprise that spiritual meanings are linked to growth. This Moon offers creativity, inspiration, passion, and new life. The Flower Moon is said to be a manifesting time, so being clear on what you want from life can be particularly powerful at this time.

Born in June

If you were born in June, you are a good planner—one step ahead and always ready with a solution. The Sun starts June in Gemini, the sign associated with clever thinking. Gemini in turn is ruled by Mercury, the planet of the mind. After this the Sun passes through the zodiac sign of Cancer, which governs mothers (those master strategists) later in the month.

No wonder you are always the first person with the best answer. You will always choose subjects, careers, or leading interests in your life which allow you to use your ingenuity. Your brilliant answers to life's questions may be small or big, but if you were born in June, your brainwaves define who you are.

You may be a visionary whose ideas may be years ahead of their time. George Orwell's prescient *1984* was published on June 8. The Statue of Liberty arrived in New York on June 17, a lady who lights the way for all.

JUNE FACTS

- June is named after the Roman goddess Juno, wife to Jupiter, king of the gods, and goddess of marriage and childbirth.

- In the Northern Hemisphere this is the month with the longest daylight hours of the year.

- Superman appeared for the first time in DC Comics in June of 1938.

- June 20 is the summer solstice—welcoming the start of this season in the Northern Hemisphere.
- Usually the Saturday after the solstice is Midsummer Day—a day when we are meant to fully appreciate nature. Historically it represents the midpoint between the planting and the harvesting. In the UK it is often celebrated at the ancient site of Stonehenge. The pagan celebration of this day is known as Litha. In Sweden it's a national holiday! Other traditions include dancing, singing, and even jumping over bonfires, which was a ritual thought to bring good luck.
- The D-Day landings of June 6, 1944, were a triumph of secret planning.
- The Apple II computer was launched on June 10, 1977. Even computers have astrological charts, and Apples are Gemini.
- June is Pride Month.
- The Civil Rights Act was approved on June 19, 1964.

BIRTHSTONE
Pearl

Pearls are often referred to as the jewel of the sea. These are very classic and classy stones, and in some cases rare—not to mention expensive. The pearl symbolizes generosity, wisdom, and purity. They are created in the most amazing way—grown by oysters to coat any hard matter that finds its way inside their shells, for example, a grain of sand. In more modern times, cultured pearls are artificially produced by putting a hard base into the oyster shell to induce the oyster to make the pearl.

In the ancient Middle East, it was believed pearls were teardrops fallen from heaven, and the early Chinese believed they were from the brain of a dragon. Because the pearl is often associated with purity and innocence, they were traditionally given as a wedding gift. But it was also said that if divers wore a pearl, it could even protect against sharks.

Pearls have often been endowed with healing properties. In Asia they were believed to fix indigestion and hemorrhages, and some Arab physicians thought that pearl powder could help eyesight and even depression.

BIRTH FLOWER
Rose

In a genus made up of more than one hundred species of flowers, roses have a long association with romance and love. They come in many different colors, and although originally thought to be native to Asia, they are now fully international. In Greek mythology the rose is linked to Aphrodite, goddess of love, who wore a crown of these blooms.

Each color rose has a different meaning. Red is for love—which is why these are given widely on Valentine's Day. Pink is for happiness and admiration, and white innocence and purity. Orange is for desire and excitement, and yellow happiness and friendship.

However, the Romans saw roses as representing death and rebirth, so they were often planted at graves. The Victorians were the ones to popularize them as a declaration of love.

EMBLEMATIC ANIMAL
African Grey Parrot

One of the most popular birds, the African grey parrot is not only beautiful, but also represents wisdom and intelligence—due to its ability to mimic speech—and, of course, communication.

The parrot has very deep spiritual significance. In Christianity, it's linked with being able to communicate with God, and in ancient Egyptian mythology, the god Thoth was often depicted as an African grey. In Native American culture, parrots are a symbol of intelligence and communication and therefore highly valued within this community. They are very sociable birds and not happy being alone.

FAMOUS ANIMAL
Hedwig

A snowy owl and Harry Potter's first and perhaps most constant companion, Hedwig was obviously a very special owl. With an impressive personality, Hedwig was sassy and very intelligent. She first appeared swooping in and out of Harry's room at the Dursleys as if she owned the place. She followed her own rules and knew that if she wanted to annoy Aunt Petunia she could do so with dead mice.

Hedwig was a key part of the Harry Potter series and much loved by fans. She was a sort of protector for Harry. In the films a number of owls played Hedwig, but the most notable was one called Gizmo.

NATIVE AMERICAN MOON
Strawberry Moon

The Strawberry Moon was thus named to mark the ripening of these berries in June, which have a relatively short harvesting time. The Europeans call it the Rose Moon. In Celtic lore this moon is the Mead Moon—celebrated with mead and festivals to promote fertility and prosperity.

The Strawberry Moon is said to bring changes to family life or the home, but also luck and love. And some suggest that it is time for a bit of self-care as it's seen as prudent to put some love into yourself if you are always giving to others.

Born in July

If you were born in July, then you go to extremes. July is the coldest month of the year in the Southern Hemisphere and the hottest in the Northern Hemisphere. It's all or nothing for you. You are fated to go through excessive and intense highs and lows in your life as a result of being a July person. Cancers and Leos are born in July. Cancer is water; Leo is fire. The extremes of the month show up in their opposing elements.

You may be the biggest or the best, for example, in a particular field, top of the class as a child, best performer at work as an adult. You also find out early on where you fail. You habitually come first in one special area of your life. You may be a top jam-maker, for example, or a regular leading scorer in football. However, you also know that when you bottom out in life, that's extreme, too. At school you had extreme results at both the top and bottom of different classes and activities.

The saying "It never rains but it pours" is true for you.

All this makes you philosophical. Over time you develop a sense of humor about life. "This too shall pass" is good advice for July people, no matter if you are hitting the heights or getting over the lows.

JULY FACTS

- July was named after Roman general Julius Caesar.
- The Fourth of July is one of the most famous holidays—American Independence Day.
- Early July is aphelion, when the Earth is farthest from the Sun for the year.

- July 15 is St. Swithin's Day in the UK. If it rains on this day, it is believed it will rain for forty consecutive days. The basis for this originates in 971 CE when the bones of St. Swithin were moved to a special shrine at Winchester Cathedral. This sparked a ferocious storm that lasted forty days. Back then, people believed that the saint was crying in heaven because of being moved. The saying "Ne'er trust a July sky" came from this.

- July 29 is the Islamic New Year.

- The second Monday in July every year is International Town Criers Day—a relatively recent celebration invented in 1997 by a Canadian town crier.

BIRTHSTONE
Ruby

Known in ancient India as the "king of precious stones," the ruby is second only to the diamond. It has long-held associations with health, power, and love as well as wealth and affluence. One of its main attributes is said to be contentment. It is sacred to Buddhists as a legend says the ruby represents the "tears of Buddha."

In ancient times rubies were believed to have mystical powers to heal the sick, mainly due to a color resembling blood. In many cultures it was also a symbol of power and youthful energy. Some believed rubies could predict danger and protect from evil by losing color. There is a story that Catherine of Aragon, the first wife of England's Henry VIII, was warned of her fall from grace by a ruby she wore on her finger.

Burmese warriors traditionally wore rubies in battle, thinking that the stone would protect them or even make them invincible. Whereas medieval Europeans saw rubies as being able to guarantee health, wisdom, wealth, and bring luck in love.

Today the ruby is associated with love and prosperity and a sought-after jewel. It is also the traditional name given to the fortieth wedding anniversary.

BIRTH FLOWER
Larkspur

A symbol of positivity, dedication, and loving bonds and sincerity, larkspurs bloom in summer and are said to have been given their name in Tudor times from their resemblance to the claw of a lark.

These are bright and vibrant flowers with an aquatic energy. A fairly popular garden flower nowadays, they come in a variety of colors. As a gift, they are often chosen for expressing love, affection, or attachment.

In Victorian times the different colors had different meanings: Pink represented fickleness. White was a happy nature. Blue was dignity. And purple was first love. Victorians also believed the larkspur could ward off evil.

EMBLEMATIC ANIMAL
Hermit Crab

Despite the name, hermit crabs can be quite social. They need their tribe to be happy. They are typically more like lobsters than crabs. They do love their homes, but they can also be outgoing. They are only mean if someone is mean to them, and they are protective of those they love and their environment. They enjoy climbing, like to eat fresh fruit and vegetables, but are also sensitive and emotional animals.

On a spiritual level, the hermit crab represents the Moon and connection with water energies. Their shell is an indicator of protection against weakness. The fact they walk sideways can also been seen as a signal that they like to avoid confrontation if possible.

FAMOUS ANIMAL
Dolly the Cloned Sheep

Dolly was born in Scotland on July 5, 1996, as the most famous sheep in the world, perhaps. She was a domestic female sheep and the first mammal cloned from an adult somatic cell using the process of nuclear transfer. She was of huge scientific and popular interest.

Dolly was a normal sheep and gave birth to six normal lambs. Ian Wilmut, the man responsible for her creation and also known as "father of Dolly," said she was charming and confident with people. Learning to work her public, she remained pretty unaffected by her fame.

NATIVE AMERICAN MOON
Full Buck Moon

The Full Buck Moon earned its name because this was the antler-growing month! Male deer or bucks grow new antlers every year at this time. Their antlers get more and more impressive as they gain maturity.

This is a period of renewal and rejuvenation. The Full Buck Moon augurs a time to embrace your inner wisdom, step into your power, and take a moment for self-reflection. Sometimes this Moon can also make you feel more tired than usual, indicting a need to rest and recuperate as well as letting go of what no longer serves you ready for new growth.

This Moon is also known as the Thunder Moon due to the commonality of thunderstorms in July.

Born in August

Named for Emperor Augustus Caesar (*Augustus* means "exalted"), this is a month for high achievers to be born. After all, Augustus did indeed proclaim himself high priest of Rome.

The Sun is in Leo and Virgo in August. Leo governs royalty who oversee their dominion from on high. Virgo rules peak performance. If you were born in August, you find something you are good at as a child or teenager and become exceptional in this field as an adult. This is where you get to rule.

Queen Elizabeth I chose August to make her famous speech when she said, "I have the heart and stomach of a king." Martin Luther King Jr. also made his best-known "I Have a Dream" speech in August, laying out his philosophy as another kind of king. Emperor Augustus himself died in August, saying, "Since well I've played my part, all clap your hands—and from the stage, dismiss me with applause."

This is who you are if you were born in this month.

AUGUST FACTS

- Although August is the eighth month of today's Gregorian calendar, it was the sixth month in Roman times. Notably, Augustus's best military victories took place in August.

- August 1 is traditionally Lammas Day, an old UK festival to mark the annual wheat and corn harvest. Mass celebrations and gatherings would occur, and a loaf of bread would be offered up as thanks to God for a good harvest. This is also celebrated in the larger pagan community. The god Lugh—the Celtic god of sun and light—is also honored on this day with Lughnasadh.

- August 17 is known as Cat's Night; it is related to a bizarre legend, whereby people who believed in witches thought that they could turn themselves into cats eight times, but the ninth they wouldn't change back. This is where the idea that cats have nine lives comes from.

- On August 2, 1776, in Philadelphia most members of the American Continental Congress signed the Declaration of Independence.

- August 26 is Women's Equality Day, celebrating the 1920 ratification of the Nineteenth Amendment to the U.S. Constitution giving women the right to vote.

BIRTHSTONE
Peridot

Peridot is known as the "sun gem," although it is normally green in color. The Greeks call it *chrysolite*, which translates as "goldstone." In Indian Vedic astrology, it represents mental stability, long life, security, and financial abundance. It can be worn to protect against anything negative. In the Bible it is listed as one of the breastplate stones and one of the foundations of the city of New Jerusalem.

It was once worn to help sleep and prevent nightmares, but during the day it could wake up creativity and also prevent depression. It also is associated with strength and courage—knowing no matter what life throws at you you have the inner power to overcome it—as well as compassion—bringing happiness to the wearer, as well as promoting health.

BIRTH FLOWER
Sunflower

The sunflower often grows taller than other blooms, so it definitely stands out from the crowd. With a gorgeous yellow color similar to the Sun, it's a joyful flower—one which can't help but make you feel happy.

Symbolically the sunflower stands for happiness, loyalty, and warmth, but it is also sturdy and definitely not a delicate blossom. In Christianity, the sunflower is seen as a symbol of God's love and has strong connections to faith. In Victorian times it stood for loyalty, longevity, and adoration and was widely used in celebrations.

EMBLEMATIC ANIMAL
Lion

Lions are fiercely protective, ambitious, popular, and generous. These majestic beasts are the king of the jungle for a reason: they are not going to shy away from adversity and challenge. They can be seen as a little vain, but are warm and loving. They also attract a lot of attention. Lions are invincible self-confident, and majestic, as well as leaders who can nurture and protect those weaker than themselves.

The symbolism of the lion has noble associations, and it depicts bravery, assurance, and an indominable spirit. Lions feature heavily in many ancient scripts and the Bible. For example, the lion is the symbol of the house of Judah, which is the house Jesus is descended from.

FAMOUS ANIMAL
Choupette

Born August 15, 2011, Choupette is possibly now one of the world's richest cats since the death of her owner: fashion designer Karl Lagerfeld. A beautiful white Burmese, Choupette was originally owned by a French model. She was one of Lagerfeld's muses and gave the cat the French nickname which translates as "cute girl."

Choupette is definitely a feline in the limelight. She is in charge of her own household. She has been on several magazine covers and even had her own biography written.

Used to the finer things in life, she traveled by private jet and dined with Lagerfeld by sitting across the table from him in their Paris apartment. Choupette definitely was, and still is, a queen.

NATIVE AMERICAN MOON
Sturgeon Moon

Native Americans found it easiest to catch surgeon during August as that was when this fish appeared in the greatest number. During this moon you might experience different energetic frequencies, and you are encouraged to connect with other people at this time. This moon is a symbol of strength, generosity, and knowledge.

The Sturgeon Moon is also known as the Red Moon because of the reddish cast it radiates in the summer month. It is suggested that you should take a long bath at this time, indulging yourself with relaxing bath oils, candles, and listening to your favorite songs while trying to be peaceful.

Born in September

The Sun passes through the zodiac signs Virgo and Libra in the month of September. Virgo is the sign associated with service, duty, and obligation to others—Virgos have a sense of great responsibility to their fellow human beings. Libra describes cooperation, balance, sharing, and compromise. If you were born in September, you always think of others before you think of yourself. Unity and harmony are very important to you. You need to know that you are both or all in something together to feel at home in the world.

This spirit of sharing burdens reminds us that World War II began in September. And on September 11, 2001, British prime minister Tony Blair offered his country's support, saying, "We therefore, here in Britain, stand shoulder to shoulder with our American friends in this hour of tragedy."

You need to be needed, it's true, but you also need trusted partners and friends you can lean on.

SEPTEMBER FACTS

- September comes from the Latin *Septem* because it was originally the seventh month of the Roman calendar.
- In Old England it was called Haervest-month (Harvest month) as the time to bring in all crops in preparation for the winter.
- September 22/23 is the autumnal equinox—the transition between warmer and colder weather.
- In September 1960 the McDonald's golden arches branding was first introduced.
- September has seen some terrible times. On September 1, 1939, Hitler invaded Poland, leading to World War II. It was the month of the Great Fire of London in 1666. And most recently it marked the tragedy of the Twin Towers in New York.
- One of the oldest English traditions—the Abbots Bromley Horn Dance—takes place on the first Sunday after September 4. Dating back to the twelfth century in Staffordshire, this folk dance consists of six deer dancers, a fool, an archer, a hobbyhorse, and Maid Marian—all played by men. They dance to music from a melodeon, which is a form of accordion, around the village of Abbots Bromley. No one is quite sure why this tradition started, but it continues today.
- The first Monday of September is Labor Day in the United States.

BIRTHSTONE
Sapphire

Normally thought of as dark blue, sapphires come in a range of colors from light greenish-blue to violet. The name came from the Greek work *sappherios*, meaning "a blue stone." It has been linked to truth, sincerity, and nobility for thousands of years as well as being associated with royalty. In ancient Greece and Rome, it was believed that kings and queens who owned a sapphire would be protected from harm as well as attract wealth.

Sapphire is the wisdom stone, helping with concentration, thought, and focus as well as having calming abilities. It was also believed to have healing properties, most notably for any eye problems and also protecting against poisons. Others believed that it would help preserve chastity and could stop any bewitchment.

One of the most famous sapphires is Princess Diana's 12-carat engagement ring. This ring went to Prince William, and he gave it to his wife Kate.

BIRTH FLOWER
Aster

Asters bloom in late summer and early autumn. There are more than 600 varieties. These flowers look similar to daises and come in a number of colors, but purple/violet seems the most common. The name comes from the ancient Greek word for star, which is a lovely reference to the shape of the flower.

They bloom around September 29, which is the feast day of St. Michael, and so they have long been associated with the transition from summer to fall. It was also sometimes believed that they could repel snakes. In Victorian England, they stood for elegance and grace which were highly regarded.

Symbolically the aster represents love, wisdom, and faith. It was linked to love in Greek mythology as a flower commonly placed on altars for the gods.

EMBLEMATIC ANIMAL
Giraffe

The giraffe is known for its intelligence and craftiness. They are quick to assess situations and weigh up how to act: they are both analytical and strategic. Giraffes are strong and determined, organized, and focused.

Giraffes are long-necked, which gives them a sense of elegance. They are also an incredibly calm animal. Symbolically the giraffe represents the fact you can reach new heights and be fully successful.

The giraffe has a presence in the Bible—notably on Noah's Ark, but also in other references which leads to the Christian link of the giraffe to a symbol of protection and provision and a divine being close to heaven.

FAMOUS ANIMAL
Peter Rabbit

Beatrix Potter first wrote about what would become one of her most famous characters—Peter Rabbit—on September 4, 1893, to Noel, the son of her friend and former governess Annie Moore.

Peter Rabbit went on to appear in books and even films, and became a hugely recognizable rabbit. He is mischievous and loves the garden—especially carrots and lettuce if he can get his paws on them. He is told by his mother to stay away from the angry Mr. McGregor's garden, but it's just too tempting!

His story has been translated into thirty-six different languages and has sold over forty-five million copies, making it one of the most best-selling books ever.

Born in October

October is the month for basketball, hockey, football, and baseball in the United States. It's a sports equinox, when all four can see big games on the same day. October finds the Sun in Libra and Scorpio. Libra is about cooperation and compromise—passing the ball—and also about tactics. Scorpio reveals passion and obsession—quite fittingly.

If you were born in October then you are skilled at sharing the space with people, but you are also capable of quite intense relationships. There's an edge to you.

You are a game-player in sports, in life, or in love.

OCTOBER FACTS

- October was the eighth month of the year in the old Roman calendar—that's why its name came from *octo*, meaning "eight."

- The Saxons called this month Wyn Monath, due to the fact it was the season of wine making.

- All Hallow's Day/Halloween on October 31 is celebrated in a number of countries. The story behind it is that this is the day that the spirits can wander the earth freely, but today it's more about dressing up and candy.

- Weather folklore around this month includes: When "deer are wearing a gray coat in October, it means a hard winter." "Much rain in October, much wind in December." And a warm October predicts a cold February.

- October is Black History Month in the UK.

- The second Monday in October is Canadian Thanksgiving Day.

- October 2 is known as Old Man's Day. This name originated in the sixteenth century when Matthew Wall, from Braughing in Hertfordshire, UK, was saved from being buried alive. He must have been in a coma when he was assumed dead, but on the way to his grave, the motion jolted him and he was able to bang on the coffin lid to be rescued. In his will he left a legacy to celebrate his escape, saying on this day the lane should be swept (as it was for his funeral procession) and the church bells should ring for him. This is still celebrated in the parish today, with children often doing the sweeping.

BIRTHSTONE
Opal

Opals are believed to have been originally mined in India, and from there they were brought to the Western world. In Sanskrit they are called *upala*, meaning "precious stone." In ancient Rome they were renamed *opalus*.

Opals have rainbowlike qualities and shifting colors, which make them beautiful, interesting, and highly sought after. In Bedouin lore an opal held lightning and fell from the sky in thunderstorms. In ancient Greece they were thought to have fortune-telling properties and also protect from illness. In Europe the opal represented purity, hope, and truth.

They are said to encourage balance and peace and help you figure out your feelings, rejecting what no longer serves you. Opals often have deep spiritual significance and can help with clarity and intuition.

In addition to being October's birthstone, opals are also associated with the twenty-fourth wedding anniversary.

BIRTH FLOWER
Cosmos

When Spanish explorers brought cosmos home from Mexico in the sixteenth century, these flowers became a favorite of Spanish priests. Cosmos are plants that love the Sun and bloom in a wide variety of colors. They have long, slim stems and blossom for a very long time. They attract birds, bees, and butterflies.

On a symbolic level, when you give someone cosmos, you are basically offering them the universe. They represent harmony, peace, tranquility, joy, and innocence. In the Victorian era they stood for joy in love and life.

Cosmos are widely used in herbalism for their anti-inflammatory, antiviral, and antibacterial properties. In folklore the flowers are said to be lucky and to attract fairies, due to the fact that the magic of the flowers makes fairies feel right at home!

EMBLEMATIC ANIMAL
Dove

The dove is symbolic of peace and love—often used in illustrations of romances and in weddings. In Greek and Roman mythology, they are associated with the goddess of love, Aphrodite and Venus, respectively.

In the Bible, the dove of Christ means salvation, the dove of David peace, and the dove with an olive branch good tidings. This iconography has led to the dove representing harmony over the years.

Doves are friendly and loyal, preferring calm environments. They also like to be helpful. Doves are intelligent and can be trained. Research has shown they are capable of recognizing themselves in mirrors—which isn't something many nonprimates can do.

FAMOUS ANIMAL
Snoopy

Snoopy first appeared in the Peanuts comic strip by Charles M. Schultz on October 4, 1950. Owned by Charlie Brown, Snoopy is a beagle who is prone to amazing flights of fancy. The original drawings are based on Spike, one of Schultz's childhood dogs. Snoopy loves books—both reading and writing them—collects fine art, and is anything but ordinary.

Woodstock the bird is his partner. After all, all Libra creatures prefer a duet.

NATIVE AMERICAN MOON
Hunter's Moon

The Hunter's Moon is tied to the autumnal equinox. When this Moon appeared, it was time for the hunters to gather up as much as they could to prepare for the upcoming winter. And at this time animals were fattening up for the cold season as well. As the fields had been harvested, it was easier to spot the animals.

Another name given to this Moon is the Blood Moon, because of the blood associated with hunting or the color of changing leaves.

Some say you should use the Hunter's Moon to connect with the outdoors and also communicate with ancestors. It is a time for spiritual growth, gratitude, and setting goals.

Born in November

The Sun passes through Scorpio and Sagittarius in November. Sagittarius is the sign associated with explorers and travelers, maps and compasses, vacations and journeys of all kinds. You are a true wanderer if you were born in November. Sagittarius is also the sign linked to travel in the mind. The iPod was launched in November, and BBC Radio starting broadcasting daily in this month in 1922. Scorpio is about passion and obsession. If you were born in November you are drawn to anything that can expand your horizons and broaden your mind—no matter if that's a new life in another place or an intriguing podcast. Scorpio delivers the intense focus. The Berlin Wall came down in November.

The word *trips* has a double meaning. LSD was first synthesized in November of 1938 in Switzerland. The first manned balloon flight also took place in November of 1783 in France. Wander near or far—or just in your mind—you are the adventurer always looking for the next fork in the road.

NOVEMBER FACTS

- November gets its name from the Latin *novem*, meaning "nine," because it was originally the ninth month of the Roman calendar.
- In the Catholic Church, November is traditionally the month to remember those who have died. November 11 is Remembrance Day in the UK, where a two-minute silence is observed at the eleventh hour of the eleventh day of the eleventh month marking the end of hostilities in World War I. The same holiday is known as Armistice Day in the United States.
- November 7 is U.S. Election Day for general elections of federal public officials.
- The fourth Thursday of every November is American Thanksgiving Day. Millions crowd the highways and airports in the days leading up to this to spend the holiday with family.
- November 5 is Guy Fawkes Day or Bonfire Night in the UK, commemorating when Fawkes tried to blow up the houses of parliament in 1605. Bonfires usually

carry a burning effigy of a person, which has become known over time as "the Guy." Traditionally in the UK children would make a "guy" and parade it around the streets asking "penny for the guy," so they could buy fireworks, before throwing it on the bonfire. The actual Guy Fawkes and his fellow traitors met a pretty terrible end: being dragged through the streets of London behind a cart before being hung, drawn, and quartered.

- An old weather saying has it that heavy snow in November will last until April.

BIRTHSTONE
Topaz

Yellowy/amber in color, topaz was one of the stones on Aaron's breastplate in the Bible, which is believed to be where birthstones originate from. The ancient Greeks believed a topaz would make the wearer invisible and give them strength. It is formed from the final stages of rock crystallization. The name originates from the Sanskrit *tapaz,* meaning "fire," and because of its color, some believed that it had the ability to attract gold.

Its health properties were said to be especially beneficial for women, but also against any lung, nose, and throat problems. It was believed to even prevent asthma and epilepsy, and it was used by soothsayers in Asia to be able to get messages from the dead.

Another widely held belief around topaz is that it attracts love. In India it was thought that if you wore it above your heart, it would guarantee long life, beauty, and intelligence. And in the Renaissance period it was believed that it would ward off black magic. Some health properties it is said to have are that it can aid with weight loss and arthritis and, if you put it under your pillow, it can stop you from having nightmares.

BIRTH FLOWER
Chrysanthemum

Chrysanthemums are hugely popular cut flowers with many varieties and available in lots of different colors. They were first cultivated in China in the fifteenth century. Chinese saw the chrysanthemum as a sign of youth that could even prevent gray hair. There is a legend that if you put a petal of one at the bottom of your glass of wine you would live longer.

The word comes from the Greek prefixes *chrysos-*, meaning "gold," and *anthemon-*, meaning "flower." They symbolize friendship, joy, and loyalty, although in parts of Europe they are seen as a symbol of death and mourning. During Victorian times, a chrysanthemum was a gift for friendship and good luck.

Traditionally this is the flower given on Mother's Day in Australia.

EMBLEMATIC ANIMAL
Scorpion

How formidable is a poisonous arachnid predating the dinosaurs, which dances when mating? As dangerous as scorpions are, though, they have many good qualities. They are very determined, brave, and loyal, although they can be prone to jealousy.

In Greek mythology, Orion boasted he could kill every animal on earth. The goddess Artemis dispatched a scorpion to kill Orion, and Zeus put the scorpion in the heavens after it won.

Scorpions are symbols of protection, independence, solitude, and intelligence as well as power and lust.

FAMOUS ANIMAL
Mickey Mouse

Mickey Mouse—perhaps one of the most famous characters in the world—was born on November 18, 1928. Created by Walt Disney in the Scorpio colors of red and black, Mickey is also inseparable from Minnie. This most famous mouse couple has made a fortune for the Disney corporation, thus mixing love and money. Mickey Mouse is adventurous, brave, and lovable, and he even has his own club!

NATIVE AMERICAN MOON
Beaver Moon

This name is said to come from the fact the Native Americans set traps for beavers during this time to ensure they had enough furs to get them through the long winter.

Some say that this Moon is time for letting go of the past and preparing for the coming new year. Because of the cold winter that is about to arrive, it is also sometimes called the Frost Moon.

It is said to be a time of giving and sharing, and in the old days it would mark the end of the hunting season.

But it is definitely a time of preparing for winter both physically and spiritually as it's the last Full Moon before the winter solstice.

Born in December

Christmas is celebrated in December, and the Sun passes through Sagittarius and Capricorn. Sagittarius is associated with the traveling done at this time as the whole world is on the move. Capricorn reveals the other great truth about December: it's about work. The end of the year brings promotions, departures, and appointments. This combination of Sagittarius the traveler and Capricorn the career or college strategist characterizes you if you were born in this month.

Francis Drake began his round-the-world voyage in December of 1577, and the first successful powered flight took place in December of 1903. Capricorn reveals great ambition just as Sagittarius reveals wanderlust. Those with December birthdays have both traits. If you were born in December you set your sights extremely high. This combination of needing to cross the horizon and also make your mark as a success story is a key part of who you are.

DECEMBER FACTS

- *Decem* is Latin for "tenth" as December was originally the tenth month in the Roman calendar. Anglo-Saxons called it Winter Monath.
- December 6 is St. Nicholas Day—he's the patron saint of children.
- This is a month of important religious celebrations, most notably Christmas (Christian) and Hanukkah (Jewish).
- December 21 is the winter solstice, the longest day of the year.
- Weather folklore tells us: "When December is changeable and mild, the whole winter will remain a child."
- The Thirteenth Amendment to the U.S. Constitution abolishing slavery was ratified on December 6, 1865.
- Old English traditions on December 31, New Year's Eve, often center around fire and have pagan tendencies. For example, the Allendale Fire Festival in Northumberland, UK, had a procession carrying tubs of flaming tar above their heads to the town square to throw on a bonfire. At midnight the church bell rang to signify Christianity replacing paganism. An adaptation of this still happens today.

BIRTHSTONE
Turquoise

Turquoise has been mined in Persia, Asia, and the Americas for thousands of years, but was also very popular with the pharaohs and rulers of ancient Egypt. The name is widely accepted to be derived from *Turkey*, through which it is thought it was first brought to Europe. In the Bible turquoise is a sign of hope.

From the thirteenth century, it was said to protect from falling, and it could even foretell disasters by breaking. The Hindu mystics believed that if you saw a turquoise stone after a New Moon it would ensure great riches.

Apache tribal lore says if you followed a rainbow to the end you would find a turquoise, and if you attached it to the end of your bow, it would improve your aim.

Turquoise mainly symbolizes prosperity, but it also offers protection from evil.

BIRTH FLOWER
Narcissus Paperwhite

Narcissus paperwhites grow best from bulbs indoors, although they are native to the Mediterranean. The beautiful white blossom signifies innocence and unconditional love. It is strongly associated with the Asian New Year because it can bloom midwinter.

In Greek mythology Narcissus was fixated on his looks and fell in love with his own reflection in a pool of water, causing him to drown. Flowers were said to have grown where he died—hence the name. Because of this there are some negative associations with vanity, but the flower has other meanings and is commonly used in making perfume.

Symbolically it stands for creativity, inspiration, forgiveness, and vitality.

In Victorian times giving someone a narcissus was saying to them that they were the "one and only." A bouquet of narcissus is said to express love.

EMBLEMATIC ANIMAL
Horse

Of many different breeds, both wild and domesticated, the horse is definitely majestic with its long flowing mane and grace. Fast and also highly sociable, horses are symbolic of strength, determination, and the drive to always move forward. Horses also remind us to be spirited, as they are playful animals.

To Native Americans the horse represented freedom, travel, and movement. The horse was always key in battle and therefore brave. In the Bible, horses are depicted as speedy, fierce, and strong. Humans have very strong bonds with horses as they are both loyal and beautiful.

FAMOUS ANIMAL
Lassie

Lassie—the classic Sagittarian dog—was "born" in a story first published on December 17, 1938. Lassie was a female Rough Collie dog and features in a short story by Eric Knight that was later expanded to a full-length novel called *Lassie Come-Home* published in 1940. Later Lassie became a film star and was first played by a dog called Pal.

Although Lassie was a female character, the female collie originally cast to play her shed too much, which was why she was replaced by Pal who had been a stand-in!

Lassie represented loyalty, unconditional love, kindness, and bravery as she always got help and saved people.

NATIVE AMERICAN MOON
Cold Moon

Unsurprisingly named, the Cold Moon for December requires no explanation. It is sometimes called the Long Night Moon as it comes closest to the winter solstice. Spiritually although it is a cold, dark time, the Cold Moon can be seen as a transition and a mark of hope for brighter things in the future. This is a good time to prioritize your goals for the upcoming year and think about what is really important.

It is also an opportunity to reflect on the past year in preparation for the new one and consider unleashing your creativity and reaching your potential. Celebrate your past successes and put a plan into action for your upcoming ones.

YOUR BIRTHDAY DAY BY DAY

Everyone has a private horoscope—a natal chart or birth chart, based on your time, place, and date of birth—and a public horoscope—a solar chart, based on your Sun sign. Just using your birth date, it is possible to spin out basic natal and solar charts, which show four important angles with ancient names—the Midheaven, the Ascendant, the Descendant, and the Imum Coeli—giving key information about who you are. The twelve houses of the zodiac and their twelve planetary rulers find their own unique places in both charts and add to the interpretation of your character, life, and challenges.

Other unique factors also contribute to making you who you are. The degree and sign of your Sun says a lot using the hundred-year-old technique of Sabian Symbols. The numbers in the birth date offer a numerology profile which supports the messages of astrology and the Sabian Symbols. Thus, the day of your birth even without a year or a time can provide a lot of detail revealing your personality and destiny.

There are over thirty house systems in astrology, but the Natural House and Solar Chart systems used in combination can show your soul's purpose and life patterns clearly. Other methods like Sabian Symbols, once channeled by medium Elsie Wheeler and astrologer Marc Edmund Jones, together with Cheiro—again, over a hundred years ago—confirm what the astrology shows.

What can they say about you? Read on to find out.

JANUARY 1

WHO ARE YOU?

You are the visionary who needs to plant their ideas—and then nurture them. If you are unable to do this, for all your inspiration you may lack the perspiration to establish your efforts. As you grow older, you become more aware of this and learn to fall back on your grounded, earthy Capricorn Sun to develop strategies and practical plans. In this way, you end up having the satisfaction of taking a picture in your mind's eye *and* making it real. Your horoscope suggests you'll travel or move or export to do this.

YOUR DESTINY

This leaning toward other regions, cities, or countries also suggests you'll be miles apart from the people who matter most to you. Your feelings are always tested and proven by long-distance relationships, no matter if this is family or even marriage. Given your yearning for other faces in other spaces, it is no surprise to find that you attract explorers, too. No matter if you are the person making the journey or receiving special visits from afar, these close connections are always proven through travel.

AMBITION AND ACHIEVEMENT

The path to glory is long, but it is also your challenge. You were born with the capacity to make it to the top, but like any true Capricorn, you also know that the mountain goat must take things slowly and be stoic about climbing higher. Your field, profession, or calling in life sets a very high bar. Before you can even attempt this kind of success, you have to manage friendships and also partnerships. This will always be intensely emotional in nature, based on feelings, as the water signs Cancer and Scorpio rule these.

GROUPS AND CIRCLES

The fixed, stubborn Scorpio rules all the groups in your life. Your greatest reward is finding the middle ground with any circle of people, no matter if this is online or in a more formal capacity, like a football team, political party, or orchestra. Discovering a way to dissolve the boundaries between your point of view and the opinions of the rest is worth the effort. You could win every argument if you tried, but the sweetest victory comes when you can manage to bring about a treaty and even lasting achievements.

WHO SHARES YOUR BIRTHDAY?

E. M. Forster, born January 1, 1879
J. D. Salinger, born January 1, 1919
Oumou Sy, born January 1, 1952
Mary Beard, born January 1, 1955

JANUARY 2

WHO ARE YOU?

You are an earth sign and also down-to-earth. You are sensible, grounded, and practical. You also know money does not grow on trees. If you want the huge amount of wealth that you can see is out there for you, it cannot remain as a daydream. You have to reach for it and bring it into your life, where you can invest it in your house, land, apartment, or garden and eventually go traveling. You may even eventually own two homes in two places. Two signs rule finance in your birth chart. One is Taurus and the other is Scorpio. Those cycles work well together in your chart so you are able to ground yourself financially.

YOUR DESTINY

The planet of visions, daydreams, and fantasizing is Neptune, and he rules your ideas. This includes your digital projects as well as your other brain waves and concepts. It is your destiny to escape from the real world by losing yourself in these notions and plans. Experience will teach you that you have to do more than be distracted by what is in your head, though. Only traveling or moving will give you what you need to plant everything where it can grow. You will relocate or emigrate more than once to realize your goals.

THE REALITY OF VICTORY

You were born with the Sun in Capricorn in the Tenth House of ambition and achievement in your birth chart. It is in your nature to try and to win. Life will reward you with plenty of triumphs, and this will also teach you about human nature. For every person who shares in your success and celebrates it with you, there will be others who do not join in. Accepting that this is not your issue is part of being a happy human being. It is also crucial to remember that coming in first does not stop questions and doubts.

THE REWARDS OF SEXUAL PARTNERSHIPS

The emotional water sign Cancer rules your zone of love, sex, engagement, and marriage. In your birth chart, this sign also rules home, household, and family—however you think of that. Your feelings rule. This does not always mean that your emotions are the best guide, but you will always be blessed with a true, deep, soulful understanding of what intimacy brings. The quest is really for equal partnership between two different (very different) human beings. You are in a great position to achieve that. Two-way alchemy is key.

WHO SHARES YOUR BIRTHDAY?

David Bailey, born January 2, 1938
Haruki Murakami, born January 2, 1949
Cuba Gooding Jr., born January 2, 1968
Christy Turlington, born January 2, 1969

JANUARY 3

WHO ARE YOU?

Aquarius rules everything and everybody that is precious to you—in other words, true friends and the people power within a group. In your birth chart, Aquarius the Water Bearer is about pooling resources with others for the common good. In your Capricorn chart, we find the same theme with all that is special and valuable that money cannot buy. You are ambitious. Your crowning achievement is always waiting for you at the top of the mountain. The main story in your life is the pure flow of friendship.

YOUR DESTINY

You are a born academic, author, or student. Less formally, you are a teacher, mentor, guide, and tutor. Virgo with all its pearls of wisdom rules your zone of knowledge. This includes the worldwide web, of course, but also college or university life, as well as libraries. It is very important that you attempt qualifications. We all know that wisdom is not on a scroll, but once you have formal recognition for your special field, it makes a huge difference to your fate in life. It also opens the gates to others.

MANAGING YOUR WORKLOAD

Your Sun in Capricorn is all about climbing to the top professionally or reaching the peak academically. You know this because the mountain is always there in the background, ready to climb. Learning to manage your workload, delegate, and even jettison your tasks is crucial. The planet Mercury in your chart rules not only your knowledge in life—but also your well-being. Awareness of a life-work balance and good health practices is essential. Your body will always tell you when you have taken on too many projects.

FINANCE, BUSINESS, AND INVESTMENT

As a grounded earth sign, you enjoy watching things grow to fruition and appreciate that even a small amount of investment can achieve great things over time. Your ruler Saturn moves in a cycle of 28–29 years and is a symbol of slow progress. Your rewards in life will come from negotiating modest sums but seeing them reap big rewards with enough time, effort, and patience. Your Capricorn Sun makes strong angles to Taurus, the sign of the bull, which also rules gold bullion and bull markets.

WHO SHARES YOUR BIRTHDAY?

J. R. R. Tolkien, born January 3, 1892
George Martin, born January 3, 1926
Jisoo, born January 3, 1995
Greta Thunberg, born January 3, 2003

JANUARY 4

WHO ARE YOU?

You are a born student for life or mentor to others, no matter if you enter academia or leave school when you are still young. You do better when you attain qualifications or even receive honorary degrees, though; it convinces more people to seek you out. This knowledge exchange in your life is also an escape from the real world. (Neptune rules your sector of internet, and so you genuinely surf the web.) The planet Mercury rules your zone of higher learning along with the detail-obsessed sign of Virgo, and these give you your gifts.

YOUR DESTINY

Relationships which revolve around intimacy and property are fated for you. For all that these partnerships, reconciliations, or budding commitments are emotional, the house, land, or apartment is always in the background. The zodiac sign ruling courtship, the bedroom, and children in your birth chart also rules joint finances in your Capricorn chart. Figuring out the dance between yourself and another—or maybe a whole sequence of dance partners—is your life path. It involves a great deal of trust.

THE TRUTH ABOUT SUCCESS

Because you were born with the Sun in Capricorn, the sign of the ambitious mountain goat who climbs to the top, winning is important to you. The truth about success is that it can set you apart from others, too. In fact, for everyone who is cheering you on, when your victories arrive there will also be those who are not on your side. Accepting that this is the reality about being on top is a lifelong challenge. There are other realities, too. When you are at the peak, you may not find it is the answer to everything about yourself and your life after all.

ESCAPING FROM THE REAL WORLD

The planet Neptune and the sign Pisces have a great deal to do with your mindset. Neptune is about holidays from reality, vacations spent surfing, swimming, cruising, or drifting. Pisces the Fish also floats in its own space, far away from everything and everybody else. This is your reward: ideas, theories, and your own realities which allow you to play at life. For all that you are a serious student of life and heavyweight in your chosen field, you have a side which is purely imaginative. There is a part of you which thrives there in a space of wide-open possibilities.

WHO SHARES YOUR BIRTHDAY?

Isaac Newton, born January 4, 1643

Louis Braille, born January 4, 1809

Michael Stipe, born January 4, 1960

JANUARY 5

WHO ARE YOU?

You are the mountain goat, Capricorn, whose next peak is never far away. You have the typical patience and fortitude of your sign and are prepared to take long journeys to get to your next high achievement. Aquarius, the sign of the group, rules your values in life. You know what people power can do and how priceless it is. Sometimes you're inside the circle; sometimes you are far outside it—but you always learn who and what you value most, as a result of those group encounters.

YOUR DESTINY

Learning meditation, cognitive behavioral therapy, or other ways to control your mind to benefit your well-being is part of your path. In your solar chart, your sector of thought is ruled by Pisces, the sign we associate with imagination, intuition, sleep, and the inner life. So you are one of the best qualified people to find ways to harness all that you think, because it so strongly affects how you feel. You will learn a great deal about your unconscious and your dreams as you live your life, Capricorn.

SUCCESS AND ACHIEVEMENT

Learning how to delegate tasks and set priorities is a constant challenge, but it will reward you with a handpicked selection of extremely successful projects. Nobody said being a Capricorn was easy, and you are ruled by Saturn, a symbol of slow, steady progress over time. Learning how to pace yourself is part of that. You are capable of juggling quite a lot, but your most impressive long-term success will come when you set priorities, choose what serves you best, then delegate or even ditch the rest.

FAITH AND FINANCE

Believing that there is enough, or more than enough, is very important. Faith and finance go together in your chart, and understanding banks, charities, and insurance companies may be part of your path. In other cases, it's a broader appreciation of generosity and philanthropy on a more personal level. Another earth sign, Taurus, rules your personal income in your birth chart. Earth signs are practical and "can-do" about life. So are you—or you will train yourself to be and to show others as well.

WHO SHARES YOUR BIRTHDAY?

Jeane Dixon, born January 5, 1904
Umberto Eco, born January 5, 1932
Hayao Miyazaki, born January 5, 1941
Chris Stein, born January 5, 1950

JANUARY 6

WHO ARE YOU?

You are the team player who is still independent and an individual within the wider group of allies and friends. Your access to the good life comes with these groups, clubs, communities, and circles. Scorpio, the sign which controls abundance, rules your sector of collaboration and cooperation. In your birth chart, Aquarius, which rules your unity with others, also happens to oversees finance. You are a joiner, but don't truly merge. A brotherhood and/or sisterhood suits you well.

YOUR DESTINY

Your relationships do not follow a conventional pattern and do not fit any category. Dealing with these complex emotional involvements is easier when you are practical about them. The water sign Cancer, associated with feelings rather than the rational mind, rules partnerships. Cancer also governs pregnancy, babies, and children in astrology. The decisions you make—no matter if you become a parent or not—are always with you. Finding a practical, sensible way to deal with puzzling emotions will always help you.

MANAGING MONEY

In your solar chart as a Capricorn, Leo points to your shared finances, business interests, property, banking, and charity commitments. Leo suggests authority and leadership so its rulership of your solar Eighth House describes your ability to hold the reins. Aquarius also influences your Second House of personal income, in your solar chart. Aquarius is about brotherhood and sisterhood and that affects your approach to all you earn, own, and owe. Second and third opinions from financial professionals can help a great deal, as your horoscope is set up in such a way that you are often spoiled with choices. Knowing who or what to invest in is a particular challenge given your chart. It can help to remember you are an earth sign. Keep your feet on the ground.

EQUAL PARTNERSHIP

Libra the Scales—known as Balance in some languages—is at the very top of your solar chart, showing that your peak achievement will be one or more equal partnerships where you achieve symmetry with the other person, no matter how different you are. Even though you can never escape the question of heirs, spares, or pretenders to your throne—whether you do or do not become a parent—it is the harmony you can achieve in a duet that is most rewarding for you.

WHO SHARES YOUR BIRTHDAY?

Joan of Arc, born January 6, 1412
Syd Barrett, born January 6, 1946
Nigella Lawson, born January 6, 1960

JANUARY 7

WHO ARE YOU?

You are a Capricorn, the patient and sometimes overcautious mountain goat who requires a long time to make decisions and take action. Saturn is your planetary ruler, and he is associated with sands through the hourglass—the slow passage of hours and days. From this comes enlightenment. You are a spiritual being who is always looking for awakening. It can't be rushed, and so through circumstance or choice, you end up stuck in time, but to the benefit of your soul.

YOUR DESTINY

Saturn, your ruler, is associated with reality not fantasy, and yet the real world will often ask you to go within to find answers. The sensitive, emotional water sign Cancer governs your relationships and partnerships. The Buddhist path of nonattachment is a wonderful idea, but the reality is that life brings loss. What you learn, across your lifetime, is that time heals most things. Cancer as the sign of the crab knows when to hide and when to come out. So do you. It soothes heart and soul.

TRAINING YOUR MIND

You have a strong imagination, with Neptune ruling your sector of thought and ideas. This can sometimes work against you, because imagination can take over and replace the real world. Learning to train your mind is important as it will help you develop your own way of meditating, controlling your mental processes, or similar. Neptune also rules sleep and dreams as well as self-hypnosis and the mysterious world of the unconscious mind. This is your challenge.

TRUE LOVE AND PARTNERSHIP

There are no guarantees in love and life, but there is always another precious partnership waiting for you. You were made for marriage or soulmate contracts with Libra, the sign of equality, taking charge of the highest point of your solar chart. This is where your highest achievements and biggest rewards will come from. Libra is the scales—or the balance in other languages—and your mastery of delicate balancing acts between yourself and the person on the other side is an ongoing gift.

WHO SHARES YOUR BIRTHDAY?

Charles Addams, born January 7, 1912
Gerald Durrell, born January 7, 1925
Nicolas Cage, born January 7, 1964

JANUARY 8

WHO ARE YOU?

Self-possessed, strong, and independent, you express the number 1 hidden in your birthday numerology by being out on your own. You are also your own first priority. Saturn rules your Sun sign of Capricorn and is a symbol of great strength and staying power. Where do you learn your ability to defend yourself so well? Your solar chart suggests this comes from the family, which is where you discover what iron willpower means. This may be because of a relative or just your upbringing.

YOUR DESTINY

Aquarius governs who and what you value most—considered to be priceless and understood in terms of all that can't be bought. Aquarius is about people power within a group. It is by being part of these communities or circles, or even by being on the other side of them, that you discover what counts. Pluto, ruling transformation, also controls the teams, clubs, bands, and networks in your life. Pluto brings endings which are also beginnings. These final and first chapters are destined.

MANAGING MONEY

The practical, productive, and methodical earth sign Virgo rules your work sector in your birth chart. You are also an earth sign with your Sun in Capricorn, so you have what it takes to earn steadily by producing reliably great output, be it hit songs—David Bowie, Elvis Presley, and Shirley Bassey all share your birthday—or excellent cakes. You are dedicated and can throw yourself into your job—and earn the financial rewards. People can count on you to deliver, and you can count on yourself to concentrate completely on what you know is so precious.

GROUPS AND FRIENDS

As you have read, people power within a circle can work with you (when you are inside the network) or you can find it challenges you (when you are against the group). Your great challenge in life is to understand the hive mind and how to deal with group dynamics. This is where the potential is, if you want all to benefit, but also where the tests are. Scorpio rules these people in your life, and it is associated with abundance and gain—or waste. Managing allies is also about managing resources.

WHO SHARES YOUR BIRTHDAY?

Elvis Presley, born January 8, 1935
Shirley Bassey, born January 8, 1937
David Bowie, born January 8, 1947

JANUARY 9

WHO ARE YOU?

You are the negotiator and dealmaker who knows how to make a little go a long way. Leo, the sign of leadership, dignity, and confidence, rules your sector of finance, business, charity, and property. You don't see money as about going to the bank or agreeing on a sale or purchase; you see it as a quest worthy of King Arthur and the Knights of the Round Table. The earth sign Taurus rules your personal income in your natal chart. This aligns beautifully with your solid, sturdy Capricorn Sun. You are patient and always plan years ahead.

YOUR DESTINY

Jupiter rules your sector of inner change, and so you always have faith, hope, and optimism about your endless incarnations. This may be tied to spirituality or religion for you. On a more practical note you transform throughout your life, and feeling born again or even being born again is quite natural. If anybody wants to know what's really hidden in your depths, though, it is a mother-child relationship. This may be your own mother or an important child in your life for which you are parent, godparent, aunt, uncle, or grandparent.

LEGACY AND INHERITANCE

Leo ruling your finance, property, business, and charity—perhaps your valuables—is about the dynasty: two or three generations who must share, give, inherit, or make even more dramatic decisions about wealth or assets. When we go to your natal chart, we find Pluto in charge of this. He is a symbol of power and how it is shared between people, young and old. This is a challenge for you in both your solar and birth chart, Capricorn: how to be fair, how to share, how to gratefully receive and to figure terms.

SPIRITUAL AWAKENING

The powerful inner self, soul, and spirit you possess make up one of your most notable qualities. A great deal happens on the inside, as you know. You have regular awakenings during your life, which some might call enlightenment and others might call moments of being born again. Jupiter with all his growth and expansion rules this area of your solar chart, where you must be alone to discover what is possible. You can be stuck for months, even years, if you are not certain about what is true for you. Then, it alters your entire life direction.

WHO SHARES YOUR BIRTHDAY?

Richard Nixon, born January 9, 1913

Joan Baez, born January 9, 1941

Jimmy Page, born January 9, 1944

JANUARY 10

WHO ARE YOU?

With Virgo, the sign of readers, writers, information, and knowledge, in charge of your education, you are a student of life or the perennial student who never stops learning. You could leave school at fifteen but always be powerfully influenced by all the world's libraries. You don't just have interests; you collect books, websites, and/or magazines. Mercury also rules your knowledge zone, and you are Mercurial by nature, always experiencing ups and downs, highs and lows, and bringing others with you on an ever-spinning wheel.

THE WANDERER

Mercury not only rules your sector of knowledge and broad horizons; he also rules your way of life. You are a wanderer who may be drawn to their own space. When we go to your Capricorn chart, we find your biggest horizons and greatest solutions come from within. You have to be alone to find that connection, which is why you may be fond of hiking or just the sort of person who regularly packs their bags. This is more than an instinct. By the time you are in your twenties, you realize that time-outs and time alone are a fantastic remedy.

EVERGREEN RELATIONSHIPS

The challenge for you, Capricorn, is the management of evergreen relationships, as any passionate partnership or marriage is never entirely over for you. It's not rational and not always logical, but then, emotional Cancer rules this side of your life and feelings matter more here than common sense. There is always the potential for someone to come back into your life, either as a friend or a lover. The Moon governs your life within a couple, and as you know, it goes through phases of constant renewal. So do you, with others.

THE PATH OF TRANSFORMATION

You are capable of transforming yourself from within and enjoying more than one reincarnation while you are still here. The planet of growth, hope, expansion, and new possibility is Jupiter, and this governs the most private and hidden areas of your life. Your soul, psyche, and spirit are forever ready to evolve. When the time is right, the world experiences you in a new way, with a new image. When we ask why this occurs, the answer is always with your mother or with your own life as a parent, godparent, uncle, aunt, or grandparent, Capricorn.

WHO SHARES YOUR BIRTHDAY?

Barbara Hepworth, born January 10, 1903

Rod Stewart, born January 10, 1945

Jared Kushner, born January 10, 1981

JANUARY 11

WHO ARE YOU?

The planet of power and control is Pluto, and he rules your groups, friendships, and teams. This works both ways in your life as sometimes it is you against a circle of people—and sometimes all of you against one. Understanding that people are far more influential and effective when they are united is part of your life lesson. The sign of brotherhood and sisterhood, Aquarius rules all that is most precious to you or priceless. Navigating situations with people and their politics is what makes you different and remarkable.

YOUR DESTINY

You are always inspired by the next great idea as Neptune with all his vision rules your sector of plans and projects. The issue is clarity and reality, though. It is too easy to be unfocused, and that can mean some of your highest potential is unrealized. Over time you discover how to use the details, research, and fine-tuned preplanning to take your concepts where they can thrive. With meticulous Virgo overseeing your sector of travel, export, and relocation, it is a down-to-earth approach which will work best with your brain waves.

THE NEGOTIATOR

You are the negotiator and arbitrator, with Libra, the sign of peace, ruling the highest point of your horoscope. One of your greatest accomplishments will be to bring two sides together or settle conflicts between two people. You don't make it look easy, but you do have the right attitude, which understands both halves of an argument or difference. This air sign, associated with fairness and reason, helps you bring a light touch to the personal or professional issues which show in your chart; you are a great peacemaker.

YOUR DUETS AND DOUBLE ACTS

It may be marriage, a professional partnership, or a duet for other reasons, but your life is also about yourself and another navigating the pathways. Libra rules the scales of balance, as you know, and it dominates the top of your horoscope. It is also associated with two people who are different but equal and who must find a way to make their relationship serve both of them. It takes time, but when you make these kinds of dual carriageways work, they can transport you and the other person to amazing discoveries.

WHO SHARES YOUR BIRTHDAY?

Harry Gordon Selfridge, born January 11, 1858
Daryl Braithwaite, born January 11, 1949
Mary J. Blige, born January 11, 1971

JANUARY 12

WHO ARE YOU?

Ambitious and always ready to take your turn at the top, you are the classic Capricorn achiever who will hit the heights more than once in your life. The numeral 1 is hidden in your birth date, and coming first and being number one are very important to you. You also understand hierarchies and how political any large organization or social strata can be. Measuring your steps and knowing when to make your move in times of change are part of your success in life. You understand the way groups operate and how to make them work.

YOUR DESTINY

Large networks of people and smaller circles within are so valuable to you that they are priceless. The sign of communities, Aquarius, rules everything that is precious. This is why you put so much thought and energy into managing your place among others and at work. You also do this in your personal life as this is where you find a sisterhood or brotherhood of similar people can sustain you. This collective may not always be in the headlines in your life, which is so full of dramatic turning points, but it supports you.

MOTHER AND CHILD RELATIONSHIPS

Your relationship with your own mother and/or your own relationship as a parent will be both your greatest challenge and also your greatest achievement. Cancer, ruling family, and its ruler the Moon, which signifies the maternal line, are in charge of your duets and duels. Partnerships or conflicts with others always lead back to the question of offspring—and what is possible spiritually. Your soul is deeply affected by this question, and it is the story of your life, even if it is a private and hidden matter.

HEALING AND THE HEALER

You will take turns at being both the healer and the healed in your life. The sign of the twins, Gemini, rules your health and well-being and also your role as a helper to others. Gemini always shows duality and double acts, so you tend to pair up with people who can match you, even though they are completely different from you. In this way you learn how the transformation of body, mind, or spirit can work. Virgo, the sign of health on all levels, governs your knowledge sector, and this process of being vulnerable or in control educates you.

WHO SHARES YOUR BIRTHDAY?

Jack London, born January 12, 1876
Kirstie Alley, born January 12, 1951
Jeff Bezos, born January 12, 1964

JANUARY 13

WHO ARE YOU?

All that you value most in life is linked to groups. Sometimes you are inside the group; sometimes you are against the group or it is against you. Aquarius, the sign which rules the hive mind, oversees everything which is most precious and priceless to you. When you are dealing with a circle of people whose ideas and opinions are pitched against yours, you realize how true that is. You also place a high price on community. This may be why your life is full of compromises, Capricorn, when you all realize unity and solidarity are worth everything.

YOUR DESTINY

Financial security and a solid footing with the bank are your destiny. The grounded earth sign Taurus rules your savings and profits in your birth chart. As you are also an earth sign, this helps stabilize you all your life, and the perfect angles from Taurus to Capricorn will help you hold on to your savings but also give you a head for business, charity, or economics. The royal Leo rules the property and money, possessions, and assets that tie you to partners or family. You are sovereign here, and your authority comes from that.

KEEPING IT REAL

Your greatest challenge in life is to keep it real. You are a fantasist and dreamer who can often confuse the contents of your imagination with reality. The confused and confusing sign Pisces—the two fish, swimming in opposite directions—rules your mind. This in turn is governed by Neptune, which shows you that often, everything you either want or fear is a projection. Once you realize that what you are experiencing is no more real than a dream or nightmare, you can get to know yourself better and become more mindful and far more grounded.

PEOPLE POWER

Once you learn how to handle group dynamics or the hive mind, you can harness people power and win precious support and backing from the group. There may be more than one group in your life as you go along: a special team, club, or band, for example. As long as you remember to treat each person in the circle as an independent individual, you can maintain what money cannot buy: special allies who together are always protective of you. You are the ambitious Capricorn who can become a leader, captain, or front person here.

WHO SHARES YOUR BIRTHDAY?

Michael Bond, born January 13, 1926
Julia Louis-Dreyfus, born January 13, 1961
Orlando Bloom, born January 13, 1977

JANUARY 14

WHO ARE YOU?

You may or may not have children over the course of your lifetime, but you have a window onto the world of children and teenagers. Leo rules the next generation in your natal chart, but in your Capricorn chart, it also rules the most precious and valuable aspects of your life. You understand how priceless childhood is and why a far younger generation than your own has to be cherished. The innocence and wonder of youthful friendship and play never cease to fascinate you, and these can be very inspiring.

YOUR DESTINY

Going back to your roots and the family tree will always help you throughout your life. It may not be easy, but remembering where you come from will ground you. You are an earth sign, Capricorn, but you can also become ungrounded and lose your balance. In your birth chart, the Moon with all her ever-changing phases rules your relatives and ancestors. As a result, it is all too easy to drift off course where your origins, history, and culture are concerned. The branches of the family tree will always give you something solid to sustain you, if you try.

TRAVEL AND FOREIGNERS

Choosing from the four corners of the world is a lifelong challenge for you. You may be a lifelong traveler or migrant. You may also have a professional life which heavily features foreigners in your destiny. The only issue is selecting who and where (and why). This comes from Neptune stretching across your zones of short and long journeys, leaving you all at sea without an anchor to ground you. It can help to narrow your choices and then use the methodical side of your earth sign nature to carefully set some global priorities.

LEADERSHIP AND AUTHORITY

You are an ambitious Capricorn who always leans toward the person at the top, but also has an eye for the next opportunity to climb in and conquer your profession, industry, or chosen field. Sometimes you can win the top role or position suddenly. This happens when the cycles of time quickly trigger your zone of success and achievement. It can feel like being crowned overnight. Just as often, you will find that when the hierarchy changes at work—or within academia or your unpaid calling—you must always know and trust your loyalties.

WHO SHARES YOUR BIRTHDAY?

Faye Dunaway, born January 14, 1941
Adjoa Andoh, born January 14, 1963
LL Cool J, born January 14, 1968
Dave Grohl, born January 14, 1969

JANUARY 15

WHO ARE YOU?

You are a spiritual or religious thinker by nature, with Pisces and Neptune ruling your sector of ideas and opinions. No matter if you accept or reject dogma, you have your own strong beliefs about the mysteries of life and death and what happens next. This may be heaven, reincarnation, or nothing at all, depending on your personal birth chart. Cancer, associated with extended families, oversees your partnerships. In your own clan and in the family circles you create, you see your doctrine played out.

YOUR DESTINY

You are a scholar, teacher, student of life, or inspiration for others, no matter if you are formally educated or not. Mercury the Messenger rules your sector of knowledge and academia. This is also where we find Virgo with all its focus on meticulous research and respect for the details. You are a natural source of wisdom for others, and what you write, publish, or broadcast carries far and wide, whether online or in the real world. Pearls of wisdom come the hard way—because you are a Capricorn and life is never simple—but the grit adds luster.

ACHIEVEMENT AND AMBITION

Your challenge in life is to pull off as many of your projects and plans as you can without overloading yourself. Saturn rules Capricorn, and it is associated with lead and all heavy weights. Taking on too much is quite natural for you, as you are so goal-driven, but life will show you how to delegate or even abandon what is not your priority. Everything you read about your Sun sign of Capricorn the Goat is true. You have a tremendous sense of mission and will patiently work very hard to make it, but you must find a system.

THE ESCAPE ARTIST

Not surprisingly, you are an escape artist, too, because life can be intense, demanding, and sometimes far too serious. Neptune and Pisces the Fish are associated with holidays from the everyday, and as they also rule your mind, you need to get away. Being on or near the water can do this for you. However, meditation, daydreaming, or even fantasy role-playing and acting can do this as well. Anything allowing you to disconnect, drift off, and remove yourself from the world is also part of your personality and your rewards in life too.

WHO SHARES YOUR BIRTHDAY?

Saint Mary MacKillop, born January 15, 1842
Martin Luther King Jr., born January 15, 1929
Jaune Quick-to-See Smith, born January 15, 1940
Claudia Winkleman, born January 15, 1972

JANUARY 16

WHO ARE YOU?

You can't buy freedom, as you know. You place a very high value on your independence, though, as a result of being put in situations where you want space more than anything else. In astrology, the planet Uranus is associated with liberty and also liberation. He rules all the things you find so precious they are priceless in your life. You are deeply intuitive and learn to use your sixth sense to help you find the way out of personal or work situations whenever you feel confined. Your extrasensory perception is a great asset.

YOUR DESTINY

It is your destiny to be wealthy if you accept what is on offer. In your birth chart, Taurus—with all its links to gold bullion and bull markets—rules your finances. Taurus is an earth sign like your own, and cycles which pass through this point in your chart always make stunning trines to your Capricorn Sun. As a practical mountain goat, you know that daydreaming about being rich is not enough. When the promise appears, you must take action. Property or travel motivate you to reach for more.

THE PUZZLE OF RELATIONSHIPS

The sensitive, emotional water sign Cancer rules your relationships. This is where you are most likely to feel all at sea. There is nothing logical about feelings. The solution is to remember you are an earth sign and to use your common sense to shift any situation which puzzles you to a place where you feel both your feet are on the ground. Neptune rules your mind, and this may explain why approaching partners, lovers, or children as a Rubik's Cube to solve can leave you drifting. Taking firm action is much better.

THE STRATEGIST

You are a strategist, like the mountain goat you are associated with. The clever sign Gemini and Mercury, the planet of quick thinking, both rule your day-to-day existence, and you can be quite cunning. Your highest achievement is actually balance, order, peace, and harmony. If that means preempting situations where you can see potential issues at work or in your personal life, then you will not hesitate. You are a one-person UN Peacekeeping Force but also something of a chess master.

WHO SHARES YOUR BIRTHDAY?

Dian Fossey, born January 16, 1932

Susan Sontag, born January 16, 1933

Kate Moss, born January 16, 1974

JANUARY 17

WHO ARE YOU?

You are a hardworking Capricorn, ruled by Saturn, which in turn rules lead weights and heavy situations. Even though you have great staying power, you learn that delegating and sometimes off-loading your many plans and responsibilities are the only answer. Without regular reviews of how and why you work—particularly as some of it will be unpaid or involve study—you will not achieve your greatest potential. Your own planet Saturn is here to teach you that responsibilities must be balanced.

YOUR DESTINY

You are an earth sign, practical and productive by nature, and will become financially comfortable, and even wealthy, if you remember that money does not grow on trees, but cultivating a growing investment is wise. The solid earth sign Taurus, which is associated with the bull, gold bullion, and the charging Wall Street bull, makes a perfect trine to your own Capricorn Sun, and the cycles of time will help you manage your business interests, property, and valuables to your advantage without losing your enjoyment of life.

THE BUILDER

You are a builder by nature and will regularly face two choices: to go back and rebuild structures in your personal or work life or to walk away and lay new foundations. Capricorn the Goat climbs to the top, and you are drawn toward the heights. Not everything in life can last forever, though, so you will regularly find that you are challenged to go back to situations and repair them or abandon what was there and start again. Like all natural builders, you know when it's worth it and when it's plainly not.

PASSIONATE PARTNERSHIP

You will be drawn toward one or more passionate partnerships over your lifetime, with the emotional water sign Cancer in charge of engagement, love, sex, living together, and marriage. Feelings, not facts, always dominate you, and so you understand poets and musicians better than most. You understand about the complexity of two hearts beating as one, for example—or just that Cure song about going to bed. When you can achieve symmetry and harmony with one so different, but equally, you truly have it all.

WHO SHARES YOUR BIRTHDAY?

Benjamin Franklin, born January 17, 1706
Eartha Kitt, born January 17, 1927
Susanna Hoffs, born January 17, 1959

JANUARY 18

WHO ARE YOU?

You are the natural bohemian who favors a more expressive, creative approach to yourself and your life. You are a Capricorn, which reveals itself in your approach to money, but you also have Neptune, the planet of escapism, in charge of your thoughts and ideas. Neptune in turn rules Pisces the Fish, which symbolize other worlds and other realities. You are tuned in to a completely different universe which you make all your own and only you understand. Can others be allowed to share your holidays from reality? Perhaps.

YOUR DESTINY

The world of children and young people is written into your chart as Leo, the sign which rules infants, students, and teenagers, dominates everything that is so precious to you it is priceless. This is where you leave your legacy, no matter if you have children, stepchildren, godchildren, young relatives, or not. The next generation—and perhaps the one after that—inherits your respect for their world. You know how to cherish and protect that private universe of innocence and play. This makes you a good parent or substitute parent.

FINANCE AND BALANCE

As you know, Leo the Lion rules over everything that is valuable to you and others in your chart. Leo is about leadership, and you associate authority with generosity, philanthropy, or charity. This can describe taxation for some Capricorns and, in other cases, good causes. You will experience being a have and also a have-not at different times in your life, but your ideas about who or what makes a suitable boss or authority are based on your values and those of others. You have what it takes to be a generous donor.

BUILDING AND REBUILDING

You are ruled by Saturn, which is an astrological symbol associated with staying power and patience. When your personal or work life is worth it, you will go back and rebuild no matter what happens. You are also practical enough to know when to walk away and start again. Renovating and returning are part of your life path, as is starting from scratch. What is made to endure in your life will be reinforced by you and become stronger because of your dedication. However, you are gifted at laying foundations for better structures, too.

WHO SHARES YOUR BIRTHDAY?

A. A. Milne, born January 18, 1882
Cary Grant, born January 18, 1904
Philippe Starck, born January 18, 1949

JANUARY 19

WHO ARE YOU?

You are an escape artist who travels or relocates to get away from the real world. Neptune rules your sector of short journeys and neighboring countries and states. Neptune is a symbol of holidays from reality, vacations from the everyday. Mars, the planet of action and impulse, is in charge of your homelife, hometown, homeland, houses, and apartments. You can be prone to leaping before you look, but that does not stop you from trying again. Mercury with his winged sandals and helmet rules your lifestyle.

YOUR DESTINY

Money will give you authority and leadership or add to your role at work or in your personal life. You are destined to rise to a position where you influence and inspire others, or you may find that you are born into that through your family. The security of having solid wealth helps you command respect from others, but as a Capricorn, you attract that anyway, as you are a grounded, mature, sensible earth sign who is patient and cautious by nature. What you end up doing with your money is the most important thing.

YOUR SPIRITUALITY

You may or may not be religious, but you are a spiritual person who will not make the big moves in life without inner certainty. This does not happen overnight, and it is often when you are caught between the present and the future that you find inspiration comes. You are a typical Capricorn, the sign of patience, ruled by Saturn, which oversees the slow passage of time. These long intervals in your life when it is impossible for you to act on family, for example, or direction give your soul its necessary enlightenment.

PARTNERSHIPS AND DUETS

The Moon rules your partnerships and duets, through the sign of Cancer, which is opposite your own. You are emotional, sensitive, powered by feelings and passing emotions when it comes to marriage, say, or even a platonic double act. Your chart is set up in such a way that the cycles of time will repeatedly put you at a crossroads in love or work pairings. Together or apart? Together but also apart? These are the questions which will follow you around all your life, particularly when two different locations call.

WHO SHARES YOUR BIRTHDAY?

Paul Cézanne, born January 19, 1906

Janis Joplin, born January 19, 1943

Dolly Parton, born January 19, 1946

JANUARY 20

WHO ARE YOU?

You are comfortable and also comforting, as you are at ease with yourself and this has its own star quality. You know you are not the same as everybody else and yet you can enjoy the difference. You are drawn to well-made clothes, designed objects, and most of all, gardens. The gorgeous appeal of nature at her wildest is something that never fails to attract you; Mother Nature has a rhythm that you understand. You know who and what to let into your world, and the invitation is irresistible to people who admire you from afar.

YOUR DESTINY

Groups, circles, communities, and networks are at the foundation of your life. People who can happily coexist because they are the same, but different, are underneath all that happens to you—and all that you make happen. You understand the need for space and separateness, even within a team, club, or similar collectives. It is this freedom to be oneself without feeling crowded that some people need, and you draw a great deal from that. Together allies and friends can feed from the same source without ever crowding each other.

FINANCIAL MANAGEMENT

The great challenge of your life is to make a little go a long way or sometimes a lot—depending on how wealthy you are at the time. How you invest what you have and where you do so is one of your recurring tests. The family tree is never far from this question nor are your ambitions. Then there is the question of unfinished business, which must be finished or even replaced with towering achievements. The longer you procrastinate, the more it becomes obvious that good financial advisors are very precious.

THE NEXT GENERATION

Your reward in life is the next generation. This may be your own child, stepchild, godchild, grandchild, niece, or nephew. It can also be children or young adults as a whole, thanks to your career or your unpaid work. The next generation with all its lack of judgment, embrace of life, and openness is always there to greet you. The cycles of time guarantee that just when one generation has passed into adulthood, another will appear. In this way you are reminded why life is worth living. You've earned it.

WHO SHARES YOUR BIRTHDAY?

Aristotle Onassis, born January 20, 1906

Buzz Aldrin, born January 20, 1930

Sophie, Duchess of Edinburgh, formerly Countess of Wessex, born January 20, 1965

JANUARY 21

WHO ARE YOU?

You prefer to move in your own world far away from other people and real life. You make a good escape artist and feel completely at home when you are taking a holiday from normality and reality. Others are fascinated by you from a distance but find it hard to get close to you. It takes a lot for you to meet people halfway and join their universe, and so if you choose to do that, it involves making the journey of a lifetime, away from your solitary lifestyle. Your life can seem like a vacation to others.

YOUR DESTINY

You are the exporter, traveler, and/or migrant who must take yourself and your plans far from home in order to find the right place for your ideas. The planet of action, Mars, rules these journeys, which you may take with bags packed or just online. You can be ungrounded, and if you want to succeed, it is important that you center and focus before you attempt these ambitious ventures to try your luck in other regions. You are an explorer at heart and often find the right reception for you is abroad.

FAMILY AND ROOTS

Your great challenge is to manage the family tree with all its tests of your judgment, time, and energy. Even in childhood it does not offer you the permanence and stability that others have. All your life, thanks to the cycles of time in the fixed sign sectors of your horoscope, nothing is forever, so different branches of your family will always require maintenance. It seems that your town, country, origins, heritage, and roots are also a work in progress or a process of never-ending change and challenge.

THE MULTITASKER

You are a multitasker with the ability to juggle several plans at once, and you have the potential to make an impact across your country or around the world. You are restless, never particularly tied to your hometown or homeland and always searching for the next horizon. This can make life feel unsettled and uncertain, as you know, but it is also true that your instincts are right about your talents, skills, abilities, or output. You are a balancer, juggler, and world citizen.

WHO SHARES YOUR BIRTHDAY?
Grigori Rasputin, born January 21, 1869
Christian Dior, born January 21, 1905
Cat Power, born January 21, 1972

JANUARY 22

WHO ARE YOU?

You are both the receiver and giver when it comes to money and will take turns at being the generous donor or lender as well as the grateful recipient in your life. The cycles of time passing through the zodiac affect your financial sectors, as the signs of benevolence are Taurus and Scorpio and in your natal chart they reveal charity toward family, partners, and friends in your Second House and philanthropy on a bigger scale with organizations in your Eighth House. You will learn a lot about human nature through your experience of charity or philanthropy. Perhaps charity begins at home for you—or always did. Maybe this is about your career or unpaid efforts, but either way it's a lifelong education.

YOUR DESTINY

You are a peacemaker who will be drawn into conflicts in your personal and professional life in order to resolve them. This comes from Libra, the sign of symmetry, harmony, and justice, which dominates your solar chart patterns. A friend to all, you have a unique gift for ending battles or differences between people, whether within your family circle, among friends, or at work. You can bring two sides together even when it seems impossible as you can also see both sides, too. This is the humanitarian in you.

DISTANCE AND RELATIONSHIPS

You have two chart patterns which connect your relationships to journeys and even relocation. Your greatest challenge is to navigate long-distance partnerships or other close connections with people. Mercury the Messenger has winged shoes and a winged helmet, and as he looms over your chart, the distances can sometimes be immense. When you cross the map to be with others, you also cross emotional boundaries, too, and the trip or move itself proves how deep the feelings run.

INTUITION AND BIG DECISIONS

With extrasensory perception showing up in your chart thanks to Neptune, you have a sixth sense, particularly about situations which put you at a crossroads. You will learn to fall back on your intuition in order to make the right decisions, because you have to. As a peacemaker you are also naturally drawn to considering both sides or feeling the pull of two completely opposite directions in an equal way. This duality can be perplexing until you realize that it is your gut feelings and instincts which will help you most.

WHO SHARES YOUR BIRTHDAY?

Lord Byron, born January 22, 1788

Jim Jarmusch, born January 22, 1953

Michael Hutchence, born January 22, 1960

JANUARY 23

WHO ARE YOU?

You live in a world of readers, writers, students, and teachers, no matter if they have a formal role or not. Uranus rules your friends and acquaintances, and this planet in turn rules publishing, education, some sections of the media, the worldwide web, and academia. As an innovator, you are personally governed by Uranus, the planet of all that is unpredictable. Life is a series of highs and lows, and you take turns at being spectator or mover and shaker. It makes you philosophical.

YOUR DESTINY

Your solar chart is set up in such a way that it is hard to own your family tree, origins, roots, history, and culture. It takes effort to find this and become grounded. The effort is worth it, because it helps to center you. Uranus is a fixed sign, just like the fixed planets influencing where you come from—your relatives, immediate family, and ancestors. You can get stuck in a mental or emotional rut until you learn to go back to where you come from spiritually. This makes every relationship look better.

ESCAPING AND RECONNECTING

You value escapism very highly, but know that you cannot buy a holiday from reality. Being in your own world, far removed from the everyday, is so precious to you that it is priceless. Your challenge is to enjoy the vacation from normality without drifting away from other people. Neptune and Pisces have charge of all that you value most, and they are associated with those who are at home in their own company, enjoying their own private world. Meeting others halfway is hard but worth it.

THE COMMUNITY

Your reward in life is the community or circle around you, which can hold other circles, too. You are a true Aquarian who can draw a great deal from the wider group. Aquarius is the water bearer, which was actually a job in Rome. Supplying the communal baths was the work of the aquarii. You give or share with your network but also receive, as these people may never be very close to you or each other, but they are the spiritual gift that keeps on giving. They will feed your soul if you want that.

WHO SHARES YOUR BIRTHDAY?

Édouard Manet, born January 23, 1832

Anita Pointer, born January 23, 1948

Robin Zander, born January 23, 1953

JANUARY 24

WHO ARE YOU?

You are the romantic of astrology, and with Gemini, the sign of the heavenly twins, in charge of your heart, you believe in twin souls—even if you find more than one person who performs that role for you. Gemini is about two people who are the same, but different, and when you fall in love, it may feel as if you are from the same spiritual family. The fire sign Leo rules your commitments, be they partnership or marriage, so there is always great heat in these double acts. The flame is very hard to extinguish.

YOUR DESTINY

With Cancer, the sign which rules houses, apartments, gardens, and towns, in charge of work, you tend to make your home—or next home—the goal. As a result you can sometimes overburden yourself with too many projects and plans, along with all the other tasks you are not paid for. This is a repeated pattern in your life, but over time you learn to delegate or get rid of the nonessentials. There is no point in carrying too much in order to have the dream of security or property when your life itself is all work and no play.

THE RIGHT PATH FOR TWO

Navigating the right path for two people is a recurring theme for you, no matter if this is your marriage or a professional partnership. Libra rules your travel and relocation, and so the scales have to be balanced between yourself and another before you can make a move. This question about what is fair between two sides, or two people, will repeat in your life every time you must choose between two homes, two workplaces, two cities, or even two countries. It's a challenge that is fated.

SOLITUDE AND FAITH

Hidden behind all these messages about twin souls in love, or two people who must find the right path, is a strong message about being alone. You are a hermit, as much as you are a partner, and it is only when you are alone that you find wisdom. Saturn rules your introspection, religion, spirituality, therapy, dreams, Tarot, meditation, and inner life. Saturn is an ancient symbol of life lessons, and you can only really uncover the deepest truths about yourself and the world when you are quite, quite alone.

WHO SHARES YOUR BIRTHDAY?

Edith Wharton, born January 24, 1862
Maria Tallchief, born January 24, 1925
Neil Diamond, born January 24, 1941
Mischa Barton, born January 24, 1986

JANUARY 25

WHO ARE YOU?

You place an extremely high value on being in your own space, taking all the time you want, and disconnecting from everything and everybody if you wish, for long periods of time. You are a dreamer and drifter by nature with Neptune ruling all that you consider to be beyond price. Neptune is associated with the ocean, so you tend to cruise through life on a permanent holiday from normality. It is a tremendous effort for you to connect with others, or for them to connect with you, but well worth it.

YOUR DESTINY

You are the craftsperson, artisan, or true professional who always has something special to offer. The issue for you is where and when, as it is all too easy for you to become so absorbed in your idea that you miss your chance. Aries rules your sector of projects, plans, and proposals. This sign has a reputation for making a bold and energetic start, but it is the perspiration as well as the inspiration which will make all the difference to you. Your concepts or products were meant to travel.

FEELING AT HOME IN THE WORLD

It is a lifelong quest for you to feel at home in the world because of the nature of your extended family tree, which has never been settled. You have to meet change with change when it comes to your relatives, and deciding if you have the time, energy, and commitment to do that is a regular challenge. It is the same in terms of your town, local area, and country. Aquarius, your chart shows fixed signs at odds with each other, leading from the sector of place and belonging. It takes work to feel at home.

SPECIAL PARTNERSHIPS

You will find a series of special partnerships throughout your life which allow you the space you need. You are also more than happy to give others the same independence. Finding different ways to be with somebody asks you both to be creative, lateral thinking, and wise, but you have what it takes to find unique pathways which have not been mapped out for you. The unconventional relationship or unorthodox double act comes naturally to you, and finding your own way together is very rewarding.

WHO SHARES YOUR BIRTHDAY?

Virginia Woolf, born January 25, 1882

John Cooper Clarke, born January 25, 1949

Alicia Keys, born January 25, 1981

JANUARY 26

WHO ARE YOU?

The power planet in your chart is Pluto, who rules your mission and position in life. You are a heavyweight who is prepared to do what it takes to get to the peak of your professional career, academic career, or the highest reaches of high society. With assertive, fearless Aries in charge of your communication, you know how to get your message across and hit all the right targets. You may not be aware of your

Capricorn nature, which is hidden in your sector of the unconscious, but you are inwardly extremely ambitious.

YOUR DESTINY

As an Aquarian, your personality and destiny are always linked to the group. This may be a formal circle of people like a team, club, union, or band. It may also be purely social or informal. Either way, how you deal with the hive mind is central to your fate. Sometimes you will be on the outside and learn crucial lessons about how people operate together. You will also see for yourself what it feels like to be part of a network or community which uses people power to achieve what would be very difficult with just one.

CIRCLES UPON CIRCLES

The ripple effect between your immediate social circles and the wider spheres connected to that influence your whole life, and your challenge is organizing this and managing it. Like any true Aquarian, you believe in tribes, but preferably with a great deal of space and independence offered to every individual. From your teenage years you learn how crucial the broader community of your allies and friends is to your soul. The test is figuring out how tribal thinking works and the way to be happy with it.

UNITY AND SOLIDARITY

Your firm belief in the right for every person in a group to be a distinct and different individual is idealistic as the reality is this can sometimes break apart unified people power. Again, this is something you realize from your teenage years on, and it will be both a life lesson and huge reward. The beauty of diversity and equality within an effective community adds to what you can all build together. Nobody said it would ever be easy—and it still won't be, whatever your age—but the results are a gift.

WHO SHARES YOUR BIRTHDAY?

Paul Newman, born January 26, 1925

Eddie Van Halen, born January 26, 1955

Ellen DeGeneres, born January 26, 1958

JANUARY 27

WHO ARE YOU?

Money and spirituality go together in your life with Neptune, the planet of faith and belief, ruling your finances. This can mean charity plays as much of a part as the church. In other cases, charity begins at home. Pisces the Fish, about compassion and sympathy and linked to Neptune, is in charge of your Second House of banking. So the most sensitive sign of the zodiac and the planet most associated with compassion both influence your approach to money. Having been helped yourself, you are sensitive to the needs of others all your life. The caring Cancer rules your sector of service. You may consider it your duty or the duty of others—even big organizations—to look after people.

YOUR DESTINY

You are destined to become a student of life, tutor, academic, author, or web writer. With Gemini, the sign of information and communication, so prominent in your chart, you are a natural teacher to your own or other people's children. Other people talk about learning or think about writing, but with Mars the action planet ruling your sector of internet, media, education, and publishing, you act. Mercury the Messenger rules everything that is precious and even priceless to you, so your particular message is your legacy.

BATTLES AND PEACEMAKING

The noble Leo the Lion with all its heroic qualities and courage rules your sector of duels and differences. Your astrological chart is set up in such a way that you will repeatedly be called upon to resolve disputes and conflicts by taking the lead. Aquarius the Water Bearer is, of course, your central Sun sign and a symbol of friendship and humanitarianism. It's not hard for you to be the peacemaker in your personal or professional life because you believe in people power. You can see the bigger picture of what is possible.

PLANTING GREAT IDEAS

The enthusiastic, adventurous, and energetic fire sign Aries rules your ideas. This same sector of your horoscope also rules travel and the worldwide web. You have always finished one mission or are about to start another, owing to the way your horoscope is set up. The issue is always the same: where to plant your brain wave or concept. Aries and its planet Mars are associated with great speed and impulse. This gets you going, but a lifelong lesson to slow down and do the research will make the difference with your success.

WHO SHARES YOUR BIRTHDAY?

Wolfgang Amadeus Mozart, born January 27, 1756

William Randolph Hearst, born January 27, 1908

Mikhail Baryshnikov, born January 27, 1948

Bridget Fonda, born January 27, 1964

JANUARY 28

WHO ARE YOU?

Your Sun sign Aquarius rules group psychology and people power in a circle. You will sometimes be up against that as others oppose you together—and sometimes you will be very much part of the community dealing with an outsider. Through this, you come to understand how people think as one and why communication is the answer to any complicated situation. In fact, it is by understanding the dynamics of a team, club, or other network that you can achieve the impossible and create unity and closeness.

YOUR DESTINY

The sign of compassion, sympathy, and understanding is Pisces and as this sign rules money for you, you do not see the usual boundaries that come with business or banks. You are a natural philanthropist and generous with family, friends, or strangers with the same amount of feeling. The cycles of time show that you will know what it is like to depend on others for help, and as a result of that, you are the first to give back. Pisces, as the sign governing your income, is associated with charity, starting inside the home or outside it.

KEEPING IT REAL

You are an escapist who is so comfortable with your own private universe that you can forget there is a real world at all. You value these holidays from reality so highly that you will put them first and leave normal life and other people far behind. You need to get away from everything that is all too real in your life by floating in your own space. This can also create issues for you with other people who find you inaccessible. It can also take you too far away from regular, ordinary life. A compromise can be useful.

COMFORT AND THE GOOD LIFE

The rich reward of all you do—no matter if it is dealing with groups, dealing with money, or dealing with yourself—is comfort and beauty. You can find this in nature, in the garden, or just at home. The grounded earth sign Taurus rules your sense of place and belonging. You tend to plant yourself solidly where you feel happiest, and that is always an environment which is both green and private. You become a different person when you are surrounded by natural beauty. Style is as important to you as your surroundings.

WHO SHARES YOUR BIRTHDAY?

Colette, born January 28, 1873

Alan Alda, born January 28, 1936

Elijah Wood, born January 28, 1981

JANUARY 29

WHO ARE YOU?

Aquarius is the sign of the water bearer who helps the group pool its resources. This is always with you, in the background, from childhood into old age. Your most transformative experiences will always come when you reach those forks in the road that liberate you to join those groups. You are an air sign and live in a world of ideas, opinions, thoughts, and theories. The sign of defense—Aries—rules this in your solar chart so you are always on guard. In your birth chart, it is Gemini which rules the same sector for you.

YOUR DESTINY

Aquarius is the sign which describes the hive mind, people power, and the community, as you know. Part of your destiny is dealing with the reality of groups. You are a strategist who is always several steps ahead, and it is your fate to manage the complications that come with networks of people. Rival teams are a fact of life, and this extends far beyond sport to politics, for example. This is where you can beat everything and everybody if you try. In fact, your ability to identify issues before they arise is a lifelong asset.

THE JOURNEY AND THE GROUP

Sagittarius rules the most important collections of people in your life. And this sign is in charge of journeys, exploration, and adventures. You understand that in order to maintain your relationships with people in a band, club, team, society, and so on you have to leave them. Your challenge in life is to honor your own need to get away by yourself (touring or even relocating) but at the same time leave things in a good place, so you can rethink the network when you come back. Thanks to the cycles of time, your life ebbs and flows.

UNDERSTANDING YOUR AQUARIUS PATH

You are a strategist, peacemaker, and communal thinker who will find the reward of true cooperation in a group—a worthwhile reward for all the time and energy required. An aquarius in ancient Rome was literally the water bearer who supplied the baths, where the community gathered from all walks of life. Diversity and equality, tolerance and space, mutual respect and shared rewards will often seem so hard to achieve in your life, but you will not be satisfied until you achieve those goals. Rich fulfillment follows.

WHO SHARES YOUR BIRTHDAY?

Germaine Greer, born January 29, 1939

Oprah Winfrey, born January 29, 1954

Roddy Frame, born January 29, 1964

JANUARY 30

WHO ARE YOU?

You are an extremely successful, determined person who carves out their niche and still finds a place at the top anyway. You can also respect the rules of a professional or academic game and follow the steps, patiently arriving at the peak. The focused Scorpio rules your career as well as your place in society. Scorpio in turn is ruled by Pluto with all his power and control. You dominate your chosen sphere and are unconsciously ambitious, as Capricorn oversees your inner life.

YOUR DESTINY

You have a habit of attracting big ideas and huge plans, which occasionally make it all the way to success. But sometimes they do not, and the lessons you learn from this make you very careful about nurturing the concepts or projects that do arise. Finding the right time and place for what you know has vast potential is not easy. However, the research you do will be worth it. Mars is the planet which has the most influence over this area of your life—linked to energy, impulse, and big beginnings. Follow-through is key.

GROUP DYNAMICS

With the Sun in Aquarius, the sign of teams, clubs, circles, and communities of all descriptions, you are most challenged by the independence and individuality of others, as these can lead to situations where it's all too easy for team spirit to vanish. More than once since childhood you will have seen the incredible potential of people power come to nothing because of a lack of organization and harmony. As a result of that, you become skilled at drawing people together and even pulling off miraculous feats of unity.

ENJOYING ALTERNATIVES

Your ruling planet of Uranus is associated with alternatives of all kinds and all that is unconventional and unique, unexpected, and often bohemian. You are two people in one body: Part of you is commanding, ambitious, and a little old before your time. You are also forever young, as a playful, experimental part of you is only too happy to operate outside the everyday, the normal, and the ordinary. Not everyone appreciates or understands that, but like-minded souls or admirers will be captivated.

WHO SHARES YOUR BIRTHDAY?

Franklin D. Roosevelt, born January 30, 1882

Phil Collins, born January 30, 1951

Olivia Colman, born January 30, 1974

JANUARY 31

WHO ARE YOU?

You like to follow what the group is doing: you trust trends, movements, and the wisdom of the crew. Aquarius is the zodiac sign associated with networks. You are a joiner and follower by nature and will leave all that you know in order to be part of something greater than yourself. You *could* do it alone, but throughout your life you will find it's just as easy to take your part in a collection of people who also share your vision. You are by nature a traveler, explorer, or migrant. You wear racing stripes all your life.

YOUR DESTINY

There are no guarantees in life, but the more often you pursue your mission in another part of the country or another part of the world, the better your odds of success are. You tend to do better with your plans when you join the equivalent of a boom or gold rush. You dislike being left behind and are often in the first wave of anything—on the spot to sign up or join in from the get-go. Sometimes it does not work. But you are always ready to go back for more adventures because, in your view, the journey matters as much as the destination.

FINDING THE RIGHT PATH

Nobody could doubt your optimism. There is so much to admire about your pioneering spirit. The way your birth chart and Aquarian chart are both set up, though, suggests the occasional risk, too. Finding the right path—the safer path—to get to where you need to be is a good idea. You have already learned from experience that if you travel, migrate, or export what you have, against the advice that comes to you from the universe, you can stumble. Sometimes it's your best friend who will warn you; at other times, it's just a friendly face in the pack. When this happens, check alternative paths.

MONEY, POSSESSIONS, AND ESCAPING FROM REALITY

Your solar chart shows Pisces, an emotional sign rather than a practical one, rules your sector of possessions, business, money, and security. You are far more interested in the destination than in what you have in your luggage. In fact, you travel light when it comes to all that you own or have earned. You are not weighed down by matters of finance or materialism and have very little attachment to property. The lure of new pastures is far more important to you than getting stuck with real estate. Life is so often a holiday waiting to happen.

WHO SHARES YOUR BIRTHDAY?

Derek Jarman, born January 31, 1942

John Lydon (aka Johnny Rotten), born January 31, 1956

Justin Timberlake, born January 31, 1981

FEBRUARY 1

WHO ARE YOU?

You believe in a sanctuary with Taurus, the sign of security and comfort, in charge of your home and household zone. Taurus is an earth sign, grounded in the real world. Cancer, on the other hand, rules your lifestyle and daily routine, and as it is the realm of mothers and grandmothers, the female influence is strong in your life and evident in your house, garden, or apartment. You form partnerships with people who believe in heirs, spares, and pretenders to your throne as royal Leo rules this sector of your chart. Who will they be?

YOUR DESTINY

You are an Aquarian, above all, and ruled by Uranus, which suggests freedom is crucial to you no matter how hard it is to find. Regular revolutions and radical, liberating, exhilarating changes are shown in your chart, thanks to the cycles of time. Only you can make this happen, and the process is psychological and spiritual, as much as it is connected to your work, personal, or home situation. You have to set yourself free, and that can only occur when you replace thought with action. These breaks for freedom characterize you.

THE RIGHT DIRECTION

You do not lack energy when it comes to your ideas, projects, and plans. The fire sign Aries rules your sector of brain waves and concepts. Aries is direct, fearless, and impulsive. This may explain why you are so quick to launch what matters to you. The only issue is the rest of the journey, as finding the right direction and the right place for your work is so important. The occasional wasted enterprise will teach you that it's not enough to push forward; you have to do the research. You need a map, some homework, and focus.

FINANCIAL SECURITY

As you know, down-to-earth Taurus governs your house, apartment, and any property investment. You also have security-conscious Cancer ruling your everyday life and routine. To complete this picture of financial grounding, we have Virgo—another earth sign, like Taurus—in charge of joint banking, investment, or business. Virgo is an astute sign, very good with detail and firmly planted in the real world. Your reward in life will always be more than enough money. You hang on and hold on rather than waste your resources.

WHO SHARES YOUR BIRTHDAY?

Terry Jones, born February 1, 1942
Meg Cabot, born February 1, 1967
Harry Styles, born February 1, 1994

FEBRUARY 2

WHO ARE YOU?

The world of children and teenagers is never very far from your own, and your window on younger people influences you. The innocence of youth and the particular kinds of friendships infants or students have with each other have an impact on who you are and what you do. This may be your own son, daughter, stepchild, niece, nephew, godchild, or grandchild. It may be younger people as a whole. You can never be part of this world and you can never go back, although a pure, playful approach to life can be tried.

YOUR DESTINY

With Libra, the sign of two sides, two halves, two parts, in charge of your travel, you are destined to always balance two places. These may be towns, cities, states, and/or countries. This balancing act may exist because of your career or thanks to the cycles of time and the way fate takes you in your personal life. This area of your horoscope is also about knowledge, both accumulated and passed on. Going between such very variable locations and trying to respect their differences educates you but also helps to teach others.

PARTNERSHIPS AND RELATIONSHIPS

Your greatest challenge in life is unique relationships or unconventional partnerships. These can appear to be like puzzles, board games, crosswords, or tests of logic. Gemini and Mercury, the planet of the mind, rule over your sector of romance and sexual passion. The babies who were born (or never born) are part of the story even when you do not consciously recognize it. The answer is always to take yourself and the emotional mystery to a place in your life where you can find a use for it. A practical approach works best.

TRANSPORTING YOUR PLANS

When you make the leap from merely admiring an idea to actually transporting it to somewhere it can thrive, you achieve your reward in life. The action planet Mars rules your sector of planning, and it is only when you realize actions speak louder than words that the potential in your concepts actually delivers. As you have read, two opposite but equal locations are written in your destiny. It may be that you have to physically move yourself and your skills, talents, and abilities in order to see them take off. This is a lifelong pattern so you may be a regular traveler or migrant, for example.

WHO SHARES YOUR BIRTHDAY?

Nell Gwyn, born February 2, 1650

Farrah Fawcett, born February 2, 1947

Shakira, born February 2, 1977

FEBRUARY 3

WHO ARE YOU?

With the royal sign Leo in charge of your relationships, you also rule them. The issue for you is the guessing game that accompanies them. With Mercury, the planet of the mind, in charge of your passions, you are drawn to overthinking your romantic desires or those of others. This same area of your chart also rules the babies who were born in the past—or who never arrived at all. It's true, there is always a lot to think about with the intricate, complex situations you face, but firm action is always the best solution.

YOUR DESTINY

You have the practical earth sign Capricorn in charge of your inner life, and you find solitude grounding as it allows you to get away from the world of people and back to your true self. You may be a meditator or walker, for that reason. The Moon, with all her changing phases, rules your daily life and routine. It is quite normal for you to feel out of sync at times, because of these fluctuating cycles in your life, so when that happens, being by yourself can be therapeutic. If you can't get to the beach or nature, you can certainly visualize it.

GROUPS AND NETWORKS

As a true Aquarian, you are supported and nourished by your circles of like-minded acquaintances, friends, and allies. The nature of the group itself may have a strong shared vision, depending on the cycles of time that you meet. Sometimes the connections are more casual and social, but you are sustained by the collective or community. In fact, something special and spiritually nourishing takes place when you allow the club, team, society, and so on to form the foundation of your world. The results can seem miraculous.

YOUR HEART AND SOUL

While Leo is in charge of your partnerships and other relationship commitments, this sign also rules the heart, and your greatest rewards will come from learning how to manage your feelings and successfully dealing with all the challenges of your emotions. Strategies that you come up with yourself can sometimes be the answer. You also gain from tried, tested, and trusted solutions for complex relationships. You are a great believer in healing and change, because you have firsthand experience of it from quite a young age.

WHO SHARES YOUR BIRTHDAY?

Gertrude Stein, born February 3, 1874

Morgan Fairchild, born February 3, 1950

Amal Clooney, born February 3, 1978

FEBRUARY 4

WHO ARE YOU?

You are a practical person who rolls up their sleeves and takes firm action at the first sight of any issue. Energetic Aries rules your sector of mind and thoughts, so you are proactive about learning techniques to take charge of your inner self. Those may be meditation, prayer, affirmations, or cognitive behavioral therapy. Practical Capricorn rules your sleep, dreams, and state of mind, so you are down-to-earth about sensible ways to harness your mind, body, and spirit. This has a big effect on your personality.

YOUR DESTINY

As a true Aquarius, pooling resources is the way forward for you, and being part of something bigger than yourself with a community or circle is always important. This is your fate, and the cycles of time suggest you will hit regular crossroads when the group is waiting and you are waiting for the group but must first make deep choices. These life-changing decisions will always show you what is possible. If you lean on your sixth sense—your extrasensory perception is priceless to you—and take action, you'll transform your life.

FINANCIAL CHALLENGES

Deciding what to do with your money is one of your regular challenges. Neptune with all his escapism, daydreaming, and duality rules your finances. As a result you can find it hard to focus on how to spend your income or savings and how to invest or negotiate. You can sometimes feel that you are holding on to a bubble, no matter if it's the property market or the value of cryptocurrency. Your horoscope suggests that when you are in doubt, it's always wise to call on second and third opinions from trusted professionals.

EARNING YOUR FREEDOM

Uranus is your ruling planet and is associated with radical action and rebellion in order to win freedom. You will have more than one revolution in your life when you break away from places, people, or situations which trap you. With your gift for understanding how your own thoughts contribute to your life as well as your deep intuition, you are always able to liberate yourself from being confined. Every time you realize you are the only person who can make a difference in your life, your reward is exhilarating liberty.

WHO SHARES YOUR BIRTHDAY?

Rosa Parks, born February 4, 1913

Betty Friedan, born February 4, 1921

El Anatsui, born February 4, 1944

Alice Cooper, born February 4, 1948

FEBRUARY 5

WHO ARE YOU?

You are able to see both sides of an issue, with balanced Libra ruling your sector of education, academia, books, the internet, and the media. You can sit squarely in the middle, which makes you a natural tutor or teacher. You may fulfill this role informally with your family and friends or find a place for yourself in a prestigious ivory tower. You understand there is no black or white and are drawn toward roles where you can use your impressive knowledge and insight to bring harmony and symmetry to the world of ideas.

YOUR DESTINY

The rather slow, stuck Taurus rules both sides of your family tree and any family you marry into. Deciding where you belong and how is a lifelong, fated challenge. The cycles of time in your solar horoscope suggest you will regularly be kept waiting by destiny until the time is right to make your move. Finding the right direction enlightens you, and no matter how delayed your decisions are throughout your life, it is only when you have played the waiting game and seen the light that you will leap into action.

BOUNDARIES AND LIMITS

With the assertive Aries ruling your communication and its ruling planet Mars raising strong boundaries, you set firm limits with others in your personal and professional life. The powerful planet Pluto is at the top of your chart, thanks to the rather intense Scorpio, which it rules. You are intimidating even when you are inviting others into your space. This combination of the firm control of Pluto and the tough, uncompromising energy of Mars makes you a force to be reckoned with, Aquarius.

FINANCIAL REWARDS

With Neptune ruling your income, savings, assets, and investments, you can find yourself frequently at sea. Neptune is a symbol of any situation which needs an anchor or at least a telescope and compass. You are fortunate in being able to balance this with your own method, order, and precision because Mercury and Virgo at the other end of your chart rule your shared finance. This enables you to bring method, order, and precision to what would otherwise be a lifetime of juggling. Mercury describes planning, facts, and figures. So you become the person who deals with uncertain financial situations with your own special technique all your life.

WHO SHARES YOUR BIRTHDAY?

Charlotte Rampling, born February 5, 1946

Bobby Brown, born February 5, 1969

Queen Mary of Denmark, born February 5, 1972

Cristiano Ronaldo, born February 5, 1985

Henry Golding, born February 5, 1987

Neymar, born February 5, 1992

FEBRUARY 6

WHO ARE YOU?

With the Sun in Aquarius in the Eleventh House of groups in your birth chart, you shine at your brilliant best when you can turn the fate of your circle or community around. With Jupiter ruling these teams, clubs, associations, or whatnot in your solar chart, your allies and friends are always looking for the next horizon. Your tribes are made up of explorers who search far and wide for all they hope for. The success or failure of the mission is down to individuals, though—and you are one of them, Aquarius.

YOUR DESTINY

Aquarius is the sign to associate with sisterhood and brotherhood. It is very much about people power with a social filter. It's your happy destiny to always be with people you can celebrate with, no matter if that's the good life, good times, or the promise of something more. You were born under the sign of equality and diversity, and that is evident in the company you keep. You also trust and believe in individual differences and can be part of something bigger than yourself without ever giving up on independence.

GROUP DYNAMICS

Pooling resources is never as simple as you would like, and the reality of always having a particular network or group in the picture relates to politics. This can even move beyond mere differences of opinion to something more challenging. Your test is to make the peace. Even if you find yourself distanced from that idea, time, patience, and an appreciation of the need for unity will help. It may be you who buries the hatchet or you who accepts a treaty, but it is the dramatic compromises which can make a group very special indeed.

TRAVEL AND RELOCATION

Libra, the sign of relationships, is ruled by Venus, a symbol of deep affection in your horoscope. Libra also oversees your travel and relocation. It's those long-distance connections which prove your depth of feeling, along with the willingness of others to meet you halfway. The sign of Libra is associated with balanced scales, so partnerships, family ties, or courtship frequently involves a fair split between your side and the other party. This is rather like meeting at a crossroads or midway across a tightrope. These tests of the heart reward you.

WHO SHARES YOUR BIRTHDAY?

Babe Ruth, born February 6, 1895

Ronald Reagan, born February 6, 1911

Bob Marley, born February 6, 1945

FEBRUARY 7

WHO ARE YOU?

As an Aquarian, you are always backed by at least one group, club, or team. These circles are a protective force in your life. Your extended family is also important, though, and the grounded, practical, comfort-loving Taurus rules your home. In turn, this same sign rules your finances in your birth chart, so you are the dreamer who looks for the pot of gold at the end of the rainbow with visions of domestic bliss—and you find it, too. Neptune offers you a strong imagination when it comes to security, and your chart can deliver.

YOUR DESTINY

It may be a charity or an ensemble cast, but you are fated to keep the right company and discover how comforting people power can be. You may be the leader, star, or front person of such a network. The planet of expansion, growth, and optimism is Jupiter, and as he rules your clubs, teams, societies, and so on, you benefit from the crowd. You have the biggest of all big pictures with these people behind you, and the only issue is remembering that every person is a unique individual and must be cared for individually, too.

DEALING WITH GROUPS

You were born with the Sun in Aquarius in the Eleventh House of people power and will deal with both sides of the hive mind during your lifetime. You will not only experience the security and help of the group, but also need to deal with groups who have conflict in mind. This is the reverse side of Aquarius energy, and your challenge is to become a strategist who can successfully head off any issues with these units or clusters before they affect you and others. Mind reading the collective plans of others is a great asset.

A WORLD OF READERS AND WRITERS

Jupiter is about the big picture, as you know, but he does not only happily influence your inner circle; he is also there on the worldwide web offering you one corner of the globe after another. You move in a fascinating universe of books, websites, media, education, academia, and ideas. Even though life does not stand still and has a random, up-and-down quality—rather like a Dickens novel, an author who shares your birthday—you always have it in perspective, partly because others are so good at reflecting it back to you.

WHO SHARES YOUR BIRTHDAY?

Charles Dickens, born February 7, 1812
Hattie Jacques, born February 7, 1922
Chris Rock, born February 7, 1965

FEBRUARY 8

WHO ARE YOU?

The sign of royalty, aristocracy, and imperialism, Leo rules your relationships. Once you have at least one solid marriage or partnership in your life, you find yourself assuming a leadership role. It doesn't even matter if love lasts; it remains evergreen long enough to support you and adds to your stability, security, comfort, and dignity. You are an impressive person, born to command with powerful Pluto in charge of your status and position in life in your solar chart.

YOUR DESTINY

For all that evergreen emotions from a relationship or marriage prop you up, it is also true that you are a loner who needs to pursue meditation, faith, spirituality, religion, or regular soul-searching with self-help. Saturn rules your sector of inner life, and discovering your soul or psyche is a lifelong mission. You are two people in one body: one is the leading light who is center stage and very much in control; the other has to spend time in seclusion looking for all that sustains you on the inside. It's deeply personal.

HIGHS AND LOWS

Your horoscope is tilted in such a way that the cycles of time can send you high and low in quite a random way. In fact, the pattern repeats so often that it's almost predictable, given that you find yourself in constantly changing and unpredictable circumstances. Pluto does rule your power and control in life, but this planet is also associated with transformation. Every beginning is always an ending even as it takes hold in your life, just as every endgame is always the start of something new taking you higher.

WHAT YOU VALUE MOST

Pisces and its ruler Neptune describe what you value most. This is quite different on your solitary, introspective side as compared to your impressive command of your own empire. You also need precious imagination, play, miracles, mystery, and magic. This is the bohemian side of your nature, and being allowed to express yourself in this way is very important to your sense of reward. There is always a group in the background, of course, as Aquarius rules communities and networks. Your circle sustains you.

WHO SHARES YOUR BIRTHDAY?

Nick Nolte, born February 8, 1941

Gary Coleman, born February 8, 1968

Seth Green, born February 8, 1974

FEBRUARY 9

WHO ARE YOU?

The vast worldwide web, but also the equally big world of bookshops, libraries, academia, entertainment, and education are the setting for your life. You were born with Jupiter, a symbol of all that is huge in scope, ruling your sector of allies and like-minded acquaintances. There is always something else to read or discuss. Your ruling planet is Uranus, a symbol of everything that is unpredictable. You become so used to your world regularly turning upside down that you become a philosopher or a comedian as a result of it.

YOUR DESTINY

Pluto rules your highest achievement, and as this planet is also associated with the afterlife, you have a strong connection to your extended circle in the spirit world. Perhaps you are aware of this, perhaps not, but people who matter to you go on evolving anyway, and what happens to you can help these souls ascend to the next level of their spiritual development. Pluto is the Roman god of the Underworld where the departed went to live under his watchful gaze. He also happens to be at the top of your solar chart.

CYCLES OF TRANSFORMATION

Pluto is a symbol of transformation in your horoscope, and through his rulership of Scorpio, the zodiac sign which is at the peak of your chart, he brings repeated cycles of endings and new beginnings at the same time. This gives your world an intensity and depth that affects your personality as well as your destiny. You are no lightweight, and through these dramatic final chapters and new chapters—always showing simultaneously—you develop your own deep understanding of matters like religion, for example.

TRAVEL AND ESCAPE

You are an escape artist by nature who values solitude, departure, and sabbaticals very highly. In fact, Neptune rules over all the things that money cannot buy, and as he is a symbol of holidays from the real world, you take regular vacations from other people. You may do this by meditating, hiking, or going it alone in other ways. The group matters to you. It always will. Yet sometimes you have to leave the ranks of friends and allies where they stand and separate yourself in order to find yourself and value them more.

WHO SHARES YOUR BIRTHDAY?

J. M. Coetzee, born February 9, 1940
Carole King, born February 9, 1942
Mia Farrow, born February 9, 1945
Zhang Ziyi, born February 9, 1979

FEBRUARY 10

WHO ARE YOU?

You are remarkably fair, evenhanded, and wise about all two-way situations. You would make a very good judge, for example. Libra, the scales of balance, rules your biggest vision of the world and your place in it. For personal or professional reasons you will be concerned with classic Libran issues like the two sexes or same-sex marriage or the class system. Race and equality are another area of interest. People turn to you for advice as you are only interested in harmony and have no other motivation except what is fair.

YOUR DESTINY

You are an Aquarian despite the Libra influence on your chart, and so you are well-known for being a friend to all. Groups, teams, clubs, societies, and all sorts of brotherhoods and sisterhoods describe your fate in life. This begins in childhood and carries on through your teenage years, and even into your senior years, you will still take your place in any party. Groups are also your gateway to the good things of life, and although you love friendships and alliances for their own sake, never forget the potential of a team effort.

FINANCE AND PROPERTY

Your greatest challenge in life comes from money, property, charity, and/or business. This can sometimes be through a partnership or a professional involvement, but your task is to negotiate, to wheel and deal. This is not easy, but with the detail-conscious Virgo ruling shared financial matters, you have what it takes to tidy up situations which require some method and order. Pisces, the sign opposite Virgo, governs the other side of your bank account and shows what happens without structure or planning. You learn.

THE POWER OF THE GROUP

Your Sun in Aquarius is in the Eleventh House of your birth chart, which rules people power within a circle and also the communal hive mind. Your reward in life is to learn just how influential people can be when they are all united. Your strong sense of fair play and justice may come to bear here or your genuine enjoyment of like-minded allies. If anyone is against all of you, or you are all against anyone, then there is no compromise. Repeatedly in your life you'll play your part in joining others to succeed.

WHO SHARES YOUR BIRTHDAY?

Boris Pasternak, born February 10, 1890

Leontyne Price, born February 10, 1927

Roberta Flack, born February 10, 1937

Elizabeth Banks, born February 10, 1974

FEBRUARY 11

WHO ARE YOU?

You are the fascinating creature who is never quite in anybody's grasp. All that you value most in life—to the point of being so precious that it is priceless—is escapist. You place a high price of being left alone to drift and float in your own world, far removed from everybody and everything back in the real world. Neptune is a symbol of the vacation from reality in astrology, and you will pay for this escapism if you have to—for example by purchasing cruises or avoiding nine-to-five work.

YOUR DESTINY

For all that you are an escape artist, you are also tied to the world of education, academia, books, the media, the worldwide web, and ideas. Perhaps this is why you need to take a vacation from reality on a regular basis. You are a natural student of life or guide to others. You can formalize this and so enjoy your time in universities or colleges. You can also pursue knowledge in your own way and in your own time. Libra governs all that you learn or pass on. Equality, fairness, and justice are big themes.

FINANCIAL MANAGEMENT

Both Virgo and Pisces rule your income, savings, investments, business plans, property, and so on. This duality, caught between overthinking and meticulous focus on details and an overload of vision, can hold you up. The planets which rule Virgo (Mercury) and Pisces (Neptune) could not be more different, so one part of you is consumed by the tiniest, most logical aspects of investments or expenses, while another part of you is dreaming or even fantasizing. Finding a balance is a lifetime challenge, but an important one.

POWER AND INFLUENCE

Your solar chart shows Pluto with all his intensity, influence, passion, and potency at the top of your horoscope. This is where you are rewarded by life and also where you hold a command position. The history of your relationships or partnerships has a great deal to do with this, as the other leading sign in your chart is Leo, who rules your marriages or commitments. There is something evergreen about your duets and romances, and this provides a secure and firm foundation from which you can rule—and enjoy your life, too.

WHO SHARES YOUR BIRTHDAY?

Mary Quant, born February 11, 1934
Burt Reynolds, born February 11, 1936
Jennifer Aniston, born February 11, 1969

FEBRUARY 12

WHO ARE YOU?

You are the ideas person and a natural teacher or guide, who is capable of leaving a great deal to future generations. This may be your child, stepchild, niece, nephew, grandchild, or godchild. However, the bigger picture of your horoscope shows powerful Pluto on the midheaven, which is where you reach great heights. You can produce plans, projects, and concepts which grow for the ages and make a difference to younger people as a whole. If you make the right choices, these simply go on growing.

YOUR DESTINY

You are an Aquarian, so friendship, allies, and people power within a group are in your destiny. This may be a political party (Abraham Lincoln shares your birthday) or a friendly crew (Charles Darwin does, too). Whoever your shipmates or partners in crime are, there is always the promise of abundance with your community. You will always be tempted to merely enjoy good company and good times, but there is also a promise of future gains from solidarity and shared effort; cooperation can deliver security.

SOLITUDE AND INTROSPECTION

Saturn rules your sector of solitude, introspection, soul-searching, and inner work. This planet is associated with the slow passage of time. Saturn is also linked to old age; the significance of the second Saturn Return, at around the age of sixty, or the third return, at around age ninety, is the source of this. Even when you are a teenager you can feel the weight of time passing, and perhaps this is why you periodically have to be alone. Only when you are by yourself can you find out what is true for you, be it a faith, belief, or inner knowing.

CHILDREN AND TEENAGERS

You have a very special part to play with those who come after you, and as you have read, this can be far into the future. If you do have children or young relatives, one will be central to your happiness and also to the shaping of your personality. You are gifted at understanding how small people evolve, and you respect the innocence and brilliance of childhood. For all that you are a natural mentor or influence for this generation, you will also find throughout your life that you can celebrate and enjoy them, too.

WHO SHARES YOUR BIRTHDAY?

Charles Darwin, born February 12, 1809
Abraham Lincoln, born February 12, 1809
Christina Ricci, born February 12, 1980

FEBRUARY 13

WHO ARE YOU?

You are the visionary and dreamer who can hold a reasonable amount of money in the bank but never fully decide where it should go. The family tree? The next ambition? Unfinished business? Neptune can leave you floundering as he rules your sector of finance, business, charity, and property. It might be called procrastination by some; to others it is idealism. You have great visions of what is possible, and it's hard to decide how to invest your time, energy, daydreams, and the actual currency. Outside advice is always useful.

YOUR DESTINY

With Pluto and all his power ruling your sector of achievement, goals, and ambitions, you know how to quickly take control of situations where others would try to keep all the control. There is a political atmosphere with many of your roles and plans because of the way your horoscope is set up. You have Mars, the action planet, in charge of your thought processes and so are well-known for being quick-thinking, highly strategic, and first to take charge of any scenario where you realize the smart solution is the right solution.

BARGAINING GAMES

Bargaining with others and yourself is part of your life, not only because Neptune and Pisces rule your own income, but because the clever, down-to-earth Virgo governs joint finance and property, business, and charity. From the first time you come into money as a young adult, you learn to lean on your grounded, practical, thoughtful Virgo side, which helps balance the other tendency of your approach to money, which is escapist. This push-pull between both signs in your chart shows in the way you bargain with others, too.

PARTNERSHIPS AND RELATIONSHIPS

As a true Aquarian, ruled by Uranus, the planet of freedom, liberation, and independence, you find this kind of space repeatedly in relationships, partnerships, or marriages. This is down to the cycles of time in your horoscope which will introduce regular crossroads into even a long-lasting commitment. In other cases more than one lover will bring questions about personal space and autonomy into your life. The reward for you is understanding love, sex, and passion the way the poets did or the songwriters do. You invent your love life.

WHO SHARES YOUR BIRTHDAY?

Peter Tork, born February 13, 1942

Peter Gabriel, born February 13, 1950

Peter Hook, born February 13, 1956

FEBRUARY 14

WHO ARE YOU?

You are the strong-willed person who can control their thoughts with action, not words. The can-do Aries rules your mind, and rather than just accept the way it leads you, from young adulthood onward you learn how to take charge of your imagination and memory. As so many of the battles in your life are conducted in your head, rather than in the real world (with Mars ruling your sector of dreams and daydreams), you soon learn techniques to help you banish what is a mere figment or projection. Often, the tool you turn to is meditation.

YOUR DESTINY

You are a true Aquarius Sun individual with the group, collective, team club, or community behind you. This collection of friends, allies, and like-minded people supports you and also protects you. You have a main circle of which you are the leader or most visible member, if you are typical of your birthday. The only cautionary note for you is that it is all too easy to treat people en masse as identical. This is very far from being the case, and a regular lesson in your life is that independent personalities need separate care.

THE BIG IDEA

You always have "the big idea" to turn into a flourishing enterprise. As you know, Aries and Mars rule your sector of the mind. You use them to take charge of your thoughts to feel more positive about life, but you can also summon up huge amounts of energy to turn brainpower into something that grows and grows. Plenty of people have inspiration, but many lack the perspiration to make things happen. As you have had the experience of seeing what happens when you don't act swiftly, you train yourself to make ideas real.

GROUNDING AND FOCUSING

With the rather heavy planet of Saturn in charge of your unconscious mind, inner life, psyche, soul, and spirit, you have to train yourself to manage your state of mind, as you know. This can be the making of you, as you have the potential to become a far stronger, more resourceful and confident person when you find methods to ground youself. It may be yoga. It may be cognitive behavioral therapy or just a self-help book solution. Hypnosis is another option. Going back to your family tree roots is another way of finding greater happiness.

WHO SHARES YOUR BIRTHDAY?

Michael Bloomberg, born February 14, 1942

Tim Buckley, born February 14, 1947

Simon Pegg, born February 14, 1970

FEBRUARY 15

WHO ARE YOU?

As a true Aquarian, your particular brotherhood or sisterhood is very important to you. In your solar chart, this community or circle of like-minded souls is ruled by Jupiter. In turn, Jupiter is associated with a higher power. You might call it God, the Creator, or the universe. Your upbringing, with or without religion, is extremely important to the shaping of your personality. All your life you will be mindful of whatever passes for a bible at the time, or even the Bible. Similarly, spiritual authority is a huge matter for you. What will you choose?

YOUR DESTINY

You value the Piscean qualities of imagination, vision, and escapism very highly. In fact, Neptune and Pisces rule over all that is most precious and even priceless to you. You know that you cannot buy a holiday from reality in a catalog. You are somebody who plays with life and inhabits their own world. Some who know you will be fascinated; some will simply not understand—but nobody could accuse you of being ordinary. This may be reflected in the way you dress. You have the soul of a bohemian, and always, always the group is behind you.

SUCCESSFUL IDEAS

Successful ideas come down to action, not words, for you. The planet Mars rules your concepts, plans, and projects, and it is associated with dynamic approaches, not procrastination or daydreaming. Yet, given your need for escapism, it can be all too easy to drift into a bubble of imagination or visions of what might be. Repeated lessons about wasted chances eventually hit home, though, and you realize that if you are going to be in charge of a successful idea drawing on your skill or talent, you have to act—and never hesitate.

GOOD TIMES, GOOD COMPANY

As with all Aquarians, you find everything comes back to your social life and social circle eventually. With Jupiter and all his expansion, growth, and hope in charge of your friendships, you will always enjoy good times in good company. There is more to it than that, though. Jupiter is also about rewards, and the particular chemistry you share with others who join with you generates incredible abundance. Perhaps some of these rewards are just for now, but try to ensure that what you all have together can feed the future.

WHO SHARES YOUR BIRTHDAY?

Galileo Galilei, born February 15, 1564

Charles Lewis Tiffany, born February 15, 1812

Matt Groening, born February 15, 1954

Megan Thee Stallion, born February 15, 1995

FEBRUARY 16

WHO ARE YOU?

The world of knowledge, education, ideas, and academia—from colleges to the worldwide web—is your domain. You are a natural author and tutor, no matter if you leave school young or proceed to publishing or life at university. Libra rules your theories and work, online and offline. Libra is about equality, justice, and fairness and balances two opposing sides. There is no black or white in your life, just the central position between both. You are wise, often sought for advice, and have a deep inner knowing.

YOUR DESTINY

For all that you are a cerebral creature, you come down to earth when you are at home, in nature, or in your favorite surroundings. The grounded earth sign Taurus rules your environment. You know how to plant yourself in beautiful places and have an eye for well-designed or made objects, and clothing, too. Your particular status in the world is partly down to one or more romantic relationship. These produce evergreen feelings no matter if they persist in your life or not. The fact is they support you and sustain you.

PARTNERSHIP CROSSROADS

Scorpio rules your ultimate achievements and accomplishments in life, as it sits on top of your solar chart. Scorpio describes sexual relationships which revolve around property or finance. There may be just one of these which characterizes your life, or there may be several. What you learn as you go along is that willpower and self-control are empowering and it takes great strength to find a path that suits both of you. You attract partners who are the same, but so different. It's your life's work.

FREEDOM AND INDEPENDENCE

As an Aquarian, you are ruled by Uranus, the planet of revolution and freedom. Your horoscope is set up in such a way that you will regularly change yourself and your life by breaking away from situations which restrict you. The turning point for you is realizing that you are your own best liberator. Only you can remove the psychological ties that bind. Saturn rules your sixth sense and also your instincts, and this planet is also linked to themes of restriction and rebellion. You were born for Independence Days.

WHO SHARES YOUR BIRTHDAY?

Pamela Colman Smith, born February 16, 1878

Ice-T, born February 16, 1958

John McEnroe, born February 16, 1959

Cathy Freeman, born February 16, 1973

Mahershala Ali, born February 16, 1974

FEBRUARY 17

WHO ARE YOU?

What you learn as a young adult stays with you for life. Having big ideas is your lesson. When they do not last, you realize that action speaks louder than words, even when the words are impressive. The plans or projects which come to nothing teach you to act quickly when inspiration arrives. Mars rules your brain waves, and Aries, associated with great speed and determination, governs what is on your computer or in your notebook. Experience shows you success comes from carpe diem.

YOUR DESTINY

Leo rules your partnerships and relationships, and this in turn for you means the world of children, teenagers, and young adults. It is your fate to never go too far into a close connection with someone new without being reminded that it's all about the next generation. This will make or break some bonds in your life, as two people will not always agree on parenthood, or even substitute parenthood. Leo rules heirs, spares, and pretenders to the throne, so it can be a complex question.

THE SPIRITUAL LEGACY

Pluto, long associated with the afterlife, rules your highest achievements. The spirit world is important throughout your life, as your extended family or friends are evolving souls, just as you are. What you do affects their path, just as their own progress can have an impact on you. Perhaps you already know about your ancestors or departed relatives. Maybe this world is hidden to you, but Pluto's command of the top of your solar chart suggests this is your great challenge in life, Aquarius.

GROUP DYNAMICS

The group, team, club, society, circle, or association that matters most to you now may be a repeat of another community of people you recognize. As a true humanitarian, your rewards come from making a success out of a shared effort. This is not easy because as an air sign you have quite separate, detached connections with others. Sometimes there is so much space that there is no unity. Your best efforts to turn things around with others and pull people together can result in slow, steady, shared success.

WHO SHARES YOUR BIRTHDAY?

Patricia Routledge, born February 17, 1929
Ruth Rendell, born February 17, 1930
Paris Hilton, born February 17, 1981

FEBRUARY 18

WHO ARE YOU?

The zodiac sign of the heavenly twins or siblings, Gemini affects your sector of children and young people. You will always have a window onto the world of infancy or school days, and the dual nature of Gemini suggests it will be siblings or cousins who teach you. This may be your own children. It is also possible that your professional life or other aspects of your personal life will make the next generation central. Observing the innocence and simplicity of a junior generation shapes your character.

YOUR DESTINY

Aquarius is the sign of the group, team, club, society, and so on. You were born near the Sun in Aquarius in the Eleventh House of brotherhood and sisterhood. This protects you throughout your life and is the backdrop to your own good fortune and happiness. You are a natural leader or front person for your circle, and there may be several collections of allies and like-minded people in your life who put you there. Understanding the individuality and independence of people in the collective will help you.

COMPLICATED RELATIONSHIPS

The Sun rules your closest ties, and these can be complicated. The Sun rules monarchy and the royal court throughout history, with all its rivalries and differences. As a result, your love life and/or family life can also be quite challenging to manage. Love triangles are not unusual for people born on February 18, but there can also be divided loyalties—say, between parents and children. Leo also rules the heart, and looking after your own feelings, as well as those of others, is part of your life.

FINANCIAL REWARDS

The sign of the gardener, Virgo describes your joint finances, investments, business interests, charity, and property. You have a talent for cultivating plans which bring security. Virgo is an earth sign and famously grounded. You have both feet on the ground when it comes to saving or making money and will find that the more focused you can be on all the details, the better off you will be—literally. Appreciating the finer points and small things in your life budget and knowing when to act could bring wealth.

WHO SHARES YOUR BIRTHDAY?

Mary I of England (Bloody Mary), born February 18, 1516
John Travolta, born February 18, 1954
Dr. Dre, born February 18, 1965

FEBRUARY 19

WHO ARE YOU?

You are the visionary and dreamer with strong ideas needing energy and action, not procrastination. Aries and Mars influence your sector of projects and plans, so your success with your special talents, skills, and brain waves depends on your being able to be proactive. For all that, you place a very high value on pondering and wondering as Neptune, with all its lack of reality, affects everything that is so precious to you it is priceless—and that includes speculating rather than acting. Achievements come when you can master this.

YOUR DESTINY

The royal Sun rules your partnerships, both professional or personal. Once you are in the right duet or double act—perhaps even a series of them—you come into your own with all the leadership and influence associated with this lord of the jungle. Any duel or contest, conflict or competition is also the making of you, because Leo also rules the battles. This adds a layer of dignity to your character, but it also means you are fated to become a force to be reckoned with all your life.

JUSTICE AND FAIR PLAY

Your sector of knowledge, education, and wisdom is affected by Libra, the sign of the scales. The scales of justice are one expression of Libra; the other is plain equality—between two opposite sexes, for example. Your challenge is to accept judgments from others and also to participate in the search for harmony and symmetry. With Aries in opposition to Libra in your chart, this is not easy, but justice will always come first. You may find yourself having to act in the interests of all that is fair or bowing to a higher power.

FINANCE AND INVESTMENT

Your partnerships, double acts, and also your duels shape your character so that you become a formidable leader with a commanding presence or top position. This also affects your finances, and with Leo the sign of royalty influencing your chart, you find yourself with rich choices about investment, philanthropy, property, or business all your life. This begins even when you are a teenager, thanks to the way your horoscope is set up. External advice from experts can be very useful if the choices are too much.

WHO SHARES YOUR BIRTHDAY?

Dick Emery, born February 19, 1915
Jeff Daniels, born February 19, 1955
Seal, born February 19, 1963

FEBRUARY 20

WHO ARE YOU?

You find your spiritual essence is replenished by your network, circle, or wider group. This may be a case of circles upon circles. They sustain and uplift you. The idea of pooling resources is central to your character, and you will see for yourself several times in your life how a community is the gift that goes on giving. Groups in general have a great deal to teach you, but some lessons are easy. What feeds the collective also inspires you because it is a brilliant example of how the life force can work at its best.

YOUR DESTINY

You are destined to cultivate not just one but many plans to make yourself money and also holding incredible potential for the future. The rest is up to you as a great deal of what you achieve financially, with charity, business, or property, will come down to timing. You have a gift for planning projects or investments which collectively can make you more than comfortable. Where it goes after that depends on your staying power, hard work, and perhaps some wise advice from professionals who know the answer to "Where to next?"

SISTERHOOD AND BROTHERHOOD

You can happily join your own brotherhood or sisterhood in enjoying the good life, as well as each other's company. This goes beyond mere socializing into a very particular kind of bonding. Everybody involved gives and receives space so that individual differences are appreciated and independence is kept. For all this, when you are with people who understand, you share something very special. You will repeatedly find that the right company is productive for you, even abundant. The trick is to capitalize on what you have.

GROUPS AND INDIVIDUALS

Your biggest reward in life will be the incredible feat of bringing people together, even when there is an outsider who is removed from the community. You will take turns at both roles. Sometimes you will be with the others, and it will be one against many with all of you dealing with the distance. At other times you will be the one against the many, and yet every time, you learn the same lesson. When ideas or opinions are so similar, then pulling everybody back together is just a few conversations or heartfelt letters away.

WHO SHARES YOUR BIRTHDAY?

Gloria Vanderbilt, born February 20, 1924
Kurt Cobain, born February 20, 1967
Trevor Noah, born February 20, 1984
Rihanna, born February 20, 1988

FEBRUARY 21

WHO ARE YOU?

The sign of leadership, Leo rules your sense of duty to others. Leo also rules the next generation and the one after that. You were born to reign and have a special dignity and authority that makes others turn to you for guidance with the young. If you do have children, you will never be just another parent. You will be like a monarch with a junior kingdom. You are a natural tutor, mentor, teacher, or head figure. You have an important part to play with the next generation, and your ideas and plans strongly affect them.

YOUR DESTINY

The groups, social circles, associations, teams, clubs, charities, teams, bands, societies, and the rest that you gather around you are fated. The businesslike sign of Capricorn rules these people in your life, so you take these communities seriously. They are never just friends or allies; they are part of the structure of your life. Rather like a CEO with their company, you have responsibilities to those who are always behind you. It is your destiny to understand that each individual must be treated separately.

PISCES SWIMS IN TWO DIRECTIONS

You were born with the Sun in Pisces, the sign of the two fish swimming in opposite directions. You are a mutable sign and could change your mind about your life at any time—and have. Not being sure about your biggest decisions is a challenge that never goes away, and you may lead a life where you are always poised to make crossroads choices, but never actually follow through. Other people may find it hard to second-guess you; you find it hard to second-guess yourself. There is a duality to your nature, Pisces.

THE STRATEGIST

The clever Virgo, ruled by Mercury, gives you a quick grasp of all situations where you must anticipate other people's tactics before you have to deal with them. Your reward is a lifetime of protection against complications you don't need, as you are extremely intuitive about the best way forward, even in potentially challenging circumstances. Like all Pisceans, you are an escape artist who can wriggle away like the fish in your zodiac sign, slipping out of any issues before they even begin.

WHO SHARES YOUR BIRTHDAY?

Anaïs Nin, born February 21, 1903

Nina Simone, born February 21, 1933

Kelsey Grammer, born February 21, 1955

FEBRUARY 22

WHO ARE YOU?

You are an explorer and adventurer who is always chasing the next horizon. Your projects, plans, and ideas are always tied to the money or the business, and with your Piscean intuition, you always follow your own radar. Sometimes you don't navigate clearly and end up on mystery tours that aren't so magical. You would rather rely on your own inner vision than any guidebook, map, or website, though. Your solar chart in astrology shows Sagittarius, the sign in charge of travel and export, also ruling your sector of success.

YOUR DESTINY

You are ruled by Neptune, the planet of escapism. Your life path is full of regular escapes, no matter if you are crossing your own country or crossing the world. The journey actually feels like home to you, far more so than home itself. In fact, even when you settle, you never really put down roots, as it seems the visions and notions that mean so much to you never really feel right unless they are planted in distant places on the map. In your birth chart, Gemini rules short journeys. It's your destiny to keep moving.

YOUR OWN VISION

You do not see life the way other people do. You may be a dreamer, an inspired visionary, a psychic. People who try to ground you in the real world need to honor your unique insights before they stand a chance. Once you have a mission, you can be quite single-minded about the journey. Common sense and practical arguments don't really have much appeal to you unless others can somehow shape these to fit your agenda. Sometimes you get it wrong—and sometimes you get it absolutely right.

THE POWER OF TWO

Your numerology shows the numeral 2 three times. Your life is about the steady flow between yourself and another. This can be you and your mother or you and your costar. (Kenneth Williams, born on February 22, is an example of this.) As a sensitive, emotional water sign, you need to feel the flow with somebody like you. It can be unspoken and intuitive. It can also be spiritual as Pisces is the sign we associate with a higher power. Virgo, the sign of healing, rules your sector of partnerships, duets, and double acts of all kinds.

WHO SHARES YOUR BIRTHDAY?

Kenneth Williams, born February 22, 1926
James Hong, born February 22, 1929
Julie Walters, born February 22, 1950
Steve Irwin, born February 22, 1962
Drew Barrymore, born February 22, 1975

FEBRUARY 23

WHO ARE YOU?

You are a natural lawyer, judge, or jury member. This applies no matter what your actual profession is. You understand fairness and justice. The scales must be balanced, and if that takes time, you are prepared to wait and do the work. Equality is at the heart of your character—whether between the two sexes, for example, or a matter of black and white. You have the gift of respecting a higher power than yourself when it comes to what is just. You are also not afraid of making "different but equal" your private motto.

YOUR DESTINY

You may or may not become a parent, but the world of children and teenagers is written into your horoscope. Just as the numeral 2 is hidden in your numerology—you believe in two equal sides or two legally balanced parties—you also have another two. This may be why young people fascinate you. They have so much to teach you about girls and boys, for example, or older and younger. Your respect for the learning process that infants or students go through on the road to fair play shapes who you become.

THE WORLD OF BOOKS AND THE WEB

All your life, you will be surrounded by the world of books, publishers, websites, libraries, colleges, universities, and schools. You are strongly influenced by readers as well as writers and students as well as teachers. In fact, knowledge is your backdrop, and it is constantly updated by the ever-changing nature of your life. More than most, you are destined to have the most unpredictable existence when every high point and low point spins around. In fact, your highs and lows inspire the web citizens around you.

FINANCIAL RELATIONSHIPS

You will take your turn at being the grateful recipient of other people's generosity and also the philanthropist or donor. So you learn a great deal about giving and receiving as a result. These financial relationships are your reward. It's not enough to be in a position to help other people. You can enjoy being comfortably wealthy for its own sake, with all that it brings you, but it is also a privilege for you to put your ideals about justice, fairness, and equality into practice. Charity begins at home or perhaps with strangers.

WHO SHARES YOUR BIRTHDAY?

Samuel Pepys, born February 23, 1633
Emperor Naruhito, born February 23, 1960
Emily Blunt, born February 23, 1983
Dakota Fanning, born February 23, 1994

FEBRUARY 24

WHO ARE YOU?

You are the hardworking artisan, craftsperson, or professional who has Leo ruling your zone of productivity, so your pride in what you produce is obvious. Other regions and countries are always in the picture with farsighted Sagittarius governing your sector of success. You are energetic, and some people see you as tireless. Once you start work, you can almost feel the heat, no matter what you do for a living. Learn to pace yourself. You are so fast—thanks to Aries ruling your sector of earning—that you must avoid burnout.

YOUR DESTINY

You are able to ground your big ideas and plans in the real world but can be slow to do so. For all that you are a speedy and methodical powerhouse in your chosen career, these grand visions fall outside that. Practical, grounded, down-to-earth Taurus rules your sector of concepts and brain waves. Taurus can also be slow to the point of getting stuck. When you discover the compromise between taking your time and actually planting your notions in the real world, you are on the road to achievement that can go on for many years.

BALANCING THE BUDGET

The balanced, harmonious Libra rules joint finances, business and taxation, investment and ownership, debt and banking. Your life is about the challenge of balancing your own budget but also finding an even two-way split with partners, say, or just one other large organization. The cycles of time affect your horoscope at regular intervals, so you periodically have to find your feet and invent a new way to be fair to yourself as well as to this partner. Doing this will save you energy as juggling is demanding.

LIBRA THE SCALES

Although you are a Piscean, Libra and the scales of justice rule your personal and professional life in terms of the deals you make with others. This can be strictly legal and so involve lawyers, judges, or juries. It can also be thematic and symbolic, so your issues may be, perhaps, with your life partner. In fact, this sector of your chart is about any deeply personal situation which might also come under the rulership of law. The reward for you is accepting what is fair but also deciding what is fair, too. Mission accomplished.

WHO SHARES YOUR BIRTHDAY?

Joseph Banks, born February 24, 1743
Steve Jobs, born February 24, 1955
Eddie Murray, born February 24, 1956

FEBRUARY 25

WHO ARE YOU?

Pluto rules your sector of big pictures and different belief systems. Pluto is associated with the cycles of endings and beginnings, death and the afterlife, final chapters and first chapters. It is about transformation. You have already experienced this in your life, and there will be more episodes which change you and also impact those around you. Through this you become a true believer, finding an explanation, a doctrine, or a philosophy to hold at the core of all you do—and who you are. As a water sign you understand emotions.

YOUR DESTINY

You are practical and productive, despite your sensitive, intense, Piscean nature—influenced by Pluto. You are energetic about making an income and can beat deadlines or meet them in a way that others cannot. You are proactive about your career or unpaid work. With Leo and all its pride ruling your jobs sector, you are content with others admiring your efforts—because you admire them as well. This is part of the motivation for your amazing ability to deliver and earn, but your dedication is also an outlet for energy.

IDEAS FOR FUTURE GENERATIONS

Your challenge in life is to make your ideas, plans, and projects not only succeed, but succeed for the heirs, spares, and pretenders to your throne. These may be your own children, godchildren, nieces, nephews, or grandchildren. It could also be a younger generation as a whole, perhaps—like a class of teenagers. You know that you have Leo, the sign of pride and leadership, ruling your sector of work and unpaid work. You have what it takes to influence and guide younger people into the future, but making the idea work is the test.

PEARLS OF WISDOM

With Jupiter and all his knowledge ruling your zone of highest achievement, you are here to learn and teach. You can do this formally by becoming an academic or advanced student. You can also achieve it through informal self-education—you never stop enrolling in courses or classes. Without a title or letters after your name, you can also become a source of intelligence and insight for sons, daughters, and so on. Less experienced, younger people in your chosen field also need your pearls of wisdom, Pisces.

WHO SHARES YOUR BIRTHDAY?

Pierre-Auguste Renoir, born February 25, 1841
George Harrison, born February 25, 1943
Chelsea Handler, born February 25, 1975

FEBRUARY 26

WHO ARE YOU?

You are the idea person who always has another concept or plan but must learn the Taurus side of your nature is there to ground you. Practical, down-to-earth Taurus rules your sector of brain waves. This sign is also well-known for its hesitation and procrastination. Over time you learn not to let this slow you down or keep you stuck, as the price you pay for being unable to move quickly enough is the failure of the idea. Your achievements in life are a tribute to your learning how to make things real and plant them securely.

YOUR DESTINY

You are fortunate to have Jupiter with all his big vision and good fortune ruling your sector of success. You also have driven, energetic Aries in charge of your income. This combination in your chart enables you to rise to the top. You are a natural boss, CEO, president, or just the leader in your field. Aries, which rules your ability to earn, is fiercely competitive and likes to be first or number one. This motivates you, and more than once in your life you will find that your horoscope helps put you up where you belong, Pisces.

METHOD AND ORDER

Pisces is the zodiac sign most linked to intuition, the sixth sense, and even mediumship. You are a channel for something greater than yourself, and you bring this insight to your relationships, your money, your ideas, and also the most challenging situations in life. Finding method and order is your great task. Neptune also rules Pisces, your Sun sign, and you can be confronted with so much information and input that you find it hard to navigate. Figuring out a way to embrace all your gifts and use what you are given is your challenge.

FAITH AND BELIEF

Pisces the fishes has long been associated with Christianity in astrology. You may or may not be a Christian, or even religious, but the rewards in your life will come from finding something and someone to follow. This can be intensely personal and may be scientism. You prefer to speak to a group or be part of a group, though, as the sign of community, Aquarius, rules your soul and spirit. A community which understands your beliefs is central to you. This is not a material reward, then, but something bigger.

WHO SHARES YOUR BIRTHDAY?

Victor Hugo, born February 26, 1802

Fats Domino, born February 26, 1928

Johnny Cash, born February 26, 1932

FEBRUARY 27

WHO ARE YOU?

You are the natural psychic or intuitive who lives in a world full of unknowns, so from a young age you learn to lean on your extrasensory perception. Pisces, part of your mission in life is to fix what you think must be managed in terms of where you come from, no matter if this is the family or the place. You use your sixth sense to do this. It helps you to keep your sense of place and your sense of belonging to your family in order—and that is a recurring challenge. Knowing your own invisible world helps.

YOUR DESTINY

You have a legal mind even if you do not work with the law. Your instinct as a strongly "two" person in numerology is to respect both sides of an argument and make them even. This is typical of Pisces, which is extremely sensitive to those who are at a disadvantage and deserve the same rights as others. This may be the climate, racism, war, the world economy, women's equality, animal welfare, and so on. Interfaith beliefs or crossover instincts about, say, Tarot may ring true for you. Equality certainly does, Pisces.

KEEPING YOUR FEET ON THE GROUND

As a true Pisces, your feet need to be on the ground. (Pisces rules shoes, boots, and feet.) It's important that you stabilize yourself regularly. You are one of those natural escape artists, as all Pisces Sun people are, and are always on the brink of quitting or splitting, so that you can always be tempted by another holiday from reality. Some of the allure of travel for you is the appeal of the unknown. You enjoy peering behind the curtain to see what's there and are drawn to the enigmas in life—and on the map.

EQUALITY BETWEEN MEN AND WOMEN

The numeral 2 is hidden in your birthday. Equality between the two sexes deeply concerns you. You might engage with this as an activist, as a true believer, or just in the way you look or act. You don't tick any old-fashioned boxes about what a lady should be or what a man is, for example. The number 2 is related to balance, as you know. You may also be sensitive to the old saying that "Two's company, and three's a crowd," and this can apply, again, to family life—all your life. You are very good at getting rid of extremes.

WHO SHARES YOUR BIRTHDAY?

Elizabeth Taylor, born February 27, 1932

Timothy Spall, born February 27, 1957

Kate Mara, born February 27, 1983

FEBRUARY 28

WHO ARE YOU?

With the numeral 2 in your birth date twice, you are a great believer in couples, pairs, and duets. In fact, these are the gateway to something else you believe in: a sense of place. Home may not necessarily be your castle—it could be any building at all—but with Cancer making a perfect trine to your own Pisces Sun, you are only really yourself when you are seeing a welcome mat. The twin sign of Gemini rules your own house, apartment, extended family, or holiday home so your "two" may be siblings or cousins.

YOUR DESTINY

You are true to your sign of Pisces, drifting and floating like the fish who represent you. You are not on the same planet for large periods of time, escaping from the real world and taking a holiday from the everyday. The cycles of time set up these vacations from reality on a regular basis so that escaping becomes part of your personality; there is a dreamy, absent, or detached side to your character that those closest to you know very well. You are sometimes remote and even completely inaccessible, off in your own world and universe.

CHILDREN AND THE NEXT GENERATION

Your relationship with children and the next generation is your great challenge in life. This may be because of actual issues with pregnancy, or there may be a child, niece, nephew, godchild, stepchild, or grandchild who provides the work in your life—and the effort. Leo rules your heirs, spares, and pretenders to the throne. It also oversees where you must put in the most time and energy on a regular basis. Sometimes this is because of your job—you are a natural teacher—but it can also be for personal reasons.

THE TRIUMPH OF YOUR IDEAS

Grounding your ideas in the real world is not something that comes naturally or easily to you, but it is worth it, Pisces, as once you make your move and find the right environment for your plans, you have the huge reward of seeing them grow to fruition. Completion and, better still, real growth are possible. The earthy Taurus rules your imagination, vision, and mental sketches. This helps you to realize that unless your brain waves are securely and firmly nurtured and protected, nothing happens. The result? Real achievement.

WHO SHARES YOUR BIRTHDAY?

Harry H. Corbett, born February 28, 1925
Brian Jones, born February 28, 1942
Cindy Wilson, born February 28, 1957

FEBRUARY 29

WHO ARE YOU?

You are a true water sign, Pisces, who merges with your circles and pools resources with the wider group. Ruled by Neptune, the symbol of spirituality, faith, and religion, you may—or may not—call yourself a believer, but you see evidence of people power throughout your life, which shapes the person you become. The sign of humanity, Aquarius, rules the sector of your chart also governed by Neptune, so there is a feeling of connection and community with others emotionally in a way that feeds your soul and spirit all your life.

YOUR DESTINY

The planet of Jupiter governs your ambition, mission, and position. Jupiter is known for its connection to excess, and you tend to take on too many projects, plans, and responsibilities. Learning how to delegate and select what matters is something that does not come naturally, but once you realize that success comes from the hard choices, you end up in a far stronger position. ("Kill your darlings" is the famous phrase for writers.) Once you learn how to work smarter, not harder, you can export your plans and perhaps travel with them.

FAMILY AND A SENSE OF BELONGING

Mercury, the planet associated with quicksilver and constant change, rules your family tree and also your sense of place, no matter if this is your idea about belonging to a region or a whole country. As a result, you can be quite Mercurial about your relatives, ancestors, roots, and origins. You can only stand still for so long before something else shifts, and as a result your great challenge in life is to try and manage what is always moving beneath your feet. The family, in particular, needs your time and energy on a regular basis.

DISTANT SHORES

Once you realize that success really comes from just a few ideas, rather than an excessive overload of them, you can find a home for your concepts in other regions. This may mean using the worldwide web to send your plans ahead of you or just exploring what is possible in other parts of your own country. Your rewards will come from successful relocation of your projects or perhaps emigration. Success in a different part of the world with an unfamiliar culture and language is a vindication of your faith in your own brainpower.

WHO SHARES YOUR BIRTHDAY?

Jimmy Dorsey, born February 29, 1904
Hermione Lee, born February 29, 1948
Jonathan Coleman, born February 29, 1956

MARCH 1

WHO ARE YOU?

You are ruled by Neptune, a symbol of deep intuition and sometimes pure mediumship. You pick up ideas and information from an invisible source, and this connection with the spiritual, invisible, or divine sphere informs everything from your relationships to your finances to your projects. You may or may not tell people you have extrasensory perception, but this sixth sense makes you a powerful transmitter and inspiration to those around you. You appear quite magical to some people in your circle, as although you do not pull rabbits out of hats, you have the ability to make things happen, seemingly with just a few words and a strong focus.

YOUR DESTINY

Complicated relationships of all kinds are in your destiny, and it will take all your ESP to help you navigate them. The sensitive, emotional, watery Cancer rules both lovers and children in your life. As you are also a water sign, it never rains but it pours, and it is up to you to find the practical answers for situations which seem all about feelings and nothing else. You really understand what all the poets, playwrights, and singers mean when they address the human heart. Time and experience are a great help, and eventually you learn to set boundaries, be firm, and replace thoughts or emotions with strong action. This improves things a lot.

GROUPS AND THE GOOD LIFE

You were born on the same day as the lead singer of the Who and a star from the TV show *Happy Days*. This should give you an idea about the hugely important role that groups, allies, friends, and circles of people play in your destiny. Yet, with the down-to-earth Capricorn ruling your social life, friendship, and fun, your lesson is never to let passing enjoyment get in the way of long-term rewards. You fall into place with others quite naturally in a community of diverse people—all happily giving each other space. This unique chemistry also offers real potential with solid work, business, or financial benefits, but it takes effort.

TWO CITIES OR TWO COUNTRIES

It would be very easy for you to live or work between two places. This may be two cities, states, or countries. The sign of the twins, Gemini, rules your homelife and property interests. Gemini also governs travel and commuting. You are more than just a dual citizen or juggler, though. Your breadth of knowledge increases the more you cross borders or even date lines. What you bring to the world as a result is a very special kind of experience and attitude. This makes you a born messenger, teacher, or guide—even if you don't think of yourself that way. Of course, there are plenty of international academics born on March 1, too, Pisces.

WHO SHARES YOUR BIRTHDAY?

Roger Daltrey, born March 1, 1944
Ron Howard, born March 1, 1954
Lupita Nyongo'o, born March 1, 1983
Justin Bieber, born March 1, 1994

MARCH 2

WHO ARE YOU?

The fortunate Sagittarius and its big-thinking ruler Jupiter are at the very top of your solar chart. You are one of life's winners, and the victories begin at school. Into your senior years you will always find that with enough positive thinking, belief, and determination you can achieve trophies, first place, or a top spot on the podium. Sagittarius by its nature is about exploring and seeing the big picture. Even though you are a Pisces, this sign dominates your ambitions, and your life is one "mission accomplished" after another.

YOUR DESTINY

Your knowledge, beliefs, and ideas about the world are ruled by Pluto, the planet which in turn governs the afterlife and departed souls. You may or may not already be aware of this, but your extended circle of family and friends in the spirit world has a direct connection with your own life. What you do affects them. As they evolve and progress spiritually, this also affects you. This is just as real as anything else in your life, and perhaps it is your own triumphs which help those who came before you move on up to the next level.

FINANCIAL MANAGEMENT

Your solar chart is set up in such a way that money needs total focus and a great deal of management. Balance is everything, with Libra, the sign of the scales, ruling business, inheritance, the bank, property, and assets. Finding harmony between the dream—Pisces is the sign of the daydreamer—and the reality is your great test. With Jupiter, the planet associated with great good fortune, in charge of your biggest achievements, wealth can even be on offer. The issue for you is trusting it, believing in it, and claiming it.

SHIPPING YOUR IDEAS

You were born to transport yourself and perhaps your ideas around your country or around the world. Your home zone is ruled by Gemini and Mercury, the planet of restless people who need to be on the move. You can do this purely online, of course, and feel that the web itself is where you are most grounded. It is common for people born on your birthday to travel or emigrate for work reasons, however. At the very least you are a born exporter, once again thanks to Jupiter with all his broad vision at the top of your chart.

WHO SHARES YOUR BIRTHDAY?

Dr. Seuss, born March 2, 1904

Jon Bon Jovi, born March 2, 1962

Daniel Craig, born March 2, 1968

MARCH 3

WHO ARE YOU?

You are the born traveler or commuter who is superbly at home with two cities, two regions, or two countries. The twins of Gemini rule your home and sense of place. This duality gives you an appreciation of different cultures, customs, or languages. You are always on the move, and as a result of constantly shifting between two work or home locations, you gather an impressive amount of knowledge. You are always welcome in both places for this reason. Over the course of your life, the two map points may also shift.

YOUR DESTINY

Libra is the sign of pairs, partnerships, duets, and couples, and it rules your search for money. You tend to pair off with others; this may be your intimate partner or your professional other half. The faces may change, but the idea of standing on one end of the scales, while somebody else so different to you is on the other, is at the heart of your quest for financial security. Do you get there? It really depends on the cycles of time. Remember you are a Pisces. Your sign shows two fish who can become confused. Professional advice helps.

SOLITUDE AND DISCOVERY

When we turn to your natal chart rather than your solar chart, we find your Sun in Pisces firmly placed in the Twelfth House of solitude, soul-searching, and the spirit. This is also where we find your unconscious and your psyche. The periods in your life when you are quite alone can happen by choice or circumstance, but you will always find yourself looking for answers. Because you are ruled by Neptune, the planet most associated with the big questions about God—or not God—and the universe, these run very deep indeed.

UNITING THE GROUP

The practical Capricorn rules the groups you are a part of or the groups which are against you. Capricorn is an earth sign, and in order to feel grounded, you will repeatedly find yourself charged with the task of setting personal feelings aside or the hive mind and uniting people. You will take turns at being both the outsider and insider and, every time, learn more about what it takes to get a community, team, society, club, association, and all the rest on firm turf. Communication is the key to everything, as you know.

WHO SHARES YOUR BIRTHDAY?

Jean Harlow, born March 3, 1911

Tone Loc, born March 3, 1966

Brian Cox, born March 3, 1968

MARCH 4

WHO ARE YOU?

You are the world citizen who is regularly tempted by travel or emigration and certainly drawn toward other nationalities and cultures in your own country. Sagittarius and Jupiter rule the top of your solar chart, and you are drawn toward countries and people whose language and history are different to your own. You are a candidate for a multicultural marriage, for example, or living as an expat. You may have a career or engaging interest which involves you with all corners of the worldwide web. Your issue? Choosing.

YOUR DESTINY

Your finances, business interests, and banking are always a matter for two people. Are two heads better than one? In your case, one of the issues is finding somebody who can bring an outsider's objectivity to your plans. The sign of the scales—two halves that make the whole—is Libra, and this is also important in your search for income or assets. As a Pisces, you are also dual in nature, with two fish representing your sign. They swim in different directions and neither of them are particularly practical or earthbound. Advisors help.

THE BACKING OF THE GROUP

The solid, comfortable, grounded Capricorn rules your group support. This may be a football team, if you are the captain or coach, or a band. It may be a large professional organization or even a collection of admirers. Your test in life is to treat each person within the wider circle as a separate individual rather than assume everybody is just another face in the community. Keeping those crucial and protective collections of allies and friends content and stable is your mission, should you accept it, Pisces.

CHOOSING YOUR LOCATION

As you know, Sagittarius and Jupiter rule your highest achievements in life and are associated with foreign people and places. Your ideas, plans, and projects must find fertile soil far from home turf, and that is one of your repeated rewards: the successful export of what is on paper or on your computer at home, but could travel a very long way indeed. Thinking globally and being aware of what is out there for you are one half of the work. The other is multitasking. Remember the Pisces duality. It's always worth juggling two ideas.

WHO SHARES YOUR BIRTHDAY?

Bobby Womack, born March 4, 1944
James Ellroy, born March 4, 1948
Evan Dando, born March 4, 1967

MARCH 5

WHO ARE YOU?

The true Pisces is always looking for the next great escape. You are a traveler, explorer, and natural migrant. Sometimes it works, and sometimes it doesn't. Even the false starts or challenges don't stop you. Sagittarius, which reigns over foreigners and foreign countries, rules your house of ambition. Your highest goals and achievements are always somewhere else on the map. At the other end of your solar chart, we find Gemini, which governs short journeys and regional exploration. This feels like home to you. In fact, your place in the world is always where you put your bag or suitcase. The next horizon is always the one to chase for you to feel secure.

YOUR DESTINY

Pisces is about the inner escape as well as travel or relocation. Your horoscope is set up in such a way that you will regularly need to leave everybody and go off on a pilgrimage by yourself—a solo sabbatical. When you come back—and you usually come back—everything and everybody looks different. The ambitious Capricorn rules your sector of groups, friends, networks, communities, and allies. When the lineup of people does not work as it could and those towering goals seem too heavy, you are inclined to go your own way. This is actually part of your lifetime pattern of success, if you can bring yourself to return, rethink, and regroup.

ESCAPISM AND REALITY

The typical Pisces Sun enjoys anybody and anything offering a way out of the real world. Who needs work and routine? You are far more interested in the champagne than you are in pressing the grapes. Your greatest challenge will be using the incredible wealth of resources you are given. It is all too easy to forget about preplanning when you are diverted by a good Friday night or Sunday afternoon, but your need for a constant weekend will mean that you have regrets later, as a harvest only lasts so long.

HEIRS, SPARES, AND PRETENDERS TO THE THRONE

You may or may not have children of your own, but you have a great deal to pass on to the next generation—and the one after that. If you do become a parent, you will lead them and teach them, and your guidance will influence them for years. Leo rules your sector of work, unpaid work, and academia. Leo is the monarch of the twelve zodiac signs, and so you may find your calling with students, teenagers, or young adults. Perhaps this is full-time parenthood for you; maybe it is a sense of mission with youth.

WHO HELPS YOU SHINE?

People who have the Sun in a sextile or trine with your own Sun will help you shine. This includes Taureans born on May 4–6, Cancerians born on July 6–8, Scorpios born on November 6–8, and Capricorns born on January 4–6.

WHO SHARES YOUR BIRTHDAY?

Rex Harrison, born March 5, 1908
Andy Gibb, born March 5, 1958
Matt Lucas, born March 5, 1974

MARCH 6

WHO ARE YOU?

You are the copilot and partner, professionally or personally, of a number of people who are the same as you, yet so different. This teaches you tolerance and the art of compromise. Libra, which rules pairs, also describes all the important property, financial, or business decisions in your life. The faces may change, but the challenge remains the same. Do you go down the same path as your opposite number, or do you find parallel paths? And how do you both decide on the same destination? Your lateral thinking around this will give you a fascinating life every time it happens, Pisces.

YOUR DESTINY

You are about action, not words, when it comes to money. With Mars the Warrior ruling your sector of income and investment, and the forthright Aries large and in charge, you are fated to be a mover and shaker when it comes to everything you own or have earned. You are a tough negotiator. Once you have decided on your mission, you don't waste any time, and your life will be full of accomplishments to show for it—whether the house or apartment, branch of the family tree or charity or business. This is quite a different side of your personality, but a series of fated events will bring it out of you, Pisces.

THE GROUP AND ITS RULES

You will be in several groups, clubs, teams, or communities in your life, and you will learn a lot about managing them as you go along. Sometimes you will be the leader or dominant person. At other times you will be the challenger. You will also play the part of the classic Pisces escape artist, who is present and yet somehow absent as the machinations of the group roll on. You will be tested by the fantastic potential of these circles and the entertainment they provide—there's never a dull moment. Unless you can use your empathy and intuition to read minds and pull people together, though, it's all a test.

THE BURNING MISSIONS

The fire sign Leo rules your work, unpaid work, and education. You have all the enthusiasm and burning passion associated with that sign when it comes to your favorite projects, plans, and ideas. That is not quite enough for you, though. With Sagittarius, the sign of exploration and adventure, ruling your success in life, you are always looking for the right place to plant your proposals or brainpower. When you manage to focus—always a challenge for Pisces—and do the research before you gallop off in search of the right home for your efforts, your achievement really is a sweet success.

WHO SHARES YOUR BIRTHDAY?

Elizabeth Barrett Browning, born March 6, 1806
Rob Reiner, born March 6, 1947
Shaquille O'Neal, born March 6, 1972

MARCH 7

WHO ARE YOU?

Intuitive but sensitive, you know exactly how others are feeling and thinking, even if it is not explained to you. Reading the room comes naturally to you. You are sensitive enough to know that life is easier when you bypass awkward conversations with friends, colleagues, family, and partners in favor of just offering what is required. So, for example, you would rather guess how to fix a work issue and produce the solutions than thrash out the details with the other person. This smooth, easy, flowing approach is learned over time—and also saves you a lot of time.

YOUR DESTINY

You are destined to pursue religion, hypnosis therapy, Tarot reading, mediumship, self-help techniques, and dream interpretation all your life—sometimes going more deeply into just one discipline over many years or at other times trying one method and then replacing it with another. You are a natural meditator or psychic. You may live alone for long periods of time as a result or have a partnership or family but create a lifestyle allowing you your solitude. A mentor or guide who understands your need for privacy but can offer you solutions—like a rabbi or a life coach, for example—will strongly influence your fate.

MAKING YOUR OWN REALITY

You have a talent for creating your own world, and it has nothing to do with reality. You could easily turn to art or photography to help you do this as these professions or interests allow you to float in a bubble far away from everyday life. You enjoy taking the visions in your head and turning them into something that can have an impact on people, proving to yourself that imagination and ideas can be powerful if you are practical about them. Learning how to do this takes years, but even as a child you are obviously drawn to creative play or imaginary friends.

SELF-DECEPTION

The biggest challenge you face is your own habit of deceiving yourself in relationships with other people You can tell yourself stories about what you are doing or give yourself excuses, but eventually you must always face the results of your actions, particularly if you are sexually unfaithful. Even if it never gets that far, your life as a partner or parent is a test of your ability to be fair to other people, whether or not you can always be strictly truthful with them. The family you grew up with and/or the family you marry into test you the most. Finding a way to get what you want and need without hurting other people is a lifelong search.

WHO SHARES YOUR BIRTHDAY?

Susan Miller, born March 7, 1947

Bryan Cranston, born March 7, 1956

Rachel Weisz, born March 7, 1970

Amanda Gorman, born March 7, 1998

MARCH 8

WHO ARE YOU?

You are the focused, determined investor or businessperson who has tough Aries in charge of your dealmaking. You may end up in any profession at all, but you have the instincts of a warrior when it comes to the money you have saved or made. The planet Mars also rules this need to treat even a basic negotiation as a mission. Mars was the Roman god of war, and although nobody is suggesting that your finances turn you into a gladiator, you can be quite uncompromising when it comes to paying other people or large organizations. This may be about taxes for you, property, or even good causes.

YOUR DESTINY

You are a true water sign, Pisces, and have all the deep feelings and sensitivity that come with that. Water rules everything that flows from you and away from you once a relationship is no more. You are also born with a zodiac sign associated with the most solitary, introspective, and soul-searching area of the chart: the Twelfth House. You need to hibernate whenever your personal life demands it, and the cycles of time suggest you will get to know yourself very well as a result. When you are alone with your own soul or spirit, you can absorb the realities of being your water sign self: it's all about emotions.

THE COMMUNITY

You are so sensitive that you do not find it too difficult to tune in to others in the many groups you will be involved with in your life. The issue is practical action, however, as the down-to-earth Capricorn rules these circles and communities. You are always mindful of the end results with your teams, clubs, bands, societies, associations, and so on. It's not enough to share the same direction; there has to be a sensible way of operating together which offers the chance to build something solid and long-lasting at the end. How easy is this? It's never easy. But however close you get is always an achievement.

GENEROSITY AND GIVING

The energetic Aries rules your personal income, which explains why you are such a dynamic negotiator. You have Libra in charge of joint finances, however, and this sign is associated with fairness and justice. As a result, when you are wealthy enough, you consider it only right to give back. This makes you notably generous, and you have the classic Pisces ability to feel compassion for those less fortunate than you. Does charity begin at home for you, or do you give on a wider basis? Times in your life when you have also seen financial justice swing your way remind you to reward others, too.

WHO SHARES YOUR BIRTHDAY?

Micky Dolenz, born March 8, 1945

Carole Bayer Sager, born March 8, 1947

Aidan Quinn, born March 8, 1959

MARCH 9

WHO ARE YOU?

Leo, which governs sovereigns, also rules your zone of daily life, work, and the system. As a result, you are likely to see more than one coronation in your lifetime. Sometimes you yourself will be crowned. At other times you will see the existing leader replaced with a new ruler. In all cases you have to accept the reshuffles that surround this kind of promotion or departure. The planet Saturn, associated with hierarchy, rules these kinds of groups around you. Restructuring the old edifice or even replacing it is part of your life, and dealing with this type of upheaval becomes part of your character.

YOUR DESTINY

You are a true Pisces, ruled by Neptune, which is associated with faith, belief, doctrine, and religion. Pisces is the sign most commonly linked to Christianity, although you may be a skeptic, of course. The central question for you, from childhood onward, is about your acceptance of authority by others who believe—or your ability to address those who hear or read you, but may also have doubts. This is the invisible world of Pisces the Fish, which we link to prayer, heaven, hell, miracles, saints, angels, gods, goddesses—and God with a capital *G*. Your individual choices about this unseen reality are part of your fate.

THE ESCAPE ARTIST

Pisces and Neptune are also associated with escapism. You are an escape artist in many ways, as you are not afraid of leaving any place that you know all too well in order to go to somewhere quite unknown or toward a destiny that is yet to be filled in. You are an extremely sensitive water sign, and so it can be easier sometimes for you to leave what or who may be too much in favor of migration or relocation. This also comes partly from Sagittarius, the sign of the traveler, which rules the highest point of your solar chart. This is where your highest aims take hold. You will learn a lot from your great escapes.

JUPITER AND ACHIEVEMENT

Jupiter rules your sector of achievement, and as this planet is associated with excess, you tend to gather an abundance of plans, projects, ideas, and responsibilities in both your personal and professional life. Jupiter is also about optimism, and perhaps you repeatedly find yourself hoping you can carry things through to completion, no matter how much you are taking on board. Sometimes you can actually achieve this, but along the way, you also learn to evaluate what is most important and come to appreciate the journey as much as the end result. If the journey means shedding a load, do it.

WHO SHARES YOUR BIRTHDAY?

Vita Sackville-West, born March 9, 1892
Walter Mercado, born March 9, 1932
Bobby Fischer, born March 9, 1943

MARCH 10

WHO ARE YOU?

You are destined to become one of the most experienced experts on group psychology in the zodiac. In your birth chart, the area of the horoscope which is ruled by your Sun sign Pisces is the same area where we find the focus on communities, circles, and collectives in your solar chart. You will always be sensitive to the power of many people acting together against an outsider. You will find that out through being one of the many, but also sometimes dealing with the hive mind as one. This shows you how to communicate, set aside differences, unite, and achieve the miracle of final solidarity, unity, and real potential together.

YOUR DESTINY

You are the boss, chief, or CEO in your chosen field. Once you retire, this may be about your family or your unpaid work. In your career or life as a volunteer, it is about your world of achievement. You are ambitious to get to the top and make it. Jupiter with all his huge vision and good fortune rules the peak of your solar chart, which is where you hit the heights. Jupiter was associated with the eagle in ancient Rome, where modern astrology comes from. Like an eagle, you can see far and wide from your privileged vantage point. Jupiter was the greatest and best two thousand years ago, and he oversees towering achievements.

FINANCIAL BALANCE

Libra, the scales of balance, rules joint finances, property, charity, and business endeavors in your chart. Your great challenge is to be fair to both sides or make two opposing interests harmonize. This may be your income and your partner's, for example. It may be your taxes and your investments. The cycles of time suggest that you will repeatedly find your country's economy or the world economy testing your ability to find symmetry. Your great lesson is to use the energy you pour into juggling this—Mars the action planet rules your own money—into a working system. You will always need to adapt.

PLANS THAT TRAVEL

Jupiter and his sign of Sagittarius, linked to other regions and countries, direct your highest goals. As you know, Jupiter helps you reach the top. Sagittarius suggests your direction will always be away from home and toward other parts of the world. Other accents or languages will appeal to you. Your reward is to make this work in a practical way, as down-to-earth Taurus rules your sector of ideas. Taurus can also be a rather stuck, slow sign, so the sense of accomplishment you feel when you act on your visions, rather than daydreaming, is enormous. Once you are grounded, Pisces, the world is open to your brain waves.

WHO SHARES YOUR BIRTHDAY?

Clare Boothe Luce, born March 10, 1903
Sharon Stone, born March 10, 1958
Prince Edward, born March 10, 1964

MARCH 11

WHO ARE YOU?

You have the numeral 1 twice in your birth date. You are the person whose life is changed by firsts. Big, bold new beginnings are part of your fate. You draw a great deal of spiritual fulfillment from the wider group. You may or may not be religious, but Pisces the Fish rules Christianity. Perhaps Buddhism draws you—or a widespread network of like-minded souls who have no interest in God or gods or buddhas and bodhisattvas but are linked by a common need to pool resources. Call it a collective, a community, or a tribe; you gain from it emotionally. You are a water sign, Pisces, and need to put your feelings first.

YOUR DESTINY

You have what it takes to become wealthy with energetic Aries ruling your sector of money saved or made. It takes sustained energy to create financial security, but luckily you were born with it. You also have Gemini, the sign of the twins, in charge of your house, apartment, land, or property investments. Gemini is the sign of the juggler and multitasker, and you are gifted with great dexterity, Pisces. This makes it possible to look after two things at once. You are also always open to the big picture of opportunity, with Jupiter ruling the top of your chart where your achievements are. Other regions or countries always call.

GENEROSITY, CHARITY, AND PHILANTHROPY

Your great challenge in life is also money. You can make it or save it in luxuriously comfortable amounts, but it is your karma to establish relationships with others that serve you fairly as well as them. You are a natural donor or lender, either with people in your circle or needy souls outside. With Libra, the scales of justice, equality, and fairness, ruling this side of your existence, you spend your life trying to balance those scales. It's never simple. When you give or lend, you set up a dynamic with others that tests them as well as yourself. Calculating what is harmonious or symmetrical takes a great deal of effort.

HUGE IDEAS

You don't just have thoughts or brainpower, Pisces. You have huge ideas with massive potential. The reward when you turn them from imagination or inspiration into reality is immense. This holds true all your life, from when you are a young adult into old age. The grounded earth sign Taurus rules your sector of the mind, so you are practical about what must be firmly planted in the real world rather than left floating in the realm of potential. This ability to put both your feet on the ground and walk your talk leads you to great success when your projects take off. You learn to research not just the timing but also the location of these launches.

WHO SHARES YOUR BIRTHDAY?

Rupert Murdoch, born March 11, 1931

Douglas Adams, born March 11, 1952

Nina Hagen, born March 11, 1955

MARCH 12

WHO ARE YOU?

You are the classic Pisces in a realm of your own removed from the real world. You are often found on a holiday from the everyday or a vacation from what's "normal." You are fascinating to people at a distance, but it can be hard to get close. It is not impossible, but it takes big decisions to leave your comfort zone of escapism to meet others halfway. The choice is always open to you to leave your usual way of life and reconnect, but there are some people born on March 12 like you who simply need to take it. You are the dreamer, drifter, and visionary who also needs to watch your reactions to medication, alcohol, and drugs.

YOUR DESTINY

Pisces is the sign ruling Christianity, so your ideas about God (whether yes or no) shape your fate. This may be because of your family or education. Your horoscope is set up in such a way that you will come to a number of crossroads involving spirituality, religion, or other doctrines. Sometimes you are the mouthpiece; sometimes you are the recipient of the message. Pisces is ruled by Neptune, so this planet looms large in your fate. Neptune is about the invisible world of heaven or hell. It is also about faith, belief, and an inner knowing that cannot be tested or shown. Meeting this in your life changes your destiny.

MANAGING YOUR WORLD

You seem very fortunate to outsiders as you are blessed with beautiful surroundings in nature or your own garden all your life. Venus rules your neighborhood or local area, and this planet is an ancient symbol of beauty. At the same time, you need to honor the rules for Pisces and work on boundaries. It is very easy for everything to end up everywhere and all over the place all the time in your life. You are a water sign, so sometimes your life is open to flooding. Your other challenge is the evergreen nature of love. If you had other lovers before your current partner, then this is an issue that needs caution and care.

CHILDREN AND TEENAGERS

You have an appreciative eye for anyone who can live in a bubble, separate from the adult realities of the outside world. Children and teenagers in your life don't even have to try. This may be your child, stepchild, godchild, niece, or nephew. There may be a professional or philanthropic involvement with the next generation, too.

As a sensitive and emotional water sign, you appreciate the delicate innocence of youth. You can never go back, but you can respect young minds and hearts. You may or may not become a parent, but there will always be another wave of younger faces to intrigue you.

WHO SHARES YOUR BIRTHDAY?

Googie Withers, born March 12, 1917
Liza Minnelli, born March 12, 1946
Dave Eggers, born March 12, 1970

MARCH 13

WHO ARE YOU?

The enthusiastic idea person who makes a fantastic start to their missions, but has to deal with the reality of seeing things through—that's you. Fiery Leo with all its confidence and energy rules your sector of work, study, and unpaid labor. At the top of your chart, the sign of the explorer and adventurer, Sagittarius, rules your goals. At first sight you may appear to be more of a fire sign than a water sign, but on closer inspection, you are a true Pisces. This is the sign that dreams and visualizes but can be unfocused. Your greatest achievements come when you ground yourself in the real world.

YOUR DESTINY

Once you overcome the Pisces tendency to escape from reality and lose yourself in your own imagination, you are in an extremely good position to take your brainpower, concepts, and notions and plant them somewhere solid. Sagittarius, at the top of your chart, rules your peak achievements in life, and these will involve travel or export, as Sagittarius rules over everything and everybody foreign to you—even if they speak the same language. Practical Taurus, a useful dash of earth in your chart, governs your plans, and if you tune in to that sensible, grounded side of yourself, you can be successful.

INDIVIDUALS AND THE GROUP

The potential to build something extraordinary with the circles or groups in your life is there from your adolescence into old age. The challenge for you is finding a way to pull everybody together working in the same direction. As a sensitive Pisces, you are all too aware of the dynamics and different personalities in a team, club, society, and so on. Dealing with this but also finding a way to join forces with those who want to unite everybody are a great test. It seems so much easier to escape into your own solo missions and attempts. Yet, if you can all set aside your independent agendas and unite with others, lasting success is possible.

WORK AND INCOME

You are partly Aries when it comes to your income. Aries rules your ability to work on productive, financially rewarding plans with sustained energy. This is the sign of the marathon runner, so you have what it takes to pour yourself into long-term jobs or projects which deliver the security you want—or even more. The sign of pride, Leo, is in charge of your skills, trade, craft, talents, and qualifications, and you enjoy showing what you can do. You are quietly proud of your efforts in a dignified way. These two fire signs of Aries and Leo have a hold on your chart which balances the escapist side of your nature and keeps you content.

WHO SHARES YOUR BIRTHDAY?

Neil Sedaka, born March 13, 1939

Adam Clayton, born March 13, 1960

Annabeth Gish, born March 13, 1971

Coco Gauff, born March 13, 2004

MARCH 14

WHO ARE YOU?

You have two zodiac signs of duality in key places in your chart. You are the person who is always on one road with one person, deciding which path you will take, together, apart, or in the middle. This is the stuff of which great Hollywood romcoms are made, but also Shakespeare's best works. You are a sensitive water sign, dominated by your feelings, and can find it very difficult to make logical, rational decisions when faced with partnership questions. Gemini and Libra both rule very different kinds of pairings: Gemini is about siblings. Libra is about romantic partners, but also former partners.

YOUR DESTINY

Your love life is part of your fate, in terms of the good life, as Libra with all its emphasis on the heart dominates your sector of lifestyle, security, and personal comfort zone. This may be because of an evergreen relationship or marriage which never stops delivering or because of a breakup which has nevertheless left you in a good place in terms of where you live—and how you live, too. You will experience this in different ways, perhaps more than once in your life, depending on the personal decisions you take. Venus is about beauty, and this planet also rules your sector of rich rewards. You're a material girl—or boy.

DEALING WITH SUCCESS

Sagittarius rules your success in life, placed at the top of your chart. This is in turn ruled by Jupiter, which is a symbol of great good fortune. Repeatedly as a young adult but also into your senior years, you emerge as the winner. What is less obvious to the outsiders who celebrate that, or even envy you, is your hidden inner response to your victories. The fact is, you cannot always square the big victories with the reality. When we look at your solar chart, we find Sagittarius squares your own Pisces Sun. Figuring out how to manage triumph is a challenge.

YOUR IDEAS AND PLANS

You have the classic vision of a true Pisces but also the lack of focus. When you get it right and do the work, prepare the ground, complete the research, and operate with a plan, the fulfillment is deep, as you know you have made it by overcoming your own tendency to go off on a tangent. This is the case when you are both younger and older, but experience teaches you that groundwork is the key. Sagittarius, which rules your position, mission, and ambition, is a fire sign. You can be mistaken for an enthusiastic, adventurous Sagittarian in your field because of that energy. The trick is to finish what you start and succeed.

WHO SHARES YOUR BIRTHDAY?

Diane Arbus, born March 14, 1923
Eleanor Bron, born March 14, 1938
Billy Crystal, born March 14, 1948
Giorgio Tsoukalos, born March 14, 1978

MARCH 15

WHO ARE YOU?

With the sign of the explorer and traveler, Sagittarius, at the very top of your chart, you are drawn to Europe, the Americas, and Australasia all your life. You are a natural migrant or tourist, exporter or world citizen. You are drawn to other accents, languages, and cultures, and your only issue is selecting just one or two at a time. Your Sagittarius rulership of the midheaven of your solar chart is there from your teenage years until old age, and you never stop being fascinated by the world-wide web and every corner of it.

YOUR DESTINY

Your heart zone is ruled by sensitive Cancer, an emotional water sign like your Sun sign. This means you really do have a deep understanding of everything that the poets and songwriters refer to when they talk about the complications of love and life. There are no simple or easy solutions for you, ever, but then you would not have the enormous depth of feeling without all that you experience. This applies to lovers, partners, and sometimes family or friends. Navigating this is part of your journey, and it can be profoundly healing.

FINANCIAL SECURITY

Balanced Libra rules your joint finances and property, business, charity, valuables, and assets. You are able to keep two sides of your budget in symmetry and can balance the scales for yourself and others. This is not easy, but the challenge of making the money go round while keeping two sides content or both sides of your planning in sync is a test you can take. Libra is about what is fair, reasonable, logical, and satisfying, in the sense that leveling the scales is always pleasing. It will take work, but you can do it.

SOLITUDE AND SOUL SATISFACTION

For all that you are intrigued by the world and caught up with your emotions, you are also a lone wolf when it suits you. Pisces rules the secluded and introspective Twelfth House of your birth chart, and there we also find Neptune, associated with escapism. This is the same house where we find your Sun, thanks to your March 15 birthday, so your personality and destiny involve solo exploration. You may be a meditator or hiker for this reason or have other outlets. Doing this restores your spirit and makes relationships work.

WHO SHARES YOUR BIRTHDAY?

John Snow, born March 15, 1813

Mike Love, born March 15, 1941

Sly Stone, born March 15, 1943

MARCH 16

WHO ARE YOU?

The sign of parenthood, children, and young people—and your life with them—is ruled by Cancer in your chart. This is a water sign like your own Pisces Sun and makes a perfect angle to your two fish. You may or may not become a parent, but the next generation is where you find rewards. You can do this as a godparent, aunt, or uncle, of course, but there may also be a special role here with younger people through your career or unpaid work. The proud Leo rules heirs, spares, and pretenders to your throne.

YOUR DESTINY

Gemini, which rules twins, siblings, and relationships between twin souls, is in charge of your house, apartment, or garden. You have a pattern of falling into pairs or couples or attracting double pairs where you live. This may be there from childhood, or you may find it takes place later on. This adds up to harmony, and in fact the sign of balance, Libra (another double sign), governs joint finances and property. As a Pisces, you always do best in or around water, too—even something as small as a pond.

BOUNDARIES AND BARRIERS

The great test for you in life is dealing with boundaries and barriers. This is classic Pisces territory as you are the two fish who swim everywhere, all the time, all over the place. What you will be shown when young and old is that there are rules for a reason. For all that a part of you is the eternal child who is fascinated by the world of the very young, you can also be hardline when you have to be. This tough approach makes sure others are aware of the boundaries that cannot be crossed, but it is also an effort. It becomes easier with experience.

THRIVING IDEAS

Looking for the good things in life begins with an appreciation of your own ideas, visions, and plans. Understanding your own need to ground this in the real world is the next step, though. This is down to Taurus, an earth sign, ruling your concepts and brain waves. This side of your nature knows that if you do not find solid foundations for your high-potential inspiration, nothing will ever last. In fact, it may never even get off the ground. When you master this and watch something grow to completion, it's a reward.

WHO SHARES YOUR BIRTHDAY?

Caroline Herschel, born March 16, 1750

Jerry Lewis, born March 16, 1926

Bernardo Bertolucci, born March 16, 1941

John Darnielle, born March 16, 1967

MARCH 17

WHO ARE YOU?

You take turns at both being the star and one of many stars in a community or circle. One moment you are heading the cast; the next somebody else is. In your birth chart, the group sign of Aquarius rules the natural domain of Pisces, your Sun sign, so you are typically committed to pooling resources, which the water bearer does best. Sharing and shining together are the ideal, but you also make it real. The only issue is the famous Pisces need for more method and order than most people; remembering that is so useful.

YOUR DESTINY

You are more about the money than you might think, reading the usual descriptions of Pisces. You have the strong, determined fire sign Aries ruling your sector of income, which might explain that to you. Repeatedly in your life you will need financial advice from tried, tested, and trusted professionals because when left to your own devices you can find yourself permanently at the start of things, but never actually able to see them through over the long term. That is where sound suggestions can really help you control your destiny.

INVESTING IN YOURSELF AND OTHERS

Not only energetic Aries but also steely Mars both rule your assets and income, so there is no question that you are a person on a mission once you have the money to invest or spend. This is also a tremendous challenge for you as there may be so many questions about the stock market, property, good causes, the family, and so on. You are very good at tough negotiations with your assertive Aries side to help you with deals, but more than most people, you also have so much to gain from professional advisors.

HEALING AND BEING HEALED

The sign of the healer and the healed is Virgo, and this rules all the pairs, couples, duos, and duets in your life. Sometimes this is a romance or marriage. However, you can play both sides of therapy, help, medicine, alternative medicine, and so on—with anyone bonded to you for that process. Understanding that it swings both ways makes you a better patient or recipient as well as a more gifted helper. Virgo has a tremendous sense of duty and service to others, and this will show and shine brightly in these double acts in your life.

WHO SHARES YOUR BIRTHDAY?

Kate Greenaway, born March 17, 1846
Rudolf Nureyev, born March 17, 1938
Rob Lowe, born March 17, 1964
Stormy Daniels, born March 17, 1979
Hozier, born March 17, 1990

MARCH 18

WHO ARE YOU?

You are a Piscean, intuitive and one step ahead of other people. You value action over words with the energetic Aries ruling everything that is precious to you. You are also courageous, with Leo the lionhearted sign ruling your work or unpaid labor. This combination makes you a strategist who is quick off the mark and gifted at removing issues before they take hold. You do extremely well in professions where you must protect your interests and those of others. Slippery as your two fish, you get away with it.

YOUR DESTINY

You are fated to be involved with one or more groups over the course of your lifetime. This may be a political party or a secret society, a band or an all-star cast. You will share the leading role with others so that sometimes you are the center of attention and at other times you take your place in the chorus as others step forward. The sign of community, unity, and solidarity is Aquarius. In your solar chart, Aquarius, the sign of pooled resources, rules your own zodiac sector. So ego-free sharing comes naturally to you and the group.

CHILDREN AND TEENAGERS

The world of children and teenagers asks a lot from you and is where your work rests, either with your sense of duty, service, obligation, or for health reasons. Leo, which is the sign associated with your heirs, spares, and pretenders to the throne, rules your job, as you know. Therefore you may actually take a professional role with a younger generation or just find that children, stepchildren, nieces, nephews, godchildren, or grandchildren are a test and also a task. This will arrive in your life repeatedly, Pisces.

WINNING VICTORIES

You are one of life's winners and will find victories, promotions, and a number of first places are written in your future. This begins when you are quite young and have your first taste of success. Even into your senior years you are capable of some amazing triumphs. Jupiter with all his good fortune, growth, and expansion rules the highest point of your chart, which is where you also hit the heights. In turn, he rules the adventurous sign of Sagittarius, which is always looking for the next challenge and the next achievement.

WHO SHARES YOUR BIRTHDAY?

Edgar Cayce, born March 18, 1877
John Updike, born March 18, 1932
Wilson Pickett, born March 18, 1941
Queen Latifah, born March 18, 1970

MARCH 19

WHO ARE YOU?

You are the sensitive Pisces soul who can exist in a bubble until you find a way of grounding yourself with both feet on the earth. This helps you center and focus. Imagination, the power of your own mind, and your interpretation of your life can sometimes take over, which is when remembering where you come from and where you belong will help you get back to who you really are. You are blessed with some wonderful people in your life—and always will be—but to fully appreciate them, you also need to feel connected to the world.

YOUR DESTINY

The sign of duos, duets, and pairs is Libra, also ruling your finances, assets, business interests, and all that is valuable to you. The cycles of time that work in your horoscope will often put you in a situation with "opposite but equal" people where you must balance each other on the scales in order to secure what you want. Libra is about sharing the task, and in your case it is about the quest for financial security.

This is sometimes about your marriage or romantic partnership but can also be about a business relationship.

THE MEDITATOR

You are a natural meditator if you work at it, and in fact your own ruler Neptune is about alternative realities found through peace of mind. Yoga may be your pathway, or you may stumble across your own way of harnessing your mind when you are a teenager. Pisces rules sleep, dreams, self-hypnosis, and consciousness, and it is in turn ruled by Neptune. Understanding how this works for you—and how to best manage it—can be a lifetime pursuit but with the satisfying end result that you discover how to properly utilize your state of mind.

FINANCIAL POWER

The other sign which rules your finances is Aries, opposite Libra in your solar chart. Libra describes the duo or duet in your life, which always leads to a search for financial promise. Aries, on the other hand, shows your personal strength. You are capable of achieving solid gains more than once in your life and over time may slowly build yourself a miniature kingdom. This sense of security and also personal influence is enough to give you the kind of clout that anyone wishing to negotiate with you has to learn to respect—or else.

WHO SHARES YOUR BIRTHDAY?

Irving Wallace, born March 19, 1916
Ursula Andress, born March 19, 1936
Glenn Close, born March 19, 1947

MARCH 20

WHO ARE YOU?

The numbers in your birth date explain why you are drawn to partners who are opposite to you. You need another person to pair up with and compare yourself to, even if you are sometimes taking opposite directions. Your numerology contains the numeral 2, and although these recurring duets in your life are complex, they also help to define your character. The 0 in your birthday suggests you are nothing without each other in these odd pairings in your life. The effort involved in meeting someone halfway is worth it.

YOUR DESTINY

You find spiritual and emotional fulfillment with a group or network of groups to hold you. These circles are the foundations of all you do and are. Even though two is your number no matter how many lessons are involved, it is also true that you find what you are looking for through a community or collective. This may be the army or an ensemble cast. Every time you find another wonderful source of pooled energy and like minds, you go through the same experience. Shared people power for you is a very special thing indeed.

SOLITUDE AND SPIRITUALITY

You are a hermit who finds meaning when you are quite alone, even if it's not always easy to be on your own. Turning away from other people can be challenging, but you also need to do it. It is the only way to discover what matters in life. Your greatest challenge will be to understand the path of the solo seeker and uncover what you are looking for. This may be religious, philosophical, intellectual, or based on something you find hard to put into words. No amount of company can take you to the real truth, and even though it is true that the group sustains you, a great deal of the hard work you do will involve you being quite alone.

THE BOSS

You are the boss, leader, or chief of your chosen field and rise to the top slowly but surely. It takes years to achieve this, but once you are there, you have stability and influence that will reward you until you are ready to let go—if you ever do. You have tremendous staying power and also respect the hierarchy, system, or establishment enough to scale the heights. This also affects the solitary path you have just read about. There is only room for one at the top. Sometimes, you are simply the head of the family, but a career fulfills you.

WHO SHARES YOUR BIRTHDAY?

Vera Lynn, born March 20, 1917

William Hurt, born March 20, 1950

Spike Lee, born March 20, 1957

MARCH 21

WHO ARE YOU?

You are a traveler and explorer whose relationships with lovers, friends, family, or partners frequently involve long distances. You have the classic NASA countdown in your birth date (3, 2, 1), and a great deal of your life will be spent on missions, if not necessarily space missions. Ignition, engines running, and liftoff are a good way to define your life and character, however, as you are adventurous by nature and never let geography stand in the way of a good romance. In fact, it possibly adds to the intensity of your feelings.

YOUR DESTINY

You are a born exporter who is destined to always need the next horizon in order to successfully plant your ideas and plans. There is no emotional barrier to stop you taking off, as you have seen. In fact, you often find that being separated from people you care about helps to strengthen your conviction. Your horoscope is geared toward cycles of time which may see you relocate or even emigrate. This may happen more than once. At the very least you are a worldwide web citizen with a yearning to explore.

AUSTRALASIA, THE AMERICAS, AND EUROPE

For all that your instincts tell you to look elsewhere for life's possibilities, it is also quite challenging for you to decide between Australasia, the Americas, and Europe. Being pulled in several directions is difficult as it can be hard to choose. You were born to love other cultures and nationalities, sometimes literally, so your passions may also pull you in different directions and that can be extremely demanding. Finding out how to discriminate, to eliminate, and to choose is a lifetime's quest, but it's worth your time and energy.

INVESTMENT IN THE FUTURE

You are headed for a lifetime of comfort, security, and investments to make. This is quite literally your reward. How to spend your money wisely and well is a test that is quite enjoyable to take, although you also benefit from tried, tested, and trusted expertise from professionals who understand the stock market, cryptocurrency, property, and—perhaps—good causes like conservation of the environment. For all your calculations, though, you can never put a price on a matter central to your character: your sexuality.

WHO SHARES YOUR BIRTHDAY?

Gary Oldman, born March 21, 1958

Rosie O'Donnell, born March 21, 1962

Rhys Darby, born March 21, 1974

MARCH 22

WHO ARE YOU?

You are strongly influenced by Mars with all his reputation for energy and being first. You have the sign of brilliance, Gemini, affecting your ideas, plans, and projects. Your challenge is to take what is so inspired and inspiring and make sure it is cultivated and nurtured. From there, all things are possible, and what begins as a concept can become the gift that goes on giving, intellectually. Aries is the ram who must always be first through the gate, and in astrology, Aries also rules the First House of the natural zodiac. He's near your Sun.

SECURITY AND INCOME

You have an easy trine between Taurus with all its moneymaking and saving and Virgo, the sign of sustained hard work. Even though you are so fiery, you are also quite down-to-earth about your craft, trade, or profession. Your skills and talents are sustainable, and enduring, so having created one revenue stream, you can repeat yourself. In fact, the nearby Aries energy helps you power through whatever must be done, long after other people may have fallen by the wayside. You're very productive.

FINANCIAL ADVICE

Given that Scorpio, a water sign which revolves around emotions, affects your joint finance, you can be led in all kinds of directions by your heart or your feelings. It may be useful to seek impartial and objective financial advice from professionals with an excellent reputation, as they can look into your situation from the outside and remove the more personal bias that you have. The family tree is always in the picture, for example, as Cancer (the sign of relatives) influences your clan, but you must find out if the numbers add up.

SEXUAL RELATIONSHIPS AND FREEDOM

Pluto and Scorpio rule your financial and property-based relationships, and your reward for working hard and following astute advice is a partnership—or perhaps more than one partnership—where you discover that sexual and emotional freedom can be yours. How you achieve this is intensely personal and will show in your birth chart, but you have a deeper understanding of physical passion than many people. How you accommodate that but also find your independence from people and situations that confine you matters.

WHO SHARES YOUR BIRTHDAY?

Marcel Marceau, born March 22, 1923
William Shatner, born March 22, 1931
Andrew Lloyd Webber, born March 22, 1948
Reese Witherspoon, born March 22, 1976
Constance Wu, born March 22, 1982

MARCH 23

WHO ARE YOU?

You are the welcoming face at celebrations and reunions of extended family and friends or the guest who receives red-carpet treatment. You were made for parties and events. Aquarius, the sign of brotherhood and sisterhood, rules your social life. You also have Cancer, the sign which rules home and family (or a home away from home), at the base of your solar chart, where you find your foundations in life. You have solid Taurus ruling your sector of income and property, and emotional security—and good homes—really count.

YOUR DESTINY

You are destined to have the kind of comfortable and beautiful environment that is suggested by down-to-earth Taurus ruling your sector of assets. We also have Scorpio, which rules sex, at the other end of the financial axis of your chart. For all that you are about the material world, you also have to factor in your libido, which can't be priced. Your decisions about money are very important to your character, and contentment, and can't be rushed. In fact, Taurus is slow to the point of sometimes being stuck.

FUNDING AND FINANCE

You are an unusual Aries in that your chart is far more inclined toward Taurus and Scorpio (the money) than that of other people born under your sign. Your biggest challenges will revolve around seeking funding or financing others. This can bring in charity or the idea that charity begins at home. There is also a deep concern with health and healing in your chart, shown by Virgo's rulership of your sector of daily reality. In fact, there is a direct connection between help, healing, and money throughout your life.

SOLITUDE AND ENLIGHTENMENT

Neptune is in charge of your inner life, psyche, soul, and spirit. Neptune is about escaping, and you do this wholeheartedly, Aries, removing yourself from everybody and everything in order to seek your own truth. You may or may not call yourself religious, but there are shades of the monk or nun about you, either Buddhist or Christian, as you suit sabbaticals and retreats. You can do this without believing in any doctrine at all, of course, but what you are looking for is the light that never goes out—what lights your path, in fact.

WHO SHARES YOUR BIRTHDAY?

Joan Crawford, born March 23, 1904

Damon Albarn, born March 23, 1968

Princess Eugenie, born March 23, 1990

MARCH 24

WHO ARE YOU?

The Sun with all its brilliance highlights the world of children and young people in your life. This can happen even if you never become a parent. The spotlight goes on a junior generation and the potential for something dazzling to be seeded once and perhaps grown forever. The Sun can sometimes be a pun. This may actually be your son, for example. Leo is about heirs, spares, and pretenders to your throne, so no matter if this is a nephew or niece or a class of teenagers you teach, you pass on your special legacy.

YOUR DESTINY

Leo also rules your heart, and this sign is associated with sovereigns, who in turn have complicated courts. The cycles of time in your horoscope suggest you will always have the most intricate situations to unravel, Aries. The other important zodiac sign in your chart is Libra, the balanced scales, which we find ruling your sector of marriage, separation, affairs, and engagement. Two is always the right number here, never three. This also applies to the family. You are destined to find out what love means and what it is.

YOUR NAME IN LIGHTS

Your name may or may not go up in lights, but it will be brightly lit online as you and a series of groups in your life have what it takes to fascinate people and draw admiration. This comes with a great many tests, of course. One of them is the classic challenge involved with egos within a circle. This is often solved by taking turns at being the star. The other issue for you, with Aquarius the Water Bearer ruling your zone of community, is how to pool resources. There is a deep commitment to that, but how can it be managed?

GROUPS AND INDIVIDUALS

You are a true Aries, for all that other signs also influence your chart. You are strong, energetic, and a survivor. You are also a warrior when you have to be. Your experiences with particular clubs, teams, societies, bands, associations, and so on will show you both sides of the hive mind. Sometimes it's one against the many—and you will be one of them. At other times you may find yourself on the wrong side of a particular circle of people. These episodes in your life empower your tribe or empower you. You'll discover both sides.

WHO SHARES YOUR BIRTHDAY?

Harry Houdini, born March 24, 1874
Steve McQueen, born March 24, 1930
Tig Notaro, born March 24, 1971
Jessica Chastain, born March 24, 1977

MARCH 25

WHO ARE YOU?

You are an impatient and sometimes quite impulsive Aries who always has a budding scheme or high-potential plan. Brilliant Gemini rules your sector of ideas. The issue for you is grounding what you believe in and making it work in the long term. Fortunately Taurus, the sign with staying power, governs everything you value most highly. Perhaps because they do not come naturally, stoicism and long-haul effort are precious to you. When you manage to apply this to your concepts, they have every chance of taking off in the right place.

YOUR DESTINY

Group politics is fated in your life, and you will take turns at being on the inside of a circle with an outsider very much apart from you all while also discovering what it is like to be one against the many. Over time you will come to see that the greatest achievement is to put the group before the individual and unite to build together. You will also discover that everybody matters in a team, club, society, association, and so on. Everything can be resolved with communication, and the end results will always be more powerful for it.

FUTURE GENERATIONS

You may or may not become a parent, but future generations have a central part to play in your life. This may be the children or teenagers of today, and their children and children's children into the years ahead. The Sun and Leo rule your sector of heirs, spares, and pretenders to the throne. If you want to be justifiably proud of those who come after you—perhaps because you taught them or led them—it will take a great deal of work. You might call this your astrological challenge in life, yet if you can master it, the rewards are huge.

HOME AND FAMILY

You are at your most identifiably Aries—ruled by Mars with all his drive and energy—with family matters. In fact, the family tree will need maintenance all your life, no matter which branches require your attention. You are assertive, proactive, and determined when it comes to your relatives and even your roots—so your heritage, culture, and history on both sides of your family tree. The ground beneath your feet is always moving, so your hometown and homeland don't give you stability for long, but they do motivate you.

WHO SHARES YOUR BIRTHDAY?

Gloria Steinem, born March 25, 1934

Aretha Franklin, born March 25, 1942

Sarah Jessica Parker, born March 25, 1965

MARCH 26

WHO ARE YOU?

You are the perpetual traveler or commuter who has twin cities, regions, or countries to enjoy. This shapes who you become. You have Gemini the Twins in charge of your journeys. This brilliant, clever sign is also in charge of your intellectual journeys, and your regular path between two very different places helps you develop a duality. You can see both sides of an issue, both black and white. As a typical Aries, you are driven, a little intimidating, energetic, and formidable. Farsighted Sagittarius determines your take on the wider world.

YOUR DESTINY

Your ruler Mars is the Roman god of war, and he governs Aries, the sign of the military. You may or may not be drawn toward that side of life, but you are destined to face repeated strategic challenges. These will always involve a group and will always require you to be faster than everyone else. That dynamic, cerebral approach to life which shows in your chart announces itself in challenging times, too. You can preempt anything by being two steps ahead. Before others know what's happened, you have already removed a situation.

YOUR FAMILY AND FOUNDATIONS

Your family tree is never stable or fixed. This began in childhood or adolescence, and throughout your life your task will be to maintain it and sometimes more than that. Your horoscope is set up in such a way that the cycles of time show regular change with either your maternal or paternal side and perhaps your own created family, too. This extends to your foundations—the geography of where you come from or where you currently belong. It spurs you on, and you are ever ready to fearlessly attack issues as they come up.

RELOCATION AND MIGRATION

You will relocate or even emigrate—perhaps more than once—according to your chart. Restless Mercury rules your shorter journeys, and farsighted Sagittarius takes charge of more ambitious moves. You will also sympathize with those who have to be on the move, escaping what they do not want. Sometimes this is a personal concern; it can also be professional. More than most you understand what it feels like to be a refugee. Your reward is the freedom to make the future your own, giving yourself or others brilliantly better days ahead.

WHO SHARES YOUR BIRTHDAY?

Joseph Campbell, born March 26, 1904
Leonard Nimoy, born March 26, 1931
Nancy Pelosi, born March 26, 1940
Diana Ross, born March 26, 1944

MARCH 27

WHO ARE YOU?

You don't just have children or teenagers in your world, you have young people to lead, guide, and mentor—and also, perhaps, to leave alone to enjoy their youth. Leo rules your children, stepchildren, godchildren, and young relatives. It also rules the next generation who inherit your care and sympathy, no matter if you become a parent or not. Perhaps the greatest gift you can pass on to juniors, as a senior, is to respect the innocence and play of life in school. Your inner child understands their universe, too.

YOUR DESTINY

The principles of justice, fairness, and (perhaps) the law rule your fate. When you were born, Libra moved into position in the Seventh House of your birth chart, which rules partnerships, but also conflicts. It describes the even balance which must be achieved between two sides or two people in a marriage or a professional double act. It also shows the need to bow to a higher authority when two sides are in opposition. It is your destiny to repeatedly deal with the issue of equality and fair play in life.

YOUR EXTENDED FAMILY

Your extended family of relatives, friends, and others is at the heart of your character. It is also never quite as simple and straightforward as you might wish. Sensitive Cancer with all its focus on feelings and moods is in charge of your clan. Your tribe is ruled by Aquarius, the sign of great diversity, difference, and independence within a group. You are likely to find a great deal of your time and energy is devoted to making things work with these people, as human nature is all too human and you have to accommodate it.

YOUR FINANCIAL REWARDS

You are passionate about your work thanks to Scorpio, which rules joint finances and property. Pluto also rules Scorpio, and this planet is associated with obsession. That can make you secure—wealthy even. It takes enormous focus to devote yourself to your career in a sustained way that guarantees one solid gold result after another. You also have the staying power of Taurus, which governs your personal income. Taurus is an earth sign, solidly planted in the real world. Practical and dedicated, your reward is also sheer excellence.

WHO SHARES YOUR BIRTHDAY?

Gloria Swanson, born March 27, 1899

Dick King-Smith, born March 27, 1922

Mariah Carey, born March 27, 1969

MARCH 28

WHO ARE YOU?

You move in a world of internet citizens, academics, authors, readers, writers, students, and teachers. This may or may not be your profession, but you are always surrounded by observers and big ideas. You are philosophical about success as well as the Snakes and Ladders of life. You have to be, because your pathway is full of extreme high points and inevitable resurrection and rebirth. Life is a spinning wheel that never stops moving as Mercury rules your daily life and routine. There is nothing predictably typical as a result.

YOUR DESTINY

You are a winner who repeatedly comes first or comes out on top. Ambitious Capricorn rules your sector of highest achievement. Capricorn is the mountain goat who climbs to the peak, and you are capable of doing extremely well within a particular system, hierarchy, or establishment. A group is always in the background, Aries, as the sign of community and diversity of Aquarius rules the wider network in your life. Nothing happens without your tribe, as you know. You share your own incredible triumphs together.

YOUR WORK AND INCOME

Your great challenge in life is to sustain your output. You are an energetic, dynamic Aries, but you also have to maintain the pace and, given your formidable efforts, that can be a real test of your staying power. There is also a second question here about your values. Scorpio, the sign of passionate intensity, rules your joint finances, business, and property. It is in opposition to Taurus in your chart, which rules your principles with money—what you will or will not sell out for, for example. Figuring out what price to pay is your challenge.

YOUR EXTENDED FAMILY IN SPIRIT

There is a natural link in your horoscope between Pluto, which governs your legacies and inheritance, and Neptune, which rules over the spiritual connection you have with your extended family in spirit. What is given between generations is not always financial. You are tied to the souls in your extended family of ancestors, friends, and relatives, and they are tied to you. When you evolve, so do they, progressing to new levels on their side of life. When they move on to new levels, this also affects you. Perhaps you know it.

WHO SHARES YOUR BIRTHDAY?

Dirk Bogarde, born March 28, 1921
Jennifer Weiner, born March 28, 1970
Lady Gaga, born March 28, 1986

MARCH 29

WHO ARE YOU?

Born with Leo ruling your relationships, you are a dynamic, determined, motivated Aries who operates in a completely different way when it comes to your emotions. Leo is the sign of the sovereign who has a complicated court and ongoing questions about heirs to the throne—those who were born or who were perhaps never born at all. This ongoing puzzle in your life may be related to just one person or a series of them. Precious bonds which don't fit any category have to be managed in a practical way; that guides your path.

YOUR DESTINY

Your global potential is there even when you are young. You have clever Gemini ruling your sector of projects and ideas; Sagittarius with all its foreign vision establishes your reach. The rest is up to you, but at least once in your life you will be fated to take one or more plans into other regions. This may require some translation or at least greater understanding of accents and cultural differences. Your aspirations are international because not everything can take off close to home. You have the mental energy to do it.

THE TACTICIAN

You are a tactician by nature who uses your Aries soldier qualities—this is the sign of the battler—to make your moves so quickly and quietly that others do not even know what you have done until it is far too late. Aquarius, the zodiac sign which rules tribes, has a natural connection to your Aries side, so you are the sole operator who can take on an entire group if you have to; your horoscope suggests you will do this repeatedly in your life. This makes you so experienced and adept that you become a powerful strategist.

INVESTING IN THE FUTURE

Your reward is not only financial; it is also the luxury of investment and possible future growth. The solid, practical Taurus rules your money. Opposite this we find Scorpio, governed by Pluto with all his passionate intensity. You have great power through your income, banking, or inheritance, and as Taurus is an earth sign, its link with your own profits suggests land, real estate, business grown from the ground up or the environment. What you can do suggests a great deal from even a modest amount, in youth or old age.

WHO SHARES YOUR BIRTHDAY?

Eric Idle, born March 29, 1943

Jo Nesbø, born March 29, 1960

Amy Sedaris, born March 29, 1961

MARCH 30

WHO ARE YOU?

Like any Aries, you will never back away from your opponents or anything which is against you. The issue all your life, though, is deciding what is real and what is not. Neptune, the planet of dreams, rules your inner life, so it is important to distinguish projection and fantasy from what is actually there. You have practical, down-to-earth Taurus in charge of your property and money, so you benefit from grounding yourself and putting both feet on the ground regarding your future wealth. That's not a dream: that's potential.

YOUR DESTINY

From childhood onward you are drawn into groups, teams, clubs, and so on where there is tremendous diversity between the individuals involved but also a lack of natural unity. This can make for really interesting end results if only everybody can agree. The zodiac sign which rules independence and space is Aquarius, and as this also rules your social life, friendships, and networks, it is important to allow yourself and others to be who you are without compromising on solidarity. That takes time and energy, Aries.

ENDINGS AND BEGINNINGS

Your horoscope is set up with simultaneous endings and beginnings in quite a dramatic way so that you will always find you are thinking about the next book of your life even as you are ending another. This is true not only for you but also for your extended family circle. Scorpio the Scorpion which rules transformation makes an exact angle to Cancer, the sign which oversees your clan of relatives and friends who are more like kin to you. This trine is regularly set off in your chart, so deep change is part of life.

FEELING AT HOME

This same angle in your chart between Scorpio and Cancer, the two water signs which describe heartfelt bonds between family and friends, also offers you a genuine sense of belonging. Perhaps because you go through so much together, the important people in your life make you feel at home, no matter if you are traveling to them or they are traveling to you. This is the real reward, rather than the daydreams about property and money which float past you. Wonderful circles of people who always welcome you are real.

WHO SHARES YOUR BIRTHDAY?

Vincent van Gogh, born March 30, 1853

Eric Clapton, born March 30, 1945

Tracy Chapman, born March 30, 1964

MARCH 31

WHO ARE YOU?

Your Aries Sun is the sign of attack and defense. Your zodiac sign is ruled by Mars, the Roman god of war. You are permanently on guard. This may have come about because of your childhood, as you have learned to be ready for anything and anybody. Your intuition is very important to you regarding this, and you may be the kind of person who relies on extrasensory perception. In fact, the mysterious planet Neptune with all its hidden depths has charge of the psychic sector of your astrology chart. It's notable; your instincts are strong.

YOUR DESTINY

Your astrological chart shows duty, service, a strong sense of responsibility, and a big work ethic drive you. You tend to take on too much. In fact, with Virgo ruling your sector of jobs, courses, and voluntary roles, it is only your overall health which will stop you from overloading yourself. Virgo governs the mind, body, and spirit in unison, and this zodiac sign is in charge of your career sector. Always listen to your body. Virgo is also the sign of method, order, and high organization. This works very well for you.

MANAGING TWO MAPS

You may be the sort of person who has a map of London as well as a map of their local county in their handbag. Or perhaps you are the kind of person who divides their life between Europe and Australia. Gemini, the sign of the heavenly twins, rules your sector of home, work, and travel. This typically means you go between two places, either because your career demands it or for personal reasons. This means you have to become a multitasker. Dealing with two different accents, cultures, languages, or customs is in your destiny.

UNDERSTANDING GROUP PSYCHOLOGY

Understanding group psychology and the hive mind is part of your journey. Aquarius, ruling brotherhoods and sisterhoods—often in combination—dominates your life. It doesn't matter if it's a political party or a rock band, you are here to learn about how people operate as a club, say, or team. Perhaps this is why you are intuitively on the attack or defense, Aries. When there is no individuality or independence within a circle of people, you need to be on guard, as you refuse to be herded.

WHO SHARES YOUR BIRTHDAY?

Johann Sebastian Bach, born March 31, 1685
Al Gore, born March 31, 1948
Angus Young, born March 31, 1955

APRIL 1

WHO ARE YOU?

You are the financial, charity, property, or business juggler who uses your famous Aries energy to make the money go round. With the earth sign Taurus in charge of your budget, it is important that you have both feet on the ground, but it takes time to develop a system that will work. Your horoscope is set up by challenging cycles of time in your sectors of banking and the economy. This means you regularly have to adjust and adapt to conditions in your country and the world, but when you master it, the reward is huge.

YOUR DESTINY

You are an adventurous soul with Sagittarius, the sign of the traveler, in charge of your sector of exploration. You may even emigrate. If you do relocate—even within your own country—you will do so more than once as you cannot resist the next horizon. Jupiter rules this same zone of your horoscope, and this planet is a symbol of optimism, positive thinking, and big thinking, too. All of this makes you characteristically upbeat, but you can also overlook the details. Researching before you pack your bags or boxes is essential.

THE HUMAN HEART

Leo oversees your close relationships with lovers, partners, and sometimes the family. This sign rules sovereigns, heirs, spares, and pretenders to the throne in astrology. If you have ever wondered why some of your most challenging bonds to others resemble a Shakespearean drama or even an episode of *The Crown*, now you know. Life is not simple or straightforward emotionally, and it will take experience and perhaps the expertise of an outsider to help you look after your feelings, Aries.

INVESTING IN THE FUTURE

Once you have overcome the need for balance and grounding with your budget, you are in a terrific position to use Pluto's powerful position in your chart to plan for the future and invest in tomorrow. Pluto is associated with great privacy and mystery, so you are a dark horse when it comes to your bank account. This old horse racing term could easily be applied to you overall, as only when you choose to reveal yourself completely to others will they know who and what they are dealing with. You're a strong negotiator.

WHO SHARES YOUR BIRTHDAY?

Ali MacGraw, born April 1, 1939
Wangari Maathai, born April 1, 1940
Bob Haozous, born April 1, 1943
Gil Scott-Heron, born April 1, 1949
Rachel Maddow, born April 1, 1973

APRIL 2

WHO ARE YOU?

You present as a comfortable Taurus as much as a driven Aries (Taurus rules your homelife), and you enjoy beautiful surroundings and well-designed clothes and interiors, as well as gardens and nature. There is a settled, down-to-earth quality about you once you have found a place you can call your own, and you may be lucky enough to do this more than once, as you have the capacity to be at the top of your profession. The real reward is being in a position to help others, of course, but you also enjoy the good life, too.

YOUR DESTINY

You are a winner and true to your Aries Sun sign, which likes to be first and come first. Making it to the top is also a feature of ambitious Capricorn, the sign at the highest point of your horoscope, where you reach the peak of your achievements. You climb to where you need to be in life, both professionally and in terms of your status. This combination of Aries, which is fearless in the face of competition, and

Capricorn, the mountain goat who ascends, makes you one of life's outstanding bosses, champions, or authorities.

FINANCIAL EQUALITY

The price you pay for being in a position to donate, lend, or help other people financially is the pressure of being responsible for navigating those relationships well and without complications. The planet of power, Pluto, rules your business interests, banking, and charity commitments. The difference between your considerable influence and control and those of others is obvious all your life. How you master that depends on experience. Every time you observe this, you learn more about handling human nature.

HELPING AND HEALING

The sign of helping, healing, duty, and service is Virgo, and it rules your sector of health and well-being. You will experience what it is like to place your trust in others but also to be the agent of change for anybody who needs you. Taking turns at being both the healer and the healed changes your life every time it happens. You are capable of turning somebody's life around through your dutiful attention to detail and care. At the same time, you are motivated to offer your assistance because you have also been helped.

WHO SHARES YOUR BIRTHDAY?

Alec Guinness, born April 2, 1914
Serge Gainsbourg, born April 2, 1928
Marvin Gaye, born April 2, 1939

APRIL 3

WHO ARE YOU?

You are the world citizen who sees the worldwide web as a portal to what really matters: which is not the computer, nor the plans on the computer, but the destination. You are a true Aries with enough energy to take both yourself and your plans to other parts of the world, or at the very least, a distant region of your own country. Your only flaw is a lack of grounding, as you are a fire sign not an earth sign, but practical Taurus in charge of your income or budget should help you put both feet on the ground before you go.

YOUR DESTINY

You are drawn toward brotherhoods, sisterhoods, or perhaps a mixture of both, as Aquarius rules your sector of groups. Aquarius is the sign of tolerance, individual freedom, independence, and diversity. You are drawn to circles of friends and allies who are very different from yourself, and together you not only enjoy life, but also find you have real potential in business, finance, or with your chosen fields. Again, it is sensible Taurus with an eye to your security which reminds you to be practical about capitalizing on success.

THE MOTHER-CHILD RELATIONSHIP

The relationship you have with your own mother—or, perhaps, the relationship you have with your son or daughter if you choose to have children—is at the heart of who you are. It can also work both ways, so your parenting transforms you as much as your mother transformed you, too. No matter which part children play in your life, you have the sensitive water sign Cancer in charge of these close bonds in your world, and as spiritual Pisces makes an exact angle to this area of your chart, your spirit or soul learns from it all.

ENDING AND STARTING CHAPTERS

Your horoscope is set up with the cycles of time showing simultaneous final chapters and new chapters, which can be as challenging as it is ultimately rewarding. Pluto rules your extended family relationships, and as this is the planet which also describes rebirth for every decisive ending in your life, there is always a powerful fresh start up ahead. Understanding this is central to your belief in life—the beat goes on—and as you will experience this constant blend of ending and beginning repeatedly, it changes who you are.

WHO SHARES YOUR BIRTHDAY?

Jane Goodall, born April 3, 1934
Alec Baldwin, born April 3, 1958
Eddie Murphy, born April 3, 1961

APRIL 4

WHO ARE YOU?

As a typical Aries you are not afraid of battles, and once you are together with your group or tribe, this can have devastating consequences for anyone unwise enough to take you all on. You are also a fiercely courageous and determined survivor in any situation where you have to fight back. This can express itself in the kind of career you choose or in your personal life. Aries is ruled by Mars the Roman god of war, and so you were born with a strong sense of self-preservation but also know how to fight the good fight, too.

YOUR DESTINY

The world of children and teenagers is important in your destiny, no matter if you become a parent or not. In your birth chart, Leo, which rules the next generation who will inherit your influence, makes a perfect and easy trine to your own Aries Sun, so you have a natural understanding of your own or other people's offspring. Your own inner child is alive and well, and so you intuitively know what the heirs, spares, and pretenders to your throne want and need. In time they will come to truly appreciate it.

BOUNDARIES AND RULES

You are tough, for all that you have a gentle appreciation of the innocence of children and young people. You are a true fire sign, and nobody can ever get close without feeling your personality at a distance. You are strong, somewhat intimidating to strangers, and know how to set boundaries. There are two reasons for this fierce authority. One is your past, as the babies who were born (or never were) have made you stronger. The other is your own family tree. You are a good gatekeeper who is open, but only just so far.

RELATIONSHIP CHOICES

You are a great potential recycler of relationships, Aries, but the choice is always yours. Your horoscope is set up so that the cycles of time will often end partnerships and other close bonds, but you are then able to repair, renovate, and relaunch what (or who) was apparently lost to you. Sometimes, being an Aries, you can impulsively kick away the traces of what you had—and walk away, too. People forget how sensitive you are. Emotional Pisces, the sign which rules hidden feelings, dominates your inner life. You already know it.

WHO SHARES YOUR BIRTHDAY?
Maya Angelou, born April 4, 1928
Anthony Perkins, born April 4, 1932
Lorraine Toussaint, born April 4, 1960
Heath Ledger, born April 4, 1979

APRIL 5

WHO ARE YOU?

Groups play an important part in your life, and this begins when you are young. Getting the group to work and also having the backing and support of a team, club, association, and so on, make the difference. You are a fearless Aries who is always up-front and also front and center. You are a natural captain or leader for that reason, but you would be nothing without the special circle of people behind you. It's not always easy and takes a great deal of maintenance and care, but with enough energy, your circle is an enormous blessing.

YOUR DESTINY

You don't necessarily use journeys to test the strength of your feelings for others, but fate has a strange way of putting miles between you and those you care about. You may have more than one long-distance relationship for this reason. Your love life is not the only place where you prove your feelings, though, and family, friends, and others who are close to your heart always seem to be at the other end of a runway or highway. The angle from Sagittarius, the sign of the traveler, is perfect to Leo in your chart—the heart sign.

CHARITY AND GENEROSITY

You have solid Taurus in charge of your income, and at the other end of the chart, powerful Scorpio, ruled by Pluto, in charge of joint finances. You will find stability, security, and even genuine wealth are on offer throughout your life. This puts you in the terrific position of being able to help others without any conditions at all. You cannot ignore the dynamic between yourself and those who need your generosity, though. It doesn't matter if this is personal or a large organization. Power has to be handled with care.

INDEPENDENCE AND INDIVIDUALITY

Rather like the Beatles (the Fab Four with all their differences—*and* George Martin, the fifth Beatle), you will repeatedly find yourself in groups which have room for your strong and fiery Aries energy as much as those who have nothing in common with you—or the rest. This intense individuality and fierce independence make all the teams in your life unforgettable, but it is the triumph of cooperation over self-interest which makes the really special people last in your memory. What you create is up to you.

WHO SHARES YOUR BIRTHDAY?

Bette Davis, born April 5, 1908
Anthony Horowitz, born April 5, 1955
Pharrell Williams, born April 5, 1973

APRIL 6

WHO ARE YOU?

You are the Aries who finds something of themselves in children and teenagers. You are never in their world but always on the outside, inspired and influenced by those so much younger than yourself. Leo rules your sector of parenthood, godchildren, young relatives, and also a junior generation as a whole. This sign is about how you guide them, no matter if you have a child or not. Your guidance is through a caring distance and an ability to let children actually be children, Aries.

YOUR DESTINY

You are strongly influenced by your mother and her relationship with you or her relationship with a sibling. In turn, you are also influenced by your own children if you become a mother or the mother of your children if you become a father. This is again the impact of Leo and the Sun ruling this sector of your chart. It is never very far from you, spiritually or psychologically, and has a greater impact on you than you might think. Maybe a psychologist or dream coach could help you uncover it.

CLOSE RELATIONSHIPS

You have sensitive, introspective Pisces ruling your sector of inner life, private feelings, and the soul or spirit. When relationships do not turn out as you would like, you can show this part of your character and become quite inaccessible to others, as you have an inclination to hibernate. In fact, this is a repeated pattern in your life. You know that going inward is the key, and once you come out of your hibernation, you are able to either recycle and renew what had not worked or simply get rid of it and walk away.

THE FREEDOM TO START AGAIN

The cycles of time have set up your horoscope in such a way that you have regular crossroads when younger and older—into old age, in fact—when you must decide to go back and rebuild what was there. As you know, you always have the choice to repair and recycle particular relationships. It is the same with work and home, as you will have to ask yourself periodically if it is worth going back and taking firm action to renew. Your person of action Aries side often wins. You just leave and restart.

WHO SHARES YOUR BIRTHDAY?

Gustave Moreau, born April 6, 1826

René Lalique, born April 6, 1860

André Previn, born April 6, 1929

Paul Rudd, born April 6, 1969

APRIL 7

WHO ARE YOU?

You are half Pisces and half Aries, as the introspective, spiritual sign of the two fish rules your inner life. You are a meditator or daydreamer who often finds it hard to move. The other half of you is all Aries, however, which creates an obvious split in your character between doing nothing—and becoming enlightened—and suddenly swinging into action. Your parents' sides of the family or your own and your partner's often become the trigger for this rapid need to make choices and act on them.

YOUR DESTINY

You are a born scholar, writer, or student of life. You may be a website manager or Substack scribbler. You may or may not enter academia, but you have Jupiter in charge of your sector of lifelong learning and knowledge, so you always want more. This may be a script in your hand or a higher degree. This works very well for you, and you have a reputation for being quite a formidable source in your chosen field. You are slightly intimidating because of this but always accessible online or on paper even if people don't get too close.

YOUR PISCES SIDE

Neptune and Pisces rule the unconscious side of your nature, so you may not even be aware of how difficult it is for people to become intimate with you. This includes partners and family. You drift and float through life, escaping from the real world. You have the soul of a surfer on an endless voyage or a sailor who never docks. Because of this, others find you fascinating, and you find it easy to disappear into your own private universe. The choice is always there to make a big move and rejoin the world, though.

FINANCIAL SECURITY

With down-to-earth, grounded Taurus in charge of your income and the fixed sign Scorpio in charge of property or business, joint finances, or charity, you are so stable it's hard to move you. In fact, Taurus is a fixed sign as well, and consequently it can be very hard to change your mind about expenditure, investment, taxation, and so on. Anybody who is trying to get you to shift your position will have to work extremely hard. You may be a hoarder or let the grass grow under your feet too long sometimes, Aries.

WHO SHARES YOUR BIRTHDAY?

William Wordsworth, born April 7, 1770
Ravi Shankar, born April 7, 1920
Jackie Chan, born April 7, 1954
Russell Crowe, born April 7, 1964
Nico Santos, born April 7, 1979

APRIL 8

WHO ARE YOU?

The sign of tourism, travel, emigration, and multiculturalism is Sagittarius, and this rules your sector of journeys and knowledge. You are the world citizen who is spoiled for choice. Will you ever settle on just one place—or even *in* just one place? Jupiter, which describes an overload of opportunities in astrology, is the planet which governs your European, British, Australasian, and American connections. You are the pioneering zodiac sign motivated by the most adventurous roaming or moving.

YOUR DESTINY

You don't just have children and young adults in your world: you mentor, guide, and rule them. This applies no matter if you become a parent or not. Leo, the sign of authority, is in charge of the younger generations in your life. Your horoscope has been set up by time cycles which encourage you to become ruler to a younger court, either sowing the seeds for your own line of succession or finding a role where those young enough to be your offspring can look up to you and learn.

DEALING WITH GROUPS

Aquarius, which rules bands, communities, circles, clubs, teams, and all networks, is in charge of friendship in your horoscope. Finding the balance between one-on-one relationships while surrounded by these collectives is your life's task. How do you keep the flow steady between yourself and another but also maintain the connection to the group? You can't separate them, as the closer friendships or partnerships are sustained by these spread out collections of people. It takes effort.

BEING A PEACEMAKER

Aries is fearless, strong, and tough, and so are you—in the name of peacekeeping. You are a one-person force who will repeatedly find themselves drawn to conflict resolution. This may or may not be your job description, but you are extremely talented at using your fire sign energy to solve people's problems. Some people born on this day do this because of family issues. In other cases, with Libra, the sign of negotiation, opposite your own Sun sign, you find that arbitration comes naturally to you.

WHO SHARES YOUR BIRTHDAY?

Kofi Anan, born April 8, 1938
Vivienne Westwood, born April 8, 1941
Julian Lennon, born April 8, 1963
Patricia Arquette, born April 8, 1968

APRIL 9

WHO ARE YOU?

You are the strong Aries person you have read about, unafraid of being up-front and also front and center. You are confident and self-assured in front of a crowd, if you have to be—or even a global audience. You are also a multitasker thanks to Gemini, the sign of the twins, ruling your sector of knowledge, ideas, plans, and projects. You can juggle two aspects of life at the same time or blend them together so that your message not only fascinates and compels, but can create quite amazing changes.

YOUR DESTINY

You are capable of transforming and healing other people, but also of trusting others enough to be healed by them. This may be literal medical or dental help, psychological therapy, or something harder to put into words: a therapeutic way of assisting that does not have a label. You are good at this because you have seen both sides, both being the one to offer your time, energy, and care and the human being who feels all too human. This gives you an empathy that comes from the Pisces-Virgo axis of your solar chart.

FREEDOM IS A STATE OF MIND

You are heavily influenced by your state of mind, thoughts, and inner world. This comes from Neptune ruling the sensitive, inward-looking zone of your chart. This can often confine you, and yet the only person who can liberate you *is* you. Being trapped by your own certain ideas about what is real is something you learn to conquer over time. You discover that sometimes the only way to get to the truth is the Aries way: dramatic action. Only when you move your mind can you move yourself and be free.

FINANCIAL SECURITY IS YOUR REWARD

You have the grounded, secure, earth sign Taurus in charge of the money that you make or save on your own merits. At the other end of your chart we find the fixed sign Scorpio describing property but also more complex relationships with others. You have what it takes to become comfortable or even wealthy. Your attitude toward all that you earn is immovable as Taurus, like Scorpio, is also a fixed sign and you find it hard to be flexible. Your instinct is to hang on and hold on, and this is a feature of your personality.

WHO SHARES YOUR BIRTHDAY?

Isambard Kingdom Brunel, born April 9, 1806

Hugh Hefner, born April 9, 1926

Marc Jacobs, born April 9, 1963

APRIL 10

WHO ARE YOU?

You are the classic Aries, ruled by Mars who likes to win his battles. You are a fast mover when you have to be and are strategically ahead of trouble, no matter if it is for other people or for yourself. Thanks to this warrior instinct, you are well-known for being quick on your feet, clever, and the master of the preemptive strike. In fact, by the time difficult people realize what has happened, you are already out of the picture, leaving just a cartoon smoke trail behind you. You are, oddly enough, a peacemaker.

YOUR DESTINY

Your solar chart is set up with cycles of time that involve your sexuality and relationships in a fated way. This may be interpreted by you as soulmates meeting or even karmic debts and credits, depending on how you feel about destiny. In fact, the people who are tied to you sexually are your teachers as independence, liberty, and freedom are the prize for being honest about partnerships, no matter if they are one-night stands or lifelong marriages. Over time you learn that autonomy is bigger than sexuality.

THE NEXT GENERATIONS

You are a natural guide, mentor, tutor, influencer, and leader with younger generations. This applies no matter if you have children or not. Sometimes it is personal, so this may be a godchild or niece or nephew. It can also be professional or in an unpaid role, with great reach over a large number of children or teenagers. This goes beyond those who come after you and stretches into the future, as their descendants can also be strongly affected by what you sow in terms of the seeds of ideas, projects, plans, or precious lessons.

THE STUDENT AND TEACHER

You are very suited to being a teacher even if that is the last profession you have ever thought about pursuing. Jupiter with all his expansion and growth rules the sector of your chart associated with college and university life. You are a natural author, academic, pupil, or graduate and feel comfortable with the word—whatever that word happens to be. It may be a sheet of music, a shelf of history books, or your own efforts online. You never stop absorbing knowledge and passing it on and are a source of wisdom, Aries.

WHO SHARES YOUR BIRTHDAY?

Joseph Pulitzer, born April 10, 1847

Max von Sydow, born April 10, 1929

Brian Setzer, born April 10, 1959

APRIL 11

WHO ARE YOU?

You have the sign of the scales, Libra, ruling all your partnerships in life, be they personal like marriage or professional. Another dual sign, Gemini, rules your ideas and opinions. As a result of this, your two-way streets often define you. You are seen in the light of the people you travel with on the same road or those you break with to follow your own path. Your duality is shown by the fact that you are the same as the other person, but also so different—and this strange combination teaches you about yourself.

YOUR DESTINY

You have all the direct, energetic, adventurous assertiveness of the true Aries when it comes to money. In duets and double acts you may find yourself stuck for a strategy, but if finance, business, charity, or property is involved, you are a force of nature. In fact, you can be a formidable negotiator. Pluto rules joint finance and property in your chart and is a symbol of power. Pluto is also quite fixed, private, and closed, so you are slightly intimidating when it comes to investment, sales, or purchases. You often win.

HALF PISCES AND HALF ARIES

Pisces with all its reputation for escapism, daydreaming, inspiration, and meditation rules your inner self. This part of your chart is also governed by Neptune, which triggers spirituality in you. That is half your story. It contradicts another part of you which is typically Aries, ruled by the action planet of Mars. Only when you are enlightened from a long period of suspension do you make your big moves in life, but when you do, it shows a complete change of direction. This pattern of waiting and wondering, then acting, recurs.

MONEY AND INVESTMENT

Once you have your financial rewards in life, you have the enjoyment of speculating on investment, shopping, growth, or even nonprofits. This is part of your earth sign side, as grounded, practical Taurus likes to know not only where the money is, but also where it can be used. This characteristic focus on land, building, the environment, floor-up business ventures, and most of all, long-term planning is part of your nature, as much as the Pisces side of you, which can sometimes mean you're mistaken for that sign.

WHO SHARES YOUR BIRTHDAY?

Oleg Cassini, born April 11, 1913

Bob Harris, born April 11, 1946

Cerys Matthews, born April 11, 1969

APRIL 12

WHO ARE YOU?

You are the classic Aries: strong, tough, determined, and fiery if you are pushed. You are extremely good at defending yourself and who or what matters most to you. You can be a person of action when you have to be but the rest of the time are content to merely set extremely firm boundaries and stand by them. You suit a position where you must protect or preserve because you are so skilled at escorting away any person or organization which would threaten that. You are quite hard to get close to for most people.

YOUR DESTINY

You are very good at acting Aries, but it is also your fate to play your Pisces side. This highly expressive, sensitive, imaginative sign rules your inner life. Underneath the surface you are quite different to your hardline self, ruled by Mars, the planet of combat. In fact, another part of you is fated to find yourself playing with life in a Piscean way: escaping from the real world, taking a vacation from reality, and always enjoying a holiday from the everyday. This may be reflected in your wardrobe, which has two halves.

THE GROUPS AND CIRCLES IN YOUR LIFE

The sign of people power, Aquarius, rules the circles in your life, which can overlap. Friends, allies, and like-minded people who share your philosophy, but also your goals, are extremely important to you. They are also challenging, and you repeatedly find that it is these networks of similar but quite independent people which test your ability to believe. The Piscean side of your nature is unconscious or covered up, but essentially about unity and harmony to a spiritual or religious level. You believe in groups, but it's hard.

YOUR PEOPLE IN SPIRIT

Pluto is the planet of transformation, and this rules your extended family in the spirit world, perhaps including friends who feel like family. You may or may not believe in an afterlife, but your horoscope shows that everything you do helps them. It works the other way, too; everything these departed generations do, spiritually, helps your own evolution. Perhaps you do know that your people on the other side of life play an active role in our lives here; in any case, only good things can come from the link.

WHO SHARES YOUR BIRTHDAY?

Tiny Tim, born April 12, 1932

Alan Ayckbourn, born April 12, 1939

Claire Danes, born April 12, 1979

APRIL 13

WHO ARE YOU?

You were born with Scorpio, the sign of financial relationships, ruling your zone of money, property, and inheritance. You are an Aries, but you have powerful Pluto and complex Scorpio in charge of your security and wealth, which dominate your personality. Your family relationships, partnerships, and the involvement of the older, middle, and younger generations together dictate how you manage your life and who you become. You may understand even when you are small that there is an inheritance waiting for you one day.

YOUR DESTINY

You are the global thinker and world citizen who has Jupiter ruling your sector of travel and also travel in the mind. Jupiter is associated with excess and, sometimes, too many opportunities and tempting choices. Once you learn how to rein yourself in and filter out one country or nationality at a time, you will lead a fascinating life where you will discover for yourself how other languages or cultures can open so many doors. In fact you find your sense of self is mirrored by what you experience abroad or on the web.

FAMILY TIES

It's quite true that the grandmother or mother relationship in the family, on either side, has a huge influence on what is decided with money or property—perhaps valuable possessions, too. This goes beyond finances, though, as there are valuable emotional and spiritual truths about the mother-child connection having a huge background impact on you. They can also be challenging. This may be about you or your sibling, or perhaps you and your own child. Through this your soul grows, but it's a very private matter.

THE BORN WARRIOR

You are a true Aries and a born warrior if you need to be. Sometimes it is enough for you to project all the fiery strength of your Sun sign without ever having to engage. There is a gift which some Aries people have of keeping firm boundaries but allowing in the people who matter most. Anyone who is kept at a distance by you is probably intimidated by you. Anyone who wants to uncover your true personality needs to understand that there is always the family tree in the background accompanying everything you do.

WHO SHARES YOUR BIRTHDAY?

Guy Fawkes, born April 13, 1570

Thomas Jefferson, born April 13, 1743

Christopher Hitchens, born April 13, 1949

APRIL 14

WHO ARE YOU?

You are partly Pisces, as well as being Aries, because Neptune and Pisces both rule your inner life, secret self, soul, and spirit. So you are a natural meditator or dreamer. A great deal of who you are does not appear on the surface. You are strongly influenced by the relationship you had with your own mother when young, but also the connection between you and your child, if you are a mother, or the mother of your children, if you are a father, and her bond with your offspring. It's always in the background and shapes who you become.

YOUR DESTINY

You are strongly influenced by Virgo, which rules your well-being, food, drink, fitness, and approach to the body, mind, and spirit. Your pure approach to this—which you were born with or must learn—is fated. You are also fated to be involved with circles of people who make pooling resources seem natural. The flow of your life is always influenced by a network, team, club, and so on. You are able to pair off with people inside the wider community and both be fulfilled by those in your world as well as pour yourselves into them.

ARIES VICTORIES

Your Aries Sun shows itself in your victories, which begin in your teenage years and repeat throughout your life. These triumphs are never just fulfilled ambitions; they involve you coming in first or winning. This is a classic indicator of your competitive, fearless side, ruled by the planet of action Mars. Yet even your success is a challenge for you, as it means you must consider the next challenge. Are you a one-hit wonder, for example, or can you repeat past glories? You also need to manage those who are part of it all.

FINANCE AND YOUR VALUES

Solid Taurus rules your money, and at the other end of the financial axis of your chart, you have Scorpio. They are about your own personal income or need for money at the Taurus end and very much about complicated relationships with others at the Scorpio end. You will be changed both by giving and receiving during your life but with care should end up wealthy enough to be a donor, generous lender, or reliable source for a charity. Understanding your values and what can't be bought and sold between people is key.

WHO SHARES YOUR BIRTHDAY?

John Gielgud, born April 14, 1904
Robert Doisneau, born April 14, 1912
Peter Capaldi, born April 14, 1958

APRIL 15

WHO ARE YOU?

You have all the drive, fierce fire sign determination, and fearless approach of the true Aries. You channel this into money, property, charity, or business. Pluto with all its power rules your sector of joint finances. You are quite an intimidating negotiator and have tough defenses. Pluto is associated with people who are hidden or private, and when it comes to your investments, you are hard to fully know or understand. Anybody who wants to understand you needs to know the intense Scorpio rules your life budget.

YOUR DESTINY

You are the hardworking and industrious creator of not just solid end results, but also solid income. You have dedicated Virgo in charge of your sector of work. Virgo is interested in method, order, detail, and solid productivity. It is an earth sign and indicates a grounded and reliable part of your nature. It shows in your career, as over the long term you have incredible energy, drawn from your ruling planet Mars. You have great staying power, and as a result, by retirement your CV shows a chain of precious achievements.

GROUP MANAGEMENT

Aries, you are a natural combatant, either with the group against one person or as an outsider against the group. You tend to attract these situations with particular communities, teams, clubs, and so on because of Aquarius, which rules the circles you are involved in as well as those circles of people who are against your ideas. Aquarius is about diversity and difference as well as independence. Your greatest challenge and achievement will be closing the gaps with others, even on opposite sides, to find harmony.

KNOWLEDGE AND WISDOM

Your reward in life is actually quite separate from your financially focused, productive side. It is about your mind and what you can achieve as a student of life or mentor and guide to others. You are a born writer, even if you are just a casual internet user and have a way of formalizing a message which gives it great weight. You belong in publishing or academia, if you have that background, but may otherwise take a completely different life path. Even if that is the case, you will always have a book to hand or tremendous wisdom to pass on.

WHO SHARES YOUR BIRTHDAY?

Jeffrey Archer, born April 15, 1940

Dodi Fayed, born April 15, 1955

Emma Thompson, born April 15, 1959

Andy Murray, born April 15, 1987

APRIL 16

WHO ARE YOU?

You are the natural businessperson or banker, no matter what career you choose. You have all the strength of Aries, but Taurus with all its solid qualities governs your finance sector. It is a fixed sign, and you have a fixed attitude to everything you have earned or saved. At the other end of your horoscope, ruling shared finances and joint property, you have Scorpio. This is another fixed sign, which explains why you will not be moved on negotiations unless they agree with your values. You're fixed on price.

YOUR DESTINY

You are a force to be reckoned with, and people do not approach you lightly, either for negotiations in your personal life or professionally. You are ruled by Mars the god of war, and although you prefer to avoid it by keeping people at a distance, you certainly have fierce and formidable qualities which intimidate those who see your invisible ring of steel. You are, of course, spiritual on the inside, as Pisces, the sign of the soul, oversees your private self. The people you let into your world must be very special.

GROUPS, CIRCLES, AND COMMUNITIES

With Aquarius, the sign of diversity, equality, and friendship, ruling your group sector, you repeatedly find yourself happily involved with allies who could not be more different from you. As you respect independence, you both have it with these people and also offer it. The challenge for you is understanding that although your various networks seem to attract abundant opportunities, it is all too easy to enjoy yourselves so much that you overlook the potential. Try to capitalize on what you all have.

FINANCIAL SYSTEMS AND LIFE BUDGETS

Your rewards in life are financial or economic and show your experience. It's not easy in young adulthood when you begin trying to balance your life, but if you can be consistent about adapting and adjusting, your reward will be a bank account that works and, more importantly, a life that satisfies your need to set your own values and income against those of others. The cycles of time dictate that changing economies in your own country and worldwide will always demand that your energy goes into this.

WHO SHARES YOUR BIRTHDAY?

Spike Milligan, born April 16, 1918
Peter Ustinov, born April 16, 1921
Claire Foy, born April 16, 1984

APRIL 17

WHO ARE YOU?

The intensely romantic Libra rules your solar Seventh House of love, marriage, and sexual partnerships. You believe in second honeymoons but also in "the one that got away," and the foundations of your life have often been built on lost love and the potential for its resurrection. The royal sign Leo has charge of your courtship rituals and also the bedroom: you don't just have brief encounters or even relationships; you have empires you reign over. This side of your personality is best expressed in front of a microphone, no matter if you are singing love songs at karaoke nights or podcasting your poetry. Gemini rules your sector of internet and media.

YOUR DESTINY

It is your fate with Libra the Scales ruling the Seventh House of duets to face regular crossroads with your twin souls. This may be a repeated number of turning points with the same person—your life partner, for example—or you may revisit the same pattern with a range of different people. You attract people, and are attracted by them, when there is sameness and difference. You explore equality and fairness in these kinds of balancing acts, because you are from the same species but recognizably of very different types. Scorpio, associated with sexual and financial relationships, dominates your chart.

HAPPY FAMILIES

You are a cardinal sign and your chart shows a Grand Cross between the other cardinal signs: Cancer, Libra, and Capricorn. We associate this combination with happy families and property—in other words, the big bank advertisement dream. For you, it is the reality not the fantasy that steers your life. This may be for all kinds of reasons, some of them deeply personal. There are two issues here: The first is how to live in a world which does not question the fairy tale. The second is about what happiness is specifically for you.

SOLITUDE AND SPIRITUALITY

The planet Neptune with all its escapism rules your inner self. You have the soul of a monk or nun. Spiritually, you need solitude. You may or may not be religious, but your need for something sacred to guide you is deep. You will spend long periods of your life alone looking for answers. Neptune rules Pisces the Fish, associated with Christianity. Your acceptance of the Christian church or rejection of it will strongly influence your path. Your own Aries Sun is associated with relaunches and second debuts. Expect many.

WHO SHARES YOUR BIRTHDAY?

J. P. Morgan, born April 17, 1837

Clare Francis, born April 17, 1946

Nick Hornby, born April 17, 1955

APRIL 18

WHO ARE YOU?

You are a strong and decisive Aries who others respect and are intimidated by. You would do well as a judge or lawyer. This comes from your opposite sign of Libra the Scales, which rules situations where you and a partner must find balance or you and your opponent must accept what is fair. You put enormous amounts of energy into this. Mars, your ruling planet, is the god of war. You use your influence to ensure that this never happens—any potential battles are avoided through the force of your character.

YOUR DESTINY

You are an ideas person, with Gemini and Mercury the Messenger in charge of your projects, plans, and ideas. The cycles of time in your horoscope ensure that these concepts or brain waves must travel in order to succeed. You often go with them, so you may relocate for work, for example, or cross distances for business reasons. The issue is focus, preparation, research, and clarity. You are a true fire sign who makes an excellent beginning with great enthusiasm and energy. The rest is down to detail, method, and order.

FINDING INDEPENDENCE

Your challenge in life is to confront your own ideas, beliefs, and emotional and mental habits. These do more to keep you restricted than you may realize. When you understand how much can be changed, though, breakthroughs arrive. This situation repeats so often in your life that you become an expert at thinking your way out of whatever keeps you away from freedom. When you do this, you can use all the energy, determination, and strength Aries is famous for to break out, break away, and truly be liberated.

FINDING FINANCIAL HARMONY

You are born into an astrological time cycle showing your national and the global economy will go through periods of instability. Your flexibility in handling this will help you to repeatedly invent a life budget that works for you. This kind of financial harmony is something that others try very hard to achieve, but for you, it is a matter of redistributing your energy and finding the balance. This is a theme right through your birthday chart. You are physically and mentally very strong. And you need symmetry.

WHO SHARES YOUR BIRTHDAY?

Hayley Mills, born April 18, 1946
Rick Moranis, born April 18, 1953
Kourtney Kardashian, born April 18, 1979

APRIL 19

WHO ARE YOU?

You are the person who in childhood has an atlas, globe, or map of your country nearby so that you can daydream or feed your need for knowledge. You were made for the worldwide web, and the worldwide web was made for you. It may be Europe, the Americas, or Australasia, but you have a relationship with particular nationalities and countries in the most personal way. Your energy is huge thanks to your chart, but you also need to control it so that you don't waste your drive procrastinating over vast choices.

YOUR DESTINY

You have all the fire of Mars and can be quite a ferocious opponent if you wish. Most of the time, though, you would rather keep anybody you don't want in your life at bay. You do this by intimidating them or showing them what might happen were they to cross the line. You are extremely protective of yourself and who or what matters to you. Somewhere in the background, a clue to this is within your family tree. A branch of the family has played its part in making you so tough, so strong.

GREAT ADVENTURES

You are an adventurer and explorer, thanks to hopeful, big-thinking Jupiter in charge of your foreign travel and tourism sector. You could easily emigrate. You don't just pack your bags; you embrace who and what is out there for you over the next horizon. Your challenge is to be a realist and not risk too much when you go. Jupiter delivers wonderful optimism, but it is very easy to overlook the crucial details and even the genuine concerns as you depart. You may already know this about yourself. Research is useful.

MALE AND FEMALE HARMONY

Your reward in life, if you work at it, is the marvelous balance between male and female that can take place when both sides listen. You were born with Libra, the sign of the scales, ruling your sector of relationships. This does not necessarily have to be romantic, though a great many April 19 people marry into situations where both partners must figure out equality. Any kind of duet or duo with the opposite sex will help you learn patience, understanding, sensitivity—and achieve fulfillment.

WHO SHARES YOUR BIRTHDAY?

Dudley Moore, born April 19, 1935

Tim Curry, born April 19, 1946

Kate Hudson, born April 19, 1979

APRIL 20

WHO ARE YOU?

You are the deep thinker and natural lone wolf who must have their own time to ponder life's imponderables. You are often a solitary figure with a need to reflect on their spirituality. You may or may not be religious, but you are always searching. When enough time has passed, you emerge from your hibernation like a creature coming back into the next season. This renews you and gives you your incredible lust for life, which you direct at foreign places or people, travel, exploration, global links.

YOUR DESTINY

You are typically fiery as you are a person of action, only stopping when you have to examine your own soul or observe your relationships. For the rest of the time you are a warrior by nature, whose response to the lack of stability or permanence in your life is to try and fix it. Your town, local area, or country is where the cycles of time suggest regular change. Perhaps this is why you turn to the one part of your foundations you can control: the family tree and all its branches.

THE BIG WIDE WORLD

The natural link between Sagittarius, the explorer sign, and your own Aries influences makes you a born wanderer. You may do this purely online where you move from Europe to Australasia to the Americas with your mouse. You are also a natural migrant who may relocate more than once in your life. You have the Mars need to keep moving, and Mercury affecting your mind and outlook makes you classically Mercurial. You find it very hard to stay still and are always looking for the next nationality to discover.

RELATIONSHIP QUESTIONS

Relationship questions are part of your personality and destiny as you never stop looking here, either. This may be just one complicated connection which keeps you occupied for years or a series of different close bonds. Their unique nature is very hard to categorize, and you can puzzle over this for a long time, as Libra the Scales influences your commitments. Should you go this way or that to achieve balance? That central issue can take up a lot of time and energy until you realize firm action is the answer.

WHO SHARES YOUR BIRTHDAY?

George Takei, born April 20, 1937

Ryan O'Neal, born April 20, 1941

Luther Vandross, born April 20, 1951

Miranda Kerr, born April 20, 1983

APRIL 21

WHO ARE YOU?

You attract partners of all kinds, personal and professional, as your teachers. These people who are just like you, but also so different to you—same species, different breed—are educational. Through your duets and double acts you discover how to negotiate. When to be together and how to be apart and how to get on the same road or how to invent your own way of getting what you both want and need by coming up with unusual ways of staying connected, while independent, are things that concern you. This makes you a creative thinker always.

YOUR DESTINY

You are productive, practical, efficient, methodical. It does not matter if you are making hit singles or bread or training star pupils. Once you have your golden formula, you stick to it and have the staying power to repeat it in an ongoing way. This gives you the financial security that helps to settle you. That stability makes you a formidable powerhouse who keeps on keeping on when everybody else has given up. You are an artisan at heart, no matter what your chosen field or profession ends up being.

THE FAMILY TREE AND YOUR LIFE PATH

There is a striking streak of procrastination running through your personality. It shows up in your life path, as when it is time to choose one direction with the family tree or another, you find yourself unable to move. This is very similar to the issue you have with partners of all kinds—your twin selves. Enlightenment and deeper wisdom on a spiritual level become part of your nature the more you face these kinds of choices. This may be about a place on the map or, philosophically, a family direction.

MONEY MATTERS

Money matters in your life constantly remind you that money matters! You can't be separated from your bank account or income and deciding what to do—spending, investment, donation, saving—puts you in a strong position once you have taken the time and also listened to advice. You are slow to move, ponderous, and comfortable with your own pace because it gives you time to think. More than that, you need time to feel all the feelings. Money is an emotional matter for you. It's not about numbers; it's about your soul.

WHO SHARES YOUR BIRTHDAY?

Iggy Pop, born April 21, 1947
Andie MacDowell, born April 21, 1958
Robert Smith, born April 21, 1959

APRIL 22

WHO ARE YOU?

You are the bringer of justice in your personal and professional life. That means equality, fairness, harmony, and symmetry on all levels. You are a natural judge, lawyer, or jury member. You are strong, somewhat intimidating, always respected. It takes a lot to stand up to you and rock your boat or unbalance your scales. You are capable of seeing that people can be completely different but always the same, in terms of what is owed to them in life. Your partnerships reflect this need for the "same but different."

YOUR DESTINY

You learn how to control your mind, body, or spirit when you are young, and this way of managing your life stays with you into old age. It may be Reiki, or cognitive behavioral therapy, or meditation. Sometimes you invent your own method, but it is crucial to you that your headspace is as comfortable as the rest of your surroundings, as it is your happy fate to always end up in exactly the right home for you. Feeling equally at home with your own thoughts is very important to you, and you learn to master it.

MONEY AND VALUES

Your life budget, value system, ethics, morals, and principles do equate to dollars or other currencies. You know two things for sure: charity begins at home and you can't put a price on good health. This may be because of your own situation or thanks to a recurring pattern in your life when you realize you must give, or give back, to those who need it most. In your birth chart, Taurus affects the bank accounts in your life. Taurus is practical. When it comes to money, you learn to be practical as well.

THE EXTENDED FAMILY CIRCLE

Your extended family circle can be composed of friends who are in the clan—for example, godparents to your children—as well as your relatives. This is your reward in life. You are blessed with fantastic people all your days who give you a sense of belonging and connection which others can only admire from a distance. There may be a special house, apartment, or particular building linked to this. You come to identify the place with the people. In this way, it comes alive for you and becomes a symbol of great joy.

WHO SHARES YOUR BIRTHDAY?

J. Robert Oppenheimer, born April 22, 1904
Queen Elizabeth II, born April 22, 1926
Jack Nicholson, born April 22, 1937
Issey Miyake, born April 22, 1938

APRIL 23

WHO ARE YOU?

You are the classic Taurus: a slow-moving, ponderous earth sign—at least when faced with which direction to take. You find enlightenment only comes when you are ready to leap into action, and that arises from energetic Aries ruling your inner self. Your family tree on both sides, along with any family you create, always sets up a square or right angle in your chart, as this is ruled by Leo and Leo cannot be squared with Taurus. West or east? One side or the other? Taking your time to choose awakens you.

YOUR DESTINY

Your solar chart shows a natural angle between your sector of foreign people and places and your own Taurus Sun. You are a natural traveler, wanderer, migrant, tourist, or explorer. This may happen where you live as you are drawn toward other cultures or languages. You could easily uproot more than once in your life. As Taurus the Bull is the zodiac sign which is hard to budge, you can be forgiven for procrastinating as you typically find choices are hard to make. What works? A practical approach.

WOMEN AND MEN

You will find equality issues about men and women follow you around all your life, for personal and professional reasons. Libra the Scales rules your sector of work but also housework. That latter may seem unimportant, but it is a classic example of the negotiations that must be done between partners, along with that other question—children and parenthood. You may have sons or daughters. You may bypass that entirely. The heart of the matter is how two opposite sexes can find the middle ground.

GROUNDED AND PRODUCTIVE

You are grounded and productive by nature, settled in your earth sign lifestyle, committed to earning a steady and reliable income, and capable of producing results with great value. Your reward in life is an income stream you can lean on, but also professional output you can be proud of. You can also volunteer your time and energy and give generously. You are not exactly a production line in a factory, but you do have the staying power to be relied upon to give people what they want repeatedly.

WHO SHARES YOUR BIRTHDAY?

Ngaio Marsh, born April 23, 1895
Lee Miller, born April 23, 1907
Roy Orbison, born April 23, 1936
Dev Patel, born April 23, 1990

APRIL 24

WHO ARE YOU?

You are the earth sign who always needs to ground themself to feel at home in the world. You appreciate your relationships more when you are centered. This can mean shifting your position regarding your family tree. In your solar chart, both sides of the family are ruled by Leo, a sign which is at a challenging angle to your Sun in Taurus the Bull. It takes time and energy to adjust and adapt, but when you do that, you find that people become more precious to you. You become happier and more content.

YOUR DESTINY

You have the exquisite taste typical of your ruler Venus, who is associated with fashion and jewelry, hairdressing and mirrors. The look of your home is usually quite striking, and you have an eye for beautiful objects and environments, no matter if that's the garden or a vintage collectors' item. The work you put into your meditation, hypnosis, Reiki, cognitive behavioral therapy, counseling, and other inner life concerns pays off as much as your careful spending or shopping. Spending on yourself works.

BRILLIANT IDEAS

To feel at home with your brilliant ideas, you have to find the right location for them as Cancer rules your projects and plans. Cancer is about the search for a place on the map: the right office, the best company. It's an emotional decision for you. It has to *feel* right. When it does, you can place your brain waves securely and watch them bear results. The challenge for you is to focus and plan ahead. This is when your earth sign nature can help you. Rather than just rush at life, you function much better when you do the homework.

YOUR FINANCES

You were born with the Sun in Taurus in the Second House of money, valuables, land, gardens, and property. Like the slow-moving bull on which your sign is based, you can spend an enjoyably long time pondering investments or simple shopping. Hidden in your chart is practical Capricorn making a supportive angle to your Taurus Sun. Scorpio and all its sexual desire are also written in your stars, as this is the zodiac sign which cannot be ignored when you do your accounts. What price is your lust, Taurus?

WHO SHARES YOUR BIRTHDAY?

Barbra Streisand, born April 24, 1942
Jean Paul Gaultier, born April 24, 1952
Paula Yates, born April 24, 1959

APRIL 25

WHO ARE YOU?

You are the true Taurus who values beautiful homes, gardens, and the glories of nature. People are extremely precious to you, too, but you tend to see this as one package: lovely friends or family, lovely surroundings. You are the welcoming host who opens the door to impressive surroundings or the happy guest who values your delightful surroundings as much as the relatives or allies at the other end. This is where your joy in life comes from. You are generous with others and value getting that same generosity back.

YOUR DESTINY

You have the sign of groups, Aquarius, at the top of your solar chart, so your destiny is tied to teams, clubs, societies, associations, and circles of all kinds. Aquarius is an air sign and associated with distant, detached friendships between people. This means you never feel crowded, but it can lead to repeated instances where the lack of close connection leads to wasted chances. Together and united, you can build incredible results for yourselves and each other. Apart it can come to nothing. This is a repeated lesson.

THE PATH OF INDEPENDENCE

Uranus is the planet which symbolizes independence, rebellion, and freedom. This rules your peak ambitions and achievements, and several times in your life, from young adulthood on, you will prove to yourself and other people that you are a born revolutionary. This is not the typical Taurus profile, but there is a part of you which has the inner strength and willpower to break free of any situation where you feel trapped. These bolts for the next horizon characterize your life.

FOREIGN PORTS

You are a world citizen from your childhood onward and never lose sight of the tempting range of accents, languages, and cultures on offer to you, from Europe to the Americas to Australasia. Gemini rules your communication, and it is opposite Sagittarius, the sign of foreign ports and distant customs. Both of these, in turn, are connected to the horoscope house which Taurus actually rules. You place a huge value and priority on traveling—even if you only travel in the mind. You may emigrate.

WHO SHARES YOUR BIRTHDAY?

Oliver Cromwell, born April 25, 1599

Al Pacino, born April 25, 1940

Björn Ulvæus, born April 25, 1945

APRIL 26

WHO ARE YOU?

As a true Taurus, you are either here to gratefully receive or to generously give. You will experience both in your life, so you know what it is like to study or struggle, for example, but also to be involved with a charity. In your personal birth chart, your Taurus Sun is in the Second House of values, principles, ethics, and morals—as expressed through money. You understand the emotional side of receiving loans or donations or being bankrolled. You also know the power and control issues that come with being rich enough to look after other people. A balance sheet is always at the back of your mind.

YOUR DESTINY

The group is part of your destiny, as Aquarius, the sign which rules circles and communities, is at the top of your solar chart. You will find that the cycles of time bring you into groups repeatedly from childhood, and every time you experience what it is like to be spiritually as well as emotionally fulfilled but also to give back. Aquarius is the sign of diversity and equality as well, and this exists no matter who is involved in your network as you are all linked by the shared need to pool resources. In fact, collectives of all kinds not only give you what you require; they also ground and center you.

HOME AND PROPERTY

Your house, apartment, and/or property investment is at the center of everything you work for, as you are motivated by the good life. At the same time, Leo rules this area of your life, and in your solar chart, it cannot be squared with Taurus. The two signs conflict, so it may be that you work so hard and carry so many burdens in order to secure your real estate or sanctuary, because the journey to what you want is harder than it should be. Virgo can help here as it makes a perfect angle to your Taurus side and is about working smarter, not harder in the interests of well-being.

THE PATH OF PARTNERS

Your reward in life depends very much on one or more partners. These people may be professional or romantic connections, but every time you are brought to this crossroads—usually by money or property—you learn about how two people can make a business, professional, home, or real estate goal work. Scorpio rules these kinds of duets in your chart, and although it will prod you in the direction of the most practical financial choices, your ability to be together or apart, or a combination of both, is not about that—it is about your souls. Figuring that out takes time, but it's worth it.

WHO SHARES YOUR BIRTHDAY?

Koo Stark, born April 26, 1956

Roger Taylor, born April 26, 1960

Melania Trump, born April 26, 1970

Amber Midthunder, born April 26, 1997

APRIL 27

WHO ARE YOU?

You are the person whose life from childhood onward is dictated by groups. Sometimes you are an insider, but at other times you will be very much on the outside—and may even find the group against you. Aquarius rules the top of your solar chart, Taurus, and this is associated with the hive mind. Discovering how people function when they are all coming from the same place is an education. In fact, even into your senior years you will be learning about power in a circle. Together, people can achieve dramatic outcomes they might not be able to alone, and you know it.

YOUR DESTINY

You are a Taurus and a fixed sign, and so are determined when you make your mind up. Understanding group dynamics, as you have seen, is part of your character. It is also part of your destiny, and experiencing what it feels like to be one against the many, but also one of the many against the opposition, is written in your destiny. The cycles of time including Aquarius at the top of your chart suggest you will have a more intense experience of teams, clubs, societies, associations, unions (even gangs) than most people. Knowing when not to be so fixed and when to compromise is a gift that takes time.

RELATIONSHIP PUZZLES

You have the cerebral Virgo in charge of your relationships, no matter if these are romantic, sexual, or eventually with your own children. Virgo is ruled by Mercury, the planet of the mind, so you don't naturally fall into partnerships; you have to figure them out. In fact, you can sometimes appear more like a Virgo in love than the Taurus you actually are. You are a great analyst when it comes to the puzzles of marriage, for example, or dating. Progress comes when you realize that not everything can be figured out and there is no instruction manual. Knowing where to place love in your life matters.

THE POWER OF TWO

The planet of power Pluto rules the relationship you have with the opposite sex. This applies in your professional life and/or your personal life. Repeatedly, you will be compelled by the other person in a way which is very difficult to resist, as Pluto shows who and what you find dominates your life. The decisions you make are up to you, but every time this happens (even at school, when everyone must learn how to deal with each other) you will realize everything else has to stop until you have found a way through. When you do, the sense of reward can be incredible.

WHO SHARES YOUR BIRTHDAY?

Mary Wollstonecraft, born April 27, 1759
Russell T. Davies, born April 27, 1963
Sally Hawkins, born April 27, 1976

APRIL 28

WHO ARE YOU?

You are the classic Taurus who enjoys design and beauty in your wardrobe and in your surroundings. This extends to the interior of your home but also your garden or the environment. Once you have secured this, you are hard to move. In fact, like the bull from which Taurus takes its name, you tend to plant yourself solidly and stay there. Venus is your ruling planet, and she describes the evergreen romantic relationships in your past you never entirely forget, which is another example of your inability to change very much. Of course, this means one marriage can renew itself for a lifetime, too.

YOUR DESTINY

Aquarius rules people power in a group, and this sign also governs your destiny, as it is placed firmly on the top of your solar chart. You will experience just how potent a tribe can be when everybody is in unison more than once in your life. You will also be shown what it is like to be an independent individual a group is in opposition to.

So you are both on the winning team which transforms everything for everybody, but also the person on the other side who must deal with the collective force of a strong circle. From this come the events which shape your fate.

KNOWLEDGE AND WISDOM

When we look at your birth chart, the Second House, which Taurus rules, shows everything you value to the point of it being priceless. In your solar chart, those precious and valuable aspects of your life are knowledge—which cannot be bought—and wisdom—which is never up for auction. This is thanks to Mercury, the planet of the mind, in charge of everything that matters to you. You are a natural student of life or guide to others. You would make an excellent academic, web publisher, or author. Even if you don't take this formal path, Mercury ensures you will be an information hub.

THE AUDIENCE

This ability to command respect and hold attention, online or in the real world, is never just about ideas or theories. You are a practical Taurus after all and prefer it when your audience, readership, or crowd can use what you offer. This makes you a fantastic source for people who need a balanced view. There is no point in just being the keeper of the keys to knowledge, you have to open the doors for everybody else, no matter if they need to know about money or relationships. You would not be a Taurus if you did not understand what values are all about, and that is part of your message to others.

WHO SHARES YOUR BIRTHDAY?

Harper Lee, born April 28, 1926
Jay Leno, born April 28, 1950
William Kentridge, born April 28, 1955
Ian Rankin, born April 28, 1960

APRIL 29

WHO ARE YOU?

The sign of duets, partnerships, and double acts is Libra, and this also rules your sector of work and daily life. You are the person who always finds themself in relationships requiring great skill and good timing. This may be marriage or a professional pairing, but you must meet others halfway and try to balance the uneven scales, Taurus. Leo rules your homelife, and as Leo the sovereign of the jungle also needs a dynasty, the question of children always hangs over every date. Your jobs, courses, or unpaid roles will often find you with your complete opposite. This makes you an artful negotiator.

YOUR DESTINY

Your life never stops changing, Taurus, as your horoscope is set up with unpredictable Uranus at the highest point or midheaven. You can and do make it to the top, but also learn to be philosophical about the highs and lows. This area of your horoscope reveals ambition, and in your birth chart, Capricorn rules the peak of your achievements. When we go back to your solar chart to look at this same sign, we find Capricorn the ambitious mountain goat overseeing academia, education, the internet, and publishing. These matters are fated for you, and the Wheel of Fortune spins you high or low as a result.

LOOKING FOR SECURITY

Some people have families and hometowns which prop up their sense of security and provide permanence in their lives. Achieving this will always be a challenge for you, Taurus, and may involve more maintenance and effort than you expect, even in childhood or adolescence when the pattern begins. You have the kind of family tree which requires an enormous amount of attention and energy if you are to take care of each and every branch. Your sense of place is also never guaranteed, even when you have settled on just one town or country, as your horoscope suggests you are never quite committed or entirely rooted.

THE NEXT GENERATION

As you know, Leo rules your home and family and is associated with heirs, spares, and pretenders to your throne. Your reward in life will be children you can lead, guide, and rule over—rather like the royal archetype that Leo is associated with. If you do not have children, you will find an alternative way to nurture younger people, perhaps through your profession or by adopting a leading role with younger relatives. Your authority, confidence, and leadership are impressive, as is the potential of every project or plan in your hand. Whatever you plant coexists with all that future generations need, too.

WHO SHARES YOUR BIRTHDAY?

Jerry Seinfeld, born April 29, 1954
Daniel Day-Lewis, born April 29, 1957
Michelle Pfeiffer, born April 29, 1958

APRIL 30

WHO ARE YOU?

Venus is your ruler, Taurus, and she is in charge of all the relationships in your life. You are profoundly affected by these and see them as the precious and priceless aspects of your world money can't buy. When you have to experience the reality of life and accept that nothing lasts forever, your need for permanence shows. This is when the other famous part of your nature comes into view as you are a great recycler and can take anything and renew it. Just as you would take an antique in need of restoration and repair it, you can also renew what others might give up on. You never give up.

YOUR DESTINY

Taurus rules wealth in astrology, and your Sun in Taurus in the Second House of abundance will deliver this to you more than once in your life. The key is believing in the money and trusting it, as your horoscope is set up in such a way that you have to accept you deserve what is on offer and be practical about how to take it. Money opens the doors to travel for you, but can also transform your home. Those are good choices to have throughout your life, and yet nothing will happen unless you use your practical, earth sign approach and turn the dream into reality. The rewards can alter everything.

SCORPIO AND SEXUALITY

There is no doubt at all that you are a true Taurus, but Scorpio, the sign of sexuality, rules your partnerships. These can be fleeting or permanent, a passionate fling or a lifelong marriage. Scorpio can also offer complicated relationships, too. You may not always be conscious of this, but your horoscope suggests it is there. You may be thinking about your bank account, for example, but Scorpio desires have an odd way of appearing, even as you are judging how to invest or save. The well-known Taurus fondness for beautiful objects, gardens, and the environment is often where you put your money.

THE MESSENGER

In your personal birth chart, it is the Second House (which Taurus rules) which shows everything that matters most to you. In your solar chart, this zone of the horoscope is ruled by Mercury the Messenger. Your reward in life will be to earn the attention of the audience, the crowd, or the class. This may be through a social media account, or it might be in academia or the media—even a literal classroom in a school. Mercury was the messenger of the gods in antiquity, and you have the ability to carry wisdom or information about something that is greater than everybody and everything, Taurus.

WHO SHARES YOUR BIRTHDAY?

Alice B. Toklas, born April 30, 1877
Jill Clayburgh, born April 30, 1944
António Guterres, born April 30, 1949

MAY 1

WHO ARE YOU?

You are a sturdy Taurus, fixed in your judgments and not given to swaying in the face of opinion. You have Libra, the sign of the law, fair play, equality, and balance, in charge of your daily life. You would make a natural judge for this reason and may find that your personal life or professional life habitually involves you in arbitration. Libra is the sign associated with harmony and symmetry. It is ruled by Venus, the planet which also rules you. You are hard to shift, like the bull from which Taurus takes its name. Solid, dependable, and grounded in the real world, you are a down-to-earth earth sign, too.

YOUR DESTINY

Just in case you thought that was quite a responsibility to bear, your horoscope has other news for you. You have a completely different side to your personality, thanks to your destiny. You are an escape artist who happily inhabits a completely different world from most other people. This comes from the groups you are involved with, which are always in the background. Your tribes and circles are ruled by Neptune and Pisces, and it is these networks which bring out your need to explore other realities. The less something looks like the real world to you, the more you want to explore it.

TOUGHER THAN TOUGH

This need to experiment with life's more unusual, creative, spiritual, or countercultural possibilities is very strong. Another reason for this is your desire to get away from challenges which ask you to be tougher than tough. This is most obvious with the family tree. This may be on your mother's side, father's side, or possibly also with the family you create. The commanding, respected, intimidating Leo rules your relatives. It also governs any decisions you make about having children or not. From this comes your leadership. You can put on a good front, and you sometimes use it with the clan.

SOLID MONEY AND SOLID WORK

The one thing that brings out your solid Taurus side is money. You have a perfect angle from the earth sign Virgo, which rules work, to your own Taurus Sun. You are capable of sustained work over a long period of time and can accumulate steadily without sometimes realizing just how much you are achieving for your bank balance. The planet Venus, which rules Taurus, also oversees your sector of routine. Venus describes love, and you are one of those people who genuinely loves their job. Jupiter rules your finances and so there is always more; you can expand your wealth steadily over the years.

WHO SHARES YOUR BIRTHDAY?

William Lilly, born May 1, 1602

Calamity Jane, born May 1, 1852

Wes Anderson, born May 1, 1969

MAY 2

WHO ARE YOU?

You are best suited to a two-city or two-country life, no matter if you do this online or commute. You can exist between London and Los Angeles, for example, or work between urban and rural areas. Existing in two spaces or cultures at once can only be achieved with confidence—and you have it. Leo reveals your leadership as it rules where you feel at home in the world—and how. Being in charge of two places on the map comes naturally, and you may never feel settled unless you are going between two places. All that you value in life is elsewhere.

YOUR DESTINY

It's your fate to be in long-distance relationships with partners, family, and/or friends. You always seem to be in the arrivals hall of life, and the area of your horoscope which is naturally owned by Taurus in astrology (the Second House) belongs to Gemini and Mercury, the messenger of the gods, in your own solar chart. You may be the traveler, migrant, or temporary resident so often in your life that you come to associate places with people and journeys with emotions. You also receive wanderers and may have one major relationship based on a flight path.

DUETS AND PAIRS

Making it work in a relationship, duet, couple, or marriage is your challenge. Perhaps because the intense, emotional Scorpio rules your partnerships, you tend to keep a geographical and also spiritual distance from others. This can be a platonic agreement between a man and woman, say, as much as it is an engagement. You can never get too far into a relationship before questions about children, stepchildren, and property dominate. As much as you like to think this is about equality and fairness between you, it's about a future dynasty—or not.

EXTENDED CIRCLES OF FAMILY AND FRIENDS

As you've read, you are always in the arrivals hall of life. Part of your reward is always being welcomed by an extended circle of family and friends. Space and distance are part of your character and lifestyle. You are spaced out between towns or cities. There is always a great deal of room between you and your emotional ties; even a marriage will contain an intimacy gap. Yet this concentrates the feelings on both sides wonderfully, and you will always give more and receive more because feelings are preserved as precious cargo, then given like a gift.

WHO SHARES YOUR BIRTHDAY?

Donatella Versace, born May 2, 1955

David Beckham, born May 2, 1975

Princess Charlotte, born May 2, 2015

MAY 3

WHO ARE YOU?

You are a solid Taurus who is practical enough to get to the top of your profession or society. Ambitious Capricorn makes a perfect angle to your sign and gives you the staying power to hit the heights. You also have Scorpio, the sign which rules complicated relationships, in charge of your partnerships. For all that you are a grounded earth sign when it comes to success, your heart is a different matter. Your personality and life will be shaped by this, no matter if your challenge is a lover or family. Scorpio is about passion, and you feel all the feelings, Taurus. It makes you stronger.

YOUR DESTINY

Your solar chart is set up in such a way that the cycles of time will always pick up powerful, sexually obsessive Pluto in your chart. You repeatedly get into partnerships which challenge you and the other person to find freedom. Uranus, the planet associated with independence and liberation, rules the top of your horoscope but can never be squared with Pluto, which rules your intimate commitments. This may be with just one person over the course of your lifetime, Taurus, or with different lovers. When you both find a way to be free, you reset your destiny every time. This shapes you.

MAKING A GROUP WORK

This same Uranus is at the highest point of your solar chart and shows the diverse tribe of completely different people who must set aside their differences to unite. The sign of groups, clubs, teams, societies, bands, and so on is Aquarius, ruled by Uranus, and it does not sit naturally or easily in your chart, as it clashes with your Taurus self. You can be quite fixed about your place in a circle of people, and your task in life will be to find the flexibility to compromise. This is the only way to really unite and welcome the diversity you all share, bringing mutual end results which are spectacular.

LIFE AT THE TOP

You operate completely differently when you find a system, business, profession, or other setup which allows you to climb to the top. Your heart may lead you into complex choices in life, but when it comes to climbing higher, socially or professionally, you know how to do it. Capricorn the mountain goat is the zodiac sign associated with ambition and patience, and it trines your Taurus Sun perfectly: once you find a challenge requiring staying power and a target to hit, you tend to relish it. From this comes your solid, settled, grounded character in later life; you make it and stay there.

WHO SHARES YOUR BIRTHDAY?

Bing Crosby, born May 3, 1903

James Brown, born May 3, 1933

Ben Elton, born May 3, 1959

Nina Garcia, born May 3, 1965

MAY 4

WHO ARE YOU?

You are born under the fixed sign of Taurus, which belongs to the earth element. You are hard to move, once you have settled on your decisions or found the right place to call home. This lends you a sturdy quality that others respect. Your solar chart shows Venus in charge of your day-to-day life. Venus is about relationships and particularly those involving children, as the goddess of love was the mother of Cupid, her dazzling son. You may or may not become a parent, but the next generation will eventually define you. Your own or other people's children are the clue to your personality.

YOUR DESTINY

Venus rules your everyday life, as you know, but she also rules the zodiac sign Libra, which nods to your sense of justice. You are a natural judge, no matter which profession you find yourself in. You have an acute sense of what is fair and this may be expressed in your personal or professional life. Understanding that there are two sides to every story is part of it. You may also have knowledge of the law, as it is your destiny to be put in situations where "equal but different" has to be accepted. Taurus, your balanced, symmetrical, harmonious approach to life helps you persuade others to accept you.

COMFORT AND BEAUTY

Taurus is associated with collectible possessions as well as nature. You feel at home with beauty and comfort, no matter if you are in a tent with designer cushions or taking your impressive wardrobe—and yourself—into the wild. Once you have found your ideal home, you tend to treat it as your castle. Leo, the sign associated with royalty, also rules your house or apartment, garden or local surroundings. You don't just inhabit a space; you command it. Even though other countries will always tempt you, there's no place like home. It's your domain.

FOREIGN PEOPLE AND PLACES

The most valuable aspects of your life—precious to the point of being priceless—are ruled by Sagittarius, the sign of foreign people and places. Other nationalities and destinations call you from childhood, and you are a natural migrant. You are also a literal internet explorer and enjoy translating ideas, customs, and even recipes from other cultures into a language you can understand. As you are ruled by Venus, the goddess of love, you find it easy to entertain the idea of relationships with other nationalities. That is your gateway to learning. Traveling in the mind or with the heart appeals.

WHO SHARES YOUR BIRTHDAY?

Audrey Hepburn, born May 4, 1929
David Guterson, born May 4, 1956
Keith Haring, born May 4, 1958

MAY 5

WHO ARE YOU?

You are a natural leader and authority figure who rules over the next generation. You may or may not become a parent, Taurus, but the royal sign Leo governs your extended family. You are commanding in your own way and people respect you. This leads to a quite natural desire to have an escape or release, and you can sometimes lead a double life, guiding and mentoring children and young adults while respecting your own inner child and their need to play. Your projects and plans, when planted, have the power to grow over time and entertain or educate generations.

YOUR DESTINY

Whenever you become involved with particular groups, clubs, teams, and so on, you find your Pisces side comes into play. Pisces is the sign of the two fish, neither of which live in the real world. You question what other people say is reality, for much of the time, by inhabiting a space where the strangest and most wonderful alternatives seem normal. This gives you relief from needing to lead or be looked up to. Your chart is set up in a fated way with the cycles of time to make these vacations from normality quite regular. In your personal or professional life, you swim in another stream.

MONEY AND SECURITY

For all that you are here to lead a younger generation, you are also a Taurus, and so you are challenged by money and property. Do you hang on and hold on or let go? Do you save or spend? Hoard or invest? These kinds of questions follow you around from your first piggy bank as a child. These matters are emotional for you and not about the numbers or statistics. The sensitive water sign Cancer, associated with real estate, also rules your thoughts and ideas. Your security comes from owning and keeping money. Your test in life is to lose the feelings and ask the experts for their advice.

YOUR OWN UNIVERSE

You have a strong Pisces streak to your character, and Pisces is ruled by Neptune, the god of the sea. You cruise and float through life, never making contact with others in the real world unless you have to. That is your reward. From a distance this can look like a holiday from everything and everybody, and yet it is so habitual that you may not always realize how far out you actually are. Groups will always be the trigger for this in your life and pooling resources comes naturally. The idea of no boundaries between others in the tribe or network feels quite natural to you. You are, at heart, an escape artist.

WHO SHARES YOUR BIRTHDAY?

Karl Marx, born May 5, 1818

Sylvia Pankhurst, born May 5, 1882

Tammy Wynette, born May 5, 1942

MAY 6

WHO ARE YOU?

You are drawn toward people and ideas which some might call a faith or belief. This can actually be religion or spirituality—but the beliefs may also be philosophical or even political. What might seem to be a private mystery or an invisible part of yourself is out in the open where it has the potential to change people, to challenge and confront them. Mars rules your soul, psyche, and spirit, Taurus. Mars is also about great energy and a dynamic approach to life. There is nothing hidden about these doctrines or declarations—they must be tested all your life, by you or others.

YOUR DESTINY

Scorpio and its ruler Pluto describe your sexual relationships, no matter if they are marriages or short-term passions. Your chart shows cycles of time which bring repeated challenges within a partnership or a series of lovers who raise the same big questions again and again. Freedom or commitment? Scorpio is certainly about desire, but it is Pluto which brings up the issue of independence. Feeling controlled by something or someone is a lifelong obstacle to overcome. Liberating yourself is just one half of it; the other person has to be liberated, too.

CLOSE AND DISTANT RELATIVES

You were born into a family which will require maintenance all your life, no matter if the people are close or distant from you. The family circle is always changing, according to your Taurus horoscope, and you will have to decide to be proactive or turn away from particular branches on the family tree. Leo rules this area of your life, and as it never sits easily with your Taurus Sun, you may find it hard to square yourself with your relatives. This also extends to your town, region, or country. It's always shifting, and securing a sense of belonging is a challenge.

GIVING GENEROUSLY

You are a true Taurus with your Sun in the Second House of banks, charities, business, and property in your birth chart. You will experience both sides of giving generously and receiving, until you create the wealth you need. On a daily basis, you are influenced by Libra, the sign of fairness and justice. This suggests that you actively need to make sure the gap is closed between yourself and others. When you are in the haves camp, you care more about the have-nots than many other people. You a natural philanthropist no matter if the giving is done personally or not.

WHO SHARES YOUR BIRTHDAY?

Sigmund Freud, born May 6, 1856

George Clooney, born May 6, 1961

Prince Archie of Sussex, born May 6, 2019

MAY 7

WHO ARE YOU?

Taurus is the sign of the builder who invests time and energy at home or work, creating security. You are the person who will go back to any situation with the family or household and restructure until you establish the stability you need. You are an earth sign and want to feel the ground beneath your feet. When you don't believe that you have it, you are capable of starting all over again, laying foundations for a new career or personal plans to give you what you want. Taurus the Bull is the zodiac sign most associated with the need for permanence, and you pursue it.

YOUR DESTINY

The planet Pluto rules Scorpio, the sign which in turn rules your sexual relationships, and this horoscope symbol is about empowerment. Either with the same partner or a series of them, you will be tested by situations which require you to find willpower, to gain the strength you need. This may be because of the chemistry you share in, for example, a marriage or the actual nature of the partnerships you choose. Self-control will give you control, and you will need that if you are to break free from who or what you feel overpowers you. This shapes who you become and what you do with your life as well.

THE FAMILY TREE

The sign of authority and leadership, Leo, governs your family tree. You are quite an intimidating person, respected but also taken very seriously by your relatives. You rule, basically. Leo is the sovereign of the jungle, and the lion is a symbol of the monarch on the throne. There is a natural distance between yourself and others, so that you control who can be close to you. The patterns in your horoscope suggest it can be hard to square who you are with what individual relatives do—or what happens to them. How you manage that is a repeated lifetime challenge for you.

WEALTH AND LEADERSHIP

You are a classic Taurus Sun person, destined to find wealth and assets—the good life, if you want it. The property market is never too far from your thoughts. Taurus is a fixed sign, ruled by the element of earth, and you are very hard to move once you have found your place in the world. As you have read, you are a builder by nature who can construct your own security over time, no matter how much sustained effort and energy is involved. You are a solid individual who has very firm views on money, and others will have to respect that to deal with you.

WHO SHARES YOUR BIRTHDAY?

Robert Browning, born May 7, 1812

Gary Cooper, born May 7, 1901

Eva Perón, born May 7, 1919

MAY 8

WHO ARE YOU?

You will take turns at both guiding and being guided in your life, no matter if you call it philosophy or religion. All that you value most highly is in the world of books and "bibles" or perhaps the Bible itself. Gemini rules the world of words, sermons, and lectures, and it also happens to rule everything that is so precious to you that it is priceless. With Libra, the scales of balance, in charge of your daily life, you are drawn to theories where there are two sides to every story. You tend to find yourself drawn to brotherhoods and sisterhoods where faith is everything along with belief.

YOUR DESTINY

Taurus knows what they put the highest price on, and it is often places, people, or concepts which cannot be bought or sold. It doesn't really matter what the doctrine is; for you it is at the core of who you are. This is interesting for you when you travel, emigrate, or deal with foreign people. Contrasting and comparing give you a far bigger perspective on other philosophies and faiths. This is not the main appeal of the worldwide web, though, or your own journeys. The sign of the explorer, Sagittarius, offers you a wealth of choices that make you feel blessed.

HOUSEHOLD AND HOME

You are a natural adventurer, as you know, so settling down and staying put with your household or family are a challenge. You are always drawn to parts of Europe, the Americas, or Australasia all your life. It couldn't be further away from domesticity and familiarity, security and settling down—but that inner conflict shows in your chart. Part of you only finds your lust for life and your freedom when you engage with another nationality or country. Leo, which rules your people and your place, is hard to square with the rest of your chart. Compromise takes work.

INSPIRATION AND PERSPIRATION

You know that particular books, philosophies, beliefs, or "bibles" are beyond price to you. This comes from the two zodiac signs Gemini and Sagittarius, which rule everything you value most. They also describe the world of ideas. Your reward in life is to have big ideas of your own, which you can then turn into thriving, long-term enterprises. You are an earth sign, Taurus. This helps you ground concepts or brain waves in the real world, rather than letting them disappear as quickly as they arrive. You have what it takes to found ongoing success, based on one idea.

WHO SHARES YOUR BIRTHDAY?

David Attenborough, born May 8, 1926

Chris Frantz, born May 8, 1951

Martha Wainwright, born May 8, 1976

MAY 9

WHO ARE YOU?

You are a true Taurus person, patient enough to invest in plans which pay dividends over time. You take great satisfaction in watching your investments or savings grow. You are an earth sign, grounded in the real world, who likes the natural rhythm of slow growth, no matter if you are on the land or not. Taurus the Bull suggests that you have both feet firmly planted and are hard to shift. Your pace is slower than that of other people, and when in doubt, you speculate, rather than act. You have the potential to become wealthy, or you may put the environment first.

YOUR DESTINY

Aquarius rules groups, friendships, networks, and communities of all kinds. In your solar chart, this sign is also hard to square with your own Taurus Sun. Throughout your life, you will find that whenever there is a choice to pool resources with others, you hit a crossroads. This is a set pattern in your horoscope created by the cycles of time. These circles of people may be professional, business, purely social, or based on particular societies, associations, or teams. As you know, you don't rush your choices. But when you do choose, it changes your life.

YOUR PLACE IN THE WORLD

A house, apartment, or other residence is never just a home to you. It is a symbol of everything you must deal with. This will happen repeatedly, as your sector of the extended families in your life is also where we find specific places which are so much more than bricks and mortar to you. All this in your astrological chart is ruled by Leo, the sign which is hard to square with Taurus. Feeling at home, in terms of your place in the world, does not come automatically and naturally. Others have their circles and their own places, and meeting them in the middle is a test.

GROUNDING YOUR RELATIONSHIPS

With the analytical Virgo ruling your close relationships, it is easy to use your mind to try and decode your emotions, Taurus. This can keep you stuck. As you know, you tend to take your time with what matters most to you. This is notable in your partnerships, partly because so many wheels are turning within. Grounding your relationships in the real world rather than overthinking them is your reward in life. When you are able to find the right place for who or what puzzles you, you can take both yourself and the situation onto solid ground. It works.

WHO SHARES YOUR BIRTHDAY?

J. M. Barrie, born May 9, 1860

Richard Adams, born May 9, 1920

Billy Joel, born May 9, 1949

MAY 10

WHO ARE YOU?

You are sometimes mistaken for a fire sign as you are energetic, enthusiastic, and always at the start of any action, especially if plans, projects, or brain waves are involved. In fact, you are a true Taurus, money-minded and ruled by Venus, the planet of financial and sexual relationships. However, you value good ideas extremely highly, and there are some concepts or campaigns which are close to priceless to you. The fiery, adventurous Sagittarius rules your sector of all that is precious. You're a one-person startup.

YOUR DESTINY

You have the sign of groups, Aquarius, at the top of your chart, fixed at the highest point of your horoscope. These groups cannot always be squared with you and vice versa. A repeated scenario in your life is outsider versus the hive mind. You'll be on both sides at different times in your life. Through this you learn that if everybody pulls together and gets the communication issues out of the way, great things can follow. It's not easy, though, because you are a fixed sign—hard to budge in a group or far outside it.

MONEY AND THE GENERATIONS

Your Taurus Sun can be found in the Second House of values, principles, ethics, finance, banking, and business in your birth chart. This is where you find your tests in life, as there are always families, extended families of friends, and several generations to consider. It's not that there is a shortage. Jupiter, with all his abundance, rules legacies and wills. It is the emotional and spiritual inheritance which is hardest to manage, though. Numbers are numbers, but it's your task to close those generation gaps.

LOVE IS ITS OWN REWARD

Passionate Scorpio with all its focus on sex rules your partnerships in life. This sign in turn is governed by Pluto, which describes the power of love. This can extend to reconciliation for many people born on May 10. The numerals 1 and 0 are hidden in your birth date. You have to look after number one, but you are nothing without another person. And not just *any* other person: you tend to fall for people who offer you a complicated relationship that the poets or musicians have been inspired by. Special deliveries.

WHO SHARES YOUR BIRTHDAY?

Fred Astaire, born May 10, 1899
Bono, born May 10, 1960
Linda Evangelista, born May 10, 1965

MAY 11

WHO ARE YOU?

The fair-minded Libra rules your work, unpaid work, or academic career. The scales of justice are always in your hands, no matter if you pursue a professional life as a detective or as a journalist holding politicians to account. Of course, there are many ways you can balance the scales between one side and the other. This may take place in your personal life, when particular partnerships or even conflicts show you unwritten laws as well as—perhaps—legal processes. Equality between the sexes and races or classes may figure in.

YOUR DESTINY

The Moon rules your short journeys, as Cancer describes your need to get away and explore. Nothing and nobody can stop you when you feel the urge, and you will go alone if you must. Beating a retreat like this is part of your nature. The planetary movements around your horoscope time this to the New Moon and Full Moon cycles. When you find even the most precious people in your life must be put to one side, you can and must be allowed to depart. Distance is necessary emotionally.

CHANGE VERSUS PERMANENCE

Taurus, you are a fixed earth sign and so very much grounded with particular family, partnership, or work structures. That is, until you are not. Uranus is the planet of radical and sudden change, and it rules your peak achievements in life. Whenever you make it to the top, either in terms of your ambitions or your personal life, you must then deal with a choice. When life is reshaped around you, as it always will be, do you walk away and start again or go back to who and what you knew and try to rebuild the past?

EXPORTING YOUR IDEAS

You have a nomad's instincts and, as you've seen, will wander off when you need to when dealing with people and situations which affect you emotionally. You extend your need to explore to work, academia, and unpaid work, too; in fact, your greatest rewards in life will come from successfully exporting your ideas. Capricorn rules foreign places and people in your solar chart. In your birth chart it rules tremendous ambition, so when you fulfill your quest to secure your plans in other countries, you win.

WHO SHARES YOUR BIRTHDAY?

Martha Graham, born May 11, 1894

Eric Burdon, born May 11, 1941

Shohreh Aghdashloo, born May 11, 1952

Natasha Richardson, born May 11, 1963

MAY 12

WHO ARE YOU?

You are the balanced voice of reason in any day-to-day situation with Libra, the sign of fairness, ruling your zone of work, housework, unpaid work, and academia. You are the peacemaker who can balance the scales of justice when two people are in conflict. You also know what it is like to be involved in an argument or even a battle. Because of this you understand how both sides feel in any difficult situation and gain a reputation for being a tactician as well as a strategist who can help clear anything up.

YOUR DESTINY

You have a chart tilted toward simultaneous endings and beginnings. Even as one chapter closes in your life, another book is already about to begin. This gives your life—and you—a certain depth and intensity. You experience these crossroads from childhood, and by the time you are an adult, you will have your own philosophy or beliefs about life as a result. Life is, after all, a series of final curtains, with the stage being set for the next drama as a result. From this comes your sense of belief in a brighter future.

MOTHERS AND CHILDREN

So many of your ideas about life, your opinions, and your theories are formed by your mother. The relationship may have been good, bad, or indifferent, but with Cancer, the sign of mothers and children, ruling your mind, you are strongly influenced by your upbringing. Should you become a parent, this is emphasized even more. This impact on your thinking applies even if you never have children. For you, there is something about the maternal bond which is central to who you are and how you function.

THE JOY OF A FULFILLED PLAN

The simple joy of a fulfilled plan is something that can take you a very long way, as life will teach you that so many projects or ideas never make it. This is where your grounded Taurus Sun comes into play, as you are an earth sign who believes that anything worthwhile has to be planted and nurtured. All that you value most highly in life is ruled by Mercury, the planet of clever concepts. In fact, for you, some achievements are priceless, because they represent what can happen when brain waves are made real.

WHO SHARES YOUR BIRTHDAY?

Edward Lear, born May 12, 1812
Florence Nightingale, born May 12, 1820
Dante Gabriel Rossetti, born May 12, 1828
Katharine Hepburn, born May 12, 1907
Tony Hawk, born May 12, 1968

MAY 13

WHO ARE YOU?

You are the negotiator and dealmaker (as well as deal-breaker) in your relationships with the opposite sex. Libra, the sign of balance, rules your sector of daily life—its scales have men on one side and women on the other. Discovering a place to meet in the middle is not fast or easy, but you regularly find yourself having to weigh up the differences between yourself and another person with a great deal of inner debate. From this comes your unique personality and some truly fascinating duets or double acts.

YOUR DESTINY

You are a leader, authority figure, and quite intimidating person to those kept at a distance. Noble Leo with all its association with royalty rules your family and household sector. Your family tree, which is a law unto itself, is never far from your thoughts. It requires maintenance all your life and never entirely leaves the back of your mind. Perhaps because of this you are a strong person who has a firm sense of boundaries. You know who to invite to become close to you—and who to keep at bay.

RICH AND POOR

As a true Taurus, you shine most brightly as a donor, philanthropist, or charity fundraiser. Your Sun is in the Second House of your birth chart, where your values and ethics are on display. These principles translate into money. The need for equality and fair play that you feel between men and women also rules your bank account. Sometimes in your life, you will be the needy rather than the needed. This shows you what it feels like to be on the wrong end of the scales. Because of this, you're generous.

LIFE AT THE TOP

Your reward in life is the top job or top position, the number one spot. This usually happens when a group is involved, as Aquarius, the sign of circles and communities, has charge over the highest point of your horoscope. It may be the team, club, society, association, or something similar which decides your success. Or perhaps those networks of people are just profoundly affected by it. Fate decrees that when you seize the day and gain the authority, there will always be people and politics around you. Understanding that can help a lot.

WHO SHARES YOUR BIRTHDAY?

Daphne du Maurier, born May 13, 1907
Armistead Maupin, born May 13, 1944
Alison Goldfrapp, born May 13, 1966

MAY 14

WHO ARE YOU?

You are a born collector, philanthropist, businessperson, bargain hunter, property investor, or trader. Your ruling planet is Venus, and she governs trade, commerce, and exchange. Venus rules the scales, too. In traditional British units of weight, there are fourteen pounds in a stone—the same as your day number of 14. Your life path is all about weighing, earning, saving, fundraising, evaluating, selling, buying, or exchanging. The number 14 repeats in your life.

YOUR DESTINY

Property means family—and family means partnerships and children. How you play this is intensely personal. You may have an extended clan or a blended dynasty. You cannot help but admire magnificent architecture, sprawling castles, and mansions. Yet these are only as valuable as the good relationships within the family circle. It's your destiny to have the keys to those gates, no matter if you are an honorary uncle, a godmother, or a bonded part of the dynasty. A special residence may be in your network of family or friends.

ONE VERSUS THE MANY

You will always find yourself in regular upheavals within your profession, unpaid work, or at a university/college as a new face becomes number one. This is the recurring situation known as "one versus the many," and it comes from the numerology in your birth date. Dealing with groups who are also on the other side to you will be part of your existence. One of your birthday numbers is 5, and this is the number we associate with the teams in the Olympic Games (five rings) as well as bands like MC5 or the Jackson 5.

ON THE MOVE

You are one of those Taurus people who gains from commuting, exporting, or going between two places, like Los Angeles and New York or London and Paris. Every time planets pass through Capricorn and your sector of distant places and faces, they create stunning patterns with your Sun. And that's every twenty-eight days in the case of the Moon! The world is always open to you on a monthly basis. It's the same with factors passing through Cancer and your sector of neighboring places. You do well in life with two cities.

WHO SHARES YOUR BIRTHDAY?

David Byrne, born May 14, 1952
Sofia Coppola, born May 14, 1971
Mark Zuckerberg, born May 14, 1984

MAY 15

WHO ARE YOU?

You are the team player whose challenge is the team itself. This is true from childhood when you may be involved with anything from a Peanuts-style gang of friends to a sports tribe. In adulthood you discover that cooperation is difficult when everybody is so different. Aquarius, the sign of diversity and community, rules your highest achievements, Taurus. Uranus, the planet of independence and individuality, is also in charge of your greatest accomplishments. When you create unity, it's wonderful.

YOUR DESTINY

All that you value most in life is the big adventure or great mission—across your country or across the world. You take repeated great journeys in your life and are a natural migrant. The sign of foreign places and people, Sagittarius, rules what money cannot buy. The planet Jupiter, a symbol of optimism and the big picture, also rules everything that is so precious to you it is priceless. You travel light when you are on the move, and what you carry with you can never surpass the value of the trip or transfer.

THE GETTING OF WISDOM

Education and academia are not simple, easy, or straightforward for you. Even though you place a very high value on qualifications—or you know others do—the tug-of-war in your chart between Gemini and Sagittarius, the signs of study and teaching, is a challenge. Both these signs describe where the real worth in your world is. You know that wisdom is not for sale in a catalog and there are no bargains where knowledge is concerned. This is a lifelong challenge for you, Taurus. How can you make it work?

THE JUGGLER AND TRAVELER

As you have read, you are a wanderer by nature. You have a great pull toward other regions, nationalities, or countries and their cultures. This is also true when it's time to work, do business, volunteer, or study. Your Taurus nature is rather slow to move, can be too fixed to the spot (Taurus is an earth sign), and hangs on rather too tightly to your projects, plans, and ideas. If you can become more flexible and faster on your feet, though, you are the exporter or intellectual adventurer who succeeds.

WHO SHARES YOUR BIRTHDAY?

Ralph Steadman, born May 15, 1936

Madeleine Albright, born May 15, 1937

Mike Oldfield, born May 15, 1953

MAY 16

WHO ARE YOU?

You are the grounded, practical, down-to-earth, money-minded Taurus that you read about in the astrology books. Solid and hard to move, you are gifted at saving as well as earning. This comes from the Sun in Taurus in your birth chart in the Second House of ownership and wealth. Taurus the Bull rules gold bullion and bull markets on the New York Stock Exchange. A natural link to Cancer, the sign of real estate, in your chart suggests that the property market is a comfortable fit for you, Taurus.

YOUR DESTINY

You have the Sun in charge of your extended family, particularly the younger members. This may be your child, niece, nephew, godchild, and so on. Whatever is planted in the family tree can grow in a wonderful way with your care and attention. Even if you don't have children of your own, it is your fate to cherish and nurture children or teenagers. The natural link to Cancer, which you have just read about, suggests there is also an easy connection to youth, from infants onward, which Cancer also rules.

REPAIR AND REBIRTH

Virgo rules healing, rehabilitation, and recuperation. These ideas about repair and rebirth are central to your life, Taurus, because of the angle Virgo makes to your own Sun sign. You are the healer or the healed from childhood on and will take turns at experiencing both. So, for example, you may become a therapeutic, helpful friend or partner but also spend some time on your own health and well-being. This process of assisting others to feel born again or being assisted yourself is a lifelong challenge.

THE HAPPY HOME

The easy flow between Cancer, which rules property and also family, and your own Taurus birth sign creates what is know as a sextile. It all comes together in your life with very special places where people feel their home is their castle but also that the extended family of relatives and friends is central. You are always welcomed. The particular houses, apartments, or surroundings that you associate so much with important people have a character of their own. They're more than bricks.

WHO SHARES YOUR BIRTHDAY?

Henry Fonda, born May 16, 1905

Christian Lacroix, born May 16, 1951

Olga Korbut, born May 16, 1955

Janet Jackson, born May 16, 1966

MAY 17

WHO ARE YOU?

Your home can be anywhere across the map, Taurus, as Cancer—which rules your sense of place in the world—also happens to govern your sector of journeys. Your ambitions to succeed with all your plans and projects are also global, with Capricorn and all its goals in charge of your foreign sector. You are a grounded earth sign, with a firm grip on all your ideas, but from a young age you will want to explore or export. Sometimes you travel with the plans, too—or they can be transported easily online.

YOUR DESTINY

Dealing with group psychology and the hive mind is a fated experience for you, no matter if you are on the inside or on the outside. This is another part of your horoscope which slowly begins to take shape by your teenage years, so it may be anything from the Scouts to a sports team that teaches you about people power within a circle. Aquarius rules the highest point of your chart where you reach for the greatest lessons. It is the sign of the outsider as well as the community. You'll see it both ways, and often, in your life.

FINANCE AND SECURITY

You are a true Taurus, and your Sun is in the Second House of your birth chart, where you deal with your bank account, possessions, and property. Taurus is a fixed sign, and you tend to be quite resistant to change where your security is concerned. It is very important that you don't lose sight of the property market with all its changes, as although you can keep your savings in the same place for years, the reality of real estate is quite different. Being open to outside advice from professionals could help with a more flexible approach.

THE FAMILY OR A DYNASTY?

You have authority, respect, and great influence with both sides of the family tree. You are more like a sovereign with a dynasty than just another relative to those who are in the clan. The royal Leo with all its dignity and leadership governs both sides of your family tree, but you will find one collection of relatives is more obviously where you rule the roost. You can seem fierce to those who don't know you well or the younger members of the tribe, but it is this approach that keeps yourself and others in a good place.

WHO SHARES YOUR BIRTHDAY?

Dennis Potter, born May 17, 1935

Dennis Hopper, born May 17, 1936

Enya, born May 17, 1961

MAY 18

WHO ARE YOU?

Groups strongly affect the person you become, Taurus, as Aquarius rules the highest point of your chart. Aquarius is all about the association, band, society, club, or other network, and every time there is a change at the top, it is the way you rejoin the circle—or not—which counts. It's rather like having a ruler crowned in place of the person who went before with a court who must adapt. In your professional or personal life, you end up being an expert on group psychology because you have to be.

YOUR DESTINY

Your Taurus Sun is in the Second House of your birth chart, which is where your principles, values, ethics, and morals exist side by side with financial questions. This brings in issues like charity and taxation, for example. Your horoscope is set up so that the cycles of time ask you to put a price on what cannot be bought and sold on a regular basis. This may be philanthropy or generosity. It may be good health on all levels. You will experience what it is like to be in need, but also to be wealthy enough to help others, too.

THE NEXT GENERATION

Your greatest challenge in life is the world of children or teenagers: the next generation. There is a pattern in your chart called a square, between Leo, which rules the younger members of your family, and your own Taurus Sun. This shows what is difficult to align or compromise with. Fortunately, the practical Virgo makes a helpful angle to your Taurus Sun, too, and as this shows your ability to guide, mentor, influence, and lead the young, there are always answers. Being open to the wisdom of others helps you with this world.

FINDING SPIRITUALITY WITH A GROUP

You already know that learning about the hive mind or group psychology can help you in your life, particularly when there are changes in your career, for example. There is also a wonderful, spiritual side to your involvement with special circles of people. You are able to find everything that is sacred—sometimes what you might call a religious experience—with these networks. Everybody is connected underneath no matter how separate they may be as independent individuals. For you it's the gift that keeps on giving.

WHO SHARES YOUR BIRTHDAY?

Rick Wakeman, born May 18, 1949

Mark Mothersbaugh, born May 18, 1950

Chow Yun-fat, born May 18, 1955

Toyah Willcox, born May 18, 1958

Taeyang, born May 18, 1988

MAY 19

WHO ARE YOU?

You are the solid, capable, dependable hard worker who is driven by goals—usually a special apartment, house, or holiday home. Taurus is an earth sign and fixed, so you commit to building your life by taking on as many projects and plans as you can. Putting one foot in front of the other, you use the advantageous angles in your chart from Virgo (which rules duty) and Capricorn (which rules ambition) to fulfill your mission. The great achievement of your life will be learning how to work differently—and better—so you can enjoy your life more.

YOUR DESTINY

You are a global citizen who has been fascinated by other nationalities or countries since childhood or adolescence. This continues all your life as you place a high value on different cultures and languages. You are a natural explorer and may even emigrate. Sagittarius rules the four corners of the world, and as this sign also shows what is precious to the point of being priceless to you, sometimes nothing else will matter as much as a foreign accent. The worldwide web is where you escape to.

MULTITALENTED AND MAGICAL

You are a multitalented multitasker who can be quite magical in terms of your influence and ideas. You may or may not describe yourself as psychic or spiritual, but with a special angle in your chart from Neptune, the planet of inspiration, you pick up concepts from a higher place you may call imagination, dreams, or just the universe. Your challenge in life, as you know, is to work better, not harder. Finding out how to roll up your sleeves and take a practical approach to all that you know is a lifetime test.

REDISCOVERING YOUR ROOTS

It is only when you rediscover your roots that you find the true fulfillment you deserve from particular relationships in your life. Cancer rules your family tree and your ancestors, culture, heritage, and history. Repeatedly in your life you will find yourself being drawn to where you come from in an effort to feel comfortable about who you are. This is a life-changing experience requiring tremendous determination and energy, but your life will prove to you that digging deep is the answer.

WHO SHARES YOUR BIRTHDAY?

Malcolm X, born May 19, 1925

Edward de Bono, born May 19, 1933

Nora Ephron, born May 19, 1941

MAY 20

WHO ARE YOU?

You are the natural loner who finds answers in solitude. You may or may not call yourself a Buddhist, an Anglican, and so on—but you are a human being in search of the spiritual all your life. You can only do this in silence and so regularly take sabbaticals from the noise and distraction of daily life to find yourself again. You are not just seeking your own soul, though; you are looking for something greater than yourself to guide you. Not everybody understands your path, but when you succeed, the results are very special.

YOUR DESTINY

You are the idea person fated to find your missions change all the time, but your quests begin in your teens or twenties. When you get it right, you export your plans—sometimes traveling or moving with them—and have the deep satisfaction of watching something thrive and prosper. The concepts urge you to seek other parts of your own country or the world to make your mark, but more importantly, to nurture budding successes in places which offer what you need. This makes you a born explorer at heart.

THE FAMILY

Some people are born into stable families where nothing much changes apart from the natural rhythms of life. Your horoscope shows fated cycles of time which will pull one or both sides of your family tree in strong directions, testing your ability to take control or play your part. This may be on one side of your family or the other, but some branches of your clan will never really be fixed or predictable. Dealing with that is a reminder that you need to pace yourself and have a plan. Life will teach you that strategy is the key.

THE ESCAPE ROUTE

You believe in escape routes for yourself and others, no matter if that is a safe haven for refugees fleeing war or on a personal level the big moves that happen in life when it's clear that the only answer is relocation or emigration. The idea of a new life in a new place is something that will call you from youth to old age, and you place great faith in the great unknown, either playing your part with migrants and new arrivals or changing your own life, more than once, by uprooting. "No Fixed Address" is sometimes your address, too.

WHO SHARES YOUR BIRTHDAY?

Jimmy Stewart, born May 20, 1908
Cher, born May 20, 1946
Charles Spencer, Ninth Earl Spencer, born May 20, 1964
Louis Theroux, born May 20, 1970

MAY 21

WHO ARE YOU?

You are the go-between who conquers two cities, two regions, or two countries. You will do this all your life, either commuting or just invested in two different locations online. You are an impressive person who has star quality, and you know how to make an impact. You are a natural explorer or traveler who feels most at home when you are between places. This gives you a special view of others, and you prefer to see both sides at the same time. An interest in different cultures or customs comes naturally to you from youth to old age.

YOUR DESTINY

Your relationship with your mother has a strong impact all your life. Sometimes it is your grandmother or a maternal figure, but it is usually your own mom. The memories of the mother-child bond or your hopes for a sacred family connection in your own future play a big part in your psyche and spirit. If it was difficult for you with your own mother, then you may idealize what is possible for yourself with a child. If this family tie was strong, then this is the spiritual source which sustains you in ways others never see.

FINDING UNITY WITH GROUPS

You will learn a lot about the group mentality during your life, and it begins in your adolescence or young adulthood. Finding unity with people even when ideas and opinions are on opposite sides of the fence is a huge task for you. It will never be easy, but one of your great lessons is that you need to focus, center, and find a sense of place before you begin your mission. As you are the natural traveler or a go-between with two homes or workspaces, this is quite demanding, but your reward is the miracle of a truce or agreement.

STRENGTH OF MIND

You have great strength of mind when you are prepared to summon up the self-discipline to find it. This changes your life and is your ultimate reward. You are a natural meditator or self-healer. Perhaps you are your own best therapist or counselor. Your inner world is a mystery to everybody else, but you learn early on that commanding your own imagination is the key to everything. You also learn that the most peaceful sanctuary is not necessarily your own bedroom: it is the quiet, still space within that makes you secure.

WHO SHARES YOUR BIRTHDAY?

Elizabeth Fry, born May 21, 1780
Fats Waller, born May 21, 1904
Mary Robinson, born May 21, 1944

MAY 22

WHO ARE YOU?

You are an escape artist who inhabits their own world. You rule your kingdom and are admired from a distance because nobody can join you. Others can attempt to get close to you, but with Pisces the sign of the fish ruling your success in life—your position and mission—you can be very hard to catch. Neptune is tied to Pisces in astrology, and this planet influences your career, academic career, or unpaid role. You drift and cruise as a result, but are always the captain of your own ship, steering your own path.

YOUR DESTINY

Groups, teams, networks, clubs, societies, bands, and associations of all kinds are in your destiny. They find you, or you change your course in life and seek them out. You have the numeral 5 in your birth date, which is associated with people power within a circle or community. Even though your decision to join new allies or fellow travelers in life is always hugely demanding, it is your destiny to repeatedly leave a life alone for a life with others united in a single goal. This comes from the cycles of time in your birth horoscope.

RELATIONSHIPS, TRAVEL, AND RELOCATION

Sagittarius, the sign of the wanderer, affects your sector of duets and duels. Relationships are the main reason you have a life path devoted to travel, relocation, and/or emigration. The phrase "moving on" might have been made for you, too. When you need to escape the complications, you set sail and put as much distance in between yourself and the past as possible. Sometimes you can make endless wandering your way of life, because it stops others from drawing too close. Packing bags removes emotional baggage.

CONNECTION AND COMMUNICATION

You were born to play with can-and-string telephones from childhood, and as an adult may find yourself with a microphone in hand as part of your career or weekend interests. One of your biggest lessons is to listen and receive as well as to be taken on board. Your occasional adventures with new crews in your life teach you that. When the lines of communication are broken with others, it is always because everything else has been lost, too—trust in intimacy or family, trust in human nature. Healing paths are fated for you.

WHO SHARES YOUR BIRTHDAY?

Arthur Conan Doyle, born May 22, 1859

Morrissey, born May 22, 1959

Naomi Campbell, born May 22, 1970

Novak Djokovic, born May 22, 1987

MAY 23

WHO ARE YOU?

You have two horoscopes in astrology. Your private or natal chart is based on your time, place, and date of birth. You have fierce Mars and combative Aries there, ruling your sector of image and reputation. Your solar chart, based on your being a Sun Gemini, shows Mars and Aries again, tied to groups. So circles, bands, communities, and ensembles showcase you as a fighter. You are light and bright, Gemini, but there is fire power there.

YOUR DESTINY

In your birth chart, Uranus rules all your networks, be they as small as a sports team or as large as an orchestra. Uranus has long been a symbol of the unique individuals within the larger whole. This is what makes the larger whole challenging for you to deal with. This is true from your childhood (say, the Boy Scouts or Girl Guides) to your senior years. You will learn, over time, how to manage the differences between people for the good of the whole.

EQUALITY AND JUSTICE

You have the numeral 2 hidden in your birth date. Finding how to balance one against one, and seek equality for yourself and another, is central to your character and life. You may be drawn to the law for this reason or find that the law has the last word on one of the most important chapters in your life. Duets and duels are shown by the numeral 2 and you know that balancing acts are crucial. Finding out how to create symmetry and harmony is vital.

THE WORLD CITIZEN

You are ruled by Mercury and he has winged sandals and a winged helmet. You don't, of course, but you do spend your life flying from one place to another, or sending your plans and projects online, to distant locations. The challenge for you is grounding yourself and your ideas in the real world so that you can actually plant these concepts in the most productive places then stand by to nurture them and watch them grow.

WHO SHARES YOUR BIRTHDAY?

Joan Collins, born May 23, 1933

Robert Moog, born May 23, 1934

Jewel, born May 23, 1974

MAY 24

WHO ARE YOU?

Once you are motivated by your group—whatever that is—you seem more like an energetic, fiery Aries than the Gemini you actually are. Your tribes motivate you, and you show a sense of mission that is recognizable to those who know you from youth to old age. A large part of you is a warrior in spirit, but it is only evident when you must take sides and either join in a collective enterprise or even lead it. Mars is the Roman god of war and the red planet. This has rulership over your teams, allies, and fellow travelers in life.

YOUR DESTINY

Your everyday life is ruled by Pluto, associated with simultaneous endings and new beginnings. You routinely experience the most dramatic transformations thanks to the cycles of time in your horoscope. These are personal or professional for you, but repeatedly put you at crossroads in your life which shape the person you become. Faced with the really big themes of release but also survival, you are much deeper spiritually or philosophically than a Gemini is meant to be. The search for meaning matters.

A WORLD OF BOOKS

Your Gemini Sun is ruled by Mercury, the planet of books, the media, and the worldwide web. Mercury is the old messenger of the gods in ancient Rome, and you are a natural writer as well as an avid reader. Queen Victoria, who shares your birthday, famously kept a diary. Depending on your life choices, you could easily become an academic. If not, you remain an enthusiastic student of life. Twists of fate and fortune, sending you high and low, make you look for wisdom and truth in the work of numerous sacred texts.

THE REWARD OF PARTNERSHIP

Jupiter with all his hope, expansion, and good fortune rules your partnerships. This is usually marriage but can sometimes be a platonic duet with the same kind of importance. Jupiter in astrology is regarded as an old Roman god, too. The Romans called him Optimus Maximus, and even when you are dating for the first time, you should be optimistic, as every encounter maximizes your own growth. In astronomy Jupiter is the gas giant of the solar system. Your partnerships take on gigantic proportions in your life. And so they should.

WHO SHARES YOUR BIRTHDAY?

Queen Victoria, born May 24, 1819
Bob Dylan, born May 24, 1941
Priscilla Presley, born May 24, 1945

MAY 25

WHO ARE YOU?

Your ruling planet of Mercury also rules Virgo, which describes you as the healer or the healed. Gemini, you will actually take turns at both over the course of your life. This is quite a powerful process no matter if it is physical, spiritual, mental, or emotional. Pluto, which is about total transformation on every level, also rules the transaction between you and the person who helps you—or you help. Major issues about trust and vulnerability emerge when you dig deeper. You understand deep change.

YOUR DESTINY

Your zodiac sign is ruled by Mercury the Messenger, who also governs journeys. Throughout your life you will be on the move. You are a natural migrant. Mercury also oversees your home and family sector, so you have a gift for helping people feel at home when they move to your town or country. Equally, when you feel you have lost your sanctuary in life, you will be the first to find a new home in a place far away. Establishing yourself in places which are a blank page—or helping others do the same—is a natural part of your life.

THE FAMILY AND BOUNDARIES

You are tough, strong, formidable, and very firm on boundaries, because life has taught you how to set limits with people. Your family tree is a regular challenge for you, no matter which branches of it need maintenance. The cycles of time in your horoscope suggest that relatives, close and far, will always give you several tests at once, as nothing stays the same forever and particular relatives will always switch direction, giving you an issue to resolve. Your past, in terms of parenthood fulfilled or unfulfilled, matters a lot.

RELATIONSHIPS AND COMPLICATED REWARDS

The planet of growth, hope for a better future, fortunate timing, and expansion is Jupiter. You have Jupiter in charge of all the duets in your life, no matter if this involves a platonic duo with the opposite sex or a marriage. At various times in your life you will explore your options with people who play different roles. Sometimes it's about an affair; sometimes it's about how men and women can work together. Again and again you will find freedom through the other person on the other end of the scales. It's always liberating.

WHO SHARES YOUR BIRTHDAY?

Raymond Carver, born May 25, 1938
Frank Oz, born May 25, 1944
Mike Myers, born May 25, 1963

MAY 26

WHO ARE YOU?

You are the Gemini ruled by Mercury, the planet which also governs your sector of home, family, ancestors, roots, heritage, culture, and history. Only when you go back there and ground yourself in where you come from do you find your place in the world. From there, relationships can be fulfilling, and you can find more satisfaction. Mercury also rules Virgo, the sign at the base of your chart. When you ground yourself firmly in your relatives' past and perhaps their town or country too, you change your life and change yourself, Gemini.

YOUR DESTINY

Gemini rules communication, learning, education, and language development on all levels, from the simple to the complex. No wonder you intuitively understand the world of children and teenagers. This is your destiny, no matter if you become a parent or not. Leo is the sign to associate with guiding, mentoring, and influencing the next generation. It also rules the chart zone which Gemini owns in the natural horoscope. You were made for this window into a younger world, and your choices here help shape growing lives.

MANAGING RELATIONSHIPS

Ever the optimist when it comes to relationships, you have two responses: recycle, repair, and renew anything which requires it or move on and don't look back. This is a challenge for you all your life, but as time goes on you become more experienced at handling who or what does not turn out as expected. This may be partners, family, or friends. Your greatest achievement emotionally is to take what you had and reinvent it. Jupiter rules your partnerships. This is the planet of hope and growth, and it works for you.

HAVE IDEA, WILL TRAVEL

You are an enthusiastic visionary who always has a plan. Your talents may incline toward the written or spoken word, as Gemini rules communication with the world. You may also be musical or have a gift for invention or the cutting edge of information. Your success comes from moving yourself and your project to a place where it can thrive. This embraces Mercury, your ruling planet, which is associated with travel and export, relocation and migration. Mercury is also the planet of brilliance, and Gemini, you have it.

WHO SHARES YOUR BIRTHDAY?

John Wayne, born May 26, 1907
Miles Davis, born May 26, 1926
Helena Bonham Carter, born May 26, 1966

MAY 27

WHO ARE YOU?

Gemini is ruled by Mercury, the messenger of the gods, and you always have a message to pass on to others. This may be the equivalent of a bible that you quote from—whether that is a recipe book or a feminist classic. You can recite chapter and verse of all that you know to be true, no matter if it's on radio, over the phone, on television, face-to-face, or across the worldwide web. You have the authority of a leader because in your birth chart, the sign of Leo the Lion, the monarch of astrology, rules your way with words.

YOUR DESTINY

Business, charity, banking, cryptocurrency, property, or valuables are central to your destiny. You may be an entrepreneur or inherit money; you may be a tax strategist, a philanthropist, or a self-made success. Capricorn the Goat rules your financial fate. In your Gemini chart this shows slow accumulation over time. In your birth chart, the same sign rules your ambition. You are quite prepared to climb slowly to the peak of your potential, and once you've made it, you will stay there.

SIGN OF THE TWINS

You are represented by the heavenly twins in the zodiac and are always pulled in two directions. One part of you may be drawn toward the West while the other is firmly in the East. Trying to reconcile two very different parts of your personality is a lifetime challenge. As you know, your audience or readership is central to you. It doesn't matter if it's in a Zoom meeting or across your desk. Articulating what you know and feel, when it is so complex, is a learning experience for you from childhood until old age.

THE QUEST FOR FREEDOM

The planet Uranus rules every revolution in your life that sets you free, and there will be more than one great escape in your destiny. You will typically travel widely or end up living far away from where you started out. Gemini, your sign rules journeys in astrology, but your horoscope also suggests that every pilgrimage is also psychological. You never just leave a place; you also leave your old self behind, when you are finally able to liberate yourself and gain an exhilarating sense of space every time you hit these choices.

WHO SHARES YOUR BIRTHDAY?

Siouxsie Sioux, born May 27, 1957

Joseph Fiennes, born May 27, 1970

Jamie Oliver, born May 27, 1975

MAY 28

WHO ARE YOU?

You are the natural student of life who never stops learning, which is true to your Gemini Sun and also your brilliant ruling planet Mercury. You are also far more interested in finance than other people born under your sign as Cancer, which rules property and home, as well as real estate investment, is in charge of your saving and earning ability. Mercury also happens to rule your sector of houses and apartments, so you channel your capacity for clever calculation into money and it pays off.

YOUR DESTINY

If your full birth chart agrees, you will become an academic or sought-after professional who is an expert in your field. Even if you leave school at a young age and never proceed to university or college, your birthday suggests a life of knowledge exchange. You are a born writer if you choose to use it. You are also deeply interested in informal education as well as, perhaps, ongoing qualifications. This input then becomes your output as others respect you for your wisdom and accomplishments and your special pearls of wisdom.

SECURITY AND STABILITY

If there is one sign associated with in-depth finance, business, and economics, it is Scorpio. This in turn is ruled by powerful Pluto. Both of these describe your day-to-day existence, and you can be quite intense about everything you own, earn, or owe. With Cancer the Crab and its clinging claws in charge of your bank account, you can hang on and hold on when everybody else has sold up and moved on. Your lifelong test is to seek the expertise from advisors in helping you to become more flexible and updated with this.

WEALTH AND ITS REWARDS

The ambitious Capricorn rules joint finances and property in your horoscope. You tend to believe in the biggest and best—once you have had enough experience to prove to you that it is possible. Trusting and then trying for what you know you deserve are the gateway to wealth. From there, all roads lead to Rome or anywhere else you like. Gemini, your ruler Mercury is the traveler of astrology with his winged helmet and sandals. For you, the dividends that life pays tend to go into new experiences in new places—forever.

WHO SHARES YOUR BIRTHDAY?

Ian Fleming, born May 28, 1908
Patrick White, born May 28, 1912
John Fogerty, born May 28, 1945

MAY 29

WHO ARE YOU?

You are the born explorer who cannot resist traveling far and wide, relocating within your own country or even emigrating. Mercury rules your Sun sign of Gemini, and he is usually shown with wings on his helmet and sandals. You tend to fly in a more conventional way, but you are also a natural hiker, rambler, or flaneur.

Uranus, a symbol of freedom, excitement, and independence, is in charge of your foreign travel sector. This also makes life unpredictable, and although you prefer to just pack your bags, remember reality has rules.

YOUR DESTINY

The zodiac sign which rules caring, compassion, and home is Cancer. This sign also rules your attitude toward money. From your childhood into old age you will learn a lot about what is so precious it is priceless. This is usually charity, simple kindness, or philanthropy. As you will both need others' generosity at different times in your life but also be able to offer it, you will find your experiences shape you. Your values—what you will and will not sell your soul for—are based on the principles you see in the real world.

THE MAGICAL MESSENGER

You are a messenger, as you know, ruled by Mercury who passed information from the gods across the universe. Your greatest challenge in life is to absorb this information—some of which might even appear to be channeled—and get the message across to others. The mysterious Neptune, which is associated with inspiration and mediumship, extrasensory perception and intuition, rules your success. Your task is to take your amazing connection to invisible wisdom and find a way to craft it into something practical and useful.

GROUP PSYCHOLOGY

Your greatest reward in life will come when you are able to understand group psychology and bring about the miracle known as reconciliation and unity. As a Gemini, you are always engaged in debates about particular opinions, theories, and ideas. These can sometimes divide a group so that there are differences which get in the way of shared potential. Sometimes you are the outsider against the many; other times you are part of the many against an outsider. When you learn how to unite everybody, great things are possible.

WHO SHARES YOUR BIRTHDAY?

Charles II, born May 29, 1630

Rupert Everett, born May 29, 1959

Noel Gallagher, born May 29, 1967

MAY 30

WHO ARE YOU?

You are the dreamer and strongly imaginative thinker who conjures up as many visions of wealth and success as you do specters and threats. As a true Gemini, you are an idea person who knows all about the potential of the worldwide web. Mercury, the traveler and messenger, rules your sign. However, you are also very good at writing scripts in your mind which seem to tell stories of tempting rewards as much as demons and monsters. None of it is real. Neptune the planet of illusion and projection needs management.

YOUR DESTINY

You are born to be in one or more partnerships where you explore what it means to be a man with a woman on any level in the twenty-first century. Your understanding of gender politics grows over time, but you cannot resist a duet. Jupiter, with all his hope for the future, growth, and expansion, rules your double acts. These can be marriages in some cases or platonic work agreements in others. You are fated to meet the people you will travel with on a dual highway, merging into one lane, for whatever reason.

GROUPS AND NETWORKS

Mars is the action planet, and he rules your involvement with groups, clubs, teams, societies, associations, and networks of all kinds. This may be online or in the real world, Gemini, but from childhood onward you learn about timing where your circles are concerned. If you move too slowly, then you will find that your groups never deliver the potential you can see. If you rush, then you can also risk the potential of those allies around you. Research and experience will show you how to handle people in your tribes.

THE GLOBAL THINKER

You are a global thinker who always has your sights set on the export potential of your plans. As a true Gemini, you typically have twin projects, but it will take a lot of grounding, preparation, and research to ensure that you can succeed with two ideas, rather than one. As you are an air sign, you can fly with your mind, even when you are barely able to walk. Take a tip from the earth sign Virgo, which rules your foundations: the more grounded you are before you move yourself and your concepts, the better life is.

WHO SHARES YOUR BIRTHDAY?

Harry Enfield, born May 30, 1961

Tim Burgess, born May 30, 1967

Duncan Jones, born May 30, 1971

MAY 31

WHO ARE YOU?

You are a Gemini and live in a world of big, potentially brilliant ideas. Mercury, the planet of the mind, rules your sign so the projects never stop coming. However, you are also money-minded and a powerful and intensely focused investor or negotiator. Scorpio, with all his interest in making or saving money, has charge over your sector of daily life, so this is part of your normal existence. In turn, Scorpio is ruled by Pluto, a symbol of tight control. You drive a hard bargain, and shares or property attracts you.

YOUR DESTINY

You are an air sign, Gemini, and sometimes the concepts come out of thin air, too. The trick for you is taking what is so inspired and inspiring and making it real. Your horoscope is set up in such a way that the cycles of time will bring you slow, ongoing rewards from just one concept or project if you can plant it in fertile ground at the right time. Neptune rules your highest achievements, and as this planet is associated with visions, you are motivated by what might be from youth into old age. Actualizing those is your destiny.

FINDING YOUR ANCESTORS

Once you find your ancestors, roots, heritage, culture, and history, you are on firm ground, Gemini. It may not be until you make the connection between feeling secure and hanging on to your family tree that you truly feel at home in the world. You tend to live in your head as Mercury the planet of the mind is your ruler. Yet Mercury also rules your foundations. Where you come from can help you emotionally with where you are going. Dig deeply for who or what makes you feel happiest, even if it's distant ancestry.

NUMBER ONE

The numeral 1 is hidden in your birthday, and you will find yourself there repeatedly in your life: coming first or being on top. Whenever this happens, you will find that the group you are part of, or surrounded by, becomes central to your journey. The decisive, assertive, competitive Aries rules your circles and networks; your societies, associations, and teams. Sometimes these people are the trigger for a rapid rise to the top for you or another. Just as often, you find that a shift at the top forces the group to rearrange itself.

WHO SHARES YOUR BIRTHDAY?

Walt Whitman, born May 31, 1819
Clint Eastwood, born May 31, 1930
Brooke Shields, born May 31, 1965
Iga Swiatek, born May 31, 2001

JUNE 1

WHO ARE YOU?

The groups in your life, which may be political parties, bands, or other networks like social media or formal associations, define you. As a Gemini, you are ruled by clever, quicksilver Mercury. Your smart tactics with difficult group dynamics train you to be faster than everybody else. The planet Mars oversees all the circles in your life. Although Mars was the Roman god of war, you never do battle with people, but you do know how to be highly strategic. Aries also governs the communities of people which affect your life. It's the sign of action, not words.

YOUR DESTINY

Mercury the Messenger is your ruling planet, as you know. Mercury can be thanked for your sharp mind but also your need to explore your own country or the world. Your Gemini Sun rules journeys. While Mercury had winged sandals and a helmet to help him travel, you usually fly, drive, or hike. The worldwide web is your natural home. However, you find real enjoyment in being on the move. You may make this part of your personal or professional life. You will also be tempted to emigrate. It's hard to keep you at home.

FINDING YOURSELF IN RELATIONSHIPS

By now you should be starting to appreciate how much you need to travel. One of the reasons for this is your relationships, which seem more fulfilling when you spend time away from them. This may be family and friends, but your instinct is to be on the move in order to spend the time alone you need to find yourself.

Rediscovering who you are without these people is important, as on your return, the chemistry changes and your understanding of people is different. This may explain your solitary interests or urge to be by yourself.

GROUP HARMONY AND UNITY

Throughout your life you will find it is your networks and circles which really shape you, rather than one-on-one partnerships. You are good at managing potential issues with groups before they happen. You also know how to recharge your connection with friends by getting away and recharging. Your greatest reward, though, is the loyal inner circle of like-minded supporters who can surround you. Aquarius, which shows that kind of cooperation, is perfectly placed in your chart. You are a good leader or front person.

WHO SHARES YOUR BIRTHDAY?

Marilyn Monroe, born June 1, 1926

Morgan Freeman, born June 1, 1937

Alanis Morissette, born June 1, 1974

Tom Holland, born June 1, 1996

JUNE 2

WHO ARE YOU?

You are ruled by Mercury, the planet of the mind, Gemini, and take a thoughtful, analytical approach to your plans and projects. Mercury had wings on his helmet, and your ideas are always ready to take flight, once you ground yourself in the real world. The issue for you is that you are an air sign, not an earth sign, so you may be more interested in what is on paper or on your computer than the practical action plans required to plant what has potential. Neptune, the planet of daydreams and visions, rules your success. Can you convert them?

YOUR DESTINY

Your heart zone is ruled by Libra the Scales. Finding out what is fair is a lifelong challenge for you with partnerships and other close relationships. If your feelings are on the line, there will always be a process of weighing and measuring. Sometimes the issue is a love triangle. Libra is governed by Venus, and this symbol of complicated emotions has charge of brief encounters but also marriages and children.

Experience will teach you that the only solution is to withdraw. If you are part of the story, then the solution is to extract yourself.

GROUPS AND TEAMS

In order to build something exceptional, you have to add perspiration as well as inspiration and cooperate with a group. Aries, the sign of action, rules all the groups in your life from sports teams to important causes. In turn, Mars rules Aries, and he is the Roman symbol of conflict. As you are gifted with communication, it may be left to you to do the persuading or negotiating when your circle needs to unite. This is a lifelong test for you, Gemini, and it begins when you are a teenager. How do very different people agree to disagree?

MOVING ON TO FREEDOM

Uranus is the planet of liberation and independence, and it rules your travel and relocation sector. More than once in your life you will break free from situations where you feel tied down and find what you are looking for in a new part of your country or the world. The idea of liberty and liberation is tied to travel or moving for you. This makes you a born explorer or wanderer although your real goal, of course, is to feel at home in a place and among people who allow you to enjoy your space. This tendency affects many lifetime decisions.

WHO SHARES YOUR BIRTHDAY?

Marquis de Sade, born June 2, 1740
Thomas Hardy, born June 2, 1840
Charlie Watts, born June 2, 1941

JUNE 3

WHO ARE YOU?

You are the person of action who is always on the move, partly because your family requires it. The other reason is the lack of secure grounding in your local area or country. This is true all your life, Gemini. You are ruled by Mercury, the planet associated with the restless traveler, the mover and shaker. Mercury also has charge of your sector of home and relatives. Nothing and nobody ever stand still for you, which may be why you are always in motion, too. The ground beneath your feet just keeps shifting, and you have to move with it.

YOUR DESTINY

Mercury, as the messenger of the gods, has a strong influence over you, and younger people will always learn from you. You may or may not have children, but future generations are important to you and your message. This is where you have authority and respect. The sign of leadership, Leo, rules all that you put into words. You have dignity as a distinguished writer, online author or presenter, or orator into old age. You are proud of the impact you have on children and teenagers, not only now, but into the future—and rightly so.

ENDINGS AND BEGINNINGS

Your horoscope is set up so that the cycles of time bring regular, dramatic crossroads for you. These are the simultaneous endings and beginnings which characterize your life. They teach you a great deal about transformation and rebirth, thanks to Pluto's rulership of your daily life sector. Accepting when chapters end and books are shut is part of your life, along with the knowledge that even when one story is over, another is already showing itself up ahead. This is intense for an air sign to deal with. Time and space always help you.

GROUPS INSPIRE JOURNEYS

Aquarius rules the circles in your life and the resources you share together. This idea of pooling everything for the community is part of your reward. You see it happen from your adolescence into your senior years and know that, together, people can discover spiritual fulfillment. From this come your greatest journeys, no matter if they are road trips, overseas adventures, or even permanent relocation. Aquarius governs your sector of distant places and possibilities. Your allies and friends are the launchpad.

WHO SHARES YOUR BIRTHDAY?

Josephine Baker, born June 3, 1906

Allen Ginsberg, born June 3, 1926

Anderson Cooper, born June 3, 1967

JUNE 4

WHO ARE YOU?

Groups of all kinds have the biggest impact on your life and personality. Through these networks you discover that people power can achieve anything, Gemini. Aquarius, the sign which rules close communities and circles of people, makes a perfect trine to your sign. It also works the other way, thanks to the cycles of time in your horoscope. You can sometimes find you are the outsider with a group and that, collectively, people can place you at a crossroads that will transform your life forever. The hive mind is a learning experience for you.

YOUR DESTINY

Gemini is the sign which rules the media and the worldwide web, libraries and writing. You are surrounded by the written word from childhood, and it will be the same in old age. You can understand your life through other people's articles, websites, and even their journals, as language is your filter. This helps with the random, unpredictable nature of your existence. Why random? Uranus is the symbol of revolutionary change in your life and its own sign, Aquarius, makes an exact aspect to your Gemini factors. Your highs and lows revolve.

THE MATERNAL RELATIONSHIP

All that you value most highly in life comes from your relationship with your mother or another maternal figure. Cancer rules this sector of your chart, where you count what is so precious it is priceless. If you did not get this from your mother, you will try to find it in other mother-child relationships. If you are a woman, for example, you may have a baby; if you are a man, you may marry a maternal type. It is different for everybody born on June 4, but emotionally and spiritually, this close family bond is at the heart of you.

INSPIRED AND INSPIRING

You were born with Neptune, the planet of inspiration and intuition, in charge of your success in life. Some people may think you are a channel for something greater than yourself. You are quite magical, in the sense that you can achieve what quantum theory tells us is true; all kinds of intriguing outcomes can be popped into existence by you through sheer force of mind and willingness to tap unseen energy. You will always have an audience or readership of some description, even from young adulthood. You translate very big ideas.

WHO SHARES YOUR BIRTHDAY?

George III, born June 4, 1738

Russell Brand, born June 4, 1975

Angelina Jolie, born June 4, 1975

JUNE 5

WHO ARE YOU?

You are the money-minded Gemini who has Cancer, the sign of the clinging crab, in charge of your bank account. Cancer also rules security and belonging and is tied to real estate. You have an emotional attachment to everything you own and earn, as Cancer is a water sign and lives by their feelings. People can discuss the stock market with you, but you have a strong compulsion about your finances which sometimes goes against what the numbers or the experts are telling you. You are a natural saver.

YOUR DESTINY

Looking at your whole solar chart, your sector of groups is influenced by Mars, the action planet. Throughout your life you will be involved in teams, clubs, or other networks of people where the pace is extremely fast. A circle of sports fans is one example. You learn through experience and come to understand that if these communities are to succeed together, you have to be proactive. You also have to understand the psychology of every different hive mind, because you cannot achieve anything alone. The action plans have to be shared.

CHILDREN AND MOTHERS

You are ruled by the planet Mercury, Gemini. Mercury also governs your sector of family life—traditionally about maternal instinct and the female line. As a result, you are pulled toward the story with your own mother, as well as deep questions about women and children in general. This goes beyond the surface as it affects your soul and spirit. What you aspire to in life is that sacred connection between mother and child which may sometimes be just a dream but, if you are fortunate, a reality. It is based on feelings, not words.

FINDING YOUR PLACE

You probably know that Mercury is the traveler of astrology, and he is also your planetary ruler. He governs your homelife as well, shown at the very base of your horoscope. When you find your true place in the world—often because you have to—you gain from the experiment. You may relocate or even emigrate as often as you have to, Gemini, in order to find that refuge or sanctuary. This makes you sympathetic to others who have to uproot, and they hold a special place in your life. A charity for children? Maybe it begins at home.

WHO SHARES YOUR BIRTHDAY?

Adam Smith, born June 5, 1723

John Maynard Keynes, born June 5, 1883

Mark Wahlberg, born June 5, 1971

JUNE 6

WHO ARE YOU?

You are the natural teacher, tutor, or lecturer who may never have that job, but still acts as an information portal. You are a true Gemini, ruled by Mercury the Messenger, and are gifted at taking inspiration and applying it to practical matters: money and business, relationships, the internet. You are intuitive and pick up insights from all around, with Neptune ruling your role and goals. Neptune, as well as Pisces as the sign it is associated with, describe the invisible universe that only a few can tune in to. Gemini, you are one of them.

YOUR DESTINY

The sign of group solidarity and shared goals is Aquarius, and this makes a perfect trine to your own Sun sign. When you find the right circle of supporters and allies, you discover security as well. Aquarius is an air sign like your own and traditionally the sign of clubs, teams, bands, unions, societies, and networks of all kinds. You are a natural leader or voice for such a community, and the cycles of time in your horoscope between Leo, the authority sign, and Aquarius suggest a round table atmosphere. Perhaps you will often play King Arthur.

FINANCIAL REALITIES

Saturn rules joint finances, business, charity, and property in your chart. Saturn is the planet of reality checks and slow results. The Greeks called him Kronos, from which you find the words *chronological order*. Everything has to happen in the right order in your life, which often means patience has to become your friend.

Fortunately Saturn also rules the earth sign Capricorn, which is firmly grounded and solid. This makes you a natural investor or saver, even though the tests of your ongoing effort and staying power are big.

YOUR FAMILY AND YOUR HOME

Mercury rules your sign, Gemini, but it also rules your family tree and your home. This may be your town, local area, or country. Mercury is never still, and there is a lack of certainty or predictability about where you come from—and the branches on that family tree—that means you must always be on the move. Sometimes this indicates greater emotional flexibility as your extended clan can change direction like the wind. At other times the issue will be your own home and sense of place. You learn to be proactive and always prepared.

WHO SHARES YOUR BIRTHDAY?

Björn Borg, born June 6, 1956

Paul Burrell, born June 6, 1958

Steve Vai, born June 6, 1960

JUNE 7

WHO ARE YOU?

You live in your own world and are a fascinating, if remote person who is far removed from reality. Neptune and Pisces rule your position, mission, and ambition in life. You are a Gemini who is strongly influenced by this placement at the top of your horoscope. The other key zodiac sign in your chart is Aquarius, governing groups of all kinds. This is the only thing that can tempt you to rejoin other people, and you are always intrigued by the idea of pooling resources and sharing the journey. If you do this, it changes your life.

YOUR DESTINY

The practical earth sign Capricorn oversees your joint finances and business. This helps ground you, and you are capable of creating steady income as a result. Sensible Saturn rules Capricorn, so you have a no-nonsense approach to making money. The cycles of time suggest you will be comfortable at least and wealthy at most. You are ruled by the planet Mercury, Gemini. Mercury also rules Virgo, the sign of hard work, method, and routine. You are an escape artist who inhabits their own space, but you know how to deliver results.

FRIENDS AND ALLIES

As you know, only a compatible crew with the right chemistry will lure you away from your unusual, solitary existence. You drift and float in your own headspace until the right group comes along. When it does, your challenge is to make the club, team, society, and so on operate as a whole. This is challenging as Aries and Mars rule your groups and there may be competition or even the chance of conflict. The incredible energy of the communities you end up with is plain to see, but finding common ground to share is also important.

THE HEALING TRANSFORMATION

As Gemini is ruled by Mercury, you are also a healer because this planet also happens to rule the sign Virgo in your chart associated with mental and physical health. The planet Pluto which shows deep transformation is also in charge of your mind, body, and spirit. This may be therapeutic in a comforting, informal way or actually involve the medical profession. You will swap places at different times in your life, sometimes being the helper—and sometimes being helped. This can be a profoundly spiritual experience as the changes come from the soul. Turning somebody's life around, or having your own life reshaped, is a rich reward.

WHO SHARES YOUR BIRTHDAY?

Liam Neeson, born June 7, 1952

Prince, born June 7, 1958

Damien Hirst, born June 7, 1965

JUNE 8

WHO ARE YOU?

Your Gemini Sun is linked to the worldwide web, the media, writing, and reading. It may be through a script, diary, or website, but your universe is populated by observers. There is a lot for them to watch as you have been born into a time cycle when the Wheel of Fortune spins in quite an unusual way. Your ruler Mercury is actually there twice, locked into a pattern with himself. Highs and lows are normal for you and begin when you are young. Life can seem like a big game of Snakes and Ladders. It makes you philosophical, Gemini.

YOUR DESTINY

When it comes to making money, you are solid, dedicated, productive, and successful. Capricorn rules joint finance and property in your chart. Capricorn the Goat is an earth sign, grounded in reality and prepared to be patient in order to get what they need. You set financial, charity, or business goals and meet them. The double appearance of Mercury in your chart also references Virgo, the sign of reliable work and sustained effort. This is one of the reasons why you understand how to serve.

FINDING BALANCE

Your emotional life is ruled by Libra the Scales. This is where you form partnerships and also look at the question of parenthood. Libra is about the identical pair who are also different. You will repeatedly find yourself in these kinds of duets from youth into old age. Being the same as the person on the other end of the scales—but also quite obviously in your own category—can make it hard to choose a path which suits both of you. Procrastination is one of your traits. Two roads, two outcomes, two choices are a lifelong puzzle to fix.

THE EXPLORER

As you know, Mercury rules your sign. This is the explorer, traveler, and wanderer of astrology. Wings are his symbol, and you may be a lifelong tourist or even a migrant. As a true Gemini, you tend to have twin cities or twin countries in your life. That duality you experience when you are in a partnership, finding balance, also emerges when you are on the move. Being pulled in two different directions on the map for personal or work reasons teaches you to see two points of view and two sides of the story. Your angle on this fascinates others.

WHO SHARES YOUR BIRTHDAY?

Joan Rivers, born June 8, 1933

Nancy Sinatra, born June 8, 1940

Tim Berners-Lee, born June 8, 1955

JUNE 9

WHO ARE YOU?

You were born with Saturn, the planet of patience, sustained effort, and solid gains, in charge of your finances. You will always succeed in a world of ideas, because you are a true Gemini who feels at home with the worldwide web. You also have a far more down-to-earth and grounded side to your character, however, and it comes from your investments and savings. Saturn rules Capricorn the Goat, who sets high goals and steadily meets them. This earth sign is also about life gardening—planting, growing, and gaining.

YOUR DESTINY

You have powerful Pluto in charge of your work, unpaid work, and academic career. The cycles of time in your horoscope will empower you and put you in firm control on a regular basis, giving you the upper hand in your chosen field or profession. Your groups are part of this. Aquarius, the sign which rules unity and solidarity among your friends and allies, makes a perfect trine to your Gemini Sun. Together you can come first in many things, but it is down to your leadership and authority in a world of ideas that spell success.

EVERGREEN RELATIONSHIPS

Your greatest challenge is understanding that love for you is evergreen. You were born with Jupiter, the planet of growth and expansion, in charge of your sector of partnerships and marriage. Even when things end between you and another person emotionally, this means there will always be more. This is really like the tree that goes on growing even when you believe it has had its time. Gemini, you may also be one of those lovers who believes that hope springs eternal in particular situations, and that is another lifelong test for you.

THE CROSSROADS OF PLUTO

You know that Pluto rules your sector of work and daily life. It is powerful and transformative. Pluto also rules the final chapter that becomes the next story. Pluto describes the most intense process of letting go and moving on for you. For most other people this is rare, but you meet these crossroads quite regularly. The death of the old and the birth of the new happen simultaneously in your life, and a new day is always dawning. This makes you stronger, more optimistic, and more empowered when you begin again and again.

WHO SHARES YOUR BIRTHDAY?

Cole Porter, born June 9, 1891

Michael J. Fox, born June 9, 1961

Johnny Depp, born June 9, 1963

JUNE 10

WHO ARE YOU?

The comfortable fit in your chart between Aquarius, the team sign, and your own Gemini Sun surrounds you from childhood. Groups, clubs, societies, associations, and circles of all kinds give you firm backing and support. You are a natural leader for these communities, or you may find yourself set apart from them but still always influenced by them. Understanding the way people work together will help you all your life as when all concerned are coming from the same place, amazing outcomes are possible. You'll know this into old age.

YOUR DESTINY

Your personal life is shown by the sign of foreign cultures and countries, Sagittarius, ruling your sector of lovers and partners. You will have a large range of choices here, as the different accents or languages on offer are all tempting. Jupiter is the planet associated with your duets, and in astrology this suggests you will always have more than you asked for in love and life. Selection is the hard part. It is through your attraction to different cultures and nationalities that you will experience the world in all its variety—and the web as well.

YOUR EXTENDED SPIRIT FAMILY

Scorpio is associated with everything that you inherit from past generations. This need not only be property or finance. In turn, Scorpio is ruled by Pluto, a symbol of the afterlife. Your challenge is to deal with the ongoing influence of your extended family in spirit. Even if you do not believe in a world after this one, it certainly believes in you. In fact, a great many of your tests in life can be traced back to those souls who are part of your circle. Their evolution on that side, spiritually, is tied to your own experience.

COOPERATION AND COLLABORATION

Aquarius, ruling groups, makes a perfect fit with your own Gemini Sun. This does not mean that organizing cooperation and collaboration is always easy. It is rewarding to make a community work, but you will also find that cooperation is an effort. True collaboration between everybody has to include the outsider. Sometimes that is you. Sometimes that is other people who have the same ideas as the community but have been set apart. Bringing everybody back together again can make everybody stronger in the end.

WHO SHARES YOUR BIRTHDAY?

Prince Philip, Duke of Edinburgh, born June 10, 1921
Judy Garland, born June 10, 1922
Elizabeth Hurley, born June 10, 1965

JUNE 11

WHO ARE YOU?

You have that double 1 in your birth date, which suggests you are best suited to equal partnership: you are both number one and come first. This also reflects your solar chart. Libra, the sign of the balanced scales, rules all the most important relationships in your life. The very first lesson about this for you may have been growing up with a sibling or cousin. Gemini rules these relationships. Later on in life, it is sexual unions, marriage, and professional double acts which dominate.

YOUR DESTINY

You are the Gemini who is always on the move and true to your sign, which rules short journeys. The best place is usually the next place. Your life may be dotted with relocation and even emigration as a result. Some of this comes from the need to leave close relationships behind—or, more specifically, what remains of close relationships which have fallen over. Communication is everything to you: the even debate, the settled understanding, that crucial process of not only speaking but listening. Your greatest achievements come when you manage to rescue and repair those relationships and reestablish communication to move forward.

GEMINI THE TWINS

Understanding the myth of Castor and Pollux, the heavenly twins who rule Gemini, can help you come to terms with those recurring situations where you are twinned with people who challenge your ideas about what is fair or just. One brother gave half his immortality to the other. All your life, measuring and weighing what is fair between you and the other person will describe your path, both professionally and personally. Gemini rules people who are poles apart but the same in the eyes of others. Twin figures follow you.

RECYCLING AND REPAIRING RELATIONSHIPS

When communication breaks down because of emotional relationships falling apart, it's the psychological equivalent of an internet failure for you. Yet, as a true Gemini, you were born to talk . . . and listen . . . and talk. One of the more interesting challenges in your life will be choosing which people are worth your time and energy if you want reconciliation and which should be left far behind. Your birth chart suggests that you usually reach this point when you are ready to travel or move again. Leo rules the heart in your chart.

WHO SHARES YOUR BIRTHDAY?

John Constable, born June 11, 1776

Jacques Cousteau, born June 11, 1910

Hugh Laurie, born June 11, 1959

JUNE 12

WHO ARE YOU?

You are the escape artist who wriggles out of the real world as often as you can to inhabit your own intriguing universe. Pisces, the sign of the two fish out of water, rules your role and your goals. Pisces is in turn governed by Neptune, a symbol of alternatives and escapism. Not fitting into the same film as everybody else is a common feeling for you. You prefer to write, shoot, and star in your own movie. Other people find you fascinating, but they may not always be able to locate any common ground with you, Gemini.

YOUR DESTINY

Your ruler Mercury actually has charge of your family tree on both sides, too. Mercury doubles up in your chart, as it is in charge of your origins and location, but also yourself. When you finally choose which direction to take—or even a combination of directions—you will know you have found out who you truly are and what matters most to you. Are you destined to follow your mother's side or father's side? East, west, north, or south on the map? This may be a literal shift or just a psychological and emotional move for you.

READERS AND WRITERS

Mercury is the planet traditionally associated with readers and writers. Once it ruled diaries and manuscripts. Today it still rules those, but it also has a connection to the worldwide web in all four corners of the planet. This is where you deal with all the tests and challenges in your life, even if it all takes place in the cloud. You are likely to face dramatic highs and lows in connection with this as the double appearance of Mercury in your chart shows him at odds with himself. Life never stops moving for you, and it takes you up and down.

CREATING UNITY TOGETHER

The group—or groups, plural—you are most emotionally involved with will teach you how to work for unity. Aquarius, which rules diversity in a community, makes an exact angle to your Gemini side. Finding a way to close the gap between yourself and others in order to achieve shared outcomes is not easy, but it is also your greatest reward. When you can play your part in helping to unite everybody, you are on your way to even more impressive results collectively, as getting there will have been a test of your tolerance and strategy.

WHO SHARES YOUR BIRTHDAY?

George H. W. Bush, born June 12, 1924
Anne Frank, born June 12, 1929
Gary Farmer, born June 12, 1953
Kendra Wilkinson, born June 12, 1985
Awkwafina, born June 12, 1988

JUNE 13

WHO ARE YOU?

You are a lifelong freedom-seeker whose independent spirit will be tested repeatedly. Dealing with this increases your intuition and self-knowledge, Gemini. Uranus rules over your journeys in life on all levels. The sign it rules, Aquarius, makes an exact pattern with your Gemini side, and so it tells a story of triumph through liberty. Liberating yourself from who or what seems to confine you is a lifelong theme, and when you achieve it, you will move yourself and your vision of yourself into a different place every time.

YOUR DESTINY

You are not really resident in the real world, thanks to Neptune and Pisces at the top of your chart. Neptune describes your tendency to float in a separate reality. Pisces's two fish swim everywhere, all over the place, all the time. Only rarely are you tempted to leave this fascinating and solitary life and join a group. When you do, this experience of pooling resources completely transports you. It's all too tempting to remain apart from the ordinary world, though. It is your destiny to drift far away from what most people would call regular life.

MOTHERS AND CHILDREN

When astrologers look for who and what you value most—what is so precious it is priceless—they go to the Second House of your chart. This is where we find Cancer, the sign of mother and child. You may or may not end up becoming a parent, but your own ideas about maternal instinct and the family are embedded in your soul and spirit. Dreams of what might be or memories of what once was are not real, but to you they represent a great truth that either takes you back to the past or gives you faith in a better future.

THE NEXT GENERATION

The theme of mothers and children has a large part to play in your private inner world, even though others may never see nor understand the process. It is also true that the next generation as a whole—from infants to teenagers—is your greatest reward. You can experience this through the family or via your professional life. Just as you know what it is like to live in a bubble, so do toddlers or school friends. Your understanding of this, sympathy for the young, and respect for childhood as a time of innocence never stop bringing you joy.

WHO SHARES YOUR BIRTHDAY?

William Butler Yeats, born June 13, 1865

Ashley Olsen, born June 13, 1986

Mary-Kate Olsen, born June 13, 1986

JUNE 14

WHO ARE YOU?

You are ruled by Mercury, the messenger of the gods and the great traveler of astrology. He had wings on his helmet and sandals; you literally fly or use the web to cross vast distances. You have the solar chart of an explorer, adventurer, tourist, and migrant. You may speak two languages or just work with two accents. It's also true that achievement for you is a holiday, business trip, or vacation. The sign which rules great escapes is Pisces, and this also rules your sector of ambition. You are frequently on a mission, Gemini.

YOUR DESTINY

You are a true Gemini and have twin sides, twin priorities, twin instincts. Gemini is named for the heavenly twins Castor and Pollux, who bargained with each other. You often bargain with yourself, because your solar chart suggests life will put you at a number of crossroads. This ability to sense both sides in a situation is quite instinctive. It may come from your childhood relationship with a sibling or cousin or perhaps with someone who was like a twin version of yourself. Right or left, East or West? You see all sides.

GROUPS, COMMUNITIES, AND PEOPLE POWER

Your life is about group chemistry and the strength of people brought together in all their diversity. In astrology this is the Aquarian vision, and this zodiac sign rules your sector of travel, migration, multiculturalism, and foreign faces and places. You have a great need to be on the move, which you know, but it cannot be separated from the temptation to lose yourself in the wider club, team, band, society, and so on. This can be quite informal, like social media or just a web of allies and friends who are separate, but connected.

THE MAP OF YOUR EMOTIONS

Sagittarius rules your zone of partnerships. Your closest one-on-one relationships are tied to other points on the map all your life. The long-distance lover is typical. Sagittarius the Archer is the centaur who gallops far and wide, and this sign is in charge of love and commitment in your horoscope. You are also a true air sign in that you go where the wind in your sails takes you, when your heart leads you. You are not the stuck, settling type and are the very last person to stay in a rut. Even if you do put down roots, you travel.

WHO SHARES YOUR BIRTHDAY?

Harriet Beecher Stowe, born June 14, 1811

Boy George, born June 14, 1961

Steffi Graf, born June 14, 1969

JUNE 15

WHO ARE YOU?

You are a natural hermit who is still capable of the most passionate and complicated relationships. The top of your horoscope shows your highest goals, and although you are a Gemini, you also have Neptune, the planet of spirituality and the soul, at the peak of your chart. You regularly escape from the real world to look for your answers as they have to come from within. This may lead you to a religious life in some cases, but perhaps you are simply looking for a light to steer by—a philosophy or deep conviction which sustains you.

YOUR DESTINY

You are a true Gemini ruled by Mercury, the planet of communication and information. You always have a special project or plan to plant. The issue for you is the timing and the conviction. You need to believe in yourself and those around you—as well as the time and place—before you can make your move. You can overthink what you have, which can mean some concepts with great potential never come to pass. Time and experience will teach you to make things happen so that you end up securing the right home for potentially great ideas.

SEXUAL POLITICS

Libra, the sign of sexual politics, equality, and the male-female balance in life, rules your relationships. This is not only about your heart; it is also about the world of babies and children, no matter if you become a parent or not. Your greatest challenge will be to face the differences between women and men and find a way through. That way lies freedom, and it is only when you understand that both of you have to be liberated at the same time that you can break free from situations which trap you. This may be personal or professional.

GREENER PASTURES

As you know, Mercury the Traveler is your ruling planet. He is usually shown with wings on his helmet and sandals, and you will find that certain journeys are your reward for everything else. These carry you to new destinations which have no guarantees but a promise of sanctuary and hope. You are a natural migrant, for example, or have a history of moving on in your own region or country. This transports you and potentially redeems your faith. You are sympathetic toward others like you, who are also born to be on the move.

WHO SHARES YOUR BIRTHDAY?

Harry Nilsson, born June 15, 1941
Xi Jinping, born June 15, 1953
Jim Belushi, born June 15, 1954

JUNE 16

WHO ARE YOU?

You are the communicator of the zodiac, Gemini, so it is your task in life to find the words to break through the gaps with others in partnerships with you. These duets and occasional duels reflect Libra in charge of the most personal zone of your chart. Libra is the sign of the scales of balance. Life is a repeated series of negotiations for you. Sometimes the issue is the difference between women and men. Closing the gap comes down to an exchange of minds as well as hearts and souls. It takes time, but it also makes you who you are.

YOUR DESTINY

You have the emotional water sign Cancer in charge of your money, so saving and making your fortune for you are not about numbers, but about pure feelings. You are fortunate in also having the practical earth sign Capricorn overseeing your joint finances and property. You may have a gift for rolling up your sleeves and making sure that your goals are achieved, no matter if you want to save all that you have or just increase it. These two signs—caring Cancer and steady Capricorn—show up in your destiny from young adulthood into old age.

MAKING IDEAS HAPPEN

You were born with the Sun in Gemini, ruled by Mercury, the planet of the mind. Ideas come and go, and they have tremendous potential. Your lifelong task is making sure that these brain waves and concepts do not vanish into thin air. As an air sign you do need to work harder on grounding your plans and projects, as bringing everything down to manageable basics is a challenge. The notions and solutions themselves are not the issue. You have the typical Gemini brilliance to thank for that. Over time, you will learn how to succeed.

THE GROUP AND THE ADVENTURE

Turning to your sector of journeys and adventures, exploration and relocation, we find Aquarius, the sign of the group. These very special circles of people are the foundation of everything you need to pack your bags and make a start. Even if you never go anywhere—which would be a wasted opportunity—the pooled resources and shared spirit of your allies and friends are very special. Aquarius the Water Bearer is about everything that gives a community what it needs. You need it, too, and from there, your adventures take off.

WHO SHARES YOUR BIRTHDAY?

Geronimo, born June 16, 1829

Stan Laurel, born June 16, 1890

Jenny Shimizu, born June 16, 1967

JUNE 17

WHO ARE YOU?

You are the Gemini who spends their lifetime looking for the words to negotiate with the opposite sex. The sector of your horoscope which rules your personal life is dominated by Libra, the scales of balance between men and women. Figuring out compromises and sometimes closure when you are aware of the differences is a puzzle that takes a lifetime to solve, but it does become easier as you grow older. Dealmaking with, for example, partners has to go beyond feelings into the right kind of language that translates across the divide.

YOUR DESTINY

You are among the most money-minded Geminis, as the solid, grounded, reliable Capricorn rules joint finance, business, charity, and property. This is where you have authority. Capricorn in turn is ruled by Saturn, a symbol of the slow passage of time. You do not like to rush your economic decisions, no matter if it's spending on your garden or considering the bigger property picture. Your values, principles, and ethics are central to your destiny—what you will or won't sell your soul for, what or who is so precious it's priceless.

DISTANT SHORES AND BUDDING SUCCESS

Your ruler is Mercury, the explorer and wanderer, and although you probably sail or fly rather than transport yourself with your helmet and sandals, you are drawn to other faces in other places all your life. You are no mere tourist, though. Being a Gemini, you always have a plan—well, two, maybe three. You are a multitasker with budding projects that are always in hand. The fact that you are an air sign helps you fly to other regions or countries in your mind, but your greatest challenge is actually taking off yourself and making it happen.

SECURITY AND STABILITY

As you know, the ambitious and solid Capricorn rules your sector of finance, business, charity, and property. You know you've made it when you have the level of wealth, comfort, and security that has you feeling you're on top. Capricorn is ruled by Saturn, which is extremely cautious over the long term. This can make you very hard to change, and you may find your lack of flexibility keeps you stuck sometimes when you most need to make your move. Outside financial advice which does not rock your comfort zone is useful.

WHO SHARES YOUR BIRTHDAY?

Newt Gingrich, born June 17, 1943

Jello Biafra, born June 17, 1958

Venus Williams, born June 17, 1980

JUNE 18

WHO ARE YOU?

You are one of life's leaders, with Leo, the royal sign, ruling your ideas, projects, and plans. In fact, the contents of your computer or notebook are never just concepts; they are tools for victory. You also have the success sign, Capricorn, ruling all your joint financial, business, charity, and property interests, so you are an impressive authority here. The competitive Aries governs the groups in your life, and you tend to gather like-minded friends and acquaintances around you for the really important missions.

YOUR DESTINY

Cancer, which describes your town, country, land, and family tree, suggests money goes into security. Cancer rules your sector of income and savings, so you tend to see money as a gateway to belonging. It is very important to you to use these fated cycles in your horoscope to make more of where you come from and where you feel you should put down roots. You are by nature a grower, builder, and farmer who understands that a little can go a long way. The family tree is always in the picture for you.

CIRCLES AND COMMUNITIES

The competitive side of your nature can't resist a challenge, and victory is always very sweet, no matter what is at stake in a contest or battle. The hard part is managing people within a group or network. You can never do anything alone, but the challenge with your birthday horoscope is understanding that people in a team, club, or other circle can be very hard to control. The number 1 is hidden in the numerology of your birthday. Coming first is normal for you, but dealing with self-interest—both yours and others'—is a lifetime lesson.

MOTHERS AND CHILDREN

You know that your family tree, roots, heritage, and ancestors are always in the picture. This is because Cancer, which rules the clan—and mothers, grandmothers, and great-grandmothers—also oversees everything you value. Your reward in life comes from the rich, spiritual, sacred side of the mother-child bond, which you may understand in terms of your own maternal line, but also any children who are born within your extended circle of family and friends. Anybody who knows you knows this feeds your soul.

WHO SHARES YOUR BIRTHDAY?

Sir Paul McCartney, born June 18, 1942
Isabella Rossellini, born June 18, 1952
Alison Moyet, born June 18, 1961

JUNE 19

WHO ARE YOU?

Some people are more concerned with money than others. The planet Mercury influences your sign, and its name is hidden in the word *merchandise*. Your financial cares and concerns go deeper than that, though. You were born with the emotional water sign Cancer affecting everything you own, earn, or need. It's never about accounting for you; it's always about feelings. Your own experiences will teach you to be compassionate for others who are looking for hope as much as help. For personal or professional lessons, you learn to give it.

YOUR DESTINY

In your birth chart, Gemini affects the Third House of knowledge. In your solar chart, the Third House is affected by Leo. This sign is about leading the next generation, and you are fated to do this, even if you have no children. One particular child may be part of your destiny, too. This may be a student you teach, as much as, for example, a nephew. You shine brightest when you accept younger people as the future, not only for all of us, but also for yourself. Understanding the part you have to play is crucial.

FINDING THE COMPASS POINTS

Discovering your direction west, east, north, or south on the map is really about knowing yourself. You can't do this until you have taken the time to find enlightenment. This is a huge test for you, and there will be times when those around you wish you would stop dangling between the present and the future. This process repeats throughout your life and is shown by Mercury's double presence in your chart. This planet influences you, too, but it also affects your family tree and your sense of place. Locating a compass point can take time.

COMFORT AND ABUNDANCE

As you know, you are one of the financially minded people who has a personal investment in money. This is always about so much more than numbers on a spreadsheet, though. For you, it is about feelings, not figures. You will be rewarded for saving or earning, investing or believing, by comfort and abundance over the course of your life. With slow-moving Saturn in charge of your bank account, life moves at a snail's pace, but even his cycle can only add to your feeling of certainty and security. You are prepared to wait, and wait, for life to deliver.

WHO SHARES YOUR BIRTHDAY?

Wallis Simpson, born June 19, 1896

Nick Drake, born June 19, 1948

Boris Johnson, born June 19, 1964

JUNE 20

WHO ARE YOU?

Your experiences make you. You are an escape artist and freedom-seeker who will repeatedly encounter quite revolutionary changes in your life if you are prepared to do the work and find liberation. The planet Uranus is associated with radical moves in the face of confinement, and it rules Aquarius, making a perfect angle to your horoscope. You are ingenious like all seekers and use your brilliant mind to get yourself out of stuck situations and into exhilarating new adventures on a regular basis. You are the original free spirit.

YOUR DESTINY

The planet Neptune and its zodiac sign Pisces affect the midheaven of your solar chart. This is where you reach furthest in your life and go highest. For you, it's all about escaping from the real world. This goes beyond wriggling out of situations or places which confine you, too. It's actually about full-blown substitute reality, and others find it fascinating, if hard to understand. Neptune and Pisces are associated with tremendous imagination and creative self-expression, and you may live that life, personally, or have that job.

TRANSPORTING YOUR IDEAS

Mercurial by nature—not given to standing still for long or being stuck—you are always intrigued by travel, export, relocation, and emigration, even when you have done this more than once. The cycles of time in your horoscope suggest that your plans are unlikely to thrive unless you take them somewhere else. You can do this at a digital distance on the worldwide web or actually join others in seeking the end of a promised rainbow. The challenge for you is managing your many ideas, grounding them, and making plans happen.

THE REWARD OF A YOUNGER GENERATION

You may or may not have children, but the next generation—and the one after that and the one after that—is your reward in life. This may be the teenagers of the future, for example, or the life of just one child you nurture from infancy, who goes on to become the person you are so proud of. The Sun affects your sector of ideas, influence, teaching, and tutoring. The Sun is associated with the sunflower whose seeds can help to grow the next garden. What you seed in your life and who will be a dazzling reward, renewed every time.

WHO SHARES YOUR BIRTHDAY?

Errol Flynn, born June 20, 1909
Brian Wilson, born June 20, 1942
Nicole Kidman, born June 20, 1967

JUNE 21

WHO ARE YOU?

The numerology of your birthday shows both 1 and 2, and you are always split between self-interest and the interests of your partnership or duet. This may be you and your brother, for example. It is commonly about you and your marriage partner. Together or alone? You can be a creative thinker when it comes to double acts. It becomes easier the more times you reach your fork in the road, either with the same person or a number of different opposite numbers. You don't always have to choose together or apart. Figuring this out defines you.

YOUR DESTINY

Born with the Sun right at the end of the sign of Gemini and the start of the sign Cancer, you are destined to always find the new beginning in the ending. You will find that life is oddly circular, so that even as one chapter closes and the book on that story is slammed shut, another brand-new book is being written. It has been like this since you were a child, and it will be like this in old age, too. For example, a period of ill-health for you or somebody important will end to be replaced by a new life in its place. The finish and restart can happen simultaneously.

THE FAMILY TREE

You were born on a day when the Sun prepares to enter Cancer, the sign which rules the family tree, your roots, heritage, culture, ancestors, and sense of place. The Sun leaves Gemini before it does this. Gemini rules the journey; Cancer rules the belonging. This unusual cusp birthday of yours means that nothing and nobody is settled, no matter if the issue is a point on the map (your family origins) or parents, siblings, aunts, uncles, cousins, and so on. You are caught between leaving and returning all your life, psychologically and often literally.

THE YOUNGER GENERATION

Your own or other people's children—infants to young adults—show wonderful results when you figure out the duality of one/two in your birth date. When two parents can agree on the journey no matter how this is mapped out, the end result can be the reward of a younger generation showing you a fascinating new world. So your children, stepchildren, godchildren, nieces, or nephews are the gift that goes on giving. You know that maintaining the family tree means organizing its branches. New growth with new generations is the outcome.

WHO SHARES YOUR BIRTHDAY?

Jean-Paul Sartre, born June 21, 1905

Ray Davies, born June 21, 1944

Prince William, born June 21, 1982

JUNE 22

WHO ARE YOU?

You are the person most comfortable in your home surroundings, no matter if this is life on the sofa, in the bedroom, or in the local park. This is where you rule. You are a commanding figure. You are respected, usually from a distance, by those who admire you, are intrigued by you, or are just intimidated by you. Respect must be paid, because you arrive at a point in your life where you have not only earned the rewards of being at home in your position, you also become who you were always meant to be—secure and solid.

YOUR DESTINY

Your life begins to offer you the emotional fulfillment you need when you remember where you come from and go back to your roots. This may be either side of your family tree. Owning your spiritual inheritance and claiming your right to feel a deeper sense of belonging sustain you. Until you do this—and you usually learn how when young—nothing really adds up. Your ancestors, heritage, culture, and history are unseen by most, but when you dig down deeply to explore the connection, it changes everything.

THE BOSS

You are the boss; an ambitious person who takes years, if necessary, to get to the top of your chosen field. This may be high society, if you are interested in status, or just the peak of your professional life. Perhaps it is your academic career. You are a towering presence in the lives of those who are still on the bottom floor and represent a kind of earned wisdom and solid achievement that reminds everybody there are no fast and easy elevators to the top. You fit the role of senior role model very easily and show this in youth, too.

THE JOURNEY BACK TO YOURSELF

You are one of those people who needs to regularly take a journey back to yourself in order to feel satisfied. Over time you learn to either go back to your family tree roots or travel alone—even if that's just hiking on the weekend—in order to rediscover your connection to friends, family, partners, and other close ties. One of your earliest lessons in life is that it's not necessarily the people concerned; it might just be you and your state of mind or understanding of yourself. Letting distance lend enchantment to the view is your solution.

WHO SHARES YOUR BIRTHDAY?

Meryl Streep, born June 22, 1949
Elizabeth Warren, born June 22, 1949
Dan Brown, born June 22, 1964
Wangechi Mutu, born June 22, 1972

JUNE 23

WHO ARE YOU?

You are the person of action who is always on the move, thanks to a constantly shifting family tree and sense of place. The branches on your family tree are always switching direction, and you spend your life choosing between acting or not. Your town, region, or country is another example of this lack of stability and permanence. You can only settle for so long before, once again, you have to change yourself and your life in order to find a sense of belonging. These repeated experiences make you energetic—and restless.

YOUR DESTINY

You will find that the cycles of time in your horoscope encourage you to take sabbaticals or solo safaris when you need to feel fulfilled. This may be as simple as cycling by yourself when you sense an urge for distance or as dramatic as leaving everything and everybody behind in a lasting way. You know yourself better when you switch location, and when you return (or not), you tend to find the issues you have with people around you disappear. Things look very different when you have taken a time-out—or just departed!

THE CHALLENGE OF WEALTH

It may sound unusual to say that the promise of a large amount of wealth—heavenly pennies from a tempting heaven—is a challenge. Yet part of the journey for you is trusting in the promise and believing that it can become real. This may involve questions about how much you deserve to be rich. It's not as simple as it looks from the outside. Reaching for wealth also involves wider questions about things like: At what price? What comes next? How does this change everything? Over time, your experience and wisdom help you answer.

THE REWARDS OF WISDOM AND KNOWLEDGE

You move in a world of wisdom and knowledge, books and the media, the world-wide web and self-education. There is always something to read or somebody to question. That makes life intriguing and you will never be bored, as there is a wealth of opinion and insight to discover from childhood into old age. Your own experiences with the highs and lows of your unpredictable, dramatic life can be better understood by filtering your own feelings through the eyes of writers. That helps you gain objective views.

WHO SHARES YOUR BIRTHDAY?

King Edward VIII, born June 23, 1894

Alan Turing, born June 23, 1912

Selma Blair, born June 23, 1972

JUNE 24

WHO ARE YOU?

You are a sensitive water sign, Cancer, and in your horoscope, another water sign—Pisces—rules your sector of travel and relocation. Your life is full of these journeys and shifts around the map. You turn to your intuition to follow the right path every time, no matter if it is for personal or professional reasons. Pisces is coupled with Neptune, describing your need to escape. Rather like Harry Houdini, you can be a well-known escapologist—but without the padlocks. Any situation where you feel tied down, though, is your catalyst.

YOUR DESTINY

You were born under the element of water, as you know. There is a perfect angle from Pisces the Fish and your own Cancer the Crab Sun sign. If this reminds you of the beach, you are correct. There is something of the permanent vacationer about you. Thanks to the cycles of time in your horoscope, you are a regular explorer of other realities—not just the great ocean, far from the city, but almost any space which appeals to your imagination and your need for other worlds. Few people really understand this part of your personality.

FINDING YOUR FAMILY PAST

You were born under the sign of the crab, which carries its home on its back; crabs also burrow deep into the sand to feel at home. When you remember your Sun sign and its gifts, you are much better off emotionally, as there is a deep need to ground yourself in your family's past. This may be any collection of branches on the tree, but there you will find shelter and a firm sense of place. You will know yourself better as a result and the relationships around you will look and feel quite different—deeper and more fulfilling.

REBUILDING AND RESTARTING

You are one of those people who can either go back and rebuild your life or roll up your sleeves and start again. The choice is always there for you in your life, and it always sets you free. You were born with your sectors of career and home in opposing signs at opposite angles. As these are periodically triggered in your life, you may take the opposite direction every time, if you wish. If you were to go back and recycle and restructure the last deep change, this time you might walk away and build from the ground up.

WHO SHARES YOUR BIRTHDAY?

St. Francis of Assisi, born June 24, 1182

Jeff Beck, born June 24, 1944

Mick Fleetwood, born June 24, 1947

Lionel Messi, born June 24, 1987

JUNE 25

WHO ARE YOU?

You were born with the Sun in Cancer in your birth chart sector of family, the local area, your country, and sense of home. There is a natural link in your natal horoscope from Cancer to Taurus, the sign of money, and Scorpio, which rules complex finance and property. You see money as a gateway to what you want in terms of the family tree as well as the place you call your own. You are a natural builder and gardener who invests not only your bank account but also your emotions in plans which build on everything you have.

YOUR DESTINY

Pluto, the symbol of powerful transformation, rules your sector of relationships. Another heavyweight planet, Saturn, rules the chemistry you have with the opposite sex. These fated connections in your life between yourself and another change you and the other person forever. Pluto is the planet which asks us to find out how much control we have or lack. Self-control and willpower are always the key to finding the balance you need so much with these people.

THE WHEEL OF FORTUNE

The Wheel of Fortune, rather like the quiz show, sends you up and down, high and low in your life. It's enough to make a philosopher or comedian out of you. These dramatic and quite random rises and falls in your status and success show you that nothing is permanent, as the Buddhists say. You also move in a world of books and websites, media or scripts. Mercury the Messenger rules your sector of communication, information, and knowledge. You are profoundly influenced by particular authors and commentators.

MANAGING THE FAMILY

As you know, you were born with the Sun in Cancer in the Fourth House of your birth chart, which describes the family tree. This applies to your mother's side as well as your father's side. This requires care and maintenance all your life. Sometimes you invest your time and energy; sometimes you live with your relatives and their ancestors in the background. The children you have, or never have, are at the very foundations of who you are and what you're all about. Life lessons make you stronger. You are a true leader.

WHO SHARES YOUR BIRTHDAY?

George Orwell, born June 25, 1903

Carly Simon, born June 25, 1945

Ricky Gervais, born June 25, 1961

JUNE 26

WHO ARE YOU?

You are ruled by the Moon, as your Sun sign is Cancer. You are sensitive, intuitive, and rely on your sixth sense when making the big decisions that govern your life. Libra rules your sense of belonging. The scales of balance pull you in two directions repeatedly about which way you should take to find security. West, east, north, or south? Your horoscope is aligned in such a way that you hit these kinds of crossroads starting when you are quite young. Your extra sense helps you decide how to take those steps.

YOUR DESTINY

You live in your head for a lot of the time with Gemini and Mercury, the planet of the mind, ruling your dreams, imagination, and unconscious. Experience teaches you to discover methods which will help you think straight and banish who or what does not deliver peace of mind. As a typical Cancerian, your home is your castle, and you decorated it and furnish it to suit yourself. Your own style, taste, and comfort are extremely important to you. Furnishing the contents of your mind with peaceful attitudes is also crucial.

THE FAMILY

You know that Cancer describes the family in astrology. You have a leading position there, as not only do you have strong foundations based on the children in your world, you also have the power to chop and change particular family tree branches. You may or may not have children, but over time, your role with a junior generation establishes you. This—together with a necessarily strong and fearless approach to boundaries—makes you quite a formidable person who is uniquely qualified to maintain that family tree.

THE PRICELESS GROUP

The groups, teams, clubs, associations, and other networks in your life are ruled by Taurus. This sign describes everything so precious to you it is priceless. People power can't be bought and sold, and you will discover just how much weight it carries throughout your life. Sometimes you will be one of the many. At other times you will be very much the outsider to discover for themself what the hive mind can accomplish. Unity and solidarity are your rewards with others. Together you can do incredible things.

WHO SHARES YOUR BIRTHDAY?

Pearl S. Buck, born June 26, 1892

Violette Szabo, born June 26, 1921

Mick Jones, born June 26, 1955

JUNE 27

WHO ARE YOU?

You are the person who tries to stay close to the top when there's a change in power. You are also a good candidate for taking the top role or position by replacing others. You are a Cancerian whose reward in life is the next generation—and the one after that. Everything you have read about passing the baton to children and teenagers is true. Yet you are also dynamic, ambitious, extremely aware of people politics, and a mover and shaker. This comes from Mars and Aries ruling your success in life.

YOUR DESTINY

The highly sensitive, emotional water sign Pisces rules your journeys. When you are not fulfilled by who or what is on offer, you leave. This could make you a lifelong traveler or even just a committed hiker. When the going gets tough emotionally, you tend to get going. This happens periodically when you find yourself at a crossroads. When you return to your people, everything looks different. Of course, sometimes you quit for good. Your spirit needs time out and time away, though—always.

YOUR PEOPLE AND PLACE

Your great challenge in life is your people and your place—or their place. You were born with the Sun in Cancer in the Fourth House of extended family and home. You may find that particular relatives—or friends who are virtually family—are your test. The house, apartment, or other residence matters quite as much as the people in that regard; you associate them with each other. Thus, bricks and mortar can have emotional connotations for you, too. Time and experience help you deal with these challenges.

INFLUENCING THE NEXT GENERATION

You were born under a sign ruled by the Moon, and throughout history, the Moon has represented parenthood, and particularly mothers. You have what it takes to pass on your knowledge to generations of children. These may be your own, a class you teach, an audience you reach. Everything that you value so much it is precious to the point of being priceless involves leading and guiding these younger faces. You are an authority here, thanks to Leo's rulership of this area of your chart.

WHO SHARES YOUR BIRTHDAY?

Helen Keller, born June 27, 1880
Isabelle Adjani, born June 27, 1955
Meera Syal, born June 27, 1961

JUNE 28

WHO ARE YOU?

You are born under the emotional Cancer, which shows up in your intimate relationships. However, groups also matter to you. Your circles define your character, because with stubborn Taurus ruling your friends and acquaintances you are hard to budge. There is an angle between Aquarius with all its diversity in the community and this sector of your chart, which makes things challenging. Together with the group, you can all build something incredible all your life, however.

YOUR DESTINY

You were born with Mercury the Messenger ruling your sector of books, ideas, the internet, the pulpit, and the microphone. You are both the person who absorbs the message and also the speaker or writer, the broadcaster or author. Neptune is opposite Mercury in the rulership of your chart. Neptune describes religions of all kinds as well as particular faiths and philosophies. This is what you take on board or not, and this is what you preach—usually to the converted but sometimes to skeptical types.

GENDER POLITICS

With Pluto and all his questions about power ruling the relationship zone of your chart, figuring out gender politics is a lifetime challenge. This applies no matter if you are a man or woman and whatever your sexual preferences are. Once you realize the real power is within you, then life becomes easier. Self-control gives you the upper hand in such situations, and you can challenge who or what dominates you so that you take command of yourself and your life. It's a lifelong mission, but you succeed with it.

FINDING A DIRECTION

When you find a direction in life, it is usually between one side or the other of your family tree. This may literally take you in different directions on the map, or sometimes the choice is philosophical or psychological. You are a Cancer Sun person born with this star in the Fourth House of your natal chart, where your relatives and ancestors hold sway. Your reward for all this deep thought is enlightenment. Your spiritual awakenings in life—and there are several—are tied to this long search.

WHO SHARES YOUR BIRTHDAY?

Henry VIII, born June 28, 1491
Elon Musk, born June 28, 1971

JUNE 29

WHO ARE YOU?

You were born with the Sun in Cancer in the Fourth House of your birth chart and take a parental role with others, acting as the authority or head. This applies to work or education as much as your personal life. You are also strongly influenced by groups all your life. With stubborn, fixed Taurus ruling your circles, you are often involved in standoffs, either as part of your circle against outsiders or actually the outsider who must deal with the tribe and the hive mind. It shapes you.

YOUR DESTINY

You were born with Pisces, the sign of religion, ruling your sector of knowledge exchange. Pisces in turn is governed by Neptune, which describes beliefs and philosophies of all kinds, and not just faith. You can be converted as much as you convert. In fact, you will take turns at this process during your life, thanks to the cycles of time in your horoscope. You probably know that the fish is a Christian symbol. You may or may not believe in God—or plural gods—but your destiny is affected by various sacred texts.

BEING ON TOP

As you know, your Cancer Sun gives you a parental role with others, assuming the authority of being the head. This strongly applies to your career, where you end up on top and have to accept the challenges that come with being at the peak of your profession or chosen field. Tough, strong Aries rules your ambition as it holds sway over the highest point of your solar chart. Mars is the planet governing Aries, and it is associated with dynamic people who succeed. With this come major tests.

THE RENAISSANCE PERSON

You are a Renaissance person with multiple assets and a direct line to something greater than yourself. This is your reward. You are a special person who stands out from the crowd. You know that Neptune rules your knowledge zone. You are inspired by what is in the ether that others cannot hear or see. Those born on June 29 can be intuitive to the point of becoming channels for something bigger than themselves. You can command an audience and hold attention with your many abilities.

WHO SHARES YOUR BIRTHDAY?

Eddie Mabo, born June 29, 1936

Gary Busey, born June 29, 1944

Bret McKenzie, born June 29, 1976

JUNE 30

WHO ARE YOU?

You are an emotional water sign, as you may know—and relationships have a tremendous impact on your feelings and mood. You were also born with Mars, the planet associated with dynamic, energetic people, at the success point of your chart. Mercury the Messenger with all his brilliance rules your sector of knowledge and ideas. All this makes you a born teacher, tutor, lecturer, broadcaster, or performer. You know how to command an audience or readership and hold it. You're a transmitter.

YOUR DESTINY

You are drawn toward the big, wide world from childhood and a natural traveler or migrant. Sagittarius rules foreign places and people and is in charge of your daily life, routine, and work. You are repeatedly tempted by different accents and languages as a result. You could easily have a long-distance relationship or leave your country to explore the map. It's possible that you will find as much success in another nation, or with a different nationality, as you do in your hometown and homeland.

PERSONAL RELATIONSHIPS

We all have to deal with relationships that do not work out. As an emotional water sign with great sensitivity, you are affected more than other people, Cancer. The numeral 0 is hidden in your birth date, and you are used to starting from zero with nothing left emotionally, then slowly relaunching. If only it were as easy as taking one, two, three steps forward—but experience has taught you that you need to retreat when things go wrong. The crab withdraws into its shell. After that, though, you always restart.

THE VIRGO INFLUENCE IN YOUR CHART

You were born with health-conscious Virgo ruling your sector of ideas, plans, knowledge, and projects. This is also where you educate yourself and others. You are drawn to precise and measured ways of being healthier, no matter if this is purely personal for you or something professional. Virgo is the sign associated with all that is pure and natural in life, no matter if it's water or a river to swim in. These principles of purity and well-being guide your thoughts, and excellent health is your reward.

WHO SHARES YOUR BIRTHDAY?

Allan Houser, born June 30, 1914

Lena Horne, born June 30, 1917

Rupert Graves, born June 30, 1963

Mike Tyson, born June 30, 1966

JULY 1

WHO ARE YOU?

You are the freedom-seeker who regularly goes through cycles which challenge you to liberate yourself. Saturn, with all his ties that bind, rules the zodiac sign opposite your own—Capricorn. Your solar horoscope is set up in a way which repeatedly restricts you and then offers you the way out. These recurring "Independence Days" (plural) make you stronger and also teach you to appreciate the exhilaration of being your own person. The numeral 1 is hidden in your birth date. When you come first, you win.

YOUR DESTINY

You are an energetic employee or self-employed worker who has incredible capacity. Mars rules your sector of success and achievement, and you are tireless. There has to be a point to all this sustained effort, though, and it is one special house, apartment, or property investment which is always in the background. As a true Cancer Sun, your home is your castle, and that is always at the back of your mind. The planet of abundance, Jupiter, rules your paid work and charity sector. Your earning potential is enormous.

FINANCIAL INVESTMENTS

Given that you have the capacity to earn a steady income stream but also fundraise, your challenge is deciding how best to spend it all. The astrological cycles you have already experienced in your lifetime, along with those to come, suggest money is more to you than just numbers. It has emotional or spiritual meaning for you, and you need to make its wise use your priority. Just as a specific house, apartment, or investment property is always in the background, so too is the family tree. Should the money you make always be spent on some branches of your family tree? It's a lifelong question.

HOME AND FAMILY

Your interpretation of home and family is personal to you. It may be your boyfriend, two cats, and a low-rent apartment; it may be a country pile in the English countryside with two sons to inherit your fortune. Cancer is the zodiac sign associated with a sense of belonging, comfort, security, and also sanctuary. At least once in your life—maybe more—you will be given the most wonderful opportunity to walk into the living dream. Finding a unique way to have a clan of some kind in your life is your great achievement.

WHO SHARES YOUR BIRTHDAY?

Estée Lauder, born July 1, 1906

Debbie Harry, born July 1, 1945

Princess Diana, born July 1, 1961

JULY 2

WHO ARE YOU?

With Mars the planet of attack and defense ruling your horoscope's midheaven, you are a tough person with excellent boundaries. You would make a good military commander even if you only use this strength of character to handle your own family. You were born with the Sun in Cancer in the sector of ancestors, roots, and relatives. This is not a fixed part of your existence, though, and this lack of permanence and stability is always in the background. So, too, are the babies you never had—or the offspring who were once infants.

YOUR DESTINY

The fixed sign Taurus rules all group situations in your life, no matter if you are the lone individual who is dealing with a circle of people around you or very much part of the community, adjusting to someone who is against you. Taurus the Bull can be a stubborn zodiac sign and will not be moved—rather like the creature the symbol represents. As it is also a fixed sign, you and others can become quite fixed in your views. Converting this standoff into unity is difficult but worthwhile, as ironically, you and the network are stronger together.

THE MULTITASKER

You are the multitasker who takes on too much and must learn to ditch or delegate if you are to enjoy life. The sector of your horoscope which rules your job, unpaid work, or academic career is governed by Jupiter, the astrological symbol of excess. Quite naturally you want all your plans and projects to grow—and they will always have that potential—but much depends on your capacity to manage your lifestyle and workload. This same zone of your chart rules your health and well-being: that must always come first, Cancer. It's crucial.

FINANCIAL SECURITY

The reward for learning how to work efficiently and productively is financial security, and just as Jupiter with all his excess is the ruling planet in charge of your roles and goals, he can also bless you with a never-ending income stream once you settle into a way of life which guarantees results and allows you to work smarter, not harder. Cancer is the zodiac sign most concerned with houses, apartments, holiday homes, and property investment, and a special place is always your incentive, even though it may be in the background.

WHO SHARES YOUR BIRTHDAY?

Larry David, born July 2, 1947

Jerry Hall, born July 2, 1956

Lindsay Lohan, born July 2, 1986

JULY 3

WHO ARE YOU?

You were born with Virgo, the sign which rules preplanning, perfected projects, and budding success, in your sector of work, unpaid work, and academia. You are the idea person who needs to ground the concept in the real world to find true rewards. The issue for you is when and how, which is usually a sign of overthinking. Procrastination can also point to a lack of proper research. As a Cancerian, you are always looking for a home for yourself and your brain waves so that you can secure a long-term situation.

YOUR DESTINY

Gemini rules your unconscious mind and you may be quite unaware of your twin selves. You are pulled in two directions at the same time, even if you don't know it—and only a psychologist could show you. This may explain why you can be equally drawn to opposite sides of the fence or polarized points of view. This duality makes it hard for you to act, as you intuitively find it very hard to differentiate between sides. Dreams can sometimes show you this as they help you get in touch with the truth.

WORK AND MONEY

The great challenge of your life is regular work for hard-earned money: routine and method, schedules and predictable output. As a true Cancerian, your need to cover costs with your house or apartment, property investment, or land is never far from your thoughts and feelings. Again, this challenge to live in the real world comes back to Virgo, the sign which has charge of your house of computers, telephones, microphones, and books. Virgo is associated with the steady crafting of reliable end results. Mastering this is worthwhile.

YOUR BRILLIANT BEST

Your brilliant best is impressive and may be characterized by qualifications, publications, or your name in print. You can grow to understand your dual nature, and instead of being pulled in opposite directions, you can find a way to appreciate extreme differences and live with them in a thoughtful and satisfying way. You may become an academic if you can satisfy your need for escapism by working hard to find the right ivory tower to climb. You are both a student of life and a guide to others, and destiny will prove it.

WHO SHARES YOUR BIRTHDAY?

Franz Kafka, born July 3, 1883

Tom Stoppard, born July 3, 1937

Tom Cruise, born July 3, 1962

JULY 4

WHO ARE YOU?

You have the instincts of a builder or farmer, renovator or gardener. You were born with the Sun in Cancer in the Fourth House of your birth chart, where plans are drawn up and visions entertained. You also have the two earth signs—Virgo and Taurus—in perfect angles to your Cancerian side. This helps you keep your feet on the ground. There is another sign in your birth chart which matters, and that's Scorpio, which trines your Cancer side. Scorpio is about an emotional attachment to money which inspires dreams.

YOUR DESTINY

In your Cancerian horoscope, Libra, the sign of the equal scales and justice, rules your foundations. In your birth chart, Libra governs two sides, two halves of the scales, duets, and sometimes duels of all kinds. This makes you acutely sensitive to the law but also the universal law that says two people can be different but equal.

Reaching that level of understanding between yourself and others is one of the great achievements of your life. Sometimes you will be called upon to arbitrate. At other times you will be bowing to laws.

POOLED RESOURCES

All that you value so much it is priceless is pooled with others. The sign of diversity within a community is Aquarius, and it rules who and what is most precious to you. This may be anything from a team or club when you are younger to more organized institutions when you are older. From this you draw what you need. The sign of two sides, two people, and two halves is Libra, as you know. This fits a perfect pattern with your Aquarian values so that you find yourself in partnerships with those who draw from a group, too.

THE MONEY-GO-ROUND

Your greatest achievement is to honor that duality in yourself with money. It teaches you a lot about balancing two sides. This may be debt and credit or your half of a bargain and somebody else's. The cycles of time in your horoscope put you in a world where your national economy, as well as the wider economy, is unstable. Nothing is ever predictable or certain for long, with Uranus, the planet of change, in charge of your banking. Yet, despite this, you can create systems which are fair to yourself and others—a huge win.

WHO SHARES YOUR BIRTHDAY?

Calvin Coolidge, born July 4, 1872
Neil Simon, born July 4, 1927
Laci Mosley, born July 4, 1991
Post Malone, born July 4, 1995

JULY 5

WHO ARE YOU?

You were born with the Sun in Cancer, the sign of the extended family and ancestors. You have a deep connection to your relatives in the spirit world as well as loved ones and friends you consider to be family. Your solar chart is similar to your birth chart, in that Pluto oversees your close relationships. Pluto shows transformation and rules the transition from this life to the next. So, as your people evolve in spirit, so do you. And when you evolve, you help them grow higher. The connection never stops, Cancer.

YOUR DESTINY

You are an authority and respected leader when it comes to finance, charity, business, or property. The noble Leo rules your values. Leo the sovereign of the jungle is quite naturally in charge of things, and the lion's place in your sector of principles and ethics gives you a certain sense of what is so precious it's priceless. This also includes *who* is so precious, too. You are destined to be comfortable, wealthy even. Part of this comes from your grounded, down-to-earth attitude toward all that you earn or own.

FINAL CHAPTERS AND FIRST CHAPTERS

As you've read, Pluto is in charge of your closest relationships. He governs the intense Scorpio, which also rules your children, any young relatives, and godchildren. This sector of your chart also has charge of your strongest emotional ties. Final chapters which become first chapters, even as you experience them, are part of this road. From youth into old age you become accustomed to tremendous transitions in your life, where simultaneous endings and beginnings challenge you to let go and release, even as you embrace the future.

THE ELEMENT OF WATER

You are a true water sign—sensitive and tuned in to the world of feelings and emotions. Another water sign, Pisces, and its ruler Neptune make an exact angle to your Cancerian side. In fact, Cancer the Crab feels at home in the sea, which Neptune rules, among the fish, which Pisces also rules. You float and drift through life, enjoying a vacation from reality, when you can. It is rare for you to break this holiday from the everyday unless you have to—you find your escapism rewarding. When you do, though, it changes your life.

WHO SHARES YOUR BIRTHDAY?

P. T. Barnum, born July 5, 1810

Georges Pompidou, born July 5, 1911

Huey Lewis, born July 5, 1950

JULY 6

WHO ARE YOU?

You are the idea person, scholar, or deep thinker whose greatest challenge is finding the right place to plant their plans. This makes you either a traveler, migrant, or ace procrastinator. Years of learning that life is not a dress rehearsal will teach you to move on your brain waves—and move with them sometimes. The planet of dreams and daydreams is Neptune, and he rules your sector of media, academia, publishing, education, journeys, and relocation. The most promising home for your ongoing self-education is always on the next part of the map.

YOUR DESTINY

Your finances and the economy of your own region or country rule your destiny. You have to learn to juggle because of the way the cycles of time have fallen—and will go on falling. Aquarius is the sign of teamwork, groups, and friendship, and it governs your bank account. What happens to your life budget is a result of those crews, and no matter how often you have to focus on your own incomings and outgoings, the group situations are always in the background. This can be a political party or a charity. Creating a system to absorb this is a lifetime pursuit.

YOUR VALUES AND FINANCES

The past, present, and future cycles of planets in Aquarius, which rules land, money, business, houses, and apartments, will always challenge you to update your values. This involves what you will and will not sell out for and who or what you consider to be so precious that it is priceless. There may be issues here about the environment for some. In other cases it is about the family tree: the ancestors or relatives. Cancer is the zodiac sign ruling the home, homeland, and clan. This is always in the background even when money matters are front and center.

A SENSE OF PLACE

In order for your family tree to keep growing and extending in a healthy, flourishing way, there is always work to be done. Your reward for being born on July 6 is the strength to manage your clan and the energy and willpower to do it. Your quest, if you choose to accept it, is to renew and improve the family, no matter if this is on one side or the other of your family tree or a new family you have created yourself. Going back to your roots is a lifelong mission. Ultimately you will discover that home is within. Lacking a firm sense of place, you find a sanctuary in your soul.

WHO SHARES YOUR BIRTHDAY?

Frida Kahlo, born July 6, 1907

The Dalai Lama, born July 6, 1935

George W. Bush, born July 6, 1946

JULY 7

WHO ARE YOU?

You are the escape artist who never settles in one place but finds two homes or workplaces keep you on the move, either on the worldwide web or by commuting and traveling. Born under Cancer, which is a water sign, you also have Pisces and Neptune in charge of your adventures across the map. This perfect trine to your own Cancerian side suggests that vacations from reality, which Neptune rules, are part of the trip—or trips, plural. Particular cities or countries, cultures, and nationalities transport you.

YOUR DESTINY

Neptune describes a particular state of mind with no interest in the everyday and ordinary. Its rulership of your sector of tourism, business travel, and migration suggests you regularly take both feet off the ground. On a less dramatic level you may be fond of the great outdoors, as it represents a giant leap away from the real world. Neptune and Pisces, the sign he rules, have a reputation for producing dreamers. You are at your most entranced when you have your bags packed. Coming down to earth is a useful asset.

MERCURY THE MESSENGER

You have Mercury the Messenger in charge of your sector of words, ideas, images, and communication. This is also where we find short journeys and commuting, and of course, Mercury is the god who had wings on his helmet and sandals. That's not how you travel these days, but your message certainly goes far and wide. You are a natural tutor, teacher, or leader by example. What you know resonates with people. What you have to transmit can sometimes seem bigger than you are. Yet you have a way of bringing it down to earth.

WOMEN AND MEN

Saturn is the planet of restriction and obstacles, and he rules the relationships you have with the opposite sex. You probably know Saturn is surrounded by rings in astronomy. Throughout your life, for personal or professional reasons, you will experiment with new ways to break free. In mythology, Saturn did just that. The boundaries and barriers you deal with in terms of men (if you are a woman) or women (if you are a man) are a great learning experience, and as you grow older, you will find it easier to liberate yourself.

WHO SHARES YOUR BIRTHDAY?

Gustav Mahler, born July 7, 1860

Ringo Starr, born July 7, 1940

Shelley Duvall, born July 7, 1949

JULY 8

WHO ARE YOU?

You are a sensitive and emotional water sign who learns a lot about yourself through your relationships. You were born with the Sun in Cancer in the extended family zone of your birth chart. In your solar chart, the powerful Pluto is in charge of your closest relationships. His sign Scorpio is associated with transformation, and your birthday horoscope gives you the ability to recycle relationships which others might consider over. This does not happen without tremendous shifts on the inside, but you can do this.

YOUR DESTINY

You are destined to be in several duets, partnerships, or two-way situations with the opposite sex, which teach you about equality and sharing. This is commonly marriage, but it can also manifest as a platonic friendship between two people who share a house or two work colleagues. Libra with its balanced scales is at the base of your horoscope, where your foundations in life are. You are extremely sensitive to the message that men and women are different but equal, and it shapes your personality.

FAITH AND BELIEF

Neptune and Pisces rule your sector of faith, beliefs, religion, and spirituality. This is different across cultures and countries, and yet you may end up exploring more than one god. Pisces the Fish are associated with the Christian church, but there are many sacred texts and also many authorities. You may find yourself preaching to the converted or the questioning at one point in your life. You are just as likely to be a follower of a particular philosophy or outlook. Pisces exactly trines your own Cancer Sun.

COMMUNITIES AND UNITY

What you value most highly is diversity in a community that also has unity. The space between people in a group, club, team, and so on also allows for breaks in the circle, however. From your adolescence into old age you will be dealing with these broken circles and discovering how much hard work is involved in bringing people back together. When you achieve this—no matter if you are in the group or outside it—you realize that what seemed impossible is, in fact, quite achievable. From this comes an even stronger set of people.

WHO SHARES YOUR BIRTHDAY?

John D. Rockefeller, born July 8, 1839

Anjelica Huston, born July 8, 1951

Kevin Bacon, born July 8, 1958

JULY 9

WHO ARE YOU?

Children are at the heart of any family, as you know—and you were born with the Sun in Cancer in the sector of parenthood and substitute parenthood in your birth chart. The Sun itself rules Leo, and this is where you seed the future. It's rather like growing sunflowers for generations. This applies no matter if you become a parent or not. There is a powerful angle in your chart, involving Pluto and Scorpio, which makes a perfect trine to your caring Cancerian side. The next generations are fated for you.

YOUR DESTINY

For all that you have an influential role to play with children and teenagers—and future waves of young people—you are also an escape artist. Pisces and Neptune describe holidays from the real world, and you are a lifelong traveler. Sometimes you will even relocate or emigrate. Even when you cannot get away for longer than a day or two, you will find a walking track or wave to take you away from everything. You are never more of a daydreamer than when you have your suitcase or backpack packed and are ready to leap.

DISTANCE RELATIONSHIPS

The emotional commitment you have to others is often tested by distance. You may fall in love with somebody who lives miles away, for example. It is also very common to find families separated by the borders in particular states or countries with your July 9 horoscope. You were born with Mercury the Messenger in charge of your sector of journeys, and although you probably use a plane and not a mysterious force that powers your winged helmet, you are one of life's explorers. It helps you investigate relationships.

GROUPS AND COMMUNITIES

All that you value most in your life is shown by Aquarius, which describes circles of people who move together toward common goals, but always with space and distance between themselves. Your lifelong mission is to make sure that the other individuals in your clubs, teams, networks, and so on remain connected. If not, experience will show you that such collective ventures can fall apart. When you succeed in pulling everybody together with the same map and compass, though, you win huge triumphs.

WHO SHARES YOUR BIRTHDAY?

Barbara Cartland, born July 9, 1901

Bon Scott, born July 9, 1946

Tom Hanks, born July 9, 1956

JULY 10

WHO ARE YOU?

You were born with Mercury the Messenger in charge of your sector of journeys and commuting. Mercury was not only the god who connected people, places, and ideas; he also flew from one location to another. You may live or work between two places for different reasons. You may seem Mercurial to others: never still, always quick to think your way through a situation, always restless. There are good reasons for this which rest with your family. You are a Cancerian, and Cancer the Crab is associated with the family tree.

YOUR DESTINY

Learning to understand the difference between your imagination and reality is a lifelong lesson. Mercury also rules another sector of your chart—where your daydreams and even your fears are constructed. Nothing is real; it is all a projection. This zone of your chart, the Twelfth House, is rather like a Hollywood studio, but where everything is scripted by you. That includes your fantasies about dream homes and money as well as your invented fear and loathing. Mercury's messages, then, are illusions. Knowing that helps.

FREEDOM COUNTS

To really understand all that you value most, you have to look at the sector of your horoscope which rules precious and priceless achievements. At the top of your list is freedom. From youth to old age, you will be shown this time and again. Liberating yourself from places and situations you find restrictive is not easy, but it also becomes your most rewarding challenge. Cancer rules the home, and you will never feel at home until you find the independence to go your own way, discover your own place in the world, and break chains.

THE FAMILY TREE

As you read at the beginning, the planet Mercury has a strong influence on your chart, and you are rather like him: always in motion, never settled, quick to come up with plans and ideas. You have also read that one good reason for this is your family tree. Cancer, because this is never as permanent and stable as you would like, you will repeatedly find yourself in maintenance mode with particular relatives. This means you can never really count on these branches on the tree to stay put; when they change, so do you. It's destiny.

WHO SHARES YOUR BIRTHDAY?

Nikola Tesla, born July 10, 1856

Marcel Proust, born July 10, 1871

Sofía Vergara, born July 10, 1972

JULY 11

WHO ARE YOU?

Libra, a symbol for duels and differences, but also duets—which can create opposition—is the key to your chart. This sign rules your home, family tree, household, security, and foundations. Your greatest achievement in life is to understand that there is no point in replaying history in your mind or imagining what might be ahead. Everybody has these kinds of battles in their background. The difference is, some people learn techniques to put them in perspective and lay them to rest—like you will.

YOUR DESTINY

You are the natural face of one or many groups, Cancer. Taurus, which shows priceless people and precious, valuable assets, also rules your sector of people power. You cannot put a price tag on a number of people who are united in supporting you. Their backing is fated in your life, and this may always be just one community or a range of different communities over the course of your lifetime. The same story about people who are worth their weight in gold shows in your birth chart, too.

THE MOON CYCLES IN YOUR LIFE

As a Cancerian, you are ruled by the Moon, and the lunar phases—particularly the New Moon cycles—bring you to regular crossroads. Are you aware of your duality? The twin sign Gemini governs your inner self. Dreams often reveal this. So might your intuition. You sense two opposite sides to your nature even when you can't see them. This private split between one side of you and another is unconscious for most of the time, but thanks to the New Moon, Full Moon, and eclipse cycles, you occasionally find it is triggered.

FINDING YOUR ROOTS

By now you should be aware of your complicated inner life. You are an extremely sensitive water sign, as you know, and your dreams, inner self, and unconscious steer you. What grounds you? Who brings you down to earth and allows you to appreciate your relationships fully? The answer lies with your roots, culture, heritage, history, and ancestry. Perhaps this is the immediate family or just where you come from geographically. This will be the great reward of your life, Cancer. Your efforts result in brand-new perspectives.

WHO SHARES YOUR BIRTHDAY?

E. B. White, born July 11, 1899

Gough Whitlam, born July 11, 1916

Giorgio Armani, born July 11, 1934

JULY 12

WHO ARE YOU?

There is a natural connection in your life between the healer and the healed. Sometimes you are the former; sometimes, the latter. You are a caring Cancerian—the word *care* is hidden in the anagram for Cancer. You also have Virgo, the sign of therapy and remedies, in a powerful angle to your own Sun sign. The transformation may be physical, spiritual, mental, or emotional. It's more than just repair work, though. When others help, your soul responds as well as the rest of you. When you help, you can achieve miracles.

YOUR DESTINY

The numerals 1 and 2 feature in the numerology for your birthday. The powerful assistance you have just read about comes from one-on-one changes. The person healing is often as affected as the person who is healed. This idea extends to other pairs, duets, and couples in your life. In times of need, it is important to remember that sometimes a two-way street or divided highway is not the best road to take. The 1-2 combination in your birth date shows you will learn about codependency and also independence.

JUSTICE AND EQUALITY

There are two sides to every story and two even weights in every set of scales. Libra, the zodiac sign associated with balance and justice, is at the base of your horoscope, which is where your foundations in life are laid. You will both accept the law and perhaps lay down the law in your lifetime. Not every legal process takes place in a courtroom, of course. There are fundamental rules about what is fair—or unfair—when two people are coming from opposite directions but must receive the same equal treatment in life.

FINANCE AND BALANCE

The 1-2 combination in your birth date is supported by Libra at the base of your chart, as you've seen. This idea of symmetry and harmony extends to money. Throughout your life you will find yourself trying to make debt and credit even to satisfy both sides of a business, banking, or property relationship. If you have ever tried to make the scales balance, you will know it takes energy, time, and effort. One of your greatest achievements will be adapting and adjusting to financial conditions needing balance.

WHO SHARES YOUR BIRTHDAY?

Henry David Thoreau, born July 12, 1817
Christine McVie, born July 12, 1943
Malala Yousafzai, born July 12, 1997

JULY 13

WHO ARE YOU?

You are the natural leader and authority figure who commands respect because of your understanding of children and teenagers—your own or other people's offspring. You are also one of life's winners. The numeral 1 is hidden in your birth date, and you will often come first in any contest, competition, or battle. The dynamic Aries and its planet of great energy and drive, Mars, both rule the top of your chart. This is where you set your ambitions, and with these factors crowning your horoscope, triumphs arrive.

YOUR DESTINY

You know that the numeral 1 is in the numerology of your birthday. You not only come first in life; you also know enough about success to support others who come first, too. Winners stick with winners. The cycles of time in your horoscope are set up to deliver drama in your career, academic career, or sometimes personal life. This is rather like a coronation or a promotion: a victory where the old is ushered out in favor of the new. Being number one changes everything for you. So does backing a number one person.

CONFLICT AND HARMONY

Mars with all his heat and Aries with all its interest in winning conflict have a strong hold at the top of your astrological chart, called the midheaven. For you, this tends to show itself in group situations where you are one against the many or actually in a circle of people pitted against somebody else. The rather stubborn, fixed Taurus the Bull governs these groups in your life. Flexibility and tolerance have to be worked for, but the reward, if you can all achieve it, is compromise, reconciliation, and powerful unity.

FUTURE GENERATIONS

You were born under the sign of Cancer the Crab, chiefly concerned with the extended family. Crabs on the beach can be like this; they move together. You may or may not have children, but you lead them and all future young generations who come after them. You achieve this by planting seeds which grow into bigger and better things. Mercury, the planet of ideas, projects, plans, and communication, rules your sector of writing, the internet, broadcasting, teaching, and public speaking. Your messages go on.

WHO SHARES YOUR BIRTHDAY?

Patrick Stewart, born July 13, 1940
Harrison Ford, born July 13, 1942
Erno Rubik, born July 13, 1944
Ken Jeong, born July 13, 1969

JULY 14

WHO ARE YOU?

You are a true Cancerian who does not actually carry your home on your back—like Cancer the Crab—but your house, apartment, or dream château is never far from your mind. A true sense of home, worth working for and saving for, is always in the background. You have strong angles to the money signs Taurus and Scorpio in your chart and, crucially, to Virgo, the sign of methodical work for steady reward. You are a craftsperson, no matter what your profession is. You know how to deliver, and financial security follows.

YOUR DESTINY

As you know, the two money signs of Taurus and Scorpio align perfectly with your Cancer side. This combination makes you a born builder, gardener, developer, or environmentalist, depending on your choices. You believe in having both feet on the ground and using the money you make to create what calls you—both in terms of the area you call home and your extended family tree. This down-to-earth, centered, productive side of your character is immediately obvious to anyone who works or does business with you.

WATER SIGN FEELINGS

You are still a water sign despite this practical earth sign focus in your chart. Water is associated with deep emotion and powerful feelings in astrology. Relationships which do not work out as you had hoped are just part of life. However, they affect you more powerfully than those born on other days. Saturn rules your partnerships but also any partnerships which do not last. Saturn also governs the slow passage of time, and you will always need to give yourself enough space to either recycle those relationships or walk away.

ANCESTORS AND THE AFTERLIFE

Scorpio is the sign which oversees finance, as you know. It does so through its ruler Pluto, associated with inheritance, wills, and legacies. The afterlife and your extended family of souls there have a powerful impact on you that goes beyond money or property, though. When your ancestors in spirit progress, so do you, if you are sensitive enough to tune in to what is taking place. Equally, when your soul also evolves, there is a deep connection between yourself and your people on the other side. Through you they move on.

WHO SHARES YOUR BIRTHDAY?

Woody Guthrie, born July 14, 1912

Ingmar Bergman, born July 14, 1918

Jane Lynch, born July 14, 1960

JULY 15

WHO ARE YOU?

Cancer is ruled by the Moon, which in turn rules mothers. Children—your own or those belonging to other people—define you. Libra rules family in your chart, and it is associated with equality. You learn about and teach fair play between male and female energies through the world of children or teenagers. Cancer governs the Fourth House of home, hometown, and homeland in astrology. It matters a lot.

YOUR DESTINY

The planet Uranus rules your property zone in turn, and as this is a symbol of independence, you will always find your freedom through the right house, apartment, and area. Many times in your life you will liberate yourself by moving or just traveling and relocating. Aquarius oversees your Eighth House of shared finances, and in turn, Uranus rules Aquarius, too. He's behind these regular revolutions.

WATCHING THE MONEY GROW

Your great challenge in life is being hardworking enough to cultivate savings or investments, then being patient enough to have them grow. Again, this comes down to Uranus, the planet of freedom, which rules your bank account. Standing still long enough to put in the effort and counting the calendar months to see interest go into your account—or debts be paid off—are something that you have to use your willpower to do.

RECYCLING RELATIONSHIPS

You are an emotional, sensitive water sign, and although you are deeply affected by the relationships which do not last as they began, you also have the ability to recycle everything, too. The solid, grounded, earthy Capricorn rules the partnerships in your life, and you can structure these, rather as a builder achieves renovations. All is never lost with you. The feelings may be intense, but every severed bond can be restored.

WHO SHARES YOUR BIRTHDAY?

Rembrandt, born July 15, 1606

Emmeline Pankhurst, born July 15, 1858

Arianna Huffington, born July 15, 1950

JULY 16

WHO ARE YOU?

You are ruled by the Moon and may have noticed that Full Moons, New Moons, and eclipses have a greater effect on you than on other people. The Moon in all her phases and moods governs Cancer, your Sun sign, and the lunar pull on ocean tides is reflected in the element of water, which also rules you. Partnerships and duets of all kinds, from professional double acts to personal bonds, affect your life path and change your personality over time. One shared journey or two separate journeys? These are emotional questions.

YOUR DESTINY

As you know, the Moon rules your feelings. She is associated with sleep, dreams, and the moods we cycle through, over the twenty-eight or twenty-nine days of a typical cycle. As you are so strongly affected by this, you learn to control your mind so that you can control your emotions. The Moon also rules memory and the past. This is where you do most of your work, no matter if it is meditation or cognitive behavioral therapy, self-hypnosis or just self-help. Mercury, the planet of the mind, governs your leading ideas. Over time, you craft these to help.

FINANCIAL REWARDS

Your Cancer Sun makes strong angles to Scorpio, which rules banking, and Taurus, which rules earning and saving. In addition, Cancer is associated with real estate. The last key sign in this sequence in your horoscope is Virgo, which governs steady work for steady results. This powerful pattern dominates your horoscope if you were born on July 16, and once you find a lifestyle and way of working which is rewarding in every way, you can master your particular career. Your house or apartment is the motivator.

THE PROMISE OF WEALTH

The cycles of time in your horoscope suggest large lump sums of money are on offer on a regular basis. This may be an inheritance, for example, or a big business success. When you realize that this level of wealth is something you deserve, it becomes an achievable goal rather than a theoretical reward. You gain when you trust what is on offer and feel that it is rightfully yours. You see the promise of wealth as a gateway to home or garden improvements or even moving somewhere bigger and better. It's your fate.

WHO SHARES YOUR BIRTHDAY?

Ida B. Wells, born July 16, 1862

Roald Amundsen, born July 16, 1872

Barbara Stanwyck, born July 16, 1907

Will Ferrell, born July 16, 1967

JULY 17

WHO ARE YOU?

You are typical of your Cancer Sun and influenced by the Moon. The lunar phases strongly affect you: New Moon, Full Moon, and eclipses. Some of the most dramatic turning points in your life will occur when the Moon is also turning. To understand yourself, you need to know that Libra, the sign of duality, left and right, West and

East, rules the foundation of your chart. You will regularly find yourself weighing up the Libra scales to figure out where to go, who to be with, what to do, who you are. Every time it occurs, it changes you.

YOUR DESTINY

You could be wealthy on a recurring basis if you use your birth chart. You were born with the Sun in Cancer making a perfect trine to factors in Scorpio (joint finances) and a sextile to factors in Taurus (your own income). Every time you see the cycles of time pick up everything you own and earn—or could have—your own Cancerian traits are triggered. Like the crab that is your sign, you like to move quickly toward what you want, grab it firmly, and take it away. It's the same with money, once you realize just how big particular lump sums may be.

MERCURY AND KNOWLEDGE

Your sector of knowledge, ideas, the media, and the worldwide web is ruled by Mercury. This messenger of the gods was often seen carrying a parchment scroll. You yourself may or may not have a scroll, but you do have a wealth of education or self-education to share throughout your life. You eventually become an expert in your chosen field and a source for others. You are a natural academic, Cancer, but even if you leave school when young, you will teach yourself and then show others. Your pearls of wisdom are precious commodities.

THE TRIUMPH OF GROUPS

Groups can be difficult things to pull together and keep together. Yet, even though you are drawn toward diverse circles of people, you have what it takes to help unite everybody. The triumph of a club, team, society, and so on, which was once in disarray and disagreement, is one of the lasting miracles of your life. Your birth date numerology gives a clue: The numeral 7—equal to the colors of a rainbow—is there. So is 1. When every different stripe of person is allowed to combine, the self-interest of one can be put aside. It's colorful.

WHO SHARES YOUR BIRTHDAY?

James Cagney, born July 17, 1899

Donald Sutherland, born July 17, 1935

Angela Merkel, born July 17, 1954

JULY 18

WHO ARE YOU?

Along with your Cancer Sun, you were born with the Sun in the Fourth House of extended families in your birth chart. All that is most valuable to you belongs to Leo, the sign of heirs, spares, and pretenders to your throne. So your personality leans toward the world of children and teenagers. This may be for personal or professional reasons. It is true even if you never have children yourself. You have a respect for their world but also a great need to protect their innocence and sense of wonder. It affects who you are and what you do.

YOUR DESTINY

You are a water sign, ruled by the element associated with deep feelings and strong emotion. Your heart and soul, not your head, rules what you do and who you become involved with. The planet Pluto, a symbol of the willpower that empowers you, governs your relationship with the opposite sex. As a woman, for example, you will find out what self-control is thanks to the control you need where men are concerned. As a man, it is women who will show you that nothing is so dominating that you cannot be the boss of yourself and push back.

THE MOON AND YOU

As a Cancerian, you are ruled by the Moon. Lunar phases from New Moon to Full Moon and eclipses have a strong effect on your chart and also on your moods and feelings. It is amazing how often you will reach a crossroads emotionally when the Moon also reaches her crossroads through the signs. You will know yourself well enough by the age of thirty to understand that you need to be alone sometimes and that you need to escape situations where you are unfulfilled. You usually return rejuvenated. Sometimes, though, you just depart.

MERCURY AND THE MESSAGE

The planet Mercury rules your theories, ideas, and knowledge as he is in charge of the chart sector where you must get your message across. He was, of course, the messenger of the gods. Mercury also rules your unconscious mind—your spirit and your soul. Perhaps others think you sometimes channel what you are telling or showing them. Even if you disagree, you have an intuition or strong sixth sense helping you convey concepts which are greater than yourself. You bring them down to earth so others can use them.

WHO SHARES YOUR BIRTHDAY?

Nelson Mandela, born July 18, 1918

James Brolin, born July 18, 1940

Richard Branson, born July 18, 1950

JULY 19

WHO ARE YOU?

The things that money cannot buy in your life are friendship, people power in a circle, and a starring role with groups. Aquarius, which rules people who pool resources, also rules your zone of priceless and precious assets. The special sense of mutual appreciation that exists in particular clubs, teams, and other networks in your life is not on sale in any catalog. Nor can you leave it behind in your will. You can, however, pass on the legacy of your shared brilliance. You all take turns at shining. However, you truly dazzle.

YOUR DESTINY

Mercury, the messenger of the gods, rules your ideas, knowledge, and life on the worldwide web. You also have messages to send, although this tends to be done across a desk, behind a podium, or on Zoom. All your life you will find that you are able to use your strong sixth sense to pass on what matters to people. What might just be in the air for others is good material for you. You are a transmitter who converts what you feel—or just know—into useful information that has practical application. You are unusual and extremely gifted, Cancer.

THE FAMILY TREE

The cycles of time in your horoscope suggest you will regularly be put in a position where you must ultimately choose to follow one side or the other of your family tree. Cancer rules the extended clan. Sometimes the choice is within your own family, created by you. Enlightenment is your reward along the way. Libra governs these choices at the bottom of your horoscope. Libra shows the scales of balance, but choosing which side to value more takes time. So do you: You are a procrastinator. Yet you always know.

THE WORLDWIDE WEB

You are an escape artist who seeks another world overseas throughout your life. Neptune rules your sector of foreign people and places. You do this online, but may also find success in planting your concepts, plans, or projects in other countries. You may learn a second language later in life in order to do this. You are a natural explorer and perhaps a migrant. If any part of your own country is foreign to you in terms of its culture or accents, that is also where you might seek a home for your budding future success. The key? Practical action.

WHO SHARES YOUR BIRTHDAY?

Edgar Degas, born July 19, 1834

Brian May, born July 19, 1947

Benedict Cumberbatch, born July 19, 1976

JULY 20

WHO ARE YOU?

Finding a place to call your own, for work or personal reasons, is a lifelong quest, Cancer. You were born with the Sun in the sign of Cancer the Crab, who carries a home around like a portable roof. This is not just about a roof over your head, though; it is about freedom. From youth into old age you will always find that the right place equates with the right independence, space, and autonomy. These revolutionary changes in your life shape you. You become a stronger person because of these crossroads but also committed to liberty, too.

YOUR DESTINY

You are an emotional water sign, ruled by your feelings and strong emotions. This makes sense when we look at your birth chart, as you have the Sun in the Fourth House of extended family relationships and these can be complicated. Blood is thicker than water, for example, but as a water sign you may find that some people in your life are all about blood, sweat, and tears. Deciding to recycle broken ties in your life or turn your back and start again makes you confident and resilient—happier, too. These crossroads reshape you.

CROSSING THE BARRIERS

You are sincere, straight, and true when it comes to all you have to offer from the heart. This is the case with lovers or family, friends or other close ties. One of the tests for you is distance. The cycles of time in your horoscope suggest that the other person—or people—will be separated from you across the map. This means you must meet each other halfway, but it is you who has to trust the journey and the destination. These regular periods in your life might see a long-distance relationship, for example, or seasonal reunions of love.

FINANCIAL PLANNING

You are a natural planner, investor, or developer who can do a great deal with even a modest amount of money. Throughout your life you will always have enough to save (perhaps) or put into your visions (more likely). The more expertise you seek, the better, as you can be emotional about everything you own or earn. An objective opinion from a financial professional can be very useful. That way you will know if there is a reality to back up your dreams, no matter if you have goals relating to property, the environment, business, or family.

WHO SHARES YOUR BIRTHDAY?

Edmund Hillary, born July 20, 1919
Cormac McCarthy, born July 20, 1933
Carlos Santana, born July 20, 1947

JULY 21

WHO ARE YOU?

Even people who know you well never *really* know you, because you spend a great deal of time in your own little world. This is where you depart from ordinary reality and take a vacation from what most people would call normal life. This is the imaginative, self-expressive side of you, which finds it hard to put on a school uniform, say, or wear regulation office attire. You are mysterious from a distance. Nobody can really fathom why you do what you do. Sometimes you don't even know yourself. You fascinate many people all your life.

YOUR DESTINY

Relationships of all kinds rule your life. You do leave room for success, as you will see in a moment, but you are strongly influenced by partnerships, family tics, and friendships. The more emotionally invested you are, the more you need to take stock when they end. You have a numerology chart which features 1 and 2. Being left alone means you have to look after number one, no matter if you chose that path or it was chosen for you. That is when you realize that the really promising one-on-one duets are always waiting.

FEMALE AND MALE DIFFERENCES

Thanks to the cycles of time in your horoscope, you will come to regular, major crossroads where you must confront the differences between men and women. You may do this in a marriage, for example, or in a platonic work relationship. It can happen with two friends sharing an apartment. Understanding the similarities as well as the gaps helps you communicate and connect every time you hit this crossroads. In fact, these cycles begin when you are a teenager. Learning lessons then (right or wrong) comes back to you later, and you learn again.

NUMBER ONE

With the numerology profile that shows the numerals 1 and 2 in your birth date, you prefer to come first and be number one, as there is no second place in a two-way contest or even a battle. If the field is more crowded in your profession, for example, you still push hard to be the leader in your career. Your weekends can be packed with entertainment or sport where there is a prize for first place or a place on the winner's podium. It fulfills a strong drive in you. This balances your more escapist, unconventional side, too.

WHO SHARES YOUR BIRTHDAY?

Ernest Hemingway, born July 21, 1899
Yusuf Islam (aka Cat Stevens), born July 21, 1948
Robin Williams, born July 21, 1951
Josh Hartnett, born July 21, 1978

JULY 22

WHO ARE YOU?

You are one of those people whose address changes for work or personal reasons more often than most. You have a free spirit and can only take being restricted for so long. This may be because of relationships which you find unfulfilling emotionally or just because you end up feeling unable to move. Your instincts always tell you to roam or even completely remove yourself. The idea of a better life in a better place is very close to your heart. Most of all, though, you are fiercely independent, and nothing and nobody can get in the way.

YOUR DESTINY

The cycles of the Full Moon, New Moon, and eclipses affect you more than other people. You respond strongly to the lunar phases, and that is when you find you reach the big crossroads in your life and have to make the decision to leave situations and people that do not make you feel fulfilled. The Moon changes phase every month, of course. So on a smaller scale you may be the kind of person who needs to remove yourself and go it alone on the weekends. Doing this puts you back in harmony with others again.

REALITY AND PROJECTION

There is a curious part of your birth chart in the Twelfth House, ruled by the two fish of Pisces and also by Neptune, the planet we associate with sea mist and fog. This is the sector of your birth chart where you project everything, as if your mind were actually an old-fashioned screen projector with slides beaming up images in front of you. When you know yourself properly, these daydreams, fantasies, distractions, and diversions—wonderful or even confronting—vanish. Understanding how you manufacture reality is useful.

TREASURE HUNTS

You have one of those horoscopes where the cycles of time will always offer you a treasure hunt. This may be an inheritance, a tax return, a business reward, valuable goods. The issue for you, from youth into old age, is finding the right professionals who can help you find what is or is not there. This does lead back to that tendency you have to imagine, daydream, and project. Finding experts who are experienced, tried, tested, and trusted can make a difference all your life. This applies no matter if it's back pay or even serious legal issues.

WHO SHARES YOUR BIRTHDAY?

Oscar de la Renta, born July 22, 1932

Albert Brooks, born July 22, 1947

Don Henley, born July 22, 1947

JULY 23

WHO ARE YOU?

You are the sincere, affectionate, straight, and true person who is treasured by those who are close to you. You are not afraid to wear your heart on your sleeve. Being open and forthright about your feelings makes others more prepared to meet you halfway. The numeral 2 is hidden in the numerology of your birthday. You commonly cover two cities, regions, or countries in your partnerships or close ties to relatives or friends. You are a born traveler and even a migrant. These journeys prove to yourself and others all that you feel.

YOUR DESTINY

Understanding the true value of money is your life path. It's really just paper and metal—unless it's cryptocurrency, then it's something else again. Challenges for yourself and other people prove to you that there is nothing as precious as good health, for example. You and the people who matter might also put a priceless price tag on charity and compassion. This can apply in a personal way: for example, in your family circle. It can also be a professional concern or perhaps a philanthropic one. What's priceless? It counts.

CHILDREN, TEENAGERS, AND FUTURE GENERATIONS

You may or may not become a parent, but you enjoy a fantastic connection to the world of the next generation. Sometimes you have to let children or teenagers take center stage in your life. For you, this happens on a recurring basis, either because of your family, your career, or your unpaid work. You may teach drama, for example, or be the proud mother of a star pupil. However, there is more to this aspect of your life than just being a successful aunt, uncle, or godparent. Future generations also inherit your influence.

EVERGREEN RELATIONSHIPS

By now, you should understand that you are about feelings, strong emotions, instincts, and above all, relationships that run deep and true. People born on other days of the year may be more consumed by success or money, but you have a different take on life. From your adolescence into old age, you will always find evergreen relationships. This may be the one that got away when you were dating. It may be a marriage that approaches its silver anniversary but still renews. Your ever-beating heart is always at the heart of you.

WHO SHARES YOUR BIRTHDAY?

Haile Selassie, born July 23, 1892

David Essex, born July 23, 1947

Woody Harrelson, born July 23, 1961

JULY 24

WHO ARE YOU?

You have an emotional investment in money, business rewards, or other kinds of treasure. Other people gather their calculators and spreadsheets, but for you, what might be owned or earned—or discovered—is really about your heart and soul. Money translates into great happiness for you all your life, but it is also a guessing game that keeps you occupied, the way board games or puzzles keep others absorbed. One of your great lessons in life, from young adulthood into old age, is to find the right experts to help you succeed.

YOUR DESTINY

You are an exceptional player in any team or group situation. You know how to let others shine, but you also know when to take center stage yourself. Together you all realize you have quite a lot of influence. You are also committed to pooling resources. Sharing what is there and joining forces to deliver results are the key to your personality and destiny. Over the course of your life you will have some brilliant, unforgettable episodes involving your friends and allies, which show you just what a tribe can do for you and also for itself.

THE COMFORT OF MONEY

You will always know what it feels like to be abundant. This may be because you become genuinely wealthy. However, your astrology chart does not show amounts; it shows feelings. The sensation of being secure, but also blessed, is something that reminds you why life is worth living. It can come from dropping out and becoming self-sufficient in your own garden. It can come from running a successful business that impresses Wall Street. Your full personal chart will reveal how you use the core elements of your horoscope. Enjoy it.

WORKING ON RELATIONSHIPS

You are always prepared to work on the relationships that you think are worth it. This is an unusual feature of your personality. When what were formerly solid gold bonds with people are broken, you will always judge who and what is worth it and change both them and yourself. It is also true that you have what it takes to walk away from those you find it better to leave behind. Your personal life is full of these kinds of dramatic transformations when you can recycle anything of real value to you—but abandon what's truly over.

WHO SHARES YOUR BIRTHDAY?

Alexandre Dumas, born July 24, 1802

Amelia Earhart, born July 24, 1897

Jennifer Lopez, born July 24, 1969

JULY 25

WHO ARE YOU?

You rule. Leo is the lion and, so, ruler of the jungle. Leadership comes naturally to you. Unlike those born on other days, you don't have to try hard to look like an authority. As the monarch of all you survey, you can also be a remote figure to others. People have to try hard to access you. You have confidence and self-assurance within your own space and on your own terms, Leo. Dealing with the real world—other people's world—may be a different matter. The dignity that is associated with your zodiac sign is there for all to see.

YOUR DESTINY

Leo is the sign associated with courtship and the bedroom. Leo the Lion is a symbol of royalty and governs heirs, spares, and pretenders to the throne—usually your children but sometimes young relatives or godchildren. The decisions you take about pregnancy for yourself or your partners dominate your life, no matter if you become a parent or not. The numeral 2 is hidden in your birthday, so marriage or partnership is also at the heart of your identity. You attract admirers, but will they ever be allowed into your world?

THE LION SYMBOL

The lion has always been a symbol of strength and nobility as monarch of the beasts. As a Leo Sun, you can also sometimes be the Cowardly Lion from *The Wizard of Oz*, keeping away from the complications of close relationships with your fellow human beings in all their complexity. It takes courage to be who you are, though. Like Richard the Lionheart, you present yourself without any disguise or apology.

You have star quality, like the Metro-Goldwyn-Mayer lion. You may remind some people of Elsa, the lioness in *Born Free*.

THE SPOTLIGHT

It's part of your journey in life to be in the spotlight—to be the observed, not the observer. It's been like this since childhood. Yet it is those times in your life when you join a group or take your place in a crew of some kind that you find out who you are. The 7 in your birth date shows the rainbow of seven colors—every one dazzling, but nothing without the others. You will know the truth of this often in your life, because circles of people seek you out and persuade you to get on board. Everyone shines together.

WHO SHARES YOUR BIRTHDAY?

Estelle Getty, born July 25, 1923

Thurston Moore, born July 25, 1958

Matt LeBlanc, born July 25, 1967

JULY 26

WHO ARE YOU?

You were born into a family that is always changing, as particular branches of your family tree can be pulled in quite extreme directions. Leo, your foundations in life, from ancestors to relatives, are ruled by Pluto, a symbol of the power to transform. You have it and will always have the choice to use it, as the controls are within reach if you want to organize your clan. This same symbol of regular change, Pluto, rules your town, local area, and/or country. You stand on shifting soil here and that can also make you a born wanderer.

YOUR DESTINY

The sign of the balanced scales is Libra, and it rules your way with words and ideas. Seeing two sides of a situation is very important to you. You are a student of life, all your life, and will always be drawn to subjects which involve questions about, for example, race, religion, or sex, because they sum up the polarity in the world and you want to invest your time and energy in knowledge that will help you find equilibrium. Taking a reasonable, balanced view of polar opposites makes you a source of wisdom for others, Leo.

THE WORLDWIDE WEB CITIZEN

The zodiac sign which rules your journeys online and offline is Aries, which is dynamic, energetic, and up-front. Mars governs Aries and is associated with the temptation of relationships, too—he was the lover of Venus. There is a great deal on offer to lure you into learning a second language, for example, or regularly packing your bags to see the world. You are a natural migrant. You can also fall in love with a culture or accent, as much as you fall in love with a place on the map. You happily take your online life offline.

FRIENDS AND CONNECTIONS

Social and lively Gemini governs your circles and your allies. There may even be a Gemini-style pair of heavenly twin types in your address book—two people who are siblings, perhaps, or who might as well be twins. You need those connections in your life in order to remind you who and what matters. This is especially true if you are dealing with the family tree blowing west and east. Gemini is an air sign, and you are a fire sign. The element of air ruling your social circle makes life feel easy, breezy, and, yes, like a breath of fresh air.

WHO SHARES YOUR BIRTHDAY?

George Bernard Shaw, born July 26, 1856

Mick Jagger, born July 26, 1943

Helen Mirren, born July 26, 1945

JULY 27

WHO ARE YOU?

Leo rules the heart. Your Sun sign also rules complex relationships. These can be between lovers, partners, or within a family. A love triangle is not unusual. In your birth chart, Leo is in charge of the Fifth House of courtship, heirs, spares, and pretenders to the throne. This is only to be expected as Leo the Lion is a royal symbol in many countries. Navigating romance is one of your challenges. Your children, stepchildren, and so on can also test your strategies later in life. You become an expert emotional tactician.

YOUR DESTINY

You are a winner by nature, and some of your biggest highlights will come from victories. These may be professional, so you come first in a highly competitive situation.

They can also be recreational, so it may be your team which wins the cup. Once is not enough for you, and success when you are younger spurs you on to seek out any enterprise or entertainment where you can be crowned in triumph. This is part of your Leo nature as your sign has long been associated with monarchs who gallop onto the field to defeat the rest.

STEADY WORK AND INCOME

The methodical, dedicated Virgo governs everything that you value most. This goes beyond the steady income stream that shows in your destiny. It's just as much about quiet pride in a job well done, as you are a craftsperson or artisan at heart, no matter if you are delivering products or end products from people who expect reliable quality. Those who only know you at certain points in your career might even mistake you for a Virgo as you are so wedded to routine and service. Then they realize: you are a Leo—and you like to win.

THE HEALING PROCESS

Virgo is not only associated with a strong work ethic; it also rules healing on all levels. This may be obvious (dentists and doctors) or it can be therapeutic, like counseling or even just strong spiritual support. One of your blessings in life is that you will never have to look very far for people to help you. In fact, it makes you stronger on all levels, because as a Leo Sun it is important that you know when to show you are vulnerable. You are justifiably proud of coming first so often, but real strength comes when you ask for assistance.

WHO SHARES YOUR BIRTHDAY?

Christopher Dean, born July 27, 1958

Alex Rodriguez, born July 27, 1975

Jonathan Rhys Meyers, born July 27, 1977

JULY 28

WHO ARE YOU?

You are the traveler or migrant who regularly finds their way out by moving on. It may be from London to the Lake District or, more ambitiously, from the United States to France. The pioneering Aries rules your sector of long-distance travel and relocation. You are a great believer in relaunches, and rather than stay with situations you have outgrown, you will always pack your bags and leave. Friends and groups support you. Gemini, which oversees your allies in your solar chart, also governs journeys in your natal chart.

YOUR DESTINY

You are a great dreamer when it comes to money, and your astrological chart shows Pisces, the sign of imagination and visualization, ruling your finances. The family tree is always a factor when you must decide how to invest or spend. So is your ambition, as the bull, which rules bull markets and gold bullion, also looks after your sector of success. Your ability to see, in your mind's eye, what could be done to increase your wealth and maximize your returns is special. It will help you achieve a great deal.

LEADERS AND FOLLOWERS

You were born with the Sun in Leo, the sign of great leadership and authority. Opposite this sign in your solar chart is Aquarius, which rules the group. The challenge for you is making the system work. At various points in your life you will be drawn into organizations and situations where the chief is nothing without their followers, yet the followers have to be in complete agreement with the chief. Understanding group psychology but also the nature of hierarchies will help you on this path whenever it opens up.

LOVE AND PARTNERSHIP

At least once in your life, perhaps more, you will be brought together with a soulmate at the right time in the right place. This is a recurring reward for you, no matter if this is a marriage which results in a chain of second honeymoons or a passionate pathway always delivering the right lover, no matter what has gone before. Your sexual relationships are ruled by Aquarius, an air sign describing independence and individuality. The space between you increases the desire as does the distance.

WHO SHARES YOUR BIRTHDAY?

Beatrix Potter, born July 28, 1866

Marcel Duchamp, born July 28, 1887

Jacqueline Kennedy Onassis, born July 28, 1929

King Maja Vajiralongkorn, born July 28, 1952

JULY 29

WHO ARE YOU?

Leo is the sign of the sovereign who inherits the crown. Sometimes the crown is also seized on the battlefield. This idea of conquering or inheriting is at the heart of your life and times. Aquarius, which rules the group, is opposite your Sun in Leo in your chart. You will often find yourself pitted against a club, team, society, association, and so on. Just as often, you will be one of the many to confront the opposition. In this way you learn all about how the community mind works.

YOUR DESTINY

You are a born teacher, tutor, guide, mentor, or influence. Leo leads a younger generation in particular. You are ruled by the Sun and so have the confidence to shine brightly and put on a brilliant display. All that you value most highly in life is intuitive, inspired, and sometimes psychic. Neptune rules this zone of your chart, and this is the planet to associate with extrasensory perception but also "just knowing" without labeling it. This helps you show the way to others and give them a practical means of using what comes.

MASTERING GROUP DYNAMICS

As you know, Aquarius with all its focus on circles and collectives is opposite you in the zodiac. There is a challenge to change yourself and others all your life when it comes to bringing these groups together. The cycles of time in your horoscope suggest it will often go either way. The community may not unite and come to nothing in the end—or you can succeed in playing your part in turning things around and collectively, your teams, clubs, societies, and so on can all reach a breathtaking outcome, uniting at last.

MONARCH OF THE JUNGLE

The old association of Leo with leading the jungle is well-known. So too is the lion emblem in heraldry around the world. All monarchs have their court, and when there is a coronation or a replacement victory, the court scatters. Loyalties have to be decided. This is partly where your long learning curve with groups comes from; you may experience it in your career, for example. Promotion is one example of this phenomenon in your chart; so is the replacement of one generation with another.

WHO SHARES YOUR BIRTHDAY?

William Horatio Powell, born July 29, 1892

Martina McBride, born July 29, 1966

Fernando Alonso, born July 29, 1981

JULY 30

WHO ARE YOU?

You are a Leo born with Taurus, the sign of money, business, charity, and property, at the top of your solar chart. You always aspire to the kind of money that you can do something impressive with; it may involve your family tree, the environment, building a business from the ground up, or creating a home. Leo is ruled by the Sun itself, and you shine most brightly when you have something to show—and show off. People forget that an earth sign rules the midheaven of your chart; you are down-to-earth about finance.

YOUR DESTINY

You are the idea person, budding talent, or potential success story who has to travel to find the right place for the end product. This energetic, fearless approach to your own efforts comes from Aries and Mars in charge of your sector of export, the worldwide web, and relocation. You are a true Leo Sun, and in order to sustain your confidence in yourself, you also have to admire yourself—or at least your abilities. The lifelong lesson here is to bring the attention back to what you have to offer and then make it succeed.

LEAPING FIRE SIGNS

The fire signs—Leo (your own sign), Aries, and Sagittarius—tend to leap forward like flames. When you have what you consider to be a white-hot idea, proposal, or concept, you race toward what you hope will be the right welcome and environment for it. Fire can also be too fast. Racing along, spurred on by your own energy, is a sight to see, but the truth about your plans is that they will only work if they are backed by research and proper preparation. Eventually experience will teach you to slow down and do this.

GROUPS AND OUTSIDERS

Leo, your opposite sign in the zodiac is Aquarius, ruling people power in a group which can be pushed against an outsider or opponent. It works the other way, too.

Aquarius can show the odd one out or the lone protester, who is against the team, club, society, and so on. Understanding both roles in your life helps you to do something miraculous: you have what it takes to reunite a network of people even when there is separation or opposition. From this, your tribes can become stronger, more successful.

WHO SHARES YOUR BIRTHDAY?

Henry Ford, born July 30, 1863
Arnold Schwarzenegger, born July 30, 1947
Kate Bush, born July 30, 1958

JULY 31

WHO ARE YOU?

Your Sun sign, Leo, is associated with children and young people. Leo is the sign of the monarch who holds court over heirs, spares, and pretenders to the throne. You have powerful memories of your relationship with your own mother. These in turn inspire all your visions about mothers and children in general. If you happen to be a mom, then this is one of the most important themes of your life: how to be queen to a prince or princess. Even if you never have children, this idea still dominates.

YOUR DESTINY

The planet Uranus with all his focus on freedom and independence rules your zone of duets, double acts, and duels. This is commonly a marriage or sexual relationship. It can also be a man against a woman at work. Uranus shows the need to liberate yourself and the other person from what binds you. Leo, this theme will repeat throughout your life in different ways. Sometimes it is just one person who tests your ideas about being a free agent. More commonly a number of people will play the same role for you.

PRIDE IN YOUR TALENT AND SKILL

Leo is known for being proud of number one, but where does it come from? For you, this is really the way you build confidence in yourself. You can't persuade others to accept your brain waves, proposals, or plans unless you believe in your own ability as well as the potential end result. This does require a healthy ego. You have it. The challenge is to move away from the idea as a flattering reflection of your brilliance, though, and toward a basic, practical, well-researched plan that will help your gifts take off.

THE BUILDER AND REBUILDER

You have Pluto, the planet of total transformation, at the base of your horoscope, which rules your home and household in opposition to the very top of it showing your career. Thanks to the cycles of time you go through regular, quite powerful changes with one or the other—and sometimes both. This sets you free to rebuild what was there or even walk away and build something completely new in your home or working life. A Leo's home is their castle and the kingdom offers a crown. That changes—and so do you.

WHO SHARES YOUR BIRTHDAY?

Milton Friedman, born July 31, 1912

Wesley Snipes, born July 31, 1962

J. K. Rowling, born July 31, 1965

AUGUST 1

WHO ARE YOU?

You are a Leo Sun born with Pisces ruling everything you find so precious that it is priceless. All that is most valuable to you is in the solar chart zone ruled by escapist Pisces the Fish and Neptune, the planet of vacations from reality. You are a fascinating person who leaves normal, everyday, ordinary life far behind for much of the time. It's shown in the way you dress. It's certainly shown in your own private universe, which very few people can relate to even though they are intrigued by all your unusual mysteries.

YOUR DESTINY

The planet Pluto—in charge of the afterlife—rules your extended family, and Scorpio is also here, with all its transformation and intensity. Your relatives in the spirit world have a profound impact on you and your life, no matter if you are aware of it or not. In turn, as you evolve, they also evolve. Their souls progress over time in accordance with what you do. Thanks to the cycles in your horoscope, there are regular episodes where those on the other side of life go to the next level spiritually, and so do you.

WOMEN, MEN, AND FREEDOM

The zone of your chart which rules the opposite sex is governed by Uranus, the symbol of freedom. Throughout your life, for different reasons, you will find it is possible to liberate yourself in a one-on-one situation with a man, if you are a woman, or snap the psychological chains, if you are a man facing a woman, in circumstances which confine you. The planet Uranus was found in a year of revolution around the world that set people free. Repeatedly, you will be offered the same scenario—sometimes with the same person.

TAKING IDEAS OVERSEAS

The adventurous Aries and the planet which rules assertiveness, Mars, both govern your travels. This is also where you find your academic qualifications, your projects, your websites, your brilliant ideas. Throughout your life you will have the choice to travel, relocate, or emigrate along with all that you have to offer. As you have the two fire signs Aries and Leo prominent in your chart, it is important that you ground yourself in the real world and remember that if you lack earth signs, you must plan and prepare even more.

WHO SHARES YOUR BIRTHDAY?

Herman Melville, born August 1, 1819

Yves Saint Laurent, born August 1, 1936

Jerry Garcia, born August 1, 1942

AUGUST 2

WHO ARE YOU?

You are the Leo who is generous and impressive; you fit the descriptions of you in the astrology books and websites you have read. You suit the role of philanthropist or Lady Bountiful, fulfilling your potential as the admired person who gives or pays up. Some of this comes from your Leo Sun, as this is the zodiac sign of royals. It is also due to Neptune, the planet of empathy and compassion, ruling your sector of finance. You know what it feels like to be in need. As a result, you act.

YOUR DESTINY

Groups of people can be as complex as families and powerful enough to change a corner of the world. With Aquarius, the sign of teams, clubs, and networks, opposite to your sign, you find you take turns at being on opposite sides of a community. Sometimes you are in the inner circle and all cooperating against one outsider. At other times, Leo, you find you are the person who is by themself, facing a number of like-minded people. The irony is, when you can all reunite and join forces, the group really is potent.

PLANNING YOUR FINANCES

You have Neptune, a symbol of sympathy, in charge of joint finance in your chart, as you know. At the other end, ruling your own income, investments, business, and property, you have Virgo and Mercury. You plot and plan, calculate and estimate, when you have money. You are prepared to do the research on how to spend what you have or make it go further. This makes you a confident negotiator. If houses, land, or apartments are involved, then powerful Pluto comes into play. You will always have the tight upper hand.

TWO PLACES, TWO LIVES

It's not that you lead a double life, Leo, but you do have Libra the Scales in charge of your journeys. You divide your time and energy between two cities, regions, or countries as a result. In this way you find symmetry and harmony, either for work or personal reasons. This pattern in your life is always there at regular intervals, thanks to the cycles of time in your horoscope. It may begin when you are quite young. Going between two different locations teaches you to respect the equality between the sexes or cultures.

WHO SHARES YOUR BIRTHDAY?

Edith Cowan, born August 2, 1861

Shimon Peres, born August 2, 1923

Peter O'Toole, born August 2, 1932

AUGUST 3

WHO ARE YOU?

You are the self-confident Leo that others expect to see, particularly in the relationships that matter most to you, but also with your own ideas and projects. You are at ease with yourself and also enjoy admiring your plans and skills—you have to, or success would never come. Long-distance relationships with partners are typical of your chart, as Libra, the sign of one-on-one connections, rules the journeys in your life. However, your whole horoscope suggests family and friends will also always involve a mission or even a move.

YOUR DESTINY

You are a fire sign, as you know, but the grounded, practical, sensible earth sign Virgo rules your finances. You are gifted at patient cultivation of your savings and income and know how to invest for long-term gains. You have another earth sign, Capricorn, in charge of your daily routine, service and duty to others, workload, and part-time or full-time jobs. This natural trine in your chart helps you have both feet on the ground and happily put the effort into giving a business what it needs—or building economic security over some years.

MONEY MYSTERIES

For all that methodical Virgo rules one part of your bank account, the imaginative sign Pisces and its ruler Neptune, the planet of mystery, also influence your finances. You are regularly on a quest to find rewards that may or may not be there. This is usually with others involved, as this part of your solar chart rules joint interests. Over time you will learn that a great deal depends on having tried, tested, and trusted advice from professionals who understand the reality; what you want may not be there at all. It doesn't stop you trying.

SUCCESS FROM PLANNING

You have all the right ingredients for success with your ideas and projects. What you need is a plan. This is true from youth into old age. You are an impressive person who persuades others to take you seriously, because you look the part and also clearly believe in your concepts or abilities. The cycles of time in your horoscope suggest that research is the key factor in finding the right environment for what you want to grow. You will always have to cast your net far and wide to find perfect conditions or risk all that potential.

WHO SHARES YOUR BIRTHDAY?

Tony Bennett, born August 3, 1926

Martin Sheen, born August 3, 1940

Martha Stewart, born August 3, 1941

AUGUST 4

WHO ARE YOU?

The zodiac sign which rules the lion—lord of the jungle—but also the lion of heraldry, royalty, and monarchy is Leo. This is your birthright, and you live up to it, particularly when you have the satisfaction of seeing your plans and projects finally succeed. You are money-minded, having sensible Virgo ruling your savings and the planet of strategy, Mercury, also in charge of your bank account. There is another side of your approach to finance which is entirely different, but this grounded part of you keeps you secure.

YOUR DESTINY

You have authority, leadership, an impressive image, and typical fire sign energy. What you actually need to rule with brilliance is research. There may also be a barrier to success here which comes from natural hesitation (should something not reward you) and performance anxiety (should you not pull off the astonishing victory that everybody expects). Once you realize that you can ask others to help, or even trick yourself in your own confidence game, the rest is just about method. Find out where projects can grow.

THE ENIGMA OF TREASURE

You know that you are on solid ground with Virgo and its down-to-earth qualities ruling your neatly calculated savings or investments. There is a completely different side to you, though, ruled by Pisces the two fish and Neptune, the planet of speculation, daydreaming, and *what-if?* thinking. Sometimes you find what you are looking for in terms of assets, finance, or even real treasure—like antiques or the hidden value in a property. There are no firm promises, though, in these quests of yours. Professional advice is useful.

TRIUMPHS AND VICTORIES

Just like the royals of old, you feel comfortable with conquests and even battles and win often enough to make these triumphs part of life. Leo the Lion is the zodiac sign which rules the spine and straight posture, as you may have read. Nobody stands as high as you do, when you are in a winning position. The only issue for you is the group around you. Aquarius rules the circles and communities nearby, and as it is in opposition to your own Leo sign, you always need to make sure you have the loyal support of the crowd.

WHO SHARES YOUR BIRTHDAY?

Louis Armstrong, born August 4, 1901

Barack Obama, born August 4, 1961

Meghan, Duchess of Sussex, born August 4, 1981

AUGUST 5

WHO ARE YOU?

There is one sector of your chart which describes the four corners of the world—and the worldwide web. It is ruled by adventurous Aries and Mars, the planet which symbolizes people with a lust for life. You are a natural traveler, exporter, and migrant. You are a fire sign as you know, and there is a direct connection between Aries and Leo, your own symbol, in your solar chart. The final fire sign, Sagittarius, also lines up. It represents abundant choice, and your only issue, from youth to old age, is selecting a nationality or nation.

YOUR DESTINY

Taurus with all its wealth, security, comfort, and property also rules the top of your chart, which is where your peak moments are predestined. Opposite, we find Scorpio, ruling the extended family around you. Scorpio also describes legacies and wills, trust funds and any family business. There are some stunning wealth signals in your chart, and you may already be aware of this. Much depends on organization, method, order, and a practical approach. Virgo, the sign of clear communication, rules your calculations.

THE PROMISE OF WEALTH

The potential for you to regularly access large amounts of money, or valuable property or items, is there all your life. Scorpio not only rules your relatives and godparents; it is also linked to Pluto, a symbol of empowerment. What you will be presented with across your days is the chance to have unusual control of your finances. This opens the gate to travel and perhaps relocation—even emigration. The cycles of time in your horoscope are set up in such a way that if you believe you deserve a rich reward, you can make it real.

THE HELPER AND THE HEALED

Virgo rules health, help, and healing. It also happens to rule everything that you find so precious it is priceless and what cannot be bought and sold in a catalog.

Throughout your life you will know what it is like to be transformed by anyone from a doctor to a therapist. You will also discover what it feels like to rescue others. Playing both roles—no matter if the issue is the mind, body, or spirit—teaches you about true strength. The strong Leo knows when to be vulnerable. Others who are not intimidated assist.

WHO SHARES YOUR BIRTHDAY?

John Huston, born August 5, 1906
Harold Holt, born August 5, 1908
Neil Armstrong, born August 5, 1930

AUGUST 6

WHO ARE YOU?

The zodiac sign of Leo falls in the elemental group of fire. It is ruled by the Sun, a symbol of self-confidence and proud display. You have all this, but you also have money. This gives you authority. Taurus the Bull, the symbol of gold bullion and bull markets, as well as the bronze bull near Wall Street, is at the top of your solar chart. You feel most on top of life when you have money, but also assets and possessions to shore you up. Leo is a fixed sign, so is Taurus. This makes you hard to move, as those negotiating with you find out.

YOUR DESTINY

The Lion, the Witch and the Wardrobe by C. S. Lewis is about a lion, but also about a deep mystery. You do not go back through the wardrobe to find Narnia in your life, Leo, but you do go on endless quests for money or rewards. The planet of great mystery is Neptune, and this rules your joint interests in business, charity, property, and currency. Part of the appeal for you is the tantalizing search for what may or may not actually exist. It is very important that you conserve your precious time and energy by finding the right people to advise you.

DOUBLE DESTINATIONS

You are at your most impressive when you are the connecting factor between two towns, two regions, or two countries. The natural link from this zone of your chart to your own Leo Sun makes you a dazzling figure, no matter if you are commuting for work reasons or find yourself in two places for personal ones. The sign of equality, Libra, governs your commitment to double destinations. Libra the Scales also shows you how there are two sides to every story and how two halves of the whole can be so different yet still equal.

CHOOSING TWO DIRECTIONS

You may have read that Libra is the sign which cannot make up its mind, as its rulership of the scales keeps it sitting on the fence. Because Libra is in charge of your travel, relocation, and even emigration agenda, you will find that life often puts you on a long pause. Choosing between West and East, for example, or one side of the family tree or the other is typical. None of this waiting is wasted time, though, as it is only when you are dangling between the present and the future that you become enlightened spiritually, Leo.

WHO SHARES YOUR BIRTHDAY?

Alexander Fleming, born August 6, 1881
Lucille Ball, born August 6, 1911
Andy Warhol, born August 6, 1928
Michelle Yeoh, born August 6, 1962

AUGUST 7

WHO ARE YOU?

Every zodiac sign has a ruling planet, and yours is the Sun—though actually a star, of course. You shine most brightly through the world of children and teenagers, Leo. Like a field of sunflowers can grow and go on for years, your influence carries through these younger generations. You are an idea person who always has a mission in hand. Adventurous Aries rules your interests in other countries. The planet of energy and drive, Mars, is always here, triggering your competitive instincts when others are also in search of places to export, travel to, or even emigrate to.

YOUR DESTINY

You may be a Leo, but your values are ruled by Virgo, the sign of health on all levels. Thanks to the cycles of time in your horoscope, you will come to understand that nothing is more precious than well-being as it cannot be bought and sold. However, it is also true that money can help with healing, and so for many reasons, it's your destiny to add up the price of recovery and help yourself and others to find the answers. What you will and will not sell your soul for is directly connected to the mind, body, and spirit.

THE NEXT GENERATION

Why does Leo rule the Fifth House, where your heirs, spares, and pretenders to the throne dwell? It is partly because of the pun in the words *Sun/son* related to your planetary ruler. It is also because Leo, the monarch of the jungle, has royal offspring along with pretenders to the throne. Even if you never have children, this could make you a strong teacher or a happy godparent. Dazzling results with children or teenagers are there all your life. This goes beyond them, though, to their children—and their children's children.

SOVEREIGNS

Like monarchs of old, you either receive moments of crowning glory throughout your life or do battle and seize the crown—symbolically anyway. When this happens, the court has to rearrange itself. Your allies and supporters, or those of the previous leading figure, are always part of the story. In fact, your opposite sign Aquarius rules circles, groups, and networks of all kinds. It is important that you maintain those relationships when regular triumphs and victories occur. This applies to your career and personal life.

WHO SHARES YOUR BIRTHDAY?

Mata Hari, born August 7, 1876

Abebe Bikila, born August 7, 1932

David Duchovny, born August 7, 1960

Charlize Theron, born August 7, 1975

AUGUST 8

WHO ARE YOU?

Why is Leo associated with star quality? It comes partly from your ruler the Sun, which acts like a spotlight in Old Hollywood. From the time you are young, you stand out from the crowd. You are also typical of Leo the sovereign of the jungle in that you tend to rule. You don't always win, of course, but you have the self-confidence, authority, and leadership to take on anybody and anything and emerge victorious. Being in charge suits you, and some observers might note that right from your teenage years you were born to do it.

YOUR DESTINY

Aquarius is opposite your Sun sign. Aquarius rules the community with all its diversity. Aquarius is also about pooling resources in order to obtain a common goal. What cannot be achieved by yourself or with a partner can be with the right group of people. You will always be able to take turns with others in leading roles or starring parts in your circles. This may be a team where you are captain with a selection of impressive players, for example. Or in a theater cast, you shine, but someone else stars.

MONEY, METHOD, AND ORDER

Born with Pisces the Fish in charge of joint finance, with Neptune ruling business, charity, property, and banking, you need method and order. You already know this, of course, but the issue is usually that you cannot control what is happening in the economy. When your country—or even the world—is all at sea, then you must adjust and adapt. The cycles of time in your horoscope suggest this happens often enough that you realize you must become the flexible DIY accountant who learns how to invent new systems every time.

KNOWLEDGE AND WISDOM

You were born with Libra, the sign of equality, justice, and fair play, ruling your ideas and education. If you enter academia, it will be with subjects where two sides must be balanced. This may involve history or science, for example, where there is no black or white, just shades of gray. Even if you are just a student of life or a natural guide to others, you do not need qualifications or a thesis—or a book deal—to impress. Thanks to the worldwide web, you scroll and others join you. This is more than information; it's wisdom.

WHO SHARES YOUR BIRTHDAY?

Dustin Hoffman, born August 8, 1937

Roger Federer, born August 8, 1981

Devery Jacobs, born August 8, 1993

Shawn Mendes, born August 8, 1998

AUGUST 9

WHO ARE YOU?

You have the self-confidence, authority, and presence to inspire respect and keep your audience. You are ruled by the Sun, which shines very brightly—and so do you. Leo the monarch of the jungle always holds sway over other people. Practical Virgo rules everything you value most in life. The planet Mercury with all his information flow and need to spread the word is also in charge of what is most precious to you. You are a natural teacher even if you have quite a different job. Your wisdom has a real-world application.

YOUR DESTINY

Right at the base of your horoscope, you find Pluto, the planet associated with the afterlife—or as it is known to mediums, the life between lives. You may or may not believe in this, but in astrology, Pluto and his zodiac sign Scorpio, which both rule your extended family, are about immortal souls. When your people in the spirit world evolve, so do you—or at least your soul makes progress. Equally, when you reach new stages in your development, your people on the other side of life welcome the change as it helps them, too.

WOMEN, MEN, AND LIBERATION

The planet Uranus is a symbol of the broken chains which lead to exhilarating new freedom. You will regularly experience this as a woman with men or as a man with women. A classic example of this is a marriage which involves new rules, new experiments, and new ways to be independent. This chart pattern also turns up at work or with platonic friendships. Uranus rules your duets and duels. Thanks to the cycles of time, it is the opposite sex which will motivate you to discover what liberation and true liberty mean.

FRIENDS AND GROUPS

Gemini the Twins rules your social life, circles of friends, groups, teams, and communities. You may be friends with siblings or cousins, for example. They are the gateway to a lifetime of unforgettable gatherings and strong networks for you. On a less literal level, there may be twin souls (married couples) who are your entry to people power, as their allies are yours, too. The worldwide web is your social home. In the twentieth century it may have been a crystal radio set. Gemini is an air sign. Light and easy, breezy connections rule.

WHO SHARES YOUR BIRTHDAY?

Rod Laver, born August 9, 1938

Whitney Houston, born August 9, 1963

Gillian Anderson, born August 9, 1968

AUGUST 10

WHO ARE YOU?

There may not actually be a crown on your head, but a good hat suits you. Leo, you are a leader who is respected and taken very seriously, particularly within the extended family tree. Your power is connected to your relatives, as Pluto, the planet of change, rules your clan. You can't stop the constant switches in direction there, but you can maintain what goes on. You need strength to do that. Leo is the monarch of the jungle, and you know how to firmly occupy your chosen chair, if not a throne. You're in charge.

YOUR DESTINY

The planet Mars is associated with great desire, and his own zodiac sign Aries is linked to fearless adventure. Both rule foreign people and countries in your destiny. You will travel all your life or just engage in language translation on the worldwide web. In fact, the internet was made for you. You may emigrate. You are also a prime candidate for a long-distance relationship or a strong bond with someone from another cultural or national background. You may first begin to show your roaming instincts when you are still a student.

YOUR OWN UNIVERSE

Pisces, the two fish who swim in another world, and the planet of escapism Neptune describe everything that is most valuable to you. You can't buy your own private universe or even bid at auction, but you can choose to spend a lot of time there. You may dress to express this side of yourself, which has no interest in what is practical, sensible, regulation—or even fashionable. There is a part of you which will always fascinate and intrigue others for this reason, though they will never, ever understand it.

YOUR PEOPLE AND YOUR PLACE

You have read how your extended family on both sides is always changing direction. Some branches on the tree will always challenge you. Pluto with all his regular transformation and shifting landscape also rules your local area or country. Nothing stands still. Nobody stays in place. Thanks to this, you may never feel completely settled, which might explain why you yearn to travel all your life or even relocate more than once. You are fearless, firm, and sometimes fast and furious when it comes to handling your relatives.

WHO SHARES YOUR BIRTHDAY?

Herbert Hoover, born August 10, 1874
Antonio Banderas, born August 10, 1960
Kylie Jenner, born August 10, 1997

AUGUST 11

WHO ARE YOU?

When your birth chart is examined, your Leo Sun dominates the Fifth House of children. Your heirs, spares, or pretenders to the throne loom over every relationship you have, even if you never become a parent. You were also born with a double number 1 in your numerology profile. You have the potential to be first with an idea and pioneer brilliant projects, plans, or concepts. What your chart does lack is earth. Grounding your brain waves, having a plan, doing the research, and firmly nurturing what you have are your big challenges.

YOUR DESTINY

Only when you can figure out your home and family can you say you are spiritually whole. Cancer, the zodiac sign which rules both sides of your family tree and your town, region, and country, is also in charge of your soul. This is your fate: to be repeated whenever you are on the verge of a great inner discovery but also a major turning point. West or East? Maternal or paternal side of the family? These processes take time, and whenever it happens, Leo, you can be in a liminal place for a long period. When you're ready, though, you really are ready.

WORK AND MONEY

When you are able to honor your work ethic—ruled by Virgo in your chart—and remember the financial motive—ruled by Taurus in your chart—you are capable of delivering, both to yourself and other people. This does not come naturally until you take pride in what you do. The idea of grand display and show is central to Leo the monarch of the jungle and the zodiac. Whatever your area of expertise and skill, it's not enough for you to achieve financial stability. You need the admiration of others and your own self-respect.

WOMEN, MEN, AND THE NEXT GENERATION

You will be in a number of educational relationships with men all your life, if you are a woman. Understanding the question of heirs, spares, and pretenders to the throne (yours or his) is central to what you decide. This can be a daughter or a godson, for example, or children en masse, for career or unpaid work reasons. If you are a Leo man, then your understanding of the opposite sex takes time—a lifetime even. Again, you can never go too far without automatically considering the next generation, and the one after.

WHO SHARES YOUR BIRTHDAY?

Enid Blyton, born August 11, 1897

Steve Wozniak, born August 11, 1950

Viola Davis, born August 11, 1965

AUGUST 12

WHO ARE YOU?

You rule your close relationships, Leo. If you are looking for your throne and crown in life (Leo is the sovereign of the jungle and the zodiac), then it is always through your heart. In fact, Leo rules the heart. This does not always make it simple, as you will see. Your leading role can give rise to Shakespearean levels of drama in love or with the family. No wonder you need time alone to find meaning. You are a hermit. The numeral 1 is in your numerology profile. When solo, you find enlightenment, answers, and what feeds your soul.

YOUR DESTINY

Aquarius rules groups in your life and it is also opposite your own Leo Sun. Dealing with who or what might move against you comes naturally. From your teenage years you learn to prevent problems before they begin. You are a natural strategist.

HOW TO RULE RELATIONSHIPS

Nobody would ever doubt that you rule your relationships. They can be puzzling, but you are still in charge of them. Always in the background are the children who were once babies—or perhaps the babies who never arrived. From this comes your greatest challenge: to lead the way but also bring yourself back to reality. The planet Neptune rules these intimate connections in your life. This can leave you all at sea, Leo. The solution is always to take yourself and the solid gold bond to a place where it can work—to ground it and center it.

PILGRIMAGE AND ENLIGHTENMENT

You have read how you need to be alone. This comes from sensitive Cancer, a water sign, in charge of your soul and spirit. You frequently need to come home to yourself—by being by yourself, too. This is very true when relationships seem unfulfilling. These may be friends, family, or partners. You have energetic Aries and determined Mars in charge of your journeys. Over time, people come to know you as an explorer, but also something of a pilgrim. It may be hiking or even outright relocation, but all roads lead to enlightenment.

WHO SHARES YOUR BIRTHDAY?

Cecil B. DeMille, born August 12, 1881
Mark Knopfler, born August 12, 1949
Pete Sampras, born August 12, 1971

AUGUST 13

WHO ARE YOU?

The horoscope you were born with gives you grounded, methodical Virgo in charge of your finances. Yet, you are also a Leo Sun, so when you do have money, you generously donate it or pay your fair share. Perhaps charity begins at home. You are respected and admired for your careful handling of your bank account and have a head for business or property. You may not have a crown or throne, but you do have a certain presence, profile, and position that impresses others. You enjoy taking your time when investing or shopping.

YOUR DESTINY

You have the instincts of a natural teacher no matter what job you take in life. You are a dynamic and energetic public speaker. You also have a significant presence on the worldwide web, with energetic Aries ruling your sector of global reach. Mars also rules this area of your destiny so you are up-front and quite content to be front and center. This makes you a powerful student of life all your life, but there is no point in holding the knowledge. For you, it has to be transmitted, and you have the charisma to do just that.

TRANSFORMATION AND HOME

Some people have settled home lives: a sense of place with their town, local area, or country. Their families or households may be quite fixed. You were born with Pluto, the planet of transformation, in charge of this sector of your horoscope. Leo, the cycles of time suggest that more than once you will relocate or even emigrate because your destiny is tied to great escapes. You never just pack your boxes or bags, you also pack any emotional baggage when you go. The map is always a magical mystery tour for you, but you believe.

GENEROUS LEO

Where does the link between generosity and Leo come from? It's ancient in origin, as Leo the monarch of the jungle is also zodiac royalty. Traditionally, leaders are patrons of others, no matter if it's musicians, astronomers, or those in need of charity. Your down-to-earth handling of money enables you to give to those you feel deserve fairer treatment. You are happy to be the person who supplies the salary or the donation and with Libra, the sign of justice, ruling your ideas in life, you see it as equality in action.

WHO SHARES YOUR BIRTHDAY?

Annie Oakley, born August 13, 1860
John Logie Baird, born August 13, 1888
Alfred Hitchcock, born August 13, 1899

AUGUST 14

WHO ARE YOU?

You are a strong leader with tremendous self-confidence, which is typical of Leo. You know who you are, especially in terms of the family. With powerful Pluto ruling your family tree on both sides, you are the person who maintains strict boundaries. Royalty—Leo is monarch of the jungle and the zodiac too—rules all the branches in your clan. Leo also rules the heart, though. In the background, partnership is always on your mind. So is courtship and the bedroom. It may be past, present, or future, Leo.

YOUR DESTINY

Aquarius is the sign naturally opposite Leo, so when you find potential opposition in life, it tends to be in a pack or circle. You are extremely good at setting boundaries, but you are also skilled at tactics which help you to successfully preempt any issues with people. Libra is the sign of the peacemaker, and it governs your ideas and opinions. You are seldom so quick and clever as when you are several steps ahead of those who would disrupt the harmony of your life—and the lives of others, too. Your conflict resolution is powerful.

THE FAMILY AND YOUR SPIRITUALITY

You find your spirituality when you must choose between one direction on the family tree and another. This happens several times in your life. It may be psychological and emotional, or even geographical. While you are caught up deciding between compass points on the map, for example—or between one side of the family and another—you find your soul. Cancer the Crab, with all its focus on your clan and your sense of place, is also in charge of your enlightenment in life. This happens often enough to change you.

THE PERSON OF ACTION

Aries with all its fearless approach to life and planet of energetic, dynamic people—it's ruled by the warrior god Mars—has a strong pattern in your chart. In fact, it is a fire sign, like Leo, and makes a perfect trine. The family with all its branches, switching direction, is your motivation. Sometimes you just have to take action, and you never hesitate. Your sense of place in the world, whether town, local area, or country, is just as prone to dramatic change as the family, with Pluto ruling this sector of your chart. Home is an ever-shifting idea.

WHO SHARES YOUR BIRTHDAY?

Magic Johnson, born August 14, 1959

Halle Berry, born August 14, 1966

Mila Kunis, born August 14, 1983

AUGUST 15

WHO ARE YOU?

You may have read that Leo the Lion is the leader of the pack, monarch of the zodiac, and sovereign of the court. In fact, Leo rules the heart more than anything else. You do rule your relationships and lead the way with them, but you also have a lifetime to develop your confidence in yourself and your certainty about where particular romances, marriages, partnerships, or family ties belong. With Neptune overseeing the most important commitments in your life, you can feel all at sea. A practical plan to ground your heart works.

YOUR DESTINY

The sector of your chart normally governed by Leo in the heavens belongs to the traveler, explorer, and migrant Sagittarius. This zodiac sign with all its longing for new horizons also makes a perfect trine to your Leo Sun. Your life is full of escape routes and adventures. You also have Aries, with all its energy, ruling foreign places and people. No matter if you set off in your own region or abroad, you have tremendous optimism and faith in the future when you go. These trips or relocations in your life make you who you are: a Sun-seeking lion.

WORK AND HOME REINVENTION

Pluto is the planet of sweeping transformation, and he rules your homelife, household, and family. He is also in direct opposition to your work, unpaid work, or academic career. Thanks to the cycles of time in your horoscope, Leo, you must regularly face crossroads in your life, when you can either reinvent what was there or walk away and start again. In order to believe something is worth preserving, you have to truly believe it is worth your time to control and recreate. If not? You are a powerful self-starter who will lay new foundations.

FINDING A FINANCIAL SYSTEM

Pisces the Fish and Neptune the ruler of the ocean both influence your finances. Stability, security, and certainty can't be purchased, especially when you find that circumstances beyond your control put you at regular inflection points. When everything is all over the place, everywhere, all the time—a characteristic of transits to Pisces—how do you pull in the net and drop anchor? Your budget must always be remade, according to the economy but also your own shifting needs. This makes you a financial inventor.

WHO SHARES YOUR BIRTHDAY?

Napoleon Bonaparte, born August 15, 1769
Princess Anne, born August 15, 1950
Jennifer Lawrence, born August 15, 1990

AUGUST 16

WHO ARE YOU?

The idea of sharing, cooperating, and collaborating is wonderful. In reality, though, only one person can really be the center of attention at any one time. Being a Leo Sun, you were born to shine and take the spotlight. Opposite your sign is Aquarius, associated with circles and communities. As a result you learn to take your turn in the many tribes you will be involved with over the course of your life. Sometimes others want to star in the story together; at other times, allies will understand that you are the miracle worker.

YOUR DESTINY

Just as Aquarius has a strong impact on your profile, so too does Pisces, with the two fish describing what you find so precious in life. Pisces is associated with vacations from reality. Its ruler Neptune opens you up to other ways of living far beyond what most people would call regular or mundane existence. You do inhabit different worlds to others, but true friends understand that. You may have your own way of expressing your personality, Leo, and if you're happy with it, that's enough.

VIRGO AND YOUR WORK ETHIC

For all that you are escapist, you also know when to work hard for what you want. This comes from the earth sign Virgo with all its sense of duty ruling what is priceless. It forms a golden triangle in your chart with Capricorn, the sign of ambition, which governs your daily routine and lifestyle. Finally, Taurus is on the midheaven of your solar chart, with all its solid, dependable, earth sign qualities, too. Your only issue is balancing your effort and energy with other priorities. When in doubt, ditch or delegate, Leo.

THE GEMINI GATEWAY

There is a natural connection in your chart between Aquarius, the sign which shows the all-star circle of people in your life, and Gemini, which rules your social media, friendship circles, and connections. This air sign pattern feeds the fire sign you were born under, and that might explain the warmth that is there. You will always find twin souls, or perhaps siblings, are the gateway to good times and even great outcomes. You know how to give space to people and use it, too. It all works so well.

WHO SHARES YOUR BIRTHDAY?

James Cameron, born August 16, 1954
Madonna, born August 16, 1958
Steve Carell, born August 16, 1962
Taika Waititi, born August 16, 1975

AUGUST 17

WHO ARE YOU?

Leo the Lion is associated with great strength. It can be found in heraldic symbols among many generations of royalty. No zodiac sovereign is superhuman, though. You also need help and healing as much as anybody else. Over time this comes to play a special part in your life, and it shapes who you become. The pure sign of service and duty, Virgo, rules the people and situations you find priceless. Of course, money can buy what you need, but it's the miracle of those who care for you that matters.

YOUR DESTINY

The relationships you have with men if you are a woman or with women if you are a man remind you that Leo rules the heart, and it can be an intricate part of you. Whatever your sexual preferences are, you must still negotiate the space between the female and the male of the species. This does commonly occur in marriage, but always with the issue of children, stepchildren, godchildren, or young relatives hanging over the dealmaking you do together. In other cases, the bonds are platonic, but the sexual politics is real.

THE CIRCLE AND THE INDIVIDUAL

The angles of your chart often show the main story, and you were born with Aquarius, the sign of people power in a circle, on the descending angle of your horoscope. The rise and fall of particular groups, clubs, teams, and so on are down to how they handle outsiders and opponents. This applies even when everybody is remarkably similar in terms of their ideas and opinions. You will find yourself in the inner circle sometimes. At others, you will be one against the many. Fixing this makes you all-powerful.

THE BUILDER AND INVESTOR

Another key angle in your chart is the midheaven, where Taurus the Bull rules. Taurus is associated with productivity, planning, and planting. When you have money, you take your time deciding on investments, purchases, or savings. Taurus is an earth sign, so this is a grounded part of your personality. Taurus the Bull also takes its time. When your feet are planted on the grass, it takes a lot to get you to move. Your family tree is always a consideration. So is your ambition. You're a builder at heart, shaping the future.

WHO SHARES YOUR BIRTHDAY?

Davy Crockett, born August 17, 1786

Maureen O'Hara, born August 17, 1920

Robert De Niro, born August 17, 1943

AUGUST 18

WHO ARE YOU?

You are the true Leo, symbolically the sovereign of the jungle. Lions are also vulnerable, however, and your challenge to those who are intimidated by your strength is to trust you enough to help you. People forget that Leo the Lion also needs assistance, despite its leading role. You inspire loyalty like all impressive and important people. Virgo, which rules healing, describes what is so precious to you that it is priceless. This may be a doctor or counselor worth more than their weight in gold.

YOUR DESTINY

You are regularly challenged to either renovate and rebuild what you have or walk away and start again. Leo, you have Uranus, the planet of change, opposite your Sun sign. Life is about reshaping for you, no matter if you dedicate the time to make a family or work structure better or take the dramatic decision to turn your back. As a result of this, you are a firm character, with all the strength Leo is known for. Your decisions prove how determined you are, no matter how challenging the paths are every time you have to choose them.

FINANCIAL CHALLENGES

Your challenge is to manage your money well enough to give you the security you need without losing sight of the property market. You tend to be emotional about your savings and assets rather than strictly practical. The water sign Scorpio, which is all about feelings, influences your approach to all that you earn, own, and owe. Another water sign, Pisces, rules your attitude toward wealth. The expertise of a professional who is all about the numbers or facts—not the heart and soul—could be extremely useful for you.

THE JOURNEY, NOT THE DESTINATION

You are a born traveler or explorer. It is all about the journey for you rather than the destination. You are divided between two places. This may be two cities, regions, or countries. The adventurous Aries and its fearless planet Mars both rule your sector of foreign places and people. You are intrigued by everything which is culturally and historically different. You may be somebody whose mind is always in two places at once, and as a result of this, perhaps you will spend large periods of your life commuting or emigrating.

WHO SHARES YOUR BIRTHDAY?

Shelley Winters, born August 18, 1920
Patrick Swayze, born August 18, 1952
Christian Slater, born August 18, 1969

AUGUST 19

WHO ARE YOU?

Your motivation is money—a lot of money. Perhaps this is in the form of precious objects that are extremely valuable or priceless. In your birth chart, Taurus the Bull, symbolizing gold bullion and bull markets, is associated with your ability to make or save small fortunes. When we look at your Leo chart, we find Taurus also rules your success, career, and ambition. The glittering prizes you dream of are always tantalizingly close. There is often an unreal quality to your visions, and so you learn how to ground the daydreams.

YOUR DESTINY

Leo rules the heart. It also rules all sorts of relationships, from courtship rituals to the bedroom. It governs pregnancy, infants, schoolchildren, and young adults—the teenagers in your life. You are typical of your sign, in that unlocking the puzzle of your own heart will take up a great deal of time and energy. In your birth chart, Scorpio rules all your valuable relationships, no matter if they involve marriage or parenthood, legacies or mortgages. Scorpio is a water sign, and it is about feelings, not logic.

MOTHERS AND CHILDREN

As a Leo, your Sun is in the Fifth House of mothers and children which rules the dynasty or the next generation. This applies no matter if it's your path to be a parent or not. This is always in the background of those relationships you've read about, which will always defy categorization. The memory of past pregnancies which did or did not happen will influence your fate, as much as the vision of some future parent-child bond. This is a spiritual matter for you. It may even be religious. Your soul is involved.

GENEROSITY AND ABUNDANCE

If you are able to make the dream real, you will end up in a powerful financial position and may become a philanthropist: the trustee of good causes or a dedicated charity donor. Charity begins at home, so it may be your reward in life to help your family or friends. Leo is associated with giving, because it is the monarch of the zodiac and royalty always bestows favors on the less fortunate. Even if life sometimes finds you at a low ebb financially, the eternal dream of pennies from heaven can turn out to be true in the end, Leo.

WHO SHARES YOUR BIRTHDAY?

Coco Chanel, born August 19, 1883

Gene Roddenberry, born August 19, 1921

Matthew Perry, born August 19, 1969

AUGUST 20

WHO ARE YOU?

Crowns and castles are associated with Leo, your Sun sign. You don't have Buckingham Palace, Windsor Castle, or the crown jewels in your life, but you do go through deep periods of questioning about who or what is at the top—at home or work. The cycles of time in your horoscope suggest quite radical changes at regular intervals. As a fixed sign, you prefer the household, family, home, workplace, and profession in your world to offer stability. Your choice to go back and restructure or walk away and restart sets you free.

YOUR DESTINY

The flower associated with your sign is the sunflower, as you are ruled by the solar cycle but also linked to the idea of seeding the future through the growth of children and teenagers in your life. This can happen even if you are not a parent, Leo. Most commonly, though, is it one special son or daughter and their own dazzling influence on another young generation which is your destiny. Jupiter with all its optimism, high hopes, and positive vision governs younger people for you—generation after generation.

GEMINI AND GROUPS

The air sign Gemini rules the groups in your life, ranging from genuine team efforts with work or unpaid work goals to purely social bonds of friendship. Gemini rules siblings and cousins. There is often a family feel to these connections. Friends can also seem more like family. With this air sign, you know how to give people breathing space, and they also respect your need to be independent. This mutual bonding is most rewarding when you can all take the resources you share and build real rewards.

THE MAGICAL MYSTERY MONEY TOUR

The zodiac signs which rule your financial sectors tell the story of your budget over time. Neptune with all its mystery is in charge of joint business, banking, and property in your world—charity and possessions, too. You find the quest for what may or may not be there fascinating. In fact it is an escape from the real world, as much as anything in a book or film. Impartial professional advice from realists in the financial field is not perhaps part of the escapism, but it will save you time—and more.

WHO SHARES YOUR BIRTHDAY?

Robert Plant, born August 20, 1948

Ke Huy Quan, born August 20, 1971

David Walliams, born August 20, 1971

Amy Adams, born August 20, 1974

AUGUST 21

WHO ARE YOU?

You are a natural recluse who has learned to excuse yourself from the noise and distraction of daily life to find useful solitude. Cancer, associated with feeling at home and finding sanctuary, also happens to be the ruler of your sector of soul-searching. You need to be alone in order to find spiritual truths. Pisces, associated with true faith, oversees the most important family or personal relationships in your life. You may be an atheist or true believer, but being a hermit helps you.

YOUR DESTINY

You are one of those people who ends up with financial comfort and even steady wealth, thanks to the way your horoscope is set up. In your solar chart we find the practical earth sign Virgo ruling your income and investments. In your birth chart (the private side of your life), we find another earth sign, Taurus, governing the same. This grounded side of your nature helps you take advantage of all the astrological cycles which encourage earning, saving, or planting in all senses of the word. Financially, you're a born farmer.

THE NEED FOR FOCUS

For all that you have a way with money, you can be all action and no focus when it comes to your ideas. The pioneering, energetic, impatient Aries rules your grasp of particular projects and plans. You are an excellent starter, but the issue is often finishing. Your challenge in life is to slow down, research your options, and then proceed. In your birth chart, the restless Sagittarius governs your quests on the worldwide web, in academia, in education, in publishing. Try exploring the destination before you set off.

THE HERMIT

The Moon rules your need to be alone and find yourself as a hermit. The Moon and her phases, from full to new, strongly influence you in this respect. When even the most precious and valuable friends, family members, and partners can't sustain you emotionally, you know yourself well enough to depart. It is not unusual for people born on August 21 to leave for years, and a long sabbatical may be part of your life story. More commonly, you may be a regular temporary hermit crab. You always return.

WHO SHARES YOUR BIRTHDAY?

Aubrey Beardsley, born August 21, 1872

Princess Margaret, born August 21, 1930

Joe Strummer, born August 21, 1952

AUGUST 22

WHO ARE YOU?

Your numerology profile contains the numeral 2 twice. The deals you negotiate with men in your life if you are a woman or women if you are a man show two sides, two sets of expectations, and two lessons to learn. This can happen with just one marriage, for example, over many years. It can also take place in a platonic situation at work, which changes you as much as it changes the other person. Finding a way to close the gaps between you and the person who is so different to you reshapes your character and fate.

YOUR DESTINY

You are a good candidate for a long-distance relationship. The cycles of time in your horoscope suggest that you will always find the gaps on the map inspiring when it comes to love. You are also destined to test the bonds of loyalty and affection with family members or very close friends who are apart from you. Mercury, as the messenger and the traveler, is prominent in your chart. Your mission is different to his, but it is part of your personality to show how sincere you are by meeting others halfway across a flight path.

BIG IDEAS AND VISIONS

You don't just have thoughts scribbled on drink coasters. You have grand visions of what might be and striking concepts which seem to arrive almost fully formed. The air signs Gemini, Libra, and Aquarius and the element of air which passes through their ruling planets of Mercury, Venus, and Uranus suggest everything that is fresh to you and others has the potential to completely change the atmosphere. These concepts can vanish into thin air, however, unless you ground them, research them, and find a place for them.

LEADERSHIP AND LOYALTY

Some aspects of life at the top ring very true for you—coronations, elections where one president replaces another, inheritance where somebody moves on up the line of succession, victory when there can be only one winner. Whenever this happens, in your personal or professional life, you always find yourself in two positions. One is actually at the peak, which means a great deal depends on the group around you. Another is within the group itself where you must decide who and what to be loyal to.

WHO SHARES YOUR BIRTHDAY?

Claude Debussy, born August 22, 1862
Ray Bradbury, born August 22, 1920
James Corden, born August 22, 1978

AUGUST 23

WHO ARE YOU?

Perhaps it is your family tree on both sides that makes you tough. You are a force to be reckoned with who keeps very strong boundaries. That does not mean you ever become the person of action that others must respect. Yet, if you have to, you will not hesitate to protect who and what matters most. You have great authority, and your position, mission, and ambition mark you out from others. In the background, though—always at the back of your mind—is the reality of a love that lasts forever.

YOUR DESTINY

You are a natural migrant who will never hesitate to exchange one place for another on the map if your heart and soul tell you it's time to go. Even in your own region or country, you never stay and put up with situations past their use-by date. You would rather chance your future and take on places and people which are quite unknown. This gives you sympathy for others who have to start from scratch in life. It also proves to you that the future is what you make it. You'll uproot more than once in your life.

THE HOME FOR YOUR IDEAS

The home for your ideas is crucial to their success, but it begins with some preparation and planning. Without a confident grasp of where those plans might thrive, you can end up always on the brink of achievement but never actually there. You are impressive, with real presence, and have no trouble drawing respect and admiration from others. The person you most need to admire is yourself, though, for taking what you have on paper or on the computer and following through in a way that delivers real results.

DIFFERENCE AND DIVERSITY

You will always be involved in teams, clubs, or other networks from childhood into old age. These teach you about the differences between people and the diversity that has to be accommodated in any successful group. Nothing is delivered gift-wrapped here; you have to be highly strategic and put time, energy, and effort into bringing people together. Even if you can only begin with one or two others and then build from there, on the occasions you do unite as one what you create together is great to see.

WHO SHARES YOUR BIRTHDAY?

King Louis XVI of France, born August 23, 1754

Keith Moon, born August 23, 1946

Kobe Bryant, born August 23, 1978

AUGUST 24

WHO ARE YOU?

The planet Neptune rules your duets and double acts, and just like the ocean that he rules, Neptune can leave us feeling all at sea. You are drawn to being part of a pair all your life—or may be born with a powerful sibling relationship, for example. The way your horoscope is set up suggests many forks in the road, every time you pair up. Neptune rules the ship that sails, and fathoming the right navigational coordinates for yourself and the other person can preoccupy you in the same duet or with a range of different faces.

YOUR DESTINY

In your solar chart, the group sign Aquarius rules your paid work, unpaid work, and academic career. Just as Pisces and its two confused fish have a strong say over partnerships, so does Aquarius govern your lifestyle with all its focus on teams, clubs, societies, and communities. Being supported by your circle is very important to your sense of self and also what you achieve in your life. You may have read that Virgo is about attention to detail. This is quite true, and it will save you repeatedly with all your networks of people.

YOUR FAMILY TREE

Sagittarius rules your family tree, so you have relatives and/or ancestors in foreign countries or born into cultures foreign to you today. Sagittarius rules distant places on the map. This is a great challenge for you, Virgo, because it can be hard to decide which direction to travel in emotionally, spiritually—even geographically. Where you come from and where you belong are always somewhere else. Where to live, where to work, and where to put down roots will be a lifetime quest for you.

EXPORTING YOUR IDEAS

It's in your destiny to always be gifted with at least one potentially productive idea, but often it will be two. The dual sign Gemini rules your success, so similar plans, always in pairs, seem to come to you at the same time. Gemini also rules journeys. Your horoscope suggests nothing works in your own town or country quite as well as it does elsewhere. This ties into the general theme of your birthday chart, which is *Where should I move to?* We could also say your question is *Where should I transplant this?* A lifelong query!

WHO SHARES YOUR BIRTHDAY?

Alexander McCall Smith, born August 24, 1948

Linton Kwesi Johnson, born August 24, 1952

Stephen Fry, born August 24, 1957

AUGUST 25

WHO ARE YOU?

You shine most brightly when backed by a group. These special circles of brilliant people cast you in the best possible light. Aquarius describes people who pool resources for a common goal and also happens to rule your sector of work, duty, lifestyle, daily routine, and tasks. You are a typical Virgo in the sense that you can pour yourself into rituals and method. Your process—be it academic, a paid job, or a voluntary position—is nothing without the band, ensemble, cast, team, club, and so on.

YOUR DESTINY

Perhaps because communities and circles are such a central part of your life, you also need to be alone. You are the hermit who withdraws in order to find what matters most. This is a feature of your relationships in and out of the bedroom. It is also a feature of your relationship with the world of babies, children, and young adults. The zodiac sign which rules your inner life in your Virgo chart also happens to govern close connections in your birth chart. So introspection and the search for meaning are part of your path.

GROUNDING YOURSELF IN THE REAL WORLD

You are an escapist who feels completely at home in the world of bohemia, entertainment, or the alternative realities of the worldwide web. This comes from Neptune, which rules your relationships. Neptune is lord of the sea and associated with floating, drifting, and sailing through life. This is a big part of who you are, as the next great escape is always just behind you. For all that this makes you fascinating, it can also remove you from the real world so much that others find you inaccessible. When you compromise, you win.

HARD WORK EARNS A SOLID INCOME

Once you find the right computer or book to lean on—Mercury the Messenger is your ruling planet, Virgo—you can invest in your own labor and patience. Virgo is an earth sign and knows how to put its feet firmly on the ground when it comes to money. And, in fact, it is one of the other earth signs—Taurus the Bull—which rules gold bullion, bull markets, and the New York Stock Exchange. Thus, with your well-starred alignment with Taurus, you have an affinity for business, banking, savings, or solid earnings.

WHO SHARES YOUR BIRTHDAY?

Sean Connery, born August 25, 1930

Elvis Costello, born August 25, 1954

Tim Burton, born August 25, 1958

AUGUST 26

WHO ARE YOU?

The element of earth holds your Virgo Sun in a comfortable way; you are grounded, at home in nature, and feel at ease with the other earth and water sign themes: the house or apartment, the garden, the good things of life. Venus rules everything you find so precious it is priceless. Venus governs evergreen love, as the mother of

Cupid, whose passion was immortal. Venus was also married to Vulcan, who forgave her for everything. Venus is both seductive and easily seduced; this is at the heart of who you truly are.

YOUR DESTINY

Neptune with all his illusions and Pisces with all its daydreams stand opposite your own Virgo Sun. Finding out who you are without the projected hopes, fantasies, and fears is very wise, as these clouds of unreality can tie up your time and energy. They can be quite persuasive; perhaps you think some ghosts or spirits have a particular power. If not that, there may be a phobia or just a recurring grand vision. When you banish the contents of your imagination in a conscious way, you can get back to the real world.

DISCOVERY AND SECURITY

It must often seem to you that you have to discover new places on the map in order to find security. This may be a genuine case of the grass being always greener on the other side of the fence. However, with Pluto the planet of transformation in charge of your journeys, you find control and empowerment only come when you can make the change and leave the past behind. With Jupiter, the planet of high hopes and eternal optimism, in charge of your homelife, you are a good candidate for repeated moves, Virgo.

THE GROUP AS A WAY OF LIFE

The chart sector actually ruling your lifestyle in the heavens is also where we find groups, clubs, teams, societies, associations, and all kinds of circles in your story. In fact, the support and backing of these people is part of your personality; you become the central figure who is surrounded by allies. This can be for personal reasons (you are involved with sport) or professional reasons (you are the leading figure in a community at work). Nothing is so habitual that it cannot be improved upon though, Virgo.

WHO SHARES YOUR BIRTHDAY?

Mother Teresa, born August 26, 1910

Branford Marsalis, born August 26, 1960

Macaulay Culkin, born August 26, 1980

AUGUST 27

WHO ARE YOU?

The angles of your horoscope show who you really are, Virgo. Pisces, the sign of dreams and illusions, is in a pattern with Gemini, the sign of the mind. Sagittarius, the sign of high hopes, is also part of the pattern. You are in the middle, sometimes dealing with fears that are not justified or fantasies about wealth or success. When you realize that Neptune, the planet of projection, stands opposite your sign, you can begin to dismantle thoughts and theories and come back down to earth. It's where you belong.

YOUR DESTINY

Home for you is not quite wherever you hang your hat, but you do feel at home when you are on the road. You are fated to take more than one epic journey in your life and may become a regular explorer. Sagittarius rules great optimism, as you have read, and it also happens to govern your sector of belonging and security. What you choose to do is not for everybody; some people do not understand why carrying luggage is the path to feeling settled. If you can't physically get away, you will see the world on the web.

TWO IS YOUR NUMBER

The numeral 2 is hidden in your numerology profile. You also have the dual sign Pisces of the two fish ruling your sector of duets and double acts. At the top of your chart, which is very important, we find Gemini the Twins. Throughout your life from youth to old age, you will always find yourself trying to balance your needs with another person's. If you can't take the same path, how do you find a direction? If there must be two paths, then what can you negotiate with each other? These questions shape you.

MERCURY AND STRATEGY

Mercury is the trickster in astrology. He is associated with quicksilver. He also rules your own Virgo Sun sign but also your Gemini midheaven. You are quick and clever when you have to be—Mercurial, in fact. You are a good ally to have because you can move your mind several hours ahead of anyone who might be an issue. You are not necessarily psychic—although you have a vivid imagination, as you know. Rather, experience teaches you that sometimes you have to be ahead of the pack and ahead of the game, too.

WHO SHARES YOUR BIRTHDAY?

Donald Bradman, born August 27, 1908

Lyndon B. Johnson, born August 27, 1908

Cesaria Evora, born August 27, 1941

Tom Ford, born August 27, 1961

AUGUST 28

WHO ARE YOU?

The angle of your horoscope which rules your household and home is where you find Jupiter with all his good fortune, Virgo. Sagittarius is also here, associated with positive thinking and broad horizons. You are an earth sign who needs to feel secure, settled, and grounded. In fact, you work very hard in the interests of your ideal house, garden, or apartment. A lovely angle from Cancer, the sign of children and teenagers in an extended household, picks up your Virgo Sun. There's room for all.

YOUR DESTINY

You are associated with a strong work ethic, methodical daily routine, and responsible attitude, Virgo. You are also the sign that astrologers link with the body and spirit, as well as the mind. Ensuring that you get the work-life balance right is something that applies to you as a student, but also as a working person later on in life. Understanding that your body is a machine (though not a robot) and needs proper care and maintenance is necessary on a regular basis. Learning to set priorities helps you manage that.

MERCURY AND YOUR MIND

Mercury rules your Virgo Sun, and it also rules Gemini, the sign of brilliant, bright communication, right at the top of your chart. You are able to take ideas seemingly from thin air and transport them somewhere solid where they can develop into projects that have long-term potential. The issue for you, as you have read, is that you need to get the work-life balance right so you do not take on too much, no matter if it's paid tasks, unpaid labors, or just everything that you are always doing for other people.

THE GROUP IS YOUR FOUNDATION

The group or network that surrounds you for years at a time—or perhaps changes faces and names throughout—is where you find your foundation. Cancer the Crab, responsible for a sense of belonging, sanctuary, and security, is also in charge of your networks. These may be as spread out as the internet is, but underneath it all, you share the same space spiritually and emotionally. It's the gift that goes on giving for you, as Cancer is a compatible water sign, and the flow with your allies and friends is lifelong.

WHO SHARES YOUR BIRTHDAY?

Johann Wolfgang von Goethe, born August 28, 1749
Ai Weiwei, born August 28, 1957
Shania Twain, born August 28, 1965
Sheryl Sandberg, born August 28, 1969

AUGUST 29

WHO ARE YOU?

You were born as a Virgo under the rulership of Mercury the Messenger. From school until your career years, you will always have projects, plans, and ideas to pass across; you might do this from pure interest or find that is where your profession calls you. Libra rules everything you value most highly. It also happens to deliver men who challenge your sense of trust, if you are a woman, and women who ask you to reach across the gap between the sexes, if you are a man. This is a lifetime quest, Virgo.

YOUR DESTINY

The planet that rules your health, well-being, daily routine, and day-to-day workload is very important in your chart, as this is Virgo's domain. It happens to be Uranus—a symbol of the revolution that sets you free. Thanks to the cycles of time in your horoscope, you are regularly involved in your own Independence Days. As Virgo rules the mind, it is your own willpower, consciousness, and intuition that you have to master in order to win your freedom. You are the free spirit who will never be tied down.

POWER AND THE UPPER HAND

A closer look at your solar chart reveals Pluto in charge of your attitude and thoughts. Pluto gives you the empowerment you need to come first. You are naturally drawn to any field, pastime, or professional area where you can find a triumph. Your ability to be the boss of yourself is part of that success. You know how to keep your hands firmly on the reins. In turn, this brings the kind of powerful hit rate that allows you to build on your last victory in order to pursue the next one. It matters a lot to you.

AN AUTHORITY WITH IDEAS

As you've read, Mercury, the planet of the mind, rules the top of your chart, where you chase your goals and also your own Virgo Sun. You are the authority figure with ideas, proposals, concepts, and brain waves to launch. Confidence is something only you can master for yourself. Planning, research, and the ability to delegate will all help you, but it is important to remember that only you can do something practical with what you hold on paper or on the computer. The key to your future is remembering you're an earth sign.

WHO SHARES YOUR BIRTHDAY?

John Locke, born August 29, 1632
Maurice Maeterlinck, born August 29, 1862
Ingrid Bergman, born August 29, 1915
Minami Hamabe, born August 29, 2000

AUGUST 30

WHO ARE YOU?

You are sometimes mistaken for a Sagittarian because of your huge enjoyment of travel. You are also one of the people most likely to relocate or emigrate—more than once. Of course, you are a Virgo and need your security as much as any earth sign, as you need to feel grounded. Yet, with Sagittarius the sign of distant places and broad horizons in charge of your home zone, you genuinely like packing your bags and finding your favorite spaces across the map. Jupiter with all his big vision also rules this chart sector.

YOUR DESTINY

In your birth chart, Virgo is in charge of the sector of daily life, regular responsibilities, and your diary. The same sector in your solar chart shows Aquarius there, the sign of the group. You are fated to be with particular teams, clubs, networks, and societies all your life from childhood. Later on, these circles begin to have a serious purpose for you. You are supported by them, and they provide a solid background for your own leadership or central role. Groups are fated.

FRIENDS AS EXTENDED FAMILY

Born with Cancer, the sign of home and family, in charge of your social life, your allies are very important to you. In fact, they can feel like relatives, and their home can feel like your home. As you know, you have Aquarius, the sign of the group, ruling your everyday life. From such groups come incredible opportunities if you are prepared to look for them. This is not your intention when you join with your friends; it's purely social. However, you are a practical Virgo and know that these people can also help.

PRODUCTIVE FRIENDSHIPS

These potentially productive friendships are there with the same group throughout or a changing parade of special circles of people. Aquarius, the sign which plays such a part in this, is about diversity within the community. It is an air sign, and you know how to circulate, of course, but also give everybody in the circle plenty of space to be an independent individual. From this comes something special; you would not be a down-to-earth Virgo unless you realized that together you can be productive and earn real rewards.

WHO SHARES YOUR BIRTHDAY?

Mary Shelley, born August 30, 1797

Warren Buffett, born August 30, 1930

Cameron Diaz, born August 30, 1972

AUGUST 31

WHO ARE YOU?

In astrology, the planets which rule the angles of your chart shape who you become. Pisces, the sign of daydreams, and Neptune, the planet of escapism, sit on one angle. On another we find Sagittarius, the sign associated with travel and even emigration. So you are not just a clever Virgo with cunning Mercury ruling you. You are actually strongly Piscean, something which those around you come to know well. That means you drift and float through life, getting away from the ordinary and everyday world if you can.

YOUR DESTINY

Neptune and Pisces are associated with people who like to inhabit their own space. This is something that others have to learn to understand and respect. You have a certain fascination for people who are drawn to you, for your imagination—which you express in the way you dress—and for your delight in evading the real world of bills to pay and correspondence to post. The cycles of time suggest you will always find yourself living an alternative existence on a regular basis and exploring your own private universe.

MERCURY THE TRICKSTER

Given your need to be far removed from the hard world of basic reality, it is quite understandable that you should use your ruling planet Mercury, with all his tricks and tactics, to have a peaceful life. In fact, you may become essential to others who rely upon your ability to remove issues before they take hold. This is rather like knowing board game moves before they are played or anticipating what others will do before they have even thought out their plans. Mercury rules your sign and also the top of your chart.

HOME IS YOUR SUITCASE

You have the soul of a natural migrant or explorer. Home is where you choose to open your suitcase or bag, and as you were born with Jupiter in charge of your sanctuaries and favorite spaces, you have all the vision, optimism, and farsightedness of this planet. The eagle is Jupiter's bird, and you also like to soar high above the map by plane. If you can't do that, you are quite content to walk your way out of the places you work or live in on a regular basis. It's the temptation of the unknown that keeps you happy.

WHO SHARES YOUR BIRTHDAY?

Van Morrison, born August 31, 1945
Richard Gere, born August 31, 1949
Tsai Ing-wen, born August 31, 1956

SEPTEMBER 1

WHO ARE YOU?

The group and its direction rules your career, success, and status in life. You are a Virgo Sun with work central to you. This also applies to unpaid work or academia. All your life you will see sudden and quite radical change at the top. Sometimes you will be promoted or appointed. Sometimes you will see a replacement of one leader with another—like lightning. When this happens, the team or community scatters, and you have to find your place with them. If it's you taking over, managing the circle is crucial.

YOUR DESTINY

Venus rules your financial sector; she also governs Taurus the Bull, the symbol of gold bullion and bull markets on Wall Street. You have what it takes to be rich on a regular basis. This is not just trickle income; it's lump sums. Venus is about valuing what you believe you are worth, so your ability to make the dream real depends on trusting that you deserve what might be yours. From these windfalls will come your ever-changing priorities for travel or home relocation, as another horizon always calls you.

YOUR CIRCLES

The group sign Aquarius has charge of your daily life and routine; as you have already read, the way people reassemble when there is a change at the top is very important your whole life through. As you become more experienced with people who are in circles or teams, societies, clubs, or bands, you also learn to play your part in bringing everybody together at the same time. Unless there is conscious navigation, such communities of people can quickly land in a heap. Like a great squadron you have to land in unison.

HOME IS SOMEWHERE ELSE

When you were born, Sagittarius ruled your home zone. It is the sign of exploration, new horizons, and often foreign places and people. Home is frequently somewhere else for you. Another reason for this is Mercury, the symbol of restless travelers, opposite this sector of your chart. Nothing and nobody is ever really settled in a permanent way for you. The family tree is ruled by Jupiter, the planet of excess. It may be large and need management, for example, or particular branches may go to excess, affecting you.

WHO SHARES YOUR BIRTHDAY?

Lily Tomlin, born September 1, 1939

Barry Gibb, born September 1, 1946

Zendaya, born September 1, 1996

Jungkook, born September 1, 1997

Tenzing Norgay Trainor, born September 1, 2001

SEPTEMBER 2

WHO ARE YOU?

You are an earth sign who only becomes grounded when you find your roots, family tree, ancestors, history, and the layers of your background—on either side of your heritage. There is a natural connection between Cancer, which rules your origins, and your own Virgo Sun. Without this, relationships can send you off-center. Neptune rules this zone of your chart, and feeling as if the anchor is missing emotionally can happen. The answer is claiming and holding your clan.

YOUR DESTINY

Your social life, groups, and networks are extremely important. Your daily routine, work, unpaid work, or academic career falls into place quite naturally when you play your part in a special circle. You are all typically very different, but you know how to give each other space. The mutual enjoyment might be enough, but there is also potential abundance to share, if you can live for tomorrow as well as the moment.

DEPARTURES AND ARRIVALS

The home, household, and family zone of your chart is ruled by Jupiter, a symbol of hope, optimism, and exploration—often as emigration. You often find yourself in the departures hall in your life because even though there are no guarantees in other places, being on the move always seems to be the most positive possibility for you. Sagittarius, ruled by Jupiter, describes your need to settle in places which promise a great deal, even if it's only on paper. You value the biggest of very broad horizons.

THE HERMIT

The Sun rules your sector of solitude. Being alone to discover yourself and the meaning of it all is something that lights your way. The Sun is one of the most important factors in the horoscope, and in your solar chart it rules Leo, one sign behind your own, Virgo—thus there is a focus on life behind the scenes for you. The force that operates behind the scenes may be God, buddhas, something you find impossible to put into words. As much as you are intensely sociable with your friends and particular circles, you also need to be a hermit in order to recharge.

WHO SHARES YOUR BIRTHDAY?
Billy Preston, born September 2, 1946
Keanu Reeves, born September 2, 1964
Salma Hayek, born September 2, 1966

SEPTEMBER 3

WHO ARE YOU?

You are the Virgo who places a high value on good health. This may be because experience teaches you that it is priceless. It may also be because you know that even if it costs you or others, there is no bigger reward than healing and help. Virgo is the sign in charge of the body, mind, and spirit. Thanks to an extended family which is regularly surrounded by money, there will always be more than enough to offer remedies and repairs. This applies to you or the people in your world. Abundance is there to share.

YOUR DESTINY

The planet Venus occupies two important places in your birth chart. She also rules evergreen love, and you have it. This may be within a long-term marriage or suggest ongoing affection for an ex. You might not always be aware of how much you lean on this perennial passion or strong feeling, yet it supports you all the time. As you have just read, money is always with you, Virgo, one way or another. With Venus ruling your shopping and collecting, your taste is impressive and important to you.

GIVING AND RECEIVING

Libra the Scales rules your income. Giving and receiving are about fairness for you—social justice or charity starting at home. You are extremely sensitive to those in need. As a result you are the donor or employer others come to depend on. Libra is a sign of symmetry and harmony. The difference between the haves and the have-nots influences your working life or personal life a great deal; you may have strong opinions on taxes, for example, or philanthropy. You identify strongly with people who have very little.

MONEY AS ACTION

A lot of people talk about helping out or paying their share, but you actually roll up your sleeves and do something about it. Aries, with all its person of action tactics, rules your shared business, charity, and finance sector. Mars is also there, and it is very much about carpe diem: good things happen when you seize the day. In your birth chart, Taurus and Scorpio, signs associated with shares, property, banks, insurance, benefits, and currency, have flowing aspects to your Virgo Sun. This all comes so naturally to you.

WHO SHARES YOUR BIRTHDAY?

Ferdinand Porsche, born September 3, 1875
Alan Ladd, born September 3, 1913
Charlie Sheen, born September 3, 1965

SEPTEMBER 4

WHO ARE YOU?

The classic Virgo signature of steady, dedicated work is written in your horoscope. You are a grounded earth sign and productive all your life. You are also a natural explorer or even migrant, with Sagittarius and its link with travel and relocation ruling your home zone. When you look for hope, you scan the map. You are always welcome wherever you land, because of your talent, skill, or ability. In fact, you are a firm believer in relaunching elsewhere and are sympathetic to those who must do this, too.

YOUR DESTINY

Virgo is the sign which rules health, well-being, mental health, and the body, mind, and spirit. In your birth chart, your own Sun sign governs the sector of doctors, nurses, therapists, and medical science. You are also a practical person who knows that the answer is always financial, through business sometimes or charity. You are also ruled by Mercury, the planet of strategy and answers. You think your way through these issues for other people who are so much in need, even as you're preparing to do something about it.

RELIABLE AND DEDICATED

You are reliable and dedicated within your chosen field or line of work, and the routine business of delivering for others comes naturally to you. In fact, the only issue to ever stop you is your own well-being. As you know, overall good health is priceless. You place a very high value on energy and life force, with Mars and Aries ruling everything that is precious to you. Others admire what you can do in a sustained way. It's not just the financial rewards that motivate you; it's a job that feels like a passion.

GROUP DYNAMICS

The groups which affect your life—all your life—teach you how to play your part in bringing different people with different goals together. Aquarius is the sign overseeing your sector of paid and unpaid achievement. This is the water bearer who motivates people to pool their resources. Uranus is also in charge of this zone of your chart, so you deal with issues about fierce independence and individuality—which this planet rules—in order to find harmony. When you achieve it, the results are astonishing.

WHO SHARES YOUR BIRTHDAY?

Linda McCartney, born September 4, 1941

Mark Ronson, born September 4, 1975

Beyoncé Knowles, born September 4, 1981

SEPTEMBER 5

WHO ARE YOU?

You were born with Venus, the planet of relationships, ruling everything that is so precious to you it is priceless. You will explore solid gold bonds with others in numerous ways all your life. Sometimes it's with partners; sometimes it's with groups. The passionate Scorpio governs the journeys you make, and a long-distance lover is a definite possibility. There are two 1s in your numerology, so you have one-on-one connections where both of you must meet halfway in order to feel equal, too.

YOUR DESTINY

Your daily life, workload, unpaid work, or study revolves around the group. This may be a network of Buddhists or a community of artists, a swimming team or a professional association. Aquarius with all its diversity in the circle rules this area of your life. This is a wonderful part of your world from your teenage years forward. It's the gift that goes on giving, Virgo, as there is a constant supply of what everybody needs on a soul level to feel fulfilled. You share a common source emotionally.

THE UNREAL REAL WORLD

The zodiac sign opposite your own is Pisces, the two fish, ruled by Neptune, in charge of all vacations from the everyday. The unreal real world is where you feel happiest. This opposition in your solar chart is one of the reasons people might mistake your Sun sign. Yet you are pulled toward the escapism of Pisces and away from who or what grounds you. Ironically, this kind of down-to-earth response can really help you, but then it would mean abandoning your essentially bohemian and self-expressive nature.

DEALING WITH ENIGMAS

You have quite a water sign–dominated chart, and feelings, impressions, and emotions have a strong pull on you. This can present you with people who are enigmas. There is no handbook or explanation for the relationship. As a Virgo, you might try to solve their puzzles with your mind, but the answer for these emotional mysteries is to do something practical and shift both yourself and the situation away from escapism and back toward the real world. The memories of babies, born or never born, is the reality.

WHO SHARES YOUR BIRTHDAY?

King Louis XIV of France, born September 5, 1638

Freddie Mercury, born September 5, 1946

Michael Keaton, born September 5, 1951

SEPTEMBER 6

WHO ARE YOU?

You were born with Libra the Scales in charge of finances, business, and property in your chart. You are the Virgo who always knows they must ground plans in the real world. However, you are also born to learn about what is fair or equal, when it comes to legacies, trust funds, mortgages, marriage, divorce, children, and inheritance. Libra's scales must be balanced. Always at the heart of this is a two-way relationship, usually between intimate partners. It's a lifelong lesson in sharing money.

YOUR DESTINY

The business sign Scorpio and investment sign Taurus both make strong angles to your Virgo Sun. Taurus in particular is about taking a down-to-earth approach to even a modest sum of money. You have the view that you can do a lot with even a little, and it serves you all your life. The power planet Pluto rules the way you think about your life, and you can be quite fixed about how to spend or negotiate, as the two financial signs making patterns in your chart are also fixed. You drive a very hard bargain.

THE POTENTIAL OF PROMISING IDEAS

You are ruled by the messenger Mercury and always have something to show and tell, even from adolescence. As you grow older, you realize that as an earth sign, there is no point in merely gazing at what is on paper or on your computer. You have to find the right environment for your idea, talent, skill, or project. This also comes partly from Sagittarius, the sign of the explorer and exporter, charged with your place in the world. Once you realize the answer is moving yourself and the plan, the success can begin.

FINDING A SHARED VISION

On the day you were born, the two fish represented by Pisces (swimming in opposite directions) opposed your sign. One-on-one relationships, like a marriage, are central to your finances. However, within group, team, or community situations, you must also find a way to allow yourself to be an independent individual, even as everyone else also wants to come first. Aquarius with all its diversity within a circle rules your daily life. When you can incorporate that into a shared vision, the results can be remarkable.

WHO SHARES YOUR BIRTHDAY?

Jane Addams, born September 6, 1860

Roger Waters, born September 6, 1943

Idris Elba, born September 6, 1972

SEPTEMBER 7

WHO ARE YOU?

Virgo, you are the alchemist who mixes partnerships and duets of all kinds in your life, drawing strength from the group. Pisces rules all two-way relationships for you, and as a water sign, it describes fluid connections with no boundaries. There is something spiritual about these double acts. They are often friendships drawn from your social circles or contributing to them. Another water sign governs your networks, and again there are no boundaries. The heart of your birth chart is Aquarius, the sign of community, diversity, and equality. There, you have the alchemical potential to turn base metals to gold.

YOUR DESTINY

The red planet Mars rules your drive to earn money or save it. This is where you are energetic and motivated, Virgo. You must then decide what you are going to do with everything you have pushed for. In your birth chart, the practical Taurus, another earth sign like your own, describes your life budget—who or what you will not sell out for, who or what is so precious that it is priceless. Grounded in your own values, you are fated to be financially comfortable, if not wealthy. Figuring out the price tags according to your own principles is a lifelong mission.

THE PUZZLE OF RELATIONSHIPS

The watery Scorpio governs your financial relationships and partnerships. Water is about deep emotion and great feeling in astrology, and although you are a practical earth sign, Virgo, when it comes to sex and romance you are often at sea. This is your challenge. Finding the right place for unique duets which do not tick any boxes is important. Babies who were—or were not—born are the backstory. Saturn with all his heavy reminders of the past rules your sector of parenthood. Love can baffle you like a jigsaw puzzle until you realize the answer is to change yourself and transform.

YOUR TALENTS TRAVEL

You are gifted with talents or skills which show huge potential all your life. Like any practical Virgo, you want to plant them somewhere they can grow. The income and business signs Taurus and Scorpio also happen to rule your regional and international travel. The sign of foreigners and foreign places, Sagittarius, has charge of your home zone. So you feel quite at home putting down temporary or permanent roots in distant locations if you have to. Seeing your budding brain waves or qualifications prosper in other regions or countries is one of your most satisfying rewards.

WHO SHARES YOUR BIRTHDAY?

Queen Elizabeth I, born September 7, 1533

Edith Sitwell, born September 7, 1887

Chrissie Hynde, born September 7, 1951

SEPTEMBER 8

WHO ARE YOU?

Your numerology suggests you will always find yourself with your opposite number on the same path but faced with two different destinations. This is a lifelong pattern, Virgo. It will be personal or professional. You were also born with the emotional Scorpio in charge of your journeys. When your feelings tell you to leave, that is exactly what you do. Pluto, the planet of transformation, rules these solitary sabbaticals. Everything changes when you go.

YOUR DESTINY

You know that the number 1 making 2 is in your numerology profile. You do face regular and repeated crossroads in your life when you must choose between west and east, left and right, or other binary choices. This can be challenging, as you are always drawn toward symmetry and harmony. Libra rules everything you value most highly. You are really like a human set of scales trying to balance everything and everybody, including yourself. When you finally choose, though, it reshapes your life.

TOGETHER OR APART

Libra in charge of what is priceless to you suggests that those duets you end up in—where both of you are the same but different—challenge you more than anything else. It need not necessarily be the obvious example of a marriage or work partnership every time. As you become more experienced, you will realize there are many creative and thoughtful ways to make twos work even if there seems to be only one way forward. Business, finances, charity, or property is usually the reason you can't procrastinate.

THE WORLD CITIZEN

Your home is the whole world. Sagittarius, the sign of the traveler, migrant, and explorer, rules where you feel you belong. Jupiter, with all his abundant choices and excess of options, also oversees this part of your life. The only difficulty for you with your journeys or plans to move is choosing. Venus governs your leaning toward distant places on the map. She is a symbol of desire, and you will often make your choices about destinations or nationalities based on who or what you fall in love with, Virgo.

WHO SHARES YOUR BIRTHDAY?

Mary, mother of Jesus, born September 8, 20 BCE

Patsy Cline, born September 8, 1932

Pink, born September 8, 1979

SEPTEMBER 9

WHO ARE YOU?

You have a gardener's soul, but you patiently grow money instead—not on trees but in your bank account. Virgo, you are a grounded earth sign with Saturn, the symbol of time, in a perfect trine to your Virgo Sun. You also have Venus, the natural ruler of finance, looking over your earning capacity, investments, business interests, and property. With care, you end up being wealthy enough to help others. Perhaps charity begins at home for you. If not, you have a professional or philanthropic calling to give or pay.

YOUR DESTINY

There is a delightful connection between Cancer, the sign of belonging and emotional security, and your own Virgo Sun showing in your birth chart. What everybody dreams of—a happy home and household—is in your destiny. It may happen more than once, depending on your complete astrological chart with time and year of birth. Jupiter with all his good fortune and abundance also rules your real estate and extended family. Jupiter offers more than enough, so this may be a big property or huge garden.

THE COMPLEX GROUP

Your daily life, routine, and work ethic come under the auspices of Aquarius, the sign associated with the complex group. Finding yourself part of a community which could go in either direction—toward the heights or in swift descent—becomes a regular part of life from your teenage years onward. It may be a team or club then. Later on, this need to unite those in the circle could be professional. You will be in collectives where people are very good at giving space to each other, but need to actually draw closer to achieve success.

THE JUSTICE OF SHARING

Libra the Scales is in charge of your finances. You may be the generous employer who pays staff in a spirit of fair play and not with an eye on the bottom line. You are an obvious candidate for a charity donor. You may feel that it is your closest relatives or friends who deserve the leveling up you can direct their way. You are prepared to be enormously patient when cultivating your assets. Once you feel secure enough—you may become wealthy, Virgo—you can only live with yourself if you help those who need it.

WHO SHARES YOUR BIRTHDAY?

Leo Tolstoy, born September 9, 1828
Colonel Sanders, born September 9, 1890
Hugh Grant, born September 9, 1960
D'Pharaoh Woon-A-Tai, born September 9, 2001

SEPTEMBER 10

WHO ARE YOU?

The numeral 1 appears in your numerology profile. You are the solo operator who is capable of great things—by yourself. You are a Virgo who does best with method and order, as well as a tidy desk and a sense of ritual. You operate in quite a different way when it comes to money. Aries, with its sense of mission, and Mars, with all its need for adventure, rule your search for what may or may not be there. Business or other kinds of treasure hunts do require a strictly practical approach.

YOUR DESTINY

You are an earth sign whose need for stability and security is at odds with your urge to relocate or emigrate. Sagittarius, the sign which rules foreign people and places—or just distant horizons in your own country—also rules your home. The family tree is also at odds with your tidy Virgo side. There's nothing particularly orderly about some of its branches, and you are fated to regularly face the choice of staying to do the work or leaving for somewhere else on the map. You take an energetic approach to either, Virgo.

WORKING WONDERS

You have what it takes to work wonders, using your dedicated Virgo Sun to take the raw elements of your plans, resources, and projects and craft them into something most people cannot duplicate. The planet Pluto describes transformation, and your thought processes are usually about making something quite new and remarkable from what is there on your desk or table. The repetition of the number 1 in your birth date suggests you are unique. You are a one-off who can create magical results by yourself.

CHILDREN AND FUTURE GENERATIONS

If you become a parent, then your offspring will fulfill your goals and perhaps exceed your ambitions. Capricorn rules parenthood for you, and it is the sign which seeks the ultimate peaks and high points. Through nurturing children, grandchildren, and so on, you achieve this. If you do not become a parent, then you will leave a different kind of legacy, ensuring that young relatives or godchildren, for example, and perhaps generation after generation of young people reward you. Youth dazzles you.

WHO SHARES YOUR BIRTHDAY?

Karl Lagerfeld, born September 10, 1933
Colin Firth, born September 10, 1960
Jack Ma, born September 10, 1964

SEPTEMBER 11

WHO ARE YOU?

You have the numeral 1 twice in your numerology chart. Coming first and being number one are a regular high point in your life. This may be number one in the bestseller lists, for example, or the first choice in an election. Being the top executive of a corporation is another example. You are frequently the ace in fields where there can be only one winner. You may be the first to earn a scholarship at your school, for example, or the winner in particular competitions. You deserve first place.

YOUR DESTINY

Juggling finances, business, valuables, property, or charity is a lifetime challenge—balancing budgets, for example, or deciding what is fair and equal. Libra, the sign of the scales, rules your sector of money. At the other end of the zodiac we find Aries, ruling joint undertakings, like mortgages or investments. This pattern in your life ties into sexual partnerships, and finding a harmonious arrangement is a lifetime quest, either with the same person or more than one. Libra is about two sides at opposite ends.

TWO JOURNEYS

This partnership or these partnerships are central to your existence. Deciding if life is to be about two separate journeys or one will create a fork in the road that changes you—and more than once. There is a huge amount of feeling and emotion when this happens, as Neptune rules your sector of marriage, common-law marriage, professional partnerships—and separation. Neptune governs the element of water and the ebb and flow of everything we feel but may find hard to articulate. Practical plans work best.

THE MYSTERY OF RELATIONSHIPS

Neptune is associated with mystery, and as you have read, this planet rules your relationships. Feeling all at sea is a common outcome with your birth date, and the solution is always practical. In fact, you are an earth sign able to put both feet on the ground if you try. When relationships of all kinds mystify you, the solution is always to move both yourself and the situation somewhere else. Trying to fathom the unfathomable is not realistic over the long term, and whenever you encounter these Neptunian situations, it is time to ground.

WHO SHARES YOUR BIRTHDAY?

D. H. Lawrence, born September 11, 1885

Jessica Mitford, born September 11, 1917

Moby, born September 11, 1965

SEPTEMBER 12

WHO ARE YOU?

Your birth chart shows the finance sign Taurus the Bull in a solid trine to your Virgo Sun. Both are earth signs, and you have a practical, grounded approach to money. Taurus rules gold bullion and the charging bull sculpture near Wall Street as well as bull markets. It is also a fixed sign. You are meticulous about your money, as any Virgo might be, with a gift for small details. You also find it hard to change your position with business, property, charity, and so on. Yet you feel more secure when you don't move.

YOUR DESTINY

Libra rules everything you value most in life. Libra the Scales describes the choice you have to make about west or east, left or right, one direction or its opposite. Libra has a reputation for producing procrastination because it is so hard to pick without disturbing the equilibrium. You are a Virgo whose destiny is shaped by these long periods of waiting and wondering between decisions. Of course, you can sit in the middle forever, but it's more enlightening to choose. Moving for work or home is typical.

PEOPLE POWER

As you know, feeling settled and secure is very important to you. You gain this sense of certainty when you find the right group to support and back you. This comes from Aquarius, the sign of the inner circle and people power, ruling your daily life. You can keep both feet on the ground as the earth sign you are when you feel you have a solid gold entourage, club, team, or committee. The numeral 1 is hidden in your birth date, so you may lead them or front them. You may be one with the many.

FIRM BOUNDARIES

The tough Aries and Mars, the planet of defensive boundaries, both show what is most valuable to you. This is what is priceless to you, and so your characteristically firm approach to life is quite noticeable. You're an authority and leader, intimidating to some. This again suits the 1 in your numerology profile. Alone, you can be a force to be reckoned with, even without that all-important group. The other aspect of life you value very highly is partnership. It's always at the back of your mind, Virgo.

WHO SHARES YOUR BIRTHDAY?

Irene Joliot-Curie, born September 12, 1897
Jesse Owens, born September 12, 1913
Barry White, born September 12, 1944

SEPTEMBER 13

WHO ARE YOU?

You were born with the earth sign Taurus in a strong pattern to your Virgo Sun; you are also an earth sign—grounded and connected to nature, birds, and animals. Taurus gives you the money to settle into the right environment and enjoy it, too. You have Neptune opposite your sign as well. Cruising and drifting through life—either actually on the water or symbolically on vacation from the real world—you exist in your own space. The only way others can really join you is with your permission to climb aboard.

YOUR DESTINY

As you've read, Taurus the Bull—who rules bull markets and gold bullion—makes a comfortable angle to your own Virgo Sun. You are fortunate with real estate and the family, too, as Jupiter governs your home zone. Jupiter is an ancient symbol of luck: right time, right place, right circumstances. You may be a gardener, natural farmer, or just good at investing and reinvesting what you own and have earned. This practical approach is in complete contrast with that other side of your personality: the escape artist.

MONEY AND THE FAMILY

The legacy you leave to a younger generation is at the heart of what matters to you—literally, what counts. This goes beyond the numbers an accountant sees. Then there is the legacy left to you. The other earth sign, Capricorn, rules future generations in your life, and again it helps to ground you in the real world where the money goes round. Saturn also oversees any children, teenagers, or forthcoming heirs to the family dynasty. This is the sign of grandparents and great-grandparents who dominate any household.

FRIENDS AS THE GATEWAY

The sign which rules Virgo's natural astrological house is very important as it shows where you feel most welcomed in life—and welcoming. This is Aquarius, the symbol of the group. The friends and allies here can feel like part of the extended family to you. They are the gateway to so much of what you want. In fact, it is only a compatible crew who can ever tempt you to jump ship and leave your own vacation from reality to join them. This helps to bring you back down to earth and gives you an anchor and others to be with.

WHO SHARES YOUR BIRTHDAY?

Roald Dahl, born September 13, 1916
Michael Johnson, born September 13, 1967
Stella McCartney, born September 13, 1971

SEPTEMBER 14

WHO ARE YOU?

You have probably read that Virgo rules work. You are a natural craftsperson who doesn't just meet expectations, you also produce solid gold results time after time, which are a tribute to your dedication as well as your commitment to quality. You can also do more than pay your way in life as a result. Taurus the Bull, which rules bull markets and gold bullion, makes a perfect trine to your Virgo Sun. You profit from being mindful of what others expect and know how to build your own rewards.

YOUR DESTINY

You may or may not have children, but your ideas, plans, and projects speak to the next generation and those which follow. The sign of authority and solid status, Capricorn, rules those who come after you and all subsequent younger people through time. Virgo, what you have to offer can be planted for the future, no matter if it is a lesson or a concept on a computer, a plan on paper, or your own words. This area of your chart is rather like a field of sunflowers, which when planted can be the gift that keeps on giving.

FINDING A DIRECTION

It is quite true that you value balance. Libra the Scales rules everything that is so precious to you it is priceless. This need to respect both sides of a situation, though, can mean you seldom choose quickly at all. You are a procrastinator, for all that you can work hard. This may be choosing between the sides of your family tree. It might be between west and east or left and right. When you are finally able to change yourself, change your life, and find a direction, you may even still sit in the middle.

GROUP POLITICS

One of the most important areas of your chart is actually linked to Virgo, and it describes daily life, routine, and your lifestyle. Here you find yourself dealing with the hive mind within a group on a regular basis. In your solar chart Aquarius, with all its focus on tribes, shows you why dealing with a circle of people is so important. Sometimes you are one against several. Sometimes you are actually inside the community of like-minded people pitted against an outsider. Through this you learn how to unite.

WHO SHARES YOUR BIRTHDAY?

James Wilson, born September 14, 1742

Margaret Sanger, born September 14, 1879

Amy Winehouse, born September 14, 1983

SEPTEMBER 15

WHO ARE YOU?

Pisces rules your partnerships with others, and no matter if this is a marriage, a professional partnership, or a unique duet, you find these double acts bring out the escapist in you. Both Pisces the Fish and its ruler Neptune are associated with holidays from the real world. As you might expect, both sign and planet are associated with the beach and ocean. Your most important partnerships keep you forever young, forever fascinating—and always a mystery to those on the outside.

YOUR DESTINY

The choice to merge with one or more groups is always there, Virgo. Your horoscope is set up in such a way that you find it tempting to lose yourself among like-minded people, no matter if this is a charity or a professional organization. You feel at home with clubs, teams, bands, charities, associations, and so on. Cancer forms a favorable angle in your chart to your Virgo Sun. Cancer is a symbol of family ties, and you find it easy to relate to a circle of allies and friends as an extended clan. Within the group, you find all that is spiritual and even sacred in your life.

THE WORLD CITIZEN

Your greatest challenge is to take your ideas, plans, projects, or qualifications and find the right part of the map to nurture them. You are a world citizen even as a teenager and well into old age and will measure your success in life by your achievements abroad. The grounded, fixed, down-to-earth Taurus rules your sector of travel, relocation, export, and emigration. This can sometimes make it hard to act:

to pack your bags and follow through. Learning how to make your visions real in other places is your task.

THE PEACEMAKER

As a Virgo, you are ruled by Mercury—a symbol of people who are clever, cunning, and quick on their feet. You are the peacemaker and problem-solver who can use their sharp mind to organize a truce. You are a one-person version of the UN Peacekeeping Forces, and this is shown by the high value you place on balance, harmony, and fair play. Libra governs everything you find precious or priceless in life, and as Libra the Scales is associated with conflict resolution, solving people's problems is your reward.

WHO SHARES YOUR BIRTHDAY?

Marco Polo, born September 15, 1254
Agatha Christie, born September 15, 1890
Jessye Norman, born September 15, 1945
Chimamanda Ngozi Adichie, born September 15, 1977
Prince Harry, Duke of Sussex, born September 15, 1984

SEPTEMBER 16

WHO ARE YOU?

You were born under Mercury the Messenger, the ruler of Virgo. You are more likely to use the media or the internet or advanced technology than a scroll and horse to get the word out. You have the same ability to reach people, though, as others are fascinated by your message. As an earth sign, you do best when you are grounded and centered. This comes easily when you claim your family tree, heritage, and ancestors. A solid link to Cancer, the sign of relatives and roots, makes a strong connection to your Virgo Sun.

YOUR DESTINY

The planet of freedom and radical change is Uranus, and he rules the most important sector of your horoscope—where both Mercury and Virgo hold sway. You are fated to have a number of breakthroughs in your life, when you also break away from who or what restricts you to find liberation. This may be for personal or professional reasons, but it is part of your fate and also helps form your personality. People come to know you as the free spirit who uses intuition and strategy to find liberty.

AMBITIONS FOR FUTURE GENERATIONS

The solidly ambitious Capricorn rules any children you have, young relatives, godchildren, younger generations, and the young people of tomorrow. You take your role and responsibility here seriously, and it is part of the reason you are so impressive. Others see you as an authority with the young. You may or may not become a parent, but you have plans, projects, or Mercurial messages to offer. These can be planted for tomorrow, the way that you nurture future adults, their children, and their children's children.

THE TOOLS AND THE TABLETOP

Virgo is the sign most associated with method, routine, and order. None of this is ever a mundane business, though, as you are deeply intuitive and seem to pick up information and knowledge out of thin air. You are a powerful communicator with Pluto ruling your sector of words, images, and ideas. You already know your own planet is Mercury, so you were made for an audience, class, or readership. Organizing your resources and pulling together your tools on the tabletop or desk begins the magic.

WHO SHARES YOUR BIRTHDAY?

Lauren Bacall, born September 16, 1924
B. B. King, born September 16, 1925
Mickey Rourke, born September 16, 1952

SEPTEMBER 17

WHO ARE YOU?

You have the numeral 1 in your numerology profile, and although groups will be a substantial part of your life, you are strong enough to be a single-minded solo operator as well. The earth sign Virgo is where your Sun falls, and another earth sign, Taurus, makes a comfortable angle to this. Security and stability are very important. Pluto rules the way you think. Dramatic, Shakespearean themes turn up in your life on a regular basis. Every final act is a first act. This makes you spiritual or just philosophical.

YOUR DESTINY

The sign of the twins, Gemini, rules your peak achievements. You go between twin cities, regions, or countries as a normal part of life. This is your destiny often enough that you become quite used to seeing two sides or two points of view. Pluto not only influences the way you think, it also governs your journeys. You don't just travel or relocate; you use these periods in your life to gain control and find empowerment. You are a force to be reckoned with, partly because of your mastery of two different places on the map.

VENUS IN YOUR CHART

Venus rules everything that is valuable to you. This planet is a symbol of everlasting desire in astrology, and through her link to Libra, the sign of partnership, she reminds you that love is for life. This applies no matter if the relationship itself does not last or the person in question passes out of your world. The truth of this perennial affection is at the core of who you are. As you know, you are an earth sign. Nature, gardens, beautiful surroundings, and a well-designed environment also make you who you are.

SOLIDARITY AND TEAM SPIRIT

One of the most important zones of your chart is under the charge of Uranus with all his rebellions, revolutionary moves, group focus, and need for team spirit. You will sometimes be one of many against an opponent in a clash of ideas. Equally, you will find yourself on the outside, pushing back against the hive mind in a particular circle. Knowing both sides of this familiar story from your teenage years forward helps you become skilled at finding solutions for solidarity. You have what it takes to reunite groups and establish consensus.

WHO SHARES YOUR BIRTHDAY?

Hank Williams, born September 17, 1923
Anne Bancroft, born September 17, 1931
Baz Luhrmann, born September 17, 1962

SEPTEMBER 18

WHO ARE YOU?

Your life is strongly influenced by money—looking for it, earning it, and making it work for you. This comes from the two finance signs of Scorpio and Taurus making patterns with your own Virgo Sun. Perhaps it's no wonder that you also want to take vacations from the real world on a regular basis. In fact, you can be mistaken for a Pisces with all your interest in your own universe. You have tremendous self-expression and may dress to suit your imagination. Others learn to let this side of you have space.

YOUR DESTINY

The cycles of time in both your solar and natal chart show that you will juggle your budget at regular intervals because of unpredictable economic conditions. This will be within your own country and in the wider world. Doing this makes you remember you are a Virgo and born to organize and restructure. Libra rules your bank account, so managing two sides, seeing it both ways, finding harmony with two accounts, people, or priorities are your task. You can and do find a solid gold income but only with effort.

POTENTIAL TREASURE

Rather like a pirate with a map, you go looking for potential treasure all your life, too. This may be a property which is just a plan on paper or an idea which you think may or may not be what you are looking for financially. Scorpio and Pluto, with all their associations with mystery, rule the way you think and schedule your life. Part of the appeal for you of these quests is the unknown. However, on a practical note, Virgo, you need to find the right professionals to give you objective advice to save yourself time.

QUALITY AND DELIVERY

Virgo is associated with a formula, recipe, or routine, and you do best, both in terms of soul satisfaction and financial reward, when you arrive at what works. This may be reels of film or football scores. Your own personal birth chart in full will reveal where your skills and talents are. As a dependable earth sign, you are grounded in the real world when you have to be. The other, escapist side of your nature can then enjoy your own reality. When working and earning, you are the solid powerhouse people come to expect.

WHO SHARES YOUR BIRTHDAY?

Samuel Johnson, born September 18, 1709

Greta Garbo, born September 18, 1905

Ronaldo, born September 18, 1976

SEPTEMBER 19

WHO ARE YOU?

Virgo is ruled by Mercury, the messenger of the gods. You are a messenger, teacher, preacher, lecturer, or voice across all mediums and media. You are a natural leader in all matters which speak to the soul, psyche, or spirit with Leo, the sign of authority, governing all that you believe. People follow you—until they don't—but you tend to have a committed base. It works best when you are reading from something or repeating something that runs deep. The powerful Pluto rules your zone of internet, media, microphone, and telephone.

YOUR DESTINY

Your sense of belonging to a family tree and a fixed part of the world is always in question. Sagittarius, which rules travel, relocation, and emigration, is in charge of the sector of your horoscope which describes your roots and foundations. You could be on the move all your life for this reason or make two or three firm commitments to new regions or completely different countries. The ground beneath your feet is never quite solid, even so, and you are destined to always have those feet turned in different directions.

DISTANCES TO CROSS

Long-distance bonds of all kinds, involving all sorts of emotional ties, are something you have to face repeatedly in your lifetime. As mentioned, the sign ruling foreigners and foreign countries is Sagittarius, and this has charge of the home in your solar chart. This raises the question of commitment on both sides. It applies no matter if this is a romance, a marriage, or even a family connection. You or the other person must always face questions about travel or relocation when you cross those emotional bridges. This is a lifelong pattern.

TWO CITIES OR TWO COUNTRIES

When you have overcome the challenges of what home should mean to you—and how far you should go to meet people halfway across the map—you will find your rewards in a settled, nomadic life. This may be because you go between New York and London, say, or just between one city and another. Mercury rules two key parts of your chart: one is your own sign Virgo, governing your sector of image, but also Gemini and your zone of success. Twin cities, twin countries, twin goals are there, if you reach for them.

WHO SHARES YOUR BIRTHDAY?

Pablita Velarde, born September 19, 1918
Brian Epstein, born September 19, 1934
Jeremy Irons, born September 19, 1948
Nile Rodgers, born September 19, 1952

SEPTEMBER 20

WHO ARE YOU?

You have natural authority and look like a leader, because you are. You are more comfortable when you have money and hang on and hold on tightly to this security as it is part of the reason you can afford to be confident about your position in life. It is different when it comes to the family tree—which can divide you—or your own plans and projects. In fact, one of the great lessons of your life is to find a system that works, even if it means delegating, so you can plant your inspiration or talent where it can grow.

YOUR DESTINY

You were born with a horoscope delivering comfortable income or savings, and this forms part of your character. As you've read, being shored up by enough investments, possessions, and everything growing makes you feel confident in your own skin. This balances the slight insecurity there when you realize that the only way your plans will ever be as impressive as you are is when you develop a method of grounding them. People who negotiate with you find you rather fixed to deal with.

THE FAMILY TREE

At regular intervals in your life you will have to choose between one side of the family tree and another. This may be either of your parents on your side or your partner's side. The choice may be spiritual, emotional, and psychological. It can also be geographical, so there is literally a choice about relocating or traveling. This also makes you who you are. There is a hesitation about your approach to life—a long dress rehearsal, if you like. This does make you enlightened, but it certainly makes you wait.

BEAUTY IN YOUR WORLD

You are drawn to beauty no matter if it is Mother Nature's design of trees and rivers or filling your wardrobe with stunning designs. It is the same with your home, where you need to have what appeals to your impressive taste. Venus has a great impact on your astrological chart. She rules Taurus and Libra and is also a symbol of what is reflected in the mirror as well as all decoration of oneself or the furniture. Venus is also representative of evergreen love. Once your heart is involved, it is involved for all time.

WHO SHARES YOUR BIRTHDAY?

Jean-Jacques Dessalines, born September 20, 1758

Sophia Loren, born September 20, 1934

George R. R. Martin, born September 20, 1948

SEPTEMBER 21

WHO ARE YOU?

You have Mercury, the planet of projects, plots, plans, and proposals, influencing both Virgo and Gemini in your astrological chart. There is no question about your having a message to carry; the only issue is how to choose and how to delegate. Another planet, Venus, holds sway over your chart through Taurus and Libra. These two planets and four signs create patterns which suggest you are not only prepared to shoulder a multitude of tasks; you are also a true romantic, no matter if you know it or not. Evergreen love never dies for you.

YOUR DESTINY

Not many people are born rich. Your whole astrological chart based on your time, place, and date of birth will reveal if that is the case for you, but you have a powerful understanding of what it feels like to be in need, as well as what it feels like to give generously or pay your fair share. A strong sense of justice and equality is behind this. As a result, you may have strong views on charity or taxation, social welfare or more personal issues. There are deeper questions about what is really owed on all sides, and time will show you that.

METHOD AND ORDER

Mercury cannot be heard, read, or understood unless he has some method and order. You need that, too, so you do not become overloaded with too many plans on paper or on the computer. You tend to put one foot in front of the other and keep going, but experience will show you that this can make the journey to your goals quite challenging. Rather than focus entirely on an objective you cannot always see, life may teach you that the road itself has to be something you can enjoy. Learning to delegate or ditch transforms you.

YOUR OWN REALITY

There is a part of you so tied to work, chores, and tasks that it is not surprising that you have a completely different side prone to escapism, at home with your own reality, and floating in a separate universe from everybody else. The mind-altering substance is yourself. This can make you a fascinating figure to others who are already impressed by your taste and style; beyond that, they also have to admire the way you are always seen from a distance. You need your separate space, and others need to know it.

WHO SHARES YOUR BIRTHDAY?

H. G. Wells, born September 21, 1866

Leonard Cohen, born September 21, 1934

Stephen King, born September 21, 1947

SEPTEMBER 22

WHO ARE YOU?

You are the success story who makes it to the top of a system—whatever that system happens to be. It may be school or university, sports or music, business or high society. Even when you are young, you appear to be older than you are. You are a serious person who makes a serious impact. You look as if you mean it, because you do. You are ambitious to be at the top, no matter if this is in your profession, your unpaid calling in life, or another way of reaching the peak of the establishment. You're a leader. You have authority and presence.

YOUR DESTINY

You may have been born into a position of influence, thanks to your family, or acquired it because of your achievements. You never lack ideas or projects; the challenge for you is planting them securely where they can thrive. In fact, you are known for being the person "most likely to" as you always have something to pitch or produce. Figuring out the strategy beyond the concept is the hard part, but it becomes easier over time. By a quirk of your horoscope, what you succeed with has to happen somewhere else—never at home.

EXPORTING THE PASSION

Nobody could doubt your passion and enthusiasm for your brain waves or plans. You hold excitement in your body and present as someone who is genuine about their visions for what might be. As you've read, it's your destiny to need to export this. The journey can sometimes preoccupy you at the start, either because you are hesitant to make a move or you race into it without preparation. In both cases the solution, as you will discover, is to look at the middle of it all. This is where strategy comes into it. The reward? Huge success.

BOOKS AND COMPUTERS

You will always move in a world of books and computers. Readers and writers, scribblers and internet citizens surround your chart through Mercury the Messenger, which rules both Virgo and Gemini. Perhaps this is why you are an idea person. Putting your theories into words is something you feel born to do. Life will show you that every high point becomes a low but every low point also becomes a high. This random and predictably unpredictable Wheel of Fortune makes you quite philosophical, taking the long view of the high points.

WHO SHARES YOUR BIRTHDAY?

Anne of Cleves, born September 22, 1515

Andrea Bocelli, born September 22, 1958

Joan Jett, born September 22, 1958

SEPTEMBER 23

WHO ARE YOU?

You are most private when it comes to relationships, and only you really understand your processes. With your plans and projects, it's a different matter, as anybody can see your intentions for children, teenagers, and the young generations which succeed them. You are capable of total transformation emotionally and are one of the few people who can recycle and repair partnerships, for example, which are no more. You are also capable of turning your back and walking away from people who have let you down, launching into new life episodes.

YOUR DESTINY

You will find you are financially comfortable with enough to invest or enjoy, thanks to the cycles of time in your horoscope picking up Taurus and Scorpio, the money signs. Understanding what money can and cannot do is part of the path. It can help with health issues but not necessarily replace the pricelessness of well-being. Money can have spiritual or even religious meaning, being a conduit for charity and kindness. You are extremely sensitive to people in need and will be in a position to help. You know how to give and give.

WEALTH AND SECURITY

As you know, the money signs Taurus and Scorpio matter in your astrological chart. Both are fixed signs, and Taurus is also an earth sign, grounded in the real world. Once you find security, you slow down so that you can stop and smell the roses but also measure your pace. As you are so sympathetic toward people in need, you are the first to help in any way you can. Sometimes it's through simple giving. On a more complex level you may take an interest in taxation, for example, or charity or insurance. You genuinely enjoy your wealth and use it well.

FUTURE GENERATIONS

The most authority and presence you have come from your own or other people's children. Even if you never become a parent, you can guide, mentor, and lead younger people. It does not just end with the current generation either, as your message, ideas, or plans can take hold and expand for years into the future. This means there will always be a youthful audience or readership for your thoughts. If you secure these and turn them into growing concerns, they will also expand over the years and still reach students of all ages tomorrow.

WHO SHARES YOUR BIRTHDAY?

Augustus, born September 23, 63 BCE

Ray Charles, born September 23, 1930

Bruce Springsteen, born September 23, 1949

SEPTEMBER 24

WHO ARE YOU?

You are a Libra Sun who also has Pluto, the planet of transformation, in charge of everything you value most highly in life. You have what it takes to reconstruct and rebuild or walk away and create. Life will often take you to that point where you have no choice but to summon up all the willpower Pluto represents and either repair a work or home situation which needs it or walk away and begin from scratch. Saturn, the planet of reality checks, influences the household and family, as much as your career. You're practical about both.

YOUR DESTINY

You will always have more than enough to work with—to be inspired by and inspire with, too. Jupiter is about the big picture, and this planet rules your communication with the world. You are a gifted teacher, mentor, guide, and tutor even if your job is quite different. Neptune rules your daily life, and it is a symbol of extrasensory perception or the use of the sixth sense. You may or may not think of yourself as inspired or even a channel, but what you pick up in the ether is translated into something that others can understand and use, too.

RELATIONSHIPS AND STRATEGIES

Close relationships are unique, don't fit categories, challenge you, and change you. Uranus is the planet governing the most valuable people in your life, but it is also a symbol of who or what needs a strategy. You rule in matters of the heart. Your own ruler is Venus, whose complicated partnerships and parenting were a way of life. However, you must find a way to hold the reins of your own feelings, and that begins with moving both yourself and any puzzling bond with others to a place in your life where it can serve a purpose. This helps ground you.

SYMPATHY AND SPIRITUALITY

Neptune describes the sixth sense, as you have read. He rules your day-to-day life, particularly at work. This planet is also a symbol for compassion and the soul. All your life you will be the healer and the healed, the helper and the helped. Reversing the roles teaches you how hard it can be to assist sometimes. You also learn how important it is to be vulnerable with people. The mysterious element to all this is the spiritual exchange, as what takes place with the body, mind, or spirit is quite pure. Neptune rules health on every possible level here.

WHO SHARES YOUR BIRTHDAY?

F. Scott Fitzgerald, born September 24, 1896

Jim Henson, born September 24, 1936

Helen Lederer, born September 24, 1954

SEPTEMBER 25

WHO ARE YOU?

You are a Libran who holds the scales of fairness, justice, and balance in your hands in relation to finance. You believe in leveling up for people in need. This will show itself in your personal or professional life. You are also a big idea person who regularly has high-potential concepts, half-formed plans, and brain waves to use. Experience teaches you that if you do nothing about these, then nothing happens. Over time, though, you become practical about this horoscope gift of Jupiter ruling your mind and learn how to make things real.

YOUR DESTINY

There is a natural link between your Libra Sun and the sign Aquarius, which describes groups in your life. Aquarius is also an air sign, like your own, so there is plenty of breathing space and room to move between people in these communities, but sometimes there is no unity either. It's your destiny to see these circles of people come to nothing or come together, depending on the others involved, but also your own willingness to put effort into uniting people. When it works, it does so in a spectacular way, impressing you with the results.

TRAVEL AND EXPORT

You were made for the worldwide web and vice versa. On the day you were born, Jupiter with all his broad horizons was in charge of your projects and plans. Jupiter is about growth over the long term, but also the long view of the map. You will always find more success in another part of your country or abroad. You may also find your biggest ideas go through stages, first appearing as inspiration, then requiring perspiration and navigation, as you try to find the right place for what you know has potential. Research and preparation are your friends.

GIVING GENEROUSLY

You express your Libran side by looking at the scales in terms of your own financial position, which is comfortable, and that of others who are in need. You can express this through your career or in your family life, for example. You may have staff or interns who benefit from your need to level the playing field economically. That is one example of this trait; another is fundraising for charity or donation to good causes. Venus, your ruler, also governs your bank account and business ethics and your interest in taxation or philanthropy.

WHO SHARES YOUR BIRTHDAY?

Barbara Walters, born September 25, 1929
Michael Douglas, born September 25, 1944
Will Smith, born September 25, 1968

SEPTEMBER 26

WHO ARE YOU?

You are the Libran ruled by Venus and your desire. This will take you into relationships with people from different cultures and nationalities, either at home or abroad. You are a prime candidate for a long-distance lover. Sagittarius, the sign of foreign people and places, governs your ideas about the world. You are also a good candidate for emigration. People who don't know you may assume you are a Sagittarian as you never stop studying the map for the people or possibilities which intrigue you. You'll have the money to explore.

YOUR DESTINY

Gemini, the sign of the writer, negotiator, planner, and messenger, is in charge of your travel agenda. At the other end of your chart is Sagittarius, as you have read; there is no interest in staying at home here. Gemini is the sign of the twins, and you are destined to have twin projects or plans at any one time. Make sure you take both with you when you export or try to find the right place for your concepts. This requires grounding and focus, preparation and research. You'll always be strongly tempted to pack a bag and go, but time it right.

INVESTING AND SPENDING

You take a long time to invest or spend your money. You will be given security financially, which enables you to take your time choosing. Anybody trying to rush you will not gain access to your world as you are quite controlling and controlled when it comes to your bank account. Pluto with its need to own a situation—and Scorpio, which is a fixed sign—both hold sway over your income, business, charity, or property. The family tree is always in the back of your mind here, but so is your career—and ongoing plans needing maintenance.

RULING YOUR FINANCES

To lovers and others, you are the world citizen who is always online and permanently tempted by particular trips or even relocation. With money, you present a completely different face. Here, you are a fixed, solid citizen who does not want to move your position at all. You are a tough negotiator who hangs on to their money for as long as possible. Your possessions, investments, business interests, and place in the world give you authority. They lend you a certain clout and influence. Anyone trying to get close to you has to understand that.

WHO SHARES YOUR BIRTHDAY?

T. S. Eliot, born September 26, 1888

George Gershwin, born September 26, 1898

Olivia Newton-John, born September 26, 1948

SEPTEMBER 27

WHO ARE YOU?

The zodiac sign Libra is as much about competition, and sometimes conflict, as it is about partnership. You are the winner who takes it all—sometimes doing so by triumphing in battle. The royal Leo with all its leadership rules the groups in your world. Every time there is a new monarch, the court scatters and loyalties must be decided. You will experience this as an insider in a circle of people dealing with a new leader—a boss, for example, or head of the family. You will also come to reign yourself and see why a group matters.

YOUR DESTINY

You have the obsessive Scorpio ruling your finances with practical Taurus in charge of your banking with others. Both are fixed signs. You are determined, focused, and disciplined when it comes to working and earning. You are extremely productive as a result and are passionate about what you do, which is typical of Scorpio and intense Pluto ruling your salary. Taurus, at the other end of your chart, is a grounded earth sign, and you know how to do a job well, repeatedly and reliably, so you can find economic stability.

INVESTING AND SPENDING

As you know, Pluto with all his intimidating power rules your budget. Nobody ever knows the real you in negotiations, no matter if you are investing, spending, or donating. Pluto is hidden for half the time, and so are you. You present a completely different face in business, for example, than you do when you are working for your own rewards. Scorpio is a fixed sign, and you can be quite resistant to people who want you to change your plans or even your values. You are a force to be reckoned with for anyone trying to sell to you.

ENDINGS AND BEGINNINGS

You are a cardinal sign, Libra, with Cancer (the extended family) and Capricorn (future goals) both dividing your solar chart. At the other end is Aries, which requires action, not words. You will always deal with simultaneous endings and beginnings in your life, affecting the generations in your clan with quite dramatic final chapters, at the same time that you realize the only answer is to start taking steps toward a fresh start. This helps you become who you are. You may be quite spiritual as a result of this or hold a rich philosophy.

WHO SHARES YOUR BIRTHDAY?

Samuel Adams, born September 27, 1722

T. C. Cannon, born September 27, 1946

Meat Loaf, born September 27, 1947

Gwyneth Paltrow, born September 27, 1972

SEPTEMBER 28

WHO ARE YOU?

The zodiac sign linked to two places, two sides, two points of view is Libra. You will always move between two towns or regions—perhaps even two countries—and, as a result of this, develop a powerful perspective on east and west, north and south, left and right, black and white, male and female. This duality is a stunning part of your character, and it helps you to make an impact. With Jupiter and his broad horizons and big picture in charge of your journeys and commuting, it's moving around the map that helps you exchange knowledge.

YOUR DESTINY

Pisces and its ruler Neptune are in charge of your daily life. You are spiritual, perhaps religious, but certainly always searching for meaning. Your soul matters as much to you as your work or your money. Neptune in particular is a symbol of solitude. You are a natural hermit. Being by yourself gives you the time, peace, and space you need to find what restores you. You can only be rejuvenated when you are alone, and other people need to understand that. The process takes time, like animals hibernating. From there, you relaunch.

BOUNDARIES AND THE FAMILY

Born with Saturn and all his lessons in charge of your family tree, you find it is impossible to ever remove it from the back of your mind. Particular branches on the family tree will always challenge you. This makes you tough, uncompromising, and firm with boundaries. Sometimes you get involved, at others you look the other way, but you are a strong person as a result. This includes your own history with parenthood, no matter if this is babies who never arrived at all or people who are now grown up. Relationships make you formidable.

PRODUCTIVE AND PASSIONATE

You have the powerhouse planet Pluto in charge of your earning capacity. The obsessive Scorpio is also here, so work is never just work for you–it will always represent what you are passionate about in your life, as the rewards go far beyond money. The other sign in charge of your finances is Taurus. This is a fixed sign, and you can be very successful with a fixed formula for your talents, abilities, and skills. More of the same is never too much with this sign combination in your chart. This also applies to charity, business, and investment.

WHO SHARES YOUR BIRTHDAY?

Bhagat Singh, born September 28, 1907

Peter Finch, born September 28, 1916

Brigitte Bardot, born September 28, 1934

SEPTEMBER 29

WHO ARE YOU?

You learn most about yourself in life because of home, household, and family situations where you feel you have to break free. You are a true Libran in that happiness is always about two sides, two people, or two halves of the whole. Yet to feel free to enjoy all that life offers, you also have to go through regular episodes of challenge and release. This is set up in your horoscope by Saturn's rulership of your place in the world. There are always restrictions or barriers—Saturn himself is surrounded by rings—but you move past them to happiness.

YOUR DESTINY

You are destined to be rich. Pluto with all his control and power rules your bank account. At the other end of your chart, the grounded and practical earth sign Taurus is in charge of joint finances. Taurus is also the sign of the gardener and farmer. You know how to plant and grow, no matter if it is seeding an investment or pursuing your own organic vegetables. Your entire personal birth chart will reveal on what level you find abundance, but it will certainly find you. It can take time. Fixed signs rule your wealth. They move slowly.

THE POWER OF TWO

You have the numeral 2 in your numerology profile. For personal reasons, which satisfy your soul, you will always find the road to fulfillment is through one-on-one relationships. This may be you with your other half or you being welcomed by a couple or partnership. These twin souls may act as the gateway to good feelings and great memories for you. You are also the person who can set aside "me" for "both of us" and, for personal or professional reasons, form duets which are also a gateway for other people.

THE EXTENDED SPIRIT FAMILY

Your everyday life is ruled by Neptune, a symbol of life after life. You may or may not believe in the afterlife, but your chart says it is a regular part of your existence. Your extended spirit family will progress when you do. This is evolution for the soul, not necessarily for other reasons, but your ancestors and relatives—and friends who feel like family—will understand it. In turn, those people in spirit also have their own upward spiral, and when they are able to go to the next level, this has an impact on you as well. Perhaps you know it's true.

WHO SHARES YOUR BIRTHDAY?

Caravaggio, born September 29, 1571

Horatio Nelson, born September 29, 1758

Anita Ekberg, born September 29, 1931

SEPTEMBER 30

WHO ARE YOU?

You learn about give-and-take, two sides, sharing, and equality from children or teenagers. You may or may not become a parent, but the balance you need always comes from a younger generation. As a Libra Sun, you hold the scales. On either end there may be male and female, old and young. Perhaps as a child or young person yourself, you learn about this. The idea of emotional exchange and "different but equal" is strong in your personality and outlook. This kind of bartering and cooperation between the young is a lifelong lesson.

YOUR DESTINY

You are surrounded by books, computers, and the media thanks to Jupiter in charge of your communication HQ. At the other end of your horoscope, Mercury the Messenger and Gemini, the sign of information, show you the global picture. You were meant for the worldwide web, Libra, with the emphasis on *world*. The ever-changing, fast-moving, literally Mercurial nature of your life means every high is followed by a low, which is already turning into a high. This is easily the most important, character-forming part of your horoscope.

DIGGING FOR BURIED TREASURE

Pluto in your chart rules the money, valuables, and assets which cannot be seen—only guessed at. Pluto reigned in the dark depths of the Underworld, which is where gold and diamonds could be found with luck. There are no guarantees for you, however, and it may help to remember that if you go searching when so much is guesswork, it pays to have experts who are professionals in the field to help. A classic example is the stock markets or cryptocurrency. Your full personal birth chart will reveal why you search, how you search, and how to do so.

SHIPPING YOUR PROJECTS

Born with Jupiter in charge of your projects, you never have just one. There may be two or three at the same time, ready to be taken across your country or around the world. Jupiter rules excess and abundance, but is also a symbol of travel and sometimes relocation. With Gemini and Mercury the Messenger ruling the map for you, there is a lifelong pattern of exported ideas showing in your chart. It pays to know which cities are welcoming which trends, Libra, as although you have a huge number of plans, narrowed-down research helps.

WHO SHARES YOUR BIRTHDAY?

Rumi, born September 30, 1207
Truman Capote, born September 30, 1924
Marion Cotillard, born September 30, 1975

OCTOBER 1

WHO ARE YOU?

You could take your talents, abilities, and skills anywhere, with Jupiter the planet of exploration ruling your plans. At the other end of your chart, Libra, you also have Gemini and Mercury the Messenger ruling your travel and relocation agenda. Of course, you can plant your proposals and applications everywhere without leaving your computer setup. You are an escapist, though, and may find the idea of taking yourself and your ideas to another place very hard to resist. You are ambitious, too, to move to places which are a step up.

YOUR DESTINY

You have the numbers 1, 1, and 0 hidden in your numerology profile. All for one and one for all! You are nothing without your friends or allies in the group. Someone will always be at the center, of course, but with the Sun—the central star in the solar system—in charge of your sector of teams, clubs, societies, and so on, you will find that together you all play your part in helping each other shine, even if one person seems to be the individual the others revolve around. You have quite good shared potential for gaining from this.

SHARED CONNECTIONS

The most personal zone of your horoscope, connected to your heart, is ruled by Aquarius, the group sign. Although you and your circles can do good business together by making the most of your shared resources, there is an emotional involvement as well. This is also spiritual for you, and from the wider network, you gain the most fulfilling sense of purpose together. It may be religious for some people born on this day. In other cases it is about your soul in a broader way; you are united by what can't be seen on the surface.

THE DAILY NONROUTINE

Pisces and its ruler Neptune are in charge of your daily routine—which never is. You are drawn to a way of life which is a vacation from reality. Wearing a prescribed uniform or wardrobe for your job, or even for school, is never going to suit your need to live in your own world of self-expression. When people try to pin you down to method and order, either at work or in study, you are far more likely to slip away into your own sphere. Anything or anybody appealing to your imagination, no matter how surreal, is so tempting.

WHO SHARES YOUR BIRTHDAY?

Jimmy Carter, born October 1, 1924
Julie Andrews, born October 1, 1935
Brie Larson, born October 1, 1989

OCTOBER 2

WHO ARE YOU?

You were born with the numerals 2, 1, and 0 in your numerology profile, and duets, partnerships, and double acts with men (if you are a woman) or women (if you are a man) dominate your life and personality. You were also born with the Sun in Libra, the sign of the scales which must be balanced between the opposite sexes. You care a great deal about your home, and it is always the end goal when you work. Your local area also draws you forward. You carry an excess of plans and ideas and learn how to handle them.

YOUR DESTINY

Jupiter in charge of your projects not only gives you an abundance of tasks and budding success stories, it also gives you a broad window on where to take them. This is always overseas, as the sign of foreign people and places, Sagittarius, is also in charge of this zone of your horoscope. Filtering out what matters is very important, and over time you will learn to jettison and delegate so that you are only left with one or two options to invest your time and energy in. Gemini the Twins rules these. Do you try two at once?

MOTHERS AND CHILDREN

At the highest point or midheaven of your solar chart is Cancer. Cancer is ruled by the Moon, a symbol of motherhood and linked to the world of parents and children. Your own relationship with your mother is never far from your subconscious. It is your first experience of bonding and attachment after all. If you become a mother or you end up fathering a child, the spiritual impact of your offspring is immense. You may or may not pray or even believe in a higher power, but the parent-child relationship is sacred.

FREEDOM, WOMEN, AND MEN

As you know, Libra the Scales is about equality between women and men. The planet Uranus is a symbol for freedom, and he is in charge of your most intimate relationships. The cycles of time in your chart suggest regular challenges for yourself with men (if you are a woman) or with women (if you are a man). Only you can liberate yourself. This may be from a marriage, for example. However, professional duets or duels—where you are both locked into the same situation—can also be important. You may do this together or just alone.

WHO SHARES YOUR BIRTHDAY?

Mahatma Gandhi, born October 2, 1869

Groucho Marx, born October 2, 1890

Graham Greene, born October 2, 1904

Sting, born October 2, 1951

OCTOBER 3

WHO ARE YOU?

You are a true Libran, in charge of the scales of justice. You would make a natural judge, but no matter what your profession is, you will respect fairness and equality between two sides in any situation. The numerals 3, 1, and 0 are in your numerology profile. It takes a third party to adjudicate when one and one are involved with zero bias. The two sides at stake may be male versus female, for example, or black and white. You are an authority figure at the center of these issues as they arise, with your Libra Sun shining bright.

YOUR DESTINY

It is your destiny to lay down the law on what is fair, but you also need to escape from the real world. You have Pisces the Fish and the planet Neptune—the symbols of vacations from reality—in charge of your everyday life. You may dress to express this. There is a strong part of your personality which others find hard to fathom even though they are also fascinated by your escapist side. People learn to leave well enough alone as Neptune is a symbol of what is hard to capture, contain, or control and you enjoy it, too.

INVESTING AND SPENDING

Pluto with its emphasis on tight control is in charge of your income. Investing and spending take time, as Taurus the Bull rules the more complex side of your negotiations. This is an earth sign and also fixed in nature, so you ruminate over everything you have earned or own. Pluto in turn governs the fixed sign Scorpio, so anybody trying to rush you or push you will be disappointed. You can be firm on price. The family tree is never far from your mind when you make your decisions—or your solid success ambitions.

BIG IDEAS

The planet Jupiter is known as a gas giant in astronomy. In astrology he describes what is big or even huge. For you, this will be those towering inspirations which offer so much for the future. The enormous concept or project with future potential is typical; the challenge for you is making sure it is secured in an environment where it can thrive. Libra, occasionally you will see even a surefire winner end up disappearing into the ether because you don't act quickly enough. Once learned, you never forget.

WHO SHARES YOUR BIRTHDAY?

Stevie Ray Vaughan, born October 3, 1954

Gwen Stefani, born October 3, 1969

Alicia Vikander, born October 3, 1988

OCTOBER 4

WHO ARE YOU?

You are the destined head of the family with Cancer, the parent, ruling the top of your solar chart. You were born with the Sun in Libra, the sign of fairness, equality, and two equal sides. This respect for balanced scales dominates your approach to life. It may be about balancing male or female, left or right, black or white, but your knowledge that everybody is different, yet also the same—and strictly equal—is very important to you. If two people or organizations are ever in competition or conflict, you make an extremely powerful arbiter.

YOUR DESTINY

Your journeys in life shape who you become. You have Jupiter with all his optimism and big thinking in charge of where you go—and how you arrive there. You can sometimes be too optimistic and need to look before you leap into other regions or neighboring countries. Experience will teach you to research more before you pack even an overnight bag. You are a natural explorer, though, and with Sagittarius, the sign of broad horizons, also ruling this zone of your chart, nothing can hold you back from the call of adventure.

MASTERING YOUR MIND

Virgo oversees the mind's impact on the body, and it can be profound, as you know. Virgo is also the sign that is in charge of your sleep, dreams, and mental health. Mercury, the planet of the mind, is Virgo's ruler. When you train yourself to master your own thoughts, you have direct evidence of the way mindfulness, meditation, or cognitive behavioral therapy, for example, can affect your entire physical well-being, too. Learning this helps you all your life, and it is worth your commitment to a plan, Libra.

HOME AS GOAL

As you know, Cancer is at the top of your chart on the midheaven, which is where you aim high. Cancer rules the family but also property, real estate investment, or your own home and surroundings. This is the goal for all your hard work, plans, and projects. Just be aware that you can take on too much. Jupiter is in charge of your journeys but also your projects, and trying to take on the biggest picture and meet the broadest horizons means you can overload yourself with an excess of responsibilities, Libra.

WHO SHARES YOUR BIRTHDAY?

Charlton Heston, born October 4, 1923

Susan Sarandon, born October 4, 1946

Alicia Silverstone, born October 4, 1976

OCTOBER 5

WHO ARE YOU?

The well-known duality of Libra, your Sun sign, is built on your understanding of two places, two sexes, two cultures. You may end up living or working between places which are different, but equal to you. Libra symbolizes the scales where everything must balance. You were also born with Mercury, the planet of the mind, and Virgo, the sign of mental health, ruling your sleep, subconscious, and inner life. When you learn how to control this—through self-help, a therapist, or just your own approach—your entire life transforms.

YOUR DESTINY

You were born to master neighboring places with Jupiter, a symbol of optimism, good fortune, and big thinking, in charge of those regions or countries which are next door. This may be Canada and the United States, for example, or Ireland and England. You can also be a city commuter. Jupiter is about places and people that take you far and wide, with a huge scope for your plans. You have authority, leadership, and a central place in the scheme of things, according to your horoscope. Part of that comes from these two special places.

THE RULER AND THE ROUND TABLE

The sign of rulership, monarchy, and royalty is Leo, the sovereign of the jungle and leader of the pack. Leo the Lion also governs the groups, teams, clubs, and circles in your world. The cycles of time in your chart suggest regular changes at the top. This may be because one side beats another or because there is a promotion or appointment. Whenever this happens, the circle must adjust. This matters quite as much as the person at the top—who will occasionally be you. The knights of your round table must choose: stay or go?

MONEY AND SEX

Scorpio is the sign associated with financial agreements and sexual relationships. It also rules your income and savings, as well as your investments, charity interests, or stock market shares. Scorpio is a fixed sign, and once you have money, you take your time parting with it—if you ever do. Never far from your thoughts, though, is your own desire. The scorpion is famous in nature for its promenade à deux, the obsessive mating ritual. This can and does influence your accounting, though it is never actually overt in the calculations or the numbers.

WHO SHARES YOUR BIRTHDAY?

Bob Geldof, born October 5, 1951
Imran Khan, born October 5, 1952
Kate Winslet, born October 5, 1975

OCTOBER 6

WHO ARE YOU?

When you were born, the Sun was in Libra, the sign of the scales which are evenly balanced on both sides. You are guided by this commitment to equality all your life and express it best in a partnership. Neptune, the planet of religion, faith, spirituality, and belief, is in charge of your daily life. On a regular basis, you must deal with sacred texts of all kinds, no matter if you accept God or not. Sometimes you will find yourself as the preacher; at other times you will be in the congregation. So much of what is under question is invisible.

YOUR DESTINY

You are fixed when it comes to your money, which may explain why you are destined to be comfortable—even wealthy. Scorpio and Taurus, two of the fixed signs of the zodiac, rule your own savings and also investment, charity, business, and property. Taurus also governs what cannot be bought or sold: the priceless environment, for example. Your values are at the heart of who you are and what you do. Sex is also a consideration as Scorpio has charge of desire. Of course, it is never in a tax return, but it is also never far from your mind.

CHILDREN AND FUTURE GENERATIONS

Freedom comes with children and teenagers, now and into the future. You may or may not become a parent, but younger generations represent unlimited space and possibility to you, as Uranus rules this sector of your chart. It is a symbol of liberation. The zodiac sign here is Aquarius: the group. These may be classes, clubs, teams, charities, committees, and so on. These quite naturally surround students, from infants to young adulthood, so perhaps that is where you will find the doors are always open to breakthroughs.

HONORING TWO SIDES

The scales of Libra first became a powerful symbol in ancient Rome. They represent a civilized way of handling the differences between two sides, two people, two sexes, and so on. In your hands, this ability to honor both parties becomes a spiritual experience. You can do this in a marriage, for example, or perhaps through your profession or unpaid work, commanding situations where there must be equilibrium. This supplies the groups around you. Those networks also draw from this example of "different but equal."

WHO SHARES YOUR BIRTHDAY?

Carole Lombard, born October 6, 1908

Britt Ekland, born October 6, 1942

Elisabeth Shue, born October 6, 1963

OCTOBER 7

WHO ARE YOU?

You have the Sun in Libra, ruled by Venus, the planet of complicated relationships with complex solutions. When in doubt, you go off by yourself; the numeral 1 is hidden in your numerology profile. You are sometimes mistaken for a Scorpio, the next sign along, because of your intense approach to money. Both Scorpio and Pluto rule your finance, business, charity, and property zone. It's emotional for you and never just about the numbers. What you own or earn represents security and comfort. It's hard to let go of that.

YOUR DESTINY

You are quite comfortable with being wealthy, and the cycles of time between Scorpio and Taurus—the other sign representing banking—in your chart suggest that your money consciousness pays off. Property is always in the background, as is the priceless value of an environment you feel at home in. The wild card in all your calculations is sex. Scorpio is well-known as the sign of desire, and this has its own space and rules in your life. It is never included in all your investments, but one way or another, it has a way of appearing.

THE BIG IDEA

The really big idea that takes off for you is not just more than you anticipated when it was a concept: it becomes the gift that keeps on giving over time. Jupiter is in charge of your thought processes, Libra, and this is the planet that is all about acorns growing into oaks. The turning point for you comes when you realize it's not enough to have brain waves appear out of thin air. As an air sign yourself, you live in your head a lot of the time, but success only arrives when you take what is there, find the right place for it, and plant it.

RECHARGING YOUR SOUL

When the closest emotional relationships that should fulfill you seem to be emptier than you would like, you learn to travel away by yourself or even move sometimes. This is a regular phase shown in your chart, and as the Moon rules your midheaven, or the highest point of your horoscope, it is often a Full Moon, New Moon, or eclipse that times this for you. You need to be alone to recharge your soul, and others have to learn to be patient. The issue, as you always know, is never the actual people; it is just your passing perception of them.

WHO SHARES YOUR BIRTHDAY?

Desmond Tutu, born October 7, 1931
John Mellencamp, born October 7, 1951
Simon Cowell, born October 7, 1959

OCTOBER 8

WHO ARE YOU?

People can guess you are a Libra because you hold the scales of justice and respect them, too. You are able to see two sides of any situation, no matter if it's male and female, black and white, north or south. This duality gives you authority, and people respect your sense of fairness. With Jupiter, the planet of excess, ruling your plans and ideas, you often take on too much. Experience will show you that overloading yourself with work is not the path to success. That comes instead when you learn to set priorities, ditch, and delegate, too.

YOUR DESTINY

You are born to have money—certainly enough to invest or spend to your intense satisfaction. You have two fixed signs, Scorpio and Taurus, ruling your financial destiny. You are hard to budge when you have made your mind up about your budget. Taurus is an earth sign, grounded and centered. Scorpio is an emotional water sign. This combination of feelings with a great need to stay put makes you a slow negotiator. However, your commitment to money and all it can do for you makes you a potentially clever investor in the future.

THE PRINCIPLE OF JUSTICE

You would be welcome on any jury and make a very good judge of any situation where there are two halves to a whole outcome. You are balanced, as a good Libra should be, and when in doubt, you will of course turn to the law to support you. Most of the time your handling of what is fair or equal is spiritual and emotional. It's psychological, not bound to lawyers or high court judges. You attract relationships and partnerships, even differences, where there must be careful and precise weighing up of two factors—always.

TWO COMPASS POINTS

Seeing it one way and another simultaneously comes partly from your habitual movement between east and west or north and south. This may be regional or international. Sagittarius with all its reputation for travel and tourism rules regular journeys between adjacent places. Gemini with its twin cities and dual nationality governs foreign places and people in your life. You will always go between two places, comparing and contrasting them but seldom deciding on one or the other. Both suit you, and they make you you.

WHO SHARES YOUR BIRTHDAY?

Sigourney Weaver, born October 8, 1949
Matt Damon, born October 8, 1970
Bruno Mars, born October 8, 1985

OCTOBER 9

WHO ARE YOU?

Born with your Sun in Libra, the sign of relationships, you spend a great deal of time and energy trying to fathom them. You will be given puzzles like this all your life, where two people—you and another—are quite clearly equal—almost the same—but on opposite sides. Venus rules your sign, and she is the goddess of infatuation and complicated partnerships, being the mother of Cupid, the wife of Vulcan, and the lover of Mars. The air sign Aquarius rules your heart zone, so you can intellectualize and overthink your feelings.

YOUR DESTINY

Understanding just how many of your life choices are illusions conjured up by you will change everything. Neptune, the planet of daydreams but also nightmares—neither of them real—is in charge of your everyday life, so you are easily fooled by your own projections. You can, for example, attribute a great deal to a partner or enemy (Libra rules both) even though it is all manufactured by your mind. Reality checks are required, as the wealth and success you fantasize about can be yours once you ground yourself in the real world.

PROJECTS AND PLANS

Life is not a dress rehearsal, and your projects and plans are best planted, rather than held in suspension. The travel signs Gemini and Sagittarius rule your ideas, and these must always be exported, regionally or internationally, to stand the best chance of success. Sometimes the answer for you is to delegate or share the budding schemes as others can help you stop procrastinating. Researching where in your country and the world your very particular brain waves are likely to take off will save you a lot of time and energy in your life.

BEAUTIFUL PARTNERSHIPS

As you know, Libra rules the scales of equal partnership and symmetry between two people, who are the same, but on opposite sides—opposite sexes, for example. Your great reward in life will be connections which are about friendship as much as affection. The pair bonding you achieve is the envy of many as you can give the other person space as much as they allow you room to move. Your partnerships will always be renewed by the wider groups around you, just as the two of you can recycle a duet into friendship.

WHO SHARES YOUR BIRTHDAY?

John Lennon, born October 9, 1940

Jackson Browne, born October 9, 1948

PJ Harvey, born October 9, 1969

OCTOBER 10

WHO ARE YOU?

The differences between men and women are shown in the scales of balance which rule your Sun sign, Libra. A large part of your life will be devoted to closing the gaps and finding the middle ground. Venus governs Libra and is a symbol of everlasting love. That is the foundation on which you rest. Your numerology involves 1, 0, 1, and 0. That adds up to two, and your gateway to happiness is always through pairs, duets, and couples. Sometimes you are one half of the whole and deliver for others. Two is your number.

YOUR DESTINY

Fate plays a hand in bringing you together with men (if you are a woman) and with women (if you are a man). It can feel as if something bigger than both of you is at work. These predestined situations may be purely professional or, more typically, marriage. Over time, you come to know what the poets and musicians were so concerned with; it may be romantic comedy or Shakespearean sonnets, but you understand the depth. The principle of equality with difference is at the heart of your most life-changing dramas, Libra.

HOLDING THE MONEY

When you were born, Pluto, the planet of power, was in charge of your income and savings. His own sign Scorpio is fixed: once you have money, you hang on to it. It's the same with your investments, assets, and possessions, which can grow up all around you. This makes you feel secure and gives you authority. It's so much more than a tax return or net income estimate. Scorpio is an emotional water sign, and you have strong feelings about holding on to what you possess. Property in particular is always in the picture.

LOVE THAT LASTS

Most people are prepared to let their first loves go; you have the capacity for everlasting love. This can make a marriage or partnership evergreen. It also means that anybody who falls in love with you and wants to commit to you will have to understand your feelings about a former partner. Venus is your ruling planet and associated with style and taste. Your wardrobe is part of who you are—far more so than with other people. Your home is also an expression of your preference for all that is designed with care.

WHO SHARES YOUR BIRTHDAY?

Giuseppe Verdi, born October 10, 1813

David Lee Roth, born October 10, 1954

Mario Lopez, born October 10, 1973

OCTOBER 11

WHO ARE YOU?

You are a true Libra who is deeply concerned with equality, justice, and fairness. You would make a powerful and impartial judge. Libra rules the scales which must be evenly balanced to achieve *equilibrium*—your zodiac sign is hidden in that word. You would also make a good marriage counselor, mediator, negotiator, or member of the police force. All your life you will be concerned with both duets and duels for this reason. You also have a gift for any relationship where you are different, yet equal.

YOUR DESTINY

Your destiny involves the fair sharing of money, property, and other assets among the generations. You were born with Scorpio the Scorpion and Taurus the Bull (and also the sign of bull markets and gold bullion) ruling your finance zones. Scorpio is about couples, no matter if they stay together or must part. Taurus is about individual life budgets. Whenever this angle of your astrology chart is triggered, you will find destiny repeatedly asks you to manage not only the bank accounts but the hearts.

THE HERMIT

Libra, the area of your birth chart which rules solitude also shows up in your solar chart as everyday life. Being alone with time to look inward is an important part of your lifestyle. This horoscope zone is governed by Neptune, which we associate with belief, faith, religion, spirituality, self-help, therapy, and psychic ability. You cannot find what you are looking for until you are by yourself, so being a hermit for some of the time is very important to you. Your numerology also suggests that with 1, 0, 1, and 1.

PLANS, PROJECTS, AND IDEAS

The zodiac signs which rule your journeys, regional or international moves, and the worldwide web are Gemini and Sagittarius. Gemini is about communication and connection, getting the big message across—and the message can sometimes feel bigger than you are. Sagittarius is about exploring your options in a foreign part of the world—or in a part of your own country which feels exotic and foreign to you. Alone with your visions, you can become disconnected from the plan, unless you reconnect.

WHO SHARES YOUR BIRTHDAY?

Eleanor Roosevelt, born October 11, 1884

Daryl Hall, born October 11, 1946

Dawn French, born October 11, 1957

Cardi B, born October 11, 1992

OCTOBER 12

WHO ARE YOU?

When you read most astrology books, Libra is shown as the sign of equality and fair play, particularly between old and young or male and female. Your education begins in childhood when you are taught this through siblings or with the opposite sex on the playground. For the rest of your life, your window into your children and young relatives is always about harmony and symmetry as a result. You may or may not become a parent, but the world of children and teenagers teaches you about equilibrium—that Libran word.

YOUR DESTINY

You are blessed with the kind of potentially big projects and ideas which can grow in the right place. Jupiter rules your plans on paper or on the computer. It also governs your way with a microphone or pen as well as a laptop. The missing element is not the opportunity or the impressive size of the project—which can sometimes be bigger than yourself. What is needed is thorough preparation and detailed research so that when you take this where it can prosper, you are able to find firm foundations at the other end. That helps you succeed.

THE WINNING SIDE

For all that Libra is associated with equality and fairness between two sides, it is also about competition and sometimes conflict. This may be with a sports team in your life, for example, or with a cause or movement. Mars, the planet of battles, and assertive, strong Aries are in opposition to your Libran side. You are a fearless person when it comes to pushing for first place. There can be only one winner when two are involved, as you know. This also comes from your numerology profile, with 1, 2 and 1, 0. There is no second prize.

THE FAMILY TREE AND BOUNDARIES

When you were born on October 12, Saturn with all his boundaries and restrictions moved to rulership of the family tree. You are the necessary enforcer of those barriers, which may be psychological and spiritual. You draw a line; others do not cross it. This may actually be family members, although it can also be people in your professional life. The attitude you need to adopt with some branches of the family tree extends quite naturally to others, too. You are welcoming but firm. This helps you keep the upper hand.

WHO SHARES YOUR BIRTHDAY?

King Edward VI of England, born October 12, 1537
Luciano Pavarotti, born October 12, 1935
Hugh Jackman, born October 12, 1968

OCTOBER 13

WHO ARE YOU?

The practical signs Taurus and Scorpio, both fixed, rule your finances. You are a natural saver who values security so much that you hang on and hold on, no matter what. The question of property investment is always there, as an ambitious Capricorn has charge of your zone of houses, land, and apartments. You can be stubborn about money. You are certainly passionate about having more than enough. As a true Libra, you are most grounded in financial partnership, and it's when you have a marriage or duet that you have liftoff.

YOUR DESTINY

Capricorn, an earth sign, rules your house, garden, land, and/or apartment, and you are destined to find a powerful sense of place and belonging once you settle on the right environment. This extends to your local surroundings; it's about more than the furniture. Your ambition, in your birth chart, is tied to your ability to find, claim, and keep the right space. It may be a village or Greenwich Village. Venus, your ruling planet, reveals why love is tied into the story. Evergreen marriage or romantic memories influence choices.

CHILDREN AND PARENTHOOD

Your great challenge is parenthood or the entire subject of children. The planet Uranus rules pregnancy, babies, infants, schoolchildren, and teenagers in your world. Uranus describes questions about freedom and these issues about independence are lifelong. It may be a younger generation who tackles the matter, or one parent in particular—perhaps you—who must decide between commitment and space. This can surface in your family but also in your professional life or voluntary roles. Where is the room to move?

THE BRILLIANT GUIDE

Your experiences with money, your lessons about emotional relationships, and a broad, wide-ranging grasp of life make you a brilliant guide. You are a natural mentor, tutor, teacher, or lecturer. The planet Jupiter rules your worldwide web, media, publishing, and educational and academic sector. This is where you spread the word or send your message. Jupiter is a blessing like no other, as he opens you up to the biggest of all possible pictures and you are a channel for knowledge greater than yourself. You're impressive.

WHO SHARES YOUR BIRTHDAY?

Baroness Margaret Thatcher, born October 13, 1925
Paul Simon, born October 13, 1941
Sacha Baron Cohen, born October 13, 1971

OCTOBER 14

WHO ARE YOU?

The symbolism of the scales of Libra goes back to ancient Rome, where it became associated with a new, civilized era. Libra is an air sign and linked with thought and debate as much as emotions. You can step back from your feelings when you must. Uranus, the planet of freedom, rules your close relationships. It is very important to you that with family, partners, or children you never feel restricted. This leads to a well-known part of your personality: you are the regular revolutionary who must always be a truly free spirit.

YOUR DESTINY

Libra is about competition, conflict, and contrasting views as much as two people in harmony. The scales have to balance, however, so your life is fated to involve these kinds of contests or even battles. With communication, goodwill, time, and good timing, too, unity comes from polarity. It's very common for you to be one of a group against one person. You will also find the tables turn, with you on your own against a circle, team, club, and so on. In this way you learn how to make both sides of a situation work together.

WOMEN AND MEN

The best-known example of the classic Libran questions about equality and harmony is the difference between women and men. You will encounter this with the opposite sex all your life and in a number of ways. The challenge of finding a level playing field between yourself and a man (if you are a woman) or yourself and a woman (if you are a man) is something any author or scriptwriter would be inspired by. Slowly but surely, you edge your way toward common ground and a genuine exchange. It's the story of your life.

YOUR VALUES

You were born with Pluto, the planet of powerful transformation, in charge of your values. You know what money can do. At the other end of your chart, your more complex financial needs are shown by Taurus the Bull, which governs principles which are priceless. This extends to charity and philanthropy for you, no matter if you ever need to receive it or are in a position to give it. At the broadest level this brings in taxation, the government, the church, and economics. One thing is certain: good health is absolutely priceless.

WHO SHARES YOUR BIRTHDAY?

Dwight D. Eisenhower, born October 14, 1890

Roger Moore, born October 14, 1927

Ralph Lauren, born October 14, 1939

OCTOBER 15

WHO ARE YOU?

You are extremely sensitive to the balance, or lack of balance, in your partnerships as well as your duels with others. You are built on the foundations of those memories, no matter if this is a marriage, a professional double act, a contest, or even a battle. This is true even when you are a teenager, and when you are much older, your history travels with you. Your birth date contains the numeral 1 twice, and that is unusual for a Libra person. Thus, we find that you judge yourself by one-on-one relationships, but by one against one, too.

YOUR DESTINY

As you know, the number 1 is hidden twice in your date of birth. You will come to know the truth about one against one situations many times in your life. Doing this makes you a peacemaker. You are here to negotiate and heal. You can only do this when you know what it is like to be in a duel yourself. This most commonly happens in romantic relationships, of course. We all have to make our bed and lie in it. The sign of leadership, Leo, rules all the groups in your life—the networks of friends who are all in it together.

TRAVEL AND RELOCATION

You have a unique chart combination of Sagittarius (foreign adventures) and Gemini (local journeys) in both your Libra horoscope and your birth horoscope, too. You have the soul of the happy wanderer and the optimism of an explorer. Sagittarius is, in turn, ruled by Jupiter, which is a symbol of big maps and high hopes. The only drawback with this astrological pattern is a lack of caution and common sense. How many times have you already taken a vacation, business trip, or even moved and wished you'd planned better?

THE GREAT ESCAPE

The unique Sagittarius-Gemini pattern in both your birth chart and also your Libra chart suggests you will help foreign travelers and migrants as much in your own country as you hope your own journeys meet with a warm welcome. The lure of the great escape works both ways for you. Libra, you understand this in other people as much as you recognize it in yourself. You may emigrate, for example. The planet Neptune rules your lifestyle, paid work, unpaid work, and academic career. Neptune describes life as a vacation.

WHO SHARES YOUR BIRTHDAY?

P. G. Wodehouse, born October 15, 1881

Penny Marshall, born October 15, 1943

Sarah, Duchess of York, born October 15, 1959

Ncuti Gatwa, born October 15, 1992

OCTOBER 16

WHO ARE YOU?

The numeral 1 appears twice in your numerology profile, and it is powerful and spiritual one-on-one relationships which will define your life. Libra the Scales, known also as Balance, shows your gift for sharing with a partner. Groups are more of a challenge and yet can also be your greatest reward. Aquarius rules everything and everybody your put your heart into. This is the sign of clubs, teams, societies, and distinctive circles of people made up of different, independent individuals. Uniting them is worth it.

YOUR DESTINY

There is a comfortable angle from Cancer with all its need for security and background in property to your finance zone, overseen by the fixed sign Scorpio. You are very hard to change or open up when it comes to money. Another fixed sign, Taurus, rules joint finance, business, charity, investments, stocks, and real estate. Once you have more than enough, you hang on and hold on, clinging rather like Cancer the Crab. Pluto with all his power, self-control, and willpower is in charge of Scorpio. What you have puts you in charge.

DUETS AND GROUPS

When self-interest, defiant independence, and competitiveness can be replaced by team spirit, the groups you are so affected by can find harmony, cooperation, and the benefits of pooled resources. You are a good candidate for being this kind of miracle worker, as you understand how two people who are in sync can supply the network or wider circle. It works both ways. When everybody is in the same space, spiritually and emotionally, it is the gift that keeps on giving, helping you to balance the scales and see one plus one.

BIG-PICTURE THINKING

Jupiter in charge of your ideas suggests big-picture thinking with tremendous optimism about what might happen to those plans with so much potential. Jupiter and Sagittarius, the sign he rules, both suggest you will be prepared to take your message around the worldwide web, but also across the map. You are more than prepared to accompany the project or concept and in fact are a good salesperson for it, as you genuinely believe in your own abilities or the possible growth that could come from the right environment.

WHO SHARES YOUR BIRTHDAY?

Oscar Wilde, born October 16, 1854

Angela Lansbury, born October 16, 1925

André Leon Talley, born October 16, 1948

Tim Robbins, born October 16, 1958

Sarah Podemski, born October 16, 1983

OCTOBER 17

WHO ARE YOU?

You are the peacemaker that the astrology books talk about; however, you will also be involved in conflicts where others play the peacemaker. Libra, seeing the situation from both angles teaches you about avoiding duels, or at least keeping the stakes low. You are most admired for being able to clean up messy situations after a contest or battle. Not only that, but with Jupiter, the planet of joviality (once called Jove) ruling your attitude toward life, you can keep your sense of humor when all around you have lost their own.

YOUR DESTINY

You aim to hang on and hold on to your money, as you have the fixed signs Scorpio and Taurus in charge of your bank account and income. It takes quite a lot of persuasion for others to negotiate with you, as you find security, comfort, and a reasonable amount of joy in everything you own or have earned. Once you have paid for the right environment—your home and local area are central to your fulfillment, with Cancer at the top of your chart—you can pay attention to something that never goes away: deep desire for sexual satisfaction.

SPIRITUAL ASSISTANCE

You are in the unusual position of having Virgo, the sign of healing, help, service, therapy, and duty, also in charge of your spirituality. This is where you will encounter Reiki, angels, prayer, and the intangible aspects of life that nevertheless can show tangible results. You will gain from this by giving or receiving. This part of your life may seem both natural to you but also supernatural to outsiders who do not understand it. The meeting of souls that can happen, even with a conventional doctor or nurse, leaves a big impression on you.

THE BOSS

You are the head of the household, the leader at home, the chief of your family tribe, and the top figure of the empire you create. Capricorn, the ambitious mountain goat who climbs to the top, rules your property and also your relatives. There is a direct connection between this area of your life and the midheaven, or peak, of your solar chart. This is ruled by Cancer the Crab with all its focus on seniority within the family tree. You are a leading figure who is respected and looked up to. You genuinely hit the heights, Libra.

WHO SHARES YOUR BIRTHDAY?

Arthur Miller, born October 17, 1915

Rita Hayworth, born October 17, 1918

Eminem, born October 17, 1972

OCTOBER 18

WHO ARE YOU?

When you were born, Mercury, the messenger of the gods, appeared at the start of your travel and relocation zone. He was the courier of mythology who flew across the universe with wings on his helmet and sandals. You are prepared to transport yourself and your feelings across the map. You are a good candidate for a long-distance relationship. All kinds of involvements from family to friends who are like family also deal in air miles or long journeys by other means. This tests your sincerity. Nobody need ever doubt your emotions.

YOUR DESTINY

You are one of those people who can train your own brain so that your comfort and happiness in life come naturally. Others succumb to their thoughts, even if it affects their mind, body, and spirit. You gain enormously from taking the opportunity to expand your horizons regarding your own cognitive behavior. This may make you a meditator, a self-help enthusiast, an expert in mindfulness, or the client of a therapist. Jupiter and all his grand solutions rule your mental capacity. With training, it's the gift that keeps on giving.

PEACEMAKER EXTRAORDINAIRE

You have no doubt read that Libra is the sign of the negotiator and peacemaker. This is true. You are particularly skilled at this, however, because of Mercury, the planet of cunning plans and clever solutions, governing not just one, but two key areas of your chart. You remove issues before they have a chance to become problems. No matter how much plotting and planning may be going on, you can suss out others who are looking for conflict and get rid of any potentially troublesome situation before it has a chance to occur.

GROUP PSYCHOLOGY

Leo rules groups in your life, and Aquarius, the sign which represents the hive mind and the outsider, is right opposite. You will often find yourself to be one of many voices in a circle of allies and like-minded people who are against a person who is both rejected and rejecting. The reverse will also happen, and it will be you who feels you are in a minority of one against the many. The transformation that occurs when all concerned can set their differences aside and restructure to find success is powerful.

WHO SHARES YOUR BIRTHDAY?

Pierre Trudeau, born October 18, 1919

Chuck Berry, born October 18, 1926

Martina Navratilova, born October 18, 1956

OCTOBER 19

WHO ARE YOU?

The idea of sharing and meeting others halfway comes naturally to you; it's a large part of who you are. Born with the Sun in Libra, the sign of the scales, you understand balance and harmony. It may be in a group where you are different but equal; it may be in relationships across the miles or where money is concerned. Children and teenagers teach you about fairness between old and young, male and female. You may or may not become a parent, but your window on the world of a younger generation shows you about exchange.

YOUR DESTINY

Your feelings are invested in groups of all kinds, from clubs to teams. Aquarius, the sign of diversity within a community, rules everything and everybody you put your heart into. Enjoying the company is the most important thing with these fated circles of friends and allies. Yet together you also have access to the good things of life: abundant possibilities for future gains, no matter if this is a professional involvement or not. The idea of harvest and celebration, but also preparation for a future harvest, is central to these groups.

FINANCE AND JUSTICE

Your Libra Sun shines brightest when you are acting on your principles, which include justice and equilibrium. Your values show in charity, for example, or when charity begins at home. When you are in a position to give, pay your way, or share, you will do so with a sense of real satisfaction. Your ideas about economics (small-scale) and society (large-scale) build throughout your life, along with your own abundance. Taurus the Bull rules joint arrangements and is the sign of ethics; it oversees what you consider to be priceless.

THE EXPLORER

The optimistic planet Jupiter and adventurous sign of Sagittarius rule your journeys around your own country and into neighboring places. At the other end of your chart, Mercury the Messenger with all his interest in air miles governs everything and everybody that is foreign and far away. You would not be a Libra if you were not prepared to take everything you feel and give, emotionally, across these borders. You may be involved in a foreign affair, for example, or have a two-city relationship. Those you love meet you halfway.

WHO SHARES YOUR BIRTHDAY?

John le Carré, born October 19, 1931
Michael Gambon, born October 19, 1940
John Lithgow, born October 19, 1945
John Edward, born October 19, 1969

OCTOBER 20

WHO ARE YOU?

The Sun reveals how you shine at your brilliant best, and when you were born, the Sun was in Libra the Scales. You are well-known for standing at the center of two sides, two points of view, the two sexes, and even two places. The fire sign Sagittarius rules your plans, and you may be mistaken for this sign sometimes as you race toward your hopes and goals with so much enthusiasm. In fact, it is only when you slow down and research the right setting for your projects that you succeed. Learning this early on saves you a lot of time.

YOUR DESTINY

You were born under a cardinal sign, Libra, and the other cardinal signs, ruling home and work, form a swinging pattern of highs and lows in your chart. You are at the top for as long as you are not. You are at the bottom for as long as you are not. This makes you quite philosophical about life; kiss the joy as it flies, perhaps? Maybe you believe, "This too shall pass." All your life, too, you are surrounded by books, magazines, newspapers, computers, and a world of words. They are mirrors which reflect your Wheel of Fortune back.

THE MOON AND YOU

You may know that Cancer the Crab is the zodiac sign ruled by the Moon and that people born when the Sun is in this part of the horoscope are strongly affected by New Moons, Full Moons, and eclipses. Well, so are you. The lunar cycle has a huge impact on how you feel, with Cancer at the top or midheaven of your chart. It is also in opposition to your sector of families and households—extended families of friends, too. When you feel out of phase, it's time to be alone and find yourself. It's part of your nature.

THE TRAVELER

Travel not only broadens your mind, it expands your knowledge and adds to your reputation. As you've read, going between two locations gives you two points of view and a symmetrical angle on the differences between the sexes, but also cultures. The worldwide web is your natural domain. When you are more established, you could easily have a career in two countries or own a holiday home. Your numerology profile contains 2, 0, 1, and 0. One plus one is two, and we are nothing without recognizing equality.

WHO SHARES YOUR BIRTHDAY?

Tom Petty, born October 20, 1950

Snoop Dogg, born October 20, 1971

Dannii Minogue, born October 20, 1971

OCTOBER 21

WHO ARE YOU?

You are a true diplomat and the negotiator who devotes themself to true, equal partnership. It may never be between genuine equals, as you appreciate the differences in your duets, but finding a way to balance the scales in a marriage, professional double act, or relationship is a lifelong quest. This helps you become tolerant—because without giving other people space to be themselves nothing will ever work for you. How are you to play monarch to a younger generation in your unique way?

YOUR DESTINY

Your birthday contains the numerology symbol 2, and much of your life and personality is about finding the power of a duet, no matter how you play it. This can be as true of a divorced pair as it is of a happily married couple enjoying a diamond wedding anniversary. Finding the flow with another person is about that tolerance and ability to extend space you have already read about. In fact, there will be times when courtship or the bedroom is as much about friendship as anything else.

FREEDOM AND INDEPENDENCE

You have read about how important it is for you to offer the other person in your duet room to move. Never too close or too much is your unspoken rule. You are an air sign after all, and you need space to breathe as much as a partner. This applies to all kinds of partnerships, not only sexual and romantic double acts. There will be occasional milestones in your life when your own need to be free changes everything. The planet Uranus is a symbol of revolution and liberation in astrology, and he is in charge of your emotions.

FINANCIAL REWARDS

You will always find financial rewards in your life with the signs of banking and property (Scorpio) and earning and saving (Taurus) influencing the money sectors in your solar chart. Figuring out how to spend what you have is a source of rich enjoyment to you, because you have the soul of an investor. The thrill of taking even a modest sum of money and ploughing it back into "the gift that keeps on giving" is something that anyone who wants to be close to you has to understand. You have the spirit of a natural farmer.

WHO SHARES YOUR BIRTHDAY?

Alfred Nobel, born October 21, 1833
Ursula K. Le Guin, born October 21, 1929
Carrie Fisher, born October 21, 1956
Kim Kardashian, born October 21, 1980

OCTOBER 22

WHO ARE YOU?

You are born on the cusp of two signs: Libra and Scorpio. Although your time, place, and date of birth will reveal which Sun sign you are, the duality in your personality might be explained by that period when you could be either and do not know. Seeing both sides, understanding that women and men are so different but equal, is part of your path. It may sometimes feel that you are fated to be faced with a particular member of the opposite sex just so you can figure out how to close the gaps between you in a fair way.

YOUR DESTINY

You will also be drawn into networks and groups, all your life, where men, women, old, young, and all cultures and nationalities share the same spiritual or emotional connection. This is genuine people power as everybody and everything is linked on a soul level. People born on October 22 may find this through faith, but in other cases there is no particular belief, except a shared trust in each other and the common source you all share. This is the "net" part of the original internet; you catch each other and stay there.

MEN AND WOMEN

You were born with the numerals 2, 2, 1, and 0 in your numerology profile. In two different ways in your life—one through travel or relocation—you will come to understand the two sexes. You will literally see how one and one can make two, or at least understand that without equality there is nothing—zero. Your horoscope suggests two cities, regions, or countries regularly pull you in two different directions. With that comes a confident appreciation of, and understanding of, how men and women can balance each other.

HARD WORK AND SOLID SECURITY

For all that you have a fascinating life with the opposite sex and the networks that hold you spiritually, you are also a down-to-earth person who knows how to work in a productive and reliable way. You are a craftsperson at heart who knows how to tailor what you do, if not to perfection, then certainly to the same high standard every time. People reward you for that, and over time you win the financial security you need. There is more to your effort than just your bank account, however; you enjoy what you do so well.

WHO SHARES YOUR BIRTHDAY?

Franz Liszt, born October 22, 1811

Catherine Deneuve, born October 22, 1943

Jeff Goldblum, born October 22, 1952

Ichiro Suzuki, born October 22, 1973

OCTOBER 23

WHO ARE YOU?

During this part of October, the Sun slowly moves from the zodiac sign Libra the Scales toward Scorpio, the sign which rules legacies and joint finance, both between partners and in the family. This draws the spotlight in the sky toward the horoscope zone where generations must figure out who and what counts. You were born into a family like this, or may marry into one or move into one in another way. Understanding that it's not about the money but instead about the value people place on one another is crucial.

YOUR DESTINY

Even though there are generation gaps between the branches of the family tree and distance between you, it is also true that your heritage, relatives, and ancestors are the answer to a great many things. It is only when you shift your position and claim your roots that you find the new perspective on people you need. Without that grounding, you may feel unfulfilled emotionally. Appreciating where you come from and why you should own both the people and the place helps you take a completely different angle on relationships.

FUTURE GENERATIONS AND YOU

Those who come after you—today's children and teenagers, but also their children and their children's children and so on—show up in your chart as a strong and reassuring story. You can enjoy this aspect of your life without ever becoming a parent, aunt, uncle, or godparent at all; however, it is more common to find one special child becomes the focus for your hope and commitment. It's rather like planting seeds which become seedlings, then flowers, then an entire garden. From that comes everything else, way into the future.

VALUES AND MONEY

Your full astrological chart, based on your time, place, and date of birth, will decide if the Sun was still in Libra or slipping into Scorpio when you were born. The world's spotlight certainly turns on finance at this time of year, and perhaps that is why your value system, principles, and ethics are so important to you. Money cannot buy good health for yourself or others, but it can certainly make a difference. Given that there is so much on offer with your family, you find yourself moved by those in need. It's part of your character.

WHO SHARES YOUR BIRTHDAY?

Pelé, born October 23, 1940

Ang Lee, born October 23, 1954

Ryan Reynolds, born October 23, 1976

OCTOBER 24

WHO ARE YOU?

When you were born, there was a stunning trine from the emotional water sign Cancer and your own passionate Scorpio Sun. Cancer also happens to rule journeys in your chart. You will meet the people you care about (family or partners) across the miles all your life. In fact, as Cancer governs your ability to feel at home, you are quite happy to pack your bags and move to anywhere on the map that will be a home away from home. Mercury the Messenger, with his winged helmet and sandals, also makes a strong angle to your Scorpio side.

YOUR DESTINY

Your destiny is shown by the zodiac sign on the midheaven of your chart, or at the highest point. This is Leo, the guardian of children and teenagers. You may or may not have children or take a guardianship role with them, but the next generation is fated in your life. Understanding that sacred time known as irreversible youth makes you respectful of younger people and their need to run their own lives. In fact, with sensitive Pisces ruling your sector of youth, you identify with them and tune in to their universe.

COMPLICATED RELATIONSHIPS

You were born with the Sun in Scorpio, ruled by Pluto, a symbol of complicated relationships. These are commonly between three people and one heart—your own. In the mythology that inspires astrology, Pluto was married to Proserpina and at odds with his mother-in-law Ceres. There may be wide variations on this theme for you—adultery in marriage is one you no doubt wish to avoid. Sometimes it's just the politics between parents and a child. In all cases, as you know by now, the answer is to withdraw your energy.

LOOKING FOR THE MYSTERY

It is only when you are alone and searching your soul for answers that you will come close to finding out the mystery of existence. As a water sign, you run deep. Pluto your ruling planet was alone for half the year, and although that is an unlikely amount of time for you to play the hermit, you do isolate yourself when you need to find out who and what is true for you. This may involve God or the rejection of God. It may be a philosophy or explanation for life, quite unrelated to any religion. Seek and ye shall find, as they say.

WHO SHARES YOUR BIRTHDAY?

Bill Wyman, born October 24, 1936

Kevin Kline, born October 24, 1947

Zahn McClarnon, born October 24, 1966

Drake, born October 24, 1986

OCTOBER 25

WHO ARE YOU?

You were born with the Sun in Scorpio, the sign ruling sexuality but also finance. You live in a world where both matter a lot to you, so you can be recognized by your zodiac symbol. The planet of escapism and dreams come true is Neptune, and he rules your home and extended family. Even though appearances can be deceptive with this horoscope pattern, they can also be wonderful to see. This is a mysterious area of your world where part of the picture of happiness at home will always be an illusion, but it is one you can enjoy.

FREEDOM AND THE FAMILY TREE

The planet Uranus is associated with the revolution that sets you free. He also rules the family tree on either side and can represent your clan and your partner's. Faced with this kind of choice, it's no wonder it can take a long time for the radical changes that liberate you, but you can be quite revolutionary about that shift in your life when it comes. Uranus also rules electricity and light bulb moments or electrical storms that wake you up. When you make your decisions, it's rapidly.

MONEY AND TRANSFORMATION

Your ruling planet Pluto is about the power to transform lives. Your Scorpio Sun governs money and property. You will find security, stability, and wealth in your lifetime and are extremely sensitive to those in need, no matter if they are in your circle or represent the cause of a charity. The difference between your position and those of others is quite striking in your chart, and with Jupiter ruling your finances, you end up in such a position of good fortune that you can afford to make an impact with whatever care is needed.

SECURITY AND CONTROL

You are a fixed sign, with a firm grip on everything you have earned, own, and save. You do not let go easily. You are also ruled by Pluto, the planet associated with control and empowerment through finance, assets, business, charity, or property. All of this puts you firmly in charge once you have achieved the comfort levels you want. Sex is always in the picture. How could it be otherwise when the story of Pluto is one of passionate longing? The scorpion itself is famous for its promenade à deux when mating. Life is a dance.

WHO SHARES YOUR BIRTHDAY?

Johann Strauss II, born October 25, 1825
Pablo Picasso, born October 25, 1881
Katy Perry, born October 25, 1984

OCTOBER 26

WHO ARE YOU?

The characteristically slow, steady, and rather settled approach to money that you are well-known for is typical of your Scorpio Sun. Scorpio is one of the four fixed signs, and you don't budge on finance, business, or investment—until you have to. Everything that you value most highly in life is tied to other parts of your country or the world. You put your faith in travel or relocation as a way of life, because experience has shown you that the great unknown is sometimes priceless. Hopeful Jupiter rules optimism and escapism.

YOUR DESTINY

There is a stunning trine in your chart from Neptune, ruling children, teenagers, and future generations, and your Scorpio side. Neptune describes vacations from the real world and one special child, niece, nephew, stepchild, or grandchild may deliver this for you. Even if you never become a parent, you may find that one generation after another comes to reward you far into the future. Neptune is about episodes which have a fairy-tale or Hollywood quality about them. Younger people can deliver that.

WATCHING THE MONEY GROW

As you know, Scorpio rules all aspects of banking and investing in astrology. It is also a fixed sign, and you can be literally fixated on watching growth in the stock market, for example, or just growth in the garden, if you cultivate your own organic vegetables. The reality of life is that it never stands still, as you also know, but when the dust settles and changes are made, you return to what you know best, which is a great passion for having more—and earning it by dedication—but also sticking fast to what you have and value most.

CROSSROADS AND CHANGES

The planet of sudden change, Uranus, rules your home, household, and family. It is opposite the career, unpaid work, and academic zone of your chart, so the cycles of time show regular crossroads when big choices have to be made. Sometimes you will go back and restructure what remains of all you had. At other times you will relish the total liberation of being free to walk away and start again. This ties in with your lifelong pattern of being on the move, when you feel the lure of the unknown is a bet worth taking.

WHO SHARES YOUR BIRTHDAY?

Hilma af Klint, born October 26, 1862
François Mitterrand, born October 26, 1916
Rita Wilson, born October 26, 1956
Keith Urban, born October 26, 1967

OCTOBER 27

WHO ARE YOU?

Around one half of your personality and path in life is about money. This fits with your Scorpio Sun as this is the sign associated with charity, taxation, investment, property, and wealth. Leo is the zodiac sign that rules your highest achievements, though. It is at the top of your solar chart and shows your starring role and guiding influence with children and teenagers, as well as the generations that follow them. You are not forever young, but some rewarding faces now and years into the future always are and see you as a leader.

YOUR DESTINY

Jupiter is the planet of abundance, and you are destined to have more than enough money to go round. He rules the sector of your chart where you build your wealth and then decide to share it. This may be through a charity or because charity begins at home. You are also a fair employer. The area of your birth chart which naturally belongs to the scales of balance and justice is ruled by Taurus in your solar chart. Taurus is about values. Some principles don't come with a price tag, and so you are generous.

FIXED BUDGETS

For all that you believe balancing the scales is about closing the gap between yourself and others financially, you are also quite fixed about what you own or have earned. When you are ready to change your position, you will, but otherwise you are very hard to persuade away from a firm approach you trust. This applies to business, taxation, your shares, property, and so on. You are an eternal optimist and trust that what you put so much effort and time into will deliver. Profits produce more profits in your dreams—and more power.

THE GROUP IS YOUR FAMILY

Aquarius, representing groups of like-minded people, allies, and friends, is also in charge of your family and household. You pool resources together and share the space. In fact, the circles you are most involved with are like relatives. Aquarius is the sign which represents people together as independent individuals who share the space but also give each other space. That is something that works for all of you. Yet you are also ruled by Pluto and need a duet or partnership, too. The right one will fit with the group.

WHO SHARES YOUR BIRTHDAY?

Theodore Roosevelt, born October 27, 1858
Sylvia Plath, born October 27, 1932
John Cleese, born October 27, 1939

OCTOBER 28

WHO ARE YOU?

There is a tradition of united effort, true community, and team spirit in your family tree. You have inherited that from a relative or ancestor. They may have been in the armed forces or a trade union, political party, or sports organization. The sign of friendship and shared goals, Aquarius, rules everything that is passed on to you in your bloodline. You believe in pooled resources. You understand the power of people who come together to make special things happen. This often becomes your work path.

YOUR DESTINY

Scorpio, your Sun Sign, is ruled by Pluto, a powerful symbol in astrology. Both Scorpio and Pluto in turn govern the Eighth House, which is where you make your most important decisions about banking, companies, good causes, houses, apartments, investments, and so on. When we turn to your Scorpio chart, we find that Gemini is placed here. You are pulled in two directions by your twin selves every time you decide your destiny. This is usually because of marriage or partnership—or separation, of course.

THE YOUNGER GENERATION

You may or may not have children, but younger generations are your true challenge in life. Leo, which describes heirs, spares, and pretenders to the throne, rules your ambitions. This may be a son or godson. It may be teenagers you teach or the reality of a young female market in your chosen field. Younger generations demand time, energy, money, and commitment which takes up a lot of space and is not always easy to accommodate. Your own childhood and perhaps your inner child play their part.

THE FAMILY TREE

Scorpio is a fixed sign, and yet there is nothing fixed about your family or your sense of place. Changing this so it becomes more secure and grounded is your reward. The part of the world that you come from is unlikely to give you firm foundations to stand on or to plant your own future. As a result, it can take a great deal of effort to find out what works for you and where on the map that might be. In astrology, Cancer rules home and clan. In your own chart, we find it is linked to journeys. Home is a journey.

WHO SHARES YOUR BIRTHDAY?

Evelyn Waugh, born October 28, 1903
Bill Gates, born October 28, 1955
Julia Roberts, born October 28, 1967

OCTOBER 29

WHO ARE YOU?

In your birth chart, Scorpio rules joint finances, legacies, inheritance, and shared property. You are recognizably a Scorpio person because your investment in people is such an important part of your life. The Moon rules your need to travel or take other kinds of journeys—local escapes, for example. The Moon is also known for its phases, and when you feel the need to do some soul-searching by yourself, you will do just that. In fact, among people you are close to, you become known for this solitary part of your nature. It's cyclical.

YOUR DESTINY

When you have more than enough money—which you will—there is a great need to benefit others who are not in your position. This can be through a charity or because you feel the need to pay your employees fairly. You can also lend or give to family members, for example, which fits the Scorpio pattern. The area of your birth chart which is ruled by Libra, the scales of balance and harmony, is also in your solar chart, and this time it comes under the rulership of Taurus. This sign is about life budgets, values, and principles.

LOOKING FOR MONEY

Pluto, your planetary ruler, was the god of the Underworld and unseen for much of the time; he was also associated with buried treasure like gold or diamonds. That part of you which is strongly influenced by Pluto can never resist the search for what lies underground or beneath a promise. This may literally be mining, for example, or a quest for what some say could reward you in business or property. Pluto does not come with guarantees, however. It will always be a leap into the dark for you.

PRICELESS VALUES

Taurus describes principles, ethics, and values which go beyond mere price tags or cost. It also happens to be the greatest influence on your ideas about what is fair between yourself and others, as you have read. Throughout your life, you will be acutely sensitive to others in need. This may lead to a professional interest in taxation, philanthropy, or just an unpaid commitment to the have-nots. Most of all, you will come to see that nothing can purchase good health on all levels and that some things count for more than shares.

WHO SHARES YOUR BIRTHDAY?

Fanny Brice, born October 29, 1891
Nikki de St. Phalle, born October 29, 1930
Richard Dreyfuss, born October 29, 1947
Winona Ryder, born October 29, 1971

OCTOBER 30

WHO ARE YOU?

As you may know, Scorpio is a fixed sign, with rulership over comfortable wealth or an abundant lifestyle. Once you have this, you tend to stay there as much as possible. What you may not know is that Saturn rules your state of mind. Saturn is the ringed planet and represents what keeps you stuck; often it is your own thoughts or imagination. Mastering this is the great achievement of your life, and regularly updating yourself on what works also transforms you. Scorpio is a powerful sign. Your willpower makes you happier.

YOUR DESTINY

Although you are a fixed sign, Uranus rules your household, family, and home at the base of your chart. Uranus is the planet associated with sudden and unexpected events which change everything instantly. You will already know about this, of course, but your chart is set up in such a way that you will always need to respect the freedom that comes with walking away and starting again. That can be wholly liberating, even exhilarating. This also applies to your career, unpaid work, or academic career, which Uranus also aspects.

YOUR HEART

Scorpio is ruled by Pluto, a symbol of love that never dies. Pluto was passionately obsessed with Proserpina, and she became his bride. Even when she spent spring and summer away from him, she always returned to be his wife. Your affection is evergreen. This means that every ex in your past is never entirely gone emotionally. Yet, Scorpio, you are also able to have a partnership over many years which does not require very much to make it come alive for you. This is rather like nature: she renews herself.

MANAGING YOUR IDEAS

Just as Saturn rules your state of mind and you learn how to deal with realities, it also rules your ideas and projects, your plans and concepts. The internet has certainly added to the load. Saturn is a symbol of everything that restricts you. Time and experience are the solutions with this planet in your chart, and once you realize that the journey is as important as the goal, you will come to see that delegating tasks or even losing what does not matter makes your pathway in life far more enjoyable and so much easier, too.

WHO SHARES YOUR BIRTHDAY?

John Adams, born October 30, 1735
Henry Winkler, born October 30, 1945
Diego Maradona, born October 30, 1960

OCTOBER 31

WHO ARE YOU?

You desire other cultures, nationalities, and countries the way other people desire a possible lover. As a Scorpio, of course, you are motivated by passionate longing. You may in fact have a foreign affair that changes your world, or even choose a life on the road, with a partner in every port. It really depends on your full astrological chart, but everything and everybody you value most highly in life is abroad—or at home, but speaking a different language or offering a different accent. It's a crucial part of your life.

YOUR DESTINY

You are destined to call somewhere else home. Cancer, the zodiac sign which rules your sense of belonging, is firmly placed on the chart sector where you go between two towns, two regions, or two countries. The saying "When in Rome" applies to you. You may even feel most at home when you are in transit, Scorpio. Relationships with all their complexity and intensity are part of the fascination for you and others. These may be other people's partnerships and affairs affecting you or complicated situations you cannot resist.

CHILDREN AND TEENAGERS

The sign at the top or midheaven of your chart is Leo. Leo is the royal who raises an heir. It is also the monarch with a younger court or generations of youthful subjects to consider. You may or may not become a parent, aunt, uncle, godparent, grandparent—but children and teenagers have a powerful impact on you. They are a reminder of the dazzling potential of youth—not just now, but far into the future. What you invest in, nurture, and hope will continue is a stunning legacy for you to leave.

WOMEN AND MEN

The story of Scorpio is also the story of its ruler Pluto. He was obsessed with one woman and at war with another. The gaps between yourself and men (if you are a woman) and women (if you are a man) are as much a part of your life story as your fascination with foreign countries and people. How you negotiate that space between the female and male of the species is something that can be purely professional or intensely personal, but it defines your character. Scorpio is an emotional water sign. Honoring feelings matters, too.

WHO SHARES YOUR BIRTHDAY?

Christopher Columbus, born October 31, 1451
John Keats, born October 31, 1795
John Candy, born October 31, 1950

NOVEMBER 1

WHO ARE YOU?

The planet of great drive and pushing power, Mars, rules your workload. You are also a Scorpio, governed by Pluto, who is associated with great self-control. Aries with all its determination also rules your paid work, unpaid work, or academic work. Your main issue is your overall lifestyle, Scorpio, because you want and need to come first—with the number 1 three times in your numerology. The journey should be worth it as well, though, and you benefit from delegating projects and dropping plans. Your load is often far too heavy.

YOUR DESTINY

The Moon rules your academic qualifications, websites, podcasts, media involvement, and general knowledge. Cancer the Crab governs this sector of your chart, and together with the Moon it is associated with the pearls found in oystershells, too. Your pearls of wisdom are not multiple: they are usually restricted to just one area of expertise or experience. As a result, others respect you and follow what you know to be true. You are, in fact, that rare thing: a natural pearl to treasure because of your fine mind.

COMING FIRST

As you know, your numerology is 111, which suggests you not only need to be first and come first, you often do. This is an interesting challenge for you, because these kinds of triumphs always promote gossip and sometimes envy. Then, there is the question of what you do after your success. Are you your own hard act to follow? With Leo, the symbol of leadership and dignity, at the top of your solar chart, you always fit the part when you come out on top, just as sovereigns of old looked natural in victory on the battlefield.

MONEY AND SECURITY

In your birth chart, your Sun in Scorpio is in the Eighth House of finance, business, banking, and property. You shine at your brilliant best when you deliver the goods and make and save the money. As you know, you have the powerhouse planet Pluto in charge of your sign, and control is very important to you. You are also a fixed sign and tend to stick doggedly to your plans. Finally, the planet of abundance, Jupiter, rules your income, so once you find your chosen field and dedicate yourself, wealth always follows.

WHO SHARES YOUR BIRTHDAY?

Lyle Lovett, born November 1, 1957

Anthony Kiedis, born November 1, 1962

Toni Collette, born November 1, 1972

NOVEMBER 2

WHO ARE YOU?

You are a true Scorpio, fixed in your approach to money and intensely guarded about all you have to save, spend, or invest. Your Scorpio Sun is in the Eighth House of joint finance and property in your birth chart. It is the world of children and teenagers which is central to your personality, though. Leo, the sign of heirs, spares, and pretenders to your throne, rules the highest point of your horoscope. If you have children, then they define you. If you don't, this younger generation is still crucial for other reasons.

YOUR DESTINY

The cycles of time in your horoscope suggest all the willpower, self-control, and rather intimidating approach of Pluto, your ruler, to money. You will be born into unpredictable times for the economy, which may explain why, when you have money, you hang on and hold on. Dealmaking and bargaining are extremely important to you, no matter if your priority is the family, property, or the things that money cannot buy, like the environment. This is when you are most recognizably a Scorpio and quite formidable.

FINANCIAL SYSTEMS

As you know, your horoscope is set up in such a way that you cannot control what happens to your national economy or the world's. This makes it necessary to regularly invent financial systems that will work for you. Gemini rules your finances at the broadest level. Gemini as the sign of the twins is a symbol of duality. Learning to juggle two sides, two accounts, two interests, two companies, and so on is your life's work. Inventing a way to accommodate change becomes a key goal.

NEPTUNE AND BELIEF

Neptune and his sign Pisces, the two fish, make a perfect angle to your Scorpio side. You are always drawn to the world of belief, faith, and particular philosophy. This may be because of your family or school to start with. Later on it may be there because of bigger ideas. The Christian Church is ruled by Pisces in astrology, but all kinds of invisible certainties are ruled by Neptune. This can be Buddhism or Wicca. It can be quantum physics. Throughout your life you will see all the sacred texts which feature spirituality, put to the test.

WHO SHARES YOUR BIRTHDAY?

Marie Antoinette, born November 2, 1755

Burt Lancaster, born November 2, 1913

Nelly, born November 2, 1974

NOVEMBER 3

WHO ARE YOU?

You are a powerful Scorpio, ruled by Pluto, the planet associated with control and the upper hand. You are an expert strategist and understand how to take issues out of the way before they become problems. Your great challenge in life is groups of all kinds. Aquarius, the sign of the club, team, gang, inside circle, network, or community, does not square with your Scorpio side. Being aware of just how risky people power can be, especially when the hive mind rules, makes you a tactician who knows how to stay several steps ahead.

YOUR DESTINY

Mars, the planet of warriors, rules your everyday life, work, unpaid work, or academic career. You don't necessarily have to act on your power, Scorpio, as showing people that you have it is often enough. Strong, fearless, and rather intimidating, you have exceptionally strong boundaries. This comes partly from both sides of your family tree. You know where you come from and who was there. Relatives or ancestors remain at the back of your mind all the time.

NEON LIGHTS

Neon lights or, in the mode of today, internet fame is part of your pathway. It may happen from adolescence, when you realize you are part of a team, club, or other group with a starring role. Later on, you may find your way into professional or other roles where your circle draws attention. You will take turns at pooling resources with these people who all have as much star power as you. It's rather like being in a union or political party, an ensemble cast or a band. Collectively you are dazzling; by yourself, you are naturally center stage.

WOMEN AND MEN

Negotiating the middle ground with men (if you are a woman) or women (if you are a man) is a lifetime challenge. How can you close the gaps in communication and understanding? The gateway to this is always pure emotion and unspoken feeling. You are a water sign, Scorpio, and know things on a soul level rather than overthinking them. Taurus and its planet Venus rule partnerships, and while these may be platonic or a traditional marriage, it is balancing the scales with the opposite sex that changes life.

WHO SHARES YOUR BIRTHDAY?

Charles Bronson, born November 3, 1921

Anna Wintour, born November 3, 1949

Dolph Lundgren, born November 3, 1957

NOVEMBER 4

WHO ARE YOU?

You are a true Scorpio who has to see past your own sexuality before you can even begin to negotiate the gaps between men and women. This applies no matter what your sexual preferences are. However, you are also a natural traveler or migrant. Cancer, the zodiac sign which rules home, also happens to govern your journeys and relocation. You find your sense of home, repeatedly, by taking your chances and leaving everything behind to move on. It also makes you sympathetic to those who seek refuge, too.

YOUR DESTINY

Scorpions can sting each other to death when they have sex, or even cannibalize each other. The ancient astrologers had a sense of humor. Nobody is saying that you have a sting in your tail, but you do find the undercurrents with the opposite sex are always there—even if you are just platonic friends who share a business together. Your awareness of the male-female divide is fated in your life, thanks to a series of relationships of all kinds where you must both try to figure out the great human puzzle of the ages.

THE FAMILY TREE

Your family tree never stands still, and the security and permanence that other people seem to have are never guaranteed. As a fixed sign, Scorpio, you try to restore what is never repaired, but this may be a lifelong mission, as particular branches of the family are always changing direction. You are a dynamic, energetic person, thanks to Mars, the warrior planet, in charge of your daily life and routine. Impatient Aries, a fast and furious fire sign, also rules your response to life. When your family needs attention, you're there.

REDISCOVERING YOUR ROOTS

You are an emotional water sign, governed by your feelings, and can be strongly affected by relationships that seem unfulfilling to you or even empty. Is it you or the other people? This question is answered when you realize that grounding yourself with your ancestors, family, heritage, history, and culture helps to center you. Like all water signs, you can drift and float until you find something to anchor you. That something is a sense of belonging to a place and particular people. After that, relationships can look very different.

WHO SHARES YOUR BIRTHDAY?

Walter Cronkite, born November 4, 1916

Chris Difford, born November 4, 1954

Matthew McConaughey, born November 4, 1969

NOVEMBER 5

WHO ARE YOU?

Your Scorpio Sun is in the finance and property sector of your birth chart, so you shine at your brilliant best as an investor. And what you invest in is personal. It may be an alternative lifestyle where you grow your own vegetables. It may be beautiful stately homes or your own business. Scorpio is a fixed sign, not given to change, and you can be quite fixed, too, when you find your happiest environment. This applies to home usually, but it can be work as well. Your security gives you control—and you really need it.

YOUR DESTINY

You may or may not become a parent, but the world of children and future young generations is your destiny. This may be because you accept the role of godparent, for example, or become a teacher. If you do have a child, they will feel more like an heir to the throne and part of a future dynasty—a prince or princess. Leo, the sign of dynasty and royalty, is at the top of your solar chart. The Sun also rules Leo and works like a spotlight. Everyone can see what you do to cultivate the next generation.

WOMEN, MEN, AND POWER

You are ruled by Pluto, the planet which symbolizes control through self-control and power through willpower. You experience this as a woman with men or as a man with women. There are usually tremendous questions about sexuality here, no matter what your preference happens to be. Repeatedly in your life you will find you can take the reins and control your journey when you find the strength to act for yourself and do what you must. It is then up to the other person to follow suit—maybe.

THE BIG IDEA

Two fire signs, Leo and Aries, rule your zones of achievement, ambition, and success. When you have the right project or plan in hand, you are not exactly "on fire," but you do find you have energy and enthusiasm—and impatience—that spurs you on. The only issue here is preplanning and research. Without a careful strategy and a thoroughly considered plan, you may find that your instincts to move your ideas are correct, but after a brilliant beginning, you do not complete things. Learning how to fix this spells success later on.

WHO SHARES YOUR BIRTHDAY?

Vivien Leigh, born November 5, 1913
Art Garfunkel, born November 5, 1941
Tilda Swinton, born November 5, 1960

NOVEMBER 6

WHO ARE YOU?

The extended family in your life, and the finances or property involved, shapes who you become. You were born with the Sun in Scorpio in the Eighth House of inheritance and legacies in your birth chart. In your solar chart, we find Gemini the Twins ruling everything you can earn or own. Gemini traditionally rules siblings and cousins, but also twins of any kind. There will always be more than enough to comfortably share or give, no matter if you are receiving or giving. This also extends to trust funds and family gifts.

YOUR DESTINY

Your ruling planet is Pluto, who was in charge of departed souls in ancient myth. He also rules the Eighth House, which is where you deal with questions of inheritance. There is a different kind of inheritance in your chart, though—it is spiritual. You may or may not believe in an afterlife, but in astrology this area of your chart is also where your ancestors are and your wider clan of relatives and friends. When they progress to the next level, so can you. When you evolve spiritually, they can move on. It's a powerful part of your life.

FINDING YOUR ROOTS

Scorpio is a water sign, associated with deep feelings and powerful emotions. These can be so strong that it is hard to gain an objective perspective sometimes. Relationships that do not satisfy you can sometimes say more about your state of mind than the actual merit of the people themselves. The answer rests with your ancestors and clan. Going back to where you come from, perhaps literally—even if just in your mind—can help you gain security and a sense of place. Grounding yourself there can help your relationships.

THE ELEMENT OF WATER

When you find yourself feeling all at sea with particular relationships you cannot fathom, it is time to take yourself and that situation somewhere else where it can no longer confuse you, but actually fit a purpose. You attract precious, unusual, and special relationships with partners, lovers, children, close friends. However, like all water signs, you can drift and float, never really getting anywhere. Neptune rules your heart. Rather than escape from what might be done in a practical way, the answer is always to act.

WHO SHARES YOUR BIRTHDAY?

Thomas Kyd, born November 6, 1558
Sally Field, born November 6, 1946
Emma Stone, born November 6, 1988

NOVEMBER 7

WHO ARE YOU?

You are motivated by money and will find security, abundance, and perhaps real wealth, Scorpio. Your Sun is in the Eighth House of your natal chart, where property, investment, business, and banking are also found. As a fixed sign, you tend to fixate on outcomes and not budge from your position until you have what you need. Once you feel secure enough to trust in your own lifestyle and financial future, you are also quite fixed. It takes a lot to get you to alter course. Jupiter with all his abundance rules your money sector.

YOUR DESTINY

Leo governs your highest achievements. This royal sign means you will often be crowned—in a kind of professional or academic coronation. It is also possible that you will do what monarchs in ancient times also did and seize the top job or top position from another. The cycles of time suggest that whenever this happens—usually through promotion, awards, or appointments—it does so dramatically and quickly. Energetic Aries rules your sector of work, unpaid work, and study. It drives you.

CHILDREN AND TEENAGERS

Leo also rules the heirs, spares, and pretenders to your throne in addition to those at the top. You may or may not have children, but their world is at the center of your life. This may be because you become a teacher or because you are appointed as a godparent. In most cases, though, your own offspring will appear, and with them comes another world that you learn to cherish and respect. Neptune rules younger people in your life, and as this is the planet of escapes from reality, you like to offer them that.

JUPITER AND ABUNDANCE

Sagittarius rules your income, assets, and ownership. It is governed by Jupiter in turn, which offers you wonderful abundance and a comforting sense of security and belonging. Jupiter will offer you more than enough and on your own terms. Perhaps you don't want to be a multimillionaire. Or you may set your sights on the kind of income that goes on forever. You tend to play a long game, Scorpio. Saturn with all his patience has charge of your ideas about life and your mindset. There is never any particular rush.

WHO SHARES YOUR BIRTHDAY?

Marie Curie, born November 7, 1867
Joni Mitchell, born November 7, 1943
Rio Ferdinand, born November 7, 1978

NOVEMBER 8

WHO ARE YOU?

You were born on November 8 with your Scorpio Sun in the Eighth House of your birth chart. Perhaps the number 8 is meaningful for you. You are a fixed sign and hang on to your money the way other people hug babies or puppies. As your Sun is in the house of finance, you cherish what you have earned or saved. This gives you emotional security, and as a water sign, for you it's all about the feelings. The only possible distraction from money for you is sex. Scorpio is associated with perennial desire and lust.

YOUR DESTINY

To feel at home in the world you often need to move. Cancer, which describes a sense of belonging, also happens to rule your sector of relocation, travel, and emigration. You will do this repeatedly, owing to the cycles of time in your horoscope. It's more than searching for a different place to be. Leaving one way of life for another is a huge, revolutionary change for you every time it happens. You find freedom. The exhilaration of liberation is worth all the willpower and self-control it takes to have it.

PLANTING IDEAS

The practical earth sign Capricorn rules your ideas, brain waves, concepts, and plans. You know that it is not enough to revel in what you have recorded on paper or a computer; you have to take it somewhere it can actually thrive. This same sector of your chart also rules journeys. Leo with all its pride rules your highest achievements. So, when you manage to plant your ideas on firm ground and develop them, you can move from the ego satisfaction of knowing you have something special to real success.

GROUPS AND POTENTIAL

You can enjoy the groups and social circles in your life on their own merits. Friends can feel like a family circle, with Aquarius, the sign of diversity in a community, ruling the zone of your chart where we find relatives. There has to be more to life than just reveling in good company, though. You are intensely sociable with the right people, but the potential for shared rewards cannot be ignored. A business venture with allies or a charity project with your inner circle is a good example of this. Together you can do a lot.

WHO SHARES YOUR BIRTHDAY?

Edmond Halley, born November 8, 1656
Bram Stoker, born November 8, 1847
Gordon Ramsay, born November 8, 1966

NOVEMBER 9

WHO ARE YOU?

You are the Scorpio who has the numeral 1 twice in your birth date numerology. When you have the financial security you want, you come first. This represents a huge leap for you, as you must learn to trust that wealth and assets can be real. They are not just a fantasy or projection. When you learn to know yourself better and stop being distracted by daydreams, you can secure what you want. You are a fixed sign, and once you have the money in your account or possessions all around you, you hold on and hang on.

YOUR DESTINY

Scorpio rules sex and the differences between men and women, as well as finance. All your life you will be put in situations where you must close the gap between yourself and men (if you are a woman) and yourself and women (if you are a man). Scorpio is a water sign, and that element is associated with deep feeling and strong emotion. The process of logical negotiation or practical planning is difficult for you, but it also gives you the progress you need with the opposite sex. This can apply at work or in your love life.

FIXED ON FINANCE

There are four fixed signs in astrology: your own Scorpio as well as Leo, Taurus, and Aquarius. In your birth chart, two of these also rule business, property, shares, and currency. Taurus the Bull, for example, is associated with gold bullion and the charging bronze sculpture near Wall Street. Leo with all its authority, leadership, and self-confidence is at the very top of your solar chart, where you achieve your highest goals and ambitions. When you finally make it financially, you do not give up easily or give in. You are formidable, in fact.

YOUR BUDGET

Scorpio rules the Eighth House of joint finance in your natal chart, as you know. You also know that this is the sign to associate with sex. As a result of this combination in your chart, you create a unique budget based on who or what is so precious to you that it is priceless. You also evaluate what you will not sell your soul for. Relationships of all kinds are always there when you add up the numbers. Your own market price on a hidden aspect of your life that others might price differently is your own business—sometimes literally. For example, you may have a love and consider them worth renting an apartment for.

WHO SHARES YOUR BIRTHDAY?

Edward VII, born November 9, 1841

Hedy Lamarr, born November 9, 1914

Sisqó, born November 9, 1978

NOVEMBER 10

WHO ARE YOU?

You are an emotional water sign who feels things very deeply and experiences life through your heart and soul, not your head. Cancer, which rules your home, also governs your travel, relocation, and emigration. You are a lifelong wanderer and will periodically look for a feeling of sanctuary and security somewhere else. Uranus is a symbol of change and new beginnings in astrology and rules your sector of hometown and homeland, as well as property, at the base of your chart. You understand refugees, too.

YOUR DESTINY

The top of your solar chart is under the charge of Leo, even though you are a Scorpio. Leo is ruled by the Sun and associated with sunflowers. You were born to plant seeds that become the next generation and the one after that. In fact, the importance of children and teenagers in your life now and in the future is at the center of your destiny. This can happen even if you never become a parent. Leo's sunflower is a wonderful symbol of what can grow in your life when you make young people the focal point.

KNOWING YOURSELF

Once you get to know yourself in depth and in detail, Scorpio, you can rethink your life so that you are never again haunted by who or what threatens you. You have an active imagination and project a great deal, as Neptune, the planet of illusion, makes angle to your Scorpio side. This can mean that your dream home, wealth, and success seem just as unreal to you as the ghosts of the past. When you are able to recognize this cloud for what it is and bring your focus back to who you really are, wonderful things are then possible.

TRANSFORMATION AND PLUTO

Pluto is your planetary ruler, Scorpio. He is associated with the transition of souls in the Underworld and brings constant transformation into your life. Every time one chapter ends, another begins. In fact, your whole life will be like a book of short stories, with one starting as soon as the last one is over. Being so heavily involved in the deepest changes shapes who you become. When you have to accept the realities of life, you tend to search for answers. What you believe, or don't believe, is a work in progress. God or no God?

WHO SHARES YOUR BIRTHDAY?

Martin Luther, born November 10, 1483

Neil Gaiman, born November 10, 1960

Brittany Murphy, born November 10, 1977

NOVEMBER 11

WHO ARE YOU?

You are a typical Scorpio as far as sexuality goes, because your relationship with the opposite sex frames your biggest challenges. This applies no matter what your sexual preference actually is. Just as importantly, you have a leading role with the next generation—in fact, all future generations. This can also happen no matter if you become a parent or not. Leo, the sign which rules the heirs, spares, and pretenders to your throne, is right at the top of your solar chart. Your highest achievement is cultivating younger people.

YOUR DESTINY

Your extended circles of friends, the groups which feel like family, and your social life are a welcoming sanctuary for you. Aquarius, the sign of diversity within the community, rules your sense of belonging. For you, these people are tied to special places. A particular house, apartment, building, or town may come to be associated with this wonderful part of your life. Scorpio, this happens repeatedly as it is a pattern shown in your chart by the cycles of time. Your club, team, or regular friendship group is your tribe.

PLUTO, SEX, AND POWER

Your numerology is echoed in your horoscope. You were born with the numeral 1 four times in your number profile. This is echoed in your episodes with men, if you are a woman, or women, if you are a man. It doesn't matter if these are purely professional or as intimate as marriage. When one and one do not make two, then it's time to set yourself free. Two of you can do this together, removing the power and control issues at the same time. These do repeat all your life. You may also learn to liberate yourself alone.

VENUS AND JUSTICE

Venus rules your duets and duels in life, as she is in charge of the zone of pairs and couples but also two sides in any debate. Justice, equality, and fairness are a strong theme for you, for all kinds of reasons. Some of this is about the way women and men relate to each other, which you have read about. In other cases, the law itself may play an important part in shaping who you become. You are able to both accept the balanced scales of Venus—who rules both Libra and Taurus—but also weigh things on the same scales yourself. You're a fair judge.

WHO SHARES YOUR BIRTHDAY?

Fyodor Dostoyevsky, born November 11, 1821
Stanley Tucci, born November 11, 1960
Demi Moore, born November 11, 1962

NOVEMBER 12

WHO ARE YOU?

The Sun was in Scorpio in the Eighth House of your birth chart when you arrived—which centers your finances. This is where you shine, brilliantly, when you master your budgets and investments. You were also born with Neptune ruling your relationships, both with partners and the world of children. This shows up in your solar chart as a perfect trine. What you achieve with your homelife and your extended family or household is a strange mixture of real and yet not real. Appearances are lovely, but not always what they seem.

YOUR DESTINY

It's your destiny to have the cycles of time delivering an unpredictable economy. This happens repeatedly in your country, or even in the world at large. Trying to balance your budget is a regular challenge because of factors beyond your control. However, this can also be your greatest achievement if you learn to update your approach to incoming and outgoing money every time there is another shift on the markets. Understanding how to create a flexible system helps you feel in control.

YOUR BUDGET

As you know, you were born with the Sun in Scorpio in your sector of joint finance, business, charity, and property. You are a fixed sign and, when you have money to spend or save, take a firm, fixed approach. You are very hard to shift and make a powerful negotiator, no matter if you are buying or trading. You are ruled by Pluto, the planet associated with power and control. Perhaps because your national and global economy is so regularly irregular, you develop an emotional attachment to hanging on and holding on.

RELATIONSHIP QUESTIONS

Neptune rules the most important relationships in your life. In astrology, Neptune is a symbol of feeling at sea and looking for an anchor or even dry land. The background story here can never be ignored; the babies who were born, or never born, are at the foundations of the relationship puzzles you feel you must solve. Actually, the answer does not lie in trying to comprehend relationships which defy categories. Your horoscope suggests the solution is to ground yourself and a solid gold bond, in a practical, useful way.

WHO SHARES YOUR BIRTHDAY?

Grace Kelly, born November 12, 1929

Neil Young, born November 12, 1945

Anne Hathaway, born November 12, 1982

NOVEMBER 13

WHO ARE YOU?

Everything you read about Scorpio being linked to money, business, charity, and property is true. You are a water sign, ruled by your feelings, and have an emotional investment in your finances. You are also a world citizen and think globally, not locally. Your intellectual or spiritual home is frequently in another country. Cancer, which governs belonging, also rules your sector of foreign people and places. Wherever you find the right environment for your ideas abroad tempts you to travel with the plans.

YOUR DESTINY

You have the planet of constant change, Uranus, in charge of your family tree, hometown, and homeland. Nothing stays the same for very long, Scorpio. That brings out your energetic, dynamic side. Aries with its fast and furious approach to life rules your everyday life. Mars, the planet of warriors, also influences this part of your lifestyle. You regularly intervene when some branches of the family tree switch direction. You are also a natural explorer or even a migrant, as conditions where you are make it easy to relocate.

FIXED WITH FINANCE

The cycles of time in your horoscope suggest you are fixed with your finances, which you probably know. After all, you are a fixed sign, Scorpio. However, you also have a broad vision for your investments or budget. Jupiter and his sign Sagittarius rule everything you have to spend. Jupiter is a symbol of big thinking in astrology. Sagittarius is the archer on horseback who stretches a bow wide to hit distant targets. You take the long view of what is possible with property, business, charity, or shares.

THE NEXT GENERATION

You are a widely respected leader and authority when it comes to your own or other people's children. You may or may not become a parent, but with Leo at the top of your solar chart, you have heirs, spares, or pretenders to your throne. This could make you a children's author as much as a mother. Whatever you plant for the future grows. This is not only about a younger generation now; there is the potential for your ideas, projects, and plans to thrive over time, in parallel with young minds which are always growing, too.

WHO SHARES YOUR BIRTHDAY?

Robert Louis Stevenson, born November 13, 1850

Gerald Butler, born November 13, 1969

Emma Raducanu, born November 13, 2002

NOVEMBER 14

WHO ARE YOU?

You have the numeral 1 appearing three times in your numerology profile. You frequently come first. The competitive Aries rules your work, service, duty, study, and daily life. Winning comes naturally to you, no matter if the issue is between two sides or just concerns your ideas and projects. Mars is the planet also in charge of your career or calling on a daily basis. As Mars is the old Roman god of war, even if you only battle yourself in your quest to prove to your own soul that you can do it, you do like to triumph.

YOUR DESTINY

You will come to understand what it feels like to be involved in a duel on all sides over the course of your lifetime. You know that Mars and Aries rule your sector of everyday life. This makes for people politics, and you will gain experience and solutions by being the peacemaker for either person on opposing sides of a conflict. This makes you a master strategist as you grow older, and if you use your knowledge of psychology but also resolution, you can become the negotiator or arbitrator who solves difficult situations very easily.

YOUR BUDGET AND THE ECONOMY

In your birth chart, the Sun is in Scorpio in the Eighth House of joint finance, property, business, and charity. You were born into time cycles which bring economic uncertainty in your country and the world. This happens often enough that you must adapt and adjust your budget and approach to finance on a regular basis. Your sign is all about hanging on to your assets or savings, but discovering that holding on too tightly is impossible in an impermanent world teaches you how to reinvent your accounting.

THE SEARCH FOR TREASURE

With Jupiter, the planet of optimism, in charge of your finances, assets, valuables, and profits, you are the hopeful seeker who is always ready to look for treasure. The reality of your chart is that it may or may not be there. Finding the right professionals to help you is important as it may not always be possible for you to take an objective and detached view of the situation. As your feelings dominate your approach to money—not your head nor your calculator—this is an emotional matter all your life. Outside advice can help.

WHO SHARES YOUR BIRTHDAY?

Claude Monet, born November 14, 1840
Charles III, born November 14, 1948
Condoleezza Rice, born November 14, 1954
Sterlin Harjo, born November 14, 1979

NOVEMBER 15

WHO ARE YOU?

You were born under the fixed sign of Scorpio, and when it comes to groups, teams, clubs, and other communities, you find it challenging to be flexible enough. Both sides in any shared situation can refuse to budge, yet when you try to unite, amazing outcomes are possible. You also know the other side of particular networks in your world. These people who are separate from each other and you are still connected on a deep emotional and spiritual level. This is what feeds your Scorpio soul most of all.

YOUR DESTINY

The planet Neptune is a symbol of inspiration and intuition and rules your daily life, unpaid work, study, and jobs. You may or may not realize you are a channel. Ideas which are greater than you are always there, and you are regularly a transmitter for knowledge. This makes you a natural teacher or tutor, no matter what your career actually is. Mercury the Messenger governs everything that is so precious to you it is priceless. You can't buy or sell life-changing information or powerful communication, and you have it.

THE GREAT ESCAPE

Another water sign, Pisces the Fish, makes a perfect angle to your Scorpio side. You can sometimes be mistaken for a Pisces by those who see your need to escape from the real world. Like the two Piscean fish who exist in a completely different world, you also need to inhabit your own universe. This makes you fascinating, though hard to understand. You are an alternative person in a conventional world and may dress to express this need to be yourself in your own space. You're suited to being a part-time bohemian.

WHO SHARES YOUR BIRTHDAY?

Georgia O'Keeffe, born November 15, 1887
Jonny Lee Miller, born November 15, 1972
Shailene Woodley, born November 15, 1991

NOVEMBER 16

WHO ARE YOU?

Your Scorpio Sun rules the Eighth House of your birth chart, where the investments, savings, property, charity, and business are. You are also a fixed sign and so can be hard to move when it comes to your finances. The planet of broad horizons and abundant opportunity, Jupiter, has charge over your money in your solar chart. You see the big picture when it comes to everything you own or have earned. Vast possibilities always appear to you, even from a modest investment. You can make it all work.

YOUR DESTINY

Jupiter reveals a comfortable excess of money on a regular basis, and eventually you may become exceptionally secure and settled. You can find it hard to let go, however, as either spending, sharing, or paying up does not come naturally. This is the fixed sign of Scorpio at work. In your birth chart, it is also opposite Taurus, another fixed sign. Taurus the Bull symbolizes gold bullion and the charging bronze bull on Wall Street. This opposition in your natal horoscope suggests the property market should be watched closely.

SOLITUDE AND AWAKENING

Scorpio, your ruling planet is Pluto. In the mythology behind astrology, Pluto spent half the year by himself while his wife Proserpina shared spring and summer with her mother Ceres on earth. He disappeared from view during autumn and winter, slowly waking up over time. This awakening for you is about your soul or spirit. You need to play the hermit in order to find meaning in your life, and there may be a period of regular hibernation for you whenever you feel the need for an inward search. It always lights your path.

EXPORTING YOUR PLANS

The best home for your ideas, projects, plans, and qualifications is in another region or even another country. The zodiac sign which rules distant places and people in your chart is Cancer, associated with a home away from home. You may travel with your concepts or skills—or even relocate. The cycles of time in your horoscope suggest that the worldwide web is the trigger, but the end results are always down to your ability to speak a second language, understand a different accent, or feel at home far afield.

WHO SHARES YOUR BIRTHDAY?

W. C. Handy, born November 16, 1873
Lisa Bonet, born November 16, 1967
Maggie Gyllenhaal, born November 16, 1977

NOVEMBER 17

WHO ARE YOU?

What you value most in life are foreign people and places. This is where you feel spoiled for choice as you will always have an abundance of options around the world. Sagittarius represents different cultures and places on the map, and it also rules your gains in life. When we look at your birth chart as well as your Scorpio chart, we find that you feel unusually at home with those who speak a different language or have a different accent. You could live abroad for some or all of the time—seduced by foreigners.

YOUR DESTINY

You were born with the Sun in Scorpio in the Eighth House of finance, business, charity, valuables, and property. You will always be given opportunities to make or save a fortune, thanks to the way your horoscope is set up. Pennies from heaven is an accurate way to describe the potential assets to come your way. They exist in your daydreams or imagination until you use your power to make the money real. Scorpio is ruled by Pluto, which in turn describes your focus, passion, and willpower. As you know, travel or relocation tempt you.

MANAGING MONEY

Your Scorpio Sun in the Eighth House is about so much more than just a row of numbers on a statement. It is about the relationships you have with partners or relatives and the price tag that commands. Taurus the Bull rules marriage, but also common-law marriage, divorce, and separation in your chart. Making these kinds of emotional calculations—although they translate into finance and property—is a complicated business for you.

YOUR POWER

You are powerful. Your ruling planet of Pluto is one of the great heavyweights of astrology. You have authority and, even as a child, were capable of impressing others. You are also a born webmaster, guide, mentor, teacher, lecturer, broadcaster, or writer. Gemini, ruled by Mercury the messenger of the gods, is in charge of the horoscope house traditionally governed by your Sun sign. You walk your talk, and people are influenced by you. Some of it is connected to money, which is always half your life.

WHO SHARES YOUR BIRTHDAY?

Peter Cook, born November 17, 1937

Martin Scorsese, born November 17, 1942

RuPaul, born November 17, 1960

NOVEMBER 18

WHO ARE YOU?

You are the explorer or traveler who puts a priceless value on your journeys. You're a natural migrant, Scorpio. You have Jupiter, the planet of broad horizons, ruling your sector of all that is precious. Sagittarius, also there, points to distant locations on the map—foreign cultures and countries. You can wander the worldwide web without ever leaving your home, of course, and you may also find some of the escapism and adventure you are looking for in your own country. Still a foreign home away from home is deeply satisfying.

YOUR DESTINY

Scorpio is ruled by Pluto, and the symbolism of this planet reveals complex relationships. In mythology, Pluto was married to Proserpina, but his mother-in-law Ceres wanted her daughter for herself. In the end, they agreed to differ and divided her time and loyalties. Pluto wanted control and so did Ceres; Proserpina was in the middle. This may explain why so often you find yourself in triangular situations with lovers, partners, close friends, or family. Over time and with experience these become easier.

GROUP PSYCHOLOGY

Understanding group psychology helps you avoid issues ahead of time. Aquarius rules gangs, teams, societies, and all kinds of networks in your life. It is also at a sharp angle to your Scorpio Sun in your chart, which means it is something you cannot square without a great deal of time and effort. As you are governed by Pluto, the planet of control, you preempt politics with people by habitually removing any potential sources of conflict before you have to deal with a group. This reminds others just how much one Scorpio can do.

FIXED ON FINANCE

In your birth chart, your fixed Scorpio Sun is in the Eighth House of wealth, property, business, charity, assets, and ownership. You do not let go easily of what you have and can be quite intimidating to negotiate with. This lack of flexibility and distrust of too much change give you stability and security, but can result in you appearing inaccessible to other people. It does, however, put you firmly in charge. It is also a useful boundary; the ringed planet Saturn rules your ideas about life. Your wealth can be your defense.

WHO SHARES YOUR BIRTHDAY?

Johnny Mercer, born November 18, 1909

Margaret Atwood, born November 18, 1939

Owen Wilson, born November 18, 1968

NOVEMBER 19

WHO ARE YOU?

You're solid and dependable. In your solar chart, the planet Saturn rules patience, slow construction, and the reliable passage of time. It also happens to oversee your ideas and opinions about what matters to you: money. Although it will never grow on trees for you, Scorpio, it can deliver what you want with measured cultivation. In your birth chart, we find your Sun in Scorpio in the Eighth House of business, property, banking, shares, valuables, and charity. You are respected for your sustained efforts here.

YOUR DESTINY

You are a winner and find being first—or coming first—comes naturally. The numeral 1 appears in your numerology profile three times. You also have royal Leo, the zodiac sign associated with monarchs, right at the top of your solar chart. You expect victory and achieve it, no matter if other people put you up where you belong or you have to do battle to achieve your triumphs. The energetic, dynamic Aries rules your working life, and Mars, the planet of competition, also appears there. You're a fearless rival.

VENUS AND THE SCALES

The planet Venus is associated with the scales. She rules Libra—known as Balance in some languages. She also rules Taurus, where the scales are used to measure anything from gold to jewelry, all that is valuable. Your solar chart shows Venus in charge of all your duets and duels. These range from marriages to professional partnerships or even legal differences. You are fated to either hand down justice or accept it. This can happen in your personal life and in a private way or actually find you dealing with the law.

TWIN LOCATIONS

The sign of the twins, Gemini, rules everything you find so precious that it is priceless. Knowing two cities, two regions, or two countries equally well is on the list.

You have a duality to your nature which comes from a double life, at least in terms of the map. You can feel at home when you are on the move, thanks to Cancer, the sign of security and sanctuary, taking charge of your travel zone. You may even make two homes at one point in your life and go between both. Sagittarius, which governs the worldwide web, also has an influence.

WHO SHARES YOUR BIRTHDAY?

Charles I, born November 19, 1600
Indira Gandhi, born November 19, 1917
Jodie Foster, born November 19, 1962

NOVEMBER 20

WHO ARE YOU?

You draw influences from Scorpio, with a fixed approach to everything you own or earn. In your birth chart, your Sun draws Eighth House patterns involving wealth, security, business, and banking; this helps you shine. You also have the numerals 1 and 2 in your numerology profile. You are frequently a lone figure, spending long periods of solitude searching for the answers. However, you pair up with people who can help you or even heal you. You also feel the two from your birthday numbers when you assist and transform another person.

YOUR DESTINY

Leo, the sign of royals and leadership, aspects the top of your solar chart, indicating your leading role in life. You don't exactly have a throne, but you do have a special place in the world. Your money adds to this position, and you are widely respected. Jupiter, a symbol of comfortable abundance, influences your bank account. You will regularly find yourself with the luxury of not just managing money, but musing over how it might be spent or saved. This does have an influence on your sexual relationships, which are crucial.

AMBITIOUS IDEAS

The most ambitious sign of the zodiac is Capricorn, the mountain goat that climbs to the top. This sign also influences your ideas, projects, plans, and opinions. You are a natural academic who could scale the heights of any college or university.

Even if you leave school young, though, you go on learning all your life, as bettering yourself intellectually is a regular temptation. You belong on the worldwide web in all cases, as you are a specialist and information hub. You were born to write or broadcast, podcast, tutor, teach, or lecture.

PLUTO AND TRANSFORMATION

You are influenced by Pluto, which is associated with transformation. You will come to know what it feels like to be dramatically changed by another person more than once. You also have the same capacity to change somebody else. This teaches you about vulnerability in others, but also vulnerability in yourself. Real strength comes from putting somebody else in your hands and taking on the responsibility for them. You also come to see it as the courage to admit you are only human, despite all your special achievements.

WHO SHARES YOUR BIRTHDAY?

Robert F. Kennedy, born November 20, 1925

Joe Biden, born November 20, 1942

Future, born November 20, 1983

NOVEMBER 21

WHO ARE YOU?

You are the person who projects daydreams about wealth, success, and the perfect home into the same cloud where you throw up everything that haunts you or confronts you. Until you get to know yourself better, you may go on being captured by the visions and even mistaking them for reality. In fact, everything is in your head, and every situation in your life can also be managed in practical ways. Finding yourself again is a regular challenge, but over time it becomes easier and you become more of a realist, which is preferable.

YOUR DESTINY

You face regular crossroads in your life, thanks to the cycles of time in your horoscope. These can be quite frequent if the people around you are not what you need; then, you take time-outs more often. Being by yourself and traveling away—or just exploring nature—nourish you. There will also be more dramatic turning points when the only option is to relocate for a while. On your return you find that everything and everybody look different. Taking a sabbatical can restore you. Once time has passed, you find fulfillment.

TACTICS AND STRATEGIES

You have a talent for developing clever tactics and smart strategies to deal with others, especially in a group. Reading the room before issues can develop keeps your life—and the lives of those around you—peaceful. You may rely on intuition to do this or just life experience, as these tests and trials with groups begin when you are a student. It may be sports or rival debating teams, but you begin to learn how a circle of people operates and to develop the preemptive moves that will serve you for the rest of your life.

WOMEN AND MEN

It may be just one relationship or several, but you are here to learn about the world of men (if you are a woman) or the world of women (if you are a man). The gaps and differences affect you from an early age. Very commonly you explore the two sexes through marriage or dating, but you can also experience platonic bonds which show you how a female perspective and male perspective have to be compared and contrasted. This gives your partnerships and even your duels great power and unforgettable intensity.

WHO SHARES YOUR BIRTHDAY?

Voltaire, born November 21, 1694

Goldie Hawn, born November 21, 1945

Björk, born November 21, 1965

Ronny Chieng, born November 21, 1985

NOVEMBER 22

WHO ARE YOU?

You are the team player who enjoys bonding with allies and friends who are so different to you but share the same good times and good feelings. You understand the need for space and the success of diversity in a community. This way, you not only share what life is all about—fun—but you also find yourself offered real rewards. These may be in business or charity, for example. You will always have clubs or circles of this kind in your life, from adolescence into old age. Knowing how to make them productive is your challenge.

YOUR DESTINY

As you have read, networks of friends or allies are in your life from your teenage years onward. These become increasingly important when you begin to let each other shine. You attract people who have star quality. They also give you a space to be the center of attention, too. You are never the leader but always the supply of what the group needs to pool resources. This varies depending on which particular circle you are involved with at the time. You are at your most impressive with these brilliant people behind you.

TWO PEOPLE, ONE PATH

Another lifelong lesson is partnership. You attract people who are identical to you on one level, but a different breed on quite another. Your horoscope is set up in such a way that the cycles of time will challenge you both to share one path—or not. The more experience you have with one-on-one relationships, the more creative and thoughtful you become about navigating together. Your numerology profile contains 1, 1, 2, and 2. Sometimes it takes two paths as you will discover with, say, a marriage.

THE WORLD OF CHILDREN

You may or may not become a parent, but the world of children—reaching forward into future generations—is your reward in life. It may be just one child, godchild, or young relative who brings you this happiness. In other cases, there may be a large number of young people involved in your fate, as you may be a teacher, for example, or a midwife. However you enjoy a younger generation, it is central to your life and character and shapes who you become. You also shape those who come after you with your great care.

WHO SHARES YOUR BIRTHDAY?

George Eliot, born November 22, 1819

Billie Jean King, born November 22, 1943

Scarlett Johansson, born November 22, 1984

NOVEMBER 23

WHO ARE YOU?

You are a natural student of life all your life and never stop learning. You are also an information hub for others. This goes beyond your special fields of expertise, though, into great wisdom and deeper knowledge. You are respected and admired from a distance, and those who are fortunate enough to get close to you automatically add to the library or you add to theirs. Sometimes the library is entirely in your mind. You know that there are only a few answers to the really big questions and remain fascinated by them.

YOUR DESTINY

You attract groups of like-minded people who appear to be the same, although on closer inspection they are all individuals. Remembering this makes it easier for you to handle your circle. This may be a sports team you coach, for example, or a religious group you organize. The actual networks will change over your lifetime, and this pattern begins when you are a teenager. As time goes by, you come to see that the collective support and backing of your allies give you more than you might always be fully aware of.

MASTERING YOUR MIND

Another horoscope pattern which shows up when you are a young adult is the need to master your own mind. You learn how to do this because you have to. It is your way to peace and acceptance, no matter if you learn Tibetan Buddhist meditation techniques or find yourself with a therapist who specializes in cognitive behavioral therapy. Understanding that you construct your own reality by lining the interior of your mind with particular images or scripts is your first step toward a lifetime of impressive mental mastery.

EVERGREEN RELATIONSHIPS

The planet Venus rules two zodiac signs in your natal and solar charts. One is Libra and the other is Taurus. Venus also governs evergreen love. It can help to know the mythology surrounding this planet. She was married to a lame blacksmith called Vulcan, but betrayed him with her part-time lover Mars. Vulcan was strong enough to overlook Mars and forgive her; their partnership went on. Venus also had a son called Cupid, who found everlasting, immortal love with Psyche. Your ex is never entirely an ex.

WHO SHARES YOUR BIRTHDAY?

Erté, born November 23, 1892

Boris Karloff, born November 23, 1887

Bruce Hornsby, born November 23, 1954

NOVEMBER 24

WHO ARE YOU?

Even if you never become a parent, you have a special window on the world of children and young people. This may be because of your job, unpaid work, or personal life. You may be the relative who plays a powerful role in the lives of the next generation, for example—or you could teach infants. You have a great respect for the unique universe occupied by the young. Its innocence and trust are something that never fails to impress you. You have a talent for encouraging these future adults to genuinely enjoy their childhood.

YOUR DESTINY

Your horoscope is set up to bring you security, financial stability, and a reluctance to change your budget or your values. This makes you an impressive if somewhat intimidating figure who others must know very well before they approach you with negotiations or requests. Your authority and presence come partly from your bank account or assets, but also from your self-confidence and self-respect. You have what it takes to accumulate through sheer effort, and beyond your actual wealth, your self-worth is priceless as a result.

WORK AND MONEY

It's not that you are in charge of a hit factory, but whatever profession you are in enables you to find a winning formula and then repeat it. You have the Midas touch with all that you produce and polish, even if you don't always perfect it. Your work ethic is strong, partly because you know you can rely on the income, but also because you are genuinely absorbed by your skills and talents. You become better over time, of course, and as long as you remain the reliable producer of what people want, the money will keep coming.

CHESS MOVES AND GROUPS

Something you learn when young is the ability to make your moves on the chess board of life some time ahead. You will always come across groups of people who create potential issues for you and others. Fortunately, your intuition is strong but so is your understanding of human nature. By the time these teams, circles, or other networks realize what has happened, you have already made a pre-emptive move and taken away any possible reason for problems. You are a natural strategist or politician, whatever your profession.

WHO SHARES YOUR BIRTHDAY?

Scott Joplin, born November 24, 1868

Billy Connolly, born November 24, 1942

Katherine Heigl, born November 24, 1978

NOVEMBER 25

WHO ARE YOU?

Everything that you value most highly is solid, secure, and built on firm foundations, as the ambitious Capricorn rules all that is priceless to you. You are a Sagittarian, of course, but it is the planet Saturn in your chart—the heavyweight of astrology—that shows you mean business. You rise to the top of any organization or particular field where it takes a long time to reach a peak that very few can occupy. It is very important that you value the company or the particular sphere you end up in; it becomes your path.

YOUR DESTINY

You will experience lows and highs in your finances, once again thanks to Saturn's rulership of your finance sector. Eventually you turn into the kind of caring, parental figure who funds other people. This may be in the family, so you become a reliable source for your relatives. You may also find what you are looking for—a sense of justice—in charities. You may end up with a bank or business which takes care of people. Cancer, the sign of parenthood, rules your money. For you, this translates into caring.

EQUALITY IN THE GROUP

You are attracted to groups where everybody is different but equal. Libra, the scales of balance, rules the teams, clubs, networks, and special circles in your life. This is an air sign, so you circulate easily and give each other breathing space. Aquarius, the sign which governs diversity in the community—but also people power—describes how you think. Its ruler Uranus, a symbol of independence, shows how you form your ideas. It is very important to you that the bonds of friendship do not get in the way of your own life.

THE POWER OF A GROUP

The particular communities you draw into your life will teach you a lot about the might of a circle of people acting as one. You will discover this from your teenage years onward. Together, you and your like-minded allies can take on anybody and anything. It also works the other way, Sagittarius. You can discover for yourself that if you are the outsider or opponent, a group can change the game in an instant. Over time, you learn which communities to be part of and why—for the very good reason that you are all so powerful.

WHO SHARES YOUR BIRTHDAY?

Joe DiMaggio, born November 25, 1914
John F. Kennedy Jr., born November 25, 1960
Christina Applegate, born November 25, 1971

NOVEMBER 26

WHO ARE YOU?

You are a Sagittarian, born to roam or even relocate. The cycles of time in your horoscope will bring you to a crossroads often, when you must decide to stay or go. It's never just another vacation or move; your horoscope suggests these decisions feel fated and alter everything. The dual sign of Gemini is your opposite in the zodiac. You are always pulled by two directions, two options, two people, two organizations when you reach these turning points. Figuring out who or what to cut out takes all your intuition.

YOUR DESTINY

Your thoughts and ideas are Aquarian: angled toward groups and communities. From your teenage years onward, you become involved in friendship circles, gangs, teams, clubs, societies, and so on. This teaches you that unless you all pull together and head in the same direction, nothing ever works. Aquarius is the sign of diversity in the community, and although you give each other plenty of space, sometimes there are so many gaps there can be no solidarity or unity. Experience shows you how to fix that and succeed.

YOUR NUMEROLOGY

You were born with the numerals 1, 1, and 2 in your numerology profile. You are regularly drawn into situations where two people are in conflict and you are the third—the peacemaker. It can work the other way, too. You can find yourself in one-against-one rifts and so dependent on an outsider to repair the situation for you and the other person. This tango of numbers becomes easier to add up over time. Eventually you may find that you are always the cheerful negotiator, as Sagittarius is the zodiac optimist.

CHILDREN AND TEENAGERS

All that is so precious to you it is priceless is contained in the world of children and teenagers. Cancer, which rules parenthood, is also in charge of your sector of all that can't be bought or sold. Young people, their innocence, and their sense of wonder and happiness do not appear in any catalog. You may or may not become a parent, but you have a special window on that world which is your reward for being here. Your ability to let youth enjoy its youth is part of your journey. From this, terrific adults can grow.

WHO SHARES YOUR BIRTHDAY?

Charles Schulz, born November 26, 1922
Tina Turner, born November 26, 1939
DJ Khaled, born November 26, 1976

NOVEMBER 27

WHO ARE YOU?

Your zodiac sign, Sagittarius, is ruled by Jupiter, which is about an excess of blessings. You are multitalented and can turn your hand to anything, impressing those around with your huge range of skills. You are practical enough to understand money, with the grounded earth sign Capricorn ruling everything you earn and own. Yet you also have a flair for communication, and your way with words and ideas first shows in childhood. Jupiter had special powers. You also tap into something greater.

YOUR DESTINY

The productive earth sign Capricorn describes your approach to finance, as mentioned. In your chart, it makes a perfect angle to Taurus, which governs your working life. Finally Virgo, the third grounded sign, is right at the top of your success zone, so the cycles of time suggest you will accumulate wealth. You hold on tight to your finances, rather like a crab hanging on to its food. Cancer rules the big picture of your finances, and you tend to be clingy with cash as it spells security to you.

TRAVEL AND RELOCATION

As a Sagittarian, you are tempted by adventure, from an overseas expedition to a long hike into foreign parts of your own country or emigration. With the Sun ruling this part of your chart, you never lack confidence about packing your bags. You are the first person to buy a ticket, and the last person to check the details of your journey. This also comes from your wildly optimistic ruling planet Jupiter. Instead, it is important that you look before you leap. Learn to research and check before you go.

THE REWARDS OF OPTIMISM

Sunny optimism is a feature of your personality, and in fact, you learn to hope for the best, as your horoscope is set up to always tilt in your favor. Since childhood, you have learned that every low point in your life becomes a high point eventually. Jupiter, your ruling planet, is also called Jove. You have a jovial attitude toward life with all its swings and roundabouts, because you know that even rock bottom means the only way is up. You will hit the heights of success many times in your life.

WHO SHARES YOUR BIRTHDAY?

Bruce Lee, born November 27, 1940

Jimi Hendrix, born November 27, 1942

Caroline Kennedy, born November 27, 1957

NOVEMBER 28

WHO ARE YOU?

You are funny or have such a strong sense of humor that natural comedians or cartoonists are your preferred company. Sagittarius, your ruling planet is Jupiter, also known as Jove. From this we get jokes, of course, and you can usually see them. You may be a natural wit, as Nancy Mitford (also born on this day) was. You were made for the internet. Your motivation, and that of others, is money. The ambitious, striving Capricorn rules your sector of business, income, valuables, banking, and all treasure hunts.

YOUR DESTINY

You will end up rich or heavily involved with somebody who is. Not only are your major goals in life tied to business, property, charity, or profit—your sense of home, security, and belonging is always tied to wealth. The zodiac sign we associate with gardening, land, and real estate is Cancer, and this sign also rules your strongest attachments. This may be your own powerful feelings for the places you eventually call your own or a potent connection to a woman who may be able to share, give, or strike a deal with you. That's fated.

THE SOUL OF AN EXPLORER

As a true Sagittarian, you are a natural explorer and feel at home in another region or country. You may spend a lot of time far away or move or make a relationship with somebody in a place so foreign to you, it recenters your comfort zone. Even when the maps don't make immediate sense, you're interested. In fact, you are one of those rare people who will set off on a search without any guarantees. For you, it is genuinely the journey. The eagle is your bird, and Jupiter, your ruling planet, is represented in mythology by flying high.

THE FAMILY TREE

Neptune rules your extended family on both sides. Feeling all at sea with your clan is common. Neptune is associated with the rolling tides. You may have been born into a family where you were always surfing the waves of change. Trying to anchor yourself with your relatives or ancestors is a regular mission for you. A lifelong lesson is that renewal and growth with the branches on the family tree cannot happen unless there is care and maintenance. Sagittarius, you always respond to a mission—a special quest, in fact.

WHO SHARES YOUR BIRTHDAY?

Nancy Mitford, born November 28, 1904

Berry Gordy, born November 28, 1929

Martin Clunes, born November 28, 1961

Armando Iannucci, born November 28, 1963

NOVEMBER 29

WHO ARE YOU?

Sagittarius, you were born with Mercury the Messenger in charge of your heart. This can result in long-distance relationships which prove to yourself and others the strength of your commitment. It may also be that the most important family or friends are separated from you across the map. As a result, you become a regular traveler, meeting them halfway with your air miles in hand. Mercury in mythology had wings on his helmet and sandals. You are more likely to fly, drive, or sail, but these journeys make you who you are.

YOUR DESTINY

In a perfect world, close relationships would last forever. Thanks to the cycles of time in your horoscope, you go through phases of choosing between repairing and recycling what has been lost or walking away and starting again. Sagittarius is known for its need to roam; this comes partly from your habitual pattern of traveling or relocating when things don't work out. Just as there is always a river to cross when you know where your heart is, you also find yourself comforted by the next destination, the next pin on a map.

LOOKING FOR MONEY

Saturn, the planet of waiting games, patience, and reality checks, rules your money. Not everything that looks like a map to buried treasure turns out to deliver the goods. Still, you are a true Sagittarian, ruled by optimistic Jupiter, always exploring where your high hopes take you. Capricorn, in charge of your bank account, brings you back down to earth—as it is an earth sign—and its own planet Saturn shows you that there are no guarantees, only the need for experienced experts who should be helping you.

TWINS ON THE SAME PATH

People born on November 29 have the numerology profile of 2, 1, 1 hidden in their birth date. You also have the dual sign of Gemini the Twins in charge of your partnerships. These are typically romantic in nature but can also be platonic: two friends, for example, or two professionals together. You will often find yourself with someone who is your nonidentical twin. You are the same, but different. The challenge throughout your life is to find a path you can both take or to invent a new map (two paths) to accept.

WHO SHARES YOUR BIRTHDAY?

C. S. Lewis, born November 29, 1898

Diane Ladd, born November 29, 1935

Don Cheadle, born November 29, 1964

Gemma Chan, born November 29, 1982

Stephanie Hsu, born November 29, 1990

NOVEMBER 30

WHO ARE YOU?

You are a Sagittarian who finds all your famous high hopes and enjoyment of life with your allies and friends. Groups suit you. There is a completely different side to your personality, though, shown by powerful Pluto in charge of your spirituality and soul. Pluto is a symbol of all the many simultaneous endings and new beginnings in your life. This makes you famously optimistic about the future, but it is also true that you are a deep thinker with strong ideas about who or what you have faith in—or truly do not.

YOUR DESTINY

You think like an Aquarian, even though you are a Sagittarian. The sign of friendship, cooperation, and collaboration governs the way you think and how you process the world. It is all done through a filter of team spirit. Your horoscope is set up so that the cycles of time will bring you clubs, teams, collectives, and communities all your life, from adolescence on. Together you can share the good things of life but also use the pooled resources to collect what you might gain from, not just now, but years into the future as well.

WATCHING THE MONEY GROW

Saturn is a symbol of staying power, and he is the ruler of your income and savings. The earth sign Capricorn is also there in your chart, enabling you to put both feet on the ground, nurture your income, and ultimately see it grow. This is really the attitude of a patient farmer or wise Wall Street investor, who has seen every high and low come and go. You gain a tremendous sense of security and comfort from this slow and steady approach. It allows you to be purely practical. Philosophy or faith does not come into it.

FREEDOM CALLS

The planet Uranus symbolizes your lifelong need to be free. This happens because you discover that life will often put you in a situation with home or work—or even larger issues—where you feel you cannot move. Experience teaches you this is not the case. It is your own willpower and intuition which can help you to liberate yourself. Uranus was discovered in a year of revolutions. Time and again you will stage your own revolution against who or what you feel confines you and find a way out via travel or relocation.

WHO SHARES YOUR BIRTHDAY?

Mark Twain, born November 30, 1835
Sir Winston Churchill, born November 30, 1874
Bo Jackson, born November 30, 1962
Chrissy Teigen, born November 30, 1985
Magnus Carlsen, born November 30, 1990

DECEMBER 1

WHO ARE YOU?

You are ruled by Jupiter, the planet of abundance, and that is your reward in life. You are also a Sagittarius Sun who happens to have the digit 1 in your birth date twice! This is played out in groups throughout your life from youth into old age. You are the one outsider against a group sometimes. At other times you will be very much in the circle against just one person. The Three Musketeers' saying "All for one and one for all" is very true for you. Through this you come to understand people power.

YOUR DESTINY

You are blessed with optimistic Jupiter in charge of your Sun sign and want the best—and the most—no matter if it's the people you share your life with or the places you call home. You have Neptune in charge of your houses, gardens, land, and apartments, and this planet is associated with bubbles. So that's property bubbles sometimes, but also escapes from the real world where you and yours are insulated from reality. This is rather like a rainbow. It seems real and delightful but it's not really . . . real. You can still enjoy it all, though.

REALITY AND ILLUSION

This Neptune effect is also there when you conjure up visions of particular houses, apartments, or people in the extended family. It's down to you to separate projection from truth. Much of the time, Sagittarius, you are looking at a cloud which is made up of imagination, memory (not always reliable), and pictures of what you think might be there. This is your great challenge in life: to come back to yourself and get to know yourself well enough to banish what are basically distractions and diversions which delay you.

COMFORTABLE ABUNDANCE

Your ruler Jupiter is associated with "more, more, more," and you will always have enjoyable, slow but steady phases in your life when you have more than enough money to go around. Saturn rules your finances, and as this planet moves at a snail's space—taking twenty-nine years to return to a sign—your progress with anything from the garden to your bank account will also be measured, rather than rushed. Jupiter is also associated with happy people who know how to show it. You are one of these. You know how to enjoy life and savor it.

WHO SHARES YOUR BIRTHDAY?

Richard Pryor, born December 1, 1940

Bette Midler, born December 1, 1945

Candace Bushnell, born December 1, 1958

Zoë Kravitz, born December 1, 1988

DECEMBER 2

WHO ARE YOU?

You are a fire sign, Sagittarius, with all the energy, enthusiasm, and can-do attitude associated with your leading element. You also have the numeral 2 hidden in your birth date—twice. You are chiefly concerned with pairs, duels, and two-way streets as a result of this. You are the peacemaker when people disagree or seek a peacemaker when you have your differences in one-on-one relationships. This also suits the position of Aries and its ruler Mars, the battle strategist, in your chart. They make perfect angles to your Sun sign.

YOUR DESTINY

The mother-child relationship is central to your psyche, soul, and spirit. In your Sagittarius chart, we find Neptune in charge of that bond. This may be about your own relationship with your mother or about all you dream of for yourself as a parent. Neptune is about inspiration. Nothing is necessarily real about what you remember or what you treasure as one of your highest hopes. They still feed you on the inside, though, and this story in your imagination, unconscious, or spirit is there all your life, no matter if you become a parent or not.

THE FAMILY TREE

You know you are a fire sign, and you believe in action, not words. This is very true when it comes to your family tree, which changes direction all the time. This lack of certainty and stability with particular relatives is also there with any family you create yourself. You have to set priorities in your life and, as you are a person on a mission, do not always have the time to fix the family. You do have a pattern of maintenance with these branches on the tree, though, and you believe in rapid solutions, not long, drawn-out answers.

MAKING A GROUP WORK

Your great reward in life is to make a group work. This may be a band, team, club, society, and so on. You have Libra, the sign of fair play, equality, and diplomacy, in charge of this section of your chart. You know how to balance the Libra scales with others, starting with just one other person inside a circle and building from there. Figuring out who deserves what in the mix—and who has what kind of role or responsibility—is something you are talented at doing. In this way you help to bring people together with potential triumphs.

WHO SHARES YOUR BIRTHDAY?

Maria Callas, born December 2, 1923

Gianni Versace, born December 2, 1946

Deb Haaland, born December 2, 1960

Britney Spears, born December 2, 1981

DECEMBER 3

WHO ARE YOU?

You are the true Sagittarian ruled by Jupiter, the planet of religion, philosophy, spirituality, and big ideas. You are easily fascinated by doctrines and can also preach your own version of what you think is the truth. Born with the numeral 3 hidden in your birth date, you also attract three-way situations. This may be you, your partner, and a child. It may be your partner and a third person who affects a marriage or sexual relationship. This is also shown by competitive Aries in charge of your personal life sector. The best way out? Withdraw.

YOUR DESTINY

You were born with the Sun in Sagittarius in the Ninth House of your birth chart, which is associated with the pope as well as religious orders. If you apply that general symbolism to your destiny, you will understand why there is a constant theme of faith and followers there. Of course, you can swap roles so that sometimes you are the true believer or disciple. At other times you will have a sacred text—whatever form that might take—to refer to. A great deal of your destiny revolves around knowing and trusting or questioning knowledge. It's your way to true faith.

DEALING WITH GROUPS

In your birth chart, Aquarius rules groups of all kinds, from societies to online circles. When we go to your solar chart, this sign turns up again, taking charge of your plans, strategies, and ideas. You regularly spend a lot of time thinking about the way groups operate—because you have to. This is true all your life from youth to old age. This makes you something of a strategist where the hive mind is concerned. The perfect trine to your sign made by assertive Aries and defensive Mars helps you avoid group politics before anything ever comes to pass.

ABUNDANCE AND THE EXTENDED FAMILY

There is always a champagne atmosphere surrounding your extended family finances. The planet Neptune is in charge of both the family and property, and it is also associated with bubbles. This may literally end up being a property bubble benefiting you or those close to you. On a more symbolic note it shows the comfortable, insulated world you all inhabit. With Cancer, the family sign, also in charge of wills, inheritance, legacies, allowances, and trust funds, your bank account is an emotional matter. Blood is thicker than water.

WHO SHARES YOUR BIRTHDAY?

Joseph Conrad, born December 3, 1857
Ozzy Osbourne, born December 3, 1948
Julianne Moore, born December 3, 1960

DECEMBER 4

WHO ARE YOU?

You were born with Jupiter, the planet of abundance and good fortune, ruling your Sagittarius Sun sign. You are blessed with big financial opportunities all your life and, with enough trust and hard work, can turn potential into delivery. As the sign of home, land, and garden is Cancer—and it also rules your bank account—what you gain in life immediately goes into the right environment for you. You are a lifelong renovator or gardener as a result; perhaps a lifelong property ladder devotee. Money is the gateway to a better home.

YOUR DESTINY

You were born with the leadership sign Leo in charge of your knowledge, qualifications, publications, websites, and broadcasting. Leo lends you the dignity and respect that you deserve, as you are a natural academic even if you leave school when you are young. You never stop learning and pass that on to others. You are a natural tutor or teacher figure to people who seek your expertise within your chosen field. Leo ruling this sector of your chart gives you poise, confidence, and a certain position in your profession or area.

A SENSE OF PLACE

For all that you believe in using money to secure a sense of place, your greatest challenge is actually doing so, as through no fault of your own, you tend to come from or settle in areas which are never settled at all. Dealing with ongoing changes to your local area or country is a lifelong challenge. Neptune and Pisces govern this area of your chart, and that can result in a rather random situation where everything is all over the place all the time. Your extended family tree is also hard to organize and maintain for similar reasons. This is your challenge.

INVESTMENT AND SAVINGS

The grounded earth sign Capricorn rules your income, savings, shares, and investments. Capricorn the Goat likes to climb toward a high goal, and you set the bar for yourself very high indeed, aiming for the substantial amounts of money that you know are there for you. Life's rich reward is to give you the comfort, security, and choice that makes you feel abundant. Capricorn is also about being grounded in the real world, and as your extended family never gives you that guarantee of security, you find it through finance.

WHO SHARES YOUR BIRTHDAY?

Ronnie Corbett, born December 4, 1930
Jeff Bridges, born December 4, 1949
Jay-Z, born December 4, 1969
Tyra Banks, born December 4, 1973

DECEMBER 5

WHO ARE YOU?

You are a true Sagittarian who will always find yourself at a crossroads on the map as major choices to travel or relocate are there all your life. However, you also have the sensitive Cancer ruling all that you find most valuable. What is so precious to you that it is priceless? The mother-child bond. This may be because of the relationship you have with your own mom or the special connection you dream of. This applies no matter if you have offspring or not, Sagittarius. The maternal ties to your child feed your soul.

YOUR DESTINY

You are destined to become the boss or a towering figure in your profession. Your chosen field will have a well-established structure so that there is only a limited amount of room at the top and it takes a long time to climb there. Understanding and respecting the system or establishment is part of the journey. You value the mother-child bond in life, but also traditional success and ambition. The reason for that is Saturn and Capricorn in charge of your sector of all that is valuable. You do what it takes to make it—and you do.

BOUNDARIES AT HOME

You were born with Pisces the Fish and its planet Neptune in charge of your home-life. This includes the interior as well as the garden or local area. Understanding the need for boundaries with yourself and others is important. In fact, it's your greatest challenge as Neptune can be rather like a flooding river or ocean. Life can end up feeling quite random, with everything all over the place everywhere—all the time. This is important with partnerships, too. The past never quite goes away for you, and that also needs boundaries.

FORKS IN THE ROAD

The cycles of time reach into your horoscope in quite dramatic ways, and every so often, you come to a crossroads where you must decide how to divide your world or carve up your situation. This always involves travel or moving, and over time you learn to develop your intuition. The eternal Sagittarian question "Where and with which people?" is not just about geography for you. It is also about the group: your circles of friends and allies. This comes from Aquarius, the sign which rules your social life, taking charge of your sector of journeys.

WHO SHARES YOUR BIRTHDAY?

Walt Disney, born December 5, 1901
Little Richard, born December 5, 1932
José Carreras, born December 5, 1946
Catherine Tate, born December 5, 1969

DECEMBER 6

WHO ARE YOU?

Sagittarius is the sign of the traveler, wanderer, or explorer. You are a great believer in getting away from it all—and away from people who do not fulfill you—in order to make life better. This can result in a job that you deliberately take, whether because of the travel or a hiking hobby. More dramatically, you are something of a lifelong escape artist who would rather be on the move or even relocate than stay and deal with emotional issues. This works well for you, Sagittarius, as when you switch your surroundings it gives you a new perspective.

YOUR DESTINY

Leo and its ruler the Sun make stunning angles to your own Sagittarius Sun. Leo is about seeding the next generation and the one after that. Children and teenagers are central to your destiny, no matter if you become a parent or not. This may be young relatives, for example, or perhaps your jobs will involve younger people. Leo is about heirs, spares, and pretenders to the throne—so it's not only your children, but also younger people who are influenced by the legacy of your personality for years to come.

HOME AND HOUSEHOLD

The planet of illusion, Neptune, rules your house, garden, apartment, household, and family. Neptune is rather like the horizon you never reach when swimming in the ocean: it seems to be real but always slips away. Neptune also governs the pot of gold at the end of the rainbow. If you have ever tried to find it, you have also observed it slips away as you get closer. Your challenge in life is to find a way of enjoying your home and household without buying into an illusion. Where possible, have objective outsiders advise you here.

EXTENDED FAMILY WEALTH

The financial and property side of your life is ruled by Cancer, which in turn governs the family. It also oversees property, which can be an investment or a proper home. This area of your horoscope is associated with trust funds, wills, legacies, and inheritance. All your life you will see how abundant the world can be when the generations come together to share or give. This also springs partly from Saturn, the planet of old age, being in charge of your own budget. It may be that older members of the family or you as you age provide the rules.

WHO SHARES YOUR BIRTHDAY?

Henry VI of England, born December 6, 1421

Ira Gershwin, born December 6, 1896

Fritz Scholder, born December 6, 1937

Judd Apatow, born December 6, 1967

DECEMBER 7

WHO ARE YOU?

You have the numerals 1 and 2 hidden in your December birth date, and you see the one-on-one relationship that a child has with their mother as central to your soul. This happens even if you never have children. It may be about "the two of us": meaning your own mother and yourself, for example. You may also hold the dream of the mother-child bond in your mind, hoping to achieve that in other ways. Cancer, the sign associated with maternal instinct, rules everything you find so precious it is also priceless.

YOUR DESTINY

Cancer is not only about maternal instinct; it is also about the family tree. Sagittarius, this sign of the crab with its home on its back is also about the extended clan, which reaches far down into the burrows on any sandy beach. When you realize that this is what sustains you and holds you, everything becomes better. Cancer governs what is most valuable to you—who or what you will never sell your soul for. The solid gold rewards you want from relationships and life itself can be found when you center, focus, and go back to your ancestral roots.

MEN AND WOMEN—TWIN CHALLENGES

Gemini the Twins rules your duets, double acts, partnerships, and also your differences. There are always two sides to every story about men and women in your life. This also takes you back to the numerals 1 and 2 in your birth date. Who comes first when there are two of you coming from opposite places? This may pan out in your personal life (marriage, for example) or in your professional life. It can even show up in friendship as Libra, the sign of equality between the two sexes, has charge of your social world and social media.

MANAGING GROUPS

Libra in your chart rules groups in general, not only the social or friendly ones. Owing to the way the cycles of time move in your horoscope, you will have to become a strategist when dealing with particular circles of people. These may be teams, clubs, bands, political parties, societies, but they all share a hive mind. A perfect angle from assertive Mars and his sign Aries—which rules speed and action—suggests you are very good at preemptive strikes. You are quick, clever, and understand people politics very well, Sagittarius.

WHO SHARES YOUR BIRTHDAY?

Tom Waits, born December 7, 1949

Larry Bird, born December 7, 1956

Nicholas Hoult, born December 7, 1989

DECEMBER 8

WHO ARE YOU?

You are a typical Sagittarian in that you like the good life, ruled by your own planet Jupiter, and enjoy sharing what life has to offer with people who have the happiness habit like you. You were also born with Cancer ruling everything that money cannot buy: what is priceless and also an inheritance. This sign governs mothers and children. This may be your own mother or a future dream of parenthood. Perhaps it is a sacred memory of a son or daughter, when they were small. Maternal instinct and this particular family tie feed your soul.

YOUR DESTINY

You find equality within a group, as Libra, the sign of fairness and sharing, governs all the clubs, teams, circles, and networks you find yourself in. You will repeatedly join societies, associations, bands, political parties, and so on, and there you will discover more than you asked for. Your challenge is to use what you all have to share; those pooled resources can go a very long way. It can be hard to think seriously about the future when there is so much to celebrate with your friends and allies, but the potential is rich. Remember it.

YOUR HOME AND REALITY CHECKS

You were born with Neptune ruling your sector of houses, apartments, land, and gardens. Neptune is well-known in astrology for situations where reality vanishes. It is very easy for you to live in a space far removed from the everyday and ordinary. It can feel more like a great escape than an actual home. This applies to your surroundings, too: the environment around where you live. Managing what is there, controlling and containing it, is a wise move all your life. Without that caretaking, you'll find hard lessons.

UNITY AND SOLIDARITY

Cooperation and collaboration come easily when life is all about celebration, but if you are collectively trying to build something together—a project, plan, or idea—it takes work. As you know, Libra oversees these communities and circles in your life, and the idea of equal sharing is very important. This can be difficult when you are all so different. Aquarius, the sign ruling diversity in a community, governs your ideas and thoughts. You know this makes sense with your many groups; the reward comes when you can act on it and unite.

WHO SHARES YOUR BIRTHDAY?

Mary, Queen of Scots, born December 8, 1542
Sammy Davis Jr., born December 8, 1925
Jim Morrison, born December 8, 1943

DECEMBER 9

WHO ARE YOU?

You are a Sagittarian, ruled by Jupiter, the planet of abundance. You will have enough excess wealth in your life to be able to give generously, no matter if this is part of your job, your relationships, or your charitable causes. Jupiter is also associated with the happiness habit, and you have it. Turning to your whole solar chart, Cancer governs everything that is so precious to you it is priceless. That is your home and/or garden. It is also any extended family member who needs your help as Cancer is the sign which rules the clan.

YOUR DESTINY

You are an idea person who always has a plan or project destined for another country. You were born with the Sun in Sagittarius, the sign of the archer who aims far and wide and often hits its targets with a spectacular bull's-eye. The numerals 1 and 2 are hidden in your birth date, and you tend to go with one concept and forget there are two. This is a numerology pattern in your life, but it also shows up in your chart. You want more from the world—and why not? The issue is grounding yourself in reality and preparing yourself.

FINDING A FINANCIAL SYSTEM

The cycles of time in your horoscope suggest that your national economy, but also the global economy, will have a direct impact on how you manage your money. You may already have gone through a global financial crisis, for example, which picked up your chart. You are more than able to beat these kinds of challenges in business, stock markets, or at the bank. However, it takes constant adjustment and change on your part, as every time you find yourself all at sea with, say, property you have to once again reinvent a system.

THE MEANING OF MONEY

You have a keen sense of what it's like to juggle income as well as debt. This makes you sympathetic to the people who are the have-nots in your world. You are not immune to the lows of the economy as well as the highs, and this makes you more sympathetic to those in need. As a result in your personal or professional life you know how to give. There is a shape in your chart called a T-Square between Libra the scales of balance and fairness and the signs ruling your finance zones. Libra is about fair play and justice, and you feel it keenly with finance.

WHO SHARES YOUR BIRTHDAY?

Kirk Douglas, born December 9, 1916

Bob Hawke, born December 9, 1929

Judi Dench, born December 9, 1934

Empress Masako, born December 9, 1963

DECEMBER 10

WHO ARE YOU?

You were born with this sequence in your birth date in numerology: 1, 2, 1, 0. As a result of this you are very single-minded about being one against the many or, perhaps, one of the many. You take turns being inside the circle against just one person, but also being the solo outsider who must deal with the group. This also shows in your chart. There are tremendous questions about what is fair or equal with the hive mind. This may be a trade union or a football team; it depends on your lifestyle. Over time you learn how to work with this.

YOUR DESTINY

You are an explorer like all Sagittarians and find traveling away or moving therapeutic. It is your answer all your life, and you use your passionate intensity within to motivate you to make the big shifts in your world. The complicated Scorpio and its power planet Pluto rule your unconscious mind, your daydreams, your meditative thoughts, and your inner life. This is really where your engine room is, Sagittarius. It is also why we find you habitually breaking free and finding a different point on the map again and again. It liberates you.

GROUPS AND YOU

One of the things you discover about the 1 in your birth date is that "one against the many" is unfair but sometimes has to happen. This does not mean the realities of groups pass you by, though. You are a clever and quick-witted strategist when it comes to particular networks or circles of people who trigger your defenses. Aries, associated with conflicts, and its ruler Mars make a perfect trine to your Sagittarius side. You can be a person of action when you have to be and head off any politics.

THE WORKER BEE

Your reward in life is being a successful and admired worker bee, who is capable of making a steady income from doing a job well. You are productive, grounded, and focused when your talents and skills are put to good use. You can become the reliable source of quality for people as you do not vary your formula but stick to what you know is lucrative but also popular. You can do this in any profession where you can see your bank account gaining; you will have wide choices all your life but what appeals most is the chance for an artisan's approach.

WHO SHARES YOUR BIRTHDAY?

Emily Dickinson, born December 10, 1830

Kenneth Branagh, born December 10, 1960

Raven-Symoné, born December 10, 1985

DECEMBER 11

WHO ARE YOU?

You were born with the numeral 2 in your birth date, hidden with 1 repeated twice. You see both sides of the story and stand in the middle. This is also shown in your horoscope where Gemini the Twins is your opposite sign. So you are the one person who can see dual perspectives on the same idea. This makes you a respected writer, broadcaster, web citizen, or academic. Even if your career takes you on a different journey in life, you are the perpetual student, Sagittarius, or natural tutor. Jupiter, ruling academia, also governs your sign.

YOUR DESTINY

You have probably read that Sagittarius is the sign associated with travel and exploration. This is true. Your Sagittarius Sun is in the Ninth House of your birth chart, where you take all your most important journeys. You measure the depth of your feelings by the distance you are prepared to travel. Your horoscope is set up in such a way that the cycles of time will put you in long-distance relationships, for example, or separate you from the people you care about in your extended circle of friends and family, so you must meet in the middle.

SOLO JOURNEYS

You are also a solo explorer or escape artist. When relationships are unfulfilling, your response is to travel by yourself or even just go for long walks. Other ways to find yourself again—and a deeper sense of satisfaction—might include fishing or golf. More dramatically, you are quite capable of moving right away from any situation you find too much to deal with. Pluto the planet of transformation rules your inner life and inner self. By going it alone, you change your point of view and on return or with distance find a new perspective.

THE FREEDOM TO START AGAIN

When your solar chart is under inspection, it becomes clear that the freedom to start again is very important to you. Uranus is a symbol of quite revolutionary change which requires a radical response from you as he rules your mindset and ideas. As this happens periodically in your life, you become quite used to stepping back from home or work and asking yourself about your own independence. The answers often challenge you to change either what was there or just yourself. Sometimes walking away is the most liberating thing.

WHO SHARES YOUR BIRTHDAY?

Aleksandr Solzhenitsyn, born December 11, 1918

Rita Moreno, born December 11, 1931

Hailee Steinfeld, born December 11, 1996

DECEMBER 12

WHO ARE YOU?

You were born with the numerals 1 and 2 repeated in your birth date. In numerology this puts you between two cities or countries. You are the one who stands in the center. The double two can also indicate being between two cultures. In your horoscope, Sagittarius, we also find a big focus on a life filled with commuting, travel, or worldwide web exploration. This may be because of your career, studies, or personal life. The impressive Leo governs all your journeys, and you are always at the center wherever you go to.

YOUR DESTINY

You are a true Sagittarian, ruled by Jupiter the planet of travel and also blessed with good fortune in your quest to be number one and come first. This is partly a result of the numerology of your birth date. You also have Virgo, the sign of the healer and the healed, at the highest point of your chart. It is your destiny to go through major episodes of help, remedy, or therapy in your life. Knowing what it feels like to assist others makes you see how purifying the process can be. Being assisted reminds you of how crucial it is to put others' health first.

COMING FIRST

When you write out your birth date in long form, you can see that one against one means a game of two sides (or a contest) and there can only be one winner. You will find that this is also a test when you triumph in all your competitions or conquests, your battles or challenges. Strangely enough, success brings all kinds of responses from the world. There are those who will have a strong reaction against your winning ways because it makes them feel insecure. Then, there is the more serious issue: How do you top yourself? Where to next?

THE FAMILY TREE

Going back to your roots with immediate relatives or distant ancestors helps to ground and center you. You were born with Neptune in charge of your family tree zone, and as a result you can feel a lack of focus in your life until you remember that where you come from is a good thing to claim and appreciate. Until this happens you may never feel as if you are really connected. Neptune is a symbol of drifting and floating in astrology, as he is the ruler of the ocean. If you ever feel all at sea, Sagittarius, your roots are the answer.

WHO SHARES YOUR BIRTHDAY?

Edvard Munch, born December 12, 1863

Frank Sinatra, born December 12, 1915

Dionne Warwick, born December 12, 1940

DECEMBER 13

WHO ARE YOU?

You are a fire sign, Sagittarius, and so a person of action. More than anything else, it is your extended family which motivates you to show others how fast and furious—and fiery—you can be. You have a similar energy when it comes to your town, local area, and/or country as all your life it will ask you to put action before words. Life is quite different when it comes to groups and friends. Libra governs this extremely sociable, easy, and welcome part of your life. Libra rules couples and pairs, partnerships and double acts; they all welcome you.

YOUR DESTINY

Gemini the Twins has charge of your own partnerships in life. You will repeatedly end up in all kinds of pairs or duets where you feel you are the same as the other person, but different. This is rather like being a sibling with a nonidentical opposite. Decisions about taking the same path, two different paths, or a combination of both will repeat all your life. The cycles of time in your horoscope will always ask you to solve this issue. The numerals 1 and 2 in your birth date also hint at the challenge. One of us or both of us?

MAINTAINING FAMILY AND PLACE

As you know, you are a driven and energetic fire sign, Sagittarius, but it would seem that you have to be when it comes to your family tree and also your place in the world. This is where Neptune is in charge of your horoscope, and life can be unsettled, confused, and confusing. Not having solid ground beneath your feet or a family to hold steady means you will repeatedly find yourself given the choice to maintain it or change your situation. Sometimes you may find you are simply tempted to leave. At other times you will actively take on the task to evolve.

NUMBER ONE

The numbers in your birth date show 1 twice, as you know, and also 2—indicating second place. Then there is 3—for third place. Sometimes coming first or being on top is all that matters, and you will enjoy those triumphs in your life. You will also learn what it feels like to be in a group when there is a dramatic rise to success for somebody else. These unforgettable victories tend to challenge those around who must decide where their loyalties lie or what the politics will be. This is a lesson and maybe a reward.

WHO SHARES YOUR BIRTHDAY?

Diego Rivera, born December 13, 1886
Jamie Foxx, born December 13, 1967
Taylor Swift, born December 13, 1989

DECEMBER 14

WHO ARE YOU?

You are the Sagittarian whose choices about travel or relocation are more pivotal than those of others. You may have read that you are the natural traveler or migrant of the zodiac, ruled by Jupiter, the planet owning the big picture on the world map. This is quite true, but you also have a strong attachment to money. This comes from the emotional water sign Cancer in charge of your finances and property. Cancer the Crab also tends to cling. Your bank account makes you feel secure, and that feeling is something you'll always strive for.

YOUR DESTINY

As a Sagittarian, you tend to be a natural escape artist or explorer. Several times in your life you will find the answers you are looking for by liberating yourself from places you feel trapped and finding your way to destinations representing a completely new life to you. This goes further than just packing boxes or bags for a holiday; journeys represent something spiritual to you. Being free is central to your ideas. The planet Uranus, a symbol of independence, rules your mind. You can only take feeling marooned for so long.

GROUPS AND PEOPLE POWER

Aquarius, the sign of people power in a group, also governs your thoughts and ideas. Your way of seeing the world is based on your own experiences as part of a community with incredible power who act as one. You are also fated to sometimes know what it feels like to be the outsider a group acts against. The numeral 1 is hidden in your birth date, and in numerology this puts the one against the many—the majority, who are all the same, against the one outsider or opponent. Being in the majority, though, shows you how effective unity is.

THE BIG CROSSROADS

Your life often ends up like the famous Clash song: "Should I Stay or Should I Go?" If you stay, then nothing improves, but if you go, then everything changes—not just your new location, but also your entire possible future. Your horoscope is set up in such a way that the cycles of time will often bring you to these dramatic points. Every time it happens, you will have to carve up the territory, and this may be between two or three places on the map, for example. What and who to cut out will be an intuitive choice on every different occasion.

WHO SHARES YOUR BIRTHDAY?

Tycho Brahe, born December 14, 1546

King George VI of England, born December 14, 1895

Patty Duke, born December 14, 1946

DECEMBER 15

WHO ARE YOU?

You are the Sagittarian who is at heart an escape artist, but unlike other Sagittarius Sun people you do not merely go on vacation—you take a holiday from reality. In fact, you are never more at home in the world than when you're not actually in it—at least the way others understand it. You also have a highly strategic side to your character, though, as Aquarius rules your mind. Aquarius is all about group psychology and understanding how people are in a circle. Knowing this means you can prevent issues before they even take hold in your life.

YOUR DESTINY

You are an authority in education, academia, the world of ideas, the worldwide web itself, publishing, and all kinds of knowledge exchange. Leo, the sign of leadership, oversees this area of your chart. If you are ever going to be crowned for your brilliant plans, it's thanks to this placement in your chart. Your only issue is self-imposed, and that's procrastination. You can be hesitant about taking your projects and concepts further, and as a result, they sometimes come to nothing. Knowing this helps you find ways to ensure they thrive.

FAMILY AND PLACE

The dual sign Pisces, the two fish, rules your extended family network and your sense of place in the world. You also have the numeral 2 in your date of birth. As a result, you will always be pulled in two different directions by couples and pairs in your tribe. Which way will you go? How to divide your time and energy? This may be your parents or the godparent of one of your children and their partner. Over time you realize that creating your own framework and structure for these two-way issues is the way forward for you.

YOUR OWN UNIVERSE

The planet Neptune and his sign Pisces are at the base of your horoscope, which is where you come from, in terms of your extended family and your place in the world. It's not always clear, as a result, which way you should go in life. From this springs the need to opt out and find your own sense of belonging. This comes from inhabiting your own universe, which has nothing to do with ordinary life as other people know it. You are a law unto yourself when you use this part of your personality, making up your own way to be uniquely yourself.

WHO SHARES YOUR BIRTHDAY?

Gustave Eiffel, born December 15, 1832
J. Paul Getty, born December 15, 1892
Don Johnson, born December 15, 1949

DECEMBER 16

WHO ARE YOU?

You are ruled by Jupiter, the figure the Romans associated with high places and top position in the hierarchy of gods. Your horoscope today is not so different: you are the winner who hits the heights, but also the mover and shaker who understands that when others rise to the top, you have to work with them. Ambitious Capricorn rules everything that you find so precious it is priceless. Capricorn is also about the peaks of life; this is the mountain goat who climbs to the mountaintop. The numeral 1 hidden in your birth date says "first."

YOUR DESTINY

Your extended network of family and friends is way out of the real world for you. Neptune governs your sense of belonging to people and places. Neptune is also a symbol for a different reality, a vacation from the rest of life. Being with these people is like going through a portal. Among your groups you have particular couples, duets, or pairs who are a key part of your holidays from the everyday. Libra, the scales of balance, rules your social life sector, and it has always been associated with partnerships of all kinds. The numeral 2 is also in your birth date.

INVESTING AND SAVING

The emotional Cancer oversees your finances, and your feelings rule your bank account, not necessarily the advice of an accountant or stockbroker. Sometimes the dream is a house, apartment, or garden; sometimes it's your local area. As you know, Neptune governs your people but also your place in the world. Despite your lack of strict business or real estate acumen, you are so invested in even a small amount of money that this may be enough to motivate you to seek objective opinions. The potential is there, but it's also a big challenge for you.

BRINGING TWO SIDES TOGETHER

Gemini the Twins rules your conflicts in life, and you also have 2 hidden in your birth date as well as 1. This central idea of one helping two sides is central to your life. You may also find that you are up against another person who is twinned with you in a fated way. Just as Castor and Pollux the heavenly twins in the Gemini constellation had to find agreement, so might you. That is when one other can unite both of you. These games of one/two help shape you, your philosophy, and your sense of humor.

WHO SHARES YOUR BIRTHDAY?

Catherine of Aragon, born December 16, 1485

Jane Austen, born December 16, 1775

Wassily Kandinsky, born December 16, 1866

DECEMBER 17

WHO ARE YOU?

You are a fire sign, Sagittarius, with all the energy and drive of that element. You take off quickly when you have a burning mission, and that can result in long-term growth, fueled by your personality. You have another side to your character, though, and that can be rather ungrounded until you remember your family tree. Going back to your roots, relatives, ancestors, and culture is healing. It's an effort, with Neptune ruling your home sector, but floating and drifting are eventually replaced by a firm commitment to where you come from.

YOUR DESTINY

You have the numeral 1 twice in your birth date, and you often come first. You will ace the competition. This can come from one idea or one qualification. The ambitious Capricorn rules everything that is so precious to you it is priceless. Capricorn the Goat wants the top job, top position, and top of the mountain. You don't have actual mountains to climb, but you do have structures to ascend. Corporations or particular parts of high society are typical. And when others are number one? You support them as you can.

INVESTING AND SAVING

You've read about how solid, grounded, down-to-earth Capricorn is in charge of everything money cannot buy. You really value being on top. This also applies to your finances. You want to come first with yourself more than anything else and find the security on an economic level that is so hard to get with some relationships. As a result of this, you can hang on and hold on to everything you own or earn. You have Cancer, an emotional and clinging water sign, ruling joint finance and property. Objective and impartial advice can be very useful.

THE REWARD OF BRILLIANT CONCEPTS

It may be a plan on the back of a paper napkin or something committed to a computer. It may be a symphony (Beethoven was born with a similar horoscope) or just a brain wave with fantastic potential. This is where you are most recognizably a Sagittarian: fired up—you are a fire sign, after all—and prepared to travel vast distances or at least trawl the worldwide web to seek the right place for your ideas. When it works for you, it does so because you do what goes against your nature: you meticulously plan, prepare, and research. Virgo rules your success!

WHO SHARES YOUR BIRTHDAY?

Ludwig van Beethoven, born December 17, 1770

Eugene Levy, born December 17, 1946

Wes Studi, born December 17, 1947

Manny Pacquiao, born December 17, 1978

DECEMBER 18

WHO ARE YOU?

You are the escape artist you've read about in astrology books. You are a natural migrant and may relocate more than once to get away from situations that have passed their use-by date. Because of this, Sagittarius, you also sympathize with anybody who is a spiritual refugee. The real heart of you is tied to the mother-child relationship, though. This may be you and your own mom or your fervent hopes and wishes for the future regarding your own or other people's children. Cancer, the sign of maternal bonds, rules all that is priceless.

YOUR DESTINY

You are governed by Jupiter, the planet which symbolizes the big picture. The eagle is his bird, soaring far and wide seeking opportunity. Jupiter is also associated with thunder and the relief and release of dramatic turning points. All this adds up in your life and your chart, because you are the person who has faith in new horizons, new adventures, new locations. You may relocate more than once, as you've read, or even find a completely new country to relaunch yourself in. You understand others who are also migrants and explorers.

THE HIVE MIND AND YOUR MIND

You think in terms of groups and hive minds, as Aquarius, the sign ruling circles and networks, is in charge of your ideas and communication. Knowing how people are when they are all clustered together in one community is extremely useful. It makes you a brilliant strategist who is always one step ahead of any collective you believe could complicate life. Reading the hive mind is one way of putting it. Your intuition and naturally astute thinking will repeatedly save the day from your adolescence into old age.

THE COMFORT OF MONEY

Cancer is the zodiac sign which not only rules everything which is so precious it is priceless; it also rules your values. The comfort of money is emotional for you, and economists and accountants may never understand what it means to you. Tremendous security comes when you hold enough and have enough to offer the luxury of choosing: How to invest or save? How to donate or lend?

How to cut deals? You are ruled by fortunate Jupiter, the planet of abundance, and will repeatedly have solid gold assets as your comforter.

WHO SHARES YOUR BIRTHDAY?

Steven Spielberg, born December 18, 1946

Brad Pitt, born December 18, 1963

Billie Eilish, born December 18, 2001

DECEMBER 19

WHO ARE YOU?

You are a Sagittarian, but ambitious Capricorn rules everything that is so precious to you it is priceless. You climb to the top and don't mind if it's a slow process to attain the peak of your profession or field. The other key sign in your chart is Gemini the Twins. This symbol of two people who are the same but different shows up in your sector of duets and duels. Two is your number, and it also shows up in your birth date in numerology. In fact, both 1 and 2 feature. All your life, making one and one equal two is your challenge.

YOUR DESTINY

As you've read, you value success, position, mission, and ambition very highly, so you are able to commit to the upward climb when you are young. It can take a long time to get to the mountaintop for Capricorn the Goat, but as this astrological symbol rules what is so precious to you, you are prepared to wait. When you are established, you find yourself with authority that others can only look up to. Another earth sign, the grounded Virgo, governs your ultimate achievement, and you are never more practical than when getting to the top.

ILLUSIONS AND REALITY

The planet Neptune with all his clouds of confusion rules your house, apartment, and homelife. Neptune is a symbol of fog and sea mist, and it is important that you realize you are imagining or projecting a great deal of the time. This may be a dream holiday house you think is just a fantasy—but could become real—and even particular situations within the extended family that you find haunt you, like ghosts. When you realize you are distracting yourself from the real issue, which is self-knowledge, you can lose the illusions and be better for it.

WORK AND LIFESTYLE

As you have read, the patient, stoic earth sign Capricorn rules everything that is beyond price for you and that is your own success. Another earth sign, Virgo, actually has charge of your ambition in life. Finally, the third earth sign Taurus describes your lifestyle, daily routine, well-being, and approach to your work ethic. Of these, Virgo is most important as it shows up twice in your chart, once overseeing your achievements and later trining your zone of health. When you manage to reach your goals by working smarter (not harder), you benefit.

WHO SHARES YOUR BIRTHDAY?

Edith Piaf, born December 19, 1915
Alyssa Milano, born December 19, 1972
Jake Gyllenhaal, born December 19, 1980

DECEMBER 20

WHO ARE YOU?

You are the adventurous person you read about in astrology books, ready to take your ideas to other regions or countries. You are the internet explorer who may or may not use Internet Explorer, but you are always ready to see where you can successfully plant your projects. Your birth date contains the numeral 2 twice as well as 1. You are the one person who can help two people reach agreement, and it happens all your life. You are often one of the two who are at odds with each other; again it is always one person who fixes this.

YOUR DESTINY

The planet Saturn influences your finances, business interests, charity, possessions, and property. Saturn is about slow and steady growth. In turn, Saturn rules Capricorn, which is an earth sign, grounded in the real world with a practical approach to money. Thanks to the cycles of time in your horoscope, you are a long-term investor with the patience to see things through to completion. You also have an emotional attachment to whatever you finance. Caring Cancer with all its strong feelings affects the other side of your money approach.

BUILDING AND REBUILDING

Your mindset is all about freedom, with Uranus, the planet of sudden liberation, influencing your thoughts and ideas. This is very important as you will spend your life building (and walking away from situations you need to be free of) and also rebuilding (and having the space to go back and reconstruct anything you believe is worth it). Every time you face this kind of dramatic crossroads in your life, you will remember that despite the revolution in front of you, from this always comes liberty. Every time you will be at liberty to choose destiny.

EXPORTING YOUR IDEAS

Your most satisfying achievements will be taking your talents, skills, and projects and finding the right place for them. You are more than content to try your luck. In fact, Jupiter the planet of good fortune is a key factor. Being optimistic about exporting your plans is part of your nature. Once you are able to remember that the issue is where and when to plant your concepts—rather than focusing on the details of the idea—you gain. Experience will teach you that the more times you do your homework on location and in the environment, the better.

WHO SHARES YOUR BIRTHDAY?

Robert Menzies, born December 20, 1894

Irene Dunne, born December 20, 1898

Jonah Hill, born December 20, 1983

DECEMBER 21

WHO ARE YOU?

You are a true explorer and your Sun aspects the Ninth House of knowledge and wisdom in your birth chart. You are an outstanding source for people but also the person who is a perpetual student of life. You also have great authority with the next generation—and in fact all the generations after that. Children and young people speak to your soul, and you have great influence here, no matter if you become a parent or not. Leo makes a stunning chart pattern, and so you are the monarch of the youth ahead of you.

YOUR DESTINY

You value the mother-child relationship so highly that it is precious to the point of being priceless. Cancer, which rules the maternal bond, also influences what you will not sell your soul for. This may be the treasured memory of your own mom raising you. It may be your dream or prayer for your own future. Sometimes it is another woman who is the sacred mother figure of your imagination, dreams, or unconscious mind. This may be your wife, for example. You may or may not be aware of it, but this powers your spirit.

THE WORLDWIDE WEB

You were always going to be a candidate for special status on the worldwide web. Jupiter rules the world; the internet rules a big world of ideas. This is your domain, no matter if you leave school young or proceed to academia or publishing. Pearls of wisdom make you important to those who need you to guide them in your chosen field. You are capable of gathering great expertise and finding a way to convey what you know that impresses but also encourages. You are not quite an open book, Sagittarius, but your books are always open.

FAIR AND EQUAL FRIENDSHIP

Libra is about the balanced scales between two people and also happens to affect your friendships, groups, and circles. Your great reward in life is finding the person who can supply you with what you need most of all—harmony between equals. You are both supplied in turn by the wider group or network. These people, who pool resources together, can also be fed by both of you, so it's a circular pattern of wonderful cooperation and understanding between like minds. It's an important theme from youth onward.

WHO SHARES YOUR BIRTHDAY?

Nostradamus, born December 21, 1503

Jane Fonda, born December 21, 1937

Samuel L. Jackson, born December 21, 1948

DECEMBER 22

WHO ARE YOU?

You are the kind of person who should really start gathering air miles from childhood, because your life is full of important journeys. You are a natural migrant, in fact. Your horoscope is set up in such a way that the cycles of time will often separate you from the people you care about. This may be partners, family, or friends. There is nothing like a long-distance relationship to bring out the romantic in you. Any kind of emotional attachment turns you into a commuter or explorer, though. Your life is spent on the move, proving affections.

YOUR DESTINY

Your horoscope reveals several themes which describe mothers and children. One is the Moon and her rulership of the zodiac sign Cancer. You may or may not become a parent, but the fascinating connection that moms share with their sons or daughters has a profound effect on you. This may be your own mother who had a complex, unique relationship with you. It may also be you yourself, if you have a child—or the woman in your life you see as mother to your heirs. Your soul, spirit, or subconscious is drawn deeply to this.

WEALTH AND PENNIES FROM HEAVEN

The interesting thing about the wealth repeatedly on offer to you during your life is that it is also a challenge for you. You may not have thought there would be anything particularly hard about accepting large lump sums when they appear like pennies from heaven. Yet this requires more thought than it would first appear. Do you genuinely trust in the process, feel you deserve the reward, and believe it can be yours? Furthermore, what happens when money is in your hands in such large amounts? All of this takes regular contemplation.

HEARING THE CALL ACROSS THE MILES

You are a born explorer because, as you know, the people you care most about emotionally are miles away from you. Crossing the great divide in your own country or overseas becomes part of your pattern. You also have many rivers to ford when it comes to the projects you are so invested in. Your chart is set up in such a way that you have to try your luck in other regions or countries; your home base is not the place. Your ability to plan, prepare, organize, and then aim, shoot, and fire—just like Sagittarius the Archer—makes you very happy.

WHO SHARES YOUR BIRTHDAY?

Robin and Maurice Gibb, born December 22, 1949
Ralph Fiennes, born December 22, 1962
Meghan Trainor, born December 22, 1993

DECEMBER 23

WHO ARE YOU?

You are a natural peacemaker in any conflict and understand that the greatest good has to come first. You are a negotiator and optimist and always lighten the atmosphere thanks to the element of air in your chart. The air signs—Libra, Aquarius, Gemini—make all the right angles to your own Sun. Changing the atmosphere is not the whole story. You also know how to strategically preempt future issues. You're quick and clever, keep your sense of humor, and your own memories of conflict help motivate you.

YOUR DESTINY

You are destined to find the right combination of people and place, however your extended family or household shapes up. The chemistry is right, but so is the setting; this may be a house you are fond of, a garden you like, a local area you have come to love. This sense of belonging can happen more than once, as your horoscope is set up with particular cycles of time that reward you for trying. For many December 23 people this is the classic white picket fence family dream. You may be different. Yet happiness is waiting.

REBUILDING OR STARTING AGAIN

Your greatest challenges in life come from sudden turning points when you realize you have two choices: you can either go back and try to recreate and restructure what you had or walk away and invent something from nothing. This is quite dramatic, and it influences your character. You have serious depths in your soul because you reach so many intense crossroads in your life. These now-or-never chapters for you challenge you to be honest about what you had—and what you could have. How much do you value old security?

UNDERSTANDING GROUP PSYCHOLOGY

The Eleventh House of your natal and solar chart is about group psychology and the team or community, as well as the outsider. In your natal or birth chart this is ruled by Aquarius. The patterns in both your horoscopes suggest that you will learn a lot about being one of the many against just one. It works the other way, too: you will sometimes be the separated and independent individual who has to figure out the group. The irony is, as you will come to see, you are all the same in terms of your ideas. Unity is worth the effort.

WHO SHARES YOUR BIRTHDAY?

Chet Baker, born December 23, 1929

Emperor Akihito, born December 23, 1933

Eddie Vedder, born December 23, 1964

DECEMBER 24

WHO ARE YOU?

Born on Christmas Eve, you understand giving and receiving from childhood. When you are older, this duality influences your approach to business, economics, property, currency, and banking—and the stock market, too. Making ends meet, keeping it fair, balancing the books, or finding a flow between debt and credit is something you could spend a lifetime trying to master. It makes you seem more concerned with money than you actually are; you are also deeply involved in groups and networks. Perhaps they meet in the middle.

YOUR DESTINY

You are grounded in your circles, and these are more than just shared social spaces or teams. There is a spiritual depth to the connection you feel between others who pool resources with you. It's not unusual to find December 24 people connecting to their groups through Buddhism, for example. However this pattern in your horoscope affects you, the soul satisfaction you need is always there, thanks to the never-ending supply of emotionally rewarding communities. You may all have your own space, but underneath you all link up.

NEGOTIATING MALE AND FEMALE SPACE

The numeral 2 turns up twice in your birth date and the numerology of these double 2s suggests that both money and the male-female divide will be on the scales in your life. Balancing the books is a two-way street, as you have read. When it comes to men (if you are a woman) and women (if you are a man), there is a lifetime of understanding ahead. Closing the gaps and finding symmetry is very important to you, even if not every attempt is successful. This is classically about marriages that educate you. It can be about friendship.

ENDINGS AND BEGINNINGS

Your reward for going through quite intense transformation in your life is a firm sense of hope about a new day dawning. You experience simultaneous endings and beginnings for this reason. Even as you are watching one chapter and book close forever, a new idea is always up ahead. The promise of a different story next time is always there, and this gives you a particular kind of faith or belief. It may or may not be spiritual or religious, but you tend to develop a philosophy about life and death, too, that runs very deep.

WHO SHARES YOUR BIRTHDAY?

Howard Hughes, born December 24, 1905

Ava Gardner, born December 24, 1922

Ricky Martin, born December 24, 1971

DECEMBER 25

WHO ARE YOU?

You were born on Christmas Day, traditionally a time for family get-togethers and home comforts. Your own tribe may or may not have celebrated Christmas like this, but perhaps the idea of domestic bliss resonates with you because every year you are reminded of your birthday at the same time that people catch up with each other, go back to their old towns, or wrap presents for children. This image of what a household could be—or what a real sense of place might mean—inspires you and motivates you. More than once, it's all yours.

YOUR DESTINY

Your sector of work, unpaid work, and study is ruled by Mercury, the messenger of the gods. You are quite Mercurial when it comes to your plans, projects, or ideas and don't spend too long contemplating them. Instead, you prefer to hit the road and find the right place for your concepts. It is usually far from home as Mercury is a traveler as well as the mouthpiece for important messages. Mercury also rules your sector of foreign people and places, the worldwide web, academia, and publishing. Success comes with planning.

THE SPIRITUAL AND RELIGIOUS LIFE

As you know, you were born on Christmas Day, the worldwide day for Christian celebration. That is not the only reason that your views on God (yes or no) matter more to you than other people. The sign Sagittarius and its ruler Jupiter are in charge of your soul and spirit. You cannot ignore this hidden, invisible part of you as it shapes who you become. You may question the sacred texts that come your way or follow them to the letter. You also have the grounded authority of Saturn, your ruler, which makes you a preacher or teacher, perhaps.

MERCURY IN YOUR HOROSCOPE

Mercury, the traveler and the messenger, rules the sign of Gemini, which in turn governs your daily life. He also has a double rulership of Virgo, the sign which describes your journeys as a whole. You are a natural explorer and perhaps a migrant, too. Your personal life may involve meeting people from other regions or countries in the middle; a long-distance relationship is typical. In your professional life as well, you have Mercury's wings on your helmet and sandals. You probably catch a plane rather than fly by supernatural means, though.

WHO SHARES YOUR BIRTHDAY?

Conrad Hilton, born December 25, 1887
Humphrey Bogart, born December 25, 1899
Jimmy Buffett, born December 25, 1946

DECEMBER 26

WHO ARE YOU?

You are the earth sign Capricorn who knows you must keep everything in your world on solid ground in order to feel secure. You will do this financially and also emotionally from youth to old age. You are born into a lifetime cycle of unpredictable economic trends in your own country and the world. Uranus is the planet of all that is unstable and subject to sudden change. This is not what you need, as a Capricorn ruled by cautious Saturn. In response you develop special systems to cope with financial uncertainties. Uranus and its sign Aquarius both sit on your Second House of lifetime financial cycles.

YOUR DESTINY

You have Leo, the sign of dynasty, ruling your sector of inheritance, trust funds, wills, and legacies. Leo the monarch of the jungle is associated with heirs, spares, and pretenders to the throne. There is no shortage of money to go round, as despite the regular irregularity of your country's economy, your own situation with the extended family is prosperous throughout your life. Learning how to share and how to give is part of the process, and yet the bigger message is relationships in your clan matter more than cash.

FINDING WHAT GROUNDS YOU

You need to find who and what brings you back down to earth in order to discover your place in the world. This means action, not words. You were born with Aries and Mars—both of which point to the need for energy—at the base of your chart. This is where you find out where you come from, who you are related to, what your ancestors did, how your place in the world pulls you back. Nothing can happen by ignoring this or putting off any firm plans. In order to feel fully satisfied and at home in the world, you must locate your roots.

MOTHERS AND CHILDREN

Cancer is associated with mothers and children. It also happens to govern your sector of double acts, duets, pairs, couples, and duels of all kinds. This strongly influences your own ideas about how two souls can be together. This may be because of your memories of your own mother or thanks to your own parenthood choices. The give-and-take of any mutually needy pair is a reminder that it all begins at birth and runs through childhood. You learn a lot from the mother and child archetype throughout your life.

WHO SHARES YOUR BIRTHDAY?

Mao Zedong, born December 26, 1893

David Sedaris, born December 26, 1956

Kit Harington, born December 26, 1986

DECEMBER 27

WHO ARE YOU?

You are the solid, centered earth sign that people tell you about in astrology books, Capricorn. You are an authority when it comes to the next generation, and your ideas, projects, and plans will be respected not only for your own and other people's children, but also for younger people far into the future. This is partly because you place such a high value on them. Leo, the sign of leadership, rules everything you find so precious it is priceless. Leo is also about guiding and influencing the young and seeding the future.

YOUR DESTINY

You are the person who meets others halfway. Libra, the sign of the scales, gives you a balanced approach to other people in partnerships and duets of all kinds. Sometimes this is literal: you will travel to be with people you care about. A long-distance relationship is typical. Double acts are about give-and-take thanks to this sign's rulership of your midheaven. Even if these emotional experiments do not always work out, you are always happy to try again. The numeral 2 appears twice in your birth date. Two is your goal.

BALANCING RELATIONSHIPS

As you know, life is a two-way street. When close relationships do not last as you expected, you have the choice of recycling them into something reborn. You can also walk away and start again. This matters very much to you, as the emotional water sign Cancer rules your partnerships and your feelings are strong. You are prepared to invest time and energy into what works between two people, two sides, and true harmony, thanks to your highest aim—which is equality and symmetry. From this come all your triumphs.

FINANCIAL SECURITY

Earth signs including your own are associated with a practical approach to money and both feet on the ground. Taurus in particular is linked to saving, earning, and investing in your birth chart. That sign, Taurus the Bull, also rules gold bullion and bull markets. It happens to make a perfect trine to your Capricorn side, so financial security is very important to you. You have what it takes to build up a comfortable and profitable life and may become something of an authority to other people.

WHO SHARES YOUR BIRTHDAY?

Louis Pasteur, born December 27, 1822

Marlene Dietrich, born December 27, 1901

Timothée Chalamet, born December 27, 1995

DECEMBER 28

WHO ARE YOU?

You are the Capricorn who is always looking for security because of your earth sign nature. You need to find what grounds you in life even though there are no guarantees. You were also born with the sign of diplomacy and harmony, Libra, at the top of your chart. Your direction in life is always toward what brings people together. Often, it is couples who do this for you, as Libra rules the scales of balance and you feel comfortable with duets. The numeral 2 appears twice in your birth date numerology, too.

YOUR DESTINY

All that you value most in life belongs to the next generation no matter if you have children or not. Leo rules the heirs, spares, and pretenders to your throne, and it also describes who is so precious to you they are priceless. This may be professional or personal for you, but you are invested in children and young people being allowed to enjoy their youth. The sign of everything that is solid gold, Taurus, rules the chart zone where you parent, guide, mentor, set an example, and sometimes teach.

FINDING THE MONEY

Life is not a treasure hunt, but it sometimes feels like one, as you go on the search for money which may or may not be there. In your personal birth chart, Pluto with all his mystery rules joint finance, business, charity, and property. Pluto reigned in the darkness of the Underworld, and you will often feel you need to carry a torch as well as a map. Finding the right professionals to help makes all the difference. Capricorn, this theme may turn up in your professional or personal life. Over time it becomes easier to master.

THE PERSON OF ACTION

Capricorn is not generally painted as a person of action in astrology books, but with dynamic Aries and impatient Mars ruling your family, you will find that particular branches of the family tree spur you on. Then an alternative side of your personality emerges, as situations which push and pull your relatives in different directions require maintenance all your life. You always have the choice to let your relatives take their own path in life, but when you want to plunge in and take charge, you will.

WHO SHARES YOUR BIRTHDAY?

Stan Lee, born December 28, 1922
Nichelle Nichols, born December 28, 1932
Maggie Smith, born December 28, 1934
Denzel Washington, born December 28, 1954

DECEMBER 29

WHO ARE YOU?

You are the ambitious, goal-focused Capricorn that people recognize as the person with a plan or on a mission. Yet you also have an extremely emotional, sensitive side and are run by your feelings. The water sign Cancer rules your partnerships and relationships. Trying to find the logic in these could take you a long time, as your heart leads you into situations which defy expectations. Remembering you are a grounded earth sign can help you to center yourself and find a place where the two of you can work.

YOUR DESTINY

Cancer the Crab is the sign opposite your own, and as you have read, it rules your most important relationships. Cancer also governs the family tree, your ancestors, heritage, roots, and culture. When you need to ground, this is where you will find everything and everybody that can give you something solid to cling to. Remembering where you come from, on either side of your family, can help you to locate a greater sense of security and belonging. This always makes relationships more fulfilling.

PLACING YOUR PLANS

Mercury rules your work, unpaid work, and study. Mercury is the messenger of the gods, and this planet is associated with brilliant ideas, plans with potential, and special projects that bring your message across. As an earth sign, you need to make sure all these are firmly planted where they can grow. Mercury is also the traveler or wanderer of astrology, and so you will often find you have to move your ideas to places where they can fulfill their potential. This often means you have to relocate, too. In this sense you're Mercurial.

FOCUS AND CLARITY

The planet Neptune oversees your mental energy and visions. Neptune can coincide with a lack of focus and clarity, yet when you learn to research the details and narrow your vision, you succeed. Your sector of foreign people and places, distant regions, and the worldwide web is ruled by Virgo, another earth sign like your own. Virgo is all about the finer points of meticulous planning which can save you time and energy when it's your moment to take your talents and skills and find a home for them.

WHO SHARES YOUR BIRTHDAY?

Mary Tyler Moore, born December 29, 1936
Ted Danson, born December 29, 1947
Jude Law, born December 29, 1972

DECEMBER 30

WHO ARE YOU?

You are ruled by Saturn, which makes you patient when it comes to financial security. As an earth sign, you need to feel centered and grounded, and you have what it takes to invest and save—then time it right. A completely different side of your personality emerges when you need to escape reality, however. Here, you might be mistaken for an imaginative Piscean, as Pisces the Fish governs your ideas and thoughts. Nobody else really understands this alternative world of yours, but you are very happy to inhabit it.

YOUR DESTINY

There is a natural link between Capricorn, your Sun sign, and Pluto the planet which rules the afterlife. Pluto also rules Scorpio, which describes inheritance and legacies. This is not about money for you; it is about what is passed on spiritually. Your extended family on the other side of life continues to influence you, just as you influence them. You may or may not believe in life after death, but your chart reveals that these special souls also grow and evolve, which in turn has an impact on you, even if you can't see it.

POOLING RESOURCES

Everything that you value most in life is shared within your circles. Pooling resources comes naturally, no matter if this is time, energy, friendship, or more practical aspects of life. Aquarius, the sign of diversity and community, has charge of all that is so precious to you it is priceless. You find something spiritual in the group that feeds your soul. Libra, which rules two people, two sides, and two equal halves, is at the top of your chart, so within these circles you will also find wonderful two-way friendships.

CULTIVATING SECURITY

Your true earth sign nature is revealed when it comes to finances, business, charity, or property. You are also a natural gardener. Cultivating and nurturing your own security come naturally to you. You have what it takes to wait for results, as your ruling planet Saturn has long been associated with the passage of time. In fact his Greek forerunner Kronos lends his name to chronological order. For everything, there is a season in your book. This rewards you steadily and feeling at home in a reliable world matters to you.

WHO SHARES YOUR BIRTHDAY?

Rudyard Kipling, born December 30, 1865
Tiger Woods, born December 30, 1975
LeBron James, born December 30, 1984

DECEMBER 31

WHO ARE YOU?

Capricorn is the sign which likes to climb toward the highest goals. The mountain goat represents you in astrology. Your peak achievements are always financial; however, you do not get there without considerable work. This suits your style. You are always looking for grounding, security, and the known as opposed to the unknown. Even though the cycles of time ensure that you have been born into national and international economic uncertainties, every time things are shaken up, you learn to invent a new life budget.

YOUR DESTINY

Your most important partnerships and relationships are ruled by Cancer, the sign of the mother and child. Your memories of your own childhood with your mother strongly influence the way your partnerships operate. It is also true that your soul, spirit, and subconscious mind are the storehouse for images of maternal instinct and childhood need. You may not even be aware of just how much this affects your day-to-day life. If you are a mother yourself, then the bond with your child is very important.

JUSTICE AND BALANCE

Libra, the scales of balance, rules the top of your chart. This is a strong guiding force, too, and you apply it to money. As you know very well what it feels like to lack certainty with finances in your past, you are the first to give generously or pay your way with those dealing with challenges. This can be among relatives (charity begins at home), or you may be a natural donor or fundraiser. In other cases you may find a profession where you can redress economic imbalance for people, fair and square.

THE COMMUNITY

The key to your rewards in life rests with Aquarius which rules the community where everybody pools resources for the common good. This sign governs everything that is so precious to you it is priceless. There is something wonderful about this, as not only does it elevate you spiritually, but you also gain from deeper emotional fulfillment of your circles supplying your partnerships and vice versa. This takes you back to Libra, the scales of balance, at the top of your chart. In duets and pairs, you find harmony.

WHO SHARES YOUR BIRTHDAY?

Henri Matisse, born December 31, 1869

Anthony Hopkins, born December 31, 1937

John Denver, born December 31, 1943

YOUR EGYPTIAN SIGN

You know your Sun sign, but do you also know your Egyptian Sun sign?

Egyptian astrology dates back to 400 BCE. The Alexandrian Egyptian astrologer Ptolemy is the founding father of this system of signs. The Egyptians used Jupiter, Saturn, Mars, Mercury, and Venus—all visible with the naked eye—to predict the future. The circular zodiac of Dendera in the Louvre illustrates this system with the familiar signs of Leo the Lion and Taurus the Bull.

What's different about the Egyptian zodiac is that they split each sign from the better-known traditional Western astrology into three sections or decans based on ten degrees of each sign's path. The word *decan* comes from the Greek *deka* which means "ten." There are three kinds of Aries, three kinds of Taurus, three kinds of Gemini, and so on. This is your Egyptian sign.

The decans are called faces in translation. So every zodiac sign shows us three faces. This may explain why as a Gemini First Decan you feel you show a completely different persona from your Gemini Second Decan friend.

The Egyptians used hieroglyphics to describe every decan. Aries Third Decan people, for example, have a couple of birds for their sign. Leo Second Decan people have a lion, and the Egyptian name for that sign is Ha-tchat.

Egyptian signs or decans must be calculated by your time, place, and date of birth for absolute accuracy. If you were born on the first or last day of a decan—the cusp—it may be that your Egyptian sign is off by a day if you are only using general information. The listings we will provide here are based on approximate dates only, so they should only be considered a rough guide.

The decan calculator available at jessicaadams.com/yourbirthday will give you the correct Egyptian sign for yourself and others. You can also pick up an Egyptian Sign birthday e-card there to send to friends on their special day.

Once you are familiar with your Egyptian Sun, your decan is also your guide to the future, and in this section you will be able to find out how the cycles of time will affect you in the coming years.

ZODIAC SIGN	FIRST DECAN	SECOND DECAN	THIRD DECAN
Aries	*Khent-kheru* **March 21 to March 30**	*Qeṭ* **March 31 to April 9**	*Sasaqeṭ* **April 10 to April 20**
Taurus	*Ārt* **April 21 to April 30**	*Khau* **May 1 to May 10**	*Remen-ḥeru-an-Saḥ* **May 11 to May 20**
Gemini	*Mestcher-Saḥ* **May 21 to May 31**	*Remen-kher-Saḥ* **June 1 to June 10**	*A-Saḥ* **June 11 to June 21**
Cancer	*Sepṭet* **June 22 to July 1**	*Ṭepā-Kenmut* **July 2 to July 11**	*Kenmut* **July 12 to July 22**
Leo	*Kher-khept-Kenmut* **July 23 to August 1**	*Ḥā-tchat* **August 2 to August 12**	*Peḥui-tchat* **August 13 to August 22**
Virgo	*Themat-ḥert* **August 23 to September 3**	*Themat-khert* **September 4 to September 13**	*Usthȧ* **September 14 to September 22**
Libra	*Bekathȧ* **September 23 to October 2**	*Ṭepā-khentet* **October 3 to October 13**	*Khentet-ḥert* **October 14 to October 22**
Scorpio	*Khentet-khert* **October 23 to November 2**	*Themes-en-khentet* **November 3 to November 12**	*Sapt-khennu* **November 13 to November 22**
Sagittarius	*Ḥer-ab-uȧa* **November 23 to December 2**	*Shesmu* **December 3 to December 12**	*Kenmu* **December 13 to December 21**
Capricorn	*Semṭet* **December 22 to December 31**	*Ṭepā-semṭ* **January 1 to January 10**	*Sert* **January 11 to January 20**
Aquarius	*Sasa-sert* **January 21 to January 30**	*Kher-khept-sert* **January 31 to February 9**	*Khukhu* **February 10 to February 18**
Pisces	*Baba* **February 19 to February 29**	*Khent-ḥeru* **March 1 to March 10**	*Ḥer-ȧb-khentu* **March 11 to March 20**

Example: The First Decan Pisces Egyptian Sign

There are three kinds of Pisceans. If you were born in the First Decan, which the Egyptian astrologers recognized as its own sign, you are different to other Pisces people. Your Sun is at 0–9 degrees of Pisces—or February 19 to February 29—and your astrological cycles are also timed differently.

What's most unusual about you? You're psychic or spiritual.

FAMOUS FIRST DECAN PISCEANS

Poison Ivy told *Guitar World* she has a psychic relationship with her guitar, which is why it stays in tune. Maybe that's why the Cramps made such amazing music.

Ian Brown, Kurt Cobain, Nina Simone, Jean-Jacques Burnel, George Harrison, and Elizabeth Taylor were also born under your decan.

SACRED EXPERIENCES

Jean-Jacques Burnel talks about "finding a communion with the audience" during Stranglers' concerts. A sense of inner knowing can help you in your professional life, as well as on a soul level.

ADOPTING RELIGION

It's common for First Decan Pisces people to adopt a religion. Ian Brown from the Stone Roses loves the Sikh religion and told *Magnetic Magazine*, "Sikh and ye shall find."

Kurt Cobain followed the beliefs of a born-again Christian family for a time. He named his band Nirvana after the famous end of rebirths in Buddhism.

Nina Simone's mother was a Methodist preacher. The first song she learned was "God Be With You Till We Meet Again," and she also performed at her local church. They called her the High Priestess of Soul.

FINDING A PHILOSOPHY

You are prone to adopting beliefs or philosophies, not just religions. Jean-Jacques Burnel took on Shidokan to help him receive the signals sent in the music business.

George Harrison was drawn to Hindu spirituality, transcendental meditation, and the Hare Krishna movement. His most successful hit was "My Sweet Lord." His ashes were scattered in the Ganges and Yamuna Rivers in India according to Hindu tradition.

Elizabeth Taylor converted to Judaism in 1959, though she was raised as a Christian Scientist, and was buried as a Jew. Her Hebrew name was Elisheba Rachel.

TRAVEL BROADENS THE MIND

Local travel or international travel has a huge impact on you if you were born with the Sun in the First Decan of Pisces. It's interesting to see the transformations that came when George Harrison went to India for the first time, for example, or what happened when Elizabeth Taylor moved from Great Britain to the United States.

Poison Ivy: February 20, 1953

Ian Brown: February 20, 1963

Kurt Cobain: February 20, 1967

Nina Simone: February 21, 1933

Jean-Jacques Burnel: February 21, 1952

George Harrison: February 25, 1943

Elizabeth Taylor: February 27, 1932

Chelsea Clinton: February 27, 1980

Example:
The Second Decan Taurus Egyptian Sign

If you were born with the Sun in the Second Decan of Taurus—May 1 to May 10—then your childhood and teenage years influence you to conserve, protect, and fundraise as an adult.

Here are some famous examples:

AUDREY HEPBURN

Sun 13 Degrees Taurus

Birth Date: May 4, 1929

Birth Place: Ixelles, Belgium

Audrey Hepburn was a UNICEF Goodwill Ambassador (1988–1993). UNICEF was important to her because she had been helped by them as a child, and she maintained this charity commitment into her last years.

DAVID ATTENBOROUGH

Sun 17 Degrees Taurus

Birth Date: May 8, 1926

Birth Place: Isleworth, London, England

David Attenborough has been a patron or supporter for a wide range of good causes, including the WWF and Fauna & Flora International (the world's oldest conservation charity), as well as the World Land Trust.

GEORGE CLOONEY

Sun 15 Degrees Taurus

Birth Date: May 6, 1961

Birth Place: Lexington, Kentucky, United States

George Clooney has been one of the United Nations Messengers of Peace since 2008. He cofounded with others, including Brad Pitt, Not On Our Watch, a charity which uses influential people to try to combat global issues. Their first priority was finding a resolution for the Darfur crisis.

BONO

Sun 19 Degrees Taurus

Birth Date: May 10, 1960

Birth Place: Dublin, Ireland

Paul David Hewson, or Bono, is not only the front man of the band U2, but also a philanthropist. In 2020, U2 donated over €13 million to the Irish COVID-19 relief fund. He was a major part of Live Aid and Band Aid in the 1980s. In 2002 he cofounded DATA (Debts, AIDS, Trade, Africa) and subsequently Project Red.

Example: The First Decan Leo Egyptian Sign

If you are a First Decan Leo, then your relationships will be very different to those of a Third Decan Leo. You have different time cycles, for a start.

FIRST DECAN LEO AND THE COMPLICATED HEART

You have a complicated heart and will always have complex relationships. Love triangles are common—"Love Don't Cost a Thing," as Jennifer Lopez sang.

First Decan Leo people have the Sun at 0–9 degrees of Leo, so their birthdays usually occur between July 23 and August 1.

FAMOUS FIRST DECAN LEO PEOPLE

Jennifer Lopez, Mick Jagger, Beatrix Potter, Kate Bush, Amelia Earhart, Jacqueline Kennedy Onassis, and J. K. Rowling are all First Decan Leos. So are Norman Cook and Yves Saint Laurent.

At first glance it may appear that First Decan Leos have very little in common. Only if you look deeper, "The Hounds of Love," as Kate Bush sang, chase you all the time you're "Running Up That Hill." Remember the Rolling Stones' song "Emotional Rescue"?

At thirty-nine, Beatrix Potter, still single, fell in love with her editor Norman Warne. He died of leukemia before the wedding. She married again, wedding her solicitor at the age of forty-seven, but wore Warne's ring for the rest of her life.

It's said Mick Jagger, a First Decan Leo, was David Bowie's lover, even though they both had wives. When Kate Bush recorded "Don't Give Up" with Peter Gabriel, rumors began about an affair.

Amelia Earhart (the word *heart* is hidden in her name) broke off her engagement to marry her publisher George Putnam.

Sometimes the sexual relationship is not a marriage but a business partnership. Pierre Bergé and Yves Saint Laurent, a First Decan Leo, created the YSL empire in 1961 when they were in a relationship together.

COLLECT A FREE EGYPTIAN SIGN BIRTHDAY CARD

As our birthday present to you, there are thirty-six free birthday cards and Egyptian sign profiles to collect once you have used the online calculator to get your decan right.

Your Egyptian Sign and the Elements

If you were born in the same decan (first, second, or third) as another person as well as the same element group (fire, earth, air, and water), you have similar highs and lows to that person. You two will go through similar cycles together. You are also compatible and have more in common with those in alignment with you than you will with other people. It's amazing how these ancient sign types and elements still work today.

The elements are simple to understand. Each Western zodiac sign is associated with one of the four elements, and these correspondences tell us something more about them.

Fire is Aries, Leo, Sagittarius. The fire signs have hot tempers which can flare up, but they are also warm people. They take the raw ingredients of a plan or project and transform them into something everyone can enjoy. They can bring anything back to life, no matter how frozen it is—and that applies to people, too. Fire signs rejuvenate us. Can you get burned by a fire sign? Of course. They can be too hot to handle. They can also be prone to burnout.

Earth is Taurus, Virgo, Capricorn. The earth signs are grounded, down-to-earth, and "the salt of the earth." They are connected to their roots in terms of their family tree on either side. Their ancestors have a strong pull. They know where they come from and never forget it. They believe in steady growth and understand that life must be about reliability and regularity. Random doesn't cut it. For success, there has to be method and order.

Air is Gemini, Libra, Aquarius. Air circulates and so do airy types. You get along together because you understand being free and easy, which gives your life a light, breezy atmosphere. Nothing and nobody too heavy is the rule. The phrase "a breath of fresh air" describes the particular energy that air signs offer. If the emotions are suffocating, then an air sign will dismiss that. These are the social signs: Gemini connects online. Libra dates, mates, and relates. Aquarius is about the group.

Water is Cancer, Scorpio, Pisces. Water describes the human bodily fluids of powerful feelings. Water is about emotions, rather than thoughts or ideas or practical needs. It is about what is irrational but strong and cannot be explained logically. Cancer is about mother's milk. It describes the family. Scorpio is about sexual fluids. It describes relationships. Pisces is about tears of joy or sadness. Water types can remarry three times against all common sense. Richard Burton (Scorpio) and Elizabeth Taylor (Pisces) did.

In ancient Egypt we find inspiration for the four elements with the Great Pyramid of Giza reflecting the four faces of the universe.

The Chemistry of the Elements

Beyond the alignment of decan and element, there are other relationships between the elements within astrology.

FIRE AND FIRE
FIRE AND AIR

Aries, Leo, Sagittarius, Gemini, Libra, and Aquarius tend to feed each other and need each other. Fire takes off and expands with air. So, for example, a Gemini can say the right things to a Leo and ignite their leadership in a situation. An Aries (fiery) and a Leo (also fiery) can warm up or heat up the atmosphere when an idea needs to leap up from nowhere.

EARTH AND EARTH
EARTH AND WATER

Taurus, Virgo, Capricorn, Cancer, Scorpio, and Pisces hold each other and benefit from each other. If the entire birth charts of friends are earthy and/or watery, they feel comfortable with each other. After a storm, the earth contains water. Rain pools in puddles or even new ponds on the soil. From this comes new life. Plants in earth need rain to grow. Without the earth, there's not much point to the rain. It has nowhere to go; it evaporates. Water needs earth to contain it or the entire planet would be all ocean!

The thirty-six Egyptian sign birthday cards to email at jessicaadams.com /yourbirthday will also show you the elemental associations and full profiles if you have the time, date, and place of birth.

Your Future from 2024 to 2043 Based on Your Decan

How else do Egyptian signs help you? Well, the decans can show you transformations in your life to 2040 and beyond with specific dates.

The most important cycle of the twenty-first century is Pluto in Aquarius. This planet of transformation moves through the zodiac sign of Aquarius in the three stages of the decans: 0–9 degrees, 10–19 degrees, and 20–29 degrees.

Pluto will be direct in Aquarius from November 20, 2024, to March 8, 2043. During that time, Pluto will make aspects, or patterns, to all the Sun signs ranging from a conjunction (same sign) to a semi-sextile (one sign away), sextile (two signs away), square (three signs away), trine (four signs away), quincunx (five signs away), and opposition (six signs away).

Any aspect from Pluto to your natal Sun can reshape your identity. The Sun shows how you shine and where you are at the center. Pluto is about deep change, so when he aspects your Sun, your profile slowly transforms. You may get a new career, for example, or you may marry or have a child.

Pluto is about the need for total control. During the years that he aspects your Sun, you will meet people, organizations, nations, or situations which try to take over. When you resist, you become stronger and more powerful. Pluto transforms your sense of self very slowly. It doesn't happen overnight. A Pluto cycle is like a gym for your mind. You will have a regular psychological workout giving you resistance training. Pluto's reward for persistence in pushing back is an increase in mental fitness.

When Pluto moves through a cycle affecting your Sun sign by decan, you can also see people or organizations you know (for example, your boss at work) go through changes which empower them and increase their strength. Your boss may be promoted, for example, or the company may rise to the top position in its field. This affects your own life, as you realize you must now match up. This also makes you stronger.

It takes about 248 years for Pluto to make this Aquarius cycle. Is this the Age of Aquarius then? It's one of them. Aquarius rules the diverse group. During these long years ahead from 2024 to 2043, the world will see people power replacing the hegemony of just a few men at the top.

The most powerful direct Pluto cycles are as follows:

First decan signs will be changed
November 20, 2024–March 27, 2029,
when Pluto is at 0–9 degrees Aquarius.

Second decan signs will be changed
December 1, 2030–July 26, 2035,
when Pluto is at 10–19 degrees Aquarius.

Third decan signs will be changed
January 11, 2037–March 9, 2043,
when Pluto is at 20–29 degrees Aquarius.

How will your own life be affected? Check your decan and the dates above and then read on.

AQUARIUS

Pluto will form a conjunction to your natal Sun in these years, Aquarius. He will also move through your solar First House of profile, identity, image, appearance, name, title, reputation, portrait, and photography. Your wardrobe and role may transform, for example, because of a powerful new position in life.

This cycle is about trying to work out who you really are and what you're really all about in some depth. This is just one example of the intense focus you can expect on your character, spirit, style, and general you-ness at this time. Pluto brings the self-analysis that comes when you ask yourself: *Who am I? What do people think of me? How do people really see me?*

The First House is about your name, face, reputation, image, and appearance. It's about your surface, as opposed to your substance. When Pluto passes through this zone of your chart, he will single out and clearly pinpoint who you are, at least as far as the rest of the world is concerned. He will show you, very clearly and obviously, how you're seen. Even famous people become overexposed now. It's like standing on an Old Hollywood film set under a giant spotlight.

This comes from Pluto's conjunction with your natal Sun in these years. In fact, there will be some birthdays (your Solar Returns) when you feel your public image has completely transformed. If you were always big, for example, you may lose a lot of weight. If you were well-known for one career, you may replace it with another.

If you are empowered now, then you're clearly projecting the right image out there or sending the right signals. Around your birthday, on the dates given for your decan, both the transiting Sun and Pluto will draw closer to your own Sun. The Sun is highlighting what you most need to pay attention to so that you can shine brightly—or even brilliantly.

Quite apart from your birthday, this Pluto in Aquarius cycle will bring other developments putting your name or face out there, where other people can give them more time, energy, and attention. You may wake up to find yourself the catalyst of events in your personal or professional life in a way that suddenly has everyone sizing you up or making up their minds about you.

This period in your life may look like narcissism, Aquarius. You'll have a lot to think about where the world of "Me, Me, Me" is concerned, because your physical appearance, your style, and your reputation—the box people put you in—is such an issue. Those big decisions about haircuts, laser eye surgery, personalized number or license plates, business cards, and so on represent new power for you.

This can make what *appeared* to be a straightforward dental appointment so much more. You will become aware of the huge impact internet sound bites and viral images can make—so much from such a little effort.

Taking back power over your face, body, or personal style could be a challenge. If you are organizing personalized writing paper, a website, a scrapbook about your life, or anything that involves paper, pens, computers, or technology promoting you, be aware of the potential potency of that. During this period in your life, if your image is part of your career, you might want to hire a professional publicist or stylist.

Commonly you'll concentrate on your hair, face, body, clothes, image, appearance, and reputation, and your public face is where you feel pressured to take a certain direction at this time. How far will you push back? It all depends on what you want to do with your outer packaging. One thing is sure, though. It will make you stronger as you realize self-control is control. For example, you may be told what to wear as part of your job or what to say or not to say.

Here's the other outcome of this cycle: a personal or professional relationship comes into focus, which has a great deal to say about your reputation. This relationship defines how you are seen and how the world talks about you or pictures you or "boxes" you. We all have labels stuck on us. Pluto will influence how things are in your image or reputation stakes for some time to come. He moves very slowly through Aquarius across your Sun.

If you marry now, for example, your life partner will be crucial in determining how you are rated and reviewed. You're the book that gets judged by its cover, and they provide the packaging. It's quite common to find that a certain someone now says a lot about how you are perceived: your reputation, your profile, your name. You may find your good name, for example, becoming crucial to somebody else's cause or case.

If you go into this cycle with a new hairdresser, makeup artist, trainer, cosmetic surgeon—anything!—then you'll know this person is fated and will challenge you to push back on certain decisions so you become stronger. Quite a powerful new image could emerge. For example, your hairdresser may want you to cut your hair, but you insist on keeping it long.

The aging process will be more of an issue now, Aquarius. How does looking older affect your potency? You may decide to schedule surgery for your eyes, chin, or body shape.

People who look after this for you are often Pluto figures: extremely powerful and rather controlling. You and that all-important person need to have a solid foundation of trust and respect to lean on for all the years that you'll be getting your Botox done or your hair colored or your professional image groomed and maintained.

Pluto always needs a channel, so you can be confronted and challenged by those who would try to take over. Resisting that makes you powerful. For instance, a personal trainer or perhaps a boxing coach may want to deliberately dominate the space in order to get results for you. You can play Pluto to your advantage; it can make you fitter and leaner.

Power? It's about how the world sees you and how you present yourself. Pluto in the First House also influences your feelings about your reputation if you are disempowered. The media or the internet, for example, can be out of your control. That means your image, your persona, and your public face seem like a space where you must always try to get the upper hand. This cycle is all about what you look like to others on the outside as a symbol of how well you hold the reins. It's a very self-involved time. At a certain point you may have to be philosophical about the worldwide web. Who can control anything on there? However, it is important that you take firm steps to do what you can, as feeling empowered is the aim of this cycle.

Many people go through Pluto's transit of the solar First House by hitting the gym or the swimming pool or their local yoga class. Many of them start walking everywhere and ditching the car or bus. These are all good tactics. If anyone or anything poses a threat to how you are seen, you'll probably feel pushed or pulled—stretched even—psychologically and emotionally. You need proven techniques for managing this kind of challenge, so meditation can help. So can hiking or self-hypnosis. You will find your own way.

For the time this cycle operates, you will be able to do more with/about your name, face, image, and reputation than you know, particularly if you gain a title or letters after your name. Your business card will probably change, so do use it. In fact, it's been more than 248 years since Pluto was in Aquarius and you had this kind of opportunity. Trade on your outer packaging now as a way of holding the reins, because it's your passport to all kinds of people, places, and possibilities. That means almost professional levels of focusing on your CV, photograph, blog, website profile, personal style, presentation, and appearance. Of course, you know there's more to you than all that, but in this cycle, Pluto is telling you to squeeze more mileage out of your surface as well as your substance. This is one transit when people take your signals as your essence. If you appear to be helping a charity, for example, in a YouTube clip, people will think you are charitable. Of course, you may be—but your advertising is now taken very seriously as a truthful reflection of who you actually are.

If there are issues about your face, body, and hair, then you will be amazed at how many possible solutions appear now. If you need surgery to fix a long-standing issue that affects the way you walk or even talk, then now is the time new options can appear or a waiting period can end.

Aquarius, be extremely cautious about doing or saying anything which might affect your reputation. Most people are discreet if you make mistakes, but if you appear to take on Pluto's controlling, dominating tendencies in public, that may be the way you are seen for some time. Gentle awareness is very useful.

You can take up more space on the stage of life during this cycle. Some people become better-known when Pluto passes through the First House—even finding fame. Your name, face, or reputation can be your calling card, taking you into areas that were previously off-limits, as you realize how powerful you have become. You can go from B-list to A-list, for example, if you happen to move in high society.

The world will be more receptive to you in this cycle. It's ready to take you as it finds you. It wants to listen to you, watch you, read you, and welcome you in . . . and at this time, this could be more influential than you expect. You may become a walking advertisement for a particular social trend or even a political trend, for example. Just your haircut, clothes, and style may represent a particular fashion.

Destiny will give you several chances to take yourself onward, upward, and outward—where a lot more people can find you. The internet is an obvious route to this kind of exposure, but so is a party packed with guests or a work conference where you're required to make a speech in front of hundreds of delegates. One big Zoom meeting could have a huge impact.

Pluto works slowly, so this may be the cycle when you begin dating an influential person, move up to an engagement (more attention), then marry (even more attention), and finally, have children. All this shows a powerful transformation of who you once were, including your name change and, of course, switching from single person to parent. This is a common example of how Pluto in Aquarius can work for Aquarians.

When Pluto is passing through your First House, which rules your mask, your performance, and your image, you can take charge by reminding yourself this is all about acting a part. This cycle has nothing to do with the person inside, but everything to do with how you are seen and how you choose to project, present, and package yourself to the outside world.

This empowers you. However, you may also be protecting your true self or deliberately building a particular persona to use this, quite consciously, for professional reasons, too. Aquarius, you will learn a great deal about self-control and self-discipline. Whatever concerns you have about how you are seen, how you appear, what you look like, and how the world rates you will encourage you to work hard on shoring up your image. You'll send signals now. A pair of earrings can say so much or a choice of outfit or a tattoo. Sending powerful messages through a clip or photograph is one way of filtering Pluto in Aquarius.

CAPRICORN

Capricorn, in these years, Pluto will make a direct semi-sextile to your natal Sun. Pluto will also be transiting your Second House of finance in your solar chart.

For some time, your financial position, your salary, your money management, your assets (possessions or property), and your debts will be in sharp focus. Your values will also be in the spotlight. That means what you will and won't sell out for and also who or what you consider to be priceless. Is this investment you made actually something worth showing off or does it need more work? Does your personal code of values pass inspection or not?

Capricorn, you will put certain things in motion where your finances, lifestyle, business interests, security, property, or values are concerned. This is a powerful time when you may inherit. You may also need to look at the power you have with other people's business or other people's income.

When you have Pluto in the Second House, the spotlight swings on the last big beginning you made or the last big ending you were forced to accept—especially in January and February of any year you see for your decan in the Pluto cycles at the beginning of this section. In all cases, this cycle finds you asking, *What do you think of me? How did I do? How do the numbers add up?*

This cycle is about singling out the most important aspects of your financial, business, and property world as opposed to the forgettable trivia. You will be dominated by something or somebody at this time. How you resist will make you stronger. This is the gym for the mind effect of a Pluto transit.

The semi-sextile to your Capricorn Sun will reshape your profile at the same time: how you are seen in the context of your paid work, unpaid work, or academic career and your status and success.

Do you have the kind of values that empower you no matter how rich or poor you are? This is the big question.

If the financial, business, or property picture falls short of your own, or other people's, expectations, use this chance to make a plan to find more control by using self-control. You need to be strong about your cash situation and security now, so if you're not, crunch the numbers—or your values—until they can pass inspection.

This is the cycle when, if you feel you are powerless to do anything, great changes will have to be made. So this is when most of the financial negotiations, business correspondence, or property transactions will occur that also transform your life. The signatures or handshakes, the question and answer sessions, and an ability to concentrate solely on the money, the house or apartment, the possessions or the business rewards can give you control. It's control born of self-control, Capricorn.

Pluto will deliver extremely powerful organizations (like banks) or controlling individuals (like tax officials) now. The Second House of cash flow, shopping, banking, profits, losses, debits, and credits presents you with intense situations on this transit. If you work in retail or trade on eBay, you will be astonished at how people can change you, even with one transaction. They are your personal trainers for firm new attitudes.

Because the general local and global atmosphere now is so different politically, there can be a trickle-down effect on your financial affairs, which means the banking system, the economy, the currency, and so on. Pluto in Aquarius at this time will bring people power into the stock markets and banks, and this will affect you, too.

If you want to feel more in control, then you really need to give full attention to what you earn, own, or owe—and make sure that you pour masses of energy into it over time. Nothing happens overnight with Pluto. It can be a gradual process of increasing self-discipline and with it—finally—control. Sometimes you will hit the most challenging situations, Capricorn, designed to make you change.

At this time, you'll find that your own progress with an important financial, business, or property goal—or something related to shopping or your possessions—is dictated by your ability to discipline yourself.

There is obviously genuine power tied up with money, houses, apartments, business, or precious possessions. Try and come up with a map you can follow—or all of you can follow in a marriage, with your family, or in your career—during this cycle. Expertise about a financial, business, or property game plan which will suit you, both of you, or all of you is a good investment if the professional advice is tried, tested, and trusted.

Turning down money can be empowering over this cycle. That can happen, too. It is also true that Pluto will make or break your financial, business, or property progress, so take this as your priority in terms of managing your life. The possibilities, in relation to cash, security, lifestyle, and all the things that make us feel rich or poor, have higher stakes now. Possessions are also about power now. That means your wallet or purse, as well as your car, favorite jacket, antiques, artworks, or heirlooms. Houses and apartments also matter in this cycle, for obvious reasons, and so do other valuable assets.

This cycle is also about the power of your value system—what you will and won't sell out for, as you've read. If it's true that everyone has their price or their idea of what is priceless, you'll be moved to act on it now, if you want to continue to hold the reins. Your principles can be expensive on this Pluto transit, Capricorn. Yet they add to your own self-worth and perhaps the value people place on your reputation.

Your old way of earning, saving, investing, or managing money will be left far behind in this cycle, as more intriguing possibilities open up. In fact, by the time this cycle is over and Pluto is on his way into your Third House, you could be on your way to vast business, property, or financial possibilities. If your goals are backed up by practical strategies and a sound approach, you will end up richer—or just feeling that way.

You may find yourself in a position of power with those who are having financial difficulties now. Your response to that, without abusing that position, is very important. This is one of those transits when large amounts of money, or extremely valuable houses, cars, apartments, and so on, can be in your hands for transfer to others.

Yet power can work both ways. You can lend money only to find somebody has control over the situation by never repaying the debt or paying it too slowly. Pluto can operate where there is a loan or donation as much as he can appear during a boom in your life. For example, the value of your apartment, house, or land may skyrocket in these years, making you more powerful.

Control can come through total transformation as Pluto aspects your Sun: A new income source, either through investment, a part-time job, a business scheme, or even a new job. An alternative way to manage your banking or accounting which would open up a lot more options—for example, by switching your mortgage type or by changing accounts. A chance to explore the stock market, locally or internationally, in a new way is likely, as influential people, books, or publications begin to educate you in what's possible. Lifestyle options which allow you to reject your old way of life and drop out—financially, at least—in favor of a more empowered existence which has nothing to do with money or status symbols and everything to do with your personal values are also on offer.

You may wake up to find that your skills, talents, or abilities are commanding a much higher price. In other words, you are your most valuable asset.

This cycle can only happen once every 248 years, so don't waste it. Professional advice is very useful with paperwork now. Of course, you need to make sure that your accountant, for example, is not playing Pluto and trying to dominate. The ideal outcome of this transit is a new position of greater financial control and influence, which you use to benefit others who are temporarily in need. Charity and philanthropy are a strong example of this Pluto cycle. Charity can also begin at home, with family or friends.

You can be broke or wealthy in this cycle, but you'll still need to get real and be extremely practical about unavoidable issues about dominance and control that come up with your situation. Try to get agreements about finance, property, business, or valuables in writing, preferably with objective professional advice. The last thing you need is a power struggle about your home, involving a roommate or tenant, for example.

I am sure you realize that Pluto's transit of your Second House is also about your marriage or common-law marriage, too. Sometimes a prenuptial is a smart idea on this transit. You certainly need to allow for the fact that the balance of power can change with your partner on this cycle. Have you factored that into your plans? Into contracts, like mortgages?

At least once in this cycle, you will be put through a Pluto test. That test will prod and poke the structure you have patiently built up in your life, as it's possible that what you've set in motion in your life is thoroughly inappropriate for you now. If so, you will also be taught something about what to do . . . and what not to do. This will always rely on your self-discipline, self-control, and ability to be the captain who steers your own ship. That takes great effort, but it is the time-honored way to deal with a Pluto transit, especially when in a semi-sextile to your own Sun, Capricorn.

The difference in your financial position, your property situation, and your attitude to what you own, earn, and owe will be quite astonishing once this cycle is over. Pluto is asking you to forget about now or later—and head straight for power. You'll be aware of this planet's background effects on you for the whole time he's here, as you will face quite dramatic questions about your income, savings, debts, banking arrangements, lease, mortgage, insurance, possessions, investments, budget, accounting, and anything else ruling your financial situation. Be aware of dominating organizations, like banks, and controlling individuals, who may be obsessed with money. Corporate takeovers are another example of Pluto at work, because he takes over on principle.

This cycle, as you know, also rules values—what you will and won't sell out for and what you consider to be above mere money. Your principles and ethics with fundraising, for example, or good causes will be in focus during this cycle, and once again, you will need to be meticulous with the paperwork and agreements. Becoming aware of the huge gap between the haves and the have-nots is very common. The former is empowered; the latter has no power.

Capricorn, it helps to periodically ask sensible outsiders for their angle on what is actually going on with your financial spoken-word agreements or your unspoken agreements. If you take pity on someone whose financial situation makes them extremely vulnerable, that is understandable, if you have the power to act as guarantor for them, for example, or promise them items in your legacy. Yet Pluto reminds you that even people who are apparently lower down the scale in terms of control over their housing or bank accounts can pull your strings. Manipulation is something to avoid on either side on this transit for obvious reasons.

SAGITTARIUS

Sagittarius, in these years, transiting Pluto in Aquarius will make a sextile to your natal Sun. In your solar chart, Pluto will move through the Third House. This zone of your chart rules brothers and sisters, cousins, short journeys (a quick plane trip, an overnight stay, a weekend car expedition), the neighbors, transport and travel, communication, the internet, the media. It's multifunctional. While Pluto passes through the Third House as well as the Sun every January and February of the years affecting your decan, life will shine a huge spotlight on all these areas of your life so that you can judge them—and make decisions.

Let's begin with your siblings. Sagittarius, your relationship with them will be much more obvious to other people on this Pluto cycle. Is the connection to your brother or sister something to be proud of or not?

Have you been doing the best with what the cosmos has given you in terms of your sibling or do you need to put more work in? The state of play with your brother or sister will be more *obvious* now and require your input. This applies to cousins, too. The Third House is also about your aunt and uncle's children.

Communication—your way with words and images or ideas and messages—is also in focus now. It's time to be admired and recognized (or even celebrated) if things are going well; your memos, speeches, website, blog, statements, essays, academic papers, letters, meetings, postcards, song lyrics, or screenplays could make you powerful.

Pluto is about empowerment through willpower. In these years, your effort to brush up your language skills, clean up your handwriting, upgrade your computer, update your web knowledge, ask advice, and so on—no matter how experienced you are—will pay off. You may switch genres if you are already a writer, or use artificial intelligence to gain more control over your projects.

The internet itself will go through a sweeping transformation in these years as social media networks are reshaped, taking power away from a tiny number of controllers and corporations and putting it in your hands as well as in your friends'. This is going to alter how you communicate, Sagittarius.

What kind of driver are you? What sort of tourist or traveler are you? How would you rate yourself on the road, in the air, or on the water? All these questions matter more now, because an important trip or transportation issue (car, bike, anything) is about to go to the top of your list—or many times, perhaps annually—in this cycle. Choose your destiny.

This is a good time to sort things out with a sibling in terms of their power or control in a situation and your own. If your sister is also your accountant, for example, you need to review that arrangement. Even though this is family, your dealmaking with a sibling or cousin may benefit from objective and impartial advice—for example, with responsibilities for older parents.

Charles III had this cycle before you. In fact, all Scorpios have. The situation he faced with his brother Prince Andrew is a good example of how siblings can be faced with deep questions about who or what has control or power.

What appears to be quite trivial in terms of your transport or commuting is far more important than it appears. Pluto with all his challenges to change is now having an impact on cars, taxis, trucks, boats, airplanes, trains, and buses—and by extension transport strikes, traffic jams, accident delays, or schedule changes. If you buy a new car, get a truck repaired, or take any kind of holiday, Pluto will be a passenger.

Be aware of that, particularly with car insurance, Sagittarius. You may also want to do extra research even if you only plan on going from London to Paris—a short trip, which the Third House rules. There is usually more to even a simple holiday or business journey than meets the eye on this transit.

A literal translation of Pluto in the Third House is "powerful motorbike" or "powerful car." Be aware of that. The road is often where people play out their power issues or need for control. Even if you normally take your driving or other people's for granted, this is a useful time to update yourself.

The Third House also rules communication, which covers a broad canvas of computers, telephones, fax machines, and mail but also your dealings with the media. The web and the press can both be towering, powerful infrastructures which seem to have the upper hand. Even something as everyday as emails can now become a Pluto story in your life, with major questions about who or what is in control of that private information or how one or two text messages, say, can hold so much power.

The Third House Pluto transit is best handled by assuming that you cannot assume anything! It's new, untried in your life, and seemingly trivial or unimportant matters, like your computer or your bicycle, which can be so much more important. Even the post office or mail—which Pluto also rules on this Third House transit—can carry stories about your need for control or others' attempts to control you.

Sagittarius, from six months to a year on this cycle based on your decan, there will be a big emphasis on planes, trains, cars, and boats. It's all about getting away for a weekend, or even longer, and also how you get around town.

This involvement may be with the local rental car firm. Maybe you'll be caught in a Pluto question about the upper hand with your boat mechanic. Either way, the whole transportation/travel issue will hinge on your ability to use self-control to have control. We could include NASA, space tourism, or submersibles in this. A short trip is a short trip.

What empowers you with communication now? It may be a second or third language. It may be the book you intend to write. Always be aware of how easy it is to take over and take charge, even when others never asked for that. Manipulation is a Pluto pitfall. Pluto can bring ended arrangements or sign-off moments with agreements, because one person feels as if they are being dominated. The worldwide web is an obvious example of how this can take place.

As this cycle rules brothers and sisters, short trips and the way you get around, and the written and spoken word, also look at how these come together.

If a sibling is acting out of character now or a cousin, step back. Look at your sibling's issue on its own merits. Forget the passion: Are they right or wrong? Do your homework on the sensitive subject of handling close relatives involved in questions about the controls. How should you proceed? Pluto is a symbol of obsession and emotion. This is not always useful in practical issues. That is when others who are tried, tested, and trusted advisors can be invaluable. Impartial and objective advice from an outsider could be useful—a wise friend, perhaps, who has no stake in the situation. Do introduce some detachment, and ask people who are sensible, intelligent, and objective.

You are right if you think the cycles can overlap. A brother, sister, or cousin may become an internet issue or a media matter. Perhaps this affects where you can and cannot travel to. The Third House is multifunctional, but it is also true that the transits can cross over.

Be careful what you say and write. Pluto in the Third House can create a big ripple effect. Do manage your words properly, especially if phones, computers, faxes, the media, speeches, radio, texts, letters, meetings, or even sign language is involved. A statement at a funeral, wedding, or similar event can carry Pluto and so seem too controlling to others. It's a good idea to check and check again before calling a printer.

A sibling relationship may have followed certain patterns or pathways to date, but Pluto will introduce a whole new set of possibilities into the equation. This may involve the internet directly through social media.

When you use your willpower on this cycle, you find power online and perhaps in the media. The time has come to explore more influential ways to get your message across when Pluto is sextile to your Sun in Sagittarius, which rules publishing, foreign languages, translation, academia, and the worldwide web itself.

The latest thing from Sony, Microsoft, Apple, or Google could give you much more scope to explore the written or spoken word. Your ideas and opinions could travel a very long way at this time and open up all kinds of doors for you. That speech, poem, blog, script, manuscript, or petition with your name attached could be your key to the most empowering possibilities. Learning to podcast is an example of the correct use of a Pluto transit. So is learning WordPress. As always, though, check the Pluto rules. You cannot strong-arm people or even manipulate now, or there may be an ending you did not want in your online life.

Pluto rules are simple, even though they take work. On this transit, someone or something will come along which compels you and dominates you—or tries to. Resisting this controlling person, organization, or situation will make you stronger. It's like a mind gym or psychological weight training. With care, this transit can transform your life for the better. It takes time, though. And it is only self-control that gives you control.

Learning to drive is a good example of a Pluto Third House transit. Issues about your car or road rules are another. We include airlines in short trips, defined by this cycle. If you feel controlled or manipulated by an airline—for example, one which has the upper hand on the fine print about refunds—Pluto will bring things to a head. Typically you will find that when you keep a tight leash, you become stronger.

Remember, Sagittarius, you are one of many people going through the same cycle together. Collectively there will be the same issues about power and control with the internet, with AI, with public transport, cars, and airlines. This is the kind of transit when it pays to source others who want to join you in correcting situations where there is a power imbalance. Astrology is like the weather or seasons: it affects millions of us at any one time. There are millions of Sagittarians in your decan, who speak your language—and who will no doubt feel as you do, should there be any question of the upper hand online, for example, being misused. That is powerful, and with Pluto in Aquarius, we are moving through an age of collective people power.

You know that, if you have a brother, cousin, or sister, this cycle will reposition you in your relationship with them. You may seek this change because the old situation no longer works for you. Alternatively, the change may be forced on you by circumstances beyond your control. It's actually not possible to hang on to the old setup with your close relation at this time, because you will either feel tremendous pressure to change or they will. What comes out of this could be very different for both of you, but also a good thing ultimately. It takes time.

Pluto is the planet which changes your world in the most dramatic way, offering a strange combination of decisive endings and powerful new beginnings all at the same time. He delivers critical moments with an overload of passion and emotion. Sagittarius, once you find out what it is about yourself that runs deepest and offers you the best chance of constructing a life which genuinely gives you control, follow it. You have everything to gain by changing. See the boxes for two famous real-world examples of this transit.

Gemini Diana Mosley, jailed English wife of Oswald Mosley, had this cycle on November 24, 1943, when her sister Jessica wrote to Prime Minister Winston Churchill asking him to keep her sibling behind bars.

Cancerian Tibetan leader the Dalai Lama had this cycle on March 31, 1959, when he took his all-or-nothing journey from Tibet to India. The trip changed his life as he went into permanent exile.

SCORPIO

Scorpio, your ruling planet Pluto will move through your family, household, home, and homeland sector in these years. Slow and total transformation is part of this cycle. Your decan will show you the years that count. At this time Pluto will be squared with your natal Sun, so your identity will be reshaped regarding the family.

The Fourth House of your chart rules your home—typically, your house or apartment, but sometimes your temporary accommodation. It also rules your family; that means parents, siblings, and relatives, as well as partners and any children. Because "home" often means roommates to people, they will also be prominent in this cycle. And, of course, the place you think of as home can also mean the country you were born in or where you live in now. In relation to all of the above, Pluto now brings slow and deep change over a number of years.

This may be reflected in the interior of your home or the garden, for example. Renovations may be dramatic. You could also find your local area changes, with property developers moving in. It is also common to see situations beyond your control—in, say, politics—altering the landscape of your hometown or homeland. Pluto represents powerful people, governments, and organizations.

Our homelife and families are often a background track. That will change now, as you find yourself staring long and hard at everything.

Read the fine print on quotes on home repairs, renovations, furniture, domestic appliances, gardening equipment, or more ambitiously, researching the property market, as a sale, purchase, mortgage, or lease will be on your agenda now. Pluto transits are the time to ask about the details regarding who or what is in control. It's the perfect time to go on a fact-finding mission, so a building quote from several sources makes sense, or there may be deeper questions about your local council regulations.

It's very important that you remember Pluto is about takeovers. If you are seen to take over a situation with, say, the local area, that may not work. Within the family, if you feel yourself wanting to have control, you also need to be aware that this will not serve you when Pluto transits the Fourth House.

If you get a new roommate now, or a new family member—or if you move in with your partner for the first time—you would be extremely wise to look at any paperwork with open eyes and obtain objective opinions from tried, tested, and trusted professionals. The foundations are there for an empowering relationship, so start from there. With work, you can create a solid bond of trust in terms of your home or domestic life, which will see you through a lot of things. It may be that someone moves into your home who changes the balance of power with your partner in your favor. That can happen, but it does take effort with Pluto transits.

This transit can also increase the value of your home so that you find yourself in a far more powerful position. It may be that your home location is also crucial to other people's plans, so once again you have the upper hand. Your local area may undergo a renaissance so that it rises through the ranks of desirable places. All these are typical outcomes of Pluto's transit of the Fourth House.

It is also common for a family member to empower you, sometimes through a legacy. Or the baton is passed among the relatives so that you rise in influence within the family circle, owing to the departure of another key person.

Your family relationships, roommate relationships, and house, apartment, or temporary accommodation will be shaped by what happens now—with long-term results. Take your time as you navigate. When Pluto transforms your life, the consequences last forever. It's quite hard to go back. Sometimes it's impossible.

Your parents, siblings, or other close relatives—dead or alive—will be an issue now as you tackle who or what has the upper hand. So will your relationship with a partner, if you live with them and any roommates in your life. People who have a direct influence on your homelife, like neighbors, builders, or cotenants, will also go to the top of your list now in terms of figuring out the politics. Pluto always brings questions about control, dominance, and self-control as well.

Your willpower will empower you on this transit. Your ability to discipline yourself and run your own world is very important, as this will put the reins back in your hands if you feel that a person, organization, or situation is taking over. The intensity of the transit, when Pluto actually squares your Sun, does not last forever. While it is taking place, though, Scorpio, you do have to meet change with change.

Pluto can be hard work sometimes. Breathe more deeply. Ask dispassionate outsiders for their perspectives. Update yourself on the rules concerning renting or owning a property: mortgages, zoning regulations, and so on. What you knew years ago may not apply, or it could easily shift on this transit.

You may also be looking at renovation, home repairs, decoration, and possibly a permanent new home now, which will bring Pluto questions. Territorialism is a sign that Pluto is at work. These cycles always end in a compromise, but you may want to keep the stakes low so that the issues do not complicate your life too much. When a roommate moves in, for example, it's important to have written ground rules. On a larger scale, there may be classic questions about who has the right to demand what in a neighborhood, given the duration of the residency in the area.

It can happen to an entire nation, too. How is the turf to be carved up or how is the territory to be divided within your own country or perhaps with other countries? This may not be evident before the cycle begins, but you will certainly know about it by the time it's over. All this affects your feelings about your own home.

Opportunities to make much more of your own power over your home-life will appear now, and you could easily move, build, emigrate, make home improvements, decorate, or renovate. Whatever gives you more clout in terms of your domestic life—even a more disciplined approach to family or roommates—will suit your lifestyle now, as Pluto encourages you to look for the reins or at least your share of the reins.

Do not overlook options like house-swapping or house-sitting at this time; it could work out extremely well for you and could give you more control, but as with all Pluto transits, you need to do careful research first. If you do move when Pluto is in the Fourth House, the new area you move to will teach you all kinds of new things about how to manage situations where you but also others want the upper hand.

Your family background or roots will empower you now. You may find you have inherited certain family talents or abilities which will give you more influence, or changes in your family situation may place you in the right set of circumstances to discover more influence. Your family can also transform at this time, thanks to new babies or the arrival of an entire network of in-laws along with a new partner. That's a common outcome. People can come and go for all sorts of reasons, and in their place, new structures are set up for all of you.

Honest agreement before marrying or moving in with somebody, coupled with impartial professional expertise, is wise. This is the kind of transit when one particular issue can end up being at the center of a power question, and it may affect your children. Even if you enter a romance in a suitably happy frame of mind, knowing the astrology can help you be a realist about what might happen later. These kinds of written agreements, vetted by experts, are prudent. Pluto is the son-in-law of mythology, dealing with his wife, mother-in-law, and brother. It is not surprising that in-laws are sometimes the issue on this transit.

You can never learn too much or know too much in this cycle. The more wide-open you leave yourself to mistakes and fate, the more challenging this cycle will be. So build a plan that works and stick to it. Situations you cannot sidestep and conditions you cannot avoid are going to make renting or owning equally important. Banks may increase the interest rates on mortgages, for example.

You were born with the Sun in Scorpio in the Eighth House of joint finance and property in your natal chart. Pluto will square your Sun during the dates that apply to your decan at the start of this section. That has a direct impact on everything you own, earn, and owe, as your profile is defined by that. So paperwork needs attention, and if there is no paperwork, you may want to consider obtaining it. A legacy or will is a classic example—both the ones naming you and the one where you name others. This is just common sense anyway, Scorpio, but it matters more on this cycle.

The advice and insights of experts or those who have been there and done that with their own families could be enormously helpful. However, as the Eighth House is about shared resources, like a mortgage or a trust fund, the issues are usually financial and legal on this transit.

Advances in the property market, building industry, mortgages, tenancy laws, and even the most basic home-related areas will affect your domestic life in these years and give you a greater feeling of being in charge of where you live and how you live. The big picture reveals a possible change of location for you, maybe more than once—if you feel you don't hold the reins. Wider changes in the community or in your country will have a ripple effect in your life, which means you will end this cycle in a very different domestic situation to the one you began with, as you've read. So check the conditions on a lease, for example. This extends to emigration, if that appeals. This is a classic example of a Pluto transformation, but you need to be clear on the laws covering your own country and nationality and those of the next destination.

How can you possibly resist a chance to go to the next level, either in terms of your domestic existence or your property interests? The answer is, you can't. Or at least, you can hang on to your old way of life if you want, but Pluto is here to give you greater strength by encouraging you to use your willpower. Sometimes it's more than encouragement; you have no choice, except to lean very hard on your self-discipline so you can run your own life and home, your own household or family. Sheer grit can make you feel you are in charge again.

The family tree needs maintenance now. Changes within these branches and around them will keep the ground moving underneath your feet. The way to play these situations is simple: recognize progress when possible. Try to avoid setting up a situation where you disempower a relative. It may be an in-law, for example. Something as basic as leaving particular family members out of wedding invitations can have far-reaching implications on this transit, because it sets up a power imbalance that lasts. Remember: everything can be forgiven or fixed.

Sometimes you will feel as if you are being swept along with masses of people to the point where resistance is the only thing that makes you stronger in terms of councils or politicians. Individuals, groups, communities, and even whole nations will now move toward something different, something new. Scorpio, that forces *you* to accept an alternative setup. This tide will have its own momentum, and if you try to stay on the shore, you may find you can't. You have to roll up your sleeves, find your psychological muscles, and use them.

The family itself might become your passport to power. Your clan could be your calling card. In all these cases and more, though, learn to leverage that influence wisely. You can get an awful lot of what you want now. So why not pursue an agenda reflecting who you actually are when you're not being the child/partner/sibling/relative in this game? Why not live a deeper, more interesting life which ends up empowering *everybody*?

LIBRA

Libra, Pluto will transform your dating, mating, and relating patterns next. This will completely change your partnerships or intimate connections over time. There may be a new partner to replace the old. People come out on this cycle, too. A child can be born or adopted; a stepchild can arrive. A godchild can be born. This transit is about your heart, but it is also about sons, daughters, and the world of children or teenagers on all levels. Work or unpaid work come up, too. Pluto in Aquarius will trine your natal Sun in the years ahead. You'll be publicly reinvented. It's powerful.

Leo Barack Obama had this cycle when he became a father for the first time to Malia Ann in 1998.

Sex is so personal, I have no idea what will come up for you now. But I do know it will be (a) vitally important and (b) your chance to become empowered. Pluto in your solar Fifth House is about courtship and the bedroom. Pluto himself is about the transformation over many years that gives you far more influence. He also teaches you to empower other people, as well as enjoy your own clout.

You might be one of those people who thinks about sex all the time—or maybe you'd rather have a cup of tea. It doesn't matter. Pluto will trine your natal Sun in Libra now, which is in the Seventh House of partnerships in your birth chart. So what is ahead is a new relationship, a marriage, a potent new phase in an existing duet. It will be quite obvious to the world at large, as the Sun shows how you shine. In Libra, the sign of the balanced scales, this will be a prominent partnership where you bring all your gift for harmony to the agreement. It's quite true that you may become engaged now. You might also reunite with your former partner, too. Pluto is dramatic.

Children—whether your own or other people's—also need a deeper look at this time. The world of children can include areas like adoption, abortion, and fertility as well as childcare and education. What happens now depends on where you're at in life—which your whole chart will tell you—but you will find that everything about your connection to a younger generation is up for general inspection and scrutiny.

This may be your child and a grandchild, for example, or your younger nieces and nephews. When Pluto is in the space, so are questions about who or what is in charge. You may need to turn to the experts for advice about parenting now or how to deal with the local school, for example. This becomes even more important if your job involves infants, schoolchildren, teenagers, or young adults. These kinds of cycles can really stretch your willpower as you have to deal with people, organizations, or situations where you feel there is a takeover.

You will be offered a far more powerful place in the world via the younger generations now. This may be marriage and stepchildren, blended extended families, or new babies, too. If you are a teacher, you may be promoted to principal or dean. If you write for teenagers, you may find your books are made into films. If you work as a midwife, you may gain a really influential new position. If you are a nanny, the family may be quite powerful.

If you find yourself doing extra homework about pregnancy, adoption, offspring, young relatives, godchildren, sex, intimacy, or contraception, you will never regret the chain of phone calls, web searches, letters, or emails about *one* of the items on this list now.

In particular, seek schools, midwives, nannies, adoption agencies, IVF specialists, and other child-related professionals to put the most recent research in your hand. Understand the full nature of the agreement in writing. This also obviously applies to sexual relationships of all kinds. What is the deal?

If you are single and speed dating, dating online, or just looking at parties, then it's a case of conscious change—a shift in your approach. Pluto is new on this cycle. You've not had these issues about control before. Try not to guess or assume when it comes to contraception, for example. Your approach to sex can and will empower you now, but you also need to be a realist about the most intense questions; unwanted pregnancies can occur.

Your adult children will also bring Pluto into situations. Perhaps you will find a child has to take on considerable power in your life following changes in your own circumstances. This is also where wise counsel from tested and trusted professionals can help.

Libra, anything which entertains and informs younger and older generations will now become more powerful. This may be football or theater. The Fifth House is about activities which bind parents and children together—grandparents, too. So that's Harry Potter and Walt Disney. What used to be just a game becomes so much on this transit. It may be that coaching the local baseball team begins to involve people politics because the team starts to win big games.

What happens in terms of your own or other people's children will help you to expand your influence in the most amazing way. A confirmed pregnancy or a big leap forward for or with your child is a very common outcome. Grown-up children could make decisions which empower you as a parent.

If you are single, destiny will line you up with a new lover—or more than one—who will take you to the next level of self-respect and self-mastery physically, emotionally, and psychologically, if you are willing to explore. Is this the *Fifty Shades of Grey* cycle? It can be.

Classically it can see second marriages where one partner's first wife or husband is concerned about the new life with their son or daughter now moving into a different family. The adoption process can involve quite obvious questions about the birth parents and the realities of the paperwork, as well as the deep feelings.

More broadly, you may find yourself involved with the Scouts or a school campaign to help a children's charity. Whenever this happens, be aware of the stakes involved. The people and issues you will be dealing with will change your life. Try to understand the reality of these commitments before you go into them.

If it's not an organization or individual changing your world, it may be a situation. Your sexuality obviously alters over time. Pregnancy can transform life in the bedroom because of hormonal changes. Menopause can also do that, and something as common as Viagra can turn a marriage in a completely different direction.

Every Pluto ending on this transit is also a new beginning. They overtake each other. When this happens, you sometimes have to be shown your own power. If a relationship chapter closes for you, then somebody new may come along who reminds you that you really are a force to be reckoned with.

What do you need now? *Your fair share of the reins.* You will not be satisfied with your old place in the scheme of things where the world of children is concerned. A strong sense of "That was then, this is now, and this is the future" will encourage you. Child custody or maintenance payments are a classic example of this transit. There can be more complicated outcomes: Godparents can wake up to find they have more responsibility than they realized. Surrogate mothers are sometimes a concern on this transit because of the nature of the deal or agreement.

Your child may move into adolescence or from adolescence to adulthood at this time, which is one obvious cause of big change, too. Another possibility? You will deal with the political realities of abortion, adoption, miscarriage, or IVF treatments and find that your old attitudes and expectations must be replaced by a new outlook because of general governmental politics or health care policies. As with all Pluto cycles, though, this one is about letting go of what ends and accepting what begins in its place. A new order is coming.

Be mindful of unwritten agreements with your in-laws on this transit, particularly if you break up with the parent of your child and find that moving away is not as straightforward as you thought. Fortunately there is a wealth of information to lean on before you take the first steps toward pregnancy.

A partnership may go through dramatic sexual phases—a start, stop, start, stop dynamic—at this time. Or you may go from one lover to another. The emotions will be intense, as Pluto rules obsession. It is quite normal for a compromise to emerge from these kinds of situations.

When people say Pluto transforms, it really is to unrecognizable degrees. You may lose your virginity on this cycle. You may reach orgasm for the first time. Your sexuality is where you will find out just how much the body influences the mind, heart, and spirit. It is quite understandable to want more time and space to deal with this.

Miscarriage or termination of a pregnancy is another scenario with Pluto's transit of the Fifth House, when it coincides with strong emotions and even stronger hormones. You are changed by these experiences and, again, need time and space to go through the phases that come with loss.

The actual loss of a grown-up child for other reasons is not unknown. It depends on all the personal birth charts involved and cannot be predicted. However, what astrology can do is give you a clear cautionary note. If you see that your child is taking risks or may be moving further away from you, you need to figure out next steps. Other parents have been there before you; other parents will have had this Pluto cycle before you.

It sometimes happens that a baby or child is at the heart of what is basically a power struggle between adults. This does have long-term consequences, even if the infant is innocent and unaware. Children grow up. Pluto changes families, and that needs to be taken into account. Putting the child first is a wise reaction on this transit, according to many who have been through it. Access granted or not or access blocked by distance, for example, is Pluto at large; try to avoid manipulating people now even if you feel compelled in that direction. This transit is associated with quite obsessive responses, but you don't have to succumb to them.

Even something as apparently artless as naming a child or selecting a surname can become a political matter on this transit as the upper hand or one-upmanship becomes the order of the day. Again, Pluto is best resisted if you find that you or your coparent are walking toward this. Whatever shifts now is usually permanent and names do not necessarily go away.

You will be capable of quite extraordinary amounts of self-control and self-discipline now, where children or teenagers are concerned. Through your efforts, young lives can be turned around or even saved. This is probably the highest expression of the transit. For years into the future, what you do is the gift that goes on giving—even if it is for students you have never met in foreign countries. Pluto can make you the difference between life and death at the most extreme reaches of this cycle.

The realities of HIV/AIDS may come home to you now. This is another example of Pluto's intensity. It is the same with highly transmissible viruses like COVID-19. This transit has an all-or-nothing quality to it when a great deal goes on the line. It really is the cycle when you understand what the poets, musicians, and playwrights meant when they created works that speak to us on the deepest level. It can be cathartic to immerse yourself in that now.

This is one of those astrological transits, especially as Pluto in Aquarius is trine your natal Sun in Libra, when you need to update yourself on love, life, sex, children, and hard realities. Remembering the way things used to be with people before this cycle, or assuming you know, is not always going to be useful. Society changes. Rather than just stumble into this long-running period in your life without preparation, do all you can to find out what's really going on out there, at all the parties, in all the bars, and in all the bedrooms.

It would be lovely if we could just dream romantic dreams or believe that parenthood was just like in the sitcoms, but this interval in your life can be intense and can also transform everything forever. Learn as you go, but don't go in without knowledge. That way you can enjoy all the extraordinary passion and depth of feeling that Pluto can bring you; the world of lovers or children can help you feel reborn.

VIRGO

This cycle is all about your work and well-being, Virgo. You will transform your way of working over the next few years, watching new power and control come your way, even as you have to shut the book on old chapters. Your health on all levels now needs more attention as the days of assuming or guessing are over for a few years. During the period based on your decan, Pluto will be in a quincunx pattern with your natal Sun in the Sixth House. This also rules your lifestyle, housework, paid jobs, unpaid jobs, academic career, and everything from dentists to therapists.

Let's consider the health, fitness, and well-being aspect of this cycle first. Everything about your body will be a lot more obvious now, particularly in January and February of the years that pertain to your decan, which is why it's classically a time for a medical checkup. The Sun reveals within a few days of this cycle beginning in late January of these years what you can be proud of in terms of your health and what is clearly in need of attention. It exposes what is central and important: what can't be overlooked.

It's a very good time to get the once-over on tooth decay, cholesterol, blood sugar levels, blood pressure, bone density, and anything else you can think of, on an ongoing basis. Even if you are already receiving medical or alternative health treatment, this Pluto cycle is extremely useful, as it can give you much clearer insights on everything. You'll get a better view of what's actually functioning or not at this moment—and that includes your doctor.

You'll be put in a position where it's easier to clearly rate treatments, diets, gurus, opticians, miracle cures, doctors, hospitals, clinics, nurses, surgeons, health insurance staff, and associated areas. Do you feel empowered or not? Do you feel in control or not?

The Sixth House is also associated with part-time and full-time work and the chores you do at home if you don't have a job, together with any outside interests which you think of as your duty—volunteer work, for example. It's about all you do on a daily basis for others rather than yourself. That includes walking the dog or feeding the cat—chickens, too. Small creatures belong to this transit.

It's very important to know that you are empowered by serving others on this cycle. When you do your daily duty by people or animals, you gain influence.

Handling that should be done thoughtfully and carefully; it is better to share the power now than use it by yourself.

You'll be involved with some kind of fact-finding mission about your health and well-being now every year. The internet will be involved, or you'll be ploughing through library books, magazines, or the phone directory as you gather sources and contacts. This is a great cycle for doing serious homework on a medical condition or lifestyle question you might have. Knowledge is power. Preventative medicine is important now because it gives you the reins, rather than your doctor, nurse, surgeon, therapist, and so on.

This cycle is also about your full-time or part-time job. If you run the home instead of working, then it applies to your daily routine in the house or apartment. All the calling, emailing, reading, web surfing, or face-to-face discussion pays off on a regular basis as Mercury catches up with Pluto in Aquarius so often. It's a brilliant time to research the state of your chosen industry or profession with a view to strategic career moves.

Cancerian singer George Michael had this cycle on November 17, 2003, when he signed a new recording contract with Sony. As is often the case with big career decisions, Pluto was in the Sixth House.

This is the period when you find yourself regularly poised to hire someone, fire someone, or find a new career. Pluto rules the pecking order at work, at university or college, or with your unpaid efforts, like doing the cooking at home or gardening. It's worth knowing about this transit so you can accommodate it in your planning. The question *Who or what is in charge of my lifestyle?* counts all the time.

Your everyday working life has its own chain of command. Even if you're self-employed or head of the home, you still have to think about your duty to other people. All work is a service, even if you're apparently calling the shots. If you're a president or a prime minister, you still have a duty to the people who voted for you, so in a way, you're still as much in service to them as a PA is to their boss. That chain of command will now become a major preoccupation for you. It may be the dog pulling on the leash and disobeying you or a more serious concern. It may be an employer who is taking over. That's pretty common on this cycle.

Confronting your own power or lack of it and doing something about it transforms your life, whenever you make these decisions.

This cycle will strongly influence the chain of command in great detail where you are, no matter if you're a full-time housekeeper with florists, supermarket deliveries, and gardeners to consider or at the head of your own company. It's about controlling yourself and strategizing when other people are clearly failing to control *their own need to dominate your day.*

There will be an interesting series of tests with doctors and dentists which examines your power over theirs. You are the client or customer after all. In typical Pluto transit style, if you use your willpower and self-control, you can change the dynamic so that instead of being a patient you are an education to them. That can happen.

Pluto rules obsession. It's very important to step back from work compulsions or the head miles you may be traveling over your health. In fact, mental health is ruled by the Sixth House of this cycle, so common issues like overthinking, anxiety, and/or depression can come up. Learning cognitive behavioral therapy is a strong and reliable response to this, and it suits the cycle with all its emphasis on being captain of your own journey. It's the same with meditation or even daily walking. You will have your own preferences for mind, body, and spirit.

Expect final chapters, closed books, and replacements in terms of health. It may be that the Reiki or hypnosis that once worked no longer does. You will transform your life by finding something else.

I know of no other cycle which opens the doors to new possibilities for healing, treatment, and even cure of conditions you have been stuck with for years. Seek and ye shall find. Sometimes you just need time or money to deal with your problems; if so, that may appear now. Alternatively, you just need medical breakthroughs, scientific advances, high-tech inventions, or new people in your world who can improve your quality of life. This is the cycle when you wake up to find there is a pill to do what you want or an injection. It pays to follow the latest medicine and health accounts online to be on the edge of this. These solutions will change your life.

People who have been stuck with depression, chronic pain, or chronic fatigue wonder when there will be light at the end of the tunnel. In this cycle, it will appear in a multitude of ways. It may be your mindset that's been holding you back or just the narrow parameters of your old doctor, your old hospital, and so on.

Very commonly in January and February of the years listed for your decan, you will get a new job in this cycle, retire, resign, or find your current position is reshaped in an amazing way. If you have full-time home duties, you may enter the workforce or just find that there is a new spin on your life at home which massively expands your horizons. At these times of year, the Sun is in step with

Pluto. Of course, it's also the time of year when people are accepted into universities and colleges, graduate, accept redundancy, retire, accept promotion, seek new jobs.

If the field you are in gives you tremendous influence and clout, then you will probably stay in it. Being an air traffic controller is an example. Being the PA to a powerful CEO is another. If you have staff, then this cycle will bring you quite a lot of control over their income, of course, and their happiness. Knowing that you have to handle Pluto with care and sensitivity is wise. Do unto others is a good rule for these transits.

This is the cycle when people receive a diagnosis for something they have lived with all their lives. It changes them forever. As Pluto will form a quincunx pattern to your Sun in Virgo on these cycles, you can expect your sense of self to transform. The way others see you can alter profoundly, and you may feel as if you are holding the steering wheel when before you were just on a path that did not always work.

Do treat your body with the respect you would give to a vintage Rolls-Royce. Your body is a machine now. Look after it, because it's going to have to carry you through some major work, academic, or unpaid labor choices.

Virgo, the regularly changing conditions with staff, equipment, hours, job descriptions, or even the industry itself will confront you. The harder you work at developing a proper set of strategies, rituals, and routines, the less of a stretch you will feel. The more you educate yourself about managing people or the realities of your business/industry or workplace psychology, the better off you will be. I know of no other cycle which depends so much on your willingness to make an effort.

Take a long look at the coping mechanisms and little structures you're creating in order to deal with what you must. We all do it, especially in our working lives. Check in every few months or so to see if these systems you've developed to manage are actually worth all your effort.

If you are unemployed or have a full-time homelife, the same issues confront you now. It may be the garden. It may be the birds. Virgo, this cycle rules the little things and the small details. Yet they have great impact. Could you believe one chicken could be such a dramatic question? Yet on this cycle, it can.

This cycle affects two areas of your life. The first covers your job, your daily routine, or the domestic work you do at home. The second area covers your health, fitness, and well-being. In both areas now, you will make progress.

To stay in the same job, working in the same conditions, or to remain stuck with the same domestic duties is not going to work for you in the years that Pluto is in the Sixth House. Equally, if you have been unemployed for a long time, that's unlikely to last for much longer, too. This cycle is about the jumping-off point between the past and the future, with distinct chapters in every book of your life you begin and end.

You may drop out of the workforce and take a sabbatical. You might switch from housework to study. You may remain in your current position, but become involved in unions or lobby groups calling for a new kind of pecking order in your workplace.

Broader changes in your field, industry, or profession or wider social or national advances, delivered by politicians or the people, may also affect you at this time. You may be swept forward by the zeitgeist or broader trends. Questions about power at the top, as opposed to power shared across all levels, are typical. Mergers between corporations may reduce competition so they have an unfair monopoly. Too much power from the peak down to your own role is common. If you go for a job interview and succeed, don't just read the fine print on the contract. Ask around. Go online to find out what the politics really are in that company.

People come out of retirement on this cycle, and their seniority grants them a huge role at the top. They can also seek asylum from their own country and transform their lifestyle and work. Pluto can be dramatic. How will you use this cycle? Remember, in astrology, there is no distinction between your health and well-being on all levels and the work you are able to do. If your body or mind becomes an issue on this long cycle, look at your true feelings about your job, housework, or study.

LEO

For Leos, Pluto is now in the Seventh House of your solar chart and will aspect your Sun by opposition. This will happen slowly over the dates given for your decan.

Your partner, ex-partner, or potential future partner will be the focus now. So will your enemy, opponent, or rival, if you have one. If you marry or become engaged now, if you break up or get divorced, or if a partner passes over, you will be able to look at your marriage, relationship, or single life or connection to an ex through the lens of power. You will also be updated. It's a wake-up call.

If you're single, a new person may come along who highlights what you need to work on in terms of your dating style/technique or shows you just how you've developed since your last breakup. It's about figuring out what you can congratulate yourself on and stick to and addressing where you need to apply more effort and learn.

Pisces George Harrison had this cycle when he married model Pattie Boyd on January 21, 1966.

You'll get an incredible amount of information about the person you want now just by talking—or googling. If your priority is your ex-partner, you'll be amazed at how much you can find out about their situation. And if you just want to scan the world of dating? Life will provide you with the sources, contacts, networks, and information if you are prepared to put in the time. Are you happily involved with a partner? An issue which is vital to the relationship or marriage will come up now, and you'll be able to do a lot of useful analysis. Are you unhappily attached or married? This period is crucial, because you'll be using your head to fathom a situation which usually affects your heart more.

This also applies to the state of play with enemies, rivals, or opponents. You are undoubtedly going to find them on your radar at this time, because various discussions, letters, emails, calls, or actual meetings will be unfolding.

This cycle will make or break the relationship you have with your ex-partner, your current partner, your potential dates for the future, and your enemies. You are about to enter a crucial phase in an existing relationship or feud—which means you can either make progress together or not at all.

Alternatively, someone new will enter your life at this time. And what do you know? It either feels like a partnership right from the start or this other person seems fated to be against you.

If you are in a battle now, that goal is usually the resolution of a dispute, difference, or grievance. You may need to be Madeleine Albright, Henry Kissinger, and the Dalai Lama, all rolled into one. Negotiate. Listen. Research.

Above all, though, this cycle is meant to be about true partnership. Occasionally this can be a business or professional double act, but the romantics of the astrology world believe you now have a chance to turn your life into *Gone with the Wind* meets *Love Story*. Pluto is about power couples. A baby, a wedding, a business, a property purchase, a holiday, a professional partnership—any of these or all of them could call you now. The goal doesn't matter as much as the fact that you're climbing the mountain together.

Tibetan Buddhist websites can help you find techniques for managing your own attack and defense mechanisms and coping calmly when other people's attack and defense mechanisms are aimed at *you*.

His Holiness the Dalai Lama, the leader of the Tibetan people and winner of the Nobel Peace Prize, is a good role model for a Pluto Seventh House transit, Leo. Somehow the Tibetan cause just gets stronger and stronger. I could write screeds of advice on handling the other side when Pluto is in the Seventh House, but the best thing I can do is tell you about Tibetan Buddhist techniques.

Can you feel compassion for the other side because they obviously feel so little peace in their lives? Or just as hard: Can you step aside from your own situation, examine the issue in the cold light of day, then admit it's better to follow the peace path yourself? That's your challenge. Sometimes your opponent, rival, or enemy at this time is your partner or an ex-partner. So that can happen now, too.

Are you happy with your partner, ex-partner, or the prospects with a future date on this cycle? That empowering person may be the gateway to the Elvis Presley Chapel of Love—more than once.

I know of no other cycle in which so many husbands, wives, boyfriends, and girlfriends look at their beloved through the lens of control and self-control.

If you are single and open to a new relationship, you will now team up with someone who can make you powerful. If, for whatever reason, dating and relationships are not possible, you will team up with a person who will be your empowering partner in other ways. This individual will open doors through work or business teamwork.

If you are already in a professional and/or sexual partnership which is basically good for your development, it will take you higher now. If your marriage or relationship is keeping you stuck or stagnating, then Pluto in your solar Seventh House, opposite your Sun, will challenge you to change.

This cycle will affect your ability to hold the reins or share the reins within your marriage, partnership, dating chances, and the state of play with any rivals or enemies. You will have to live in the real world at this time, as the facts about yourself and your situation will need to be dealt with in the most practical way. To build the kind of relationship, the kind of single life, or even the kind of status quo with your opponents doing the most to elevate your position is Pluto's task now.

This cycle will ask you to draw on your experience, make a plan, put everything together, then roll up your sleeves and do what is necessary.

It's really important to be clear about the sort of relationship or the kind of single life you are now building. Equally, if you are trying to structure your world a certain way in order to deal with enemies, you need to be fully conscious of what you're creating. What do you think you're doing here?

Stand back and take an objective look at what you are putting together for yourself now. Cancerians had this cycle before you. People who are older and wiser and have been there before you will be excellent sources of advice now. Hit the books, courses, and whatever else you have to, to check if your hard work is worth it.

It's also important to leave time and energy for other things apart from this love life or feud which is constantly under reconstruction, even if it is the transformation to empower you.

You're likely to take a far more intense approach to your partner, former partner, or love life at this time—or you may find that a certain someone wants to take a really intense approach with *you*. Pluto is about sexual obsession.

Pluto can and will appear in the shape of a new person of interest in your life if you are open to it. This person will be an agent for change in some way—your chance to take the great leap forward in terms of your upper hand in life.

Typically, you will want the ability to move ahead in your love life, now, without being confined to where you were last year or even last week. The changes you make will also force others around you to change, though, so be prepared for the consequences of that.

If you are determined to hang on to your old love life, your old sex life, and your old relating patterns, then you may be left behind as Pluto makes a U-turn around you. It's your destiny to be surrounded by people who are searching for more empowerment now, and they are seeking it through the world of relationships and partnerships, which is why this aspect of your existence probably feels so dramatic. This Pluto cycle will have a ripple effect on your partner, ex, or future date as well.

What happened to the usual dating, mating, and relating setup? The answer is that other people's desire for whatever or whoever suits Pluto's intensity is now forcing your world into a dramatically different shape. The choice is yours: move with the times or not.

The Seventh House Pluto transit is long, steady, and always in the background now and rules the necessary compromises and new deals you strike with your life partner, current relationship, and ex-partners. It also rules your enemies and opponents, as you know, and over time you will find that this game also transforms.

It may sound strange to hear that you can be empowered by an enemy, but it can happen now. Explore ways in which one or both of you can lose the old enemies game.

Happily, this cycle can also produce the most intense, passionate new phases in relationships that appeal to your need for a completely different sort of partnership. There is always something compelling, if unfathomable, about the marriages, affairs, business partnerships, and working relationships which turn up when Pluto is in the Seventh House. How can two souls connect so fully? It's like a film, song, or book—dramatic, Shakespearean, life-changing.

This cycle is all about accepting the ongoing shape-shifting in your marriage, relationship, former partner or current/ex alignments, work or business partner in order to experience what it feels like to be one half of a power couple. It is also about anyone who is against you—an opponent, rival, or enemy—teaching you how to become more powerful.

The effects are the same no matter if you are madly in love, getting married, divorcing, dealing with bereavement, or managing a feud. Pluto's challenge to you now is to dig deeply inside yourself for the aspects of your personality that have been ignored, neglected, or buried. You'll do this because of an ending (a departure or other dramatic change) or a beginning (a new relationship or a new level of commitment). This transit is rather like a book with distinct chapters.

The endings may arrive as a marriage or relationship fails, as one partner passes on, or as the partnership changes shape for other reasons. The endings may also come when an enemy, difficult ex, rival, or opponent gets the controls and you realize that you are now required to pull the reins back to your side. Other variations on this theme include a dramatic shift in the dynamic of your relationship or marriage which makes you feel as if you're finishing a chapter even as you are writing a new one.

In the case of a love life ending or final chapter, you have only one choice if you are going to find your power. You must now forget about the person you were trying to be and the relationship game you were trying to play and get on with the business of finding out *who you really are*. That will require some digging. And in the meantime you must feel Pluto's big emotions. Let them come, then let them go. Then find the undiscovered parts of yourself you have to bring to your new love life: the one you want next time round.

You'll win now, too. You'll reach a point in your partnerships or even in your battle with an enemy where you are top dog. Pluto rules dogs—he owned one called Cerberus.

Gemini actress Nicole Kidman had this Pluto Seventh House cycle on August 8, 2001, when she split from her Cancerian husband, actor Tom Cruise. The early twenty-first century—when Pluto dominated Gemini's Seventh House of marriage—was also decisive for other Geminis like Paul McCartney and Angelina Jolie. More recently, Cancerians had this cycle. Prince William married Kate Middleton on it. He entered into a dispute with his brother Prince Harry during it, too.

In astrology, knowledge is power. This is a powerful cycle, as you have seen, but just knowing what to do and what not to do can help you navigate Pluto in the Seventh House successfully.

CANCER

This cycle is all about your finances and property, Cancer. Total transformation is coming over a number of years. Pluto in Aquarius will form a quincunx pattern with your natal Sun. It will also pass through the Eighth House of your solar chart. This rules the legacy you leave to others as well as the legacy left to you.

Mortgages, taxes, inheritance payments, partnership investments, commissions, loans, settlements, debts, joint assets, and shared resources come under the rulership of the Eighth House. It's about what you own, earn, or owe in relation to a second or third party. The Sun will single out all the important issues for you every January and February in the years listed for your decan, so you have a chance to sort out what or who is making you feel in control or not. However, it can also expose issues about the balance of power. If it does, don't ignore them.

A classic example would be a couple with a child who each have different salaries or one income and no income at all. Another example might be Wall Street at its most intense.

The Eighth House also rules sexual and financial relationships—commonly, the marriage and mortgage. The part of the wedding vow that states "until death do us part" is in this cycle.

Death and dying are other Eighth House concerns, in the context of bank accounts, houses, valuables, or apartments. A lot of people never think about these things. Either way, fate will have a funny way of steering you toward these issues at this time as the cycle rolls on. A common example might be an older family member who is unlikely to be here for much longer, so their will is an issue.

If the transition from life to the afterlife directly and *personally* concerns you when this cycle comes along, it will illuminate and clarify what's effective and what's not about the way you've been managing things so far. Pluto comes along to show us that we should never guess or assume about death. Empowerment comes from willpower and self-control in this cycle.

It's quite true that money, property, and business can bring out the need for total control in people. In this cycle, you must learn to make money, property, and business your excuse to become the greatest fact-checker of all time. For a few weeks every year going forward, you'll have plenty of paperwork, meetings, correspondence, contracts, or emails to deal with. But at every stage, the deal is to find out. Tried and tested legal or financial professionals can save you a lot of time.

There is rather a lot at stake, because Pluto is now emphasizing cash, houses, apartments, possessions, taxes, settlements, investments, debts, assets, loans, and all the rest. In the big picture of your life, though, the number crunching you're doing at the moment is much less important than the power-based relationship itself. You might think this period in your life is all about how rich or poor you feel, but it's actually about the quality and depth of this specific relationship where you and the other person—or people, plural—must be honest about the upper hand. If you both or all get it right now, *that's* solid gold. A power couple contract based purely on the two of you, say, being philanthropists is a strong outcome.

On occasion, people who should not be in your life or anywhere near it will turn up. The power that other people find in money, they are now finding through sex as well as money—or your house or apartment. Occasionally, during this cycle your radar will twitch. Listen to it and get out of there! Pluto can show up as controlling people who make you obsessive or who are obsessed with you. It's never just about the bedroom. It's usually about your bank account as well, or your assets like a shared home. It's not common, but it's worth knowing about.

Income tax is part of this cycle. So are big and small business. Going into this Pluto transit means your old assumptions can be challenged. Rather than be caught out by difficult questions about who or what has the upper hand, find out how areas like taxation, for example, have changed.

The money, property, possessions, or assets belonging to people in your immediate circle—or to big organizations or government departments—are now your key to having real clout and influence, Cancer, but this will only come when you summon up the willpower.

What is given, paid back, loaned, or shared could now give you enormous scope for greater control and offer you a new pathway which simply was not there before. What's out there for you now? Just remember the golden rule with Pluto: never use your position to manipulate situations if you can avoid it or take over other people's space.

It can work the other way, too, strangely enough. Don't lend money or give cash-in-kind favors, like free or cheap accommodations, to people who control your life. They may ask for all kinds of reasons, but power can't be poorly handled on this transit or Pluto has an odd way of ending a setup quite dramatically.

If you're prepared to learn rapidly, try everything within reason, and exploit each deal, arrangement, or offer as it emerges, you should take giant leaps in your own financial control now. What seemed outside the realm of possibility just twelve months ago can now become a reality. You will not have this fork in the road in quite this way for another 248 years, so it's wise to follow all the clues, signs, tips, and lucky breaks now.

It may not be until this cycle has finished that you are able to appreciate just how narrow your view of death or sex was or how completely inexperienced you were. This cycle will broaden your horizons and give you a chance to develop your understanding and become much more worldly about these vast, complicated areas of human experience.

You see this with bands: The lead singer is apparently the one with all the power, but it's actually the drummer who writes the hits. The guitarist thinks they are the uncredited reason the song goes to number one and the rest is . . . Pluto in the Eighth House—particularly if the guitarist is sleeping with the lead singer.

Cancer, this cycle can be global. If you are picking up the zeitgeist or the mood of the times, you may even find that you are part of a larger trend where people en masse decide to leave their old financial, business, or property setups behind and go to the next level of control. Out of this could come lasting local, national, or even worldwide change. The rise of cryptocurrency is an example of what is to come as applied to people as a whole and not just bitcoin investors. Then, there is the likely arrival of the new banks, the new crowdfunding, and so on. Pluto in Aquarius is about people power.

Sometimes financial, property, business, or economically led changes on a large scale will force you to move forward because you see it as the only way to have control. Surf the waves and stay ahead. Anything from new ways of internet banking to changes in the property, business, or taxation laws where you live could have a huge impact now. They could transform your life.

The changes will come as a result of dramatic turning points involving other people's stake, share, debt, or other position. Expect some final chapters which will alter everything forever. And expect some amazing breakthroughs, too—the kind giving you solid new status and influence.

What doesn't work out now, in terms of finances and security, will have a feeling of intense finality about it. Don't be fooled. Although one situation in your life is over, *you* are not and neither is your bank account or investment. Once you have dealt with some final chapters in these years, remember a new book is being written on top of them. It's your whole self that Pluto is interested in, not the version of yourself you were trading with before. That whole self is what you must now take forward into a new life. Release the past if you do hit the end of a chapter—like the end of a job or income source. Then set the coordinates in a direction that will serve *you*, rather than other people or even the world at large. Steer your own ship on your own course.

Cancer, most people going through this cycle become rich or at least secure and are smart enough to use their new position to achieve something good—as in, good for everyone. If you don't—for example, if you use your influence in ways that make others feel they can do nothing—you will have to take your karmic risk and live with it. The point at which others' cash, home, possessions, or other resources puts you up there on the winner's podium is the point at which you need to use that position properly. That means taking the larger picture of others' lives into account, but also promising yourself that now that you're in control, you'll start living a life which honors all the aspects of yourself and not just those which so successfully got you where you are now.

Being honest about the nature of the deal between yourself and others who lack your economic clout is a good start. These things can happen quite naturally during a Pluto transit of the Eighth House.

Your Sun in Cancer is in the Fourth House natally, in your sector of family, property, real estate investment, house-sitting, tenancy, mortgages, and so on. Pluto's angle to your Sun will make your situation very clear to yourself and others, and the dynamics of power—even if it's just with the bank—will be obvious. You may inherit, for example, from a family member, and this affects your own family, too.

Charity or philanthropy is just as much a vehicle for this transit as a mortgage. Be really careful that you read the fine print and understand the full picture with those involved. Just because there are good feelings here and good intentions (from you) does not mean that you can avoid people who want to take over. In fact, the word *takeover* is appropriate for most things happening on this cycle. Your bank may be taken over by another bank. There may be a corporate takeover which affects the price of your shares.

Pluto was discovered in 1930 as it became clear that a few people—and countries—wanted total domination. This is a good reminder about this cycle, which can result in some complicated game-playing if you enter into it at the lowest level. Taking advantage of people in a situation where they have no recourse, in terms of their finances or their home, is one of the pitfalls of this transit.

At its highest expression, Pluto in the Eighth House is about understanding what you can do for others because you can—and not because you have any particular expectations. Nevertheless, it is very good to have an impartial professional on hand to advise you, as even the best of intentions still require rules.

Be alert, too, with situations where you are obviously receiving something for nothing, if those responsible fail to put anything in writing for you. What is the actual arrangement? What is the expectation? Nobody likes to look at these things under the microscope if a friend, partner, or family member is involved, but talk to a Gemini if you want to know how these cycles can pan out.

A prenuptial agreement is not exactly happily ever after thinking, but it could make perfect sense to you now. Looking at the reality of child maintenance is another example. If there is a stepchild involved who is not your legal responsibility so far but you have a definite responsibility to put food on the table, then this is the kind of thing that really calls for the professionals as early in the cycle as you can organize advice.

Sometimes there are contracts between husbands and wives where there is a clause—about his drinking, for example, or her addiction—which is highly unusual and by no means romantic, yet important to both of them, as the nature of the deal is clearly laid out. Both feel empowered by it.

You will have your own stories on this cycle. Pluto rewards you with great strength and tremendous influence if you remember the Pluto rules.

GEMINI

This cycle is all about your involvement with foreign people and places. You may learn a second language. You could emigrate. A person from another culture is likely to transform your life. Years spent working or studying overseas are also a common outcome of this cycle. In the dates for your decan, Pluto in Aquarius will trine your natal Sun. What happens will give the worldwide web new power in your life. Translating other ideas or hearing different accents and global viewpoints can empower you, too.

This cycle is about self-education and academia. You could pick up a diploma, a degree, or an award. Your ideas and beliefs regarding international matters or foreign issues could win you admiration, recognition, and respect in January or February of any year in your decan cycle, if you work at it. The Sun turns a spotlight on this aspect of your personality and achievements now, so if you have truly become one of those people who has something special to offer, you can now pick up some credit. More important, you'll know you're on track—which will help you plan for the future. Pluto rewards willpower with far greater strength. It's like training a muscle.

The Ninth House used to rule sea voyages a few centuries ago. Now it rules long-haul flights, foreign countries—whether to visit or to live in—and people from other countries and cultures. It also governs any part of the internet you find foreign. What happens over the next few years can give you unusual control, if you have the self-control to try for it.

It can happen because you're actually traveling or because you're in closer contact with people from Europe, Australasia, or the Americas. It is a life-changing cycle for anthropologists or those in academia whose worldview is global.

You know what you want now, in terms of travel, education, the web, or publishing. Or perhaps you have certain goals relating to people from other countries, regions, or cultures. There's no travel involved, but you need to pursue a specific ambition in relation to someone who seems foreign to you.

Your passport is now a person. That person may have been with you for years, or you could meet them for the first time within months of this cycle beginning.

Destiny will shackle you during this period. It will either pull you into a close, one-on-one game with someone you're already involved with or present you with a new player whose goals are the same as yours or, at least, compatible. Together, you and this all-important person will do more than you ever could alone. You empower each other.

Tremendous questions about cultures or nationalities and nations with respect to their history with each other come up now. You may find that the Commonwealth is in question or the United States and all its backstory with different nationalities and religions. The Ninth House is about the big picture. It is also about the power question there. It may pick up your life in quite a personal way.

If you do find yourself feeling dominated by foreign people or countries for any reason, the answer is to push back. Resistance is a way of developing your own strength, and you can fix many issues with sheer willpower now.

Pluto is the planet which brings final chapters in your life and forces you to confront yourself as you really are. This always results in a new beginning and a new kind of life—usually one which gives you the reins.

In this cycle, you will experience the endings and beginnings of Pluto through travel, relocation for work or home reasons, study, teaching, publishing, and the world of the internet in translation. That's quite a mixed bag. But it covers every situation, place, and person with the capacity to expand your horizons—geographically or intellectually. During these years, fate will make sure that you travel or just travel in the mind. Either way, the biggest endings—and enforced new beginnings—will come when you are on the move or drawing people and plans into your life which promise to fill out your understanding and knowledge of the world.

Each critical moment you experience with travel, relocation, study, academia, publishing, and your life online will force you to reject the old game of life you were playing and search harder for who you really are, from your core to your shell. Let the old setup—the old rules and roles—disappear. In time it will seem irrelevant, except as a learning experience. What is far more important is that you set a new agenda and play a new game, preferably using your whole, authentic self rather than the version of it you were relying on before.

Sometimes this transit seems to know more than you do about who and what are good for you. Just as Pluto will send you crashing out of various situations in these years, it will also stand you back up when the time is right. Except the next time, you will emerge at a far higher level. Don't spend too long regretting anything or anybody going out of your life now, as it was never going to empower you enough—not for Pluto's liking, anyway. This strongly applies to travel and travelers.

Publishing in all its forms is a function of this transit. It may be digital or traditional. An author-publisher-agent contract is a good example of power sharing. The rise of artificial intelligence puts that in question as these Pluto transits grow.

Aries actor and writer Robert Downey Jr. had this cycle on July 7, 2006, when he signed a book contract with HarperCollins for his autobiography. That is a common example of how Pluto in the Ninth House can deliver.

Vast subjects from any university or college website show you the terrain covered by this transit. It may be religious studies, Latin, Greek, philosophy, quantum mechanics. If you decide to go back and finish your degree or accept a higher degree, that's a strong Pluto outcome.

Education is sometimes formal in this cycle—you enroll in courses, seminars, or workshops—but it is commonly informal. Your knowledge base will change radically through books, the internet, DVDs, radio, and television as much as it alters through classes or lectures. Lots of people will be your teachers in disguise, too—especially if their angle on the world is different from your own. You may be asked to teach, tutor, or just give a casual talk on this transit, even if you have never considered yourself the kind of expert who is asked to appear behind a lectern or on Zoom.

Your mindset is the product of your education, your family, your community, your country, and your own ideas and theories. The difference between your perspective *before* this cycle begins and *after* it has finished will be extraordinary. This Pluto transit can transform your views on yourself and the world. If you have a fixed and unchanging angle on how things are, you will be a prime candidate for just this sort of rebuilding of your outlook.

If you feel your knowledge base is too limited at this time, you will take steps to change this, as you open yourself up to new ideas, techniques, and methods to take you to the next level. You could end this cycle with certifications, but the subjects you study are unlikely to be too safe or easy. A lot of people begin learning about astrology when Pluto travels through the Ninth House.

If you visit other countries or even emigrate now, you are unlikely to play it safe and take your old views and habits with you. Even if you wished to stay where you were, in terms of your former ideas and beliefs, destiny will have a way of asking you to evolve. The places you visit or move to now have a fated part to play in taking you to the next level. One specific foreign connection in your life could do more to alter your theories about yourself and the way the world is than any number of books or university lectures.

This cycle is actually about the expansion of your horizons. It's about stretching your usual limits, geographically or mentally. That's why it covers the world of books and learning as well as travel, relocation, and your dealings with people from other cultures, belief systems, and accents. Knowing how much stronger you become after resisting anybody or anything trying to take over is a good start. Migration, borders, passports, and visas are sometimes where this plays out.

People become authors on this transit. They spend a sabbatical in a foreign country and become part of the local scene, either eventually moving there or just forging a strong lifetime bond. Flights and cruises, sailing and adventuring in other ways—even to space—are a Ninth House concern. How you get from A to B, as well as why, can send a strong Pluto control signal to other people. Flying first class can do that, too.

The upper hand is often played out through the first handshake with a traveler, tourist, or new arrival. They may be visiting your country or a resident here. Alternatively, you may be dealing with them on the other end of a phone. Nevertheless, there is nothing and nobody so foreign to you that you cannot do some research. Educate yourself about how to communicate, how to cope, and how to manage. Update yourself on what's going to work best. For the next year or so, you're going to need a plan. Make it the best one you can find and then stick to it.

This cycle affected Queen Elizabeth II when Prince Harry married Meghan Markle. The United States entered the game.

As always with Pluto, older and more experienced people can be very helpful. You cannot change who you are nor can you alter aspects of what is taking place abroad or with foreign people in your own country. Nevertheless, you can create and control your response to all of that. Gemini, it's usually the "sensible" and time-honored approach that works best at this time. But it's your choice. Once you've asked enough questions, just go with the system that you trust.

Ask the experts, and when you can't do that, scan professional organizations or community forums. Then roll up your sleeves and get on with your best bet: your smartest plan. Pluto does reward you toward the end of the cycle with solutions you did not know could possibly exist. They will always involve great willpower, however.

Having access to knowledge which others do not can empower you now. However, you need to be aware that they may really *feel* that lack of information in their lives. It is important on any Pluto transit of the Ninth House not to appear to have the upper hand because you know something they don't. Not everybody can be an expert on what intrigues you.

You are likely to find your power base with a foreign person, group, or even a particular country in a symbolic way now. Once again you have to measure that with the reality of being a local in your hometown or homeland.

Pluto is associated with dogs because there is often a feeling that someone is leader of the pack. Cerberus was of course Pluto's own many-headed dog who guarded Hades, the Underworld where he dwelled with his wife Proserpina. This idea about being top dog or not is central to this cycle. You will probably see it before it really takes shape in your life, and of course you are free to avoid it or drop it.

Given that academia, the worldwide web, and publishing are hierarchies with a great many dog-eat-dog scenarios involved, these are places where you may hear Pluto or at least Cerberus.

If you emigrate or even just spend a long amount of time in another country on a regular basis, you may find it gives you a greater and more detailed understanding of how people politics works than any amount of books would. There is the official explanation of how authority or government operates in those places, and then there is the reality—the unofficial power game. It is a good idea to research the details on the ground of emigrating or even temporarily relocating as much as the book or internet reality. What people tell you firsthand can save you a great deal of time, should you move.

Sometimes this cycle can coincide with global conflict, which quite naturally brings in intense questions about nationality, race, religion, and so on. Pluto can teach you an enormous amount if so, but you have to begin with self-discipline.

TAURUS

Pluto will transform your career, unpaid role, or academic ventures in the time frames listed for your decan. There will be a complete change in the balance of power in your chosen field, industry, or profession with life-changing promotions, demotions, and mergers. Every ending you deal with is also a new beginning, Taurus. Pluto will square your natal Sun at this time. He will transit your Tenth House of success and status, and you will see some unforgettable departures and arrivals which will change everything for you. If you use your willpower, you may also wake up to find you have quite incredible new influence.

You are more than your career, your social status, or your position in the world, of course—but control comes from your business card, your achievements, your success, and your mission on this cycle. Are you a full-time Mr. or Mrs., with a partner whose money, power, and/or children defines your own status? That role, too, will be up for transformation. This cycle is well-known for taking people from the bottom to the top.

Do you have any idea about what you're well-known for in your particular industry or field? Do you know what you're "famous" for in your social circles? That's what the Sun will single out now. Its brilliant, relentless spotlight will sweep around your name, reputation, CV, and success rating for around twenty-one days, from the final week of January to the third week of February, in every time frame for the three decans—showing you the score.

The same trends apply to you if you are retired, unemployed, or have full-time home duties, but this cycle will be about the roles and goals you have on your own merits. Other people's feedback will give you a useful yardstick for measuring yourself and your life at this time. Are they seeing all of you? Of course not. Their view is restricted to your most outstanding features—the aspects of yourself and your life you're best-known for. January and February are times of promotion, demotion, departure, and arrival, and you will see profound changes in the years for your decan.

Everything about your performance at work will now be much more obvious for better or for worse. Projects, plans, and people will come along to expose how astonishingly marvelous you are or how much work you have to do. If you want power, you have to earn it.

Honors, letters after your name, and other power signals can arrive now if you have earned them. You'll feel obsessive now and passionate! Alternatively, it may be your boss, client, colleague, or professional rival who starts obsessing. In your career, your status, and your success, you will find vindication for your willpower.

When it comes to people politics now, every action provokes a reaction. Equally, if you are pushy about your career without being sensitive enough to take other people into consideration, that too will have a domino effect—around the workplace, around your community, and even around the planet, depending on your job. Takeovers are common. And people trying to take over are also common. Don't be one of those; it will not work on a Pluto transit—at least not in the long term.

What if you are dealing with other people's temporary compulsion? Remember, you don't necessarily have to react. Just because your boss is fixated or a colleague is momentarily seized by some big plan doesn't mean you have to take them seriously. If the issue has any validity at all, it will still make sense and carry weight later. Pluto is linked to the idea of a great longing that knows no obstacles, but that is not appropriate for every single project or role.

If you are retired, have full-time home duties, or are unemployed, Pluto will deliver the same scenario, but channeled through other areas of your life related to your role and your goals. Be aware of the pecking order at home, for example. Whether you call your success in life your spouse, your children, or the house, it will be there that Pluto works.

Even if something—a new job, a professional coup, a union demonstration—is actually an excellent idea now, it's important to try and ask the Pluto questions. Are you controlling others or manipulating a situation? Are you yourself being played?

Your ambitions, your ideas about success, and your mission in life will trigger a journey of deep soul-searching now and result in dramatic changes in your path. A complete change of position, status, or employment is possible. So is a new place in the world, which gives you extraordinary power. As you know, endings become beginnings now. So there may be a final chapter and closed book that prompts an entirely new book appearing at the same time. These stories of your life are big.

This cycle will give you some critical, extremely intense times when you are forced to accept how powerful—or utterly powerless—you have become, in the particular game of success or achievement you have been playing. The end results for you will be exactly the same, no matter if you feel you are out of the game or on top of it. Taurus, you're going to have to dig deeper inside yourself and change course.

This planet wants you to delve for your substance—the stuff you are really made of underneath, which will empower you and give you control of yourself and your life on your own terms. This process is slow. It may take months or years. But in many ways you have no choice. If you continue to live your life on the surface now in regard to your ambitions, career, or mission, you will pay the price, as what this transit is really about is power.

If others feel you have trampled them in any way, then they will attempt to push back, and you have to take that into account if you are going to take shortcuts to the controls. Nothing that happens on this transit is ever let go.

So, win or lose, you must now dig deeper and begin a new game, with a new role which suits who you actually are beneath the surface. You will need time and space to go inside yourself at this time in order to start the search. What is it about yourself at the deepest layers that could genuinely give you the reins in your life? Plot your own path now by operating from your soul, not the name, face, or title that either worked or didn't. A new life is offered repeatedly on this transit.

Do check the fine print on the contract with any new project or role and arm yourself with as many facts as you can—not only about your employers, but also about the state of your business/industry. You must now inform yourself, educate yourself, and update yourself as much as you can about the work that you do or the position you're about to take. If you don't, you could be setting up some intense situations later.

People can and do constantly want to be top dog on this cycle. The more you can live in the real world about the particular profession or position you're choosing, the better off you will be. Ask the sign just before yours about this cycle: it happens to be Aries. They had it before you for years of their life. What happened? What did they learn?

The hierarchy or chain of command within your chosen field will be reshaped now. People may go for all kinds of reasons, leaving the scene or departing in final ways. This affects you. Allow for these possibilities when you plan your ascent.

Be clever. You will need to build up some kind of psychological stronghold now as you manage this rather intense cycle. It may be psychological—a need to think a certain way or respond a certain way to feel you have the reins. It may also be practical and hands-on—a workplace system or professional routine, which will take care of what you are most concerned by in terms of others taking over or having too much power.

Retirement is never actually retirement on this transit because puttering around and pulling up weeds just do not offer enough empowerment. In fact, people who retire now may find they have more influence than they ever did when working for a salary.

Your CV can feel as if it is always shifting on this cycle, Taurus. So you may be researching a future job, analyzing the consequences of retiring or resigning, or just doing your homework on a boss, client, colleague, or professional competitor regularly.

This is probably *the* networking cycle for ambitious people. Keep every business card, and reply to every email. Information about your career or industry which is hard to get at other times will be parked right under your nose now. It is an excellent time to gather your sources and examine your options. If you are a student, a full-time home duties person, retired, or unemployed, then this cycle will affect the goals, ambitions, and missions most important to you. Expect the same scenario: a lot of networking, information gathering, and analysis.

This cycle has a lot to say about your nonprofessional and intensely emotional relationships with bosses, employers, clients, and colleagues. If you don't have a job of any description, it's about your relationship with people who have an impact on your work at home or your duties in the wider community. Pluto does not do logic; he does obsession or feelings.

This cycle, which can only happen every 248 years, is going to open up new possibilities for success and achievement that are a direct result of your self-control and self-discipline, beyond all the feelings. Expect an invitation to go forward, explore, and trade on your gifts which may be almost impossible to refuse. Taurus, almost everything on offer now promises to take you away from what you know and introduce you to possibilities delivering to you the upper hand. You may be pulled into the orbit of the most powerful player in your field at the time—or close to it.

Pluto is passing over the midheaven, or the highest point, of your solar chart now. Symbolically and literally, it is telling you to look up and then look out. If you stay where you have been before this cycle begins or even attempt to go back, you will be turning away from a unique set of circumstances which may never be there for you again. This cycle can make you. It can produce the big hit or stunning victory that nobody ever forgets, Taurus.

Ambitions and goals do not have to relate to careers, of course. This cycle will dramatically alter your path no matter if you are retired, jobless, studying, or occupying a full-time role in the home. Then there are your goals outside work—the weekend and evening pursuits you count as your *real* calling in life and vocation. If you are a rich widow with a needy little dog, then the local vet may place you on their A-list. Status is not necessarily about a job now.

Of course, Pluto is notorious for producing firings, resignations, and redundancies. His effects are always the same, though. No matter if you think of a particular professional turning point as good or bad, this planet's only role is to take you further. Career downturns at this time often tend to be disguised upturns: your destiny will be reshaped and Pluto will take you higher in the end—and toward new places and possibilities your old life never permitted.

This may happen because a larger trend sweeps you along—for example, a change in government policy or in your particular field or industry, which suddenly makes a step forward possible. It is very likely that you will wake up to find out that you have become invaluable to those who have far more power than you. This is your reward if you harness your determination, Taurus. You can, for example, be the controlling force behind the throne.

Machinations and manipulation will tempt you and test you. How far do you want to go into that world, Taurus? Pluto will form a square to your natal Sun in the Second House of finance, values, ethics, principles, banking, and price tags during these years. That will be seen and judged by the world at large as a definition of your character at that time. Knowing the square is coming will help you check on your balances, so to speak.

ARIES

Your main group or network will transform in this cycle and never be the same again. Expect a restructure. There will also be new groups to replace the old, Aries. These will redistribute the way the controls operate. This applies no matter if you are heavily involved with a sports team, committee, trade union, online community, political party, rock band, dance troupe, and so on. Pluto will form a sextile to your Sun in Aries at this time, so your profile will be power-boosted.

Friends are often in the background of our lives, but not in this cycle. During this cycle, in January and February of every year affecting your decan, the Sun will illuminate your own performance as a friend. You'll be thrown into situations which highlight exactly what you bring to your friendships. Are you getting it spectacularly right? If so, you'll feel a warm glow. If your friendship skills could do with some work, though, one episode will make the problem very clear. The start of every year in your Pluto cycle will be about the way power works within the circle.

Social events will come along now throwing you and your friends together. Or they get caught up in their own little life episodes which suddenly directly involve you. Everyone is watching—so how will you perform? More important, how effective have you been, over the last eleven months, as a friend? That's what the Sun will really expose now. Aries, just as Rome wasn't built in a day, it's clear that this particular friendship wasn't thrown together in a single afternoon either. So look back and *back*, and you will see that everything about this three-week period is actually about the last few months or even years.

You now have a rare chance to understand what's worked best for you, in terms of your friendship with a certain someone, and what you know you've let slide. Either way, you win. This cycle is also about group chemistry. Together, you can shine at this time. If things are shaky, that will be obvious too, but at least you'll have clarity.

Pluto in the Eleventh House can find you leaving your group. It can also find you making your debut with a particular community or circle as well. Power changes hands.

Hillary Rodham had this cycle when she became president of the Wellesley College Young Republicans.

If an old friend reenters your life now, they will connect you to a large network of people who are quite powerful socially or professionally. If you make a new friend at this time, this person will also open up your world either online or through a whole chain of invitations and introductions. The Eleventh House is also about existing friends, of course, which might explain why that person who has been there *forever* suddenly goes to the top of your list and you find yourself with a larger phone or internet bill. Your friend is likely to make strong waves in your life now, and a lot of time will be spent accepting that people power is not a myth: it really does deliver.

An ever-changing group, club, team, organization, association, or social network will also take up your mental energy now, as it never stands still. This may be outside the central circle that you begin this cycle with according to your decan dates. You will be amazed at the number of resources and sources which suddenly become available to unite with others and make a difference. And it will be a big difference, Aries.

Even if you're not a joiner and can't stand group dynamics, you will still find it hard not to cross paths with some kind of people-pack now. You will realize that collectively you can transform a corner of the world far more effectively than you ever could with just a partner or by yourself.

If you make a new friend now, this rather interesting person could turn out to be of lasting importance in your life. It all depends on how much you are prepared to give to each other in terms of time, tolerance, and tact. There'll be a natural sense of closeness to a seat of power—which happens to be theirs. What is now required is a combination of strength and sensitivity, telepathic understanding and clear communication. They will act as a catalyst for total transformation for you if you allow yourself to be reshaped. You will be shown that by being their friend and befriending the inner circle you can be part of something greater than yourself.

Pluto rules obsession. So there may be a group around you—a book group, a website forum, and so on—where one or more people are feeling the compulsion. Keep an eye on the networks, teams, clubs, associations, organizations, classes, and other assortments of people who are in your world or on the fringes of your world at this time.

Friends can be made or lost in this cycle. It's all about being human, really, but the basic rule with Pluto transits is that if somebody is cramping your style or taking over in dominating, then you will likely leave or fate may ensure they go. This cycle has a dramatic impact on athletes and team players in sports. It's not just about the medals or trophies; it's about the politics.

You have a friend who is about to trigger certain basic issues about who or what is in charge of the friendship at this time. They may be an obvious conduit for Pluto in the first or second year of this cycle. You may have known this person for years, or you may find the friendship takes off while this cycle is running. Nevertheless, this person is about to push more buttons than you knew you had. And you can't really do anything to change it. For one reason or another, you're stuck with a situation which means you must now live with the *realities* of being this person's friend. Is it their personality, the changes in their life, or their circumstances?

Perhaps you need to give them your blood as you share the same rare blood group. Pluto offers up all kinds of scenarios. Maybe you know their secret, and it affects the whole community. Perhaps they know yours, and it would change the family.

Be practical and make a list of what you trust will work best. Go to good books, trusted advisors, or older, wiser people if you must. And give it time. The system that is going to work best now is one that necessarily involves a long stretch of patience and effort on your part.

Destiny will line up the people you need most at this time to teach you the most about your own willpower and self-control in situations where you must discipline yourself in order to push back. There may be a friend who takes over or a whole group which tries to take over. Or the group itself may be dominated.

Pluto trains your inner strength through a period of pushing, pulling, and testing. The answer is, of course, to push back yourself. Resistance is useful on a Pluto cycle, as you gain so much self-respect but also genuine improvement in your situation.

Pluto often disturbs your position; in fact, it can make it almost impossible to hang on to the way things used to be as well as to the way you view your place in the group or with a particular friend. Be aware that if you engage in game-playing it does not just end there. It is very likely that you will see the consequences of this taken to the last degree. Be cautious before you go into a Pluto transit doing that. Friends or others in the group will be very sensitive to any Shakespearean-style dramas among your happy band.

Pluto can deliver much deeper, much more satisfying, and far more promising friendships and group alliances than the situation you were in before. That was a basic game. But your new social life will allow you to set a totally new agenda, and this time your involvement with any kind of group will hopefully do a better job of serving who you actually are. Frankly, that's a person looking for empowerment.

If you all have to call it a day in order to find your own upper hand, then that may have to happen. Even if you have to go solo, departing the old circle, Pluto rules suggest that if this is the only thing that will correct a lopsided hierarchy, then it's the answer.

As Pluto is in Aquarius and the Eleventh House of your natal chart, what you experience with your friends and allies will be reflected in wider changes in your country and the world. The control now belongs to the diverse community where men and women are equal and where everybody pools resources together, no matter what their age, race, class, and so on.

An Aquarian type with that sign prominent in their horoscope may move into a central position in your life and bring their circle along, too. This will be an incredible education for you. One of the reasons for this is the space, tolerance, and freedom extended from one person in the circle to the others. There is no crowding or game-playing—no complications.

This kind of association may be the main one for this entire cycle, or there may be a series of them. Every time you learn how people power works. There has to be room to move and breathe as well. Aquarius is an air sign. Anything or anybody trying to control things is quite normal on a Pluto transit, but it is against the nature of the way this network should actually operate.

You can also play the outsider or maverick with existing groups at this time. Moving freely around them and sometimes among them, you realize you have more clout that way. You don't always have to be an insider in order to supply a group with what it needs. Aries, if you have Aquarius factors in your natal chart, then at some point Pluto will form a conjunction with them. This is like being plugged into the mains. The friends you unite with then will transform you and themselves, and the transformation will extend to where you all operate.

A good example of this is a charity. Another is a professional venture based on everybody sharing. The notable feature of this is the equal control taken by men and women. Even if your previous circles were mostly male or mostly female, this transit will change that. Pluto is the bringer of sweeping transformation.

If you have to give up something or someone, then accept that it was an obstacle to your own potential. Your influence and reach will grow as a result of what or who is replaced. Any friend or person in a group who tries to dominate you is not going to last on this cycle.

One great truth about this transit is that a friendship can be as powerful or even more powerful than a marriage or a child. A platonic bond between two true friends can be of central importance and life-changing consequence. You can also, of course, have friends with benefits on this transit and enjoy a bond but not a relationship which also takes place in the bedroom.

The Pluto in Aquarius ideal is really everybody together, however, sharing the combined talents, skills, abilities, contacts, and resources they possess. Often, also the money—but not necessarily. Sex may or may not come into it; the kinds of bonds that this cycle produces tend to be quite hands-off in general. It is the distance which tends to work at this time, not the intimacy.

Becoming involved in power games within your circle will not end quickly or easily on this transit. Be aware of taking sides or getting into complex situations, as Pluto is a long-term planet when he moves through your chart. Nothing is ever wrapped up. The wise Aries will avoid that and instead focus on Three Musketeers thinking—one for all and all for one.

What compels people now will be the huge differences between you all. It may be gender, skin color, sexual preference, age, class, and so on. These kinds of circles do best online, as the anonymity offers a lack of labeling quite liberating for everyone who just wants to feel like part of the gang or the crowd.

Sometimes it's accents or height, the plain and the plain gorgeous. There is a great need in society and the world at this time to embrace diversity within a small collective. The more that your collective challenges the status quo of power, the more you will find it succeeds with people.

PISCES

This is the cycle which is invisible to others but transforms you on the inside. Pisces, in the years affecting your decan you will find that your belief in God or rejection of God changes you. It puts you in psychological and spiritual control, no matter which way fate takes you. You may explore Tarot, paganism, or even scientism—the scientific rejection of religion. You could just as easily find that it is Christianity, Islam, Judaism, Buddhism, and so on which empower you. Then there is self-help—whether hypnosis, mediumship, or psychology. During this transit Pluto will semi-sextile your natal Sun from the zodiac sign of Aquarius and transit your utterly private Twelfth House.

You'll become better-known for what you do behind the scenes now than what you do for the up-front stuff. The Sun's spotlight will swing onto all the things you achieve privately or by yourself away from other people's attention in January and February of every year of influence for your decan. Have you privately been seeing a therapist? You'll share it with others now. It's all about what you do *quietly*.

The Sun is neither negative nor positive; it just works like the real Sun illuminating whatever it touches. When it moves into the Twelfth House, along with Pluto, every January and February, it lights up anything and anybody you have been keeping to yourself so that everyone else can see it. Often people get attention for their religious or psychic secrets at this time. Whatever has been covered up so carefully is finally exposed.

The Sun always hones in like a laser beam on those aspects of yourself and your life that are outstanding and special, the bits and pieces in your personality, and in your world that are characteristic and unique. The fact that it's all under wraps is irrelevant. Now is the time for you to inspect the hidden projects and plans of your true, secret, inner self.

Pluto tells you that real control comes from self-control, but nobody may see that apart from your priest or therapist.

You can feel exposed at this time—as if you've suddenly been made aware of everything that you've been covering up or even *forgetting* about yourself. The exposure is useful, though, as it will enable you to get in touch with who you really are when nobody else is around. What's inside your clockwork? The Twelfth House is about the subconscious. That is why so many people pursue therapy now.

This empowering self-examination can happen through meditation, dreams, psychic experiences, astrology, counseling, therapy, or keeping a journal. This cycle sheds light on the person you actually are when you're not out there being someone else's friend, sibling, parent, child, partner, boss, colleague—what have you. There can be a conversion experience or epiphany. It happens.

You will feel quite literally self-conscious now—conscious of your self as it really is. You only get one chance every 248 years to see the real you on this level and find the power, but if there is anything that needs fixing about your inner self, it will be impossible to ignore. Your secret self is known to Jungian and Freudian psychologists alike as your unconscious. Mediums call it your spirit. Right now, it may feel as if it's all of you. Pluto takes years to work through the Twelfth House, but transformation can take years, too.

This cycle can also bring a period of hibernation, as you remove yourself from the outside world and turn your attention to your inner world instead. You might take a sabbatical, claim sick leave, check into a spa, or just spend a lot of time sitting in your room with the door locked! You may also be *researching* a retreat of some kind—a period of time in your life or a special place where you hope to find some solitude and privacy. The Twelfth House rules the time we spend by ourselves, when we discover who we really are without other people. It describes a private encounter with your own soul. It often takes place in a church or on a therapist's couch. It can happen in bed when you are dreaming or at a card table with a Tarot spread out in front of you.

You will now find yourself in a relationship vital to a confidential spiritual plan or a secret psychic agenda you have. The relationship may just hit a phase where everything suddenly has to become hush-hush. Or you could begin a new kind of connection with someone who enters your life at this time to help you move forward on a Project X or Plan Z. This will take up quite a lot of this cycle as this confidante is important.

Here are two examples: You decide to give up smoking and book time with a hypnotist for private after-hours sessions. Another example? You begin your conversion to Roman Catholicism.

What matters to you now is undoubtedly deeply private and sensitive, to the point where you must exclude almost everyone from your most personal plans and concerns. The remaining confidante is now the person you must negotiate with and hold hands with—symbolically or literally!—as you go forward. What's in front of you now is, shall we say, a most delicate matter, a sensitive subject, not for public airing. All the more reason, then, to make sure that your confidante is someone you can truly feel empowered by.

Like Greta Garbo, you *vant* to be alone. It's possible that your idea is a very good one: a health farm holiday, weekend in the mountains, or secret retreat is just what you need. If you give up drugs or alcohol now, it will transform your life. It happens. You can turn to God again on this transit, having left this behind years before. You were born with the Sun in Pisces in the Twelfth House natally, where your soul or spirit resides, and Pluto in Aquarius is now transiting your solar Twelfth House.

You will explore your inner self in order to gain control over what you feel has control over you, but this will mean keeping some things secret (your therapy? your psychic readings? your diary?) so be prepared to live a double life when this cycle affects you. You may have peered into your soul before this cycle, or you may not even have known you had one. It doesn't matter. It's the private, secret core of yourself which now offers the most room for the upper hand. It has nothing to do with money, sex, or work, and everything to do with who you really are when nobody else is watching.

Meditation, which encourages you to turn inward, can permanently change your life for the better now. So can yoga. Any discipline which encourages you to turn in on yourself—writing poetry, making deeply introspective art or music—will help you find your power.

It's about looking in the mirror or disappearing into inner space—of dreams or automatic writing, for example—and finding out who's in there. What are you all about, and who are you, really and truly? The search for those answers may take you the entire cycle, but you will discover that there is an awful lot more to you than you ever knew was there. And it puts you in a different place, so you no longer feel you cannot control particular outcomes. Of course, you can. You are your own pilot, your own captain.

Taking a voyage around yourself can be a mind-blowing experience at this time and one not to be missed. You will never see yourself or other people the same way again if you allow yourself the time to take this inner journey.

Who are you when there is nobody else around to react to? What are you made of? Pisces, you may need to be alone now in order to find this out. You will now see yourself as you truly are in the privacy of your own space, in your own time, and in your own way. This confrontation with the way things *really* are may not be easy, but it will help you set about the task of carefully building up a private world inside your own heart and head, which goes some way to putting the reins in your hands where your soul, spirit, or psyche is concerned.

The whole process may well feel like an endurance test. It's certainly not going to be easy or fast! But by the time this cycle is over, you will have new psychological bones inside you. Like a building, you'll be under construction now, even though nobody else will be able to find out what is actually going on. Perhaps it will be reconstruction. Phobias can be overcome on this transit; so can addictions.

Whatever it may look like on the outside, your inner life could be dramatically different now. The most advanced stuff in your life—the truly progressive experiments and U-turns—is likely to happen in a locked room or an isolated place. Partners may have to make way.

The old astrology books associate this cycle with prison or mental hospitals. Quite wrong. Sometimes people just move out of shared households and get single apartments to leave the world behind, and thus you can have a relationship with yourself—*by* yourself.

Your conscience, soul, and spiritual convictions all matter more now. You have to find out what you believe and have faith in.

This zone of your horoscope is famously off-limits to everybody, even your favorite psychic, so there is no point in trying to categorize it any further. Suffice it to say, for the years that Pluto is here, you will be submerging large chunks of yourself and your life to the point where the neighbors begin to wonder where you are. Classically, though, this is the cycle in which people find you either (a) elusive or (b) unknowable. You may be keeping powerful secrets. So, in the secrecy of the confessional, bombs can be dropped.

Your confidantes do hold the keys. Be aware of the fine print on those bonds.

If what you've been up to does not truly serve who you are, then Pluto will firmly remove it. This will not be easy. After all, you've had your reasons for being attached to this situation—and you probably thought that if you could win the game you were playing, you'd get the kind of control you've always wanted. Sometimes people leave the church or therapy. They reject their psychic side.

If you bottom out of your secret life now, treat it as an excuse to find out who you actually are when you're not playing that particular game. Once you know, relaunch yourself. What on earth is the point of being who you're not in order to gain "control" over a game of life which isn't really you? That is Pluto's message to you now.

As your current position rests on the fact that you've been trading on certain aspects of yourself while burying or forgetting others, you may want to start by bringing *all* of you into the picture. As that's the only way you're going to feel *genuinely* in control of your life, it may be worth a try.

Hypnotists who see your secrets have power now, so be aware of that. Yet there are sensible rules in place for all these kinds of contracts. It's the same with a psychiatrist or psychologist.

It's hard to keep things under the floorboards on this transit. Your subconscious has a way of running the show. Becoming aware of how you unknowingly program yourself will transform you. If you have always felt at the mercy of, say, a compulsion or obsession, this is the cycle when you will take your power back if you try.

Your childhood and adolescence, in terms of your religious upbringing with the family or school, will be in focus now. It's the same with teachers or parents who believed in nothing except science. Pluto transforms and it takes years, but you may well find that you are ready to change on the inside. This can happen if you felt God or religious intermediaries were in control or as if the spirit world or universe were in charge. On this transit you can reclaim your own upper hand over yourself.

YOUR INDIAN OR MOON SIGN

Indian or Vedic astrology is ancient and completely different from what we use in the West. The Nakshatra or Moon Sign in India gives a short insight into how you would be seen in that culture. There are twenty-seven Indian Moon signs, known as the lunar mansions, which each correspond to approximately thirteen degrees along the ecliptic.

Once you know your Indian Moon sign, you can check the following brief profile to find out what it says about you. Only a calculator can accurately pinpoint your Nakshatra or Indian Moon sign based on an accurate time, place, and date of birth. Visit jessicaadams.com/yourbirthday to use this free Indian or Vedic astrology online service.

Special thanks to the late Keven Barrett, from the American Council of Vedic Astrology, for his help with this section.

Ashvini—The Horse Owner

You're more popular than the winner of the Grand National, Melbourne Cup, or Kentucky Derby. Is it your good looks, your coordinated wardrobe, or your skillful work?

Bharani—The Bearer

This sign is about bearing children or birthing a creative brainchild of some kind. You're born for success, and your karma suggests a generally lucky life.

Krittika—The Cutter

You're sharper than a complimentary set of steak knives, and perhaps that's why you've become so well-known. The tools of your trade are important to success.

Rohini—The Cart

No matter how long it takes, you are always transported to greater heights or more interesting places. Your tactful style and honesty help you get there.

Mrigashira—The Deer's Head

Like Bambi, you are good at digging your hooves in, but rather timid. You may have a connection with animals in your professional life or be a pet lover.

Ardra—The Teardrop

You're an emotional person, and there may be a connection with liquid or fluids in your career—pharmacists, for instance. Every ending is a new start for you.

Punarvasu—The Arrows

Like arrows which can be aimed in all directions, your opinions don't always go the same way, either. You always hit your targets in life, though—a definite plus!

Pushya—The Cow Udder

You give and give—like a cow providing vats of cream. Your generosity is best served through donations of time, energy, or money to charity or needy pals!

Ashlesha—The Serpent

Strangely, there may be a link to snakes in your life! You are cunning and clever and can be tricky if you have to be. Mahatma Gandhi shares this sign.

Magha—The Royal Throne

You'll have servants in this life, or maybe just roommates or lovers who do the dishes for you! Your ancestors really matter to you. Expect a VIP job.

Purva Phalguni—The Hammock

You could easily work in industries which promote pleasure, rest, and relaxation. Like a hammock, you give your friends real comfort and joy.

Uttara Phalguni—The Bed

An easy life is your birthright—permanent breakfast in bed, perhaps, or lounging by the pool? Some say you could even end up as a celebrity.

Hasta—The Hand

Needless to say, tradition states that you'll end up in a hands-on profession. Be it massage or palmistry—or even magic—your light touch is noticeable.

Chitra—The Jewel

Beauty and adornment are your thing. You may be good-looking or just have more than your fair share of charm and glittering 100-watt charisma.

Svati—The Sprout

Like a real sprout, you start small. Nevertheless, your whole life is dedicated to growing and evolving and improving. You just need time and space to do it!

Vishakha—The Gateway

The gate is open to money for you. You are powerful and goal-driven. You could easily become the boss of your company or be in business for yourself.

Anuradha—The Second Gateway

Your symbol is the same as Vishakha, and like this sign, you also attract money. The door is always open to travel and networking for you—it never closes.

Jyeshtha—The Talisman

You may protect other people in your career or end up with a life where others' karma with you grants you protection! You are a positive person.

Mula—The Root

Your tentacles stretch below the surface, and you have a talent for getting to the hidden depths. You could be a healer or even an investigative journalist.

Purva Ashadha—The Fan

When life becomes too hot to handle, you are prepared to wait for things to cool down. You are patient enough to stay the course for whatever you want from life.

Uttara Ashadha—The Elephant's Tusk

Do you feel an attraction to Ganesha, the elephant-headed god? Maybe this is why. You may have a destiny connected to large animals—of all types!

Shravana—The Three Footprints

You put one foot in front of the other and walk the path of learning. The world of media and education may play a fated part in your destiny.

Dhanishtha—The Drum

As you might suspect, you are musical or will have strong links to musicians. Anything rhythmic, like poetry or mantras, could also be in your destiny.

Shatabhisha—The Circle

The circle of the heavens is in your destiny, so you could be a pilot, an astronomer, or . . . wait for it . . . an astrology fan. Science could attract you, too.

Purva Bhadrapada—Two Faces

You have one face you show to the world and one face which only you get to see. There are two sides to you! Only you know what you really feel and think.

Uttara Bhadrapada—The Cot

The mysteries of birth, life, and death are on your karmic path. Perhaps that's why your spirituality is so important to you. It helps you deal with life as it is.

Revati—The Timing Drum

Any career or hobby which involves the clock or calendar is part of your destiny—from selling antique grandfather clocks to logging on/off as an airline pilot.

For an extended interpretation of Indian Moon signs, please confirm your time of birth to know more. You'll find twenty-seven profiles at jessicaadams.com/yourbirthday.

Adapted from
Essential Astrology for Women,
with permission.

YOUR ASIAN ZODIAC SIGN

Asian signs are sometimes called Chinese zodiac signs, but they are not exclusive to China and evolved in many different countries along the Silk Road between old China and Rome centuries ago. They are based on the planet Jupiter, which in the West is still known as the lucky planet.

The Asian system of a repeated twelve-year cycle of animal signs (like the Dragon in 2024) is based on the orbit of Jupiter. Jupiter is also known as the Year Star in China. Astronomers in that country followed Jupiter's transit around the Sun and divided a zodiac circle into twelve sections, rounded up to twelve years, which is this fortunate planet's approximate cycle.

So every twelfth year, a particular animal repeats, and we find ourselves in Year of the Pig, for example, or Year of the Rat.

The actual starting dates of any new Asian zodiac year are decided by the New Moon. This is why the "Chinese New Year" is better described as the Lunar New Year. The festival that begins every new Asian zodiac period starts with the first New Moon on the lunar calendar.

What's your Asian zodiac sign? You can use the online calculator at jessicaadams.com/yourbirthday to be sure. The date of the Lunar New Year doesn't align with the new year of the Gregorian calendar and shifts from year to year, so do double-check.

The Rat

1936 / 1948 / 1960 /1972/ 1984 / 1996 / 2008 / 2020 / 2032

Rats need partners more than any other signs and are looking for soulmates who can share work commitments or weekend pursuits, making life a two-way street every day of the year. If you are with a Rat, be prepared: they don't date, mate, and relate the way other signs do. They are looking for a deep bond that can last a lifetime, and they will have enormous issues should a partnership ever fall apart.

If you are a Rat, then you may have fallen in love with a soulmate when you were very young. If so, this person's influence will never entirely leave you. It is interesting to note three famous Rats of our era—King Charles III, Bono, and Alan Turing—formed youthful attachments which lasted. Charles eventually wed his sweetheart Camilla Parker-Bowles. Bono is still married to his early love. And Turing, who tragically lost his boyhood love, remained influenced by him all his life.

Just like his father, Prince Harry is a Rat.

Every Rat needs a partnership of some kind—and these have a spiritual dimension. It may be the relationship between an artist and a muse. It may be a Bert and Ernie–style bond. For the record, Muppets creator Jim Henson was a Rat.

It is too simplistic to say that Rats are romantics and just want a forever bond. What they are actually seeking is any kind of partnership—no matter how hard, no matter how complicated—that will teach them what they need to learn on a soul level.

For every Bogie, there has to be a Bacall, and perhaps it's no surprise that Lauren Bacall was a Rat.

Equality, fairness, and justice fascinate the Rat—perhaps even the law. It is part of the Rat's life path to examine what is fair in terms of balancing the scales, and their partners are their raw material. At heart, the Rat seeks to be one half of a power couple. It is a Rat's greatest moment when they achieve that.

Behind every Chris Martin, there is a Gwyneth Paltrow—another Rat. In the Year of the Rat 1984, George Orwell's publisher Penguin relaunched his book *1984*, which is the story of two lovers who try to beat the system together. If you are a Rat, you can never read it too many times. Shakespeare, creator of *Romeo and Juliet*, was a Rat.

The Ox

1937 / 1949 / 1961 / 1973 / 1985 / 1997 / 2009 / 2021 / 2033

The Ox is the most fiercely patriotic sign and strongly relates to their roots. If you are an Ox, then you are typical of your hometown or homeland—your ancestors and family. It is very hard for you to switch social classes, cultures, or countries. Rather like your namesake, you belong to your own patch of turf. You have your field, and there is some far corner of it which is forever yours.

The Ox is tremendously proud of their neighborhood or country and always flies the flag in some way. One parent, much more than the other, is a tremendous influence on the young Ox. Sometimes an aunt, uncle, or grandparent can play that role, but it is usually a powerfully influential father or mother who shapes the Ox's destiny. Former president Barack Obama is an Ox.

Richard Burton and Wales, Walt Disney and Disneyland—these are just two examples of Ox men who psychologically and spiritually "owned" their patch. Disney of course created his own miniature nation, which still stands today—even in Paris. Where is your turf?

It is very important to an Ox that their partner shares their passion for home, and property can be a very persuasive bargaining chip in the search for love and commitment.

The world's most famous Ox is Princess Diana who flew the flag for England no matter where she traveled. Former British prime minister Margaret Thatcher is another well-known Ox. It does not matter how far an Ox wanders across the globe, they always take their roots, country, culture, and accent with them, and there is a sense that they are always secretly homesick and just longing to return and unpack.

If an Ox has a bad experience with their hometown or homeland, they will seek another to adopt. It can happen. Just like the animal, they can be stubborn about emotional issues. It can be impossible to change an Ox's mind once they are past this point. As Thatcher once said, "The lady's not for turning."

The Tiger

1938 / 1950 / 1962 / 1974 / 1986 / 1998 / 2010 / 2022 / 2034

Tigers need tribes of friends and allies, and their friends and allies need them, too. Still, the Tiger must keep a little apart if the group is to remain united. Tigers typically have several teams or networks but are always outsiders. Think of Queen Elizabeth II and the group of nations in her Commonwealth. She ruled this global network, but necessarily held herself aloof from it. Also try Tigger in *Winnie the Pooh*. Tigger is one of the most famous tigers in the world, but he has nothing in common with the other animals in the Hundred Acre Wood.

Tiger Germaine Greer helped create the Women's Liberation movement but is fiercely independent within it. The same might be said for Tiger Robert Bly who created the Men's Movement but is apart from it. At the other end of the scale think of Tiger Hugh Hefner—whose tribe consisted of Playboy Bunnies while he was never exactly down among the women.

If this is your Asian zodiac sign, then your life path is about making a circle of people work for you—and helping this circle to hit the heights—without giving up your own space, territory, and personality. If you think back to your school days, you will see how the pattern started when you were young.

In Year of the Tiger 1938, the League of Nations met its most critical test of keeping world peace—and fell apart. Why? Because not every nation would fall in line. Perhaps it's not surprising. The League of Nations was actually founded in another Year of the Tiger, too—back in 1914.

Tiger Emily Brontë of *Wuthering Heights* fame was part of the tribe of Brontë sisters but went her own wild way. Fortunately, her siblings understood and made space for her. Tiger Victoria Beckham made her name in the Spice Girls then became more famous than any of them. Think of Tiger Kenneth Williams in the Carry On films: he needed that comedy tribe, but he did not belong to it. Robbie Williams is another ferociously independent Tiger who found his power through a band then went his own sweet way. Tiger Tom Cruise is the Scientologist who is in the tribe but apart from them, too. Agnetha Fältskog from ABBA is another Tiger who needed her group—and they needed her—but the structure of ABBA based on couples did not work for her and she flew solo. The group collapsed.

In the wild, the tiger is a solitary but social animal. This is how tigers survive, and if you are a Tiger, it is how you will succeed, too.

The Rabbit

1939 / 1951 / 1963 / 1975 / 1987 / 1999 / 2011 / 2023 / 2035

The Rabbit—also known by some Eastern astrologers as the Cat—is one of the few Asian animals to be directly associated with business, finance, and trade. Rabbits are a commodity in Asia today just as they always have been and are sold as food and clothing. Angora rabbit fur is particularly valuable. Cats—the Vietnamese version of the Rabbit sign—have long been the protectors of precious food cargo on long sea voyages. Around five thousand years ago the Chinese were also using them to guard grain from rodents.

If you were born in the Year of the Rabbit, your personal life will be profoundly affected by questions about money, property, business, and valuables. Sometimes this occurs because of divorces or separations along the way. The breakups can also be on a purely professional or business level. If you are a Rabbit, then you are keenly aware of the power that love and sex can have over the human soul. Johnny Depp is a Rabbit. Angelina Jolie and Brad Pitt are both Rabbits.

One way for Rabbits to navigate the complex world of finance, property, and business is to channel their funds or energy into good causes, nonprofits, and charities. In this way they can act out the power issues which come with money but keep their personal and business lives well away from the action.

You will find your own potency, influence, and effectiveness in the world through your own very particular way of handling money. The training starts when you are young, no matter if it is a parental allowance, student debt, or the fact that a partner must pay your way as you try to switch careers.

Goats are the only other sign in the Chinese zodiac to be so deeply concerned with what is earned, owned, or owed. Both these signs have a very strong sense of values—what they will, or will not, sell out for.

You might identify with pirates or with Robin Hood types who rob from the rich to give to the poor. Perhaps you are a big-spending philanthropist. You may be a tax exile on principle or a born-again aristocrat thanks to a good marriage. Money is never straightforward for your sign, but it will also help you find who or what is most precious and valuable to you.

The Dragon

1940 / 1952 / 1964 / 1976 / 1988 / 2000 / 2012 / 2024 / 2036

A dragon is a mythical creature, and those with this sign are also drawn to myths and legends. In fact, you become a legend yourself, when you make your dreams and visions real. John Lennon is a good example of a Dragon. When he wrote and sang the words to his biggest hit "Imagine," he described himself as a dreamer. Dr. Martin Luther King Jr., famous for his "I Have a Dream" speech, is another Dragon. Tracy Chapman is yet another idealistic Dragon.

Sometimes the visions and dreams are artistic or literary. Dragon Salvador Dalí, the surrealist, saw melting clocks and put them on canvas. The key to understanding people born under the Asian sign of the Dragon is to respect the pictures inside their heads. These pictures of alternative realities can also fascinate and hypnotize the whole world if the Dragon works hard enough. If you are a true Dragon, then you can bring mental images into the real world.

Who could say Dragon Sigmund Freud's theories about the unconscious mind and dreaming were real until he cured people's psychological problems? Famous mythologist Joseph Campbell, another Dragon, also lived in a world of myth and archetypes, which he gave cultural weight to. Melinda Gates has that same vision, using her millions for a better world. What is different about Dragons is that the idea at the back of their mind, which most people would call impossible or too hard, can become a physical reality.

Dragons feature heavily in the books of J. R. R. Tolkien, where they have a hypnotic power called "dragon-spell" which can sway people. Writer Terry Pratchett immortalizes dragons in his Discworld novels: his noble dragons can be created with magic and imagination. In J. K. Rowling's Harry Potter series, dragons have magic in their blood. In the work of Emily Rodda, dragons have virtues like strength, honor, luck, faith, hope, joy, and truth.

In the Year of the Dragon 1964, Nelson Mandela gave a three-hour speech in which he told the world that he was prepared to die for his ideals. He was sentenced to life imprisonment. In that same year full of Dragon energy, Lennon announced that the Beatles would not play to a segregated audience in the United States, and fellow Dragon King won the Nobel Peace Prize.

In Dragon years, you can also take your vision, ideal, or dream and make it so. You may be a druid, witch, artist, politician, activist, psychologist, or mythologist, but you have what it takes to sway others with what only you can see. Barack Obama saw his campaign through to victory in the Year of the Dragon 2012. It is often a Dragon year in the Asian zodiac when the unreal is made real.

The Snake

1941 / 1953 / 1965 / 1977 / 1989 / 2001 / 2013 / 2025 / 2037

The flickering tongue of the snake and its famous hiss and occasional rattle tell you the first thing you need to know about this sign. Snakes need to be heard and fully understood. This is the wordsmith of the Asian zodiac. If you're a Snake, you have a way with quotes.

Did you know Apple Macintosh computers got their official start in Year of the Snake 1977? If you are a Snake, then your life may revolve around the internet. Even if you reject computers, you must still have a venue for your way with words—whether sung, written, or spoken. Bob Dylan is a Snake. John F. Kennedy, whose speeches are legendary, was a Snake.

As children, Snakes should be encouraged in English and language classes as they have tremendous potential as writers.

You will never have a dull postcard from a Snake, and many of them are extremely witty or natural poets. They have a way of presenting the facts or selling their message which is irresistible. Even if all you do is keep a diary, it will be well worth reading years into the future. Investigative journalism may draw you, as it did Snake Jessica Mitford. Alternatively, you may be a children's writer like Snake J. K. Rowling, who named her own daughter after Jessica Mitford, too.

In the age of Instagram and YouTube perhaps your preferred medium is photography or film, but Snakes have a way of sharing what they want to say in a powerful and effective way, even if no words are involved.

Snakes are natural teachers, readers, and writers. Language is a virus, and you understand it.

The Horse

1942 / 1954 / 1966 / 1978 / 1990 / 2002 / 2014 / 2026 / 2038

The loyal horse is the most patient of animals, plodding to the top of the mountain or taking its rider as far as they want to go. Horses are the animals most associated in history with conquest, as without the horse, the Romans would not have had an empire. President Joe Biden is a Horse—he began his political career at the county council level and then climbed.

Perhaps it is not surprising that Horses are the most ambitious sign in the Asian zodiac. They might begin with very little in life but within three or four decades—often using each Year of the Horse as a stepping stone—the Horse will have reached the top.

Horse Paul McCartney grew up in a very simple house in Liverpool. There was no private music tuition for him, but he had become one of the most successful musicians in the world by 1966, one of his luckiest Horse years. McCartney shares a Liverpool background and also songwriting credits with Elvis Costello, another Horse. Costello began his working life at a bank, and then spent time in the computer department of a cosmetic company. From there, he ended up in more than one musical hall of fame.

Helena Bonham Carter, another Horse, was never trained as an actress but ended up playing the Queen Mother in *The King's Speech* and then being awarded the CBE for her services to acting by Queen Elizabeth II herself.

It is the ability to keep going no matter what, under the worst possible conditions, that makes Horses succeed in the end. They try harder than other people and are perhaps more driven—just as their namesake animal is driven by its rider, there is something about this sign which is quite relentless.

Another Horse, Jimi Hendrix, took a broom to school in lieu of a guitar because there was no money in his home for a musical instrument. Later on, he found a ukulele in the trash. It had one string, but Hendrix taught himself to play on it anyway.

Horses tend to bounce back faster and more confidently than other signs. Perhaps because of this, they achieve more in the first four decades of their lives than other people do over the course of their entire CV. Greta Thunberg is a Horse. The first man on the Moon—the ultimate climb to the top of the universe—was a Horse: Neil Armstrong.

The Goat

1943 / 1955 / 1967 / 1979 / 1991 / 2003 / 2015 / 2027 / 2039

Goats develop their own value system in their teens or twenties, and most of them stick to it for the rest of their lives. If they do dramatically change their attitude toward money and the material world, it has profound consequences and will alter every other aspect of their existence as well. In most cases, though, Goats decide early on if they are capitalists, socialists, collectors, hippies, tax exiles, or communists. This then becomes the light by which they steer their journeys.

To understand the Goat, read *Pride and Prejudice* by Jane Austen, who was born under this Asian sign. It is not just a love story; it is a love and money story.

In the real world, goats are one of the few animals to steer African rural economies. A goat makes the money go round. Not a lot of people know that it was a Goat—George Harrison—who wrote the Beatles' classic "Taxman," about his objection to paying heavy taxes with the Beatles in 1960s Britain. Harrison's contemporary Mick Jagger, another Goat, became a tax exile.

Goats can be anti-materialists or total capitalists, but they all hold such strong beliefs about money it can make or break relationships.

It should not surprise you to hear that billionaire Bill Gates is a Goat. Or, perhaps, that Coco Chanel, who created wardrobes for billionaires, was a Goat, too. Coco came from poverty, and her values revolved around the creation of costly collectibles—to keep (and keep their value) forever. Eventually, this became known as investment dressing.

How do Goats decide what is precious and valuable to them? Some find it by developing a relationship with nature and becoming environmental activists who reject the tenets of big business, which seeks to destroy the wilderness in order to accumulate profit. Then there are the Goats who are at the top of Wall Street and any New York skyscraper you wish to name, who have no issues at all with selling their souls for the right price.

Steve Jobs was a Goat. So is Tim Berners-Lee, who invented the worldwide web and gave it away for nothing to make the world a better place.

The Monkey

1944 / 1956 / 1968 / 1980 / 1992 / 2004 / 2016 / 2028 / 2040

Does the mind rule the body, or does the body rule the mind? Monkeys are more strongly affected by their physical condition and state than any other Asian zodiac sign. The Monkey's relationship with their body is extremely important to them.

It would be a mistake to assume that a Monkey is all about health and fitness, though. There are some very famous Monkeys, like Timothy Leary and F. Scott Fitzgerald, who pursued drugs and alcohol, respectively. It is more accurate to say that Monkeys believe that their bodies are the path to everything else. Leary's career and life revolved around LSD after all.

Former prime minister Theresa May has diabetes. Professor Brian Cox is a runner who is also well-known for his boxing workouts. Monkeys place a huge emphasis on the physical, along with the mental and spiritual, and find it hard to understand people who live as if they were cut off below the neck.

Perhaps it's not surprising that the Year of the Monkey 1980 began a decade of obsession with mineral water and gym memberships. It was also the decade that vegetarianism became mainstream after only existing on the fringes of hippiedom. Finally, the eighties was the decade that HIV arrived, making everyone body-conscious for completely different reasons.

If you were born under the sign of the Monkey, then your journey in life is to understand that your body will often serve your soul. In other words, if your body stops functioning as normal, it is time to ask your soul what your physical being is trying to achieve for you. It works the other way, too.

The Rooster

1945 / 1957 / 1969 / 1981 / 1993 / 2005 / 2017 / 2029 / 2041

Roosters are people who are not bothered by labels like old/young or male/female. This also goes for questions about their racial heritage. Roosters are here to express their personalities first and foremost, without worrying too much about the way the world stereotypes them.

Roosters are ageless and will dress exactly the way they did forty years ago with just a few twists to modernize their look. Even when young, they have the peculiar quality of seeming timeless. Sometimes they achieve this by adopting a retro look. A classic wardrobe or haircut achieves the same thing. By tailoring their image in this way, Roosters cleverly seem to be the same age forever.

Joan Collins and Debbie Harry, both Roosters, are perhaps the best examples of this. This sign is not just about appearances, though. A much deeper issue is the Rooster's need to be accepted without prejudice, which is why they work so hard to cultivate an image which lets their soul shine through all their life. Yoko Ono is an ageless, timeless Rooster.

You are all about self-interest, self-confidence, and intense individuality. People born under this sign do not accept gender stereotypes. In 1981, a Rooster year, gender benders like Marilyn and Boy George were tapping into this energy, which is all about the free self—expression, not boxes on the basis of gender, age, race, or anything else.

If you are a Rooster, you are here to confront, challenge, and provoke us into accepting your spirit, not your exterior, and to demand acceptance for your personality, talents, and strengths—without any of the obstacles that labeling presents.

The Dog

1946 / 1958 / 1970 / 1982 / 1994 / 2006 / 2018 / 2030 / 2042

Dogs—the kind you grew up with or own now—seldom stay with their birth families. They are adopted by human families instead and quickly switch allegiance. The average dog ends up a long way from home and with almost no connection to their original litter unless puppies are taken together. Dogs are used to moving on. In Asian astrology they are also mobile and can end up a very long way from the original place of birth and family. This sign finds it easy to disconnect from its roots. If you are a Dog, you may take a job which involves being on tour or dealing with foreigners so that you are on the road.

Family loyalties can be flexible. Even a Dog who creates their own family may reject that as well. It can happen. There may be a dramatic cutoff point or a subtler separation, as the Dog goes their own way and family members head off elsewhere. Close bonds loosen to the point where they no longer bind, or sometimes the Dog snaps both collar and chain, so to speak, and is gone. Freedom's just another word for nothing left to lose for many Dogs. They sometimes stray. A stifling marriage can be very tough for them.

Dogs can take on a whole new country or culture very easily. Alternatively, they can remain in their own hometown but spend a lot of time traveling physically or in the mind. It's another way of breaking free. Foreign relations are important to these people, and they often acquire a second language. Winston Churchill is one such example. Former U.S. presidents Bill Clinton and George W. Bush had to make foreign diplomacy their way of life. Dogs do well in other countries.

They find it easy to decamp and make a new place their own—or even to wander the world for the rest of their lives. Dog David Bowie famously went to Berlin, then ended up in New York, a long way from his native Brixton. Jack Kerouac went *On the Road*. Dogs like Queen Latifah have international reach and a global connection.

Dogs can be lifelong nomads who adopt some far corner of the world as their own and go back and forth between their roots and the new home. Sometimes it is a surprise to others when they discover a Dog is related to you; Dogs can act as if those ties simply don't exist.

If a Dog grows up in a town or country where there is too much restriction—too many rules, too many limitations—they will be the first to leave if they can. If this is impossible, they may become a lifelong escape artist instead, always awaiting the next getaway vehicle. If the getaway is inside their head, via a computer screen, so be it—but one way or another they will find a way to get out even if that is only to travel in the mind.

The Pig

1947 / 1959 / 1971 / 1983 / 1995 / 2007 / 2019 / 2031 / 2043

The Pig is defined by their relationship with the world of children and teenagers. Becoming a parent or not affects the Pig far more than the other eleven Asian zodiac signs.

The parent-child relationship is key to understanding what a Pig wants from life, as they must have some sort of involvement with a younger generation to feel fulfilled. If they are unable to have children, then there may be fostering, adoption, teaching, mentoring, and so on. If partners are unable to have children with them, then they may reject those partners. That can happen.

There are usually substitute offspring in the life of a Pig, rather like an extended family of godchildren, nieces, and nephews—maybe even a whole global classroom or younger global village.

The younger generations as a whole can end up inheriting the legacy of the Pig's personality. Pigs are usually identified by their children and grandchildren, but if they skip parenthood—as His Holiness the Dalai Lama has done—there will still be an attachment to youth en masse. Young Tibetans, for example, see the Dalai Lama as a father figure. Elon Musk could be considered father to a generation of teenagers on social media through his platform X (formerly Twitter).

Pigs are forever young and have a childish quality about them, which means children and teenagers can relate—and they relate back. Stephen King understands his younger audience, no matter how old he grows. Hillary Clinton has a younger fan base of millennial women.

The path of the Pig with the younger generation is never straightforward for some reason. There may be complex relationships with stepchildren. Sometimes the issue is a partner's infertility or unwillingness to become a parent. Occasionally a child may turn out to be someone else's—it happens. There can be IVF surprises or fated adoptions. Elton John is a good example of the latter. John and his partner David Furnish both used a surrogate mother to give birth to their sons Zachary Jackson Levon Furnish-John and Elijah Joseph Daniel Furnish-John.

Should pregnancy come, it tends to be a very big deal. Often the children are, too. They are often acutely aware of the Pig parent's expectations and the strong influence of their personality. This produces a fork in the road when the child will either decide to follow in the Pig's footsteps or veer off wildly in another direction.

Pigs can sometimes choose much younger partners so that there is a parent-child dynamic. These unusual arrangements seldom pass without comment, but perhaps the Pig has found what they are looking for. Sometimes it lasts; sometimes it's just a temporary need.

Adapted from an original feature in The Express *by Jessica Adams, with permission.*

YOUR BIRTHDAY TAROT

The Tarot itself is ancient, but the most popular deck in the world was created in 1909—for all time. The Smith-Waite Tarot deck has sold over six million copies and was created by two trained astrologers: Pamela Colman Smith and Arthur E. Waite. These seventy-eight cards contain many astrological symbols and clues. Tarot decks are divided into the Major and Minor Arcana.

The Major Arcana cards represent significant life lessons and the big themes in your life. The message in Major Arcana cards is always complex. When you see a Major Arcana card, you are being told about major landmarks in your life—things you won't forget.

The Minor Arcana cards are divided into four suits: Cups, Swords, Pentacles (or Coins), and Wands (or Staves). Each represents a particular area in life: Cups are emotion and matters of the heart; Swords, action and potential conflict; Pentacles, money and business; and Wands, ideas and communication. The Minor Arcana shows less life-changing aspects of your world, as opposed to the Major Arcana which shares major turning points.

Tried, tested, and trusted by millions, the Smith-Waite Tarot offers powerful insights into what and who matter most in your birthday year. It's yours to use for life; the gift that goes on giving.

The insights provided by these Tarot cards can help you orient yourself for the year with a birthday reading. If you would like to give yourself a birthday Tarot reading, there are two popular spreads which can reveal the next twelve months. A really simple way to forecast the coming year is just to draw one card to ask: *What is the main story in my life until my next birthday?* You can also draw three cards for past, present, and future based on your last birthday year, your birthday today, and your next birthday year.

Then use the following guide to the Smith-Waite cards to find out what is in store for you. You can also employ the free deck online at jessicaadams.com /yourbirthday or try other websites and decks, too.

If you own a Smith-Waite deck yourself, you may want to keep it in a special bag or box. If you are using the online version of the deck, then you may want to light a candle or burn some incense or aromatherapy oil to establish a sacred space for your reading.

THE MAJOR ARCANA

THE FOOL (0)

Quick Look

We see a person leaping into the unknown. It is about taking risks unless one heeds a warning which offers safer travels. This card is full of the excitement of adventure—exploration, travels, or relocation. However, you need common sense and caution—after all, fools rush in and may fall off a cliff.

Description

This card depicts an adventure about to unfold. This can be a major trip, relocation, or a more symbolic leap into the unknown. It could work, but at the same time it would be crazy to set off without a map. The Fool is a warning: don't charge in or set off on the wrong path. The message here is take your time.

The Fool is "The Happy Wanderer" of the song, or maybe Jack Kerouac writing *On the Road.* It's the Durrell family moving to Corfu or the student taking a gap year. It might not be what you want to hear, but you can't just take off blindly and hope that someone will rescue you if it all goes wrong.

So keep the spirit of adventure, but lose the blind trust.

If you look at the card, there may be a map and guidebook in the backpack, but the Fool is not looking. Instead this character is about to go careering off the cliff. Just in time, the white barking dog alerts him. The dog's "woof, woof" might translate to "Watch out!" in this card; the dog saves the Fool. It's reminiscent of Tintin and Snowy. As fans of *Tintin* by Hergé will know, Snowy was ever willing to raise the alarm and save his master.

Bear in mind the journey here may be symbolic. It is representative more of a leap into the unknown—a magnificent love affair, the thrill of finding a new job, or even a giant leap into a NASA internship.

With Major Arcana cards, there is a major potential outcome. As always with Smith's illustrations, you can move the Fool around like an actor. He can return home having heeded the dog's warning or turn in a different direction—the Fool has so much potential, you can decide what to do with it. So, interesting question: Who or what is the Fool actually racing toward? The thrill of the unknown, the adrenaline high of the great departure, or a very specific destination?

Beware: the crumbling cliff won't take much weight. There is a real sense the Fool is going to behave like some kind of cartoon creature and leap off the edge, only to run frantically in midair before crashing down below with his worried white dog looking on.

The lesson of the card is that *you decide* what kind of universe you want to end up in. There are ways to make your adventure and ways to avoid it. It's down to you now, but the possibilities are there.

Pamela Colman Smith & the Fool

The little white dog in the card was probably modeled on actress Ellen Terry's favorite pet. Terry was Smith's host at Smallhythe where she created her Tarot illustrations. So when considering this dog, think about those like Lassie who save the day or a St. Bernard who can come to our rescue in the snow.

Astrology & the Fool

The Fool is lit by the Sun—which may be an astrological symbol to consider here. Again we must also note the dog. Dogs are employed as guards after all. And within astrology, Pluto owned a dog called Cerberus who guarded Hades. If you read the Tarot alongside your birth chart, there might be a clue there.

There is also a fair amount of denial in this card. The Fool's hose and boots are yellow—the color of fear: think cowardly custard and Saturn, the pale yellow planet which is a symbol of hesitation and caution provoked by anxiety about the future.

THE MAGICIAN (I)

Quick Look

We see a multitasking Renaissance man who is channeling something greater than himself. This is an impressive tutor, teacher, guide, mentor, or leader. There is a balanced emphasis on money, ideas, relationships, and action all spread out before the Magician. The message is that everything is possible once the magic rolls.

Description

A strong card and one that seldom turns up. There is so much power in the Magician. The musician Steve Kilbey has painted himself as the Magician in his own illustrated deck.

There is a lot going on in this card! Pentacles, Cups, Swords, and Wands are on the table, so this person has interests across money, relationships, people politics, and big ideas. He is all-powerful because the entire known Tarot world of Cups, Wands/Staves/Rods, Swords, and Pentacles/Coins is laid out there.

The Magician is measuring reality with both arms, and using them as the yardstick, he judges what there is to choose from. Magic is about measuring reality and watching it unfold, of course. It is like quantum mechanics—there is no single reality. There is no "correct" or "real" universe; it is only when we observe that we find out where we actually are.

You can see the dove of peace etched into the wood on the table. Red roses and white lilies surround the frame. Ask yourself if these symbols mean something to you.

The Magician is perhaps channeling something divine with the curious object in the left hand. The right hand points down to earth, grounding the magic.

This is Harry Potter, with his glasses hovering a few centimeters above his head. The bandage hides his lightning scar. There is something magical about J. K. Rowling's own story: a single mother, writing in an Edinburgh café, inspired by visions on a train, sets out on the path to fame and great wealth.

When this card appears, there is magic in the air of one's chosen universe. It takes tremendous self-confidence and certainty to be able to reach for what is there and discard all other known parallel universes, however.

The Magician also represents infinity: the figure eight of scientists, the snake biting its own tail on the belt, also suggests eternal time and no beginning and no end. Everything is possible in this card, once someone harnesses their energy and gets down to work. It is a card of manifestation—success is there for the taking but you have to believe in it and be committed.

A huge factor of this card is that so much depends on the state of mind of the person asking the question or the person at the heart of the action. If one is focused, certain, clear, confident, and aware of the way parallel universes work, then it's a question of believing, knowing, measuring, and receiving.

Pamela Colman Smith & the Magician

The Golden Dawn—the secret society where Smith learned astrology and where Waite, her partner in the cards, pursued his dreams—was genuinely magical. In fact, its most famous member, W. B. Yeats (who inducted Smith), got everything we might assume he wanted from it. His rival in love was executed. Yeats himself won the Nobel Prize for Literature. Was that mere coincidence or was it Magic with a capital *M*?

Astrology & the Magician

There is a lot of astrology in this card. The measuring comes to us from the famous double-slit experiment, but actually in astrology it is done with geometry. Astrology is a numbers game, based on a 360-degree circle, twelve zodiac signs, twelve houses, and so on. The measuring is real. Aspects are geometrical patterns, like a sextile, square, trine, and so on.

The Magician's arms form an opposition. He is illustrating two opposite signs of the zodiac perhaps or the MC (Midheaven) in opposition to the IC (Imum Coeli). This may be a clue if you are looking at an astrological chart.

The snake belt is similar to the Dragon's Head and the Dragon's Tail on astrolabes, beloved of Geoffrey Chaucer among others. This is the North Node (head) and South Node (tail) which go in a constant loop. This may be another astrological clue.

The asteroid in your personal birth chart, shown by a snake (coiled on a staff) known to the Romans as Aesculapia, is also here. The snake belt is a hint of that symbol in your chart, which is about miraculous resurrection and rebirth.

THE HIGH PRIESTESS (II)

Quick Look

The High Priestess in the card is professional and/or an academic woman. It could be Margaret Mead, Oprah Winfrey, Germaine Greer, or Annie Horniman, to name a few. Either qualifications, a book, website, blog, or journalism is illustrated by the scroll. It is a card of intuition, knowledge, feminine power, and the subconscious mind.

Description

This card is instantly recognizable as a female academic or professional. There is no sexual ambiguity here. This woman has strong ideas, powerful convictions, and you may disagree or agree with her, but you have to respect the intellectual power.

There is also a sense of mystery with the High Priestess, because she sits in front of screens. On either side of her are two columns which mark the entrance to a sacred temple. One pillar has the letter *B*—which stands for *Boaz* or "in his strength." The other pillar has the letter *J*—which means *Jachin* or "he will establish." These are from the mystical Temple of Solomon. The black and white pillars are duality, darkness/light. It suggests you need to accept the function of opposites before you enter the space.

Behind the High Priestess, herself a symbol of the asteroid Minerva (wisdom), we have pomegranates, which are a symbol of Proserpina. She was the go-between who connected her husband Pluto to her mother Ceres—and perhaps they are also represented by the black and white columns. Pluto and Ceres were both very black/white about their lives. They were passionate, obsessive, and not given to compromise.

The story goes like this: Pluto fell in love with Proserpina. He lived underground in Hades and broke the rules, splitting the earth apart to rise up and seize her. Her mother Ceres mourned her daughter after the abduction and then, enraged, went on strike. The four seasons under her rulership ground to a halt. Eventually Jupiter intervened. He asked his brother Pluto to take part in a test of what was fair and just. Thus, Jupiter needed to know if Proserpina had eaten pomegranates—a Roman euphemism for vaginal sex—during her stay in Hades. Proserpina replied she had eaten half a pomegranate. Very likely, she had gone halfway. The Romans had a very basic sense of humor about sex. As a response, Jupiter decreed that Proserpina should spend half the year with her husband—when it is winter and autumn—and half the year with her mother—when it is summer and spring.

The High Priestess usually studies and gains qualifications. Or she is a writer. She may have a website or blog. There may be journals or books. This card always turns up when someone is enquiring about a university or college degree—if they want to know if success is possible, this card is a firm yes as you can see by the rolled degree in hand. It is also a symbol of a brilliant female lecturer or professor. There may be degrees here, ranging from BA to PhD. This card is about learning and being taught at the highest level. The pearl of wisdom rests in the High Priestess's crown. The Christian cross symbolizes her faith.

This card also tells you that answers come on the deepest level and it is to the books you must turn—or the experts and perhaps your subconscious or higher mind.

Pamela Colman Smith & the High Priestess

The large cross is important. Smith converted to Catholicism later in life; Waite started as one. The Golden Dawn, the magical secret society to which they both belonged, was notable for the number of intelligent, powerful, accomplished women in its ranks. Annie Horniman, who bankrolled the Golden Dawn with her family money, started the Abbey Theatre in Dublin on the strength of a Tarot card reading. She later became an academic in England and is a good fit for the High Priestess, though of course it could have been any of the women in the Golden Dawn—like Florence Farr.

Astrology & the High Priestess

This is a symbol of the Third House and Gemini (the scroll is indicative of a newspaper or press release). However, it is also a symbol of the Moon, which you can see in the foreground. The Ninth House of academia and education is suggested here. There are quite a few astrological clues in this card.

It is important to ask yourself who the go-between or middle person is, in any situation where there are two sturdy polar opposites. A Pluto and Ceres figure. Look at the New Moon cycles too, because that lunar symbol at the bottom of the card is not there by accident.

THE EMPRESS (III)

Quick Look

This card is about lying back and enjoying a rich harvest—illustrated by a lush garden, a luxuriously comfortable house or apartment, or money rolling in. However, there are some cautionary notes about not letting things go to waste. For all that the Empress is loving her space and her place in the world, care is required to keep it this way.

Description

Here we have the very image of domestic bliss. The Domestic Goddess, perhaps a Nigella Lawson type or Vita Sackville-West, is immortalized in a lush English garden. Perhaps this is a bohemian who has dropped out of big-city pursuits or a hippie who has decided to redefine success as life on holiday.

The Empress is more than just a woman of leisure with stars on her crown and a Venus (desire) symbol in stone at her elbow, though. She is also reminding us of Ceres and the need to reap what you sow from a rich harvest so that you can prepare for the future. Summer does not last. It turns to autumn and then winter. The Empress tells us that you can live for the moment, but you also have to prepare for the future.

In the original story of Ceres, Pluto, and Proserpina, it was accepted that whenever Proserpina, the beloved daughter of Ceres, was on her annual six-month departure from Hades and her husband Pluto, the earth laughed in flowers. Ceres was overjoyed to have her daughter Proserpina back with her, and so autumn and winter were left behind, along with the lonely dark days of sole motherhood, to be replaced by sunshine, warm weather, and the harvest.

Thus, the Empress is a cautionary tale as well. Unless you leave the sofa and get to work, cutting the wheat and corn and grinding it for flour, you may find there is precious little to feed you when the seasons change. You can literally interpret this card that way, thinking three or six months into the future.

A river is pouring in. This is abundance! But it needs to be harnessed, used, managed, and not left to fall away. This, together with the wheat which must be processed, is the second cautionary symbol in the card. This is a beautiful waterway and will supply the garden all summer, but what if it floods?

The Empress is holding a golden spoon, which is open to your interpretation. For some the spoon is a nod to the Who and their song "Substitute." (Referencing birth, plastic spoons, and destiny.) Other people do not see a spoon at all. They see a microphone. Maybe the Empress is a podcaster.

The Empress is a delightful symbol of a woman who has tremendous comfort, luxury, peace, quiet, solitude, and harmony. She is not feeling remotely alone, though, as she has that rather interesting symbol of love, sex, and seduction which is evergreen. Clearly a relationship or a phase in a marriage is there to be revived and recycled, if she wants to do it!

Pamela Colman Smith & the Empress

The only thing to say about Smith's illustrations of fertile times and "the good life" is there is a need to stop lounging around, roll up the sleeves, and get to grips with what needs to be harvested and set aside for the future. This is something Smith understood from her personal life as a single woman making her own way in a time when that was much harder to do.

Astrology & the Empress

The stars on the crown of the Empress will have special meaning for you. Perhaps astrology is her crowning glory. This may also be an old wedding tiara—the Empress still wears the triumph of her big day on her head. Maybe it is astronomy which rules her intellectually.

The Venus symbol is on the heart—a strange concrete heart—wedged under this woman's chaise longue. We also see Ceres, the dwarf planet, symbolized by the corn at her feet. There is plenty of astrology here.

Ceres was the goddess of Roman agriculture who ruled the four seasons. This dwarf planet was discovered in 1801 when *The Seasons* by Joseph Haydn made its debut. This composition reflects the synchronicity of the year. Ceres was in charge of spring, summer, autumn, and winter. She ruled the harvest of corn and wheat, which depended on regular seasons.

The cushions are beautiful and expensive—probably velvet. You can see the Venus symbol repeated on the final black-and-yellow cushion. As we have spoken about Ceres, it is only fair to mention the other Roman goddess Venus. Both were intensely feminine archetypes. Venus was beautiful and vain. Her symbol in astrology is a truncated hand mirror. For some people, the spoon in the card is actually a strange little looking glass for a dressing table. Venus was jealous of women who were as beautiful—or more so—than she was. Venus seduced men, but was also seduced by them. She was married to Vulcan the Blacksmith, but had sex on the side with Mars the Warrior. Venus is very 20th Century Fox. You will see her in a lot of Hollywood films.

You should look at both Ceres and Venus if examining an astrological chart.

THE EMPEROR (IV)
Quick Look

Here we have an old man at the top of the business, firm, company, or organization. He is gray/white-haired. Perhaps he is nearing retirement or has stubbornly continued to operate past that age. He likely has Aries and Capricorn strong in his horoscope, or their ruling planets, Mars and Saturn. He's hard work, authoritative, and a father figure.

Description

This is a boss, senior official, corporate male, or perhaps your father or husband. It may be you, if you have risen to the top of your profession and are senior. Some people think the Emperor is holding what might be a Christmas bauble in his hand. Other readers over the years have seen his golden helmet as a propeller head. Is this the CEO or manager in a high-tech company? Are we talking Steve Jobs here or Bill Gates?

Intimidating, powerful, influential, and forbidding, the Emperor is quite alone. He's made it to the top, but what can you do for him? What can he do for you? He seems uncomfortable in his position, so perhaps he is ready to give it or share it with you, if you strike the right chord or make the right approach.

Thus, this card can turn up when you are seeking a promotion or an extension on your exams. It can turn up when you have to talk to your father about a loan or your girlfriend's father about her hand in marriage. There is a suggestion of the job interview about this card.

In China of old the emperor was the supreme ruler and surrounded by all kinds of walls, gates, doors, and locks—all kinds of protection. There is something so challenging about men represented by this card. They are inaccessible, and yet, here he seems available to you, primarily because nobody else is there. The question is, do you have what it takes to get up to him—onto his level—to begin the conversation?

This card is about classic male power in that it can feel quite isolating to the man who has it and in turn he can be very hard to reach. There is a great deal to be gained here by reading this man's mind. Put yourself in his shoes. Does absolute power corrupt absolutely? Is it a long way to the top, as AC/DC thought? Is it lonely at the top?

Of course, this may also be you! If so, you need to ask yourself what success means to you, what has it delivered, and what has it denied you. What might success be like after this, and what would it take to bring it to your door? Maybe you need another new mountain to climb or you'd rather like to retire or resign from this one, or delegate or restructure, perhaps, so that authority is not so isolating.

If the Emperor does happen to be you, then you have a great deal of deep thinking to do about next steps. Understanding the psychology of power and ambition is part and parcel of understanding the Emperor.

Pamela Colman Smith & the Emperor

Smith drew from tradition with this card. She also may have been influenced by the Emperor from the Visconti-Sforza Tarot from the fifteenth century, which depicted a ruler with a long white beard holding an orb in his left hand. But the Golden Dawn is prominent as well, especially with the color red. It attributed red to Aries and Mars—and red is also the color of transformation in alchemy.

Astrology & the Emperor

Capricorn and Aries are both shown here—two masculine signs to be reckoned with.

Capricorn the Goat climbs to the top and is a social mountaineer but also king of the mountain (usually a skyscraper). Whenever we talk about Capricorn types, we are looking at some kind of system, structure, traditional pyramid-tiered hierarchy, or towering organization. It frequently occurs when the headquarters is multistory, because the Emperor makes it to the top and can often literally be found in the penthouse office.

Aries the Ram decorates the throne. The red color suggests Mars, the aggressive ruler of Aries. The mountains are pure Capricorn the Goat, as we've seen, but Aries the Ram butts heads and can be a battering ram on the way to the top. This card is really telling you to look deeply into the soul, heart, and mind of this man to figure him out and strike a deal. He is obviously receptive even though he is intimidating. And if this is you? Ask yourself if you want to stay at the top and why. And how do you intend to do that?

The Mars/Aries and Saturn/Capricorn combination is clearly seen in the symbolism of the mountain, but also the rams' heads and the blazing scarlet robes suggests someone tough, determined, stoic, rather aggressive, fearless, and persistent. This is a man to be reckoned with, but the reality of these kinds of structures or organizations is that there is always some young blood, pushing their way up from the ground floor, past middle management, and into the upper corridors of power. Perhaps this is what is so lonely about being the Emperor. You know that the system you have served for so long—and supported and ascended—is the same system which encourages your replacement.

THE HIEROPHANT (V)
Quick Look

The Hierophant is like the pope, or may actually be the pope if a Roman Catholic is involved in your situation. In any case, this is the head of a belief system, religion, or pseudo-religion. A Bible or good book is prominent here. The word is the law. The monks suggest questions about accepting or rejecting that. It is conventional thinking and a question about morality and tradition.

Description

This is the pope with two monks. I always think the monks have enormous Y-front underpants patterns sewn onto their garments. You can't avoid thinking about sex when you see the Catholic Church on a card, and this is the pope laying down the law about celibacy and perhaps about the holy vows of matrimony.

The two fingers may be about to make the famous V for Victory symbol of Winston Churchill or perhaps the peace sign which became popular during the Vietnam War. The crossed keys show the Vatican. There are lots of questions here about what is right and wrong, good and evil, ethical and unethical, moral and amoral. Who or what is in charge and who or what must obey?

The Hierophant has been seen by Tarot author and expert Sasha Fenton as a symbol of conventional marriage as opposed to living together. This is true. After all, this is the pope we are talking about! In general, this card is a symbol of any orthodoxy or system which represents the establishment, with the man at the top and the rest at the bottom.

In this card we also see patriarchy: male leader, male followers. Not a nun to be spotted anywhere! It all hinges on faith and belief, and perhaps pledges or commitments. This card can be applied to a corporation or government as much as the Church.

There is an established order in this card, a tremendous emphasis on belief and trust, but also a question about loyalty or disloyalty. In the end it comes down to faith, but perhaps it's also about practical reasons. Can one afford a departure or break with the leadership and the system? Can one afford to go out on one's own? Do you need to learn a new belief system or, if you have mastered it, take on the role of a teacher?

Given the strict rules of most religions on sex, drugs, alcohol—and even particular kinds of food—the Hierophant always comes with a message about temptation and freedom. There is a choice here, either immediately or eventually. It is principally for the monks in the situation, but it is also true that the Hierophant himself can have a crisis of faith. What happens when, to quote Michael Stipe in R.E.M., you are losing your religion?

Pamela Colman Smith & the Hierophant

The Roman Catholic Church was important in the lives of both Smith, the Tarot artist, and her mentor Waite. He rejected it; she turned to it.

Smith was friends with G. K. Chesterton, who created Father Brown, and this card reminds us that priests can sometimes get into trouble with the Church if they don't follow the rules. You have to ask yourself about the system with this one. The monks are below the pope, but they are also powerful, because without his monasteries, he is nothing. Neither is the Vatican.

The Golden Dawn, the magical secret society into which Smith was inducted by W. B. Yeats, had a rigid set of rules and its own leadership. Waite was one of its leading lights.

Astrology & the Hierophant

A symbol of Jupiter and the Ninth House, but also—perhaps—of Uranus, is in his hand. Uranus has a very similar glyph, and it is a symbol of the revolution that leads to freedom and independence.

THE LOVERS (VI)

Quick Look

What therefore God hath joined together, let not man put asunder. Here we have a man and woman—Adam and Eve in the Garden of Eden, naked and exposed. This card is about the sexual attraction that leads to engagement and marriage—adultery, too. It can also show reconciliation between divorcées. In its purest form it is all about relationship and connection.

Description

There is a higher power at work in this card, embracing the mere mortals who are in love or rediscovering love. This goes beyond sex; it is about something far deeper and more emotional—more complicated, too. The Lovers can show a second honeymoon in a struggling marriage. It can also show two people who have discovered each other, want each other, but are wondering, *When, how, should we? How do two people figure out their relationship?*

The angelic figure in the background is like God or another divinity, bringing the two together. It can also be a pagan figure. This *is* sexual as well as spiritual or emotional. The rather prominent volcano in the landscape is a geographical erection about to explode. The snake on the apple tree is the serpent in the Garden of Eden, and here you find Eve and Adam wondering when to act, what to do, how to do it, and what the repercussions will be.

The benign figure tells these two: "This thing is bigger than both of you." And the calm smile suggests everything is in hand.

There is confusion, though. The billowing clouds indicate things have to be cleared up before these two can hold hands and venture forth. The path of the Lovers is not straightforward, perhaps.

This card is a call to action. It always turns up when two people have just met and feel Cupid's arrow strike. The Lovers also turns up when two people are thinking about breaking up. It brings to mind so many songs: "If You Leave Me Now," "If You Leave Me, Can I Come Too."

The answer with so many of Smith's cards is to cast yourself in the role of the man or woman and move the action in the card as if it were a stage set and you were directing a play. Smith was, among her many gifts, a set designer for the Abbey Theatre in Dublin. These two actors have prepared lines as yet unspoken in their minds. They are on the verge of talking seriously or at least finding the words. Choosing a particular world to inhabit is often a case of directing the action in the Tarot stage set. So now might be the time to look at different scripts.

There is a tremendous need for communication with the Lovers. Nobody doubts the passion. Everyone can see God or something like him, bringing these two together. You would expect there to be important astrological transits in the Fifth and/or Seventh House of either chart, which time things.

The snake or serpent in the tree is visible, as are the apples. Forbidden fruit. All the imagery and symbolism is there, and it makes sense in the context of *Romeo and Juliet* or *Pride and Prejudice*. This is Mr. Darcy and Miss Elizabeth Bennet searching for the words.

Sexual attraction or mixed emotions can make communication difficult, but here on this set the words are the thing, not the props or the actors. Listening carefully and talking just as carefully will be the key to the breakthrough both of these Lovers require.

Pamela Colman Smith & the Lovers

Forbidden fruit in the time of when Smith created this card was often sexual. A more permissive society would come about fifty years later. She knew W. B. Yeats, whose love life became the inspiration for so many poems and stories. He was obsessed with Maud Gonne, although they would never be permanently together. Smith was also aware of other interesting lovers in the Golden Dawn circle, like Florence Farr and George Bernard Shaw.

Astrology & the Lovers

You can see the Sun in the card—Sun signs or Sun transits may be important. This is, however, ultimately a card of Venus (who rules apples) and the Seventh House of sexual union, engagement, marriage, and common-law marriage. If you are looking for clues in either astrological chart, look to Venus herself, Libra as the sign she rules, and/or the Seventh House.

In the astrological chart, you might also look for the asteroid Cupido as well as his mother Venus for clues. The zodiac sign and aspects of Cupido and Venus can help fill in the gaps in information with this card.

THE CHARIOT (VII)

Quick Look

Someone is traveling between two cities or countries or relocating. As this is a Major Arcana card, it is a major journey or move. The charioteer brings knowledge, spiritual or esoteric wisdom, and the known world to the new destination. This is a splendid arrival and will change the residents, too.

Description

You can see the symbol for the Royal Air Force (RAF) on the front of the chariot, which foresaw the air force so important to Smith's country some thirty years after she created this card. Many people identify a red spinning top just below the RAF wings. This is a tale of two cities or two countries. Someone once told me, "The Charioteer has knowledge under his belt." And so he does.

There are also two New Moons hidden in the epaulets. This is one of those cards you can take apart, detail by detail, and it usually reveals an intensely personal message which can't be found in a book.

The reflective square on the tunic suggests a television, radar, or computer screen. This is someone who is going places. It's a trip but also a head trip. This card is full of so much symbolism for you to interpret in quite a personal way. The black and white sphinxes on either side can suggest questions about race to some people. There may literally be Egypt in the answer. I was once given a reading by a person who told me I would be traveling (true, the Chariot is the old-fashioned version of a long train trip) and that I had astrology under my belt (also true) as the man in this card has those symbols right there.

This is the Eagles' "New Kid in Town." It is also Jimi Hendrix bringing Black American culture to London in the sixties. We think about two cities or two countries with the Chariot, and it can turn up when we have a NYLON resident (New York/London) or someone who is used to living between Los Angeles and New York.

A Tale of Two Cities is suggested here. It is important to note that the charioteer has to submit to a two-way process of education, if he is wise. Life is not just about landing somewhere and lecturing the population. It is about listening and reading, absorbing and appreciating.

This is rather like Larry Durrell moving from England to Corfu with his family and bringing his typewriter and English book collection with him in the BBC series.

It was never going to be a one-way street, and he ultimately drew as much from Greek culture, literature, and language as the local villagers did from him. An important lesson for us all to learn is in this card.

Pamela Colman Smith & the Chariot

There is an Egyptian in this card for academia which was central to Smith. The British Museum is represented, where the Golden Dawn gathered.

Astrology & the Chariot

This is a great symbol of the Ninth House as it suggests astronomy and astrology (stars on the canopy) and the Egyptian symbolism suggests academia and foreign journeys.

The Chariot can show up as a Gemini-Sagittarius opposition in the chart and Third House and/or Ninth House transits. The aspects will tell the full story.

STRENGTH (VIII)

Quick Look

This card points to help and healing—perhaps a dentist, surgeon, or doctor. A therapeutic presence might also be a sympathetic nurse figure or a Reiki practitioner. However, there is a dual message. It takes strength to overcome the fear of who or what intimidates you and to offer help. Strong people also know when to show vulnerability or inner strength.

Description

The card shows absolute trust. The lion could maul the healer. The healer could hurt the lion. Instead something miraculous is occurring. This is a two-way street. There has to be deep tolerance and understanding on both sides if relief and release are to arrive.

This is a very encouraging card to see if you are about to have surgery or dentistry. It means the right person for the job is at hand. If you are in the medical or healing profession, you just know that your next patient is going to be more than just another customer. There will be a profound interchange here, and you may effect a transformation. You certainly won't be forgotten. There is always the risk of the "ouch" with this card, though! Both must be aware of it. Rather like a vet taking a thorn out of a cat's paw, it can hurt and there has to be great, great care.

Therapy is associated with this card, and people may find it's about a psychological process with a counselor, for example. If there are issues with fertility,

IVF, or virility, then Strength is a sure sign that some of Marvin Gaye's "Sexual Healing" might be on the way or perhaps a way through struggles with parenting.

As the rather angelic creature offering help does not seem to belong to this realm, Strength is also associated with spiritual healing.

Pamela Colman Smith & Strength

On a broader level, Strength is about the British Empire, and the healing process required for Britain in both the world wars after Smith first launched these cards around 1910. It can be read on the broadest, national level for a country in trouble or in an intimate and personal way, if you just happen to be looking for the right doctor.

Astrology & Strength

Leo the Lion is front and center here. The Sixth House, which rules doctors, nurses, surgeons, dentists, and healers, may also tie in with Strength. The word itself is a Virgo and Sixth House concept—getting your strength back after surgery or an illness, for example. The healing here may also be for depression or anxiety. Perhaps there are other mental health issues. Strength is about a heart surgeon or a psychiatrist, a hypnotherapist or an acupuncturist.

Leo is about leadership, particularly of the young, and if you have Leo planets, asteroids, points, or angles in trouble (you are going through difficult aspects to these), then Strength may turn up to guide you through this transit. Good astrology can show you when the transit will end and the ailing lion within can return to full strength.

THE HERMIT (IX)

Quick Look

The Hermit is alone, with a lit lantern. Solitude brings illumination. It's a card of introspection—being alone brings a spiritual or religious breakthrough. It can also be scientific—a slow "eureka" moment of truth. Without the noise or distraction of other people you can find what you need. Still haven't found what you're looking for? Maybe alone you actually can focus on some soul-searching and seeking inner guidance.

Description

Quite alone, an old man or someone presenting as an old man looks down at the snow while holding an unusual lantern with a radiating star, suggesting something bigger than just a candle flame. Perhaps this is near Christmas in Europe and the birth of the savior Jesus Christ. In other cases, it could be the eighteenth century and the Enlightenment of science against religion. The Hermit is personal. It really depends on how "light dawning" is defined by the reader. For some people it's God. For others it's philosophy or multiverse theory.

The Hermit is honoring the bright star in the lantern without looking at it. What is in there would melt the frozen snow. It's warm, brilliant, glowing, and the only point of color in an otherwise bleak card.

The man is holding a stick, or possibly a mirror or a very thin laptop. When Smith created this image, laptop computers were not even thought of, but here it is, as clear as day. The internet contains a lot of illuminating information about the Roman Catholic Church, Buddhism, humanism, Judaism, Hinduism—all the isms in fact. This is a person searching the prism for the right ism.

The Hermit is often literal, so there is a period of solitude or even a whole life which is spent alone at play here. I once read for a person who had decided to get his own apartment, avoid relationships of all kinds (quite happily), and devote himself to meditation and study. Sometimes this card can appear if a person needs to take a sabbatical. They literally need to go off on a retreat or on a solo holiday and find out who and what matters most.

As a person, this is a monk or a loner of some kind. As with all of Smith's cards, you can see the whole illustration as a dynamic stage set. If the Hermit finds what he is looking for, spiritually or intellectually, he can do other things. He might shave his beard off and leave this place, find some new clothes for a warmer climate, and restart his life with other people.

The card is there to be worked with. Sometimes people are content to let the Hermit be, though. They know they are meant to be alone—for example, in isolation in quarantine or on a Buddhist retreat or moving into an apartment after the end of a marriage. They also fully expect and welcome the process of finding themselves, which can only come when the dialogue stops with other people.

Listening to yourself, hearing your own thoughts, seeing yourself without the reflected mirror image that others project are a huge process. The Hermit is a Major Arcana card because it represents a deep and important journey of self-examination and soul-examination. To quote Kate Bush: What is the "Deal with God" here? Perhaps there is no God for the Hermit. Maybe this is the search for meaning which ends with the conclusion that there is none!

The idea of being guided is also close to this card. Being lost and found or finding oneself often happens in solitude.

Lanterns are important symbols: they provide a protective enclosure for the light source. The Hermit reveals protection. You are never alone. A higher power is always with you, no matter if you call this God or the universe or All That Is. Wind and rain cannot extinguish the flame. Morrissey (The Smiths) sang about those lights that can't be extinguished.

There is a strong question about communication and signaling because, as well as protection, the lantern was used to communicate, for example, on ships. Is the message from the light being received and understood? Is the Hermit hearing the spiritual, religious, or philosophical message?

The staff or rod that the Hermit leans on is his prop. That is the practical side of his life. He needs a walking stick to help him through the snowdrifts. That's fine as far as it goes, but he is searching for the spiritual or meaningful. That is also fine, as far as it goes, but the inner search can only work if there is also something or someone to lean on—a voice on Zoom, perhaps, or a letter from home.

Pamela Colman Smith & the Hermit

In Christianity—Smith became a Roman Catholic later in life—oil lamps are referenced in the New Testament and were used in churches to illuminate icons in the corner. In Hindu temples, oil lamps have deities embossed on the back. Lanterns transport Holy Fire from the Church of the Holy Sepulchre on Great Saturday during Holy Week. Also, in Smith's day, an oil lamp or lantern was a symbol of lighting the way for Jewish people. Jews used oil lamps in spiritual rituals. The Temple Menorah is a seven-branched oil lamp.

Astrology & the Hermit

This card relates to the Twelfth House of solitude in astrology and the Ninth House which rules beliefs of all stripes. The Twelfth House is ruled by Pisces and the Ninth House by Sagittarius, and sometimes a square from a planet in one sign to the other is reflected in this card. How do you square yourself with the truth?

WHEEL OF FORTUNE (X)

Quick Look

The Wheel of Fortune tells us that life is random and every high is a low in the making just as every low is a high in the making. Philosophers have written books about the endlessly spinning up-and-down nature of existence. There are books in the corners of this card. Here we have both readers and writers as well as four hidden zodiac signs. It's the cycle of life.

Description

On the Wheel of Fortune, every low point becomes a high point at some stage. Every high point becomes a low point at some stage. If you are going through a hard time, the Wheel reminds you that this will turn again.

This is a card full of imagery, so it is important to take a close look. Some people believe W. B. Yeats, who inducted Smith into the Golden Dawn, was the secret third contributor to this Tarot deck, hinted at by Waite. His most famous poem is "The Second Coming," written ten years after Smith's deck arrived.

Yeats' imagery in the poem, including the widening gyre, the falcon and falconer and the centre, can be seen in this Tarot card. The Wheel of Fortune has that sense of life without any stability or structure, which Yeats referred to.

There may be a falcon in the top right-hand corner. The half-lion, half-man in the poem may be seen at the top of the wheel, as indicated in the poem. The shadows of the birds are there too. Tarot readers have speculated for years about the involvement of Yeats in the creation of Pamela and Arthur's deck of cards. Perhaps The Wheel of Fortune has some of his imagery and even his inspiration.

The world of books may affect you as a librarian, student, author, teacher, editor, academic, and so on. The other creatures in this card are also rich with symbolism. The Egyptian sphinx—the keeper of riddles—is at the top of the wheel. She is holding a sword. The snake is said to be Typhon by some, but it could just as easily be the serpent entwined around the Rod of Aesculapius.

A canine creature with human and devilish stylings—an Anubis—supports the Wheel at the bottom, just as the sphinx holds it at the top. The Wheel itself resembles a horoscope of sorts, but you can also see some capital letters here. *O*, *R*, *A*, and *T* are spaced in the First, Fourth, Seventh, and Tenth House positions of the traditional horoscope.

The Four Evangelists are the source of the lion, ox, man, and eagle in the four corners of this card, but for you these might have quite a different meaning. It really depends on your religious background. This is one of Smith's illustrations which lends itself to being moved around or stage-directed. How might you spin the Wheel in your favor? The snake, falling downward, is a reminder of the game Snakes and Ladders. In the game of life, there are ladders to take you higher and snakes to take you down.

The clouds are heavy and gray. Into every life, a little rain must fall—but rain also makes fertile soil for later growth. The world turns, and nothing stays the same.

The readers and writers in the four corners are the real clue to the Wheel of Fortune. The hurdy-gurdy nature of life leads us to turn to our astrology books, Tarot journals, philosophical tracts, sacred texts, self-help libraries, or even Shakespeare—

who referenced Fortuna in his work. This card should send you to your personal birth chart for clues. The two fixed signs in particular which are shown at the bottom of the card—Taurus the Bull and Leo the Lion—may be important to you when this card appears.

Pamela Colman Smith & the Wheel of Fortune

W. B. Yeats is a big clue here as discussed above, as are Smith's often uncanny references that make so much sense to us today in relation to computers and quantum physics. Smith seemed to be a true pioneer in so many ways, and this card, if studied closely, really illustrates that.

Astrology & the Wheel of Fortune

You can see Taurus, Leo, and Jupiter (the eagle) in this card, just as you do throughout Smith's deck. Aquarius, the wavy line logo, is hidden at the bottom of the Wheel. The snake is a symbol of the asteroid Aesculapia in astrology. You can also see Virgo the Maiden in the top left-hand corner.

The books suggest the Ninth House or Third House. Most of all, the asteroid Fortuna (daughter of Jupiter) is what this Wheel of Fortune is all about.

This illustration by Smith is laden with symbolism. Where do you start? It's for personal interpretation. You may be a Leo (bottom right-hand corner) affected by a Taurus (bottom left-hand corner). Perhaps you are experiencing transits by Jupiter (the eagle in the top right-hand corner) or you have planets in Virgo under transit (top left-hand corner).

JUSTICE (XI)

Quick Look

In some ways the Justice card speaks for itself. This is about the law being handed down from on high. It may be the natural law of what is fair or correct. It may be the Law with a capital *L*, which can take you to the Supreme Court. This is a reassuring card, as it says both sides will be level in the end. Without fear or favor, a higher authority or power is in charge.

Description

Sometimes the law—whether in terms of karma (ancient justice) or the legal profession—is bigger than you are. There is something comforting here about these meticulously balanced scales. The scales seen here are almost exactly aligned. The judge, lawyer, or mediator is threatening anyone who dares to challenge the outcome.

There are some curious little symbols here, typical of Smith's odd details. Is that a computer screen or hidden camera in the crown? Is that the Japanese flag on the gown? Why is only one shoe showing and why is it white? What is behind the brown curtain? You will interpret these bits of information for yourself and perhaps in very different ways. It is one of Smith's richest symbolic cards, and it will say something different to every person who reads it.

Of course, it turns up when a legal process is ahead, and if so, one has to bow down to the power of Justice herself. Look at the tiny details to see what you are being told.

This card operates on two levels. It indicates lawyers, juries, and judges—in which case justice will be fair and square, those scales are so finely tuned. It can also operate when you are going through a personal situation which is patently, blatantly unfair. I once read for a woman many years ago whose friend had slept with her former boyfriend just weeks after the breakup. Justice turned up, and she yelled out in triumph when she saw it. The friend was shed by both of them, and actually her whole social circle, and never darkened anybody's door again!

There is a strong message here to respect the law in all its forms. When Justice arrives, imbalance is corrected; injustice is repaired; unfairness is dismissed. If there is/was a marriage, professional partnership, or two-way sporting contest—tennis at Wimbledon, for example—then here we have an umpire or referee's verdict. Justice often turns up when a verdict is close. Would anybody argue with the crowned figure who presides over proceedings? I think not.

Pamela Colman Smith & Justice

In the Tarot, we see art imitating life. It is fascinating to note that this most famous of all Tarot decks, the Waite-Smith, was a two-person endeavor, but for many years Smith was never credited on the deck, even though it was her vision which dominates the cards we see today.

Well, in the twenty-first century justice prevails! Stuart R. Kaplan and U.S. Games Systems, now producing the many variations of her deck, have ensured that Pamela Colman Smith is properly recognized. Sexism is an expression of the Justice card, and Smith had to deal with plenty of it at the start of last century, which put her very much in second place on this Tarot project despite her doing the lion's share of the work. She was involved in the women's suffrage movement, volunteering her talents for their publicity campaign. She was also of mixed-race parentage, and so we need to talk about racism with Justice as well as sexism.

Astrology & Justice

It's interesting to note here that Waite, who commissioned Smith to create her cards and guided the project, successfully taking it to the Rider publishing company, was a Libra Sun man. This is a potent symbol of Libra the Scales which oversees the Seventh House of partnership, separation, and divorce and in turn is ruled by Venus. (Scales can also be seen in the Six of Pentacles as a symbol of Venus in her rulership of Taurus and the Second House of money.) It is very common for this card to appear when there are transits in the Seventh House or aspects to natal factors in the Seventh House.

THE HANGED MAN (XII)

Quick Look

Dangling in midair, caught between two directions—west and east or left and right, shown by the branches above—the Hanged Man does nothing but procrastinate or wriggle, but the light around his head shows enlightenment comes during this waiting game. It's about taking a minute and pausing and surrendering before looking at new directions. Eventually he will untangle himself and take action.

Description

Here we are dangling upside down, stuck for the moment and going nowhere fast. When the time is right, things move on, but first there has to be illumination and enlightenment. The eureka moment of truth is suggested here. So is the Sun or aspects to the Sun as the human head is radiating golden light.

This is rather like being forced to wait for an outcome with property, family, or citizenship as a few examples. The roots and branches of the foliage above the Hanged Man suggest where he has come from—either side of the family tree—or where he is going to. This is one of the "absolutely male" cards in Smith's deck. Unlike some of the more ambiguous people illustrated, this is quite clearly a man.

I always think of the phrase *cooling-off period* when the Hanged Man appears, as sometimes a house or apartment purchase comes with that option should the purchaser change their mind. The enlightenment can be a brilliant breakthrough or realization which changes the original plan.

On a more serious note, I was reading for a woman whose boyfriend had disappeared when this card turned up. She feared he had hung himself—taken his own life—but none of Smith's cards ever show death, unless it is a known factor already. In fact, he was instead just "dangling" without a fixed address and had lost his telephone. (The Hanged Man is upside down so things fall out of his pockets.) Eventually, he turned up.

When the time is right, this person will get untangled, reach up, and start moving. The whole purpose of the waiting game would appear to be a spiritual or mental wake-up call.

Look beyond the title; observe the actual figure who is all tangled up. This card reminds me of Bono and U2 and their song about being stuck in a situation you can't get out of. It takes the most tremendous effort to do so, but it can be done. This card is also rather like Shakespeare's expression "hoist[ed] by your own petard." You can be your own worst enemy here—or someone else is—sabotaging and stuck as a result of it.

The planet Uranus is associated with the world turning upside down. In mythology, Uranus was thrown off his wife Gaia (the earth) while having sex with her. He turned her upside down. The shock of hair on the Hanged Man and the suggestion of electrocution with his hair standing on end are a good pointer to a recent or current Uranus transit.

Uranus is also the symbol of independence and liberation. At some point the Hanged Man will stop this state of suspended animation and find the strength and willpower to free himself. The sense of space and autonomy after such a long time spent trapped in midair will probably feel quite Uranian: A revolution. A revelation. Liberation!

Pamela Colman Smith & the Hanged Man

As noted, Smith's cards were full of clues, and this does not depict death. The tree, the formation of his legs, and the look on his face give us lots of Smith's symbolism to work with.

Astrology & the Hanged Man

The Hanged Man is a symbol of any retrograde planet. *Retrograde* means that normal motion is obstructed; the planet appears to stand still and go backward. Mars Retrograde means action is reversed. Mercury Retrograde means communication is reversed. Do check your astrological chart if you see this classic symbol of a standstill.

The family tree on either side is suggested (Cancer and the Fourth House), and the *T* shape of the tree may be a classic T square, which in astrology is a point of tension when three factors form 90-degree squares to each other.

DEATH (XIII)
Quick Look

The beginning of the end. Smith's cards never show actual death, unless it is expected—with a terminally ill person, for example—so this card means a merciful release for the questioner. Death here is symbolic. The end of the old and the promise of the new are up ahead, with that dazzling Sun rising in the distance. It points to endings, changes, and transformations.

Description

Sasha Fenton, a very good Tarot reader and best-selling author, once observed that Death confronted people when it turned up in a reading. It certainly does, and it also confronts the Tarot professional. It is a rare card showing a major ending, but that is not necessarily bad.

This card shows Pluto, the ruler of the Underworld and Roman judge of the dead, with skulls and crossbones on his horse's bridle. Pluto is associated with the color black, because he was the god of the Underworld, or Hades. It was where the coal was, deep underground, and sunlight never crept in. Pluto also rode on a carriage led by horses, usually also shown as black. Check your chart. Is there a Pluto transit? Or a transit to natal Pluto?

New York readers saw the Twin Towers shown here in the Death card on September 11, 2001. Smith's Tarot can be uncanny. It represents the death of a ruler—in this case it would eventually be Osama bin Laden but also Saddam Hussein—and the reaction of the families. When you look at the figure on the ground and the grieving children, you are shown patriarchy symbolically or the end of male leadership.

Death can be a political or a philosophical card. It can show regime changes—for instance, the passing of the Reagan era of politics or Thatcherism in the UK. When you look deeply into this card, you can see the immediate drama and loss, but also a vast space of middle ground, which must be crossed by land and sea—symbolically a big voyage—to get to the brand-new day and the brilliant promise of the Sun up ahead. The Sun has a double meaning here. Death hints that the Sun may once again turn up months or years into the future.

Of course, this card is open to personal and wide interpretation through the ages. This card played its part in what must have been millions of readings during the Spanish flu, the two world wars, and Vietnam. The dead king in the card may be King Edward VII who passed away in 1910, one year after this deck went on sale. Perhaps Smith had him in mind.

Death is typically more a symbol of death of the old and birth of the new, which can be about either house renovations or the end of an era. Yet any renovations would have massive emotional impact on the owners. Death is not just about mere endings: it has a pull on the soul. You will find in this card exactly what you need to see. The tiny details of the imagery are the clue to everything, as Smith had a gift for sending messages in even the angle of a child's head.

You can see the "golden dawn" between two towers up ahead. Even as one era is closing, a brilliant new one is in store. There is always hope and new life. The key to this card is to note the dazzling sight of the Sun rising in the far distance. That is the future—and it is bright. Every journey begins with a single step. Yet you would be remiss not to pay attention to the middle ground. This is a voyage. You don't get to the horizon until you cross the river. There is a necessary and long transition.

There is a great suggestion in this card to lower the histrionics and reduce the drama, attention-seeking, or reaction. Perhaps someone is being childish. A huge reaction of grief at the beginning is understandable, but if a situation is being milked in a theatrical way, perhaps it's time to be mature about it. Death is a fact of life, and much as we would love to avoid it, we cannot do that. It is as natural as birth.

The answer comes here from religion, spirituality, or philosophy with the figure of the bishop. You cannot negotiate with Death because everything has its organic ending. Yet you can bring peace and calm to a situation by drawing on ancient wisdom. This may be Buddhism or a simple note of philosophy. The Sun also rises. Life goes on. Tomorrow is another day.

More than anything else, this card is a reminder to let Death ride on. He's on horseback, you see. Let him go and he will vanish from the landscape. Bury the past or recycle it. Then begin the journey. The future is bright.

Pamela Colman Smith & Death

The Golden Dawn, the secret magical society which drew Smith and Waite together, is symbolically pictured here. The towers Smith shows are a common theme in the entire deck and can also be seen in the Moon, another Major Arcana card.

Astrology & Death

The grieving children are ruled by Leo and the Fifth House. The inheritance of the crown, which they may or may not collect, is Scorpio and the Eighth House. The bishop is one of many Christian icons in the deck. You will have to decide what he represents to you. The Tudor Rose on the flag reminds us, again, of war. Possibly the Wars of the Roses. This is the end of a battle sometimes. It can show a divorce and a decision made about child custody. Thus, the father is "dead" to the children, and they are responding.

TEMPERANCE (XIV)

Quick Look

This is a card of good mental and physical health. Temperance in Smith's day was abstinence from alcohol. Temperance is a great card, invoking moderation, balance, and patience: it's inviting you to calm.

Description

This may be a doctor, surgeon, Reiki master, nurse, or any type of healer/medical worker. The yellow iris in the picture is also known as yellow flag or water flag. That may be another clue for you. The crown above the mountains shows potential victory or special status and position above Capricorn the Goat's Tenth House peak of achievement, but it has to be reached after a long journey. With Temperance, you begin right now with help from a friend or group—one which helps your good health, mental health, peace of mind, well-being, or happiness on some level. Then you set forth. You can't conquer the world unless you are in good shape.

Look carefully at the feathered wings for more typical Smith clues and signs tucked away in the folds. I really recommend that you go to these cards with a magnifying glass if you have one. Also consider holding the cards sideways and upside down for a better look. What is tucked away in the dense, inky illustrations? This is another really rich and complex card.

The phrases *testing the water* and *getting your feet wet* may also apply here.

It frequently turns up when people are asking about a year off work or time to recuperate. You also see it when people are coming off alcohol and joining Alcoholics Anonymous. It can turn up if someone has been through an awful period of mental or physical health problems and is a lovely sign that they are now in calmer waters. Less dramatically, Temperance turns up when you are detoxing or doing a Dry January.

Pamela Colman Smith & Temperance

Temperance societies of the past remind us of Aquarius, and the wavy-line logo of the sign is hidden in the card pattern. This is a terrific card to see. Smith herself was also an Aquarius Sun, fond of groups devoted to good causes.

Astrology & Temperance

If you are looking at your astrological chart, you will be focused on Aquarius and the Eleventh House of societies, groups, communities, clubs, teams, and associations. This is a pure Aquarius symbol as we have a water bearer pouring the liquid from cup to cup with the wavy Aquarius logo. The pond below hints of pooled resources and Roman baths, which gave the whole community a place to gather and was, in fact, fed by *aquarii*—literally the water bearers of the time.

This is also a Virgo and Sixth House card as it shows healing. It indicates mental or physical health as well as balance and harmony, so it is a wonderful card to see.

Note the yellow triangle, or Grand Trine shape, on the angel's robe. This is another astrological symbol, as a *trine* means "flow" in astrology and this whole card is about flowing. A trine connects fire signs (Aries, Leo, Sagittarius), earth signs (Taurus, Virgo, Capricorn), air signs (Gemini, Libra, Aquarius), and water signs (Cancer, Scorpio, Pisces).

Perhaps there are others born under your element or in this group, or perhaps the friendship shown by the Aquarius symbolism is also joining you with someone born under a compatible element. The fire signs and air signs help each other flow. The earth signs and water signs do, too. So, for example, you may be looking at a group of friends and acquaintances with fire-air alignments, which helps your fire sign self go with the flow. Aries, Gemini, Leo, Libra, Sagittarius, and Aquarius may all be involved or perhaps just some of those signs—but there is a feeling of everybody pooling their resources.

THE DEVIL (XV)

Quick Look

You and your former, current, or potential sexual partner need to break free. It is not so hard to do, but both of you are overwhelmed and intimidated by something or someone "evil." In Smith's day this was the sin of adultery, but it can also be morally wrong, perhaps, to stay in a bad marriage in which you feel trapped.

Description

This card speaks of marriage, sex, and money. The Devil as an archetype has a huge list of interpretations, but this card is best understood personally. Who or what is this devil to you? Who or what is evil? Who or what represents sin? This is about your own soul.

We do have a Pluto archetype in the Devil. The Devil dominates—he has taken over this trapped couple, or has he?—and Pluto also sought to dominate. But the reality of Pluto is that he is always demoted! This happened to him in astronomical circles in 2006. Don't be fooled by the Big Bad Wolf. I know it looks rather scary in a twentieth-century cheap-TV way, but in fact, this vision of Pluto dressed up as Satan is a reminder that nothing is that powerful.

If you *give your power away*, then you become disempowered. This couple appears to be doing that. They have promoted Pluto by refusing to own their own potency and strength. If you take back your power, then you are free. You can flee the scene. The chains binding this couple look to be surprisingly easy to slip.

Pluto was and is associated with sexual obsession and naked passion in astrology because he fell in love with Proserpina and had to own her at any price even if it meant breaking the rules of nature. This is one of Smith's few overtly sexual cards. The card shows sexual bondage, and as sex and money are both ruled by the Eighth House and Scorpio, this card links to them as well. Perhaps it's time to shed the mortgage, the bank, and the bad marriage.

The Devil is of course about sin and evil, and in early twentieth-century Christianity, adultery was certainly a sin. This card also tallies with the Seventh House which rules marriage and affairs. The trick here is for both people to realize that "the devil" is just a point of view, an attitude, or a belief.

What we have is two people, naked and chained, before Satan himself. Yet, as I mentioned, this card is for personal interpretation. Today gay, lesbian, and bisexual people in much of the modern world are treated completely differently. The phrase *better the devil you know* is suggested here. So how does the Devil pan out in real life, in a Tarot reading?

I have drawn it for clients when two people are unhappily married and need to break up but are too frightened to do it because of the children and the apartment. It also turns up when a married woman is having an affair and does not know what to do. Alternative definitions of freedom, to quote "Me and Bobby McGee." The truth is, these two could easily walk away whenever they want. If you really examine Smith's drawing closely, you will see that it hardly takes much effort at all for the woman (say) to liberate herself from the clanging metalwork and then liberate the man as well.

This is the interesting part: What happens then? Do they sleep together? Separate and go in different directions? Seek a therapist to help them sort out their ideas about sin? In Smith's day, the Golden Dawn was full of intriguing women who had the most complicated relationships—at least in the eyes of polite society. The time has come to examine what and who is so wrong with this card. And above all, look at how to get away, how to break free. How can you come to understand that nothing and nobody has ultimate power over you—unless you hand it over?

Pamela Colman Smith & the Devil

When Smith created this card, homosexuality was against the law, and of course the Catholic Church recognized it as a sin. She could not even illustrate these two past, present, or potential lovers as the same sex because that was still "the love that dare not speak its name." Oscar Wilde, whose wife Constance was involved in the Golden Dawn along with Smith and Waith, was jailed for his passions.

Smith herself was involved (perhaps intimately) with high-profile lesbians in the British theatrical world of the twentieth century, but the closest she ever comes to showing lesbian love is the Three of Cups. She did, in fact, know the major players in a ménage à trois, and all three women had their own cottage within the grounds of Ellen Terry's property of Smallhythe, where Smith probably drew the cards.

Astrology & the Devil

This card speaks of Libra (marriage) but also Scorpio (sex and money). Uranus is suggested here, as he is the 1781 symbol of liberation, freedom, independence, and the beginning of the end of slavery in the United States. If you look at your chart, you might find Uranus in transit or being transited. However, you also need to look at Libra and/or Scorpio, as discussed, and possibly the Eighth House, which is governed by Pluto, who in Roman times ruled Hades or the Underworld. For Christians after Emperor Constantine the myths meant nothing, but the idea of darker realms came to mean hell.

The Devil has the horns of Aries. The woman has Bacchic grapes in her tail. Fire signs (Aries, Leo, Sagittarius) are suggested by the blazing torch in the Devil's left hand. There is a great deal to work with here, if you look at your chart.

THE TOWER (XVI)
Quick Look

A sudden bolt from the blue or shock and a home or workplace falls apart. Sometimes the Tower can be another sort of structure, like an institution, a dynasty, or a belief system. More often it is a house, apartment, or office, and the lightning strike sets everyone free once the world has finished turning upside down. Chaos, change, and upheaval are all in this card.

Description

The Tower confronts people because it looks like a disaster striking. However, it is a great deal more than that. Still, if you are asking something like, *Will my business succeed within twelve months if I launch it today?* the card is unequivocal. Do avoid this!

The Tower is useful as a portent of doom if you are asking about, say, a forthcoming engagement or the purchase of a property. Yet it can also be so useful if you ask about an event after it has happened, seeking meaning or guidance. I am sure you realize how often the Tower might turn up in a year like 2020, for example, when we were all confronted with COVID-19 for the first time and its sudden, shocking impact on our lives. In 2020 we saw the British prime minister Boris Johnson contract the virus. The American president Donald Trump and his wife Melania both did as well. Prince Charles . . . it was one shock after another in a year of many such shocks. This is also the card so many Tarot readers claim to have seen before the dreadful events of 9/11.

So what are we to do with the Tower? If you look closely, you will see the actual tower is a gray, depressing, heavy, bleak structure. Sure, it represents the known world to its falling inhabitants—one of which has the crown of a head or leader of the family or business—but is it really so bad?

What if the characters here—one of which represents you or the people in your world—fall safely on the ground? What then? They can go back later and rebuild what they had or walk away and start again. It is amazing how often the Tower appears when people realize with a start that they have no desire at all to go back to what was there and relish the chance to break free and create completely new worlds of their own.

And then there is the option for the ejected residents to just turn their backs and leave the scene. Maybe they were never particularly happy in the old world. This edifice can be a fortress which imprisoned as well as a concrete affirmation of success. We all know very successful families with impressive homes who have never felt free: the whole time they have been under lock and key. We all know about rich corporations with miserable staff.

Uranus is a symbol of the song "The World Turned Upside Down," and the person on the right is inverted. This is a flip, a dive. People often do flip during a Tower card experience or find themselves diving for cover. Once the blood has stopped pumping so fast, though, and there has been time to calm down, it is clearly the moment to start again. That is actually the really interesting question here: What comes next?

The other obvious issue is that whatever "towers" in one's life has to be built to last. The situation, place, organization, or person indicated by this card could not take the forces of nature. It was inherently unsound and was just not built to endure. The message of hope here is to rebuild, repair, improve, or move on and build again. This structure was just far too vulnerable to the vagaries of fate and fortune, and so it was never really secure at all. What seemed to be watertight and cast-iron never really was, so look to the astrological chart to see what is transiting Uranus or how Uranus is transiting. That will give you an enormous wealth of information to work with as you make the choice to go back and rebuild or just walk away and invent something quite new—something better.

Do you reset, rebuild, recycle, restart? Perhaps you do—if you think the original structure is worth the massive effort involved. It is just as valid to reject what was there before, though, and instead of a *reset*, think about a *revolution*. I find it really interesting that so many of my readers swept up in the drama of COVID-19 in the year 2020 wanted a radical new beginning. They wanted no part of the old system at all!

Pamela Colman Smith & the Tower

Smith had a great gift of drawing figures halfway through a scene. It's rather like a play which has been interrupted. Yes, the inhabitants of this uninviting, sterile building are falling. They are reeling in horror as they are thrown out of what used to be their castle. (And we all know everyone's home is their castle.) Lightning has struck the peak and the crown has come off. Everything is on fire. If this were your play, what happens next?

Astrology & the Tower

Moving away from the literal to the symbolic, the lightning bolt or thunderbolt suggests both Jupiter—who threw them and is a sign of great opportunity—and his grandfather Uranus, who is linked to electricity and lightning. It is terribly important that you check your astrological chart for Uranus in particular, either by transit or in terms of transits to the natal placement. Shock is his calling card, and it can feel like a jolt.

We have both planets in this card, as Jupiter is the thunderous sky and Uranus is the jagged bolt of electrical phenomena—so there is shock, upheaval, and quite revolutionary change (Uranus) but also an opportunity (Jupiter) to rebuild a bigger, better structure or commence something new and superior.

If the characters do return to the Tower and start again, perhaps they might paint it a more cheerful color. Maybe they will add greenery, solar panels, festive curtains, and a waterfall. Maybe they will fill it with interesting new people.

THE STAR (XVII)

Quick Look

This is a very special circle of people with one superstar or shining light and dazzling people power. It's a good card for joining a group or launching a project. Think hope, renewal, and possibilities within a group which together can literally reach for the heavens.

Description

If you were a member of Pussy Riot in Moscow a few years ago wondering how your quest for world fame might go, the Star would have vindicated you. It's the same even with largely male organizations like builders' trade unions. The Star tells you that people power is a remarkable thing once you all work out who the *star of the show* is—but you are all twinkling lights.

The blonde figure in the center of the card often quite literally shows up in your life. For example, the flaxen-haired maiden might have been Linda McCartney and the circle of stars might have been Wings. It is amazing how often we find a fair-haired person playing the central character with this card. I have seen it turn up in readings for members of the UK Conservative Party and the blonde has been, hilariously, Prime Minister Boris Johnson—or at least his sister Rachel.

In Rome, this impressive maiden would have been an aquarius (water bearer) supplying the communal baths. Aquarius is very much the sign to associate with those who feed the needs of the group without ever actually getting too involved.

There are questions here about who the central light within the group is and who are the satellites. Yet, with care, this collective can work together. Ask yourself what the bird in the tree represents. Smith's birds are always important. Perhaps this is X (formerly Twitter)—after all, birds tweet—and the circle is purely online. Maybe the phrase *a little bird told me* means something to you with this group of friends. Birds have intensely personal meaning. Really look at this winged messenger and give it some thought. The bird may be a guide or voice of wisdom if you let it speak to you. The Star is one of those cards you really have to decode for yourself, and it can defy any book of interpretations!

The naked woman may also be meaningful for you here purely because she is naked. This is one of Smith's sexualized cards. It really depends on you and your circumstances: Perhaps she is your lover. Maybe you can see the potential sexualization of a situation, but in the end it is bypassed.

The Star is also about how a group functions. One person must always be up front, front and center, like the brilliant Star here, yet everybody shines together.

This makes sense. England did not win the World Cup in 1966 without blonde captain Bobby Moore. So many groups need a leader. The Spice Girls might have tried for democracy, but Geri Halliwell invariably ended up wearing the platform boots.

This is a really encouraging card if you are involved with a team, association, society, club, ensemble cast, or something similar. It shows pooling resources, and in fact there is abundant supply here of whatever the group needs. Both jugs are flowing. Her cup runneth over. The dazzling, beautiful, bright, brilliant background must surely be a reflection of Smith's own joyous experiences with her friends—and she had many. The trick with this card is to understand that constellations depend on the individual stars within to make any patterns at all. Everyone must shine, can shine, and does shine.

Accepting an Oscar, the sensible actor thanks the cast and crew. They know there is more to this than just one voice or face. Kurt Cobain was the blonde star in Nirvana, but he was a generous musician, writer, and singer who shared the space with his bandmates. When you listen to Nirvana, you hear all three of them.

The water in this card is flooding the space. That is quite important, for as much as the Star is about Aquarius and the Eleventh House, it is also about Neptune. Neptune has no boundaries. It rules rivers, the ocean, and the sea. It can also reveal floods and a lack of boundaries.

Smith's cards are to be worked with, using active imagination and focused intention. How could this water be managed better? How could the resources be saved? Perhaps the bird has some advice. It is not enough to keep pouring; at some point you have to start observing and acting. Pouring (time, energy, talent, money, goodwill, ability) into a shared pool is a wonderful thing to do, and it can be an oasis in the desert (or a band like Oasis in the music industry).

Pamela Colman Smith & the Star

This is another Aquarian image reflecting Smith's own Aquarius Sun. And she was a friend to many and a member of Britain's most famous secret society, the Golden Dawn, so she lived her Sun sign and put it into her cards. The light in her firmament was future Nobel Prize winner W. B. Yeats, but some might say she herself was the true star.

Astrology & the Star

Feeding a community with what it needs is essentially the role of an Aquarius type. That sign is likely to dominate your chart in this reading, or perhaps somebody else in the community has an Aquarius chart signature. We think about Germaine

Greer and the Women's Liberation movement of the 1970s, for example, or Yoko Ono and her Plastic Ono Band (she is also an Aquarius Sun). John Lennon had an Aquarius Moon, so the Star might just as easily be about the Beatles.

Have a look at the way Smith has illustrated the water in this card and start to think about Neptune by transit or transits to Neptune, as this is a clear message about dissolving boundaries and that is very much the astrological territory with this planet.

THE MOON (XVIII)

Quick Look

A choice about where to live or to work faces two people who are the same but different. Do they travel or move together? Do they part company? There are many paths to the future here, and diverging is possible. Financial, business, charity, or property questions are not far behind. Time is of the essence.

Description

The Moon itself is the biggest clue in this card. This is a Full Moon but rather a serious one. On a Full Moon, the Sun and Moon are in opposite zodiac signs. Here the two dogs are opposite each other—at cross-purposes even though they are the same. The dogs are different colors yet identical. Think of the same sort of person who is at the same time a different type of person!

This card commonly turns up when people must decide to get married, move in with each other, or separate. It is the property market and the financial realities that make them say yes or no—thus Scorpio snapping at their heels. If they dither for too much longer, the value of their apartment may drop. If they "moon" about for too many more weeks, an incredible job offer for one of them (perhaps in a distant high-rise building) may vanish.

This is a good example of the quantum mechanics in so many of Smith's cards. The dogs can take the same path together or go in opposite directions. Quantum uncertainty is explained by most scientists as a multiverse—multiple universes rather than one, but absolute "reality" to live with. You and another must now choose where to live or where to work.

Parallel universes are based on parallel choices: left and right, yes and no. This card is associated with some stuck confusion, especially if a couple does not know if they should stay together or break up. You will get so much more from this card if you realize the dogs can do *anything*. They do not have to take the obvious, central path. There is nothing stopping them from exploring other possibilities. And they do not even have to stick together.

As with so many of Smith's cards, you can work creatively with this, applying your imagination to visualize different outcomes. The card is showing you actors: How would you direct that action? What would the dogs do? What about the scorpion/lobster? It really depends on your situation. This may be a divorcing couple who have forgotten they promised "until death do us part" or that breaking up can be so expensive. It can also be the passion, intensity, and obsession of Scorpio love, which risks everything. What is interesting is that this scorpion lookalike is so close to the dogs, but they seem blind to it.

You also see the Moon turning up when people have just fallen in love and cannot decide which apartment should be the nest or if there should even be a commitment toward just one property.

The Moon in all her phases is also about menstruation and pregnancy, so that may be writ large when this card turns up. The lunar cycle of twenty-eight to twenty-nine days is the same as a woman's period, and of course periods stop when babies arrive. This card can also appear when a child is on the way and it's time to think about a better-paying job or a bigger home.

Pamela Colman Smith & the Moon

Smith often put blind eyes on her subjects. Here we have two rather blind dogs who can't see each other, can't see what is coming up behind them, and are thus unable to make a move. There is a great need here for communication, honesty, and probably a wake-up call, if the situation is to be sorted out.

Astrology & the Moon

The lobster here is often taken for a scorpion and thus the zodiac sign Scorpio. Scorpio rules sex and money (marriage and mortgage) but also death and property (until death do us part). This looks like a scorpion waiting to bite. The two dogs cannot see it and are quite unaware of the pressing urgency behind them. I strongly recommend looking for factors in Scorpio in your chart or somebody else's when you pull this card. Scorpions kiss and kill. When they breed, they can cannibalize each other or sting each other to death. The old astrologers had a sense of humor and knew that marriage was so much more than romance.

The two towers and two dogs suggest Libra—pairs and partnerships. The dogs are identical in shape and breed, so another option is perhaps Gemini the Twins (the brothers). It's all highly symbolic of twos, and your chart will reveal if you are looking at Libra and/or Gemini in terms of transits.

Looking at the Moon in your chart or someone else's and also the transits of particular Full Moons and New Moons to either chart can be very useful.

THE SUN (XIX)

Quick Look

A child—or a person (it could be a grown-up, too) who is old enough to be your son or daughter—has brilliant tidings or brings wonderful breakthroughs. This is your new godchild, perhaps, or the joy of teaching a class of university students, if you are a senior academic. It's Harry Potter or Beatrix Potter, in fact. There is fun and vitality—it really is a positive card.

Description

Whenever this card turns up, it puts a smile on your face or your Tarot reader's, because it is a shot of pure joy, delivered by Pamela Colman Smith all the way from 1909. So much energy is poured into this illustration it radiates years later.

It is, of course, about a child. But it can also be about someone old enough to be your own child. So you could be sixty while this younger person is forty! This is unusual, though. Mostly, we have a message here about welcome turning points and celebratory moments involving children or teenagers. Sometimes—a pregnancy.

We also associate sunflowers with a "son flowering" and the blossoming of youth. This card appears when children do well at school or a girl becomes the captain of her soccer team. It can be quite literal, in that a nephew does well at the local gymkhana. This card rules the next generation: sons, daughters, godchildren, young relatives or just younger faces to be mentored, guided, or entertained.

It dazzles with its radiance and happiness. Look at the horse, the flowing red fabric, and the wall behind for clues. Also consider the face inside the Sun and the child's headpiece. Smith's cards work best when used as psychic triggers, so just sitting with the imagery here and letting it speak to you can be helpful.

This card has traditionally been associated with a yes answer if the question is about pregnancy or adoption, as I've mentioned—particularly with IVF. It can also show up when a branch of the family tree turns up again. This card has a summery, celebratory feel.

Pamela Colman Smith & the Sun

This card is also "the golden child." Children can make everything seem new and different—exciting—and there is such joy oozing from this card. Smith never had children, but she had a flair for communicating in a childlike way and a gift for understanding folk stories and myths.

Astrology & the Sun

This is pure Leo and Fifth House symbolism. Leo is ruled by the Sun—which shines here among sunflowers. The play on words is also evident. The Sun can be "the son" and so the son and heir. It is amazing how often this card will turn up when a couple are going through IVF treatment and hoping for good news. The son and heir is on the way, even if this is an adoption.

Leo is associated by rulership with the Fifth House which rules the heirs to the throne. The British royal family has a high Leo count. The son or daughter could also inherit the kingdom or influence, insight and inspiration of a parent, godparent, grandparent, stepparent, aunt, uncle, and so on. It is interesting that both J. K. Rowling and Beatrix Potter were born under this sign.

The sign of Sagittarius is hinted at, too, with the horse. In fact, all the horses in Smith's cards can reveal a Sagittarian theme of exploring and having adventures, learning and growing. Sagittarius rules the Ninth House of the chart, which is associated with education and academia, books and libraries, websites and the expansion of the mind. Perhaps you have factors in Sagittarius under transit now, or you may be experiencing a Sagittarius transit.

JUDGEMENT (XX)

Quick Look

Your family and friends in spirit go to the next stage of their soul's evolution. This is about people judging themselves ready to move on, but also a higher power (the angel) judging them suitable for the next spiritual step. This has a corresponding impact on you on the earthly plane. Their fate is tied to yours now if you accept a higher level of consciousness.

Description

This card confuses Tarot readers who don't accept mediumship and life after so-called death, because to understand it, you have to be open to the idea that we don't die! Perhaps you know this to be true already, in which case Judgement informs you that there is a huge shift taking place with your family or friends (perhaps partners) in the spirit world. There may be a transition taking place, so someone has just passed away—or crossed over, to quote my friend John Edward.

What you see is what you get with this card.

Two families rise from their coffins to embrace an angel judging them from heaven. This card is linked to the Eighth House, home of the last will and testament, legacies, and any inheritance.

The trumpet was often used by mediums in the early twentieth century to communicate with the spirit world. This card is a powerful symbol of transformation, redemption, and rebirth. The asteroid Aesculapia may also tie in here as a symbol of what lasts forever—what resurrects and returns.

Judgement can sometimes be quite literal as a card, revealing a judgment to be made—perhaps a spiritual, ethical, or moral judgment, rather like being assessed at the pearly gates. Your soul is weighed as you rise from the coffin; you are measured by a greater force.

Note the red cross here, too. That may have personal meaning for you. It can be seen as the Red Cross aid organization or St. George's flag of England.

You have to return to the people rising from the coffins, though. This is about new life from old. And it's about families. Ancestors are very important when Judgement appears. You come from a long line, but a long line of what and which people? That lineage is now having an impact on your life here in the real world as a substantial transformation is taking place with those who came before. As you can imagine, there are sometimes really heavy karmic stories played out with Judgement. It may be the case that a whole generation of souls tied to a particular religious group, family tree, business organization, or similar, is now going to the next level—because events on earth make it possible for them to ascend.

Judgement is a dramatic card which will have intensely personal meaning for you. I am sure you can see how it might turn up in situations when a great many people have lost their lives in one single tragedy (thus connecting all of them) and have been waiting for an event here on earth to set them free. This all sounds rather morbid, but actually Judgement is about liberation. The angelic realms are calling. Heaven is ahead and on high, and at last the signal has come. The idea of release and relief is close to this card. Depending on your belief system, there can be reincarnation, too.

Pamela Colman Smith & Judgement

As part of the Golden Dawn Smith would have studied the occult. But interestingly she converted to Catholicism, and this card contains many symbols and clues which were personal to her.

Astrology & Judgement

The asteroid Psyche—a symbol of what lasts forever in your astrological chart—was named for another human being who was given immortality. This is a card of the next stage in a soul's development as part of a family group of souls—perhaps two of them—and thus suggests people who incarnate and reincarnate together as family groups.

THE WORLD (XXI)

Quick Look

So many choices for the world traveler, or just the armchair traveler, come with this card. Which way do you turn? Europe? The United Kingdom of Great Britain and Northern Ireland? Australasia? The Americas? It is a Major Arcana card, so the outcome is important. Grounding, focusing, and concentrating are required.

Description

This card is really about too much choice, and it's international in nature. Just as much as the central character (probably yourself) must select from countries, this card is about choosing nationalities. Perhaps it's the worldwide web, world travel, and "the big wide world." Thus we can interpret the symbols in geographical terms. The lion stands for Great Britain, the bull for Spain, the eagle for the United States of America. And who is the person in the top left-hand corner? A symbol of Australia and Asia together? This face has an Australian's sun and sea-bleached hair, but more Asian features. Perhaps we are looking at Oceania.

Smith's characteristic clouds surround the four corners of the earth. They are a symbol of cloud-based computing which teaches us about quantum information. Everything is a possibility! Science has proven that quantum uncertainty is our reality. There is no single objective standard. Everything is a cloud of potential until we make it so. This is true of all Smith's choice cards, and you are being shown a place where all worlds are possible and actually unfolding right now—in another country.

The World is an incredible card that never fails to impress in readings as it can be so literal. I have seen it turn up for clients who almost fall off their chair, because they have only just bought tickets to Barcelona or London. You see it when people are confused about emigrating or uncertain about an import/export program. The trick is always to bring the attention back into the self, away from the distraction of who or what is in another country.

It's a fantastic card to see if you want to expand, explore, and emigrate or take a gap year. It can even be about going deeply into a new relationship with somebody from a foreign or unfamiliar culture. What does this card say to you? It can sometimes raise the issue of sexuality and female seduction. This may be Lady Gaga or Madonna, wooing the entire world and having fun doing it.

The person at the center of the card is you or someone you know. The primary relationship has to be with the self, and not with the World, in the first instance. Unless you know yourself and have sorted yourself out (stop dancing and start thinking), nothing can really shift here. Everything remains an untapped possibility and none of the four corners of the world can be explored. There has to be a commitment, because you cannot be in four places at once. Nor is it necessarily possible to travel to four places at once. Choice means rejecting some outcomes, but you cannot really reject what you do not know—or a person you do not know.

This card is about settling down, taking a deep breath, doing some research, but also very much about that old maxim to know thyself. There is no point in just grabbing at the first face, space, or place overseas that beckons. It's time for self-knowledge and clear intention. That way, the choice is made with full awareness of the repercussions. It is useful to look at the faces of the bull, lion, eagle, and angel figure, too. What can you read into each expression? Your psychic ability should give you some inside information here about the United Kingdom, Spain, or perhaps Europe or the European Union.

Pamela Colman Smith & the World

Smith only put a very few naked people into her cards, but this is one of them. The image was very likely copied from one of the saucy postcards of 1909, showing actresses in various states of undress with only wispy scarves to cover their modesty.

World travel in Smith and Waite's day was not on budget airlines. Embarking on a world-circling trip was overwhelming, which may explain why the central woman on this card does not know which way to turn. As you might imagine, it is a time for concentration and focus, which can aid a smart decision. Smith and Waite were both migrants, and later on in her life, Smith in particular became tied to London as much as New York. So even though this card was created in 1909, it has a very modern feel, as the world emerges from an age of globalization.

Astrology & the World

This card relates to Jupiter (the eagle), Leo (the lion), Taurus (the bull), and the Ninth House (travel and foreign people and places). You would certainly be looking at transits to Sagittarius factors in the Ninth House or transits from Sagittarius factors.

THE MINOR ARCANA

The Suit of Cups

Cups are love, feelings, and emotion in the Tarot. The element associated with Cups is water, and thus represents the signs of Cancer, Scorpio, and Pisces in the tradition of the Tarot cards.

ACE OF CUPS

Quick Look

This card shows an abundance of fulfilling emotional outcomes. Your cup runneth over. This is about your soul, spirit, and heart overflowing. There may be a group, community, or movement in the background. Center stage is a very special relationship. It may be child and parent at the christening font or a very pure partnership.

Description

This is one of those cards which makes every heart leap because at first glance it transmits so much joy and energy. It is a terrific Tarot card to see if you have been going through a hard time. It often turns up before a baby is christened, but it can also appear when there is a relationship phase, a friendship phase, or a brand-new involvement that will be the gift that keeps on giving.

Look at all the symbols closely here. The letter *W* is on the Cup. The Christian cross is on the communion wafer. The dove of peace flies overhead. The Holy Grail is certainly hidden in the Cup symbolism, so perhaps you are involved with Arthurian mythology or even Monty Python! The Buddhist lotus flowers dot the water—which may have particular meaning for you if you are involved with Tibet or Thailand. As always, with Smith's cards you should interpret the symbols in a personal way.

The Ace of Cups is brimming with potential unrealized to date. You have to make this happen by trusting the Tarot card and believing that the moment is right to take what is on offer. It is yours to enjoy, but time is of the essence as it's not certain how long the offer will remain. Although the card is so joyful, it is still all an unpopped universe. There is a spiritually fulfilling and rewarding relationship or family situation, which can feel as if something has been christened or blessed. It's refreshing, promising, deep, and complex. Reach for what you see. Something sacred is on offer here, but it must be brought down to earth and integrated into your life.

The tremendous emotional and spiritual surge of the Ace of Cups is profoundly moving, because it describes something that is so deeply felt between two or more people. This is the stuff of great music, poetry, or art or spiritual experiences. It is also of tremendous religious importance to some Roman Catholics, as this imagery ties in with Sunday mass.

On a more basic note, a gold chalice is a gold chalice. This can be the sports victory held aloft, no matter if we're talking the World Cup in soccer or the Grand Prix. The winner of the Melbourne Cup or any other award is suggested here, depending on who you are and what your question is. This is so much more than a win on the board, though. This message transcends the metal in hand and becomes so much more spiritually. You might say England's 1966 World Cup, in Bobby Moore's hands with the queen in attendance on British soil and against Germany, twenty years or so after the war, had that kind of resonance.

Pamela Colman Smith & Ace of Cups

The cloud is classic quantum uncertainty, and Smith's cards are full of them—billowing clouds of potential delivery and hypothetical reality. Nothing can occur until this is made real. This is a central part of the Tarot experience: there is no point drawing cards in a cynical way, as the trick with quantum reality is to accept, trust, and *know* things to be true. When you step into Smith and Waite's world of Tarot, you have to commit completely. There is no point distrusting the experience or being skeptical about what is there. This card is about buying into what and who is on offer.

Astrology & Ace of Cups

The Cup itself is about emotional or sometimes sexual fulfillment, and this one is overflowing, as we've seen. There is no end to what pours forth. Cups were associated with water signs in the original Tarot—so Cancer, Scorpio, Pisces. And watery imagery carries over into them: Cancer is mother's milk. Scorpio is the blood, sweat, and tears—and other bodily fluids—of a passionate marriage. Pisces is just tears.

TWO OF CUPS
Quick Look

This suggests a reconciliation between a couple who have separated, divorced, or just had problems. It is also the first gesture of trust between two people who want to be lovers but have not yet made the leap. It's rather like the Cure song "Let's Go to Bed" or the Smiths' "Ask."

Description

We all recognize this moment between lovers or potential lovers in this card. A couple who have argued are about to make up or two people who are attracted to each other need to cross the bridge between them to find intimacy and trust. This is about unspoken communication as much as it is about finding the right words. Yet there is so much potential for happiness in this card—an engagement or marriage, possibly a child.

Perhaps, though, it is just an amicable split if the relationship is on the rocks and needs a decision. Agreeing to differ can be one outcome of this Two of Cups card. Getting together is another! It really depends on what your question is and where your life stands when you pull it.

Leo the Lion is about sexual relationships which might produce babies or lead to stepparenting. It is also about decisions made not to have children, but instead to adopt nieces, nephews, or godchildren as one's own. The pretenders to the throne, as well as the heirs to the throne, are indicated by Leo. Thus, this card can appear when a couple is deciding to spend money on IVF treatment or if child custody in a separation is a key question. Then there is the matter of having babies at all and making the commitment of marriage. The lion hovers over this couple, impossible to ignore.

We also associate kings with a court, and thus courtship and being courted. This is a card of courtship, as one person tries to pay court to the other. Just look at the body language. There is tremendous hesitation here, but also the sense that something/someone bigger than both of you is dictating what will happen.

It's also about rulership; the entire situation is surrounded by a Leo and Fifth House question: Who succeeds either or both of you on the throne and how is that to happen? Will it be a godchild or your own sons and daughters?

The asteroid Aesculapia is shown by the snakes entwined on the rod which also looks like a DNA symbol—the double helix. This asteroid is about what comes back from the brink—who or what has been written off, but comes to life again, rather miraculously. Thus, this card can also show reconciliation. Two people have parted company but, amazingly, given all that has been said and done, they are now ready to talk about making up.

As with all Smith's cards, the illustration is a stage set with props, actors, and a supplied scenario. You are free to improvise and direct your own life by moving all these elements around until you get what you want and need.

Pamela Colman Smith & Two of Cups

A characteristic Kent cottage is in the background, representing a lovely home. (Smith created her deck in the countryside there.) Background details always matter in these cards. The question of property is part and parcel of what must be discussed or agreed to. Thus, we have the association of this card with two people moving in together or breaking up and selling the apartment.

Astrology & Two of Cups

The zodiac signs with associations here are Leo, Gemini, and Libra.

Leo the Lion is overhead with his rulership of the Fifth House, which in turn describes pregnancy, stepchildren, shared godchildren, nieces and nephews, adoption, and parenting. You should look to Leo and the Fifth House in your chart or the other person's.

This card also works as a Gemini symbol—the glyph is the Gemini sign and all pairs or twin souls are Gemini. One person stands firm. The other is hesitant. Gemini is a pair, just as Libra is a pair. The difference here is that Gemini is about communication or a lack of it! Perhaps it is Gemini-based Third House communication issues between both parties that got us here in the first place.

This card may symbolize the Seventh House and Libra—couples who have to negotiate having a child, moving in together, separating or reconciling. Libra is about the scales of literally two bowls (or Cups?) held on a single chain or stand and how to make them symmetrical.

Using one or both horoscopes can really help if you are looking for zodiac sign or house clues. Is this a Libra question about equality and the law, or a Gemini question about communication? Perhaps it is both. You would certainly be looking at Leo and the Fifth House in either or both charts to see what the bigger story is. There may be a transit to a Leo placement or there may be a transit in Leo.

THREE OF CUPS

Quick Look

Three people, probably female at first glance, celebrate their friendship, their achievements, and a harvest of some kind. There is rich and ripe fruit all around, and the champagne is flowing. The only caveat is that unless everything is used—preserved, cooked, and enjoyed or employed to seed future growth—it's wasteful.

Description

Here we have an archetypal experience of feminine triumph known to Bananarama, the Supremes, the Slits, and other all-female bands. It reminds me of the days when our anthology of short stories *Girls' Night In* beat both J. K. Rowling and the Beatles in the bestseller lists. It was edited by me, Jessica Adams, Chris Manby, and Fiona Walker—three women who liked a glass of wine or two. We did in fact use our harvest, and the books kept on coming for years. This card has personal meaning for us, but it will also have an intensely personal meaning for you. Which group of women is this?

This is also an image of female solidarity so it may bring in the Eleventh House. Cups are related to sex and feelings so this may be a solid bond of sisterly friendship or something more.

Halloween is suggested by the pumpkin. Perhaps these are witches. This card is suggestive of *A Dance to the Music of Time* (Poussin) and astrology itself as the women could be moving in either direction, hinting at Retrogrades in the chart. The mood here is happy, celebratory.

Smith's card is quite pure. There is nothing lurking. The harvest has been picked, and this might be the CWA (Country Women's Association) in Australia enjoying a good year for the roses. There is no competition between these women. There is no secret agenda, just honest solidarity and sisterhood. This is a delightful card to see if you are hoping for a good outcome with an all-female project.

Of course, it is possible that not every person in this circle of three is female. There may be room for a man here with longer locks with his back to us. We may be talking about Boy George in Culture Club celebrating fame and fortune with female friends after the success of "Do You Really Want to Hurt Me?"

Just remember that if the champagne is to keep flowing, there has to be continuity. That pumpkin should be made into scones, perhaps, or soup—but the seeds should be carefully replanted so that the harvest is ongoing. It really can be, as I found out for myself, all the way back in 1999 when *Girls' Night In* first appeared as an exclusively female venture with writers who went on to become very famous, like Marian Keyes. Today it survives as a spin-off series for children called Kids' Night In, but the e-book goes on making money for the children's charity War Child.

This is a Minor Arcana card, so it may not transform your life, but its impact can be substantial all the same. There is abundance here: a sense of "there's more where that came from" and the fruits of the women's labor spread out all around them suggest that what is gained could become the first step toward something that returns every season. Minor is not always minor. What starts small in Smith's Tarot can grow, with care, attention, and tremendous patience, into something really big.

We can also see these women as three bridesmaids at a wedding banquet who have something special: loyalty, friendship, trust. From that could come anything at all in the years ahead.

This card is about planting the right things at the right time in the right place, then attending to them until they come to fruition. Life gardening is very important, though, as it's not enough to just celebrate and move on. What a waste of vast potential that would be! What is all around these three women should become the basis of something much more.

Pamela Colman Smith & Three of Cups

Tarot designer Smith was close to theater world suffragette and lesbian Edith Craig, who from 1916 was in a ménage à trois with Christabel Marshall and Clare "Tony" Atwood. The three women here may well be feminists or lesbian lovers. Also, so many of Smith's cards are agricultural in nature, perhaps because she created them partly or wholly at Smallhythe in the Garden of England—Kent.

Astrology & Three of Cups

The Eleventh House is of course ruled by Aquarius, and Smith herself was an Aquarius Sun. She created illustrations for the nascent suffrage movement at the turn of last century, and of course her sisters did indeed win the vote. This zodiac sign is associated with community, equality, and diversity. Also asexuality!

Consulting astrological charts could be useful here if you are watching the transits of Jupiter, which is associated with abundance, reward, and happy endings. He moves in twelve-year cycles, so perhaps this is a twelve-year program. Maybe it is just the conjunctions, sextiles, or trines of transiting Jupiter you need to watch. The chart itself will give the clue. Has there just been an exact aspect involving Jupiter? If so, you can set your watch by it, as this planet will move around the horoscope, always referring to the original harvest.

The Romans associated Jupiter with the oak tree and the acorn. From little acorns, mighty oaks do grow. There is a suggestion of this about the pumpkin that comes from the seed. To really work with the potential in this group, look at the Jupiter placements.

FOUR OF CUPS
Quick Look

The problem is, nobody and nothing is good enough—not emotionally anyway. There is nothing here that satisfies or fulfills. Yet people are solid gold and rather precious and valuable. So perhaps the problem is the disgruntled, rather flat figure under the tree. This may be you or someone with mild depression.

Description

Cups represent emotions, feelings, or sex. Here we have someone who is being offered a potential relationship of whatever kind while being quite blind to the three solid gold relationships already there.

It's so easy to blame everything on the quality—or lack thereof—of particular friends, lovers, potential dates, work colleagues, or family members. Here we have a clear case of someone being quite muddled about the fact that the issue is their own state of mind. They are rejecting who and what is there because they are ungrounded (note how the figure appears to hover several feet above the air) and very closed off. Notice the body language of the crossed arms and legs: they are on the defensive.

Also consider the tree (family tree) behind. This is one way out of the whole problem. This person needs to get back to their family roots—to ground, to center, to focus, to feel the earth beneath their feet and take shelter in the family itself or at least to grasp their origins. Remembering who you are is about keeping in mind where you come from. Perhaps the family is the hidden core of the issue. A bit of digging might reveal that. Or is going back to the family the solution?

This is blocked energy, in terms of Reiki, which requires you to be open with palms facing upward to receive healing.

There is work to be done with the Four of Cups. Smith's cards are really about transforming reality by reshaping attitudes. Everything here can be changed with effort. The rather unimpressed, flat, somewhat sad figure could open up, relax, and unbend. Surely this is a candidate for yoga or sports. This is mild depression as a *physical* condition, because the person is so removed from the real world and so distanced from other people, tying them up in knots. Smith occasionally portrays people caught in such a way: the Hanged Man is another example.

It's time to stop sulking or wallowing and start getting physical. Going for a walk is enough. The countryside all around is lush and inviting. Perhaps then it is time to go and talk to a medical professional or just to understand that mild depression or a low mood can be addressed by all sorts of alternative methods from Reiki to running.

The person, in short, has to work on themself before we even get to the three or four relationships/friendships on offer. The tree is a tremendous clue. Look to Cancer and the Fourth House, which is associated with the branches on the family tree, as well as one's historic, cultural, and local roots. Literally, where you come from. There are some real questions here about the parents, siblings, aunts and uncles, cousins, nieces, nephews, and grandparents in this story.

You can see how much happier this figure under the tree would be if their arms and legs were uncrossed, their feet were on the ground, the family tree could be recognized as a shelter (not just looming unseen in the background), and the glittering Cups (three people, with a fourth potential face) could be enjoyed, appreciated, and examined for all they offer. The inviting landscape is there to be explored as well.

This is a card which shows someone who does not appreciate all they have been offered in life, because of a lack of perception and grounding. An action plan is called for with the Four of Cups, far more so than with many of the cards in the Smith-Waite Tarot.

Pamela Colman Smith & Four of Cups

This archetypal experience is shown clearly in Smith's vision, perhaps of herself, but certainly of other people. A lack of enjoyment, a lack of appreciation, or a lack of gratitude, awareness, perception. Everything is shunted onto the emptiness of particular relationships or friendships (empty gold Cups), but the fact is one never knows if the Cups are full or empty until there is some effort and investigation! How can you discover anything or anybody when you are not even on planet earth with the rest of them?

Astrology & Four of Cups

There is Neptune symbolism in this card as he rules both clouds and blindness. You might look for Neptune by transit in the chart or transits to natal Neptune. There is a certain unreality about this person. How can they be so blind to such solid gold potential?

FIVE OF CUPS

Quick Look

Solitude and mourning, as three relationships have fallen over—a loss of some kind. There are two more, solid gold, but they are out of the line of sight. However, there is hope here: a bridge to a different future or a new home (or a return home). Within that home, anything and anybody at all could be created. First, though, there must be an emotional cleanup.

Description

Cups describe love and sex, and sometimes bodily fluids. Here we have three fallen over—maybe kicked to the ground—and we can see toxic green fluid (poisonous emotion or bile perhaps) on the ground along with blood.

This might be a woman getting over the end of a marriage (one person) and a complicated situation with two children. It might be a man who has been let down by three former friends. Smith did not randomly create these cards. Here we have blood: a dramatic symbol of "that bloody person."

The Five of Cups can sometimes show bereavement, so you have to take that into account as well. This may be an accident which has taken someone or more than one person.

This card has an awful lot encoded in the illustration. First there is the relief and release of the river, which might wash the Cups (clean up the relationships) and return them like new, sparkling and solid gold. There is also the option to just get rid of what remains, to turn one's back on what did not work out emotionally, no matter if it is love, children, family, or friends. This character in black could kick the Cups into the water so that they sink to the bottom, forgotten.

The cloaked figure is downcast, hidden, and apparently in mourning—or a vampire! Vampires do feast on blood. Emotional vampires feast on other substances. Perhaps you feel you are one of the solid gold people here, kicked to one side or waiting ignored in the background, while some kind of Count Dracula prepares for the next victim. This card can really be open to wide interpretation. Maybe you feel like a bit of a vampire! Do you eat people up? Chew them up and spit them out?

What does the green fluid mean to you? This is Chartreuse, perhaps, or absinthe. Maybe it is poison. Sometimes poison is released when a relationship falls over.

Two glittering Cups—solid gold, precious—are still upright and intact as we've discussed, but the brooding figure cannot see them yet. The bridge and castle are also important, for their sheer potential. So is the river. The Cups are just waiting to be cleaned in the water—or will this figure walk away altogether and cross the bridge to a new life?

There is emptiness here. The Cups contain nothing, though they once did. There is also a sense of someone just waiting to shed a skin—to get rid of an outer layer of depression or grief or perhaps dark thoughts. The sense of self has gone. We cannot even see this person's face: all we see is the black robe.

This process of mourning, adjustment, and "the journey" will take time. It may require months or even years. There is no set universal schedule; the response to loss can only be dealt with individually. In this card, we might see someone who acts very quickly, hurling the stained Cups into the water, pulling off the robe of mourning, turning to gather the two remaining Cups (solid gold people) behind, and racing across the bridge—pelting toward a new future.

Other people can stay stuck in the mourning, grief, or loss stage for a very long time indeed, but that seems like a waste when everything one could possibly want to make good and start again is right there. This is one of Smith's cards which just cries out to be worked with. Whatever is therapeutic and healing could be the difference here, as it can be hard to shed the dark, heavy robes of grief by oneself. A counselor might be really useful or perhaps a Reiki master or yoga teacher.

Pamela Colman Smith & Five of Cups

Smith knew Bram Stoker, author of *Dracula*, well, and he may have been a member of the Golden Dawn, the magical secret society which also included her collaborator Waite.

There is strong visualization potential in this card, which can be stage directed like all of Smith's work. She was a set designer as well as a powerful psychic. Much of what she was picking up in 1909 would become the new science of quantum mechanics. Everything is a cloud of potential until we enter into the experiment and make it become what it will be. These cards are interactive. Move the character and the Cups with your mind. Cross the bridge. Enter the new potential home. Find out what happens when you do.

Astrology & Five of Cups

Aquarius the Water Bearer is the sign we associate with rivers, but there is also Pisces ruled by Neptune. A bridge is Libra, because it connects two sides. The blood might be Scorpio, associated with death and sex. The waiting castle is Cancer. Take the card apart and see what it means to you, as each of the signs will have a very particular message, depending on your chart and perhaps the charts of the other people involved.

SIX OF CUPS

Quick Look

This is about two children or teenagers and their own delightful private world. You can enter and learn from them or play a more important role—teacher, perhaps, or just more committed parent or godparent. Child's play is shown here, and it has its own innocence and charm. This card is usually literally about the young.

Description

This is one of Smith's children cards, the Sun being the other one that people know best. Here we have the innocent exchange of feelings carried out with pure charm and trust. Children like to go to birthday parties and give each other presents, but also to swap objects. When I was at Mowbray Heights Primary School, we swapped playing cards, but also our Christmas presents. The idea here is "one for you and one for me."

This card is usually about children in a literal way. So we might be talking about your niece and nephew here or two children in your class. It sometimes turns up if there is a childish adult relationship. So, for example, it can indicate two people are all about little presents and innocent friendship, even though the Cups are involved and always about stronger emotions—being linked to Cancer, Scorpio, and Pisces. This card can turn up if a woman wants a man sexually but he wants to play at being pals.

If we take this card purely as a child's world or a teenager's universe, then we can see the escapism of a youthful reality. This is a bubble for these two younger faces. They are completely removed from the adult world with all their flowers in this little corner of the garden in what appears to be a very grown-up estate.

This might be the young Prince Charles and Princess Anne at Buckingham Palace in the 1950s or '60s, left to their own devices and getting on with childish or adolescent pursuits while the adults are involved in the very serious business of managing the royal property and business.

Look at the man with his spear striding off to the left. Why is he leaving the scene? Your answer to that will be quite important as this card is open to such personal interpretation. Is this the father of your children who has dropped them off with you for the weekend? Perhaps you get from the children what you do not get from the man. This card tells you to really relish and appreciate the little ones here, because they are not young forever.

Take into account the blossoming flowers in the Cups at the front of the card. What is growing? How can growth be encouraged? There is something so promising about all that you see before you: The two young souls, who look as if they have escaped from a fairy story. The trust between them. The solid gold vessels, which always show precious and valuable relationships. The rather impressive surroundings—is this a school, a house, or a future university? There is a coat of arms as well, and perhaps it means something to you. I have seen people take it as a symbol for Scotland.

If children or teenagers do not ring a bell with you, then this may be about your own inner child. There is nothing adult here at all—no grown-up intimacy, no money, no mortgage, no mature dialogue, no sex at all! It's all playful, naive, heart-to-heart contact.

What is this card telling you? There is so much here to enjoy if you are an adult who is watching the children or teenagers from a distance. With appropriate timing and care, you could ask to be included in their game, their child's play.

Astrology & Six of Cups

In your horoscope or that of another key person, we find something familiar. This card represents Leo and the Fifth House. The Fifth House describes the entertainment, education, and activities which bind the generations together young and old. This is where we might find theater, music, riding, or a particular kind of book, like Harry Potter, which can be read by all the generations.

This can sometimes indicate the Second House or Eighth House. There is an exchange—what one gives to another, just as one sibling leaves to another or swaps with another. Most of all, the signs here are Cancer (the property and perhaps the siblings in the family) or Leo (children, or teenagers, as a whole).

SEVEN OF CUPS

Quick Look

Everything is in your head: the house or apartment, the money, the success, the toxic people, the terrifying situations. You are projecting everything from your imagination. You can still have the good things and lose the bad by working on your mind. Conscious awareness of your projections will fix it.

Description

This is the most important card in the Tarot created by Smith and Waite. That may surprise some professional Tarot readers, because it is a Minor Arcana card. It is also less striking, say, than cards like the Two of Cups or the Ten of Wands.

The card shows a person in silhouette, in the shadows, who is confused by a billowing cloud of rich symbols, ranging from diamonds and pearls to a skull and snake. (That is the first clue: everything and everybody is a shadow projected on a wall.)

The card is dominated by a cloud. Unpopped possibilities, competing parallel universes, a multiverse full of ghosts, poisonous people (snakes), palaces, diamonds and pearls, victory and dangerous dragons—none of it is real; it is all a projection. They are the imagination, hopes, fears, and daydreams of someone living in a quantum world. Time to manifest what you want rather than what you don't want. Nothing is real until you look for it and measure it. It is the act of measuring that decides which universe you get, and so the measurements you use (astrology, perhaps?) become extremely important. The most obvious measuring device nonastrologers use is memory, based on apparent years or months, birthdays, old calendar dates. Time is a construct. There is nothing real about it.

So, if you really want to get into this card, you'll begin by considering what you assume to be true about the past and your past measurements of time. It is on this that you base your projections of the present and future, so it's worth a much closer look to find if you are projecting all these rich fantasies and horrid visions!

The person in silhouette here is nothing to themself—just a slide projector whirring in the dark while the show takes place on the facing wall. The trick with this card is to "know thyself" and to understand that nothing is real. There are only realities to find. You may want to use measurements that serve you, when judging what is "there" for you.

Pamela Colman Smith & Seven of Cups

It took me several visits to Dublin before I understood this card. Smith was mentored by W. B. Yeats, and both were involved in magic. Magic spells and their outcomes are expressions of quantum reality. In other words, there is no single, objective reality. Science tells us—in fact has proven—that until we measure what is "real" it can exist in at least two states at once, and logically, many more. It's like *Doctor Who*: many worlds, many universes.

The realization of dreams, wishes, and hopes by supernatural means is one way of defining magic.

W. B. Yeats—very likely the third man to work on the Smith-Waite Tarot—lived a few doors away from an outstanding scientist whose emerging twentieth-century field of quantum mechanics was also about mystery in the form of quantum uncertainty.

Across Merrion Square, in the heart of Dublin, there is a plaque to Oscar Wilde, whose wife Constance was a magical acquaintance of Yeats in the Golden Dawn.

Across Dublin itself was the theater impresario Annie Horniman, who founded her company on the back of a Tarot card reading—more magic and mystery. The Golden Dawn members had extraordinary lives. It could be said that Yeats used magic to win a Nobel Prize. Who knows? Only Yeats.

Astrology & Seven of Cups

What you measure with defines what you find. What you measure with is in your head. This is how astrology works. So many people do not understand that astrology is related to quantum mechanics and the multiverse theory, which proposes that what we get is what we see. It's a flipped version of the famous saying.

Astrology, which rests on angles and aspects divided from a circle of 360 degrees, is a yardstick for a particular sort of reality, a certain kind of universe. It's quantum uncertainty writ large. No wonder astrology has not just survived but thrived over the last 2,000 years or so. It's a beautiful fit for multiverse theory.

EIGHT OF CUPS

Quick Look

When you beat a retreat from empty and unfulfilling relationships—partners, former partners, friends, family, colleagues—you are halfway to healing. There is an interesting choice here. Does one step away forever and never return or is a hiatus enough to "let distance lend enchantment to the view"? Your choice.

Description

"Just Walk Away, Renee!" This card brings to mind a lot of songs, including this one by the Left Banke. "She's Leaving Home" by the Beatles is another. This is an archetypal experience: breaking up with a shared household, breaking up with a social circle or an organized group of people, even a family, perhaps leaving "everybody and everything" behind.

The downcast face of the Full Moon suggests that the lunar cycle has reached peak squeeze. The Sun is always opposite the Moon on a Full Moon, and here we have someone who is not exactly leaping for joy on their journey, but going because there is nothing left emotionally. This is a classic case of there being quantity but not quality. There are people all around, but as Cold Chisel's Jimmy Barnes observed, he neither wanted or needed what was on offer. We might also think of Elton John and Bernie Taupin's classic "Goodbye Yellow Brick Road," where a disenchanted man, probably gay, tires of big-city life and goes back to the countryside.

When this card turns up, look at the lunar cycles, aspects to the natal Moon, and in particular eclipse cycles going back months or years in the same zodiac sign. The Moon is a symbol of mothers, breast milk, and fed babies. Here we have someone who is not being fed emotionally. In fact, they are being starved. The Cups should be full and fulfilling. They are stacked high, but there is nothing there that we can see. There is certainly nothing there for this departing figure.

The eight Cups here symbolize friends, family, lovers, or former lovers and show solid gold people. The issue is the emotional climate—the lunar cycle and the times. When this person returns, it may be a New Moon, a sunny day, and things may look and feel so much happier. This case of mild to severe depression, anger, or even deep rage could become history by the next turn of the lunar cycle. Conditions can change.

Ask yourself this: *Who is not fulfilling promises or potential? Who is an empty vessel?* These Cups say it is not just one person, but all of them. Yet times change, and people can fill up again. They can become fulfilling.

For all that they are empty on departure, the Cups are still solid gold. These are precious people or valuable relationships with enormous worth—and could return so much more, another time perhaps.

Will there be a return? Sometimes people don't come back. Some authors feel Smith, the creator of the cards, was depicting a famous 1909 eclipse in this card. An eclipse is a blind spot. This person cannot see how precious and valuable these eight relationships or friendships are. Their back is turned. Perhaps never to turn back?

Pamela Colman Smith & Eight of Cups

Smith turned her back on British literary, artistic, and bohemian society and left for the coast and a simple life away from Yeats and his family. Her visitors' book in London, once so full, emptied, and she departed for the sea and the countryside, Catholicism, and anonymity. Very few people in the village of Bude, where she passed away, knew who she was. So given that Smith herself is the creator of this card, we have to say there is a decent chance that you or someone else will never go back.

All Tarot cards can be directed like a stage set, however, as Smith was also a set designer for the Abbey Theatre among others. Now you are the director. Perhaps you want to change the lighting. Bring other cast members onto the set. Urge the central figure to alter the script. This card has tremendous potential for redemption, final reward, and reconciliation. If you want clues about how this could happen, then pull another card.

Astrology & Eight of Cups

Cups are water signs in the Tarot. That means Cancer, Scorpio, Pisces. Mother's milk comes with Cancer. Then there is the sweat, semen, and occasionally the blood of Scorpio sex. The tears of sympathy, sensitivity, and compassion speak to Pisces.

NINE OF CUPS

Quick Look

This is the solid backing of some solid gold people—friends or family, perhaps a political party lined up behind a beaming leader. Is the rather self-satisfied, well-fed character on the chair you or somebody else? Pay attention to the semicircle of Cups. At the far right-hand side, one is slipping. Who needs help?

Description

This card is a warning. Given that all the Cups cards are Cancer, Scorpio, Pisces—the emotional water signs—it may be that these signs are actually involved. There are many of them, and the Cups all look the same. But that's a trap. If you regard people as a faceless mass and make assumptions that they are backing you, sooner or later one of them may break from the group, and when they fall, the rest can topple as well.

Attention must be paid, to quote Arthur Miller. No matter how self-absorbed and self-congratulatory someone feels about "all this" and "my people," it really is time to get off the chair and pay singular, individual attention to each solid gold person behind. Treating people on a case-by-case basis—checking that they feel fulfilled, have all they need, are in a sturdy position—averts what could be quite disastrous, at least at one end of the group or the family.

Let's look at Smith's card from the outside in. A smug, rather fat man poses in front of his nine trophies. These are Cups, which represent sexuality or emotions. Water signs, as I've mentioned. Look again at the Cup in the right-hand corner which is about to fall off. This man is so wrapped up in his own achievement, he is not paying attention to the individual people who "have his back," and one of them does not! Like "Ten Green Bottles," if one should accidentally fall, it means many of them might. The fabric can be pulled away and other Cups can crash down. So much depends on just one person, but this one person is not even on the fat man's radar! The key to success for the person at the front, who may be you or another, is to remember that such a wall of solid gold support does not happen by itself. Don't take it for granted.

At some point you have to stop basking in the backing and actually actively pursue each and every one as an individual. Put back into these people what they need. Try to enrich, expand, and improve the separate relationships and people. Of course, this may be a message for quite another person and not you! The ability to stop basking, start rolling sleeves up, and pour time, energy, and attention into the individual is enough to turn this picture around. With care, sensitivity, time, and effort, this impressive wall of support and backing can indeed become hard to topple.

The central character needs to remember that they are the first line of defense. "This far and no further" might be the message. Every group needs a leader, protector, and defender. That is really the purpose of this person. Less smugness and more sharp awareness of this huge responsibility will also help turn things around. That wobbling Cup on the far right-hand side of the picture can be realigned and the whole returned to completion.

Pamela Colman Smith & Nine of Cups

Smith and Waite were in the Golden Dawn for long enough to see the membership fractured and divided. Smith also worked with Ellen Terry and was familiar with Shakespeare. This card is not unlike *Henry V*, with its band of brothers. It is an archetypal experience; how often have we seen prime ministers or presidents get so lost in their own position and magnificence that they forget about the individuals behind them? This is a great lesson for our times, as we go into Jupiter, Saturn, and finally Pluto in Aquarius—the sign of group solidarity and the orchestra of community.

Astrology & Nine of Cups

This card hints at Aquarius and the Eleventh House, with its emphasis on the group. This card reminds us of the phrase *they've got your back* and is very much about being supported.

TEN OF CUPS

Quick Look

The absolute best outcome, with two parents and two children, the rainbow and the pot of gold, the beautiful surroundings and the family home. It all seems too good to be true, but it happens every day. I've drawn it once, for a reader, who had divorced a drug addict husband. She went on to marry a real estate agent and become a mother.

Description

As we know, Cups are sex or emotion, and here we have ten of them forming a rainbow. (Think "Somewhere Over the Rainbow" and "The Pot of Gold at the End of the Rainbow.") A rainbow is a peculiar thing: a beautiful illusion. Walk to the apparent end and it vanishes out of your grasp.

The couple is close; the children are happy. The house looks like a cozy dream cottage. There is celebration here. The couple throws their hands in the air; the children are dancing.

This is a classic card for family and property joy. I have drawn it very rarely in readings for clients, but every time the woman concerned has gone on to marry, have children, and establish a happy home and garden. As I mentioned, I read it once for a woman who had divorced a drug addict and she went on to meet the man of her domesticated dreams, settle down, enjoy a stunning house, and in fact had three children, not two. Remember, a rainbow is an illusion, but the rest is real.

This card is fascinating because it's all about the space. The environment, rented or owned, lent or mortgaged, is part of the family. You cannot separate husband and wife or children from the garden, the local area, and/or the home. It's a part of them. It has an emotional presence. So we'd have to say that the zodiac sign of Cancer and the Fourth House really matter. This goes beyond falling in love with a partner or giving birth to sons and daughters. The ecstatic response of the couple to the home and the joyous children suggests the material world is a really big part of the relationships between all four of them. You cannot do this without taking into account Mother Nature but also priceless or expensive security and beauty.

This card is a beginning and not a midway or end. It is the very start of moving in together, buying a property, inheriting a property, or finding a dream space to rent. The rest comes later and is ongoing. The children will become teenagers and young adults. The couple so tied to being parents will find different roles in twenty years or so, and that could mean massive shifts in the marriage, as the whole point and purpose of them coming together in the first place was a child or two to start and then more.

Let us not be cynics, though, and say that all good things come to an end: life doesn't become less than it was; it just becomes different. The celebration, radiance, and joy of the very start of married life is here. The rest is a journey, to be sure, but eventually it becomes the memory of something so precious, rare, and unforgettable that it helps create the bedrock on which the future emotional life of this couple rests. Into old age, with a little luck, they will never forget this moment.

Astrology & Ten of Cups

In astrology we associate this card with the Fourth House of property and clan—thus "my people and my place." You might also find here the Fifth House (children), the Seventh House (partnership and marriage), or the Eighth House (property as family legacy). Perhaps you, the other person, or the children are going through transits to all these houses.

Cancer is the crab who carries the home on her back. Taurus is the valuable real estate. Leo is the children. Scorpio is "until death do us part."

PAGE OF CUPS

Quick Look

Here we have a young man, effeminate, bohemian, and definitely in his own camp. He has Pisces emphasized in his personal birth chart. He has caught the fish but is playing with it. Maybe he is not sure what to do with it? There are probably plenty more fish in the sea, but until he takes a focused, mature approach, he'll never catch any.

Description

Here we have a fascinating, original, interesting young man with Pisces and the Twelfth House emphasized in his horoscope. He may be spiritual, religious, interested in astrology, the Tarot, mediumship, Buddhism, or some other ism that is his personal belief system and philosophy.

He floats through life, dancing with the moment, never really settling down or growing up—at least for now. In Tarot we traditionally accept the Pages as the most junior people in your world, but sometimes you can enquire about a childish man (even a childish man in his senior years) and the Tarot will joke with you and show you a perpetual adolescent or schoolboy.

Pages are always younger than you, so this boy/man is your junior. He is showing Pisces (the fish in the cup) and Neptune, the ruler of Pisces (the sea behind him). He is in touch with his feminine side, thanks to the pink and blue outfit. He would understand the Blur song "Girls and Boys."

He has something to give sexually or emotionally, as Cups rule both. The fish itself is associated with the phrase *plenty more fish in the sea* with respect to the dating game. There is something lacking in commitment here and certainly seriousness. This is not someone to settle down and have children with, because he is himself a child.

He's fun, never dull, not remotely in the real world, and you need to know what to do with him!

This is a puzzling card, but there are some clues. The sea behind him is also the usual Aquarius pool, and people pool resources there. Yet here we also find Pisces (the other fish of the pair in the zodiac sign) and all its spiritual depths. This may be Christianity, or it may be another philosophy he holds.

This is not a suit and tie man or schoolboy—no uniform for him. A creative dresser with a tremendous feeling for color and style is in front of you. He may be musical, artistic, or theatrical. He is inviting you to join in the dance of life, rather than make any proper attempt at harvesting abundance—yet the possibility of abundance is there. One fish may be part of a salmon source or perhaps a nod to beluga caviar in the depths.

You have to wonder if he cares at all about catching anything, as he seems more caught by the moment. It would be up to someone else to stride in and start talking seriously about business.

You may know men who are keen on fishing and always throw their catch back. This Page seems to be on the verge of doing just that; meanwhile the fish is gasping. There can be something cruel about playing with fish like this—or people, come to think of it. Not taking anything or anybody seriously can be an issue with strongly Pisces men who have not grown up in the real world, and it can be tricky in a sexual relationship.

Escaping from the real world is what the Page is all about. He's about the vacation from reality. The fish is "a fish out of water" and needs to go back in. Ask yourself who or what the fish represents in this card. He could keep it and cook it, but you have to wonder if he has any interest at all in getting into a kitchen or anywhere near a recipe book.

With time, maturity, life lessons, and the encouragement of other people, the Page of Cups can develop into someone who has so much to give. There can be a leaning toward conservation and the environment here—perhaps Sea Shepherd or Greenpeace. The Page of Cups is entertaining, but there is tremendous untapped potential here, too. I am always reminded of Kurt Cobain (who I interviewed) when I see the Page of Cups, not necessarily because he was younger than me (he wasn't) but really because he was a Pisces who played with life. He was an incredible dresser and a musical genius, but had no interest in the material world. The swimming pool with the baby on the cover of *Nevermind* is a variation on the theme you see with the Page of Cups.

Pamela Colman Smith & Page of Cups

Within a family this is Peter Pan who never grows up. In fact, Smith's world was populated with people like J. M. Barrie, and she certainly had her fair share of creatives and bohemians around her when this card was created.

Astrology & Page of Cups

As well as indicating a Pisces figure, this certainly speaks to Neptune transits to the astrological chart if this card appears, but also transits to natal Neptune. There is something not quite real about the world represented by the Page of Cups.

KNIGHT OF CUPS
Quick Look

A man on a mission is traveling locally, or perhaps internationally, with sincere affection or something deeper. It really depends on the relationship you have with him. Is he a friend, family member, or a former, current, or potential partner? He is sincere and determined, and you should probably meet him halfway if you can.

Description

The Knight of Cups is always good to see in the Tarot. Here is someone who is solid gold and also steady. He has stamina, a sense of purpose, and something valuable to give you. That is, perhaps, why you should do at least half of the running here so that he is not forced to make the journey to you unsupported. He's come a long way, but also has rather a long way to go—and a chap needs help sometimes.

Cups are always a symbol of sex or emotion. He has something to give, but he needs to get there to give it. This man could be courting you or off to meet you for the first time after a period of internet dating.

In some cases the Cups have nothing to do with the heart or romance but everything to do with a family relationship. This is the young soldier returned from combat on his way with presents to put under the Christmas tree. Unlike some of the men Smith created in her illustrations, he is firm, focused, and steadfast.

He is a man on a mission. The Third House (short journeys) or Ninth House (global travel or emigration) is suggested here. Will he settle down? He might. If the exchange was the right one! There is a suggestion here of a new relationship or a renewed one.

This may be the backpacker on a gap year who wants to resume a holiday affair. It can be the new face hired by your company who is moving from another state or county. This is an attractive, interesting man. Nothing can really be decided until he has reached his destination and settled down. You have to ask: Is his whole life like this, shifting from place to place? Or is this the last leg on something that looks like permanence for both of you?

You might say there are "many rivers to cross" for the Knight of Cups as he has had quite a journey. Like all Cups in the cards, this is a solid gold symbol of something special emotionally, which is being offered up either for exchange or as a gift from the heart. This is an archetypal image of quest and delivery; he might be Walter Raleigh returning to Queen Elizabeth I or the young Prince Philip returning to Queen Elizabeth II after his travels.

Astrology & Knight of Cups

Straight and true, the Knight of Cups is on a mission, wearing Mercury's characteristic wings on his helmet and shoes. Sagittarius is suggested by the horse, but Mercury is riding it. There is a lot of astrology hidden in this card. This may literally be Mercury in Sagittarius, natally or by transit.

There is the wavy Aquarius logo but also Pisces the Fish on the armor. So we are talking potentially three zodiac signs here and one planet.

QUEEN OF CUPS

Quick Look

This rather impressive woman has a relationship which is solid gold, unique, valuable, and quite confusing to her. She needs to stop procrastinating and do something practical with it—planting it on solid ground would be a start. This is a family relationship, romance, partnership, or friendship which she finds baffling because it escapes categorization.

Description

I have seen women change their lives when they draw this card, as they recognize that all their dithering is getting them nowhere and something or someone must be physically moved to a space or place where there is a purpose. Women who are affected by drugs and alcohol or even prescribed meditation can sometimes feel quite spaced out, dazed, and confused—and be vulnerable to the sort of scene we see here where everything and everybody are "all at sea." The sea is self-evident in this card, and getting in over your head is one outcome of wasting time puzzling over a particular person, without doing anything about them.

This is clearly a woman worth our respect (a Queen) who has a precious, unique relationship she does not know what to do with.

The Cup here is not like any Cup you have ever seen. It is fine, detailed, rather odd, and we would suspect a one-off. If it were on *Antiques Roadshow*, it would be priceless. So this person in the Queen of Cups' life is not commonplace or everyday. Nor is this person particularly easy to come to grips with, but something must be done here, or the tide may turn.

In her past we could find pregnancies that did not come to term or the baby phase of her grown-up children. She is unconscious of this, but it is the foundation upon which she rests. These babies are above her and at her feet cast in stone. This is a woman who is quite unconscious about her abortions, miscarriages, the stepchildren she never took on, or the orphans she never adopted. More commonly, this is a woman who has built her world on being a mother, but is quite unconscious of the fact that she has permanently parked her adult son or daughter in infancy somewhere at the back of her mind.

The Queen of Cups is cast adrift, not living in the real world, and far removed from what people back home would call normal living. This might be the late Elizabeth Taylor pondering Richard Burton or the late Princess Diana wondering what on earth she is going to do about her latest admirer.

Of course, the Cup here can be a friend, family member, or colleague. The solution is to stop just gazing at the Cup and go back to the village or town with it tucked under one arm, where the relationship (a Cup is always a relationship) can find an appropriate place. At the moment it is a distraction from the real issue: babies that came/didn't come quite some time ago. The Queen would be happier with dry feet.

This is a trophy or a collector's item. It may, in fact, be a trophy boyfriend or husband who is good-looking, rich, or successful. If it is the woman's son or daughter, there is something here that is so hard for her to deal with or come to terms with, but still very special.

Actual movement—taking action—gives the Cup a home somewhere in one of the villages or towns up on the cliffs. The Queen needs to gather up her skirts, hold the peculiar but golden relationship fast, and set about finding the right environment for it.

This may be a museum. Perhaps this is a former husband or live-in partner who belongs to the past, not the future, and until the Queen of Cups puts him behind a glass case, she will never get on with her life. Perhaps she needs to pass the Cup on! Maybe there is someone in the nearest town who would make far better use of this than she ever would. Maybe it is time to let go of a valuable but puzzling friend who one never quite moves into sexual territory with. This sort of platonic pal might be the ideal wife for a single man out there, but until the Queen lets go, nobody will ever know. The trick with this card is to realize that it is about *the environment* not the Cup itself. It is about finding the right place for such a person or relationship and that requires some common sense, self-discipline, and a bit of shoulder to the wheel.

Pamela Colman Smith & Queen of Cups

This is a picture of Kent with its beautiful white chalk cliffs, where Smith created her card. Our Queen is drifting further into the English Channel as the water laps against her feet and she forgets about the real world.

Astrology & Queen of Cups

The Queen is herself likely to have the water signs Cancer, Scorpio, and/or Pisces prominent in her birth chart, which is true across the suit of Cups as well. Also, this is a card showing the Fifth House of parenthood and relationships and also Neptune, that symbol of drifting unreality. Look for a Neptune transit, but also a transit to a natal Neptune.

KING OF CUPS

Quick Look

This is the card that appears when a man is out of touch with reality and inaccessible. He may be affected by drugs, prescribed medication, or alcohol which makes him spaced out. Even if this is not the case, he is drifting, floating, cruising, and in a world of his own. If you want to join him, he will have to make room for you. The ship in the background is the key to this card.

Description

Communication is the key to this man. If you can make him listen or read and engage him in a conversation about changing his position in life, you'll get what you want, which is presumably some action and outcome. The ship in the background could be nearing his floating throne at any moment, and he could jump aboard. You could join him. That ship could take the pair of you anywhere, into a whole new life. Yet so much depends on him. The King of Cups can be infuriatingly detached, and if he is not interested in listening to you, it is hard to see how he will ever organize himself.

This card appeared in a reading about the 2018 World Cup on my website and one powerfully psychic reader immediately predicted France would win. The Jules Rimet Cup is in hand! Perhaps we have a soccer-obsessive here who cares more about his favorite team losing on the weekend than he does about the fact that your son needs his homework checked. You can also see why fishing could be the obsession with the King of Cups or sailing, surfing, scuba diving, and so on.

Soccer or aquatic pursuits aside, this card is about a man who does not inhabit the real world because he does not have to. He is all at sea, but he appears well-fed, and so has everything he needs. He may be fishy—so slippery, hard to catch, elusive. Very likely, the only environment he would accept is an island or perhaps that ship, almost out of sight. Whatever environment he wants, it will have to accommodate his tremendous need to escape—to go with the currents.

He represents a holiday from reality for you, which Neptune also does. Perhaps it is you who has the Neptune transit to your chart, or natal Neptune under transit. Women often fall in love with this King because he has nothing to do with mortgages or the housework, but everything to do with a vacation from the ordinary and the everyday.

If you want to get close to him you will have to come over to his side of reality, which is the trick to communication between you. You cannot possibly swim up to the King of Cups and start chattering about the price of milk or the Dyson not working, because he has absolutely no connection at all with the mundane or the "too real."

Note, too, the fact that he has left no room at all on his floating throne for a partner. It's all about him—and he takes up a lot of space. He is impressive, substantial, intriguing. Can he accommodate a life partner or another type of relationship? Perhaps for a short time, but as I've mentioned, your best bet here is the ship. This is a symbol of an environment and a journey that you can both enjoy. It would be a massive departure for everyone, a real commitment for both of you. That takes communication and a lot of luck.

Does he want to get off his floating throne when he finally sights land? Will you be there to greet him on the shore? Can you see this current drifting period in his life as just an episode?

As I've mentioned, the big Cup also suggests alcohol, or this may be a mortar and pestle to grind drugs. Pisces and Neptune have long been associated with substances that alter reality.

The other possibility here with your King of Cups is that he is just going to dive straight into the ocean. His toe is already pointing toward the water. Maybe he's about to throw it all away in favor of immersing himself in something else. Is it practical? Of course not. But there is a certain sort of King who is on the verge of total escape or complete disappearance. I need to mention this to you. Perhaps the King's face will speak to you with this card. You do sometimes get this with a minority of heavily Pisces/Neptune types, who are so completely drawn to the other world of nonreality, or even oblivion, that they are forever on the point of suddenly disappearing from view.

Pamela Colman Smith & King of Cups

The King of Cups can float forever. Our Tarot creator Smith was identifying someone here who was either going through a Neptune transit or having transits to his natal Neptune. Perhaps it was someone she knew from her close-knit group?

Astrology & King of Cups

The King of Cups is pure Pisces and Neptune. The Cups are symbols of the water signs anyway: Cancer, Scorpio, and Pisces. He probably has one or all three signs emphasized in his natal chart. He has a lot to give emotionally or sexually—perhaps just spiritually. However, he does not inhabit terra firma as the rest of us do, and he is very hard work if you want cooperation and collaboration. He is living proof that "no man is an island" is quite wrong: he actually is the entire island all by himself.

The Suit of Swords

Swords often deal with the intellect or mind. Swords are sharp and also often double-edged. Air is the element here, relating to knowledge, change, power. The associated zodiac signs would be Gemini, Libra, Aquarius.

ACE OF SWORDS

Quick Look

The crown, top job, top position, or highest role has been seized. A Sword cuts through situations quickly and often aggressively. This can be disempowerment for one person, empowerment for another. It can be official—so a demotion and replacement or election results with loss and victory. Or it can be informal.

Description

This card is full of power, strength, and energy. *The Crown* on Netflix is a good way to think about it. It is full of changes in the balance of power. Some are there to be seen (the coronation of Queen Elizabeth II after the passing of her father), and others are less obvious. If you think about the transfer of power when Prince William was born, establishing an heir to the throne, that is officialdom—yet subtle developments like the increasing popularity of Diana, Princess of Wales, in the media against Charles, Prince of Wales, are less visible.

This is a card that tells you exactly what it is. A crown has been taken by force and is there for the choosing. It's pure potential with all its promise of new power and prominence for the taker—and it has to be made real.

There is a sense of anticipation, liberation, excitement, and tremendous challenge with the Ace of Swords. The Queen is dead, long live the King, but how are things to proceed now that there is a transformation at the top? So much about this card is potential to be filled. How are you going to play this particular part of the drama?

Here, a statement is being made or a pose has been struck. The cloud is the giveaway: it's all hypothetical until you put it to the test. What you compute about this card is what you will find. Was there a change in the line of succession or not? Did power change hands or not? Will anyone take the crown or will it remain hanging?

The challenge for leadership or the top job is not real as such; it's a maybe situation. And perhaps it happened and perhaps it didn't—it really depends how much you can see through the clouds. It's amazing how often the machinations over power at the top are covered up. It takes years for voters or the general public to discover what was really going on.

Victory is possible, but this is a picture of quantum reality. The big win is an unpopped possibility or unchosen universe at the moment. We are in the rather odd position of seeing something that has happened—a leader has been deposed and their title is up for grabs—and yet the clouds tell us we have to believe in it, and accept it, before it becomes historic fact.

The laurel leaves you see here meant a military victory to the Romans. To be crowned with laurel leaves was the honor bestowed on a conquering commander. Swords are about battles and perhaps wars. This is Oliver Cromwell but also Margaret Thatcher. It is the English Civil War, but also the Wars of the Roses, World War I, World War II, the Vietnam War. It is interesting that there are no people in this card. It's all about the honor, the title, the position.

Pamela Colman Smith & Ace of Swords

Smith worked with images of quantum uncertainty, and her clouds are everywhere in this Tarot. Cloud-based quantum computing, as seen from an artist in 1909! Clouds can also mask things so that nobody is really sure about what is going on. If a foreign power takes over the presidency of the United States by secretly blackmailing or threatening the leadership, there will most certainly have been a dethronement but nobody will ever know, because it has been covered up by clouds of "masking" public relations.

Astrology & Ace of Swords

The crown, symbolizing the top job or leading role, can only be taken here by force. Swords are symbols of aggression. There is a Tenth House connection here, backed up by the mountains (Capricorn the Goat rules the Tenth House).

Mars rules the Sword itself. Aries is ruled by Mars, of course, so there is a cardinal sign Aries-Capricorn focus on this part of the Tarot. We might be looking at William the Conqueror and the Battle of Hastings. We may be looking at the liberation of Paris by Allied troops against the Nazis. What happens is swift. If we go back to 1781 and Yorktown, the Americans dispensed with the British rapidly.

The scattered yellow leaves may describe the group around the situation, which is the Eleventh House ruled by Aquarius. This card is so reminiscent of any election for prime minister, president, or premier. Losers lose, winners are victorious, and the political parties involved break apart with reshuffles and departures, elevations and arrivals.

This card can describe Pluto as well as Mars. Pluto is always about a change in the balance of power. Astrologically, it is a mixture of signs and planets if you are looking for clues. Yet, a Pluto transit, perhaps a transit to natal Pluto, is very likely. The crown can be Leo, monarch of the jungle, or you can see it as a crowning achievement or the peak/pinnacle of a career, so we may be talking Capricorn, as I've mentioned.

TWO OF SWORDS

Quick Look

A decision must be made to cut out someone or something from this woman's life. She is on the defensive. This is like the Stealers Wheel song "Stuck in the Middle With You." Where jokers are on one side and clowns on another. It's also the Magazine song "Shot by Both Sides." Nothing can improve here until the woman is either rescued or, better still, takes off the blindfold.

Description

Decisions, decisions. Is this woman right to be on guard, likely quite paranoid, about both sides in a situation where she is stuck in the middle? She has no idea because she cannot see. It may be that there is no threat at all, and she really needs to put down one or both Swords, at least long enough to take off the blindfold so she can get the true measure of the perceived threats.

She may very well be at risk from people against her on either or both sides of her life, but if so, it is imperative that she be quick and clever. The blindfold needs to be whipped off, both Swords handled swiftly, and a battle plan followed. There is huge emphasis on plotting, planning, and strategy with this card. Rather than just sitting there paralyzed by inaction and trepidation, this woman would be far better off tuning in with her remaining senses—including the sixth sense—and coming up with a game plan to get away, fight back, or perhaps put her weapons down if there is no threat.

It is not unusual for the quandary to be about having a baby or not or the role of motherhood with a particular child. The two sides can be her side of the family and her husband's. Yet, the Moon can also indicate the mother figure in a corporation, business, or company. This may be a caretaker or employer who finds herself in a very heavy and rather tense situation. There is always a sense of playing Keep Away with this card. In some cases it can show Proserpina in the chart, or transits from Proserpina, as she was in danger of being "shot by both sides" with her husband Pluto and her mother Ceres each holding on to her in their lives for half the year.

As discussed, this woman needs to take her blindfold off so that she can see where to head next. The rocks will give her a path to the promising landscape in the distance. She can leapfrog her way forward. Yet nothing can happen while she cannot see.

To see, the lady in the Two of Swords needs to come up with a strategy whereby she puts one weapon down, defends herself with the other, and quickly takes her blindfold off. At least then she can move left, right, to the front or behind, and protect herself or get away. She could even smite her opponent.

The other fascinating part of this card is the potential for fantasy and illusion. Perhaps there is nothing and nobody there to threaten this woman at all. She may be imagining or projecting a problem which does not exist. She will never know until she puts one Sword down and leaves herself defenseless on one side so she can take away what/who is blinding her to the truth of her situation.

You can also see how heavy the Swords are. She would be so much happier hurling them into the sea and going for a swim. There are so many options for relief, release, and recovery in this card. What would happen if she called for help—yelled for assistance? Perhaps other people could fight her battle, if there are genuinely enemies on one or both sides of her life.

There is more empowerment in a silent strategy, though, and this is the best way out of a very testing and difficult situation. She can't sit there forever, weighed down by all that metalwork. At some point, acting has to be better than not acting. A woman who is embattled can sometimes find this Tarot card speaks to her about what to do and when to do it.

The large body of water behind her suggests Aquarius the Water Bearer might be useful in her chart or people with Aquarius planets could be of assistance. Here we have the queen at the passing of Diana, Princess of Wales, with her media critics against her on one side and members of Diana's family against her on the other. Flying blind or "feeling your way" at such times isn't really useful and just prolongs a rather stuck and difficult situation. It is far better to have some kind of battle plan and be proactive. Then the guesswork can end and action can begin. The sort of action required really depends on staring the apparent opposition, threat, or enemy in the face on both sides and understanding who and what is there.

Astrology & Two of Swords

The lunar cycle is important here. This is a New Moon, emerging or just recently gone. Thus, it is a new beginning, but things are on hold. Have a look at the Moon's transits to your chart or transits to the Moon. The Moon is about maternal instinct, mothers, babies, and its root *mo* can be found in *mom* and *mother*.

This is a card of chopping and changing, so it suggests Saturn who castrated his father Uranus, or Uranus himself, who was chopped and changed. It is also a Libra card as Libra describes both sides of a situation.

THREE OF SWORDS

Quick Look

This is about a love triangle, commonly with a marriage and an affair, but it can also be found in families or even friendships with one against two. It is as painful as it looks, but can be fixed. The trick with this card is for the reader (you) to extract themself from the situation. This leaves the other two to do the same—or not. You can at least control your own circumstances, though, and pull out.

Description

Three can be very difficult when the heart is involved—a love triangle, usually, with two partners in a painful situation with a third person or perhaps an ex who will not go away, a mistress, or a romantic rival. This card can also describe two parents and a child in a bad marriage. I have seen just that with a father whose wife and daughter were ganging up on him.

The perfect cure is the extraction of all three Swords at once to promote heart healing. This is the marriage of Diana, Princess of Wales, and Prince Charles with various third parties. Camilla Parker-Bowles was the most famous face in the painful saga, but of course Diana also had lovers.

It is unusual for three people to all simultaneously resign from a painful situation for the human heart. Yet, if you are the questioner here, it is clearly you as the third Sword and you can act alone if you must. Perhaps encourage at least one other person to leave with you!

The trick, yes, is all three antagonists acting in concert, but to reach that point involves tremendous communication breakthroughs, trust, and transformation. Much as we would wish that were the case, it is not always humanly possible. If all three withdraw from this unhealthy emotional situation, at least the wounds could be healed and life could move on.

Time is of the essence here, so the card invokes Mars. Have a look for that in any of the three astrological charts, either by transit or by aspects to natal Mars. Mars is the god of war and the phrase *all's fair in love and war* springs to mind, though it frequently feels so painful it can be like heart surgery.

Unless surgery is actually performed at least emotionally, spiritually, or psychologically, this heart will fall or fail. We also think about *bleeding hearts* with this card, and sometimes there can be one of the three people begging for sympathy and wringing things out emotionally. That has to be said. It can happen.

The word *withdrawal* comes with this card as well. Withdraw your sword or withdraw the swords, plural. You really have to step back and look at the wounds and the potential for healing. Healing is going to take time for this heart, isn't it? But whose heart is it? Yours or the second person's or the third person's involved?

One thing is sure: This is not a happy heart. It is not a healthy heart. There is something utterly doomed about this if all three continue. The only hope is extensive recovery, and that will take time. Nothing and nobody can heal until one, two, or all three of you remove the aggression, attack, or defense from the situation. Swords are a symbol of a battle, a fight, a war. That can be as engaging as love, can't it?

Yet, once you step back from this card and look at it dispassionately, you should be able to gain the detachment that tells you this is never going to function well. It is utterly dysfunctional in every way, and even though what you three have is the stuff of rock ballads, operas, soap operas, and French literature, it is hardly what you want in your lives day in and day out.

Pamela Colman Smith & Three of Swords

Closer in time to 1909 when Smith illustrated this card, Alice Keppel was the most famous mistress of King Edward VII. Perhaps there is something of that in this card.

Astrology & Three of Swords

The Seventh House is the house of marriage but also divorce and separation—suggested by the card. I have seen this card appear when three people are stubbornly fixed in a toxic three-way situation and nobody will withdraw or pull out their Sword.

You might also look at Vesta in the charts or by transit, as in astrology she frequently turns up when one man plays two women against each other so he can stroke his ego or gain some kind of power. This card is often a sign that the asteroid Vesta is around. She is a symbol of the Temple of the Vestales in the Roman Forum, where one man—the Pontifex Maximus—controlled all the virginal priestesses. The gender politics were quite toxic.

FOUR OF SWORDS
Quick Look

A period of rest and recuperation. What is fascinating about this card is the stained glass window in the corner showing a mother and child. What is that picture saying to you? This is an intensely personal card to be read individually. The woman and infant hold a message.

Description

With enough time, everything and everybody can heal, and that is what this card is all about. There needs to be a long period of rejuvenation before life can begin again. This is not unlike the Doctor in *Doctor Who* between incarnations, is it? Waiting for Jon Pertwee to become Tom Baker. There is also a bright message of hope and renewal coming from the mother and child in the stained glass window, as I've mentioned—where the light is getting in through the cracks.

Now, this might be you as a child with your mother. Or it may be you one day having a child of your own or teaching an infant or teenager. Rest, repair, recovery, recuperation, and resurrection are the rules now.

The Swords are heavy and hang all round the sleeper. There have been attacks here—perhaps one on the immune system or surgery, as a surgeon goes in with knives to remove what ails you. The attacks may have been from critics, opponents, or even on the level of psychic attack.

It's all a memory now; it's all been turned to stone. Like memories of battles past in Westminster Abbey or St. Paul's Cathedral, here we have memorials of long-ago feuds and conflicts. All the Mars—the Swords of conflict or aggression—rests in the past, so you may be looking at past Mars transits to the natal chart or transits to natal Mars which are now behind you. Now it is time for a rebirth.

The stained glass window holds the potential for a rich and colorful adult-child relationship—teacher and pupil, mother and child, godparent and godchild, and so on. Yet nothing can be made real until the transition is complete.

Pamela Colman Smith & Four of Swords

The image is like all of Smith's glass and light—here to be actualized and made real. Prayer can be powerful with this card. She did, in fact, create the deck within walking distance of a tiny local church at Smallhythe and, later in life, converted to Roman Catholicism.

Astrology & Four of Swords

The Fifth House is implicated here, ruled by Leo and the Sun in your chart. The Fifth House is about your own and other people's offspring, from babies to young adults—millennials who are old enough to be your own children if you are the right age.

This card also tallies with the Twelfth House in astrology, which is ruled by Neptune, discovered in the same year that anesthetic was first used in public. Have a look at Neptune, Pisces, and the Twelfth House in your chart, as religion, spirituality, Reiki, meditation, Buddhism, Christianity, and so on often link to this card. "I am the life and the resurrection" is a statement that springs to mind. In Buddhism, reincarnation is of course suggested by this sleeping survivor.

The Fifth House and Leo, shining in the window, remind you about this part of the horoscope as home to the teacher, mentor, and guide who sets an example for—and leads—a younger generation. Nothing can happen unless there is a deep and powerful turnaround for the sleeping or resting figure, though.

Aesculapius, which is an astrological symbol of resurrection, can sometimes be implicated with this card, too. The Romans took people on the brink of no return to his temples, and overnight, those who were in desperate need of healing found recovery, resurrection, and the miracle required for restoration. The asteroid Aesculapia may also be worth checking in your chart, by natal placement under transit or by actual transit.

FIVE OF SWORDS
Quick Look

This card turns up when there have been battles. They may be emotional, psychological, physical (illness), or intellectual. Someone—probably you—needs to take the time to rejuvenate. It might be over, but all is not well yet . . .

Description

There is a great need here to escape from the reality of recent conflict. Someone is hurt. In the foreground a fiery type (Aries, Leo, or Sagittarius chart signatures, shown by the ginger hair, red shirt and trousers, and mustard boots) takes the Swords away smiling! This card is wide open to your interpretation as the action could go anywhere. How will this resolve? A sense of humor and a cheerful outlook can remedy most situations, no matter if there has been conflict. You may feel defeated but how are you going to move on? Now is the time to figure that out.

It's rather like a grown-up striding into a situation where children have been fighting and have hurt each other. "Now then, now then, what's all this about?" is the classic question shortly before things are sorted out and the children are playing happily together again. On a more serious, adult note, here we have a wounded person, the antagonist or attacker, and the peacemaker. The key thing is that the Swords are removed or it could all start up again.

Astrology & Five of Swords

Mars is at work in this card as the god of battle and war. You can also see Neptune in the sea.

SIX OF SWORDS

Quick Look

You or people who matter to you relocate. This may be long-term travel or emigration—perhaps a move across town or across the country. The future is a blank canvas. Using the problems of the past to prop up the escape to the unknown future is the way forward, but at a certain point that baggage must go. A group, club, team, society, or other circle is supportive.

Description

This is a classic picture of a family who has had enough of "the slings and arrows of outrageous fortune" and decided to emigrate to a country they have never visited. A lot of British families did that in the 1970s. This does not have to be a family, of course. Those people in the boat are really symbolic, not literal.

Emigration, travel, or moving away often happens because it has come to the last straw, the only option. The body language here suggests downcast people or even depressed people. Refugees, perhaps? Maybe you are in the boat or just assisting. This card can turn up when you are helping a friend leave a bad marriage with her children.

It is always good to look at what is literally shown in Smith's illustrations.

Here we have a miserably huddled woman and child being helped across the water, hopefully to better times—they are downcast as the body language is clear—by someone who has the strength. This may of course be the husband and father, yet it may also be an outsider. Note the Aquarius symbol to the right. A group, team, community, or club is close by. This can easily be new friends or old friends helping a move, too. This is the case when people switch countries and are given a list of phone numbers and names to contact at the other side. Friends help friends, by introducing friends of friends. When one moves, starting again is made easier by the immediate joining of, say, football or cricket teams.

The future (the destination) has no color. It is for the woman and child to fill in. Thus, there is the idea of a blank canvas. The distant shore reveals nothing. Smith left it almost white. In time, other Tarot cards may show the possibilities and potential of the new hometown, the new homeland. It is there to be painted.

Look at the Swords in the wooden boat. If they were removed, the whole thing would sink. Thus, the Swords—always a symbol of conflict, and possibly Mars by transit or transits to natal Mars in this card—are serving a purpose.

They are being used to help carry the people away from what has obviously been a dismal situation. I have seen this card turn up when a woman has left a bad relationship in a hurry and flown to another region to start a new life. The Swords have hit the boat, but they also plug the holes in the boat!

The biggest focus in this card should probably be the mental health of those moving or escaping. There is depression here—possibly anxiety. Apart from anything else there needs to be tremendous focus on medical help, healing, Reiki, hypnosis, exercise, yoga, therapy, meditation. Something on this list, or even new to this list, will get the escapees into the right frame of mind to make a go of it in the new place.

This card can occasionally turn up if there has been a rotten experience with an employer or business, and thus all concerned are moving to a new workplace or even an entirely different industry or business. It is more commonly associated with personal or family departures, but it can happen.

The Beatles' song "She's Leaving Home" is one way to think about this card. An unhappy daughter leaves the family after feeling alone for years.

The great thing about this card is there is not far or long to go. These people are going to make it, just in the nick of time. The Split Enz song "Six Months in a Leaky Boat" might also point to themes in this card. They are lucky just to be afloat—but these people *are* afloat, and the future is calling.

Pamela Colman Smith & Six of Swords

Smith repeats the idea of Swords serving a practical use in other cards. The "slings and arrows of outrageous fortune" have a function. Without them, there would be no travel or transport in this card. The boat would leak and sink. So, for all that the people escaping feel they have been threatened or attacked, they are in one piece, and the Swords now help the departure and relocation.

Smith herself fled London after miserable experiences that we will never know about: she kept the story to herself. She found a very happy new life, as far as we can tell, living on the coast.

Astrology & Six of Swords

The Aquarius wavy lines are prominent below the boat—the famous logo shows circulating air, as Aquarius is an air sign, but also the "pooling of resources." Aquarius is actually the title of a Roman water bearer who supplied the communal baths. Note how Aquarius carries the load.

SEVEN OF SWORDS

Quick Look

This card shows a positive, practical person preempting a problem. There is risk here, because a dark little group is plotting and planning in the distance. Yet, with the right timing and approach, this individual—you, perhaps?—can swiftly take away anything that could be weaponized, any future means of conflict. This is an image of strategy. The tents suggest questions about territorialism and staking claims.

Description

Removing the means to future conflict can be a breeze, which is why the person in this card is grinning. How can there be a battle, feud, or even a war if there is nothing to fight with? It is unclear if there has already been a brawl or if there is only the potential for one, but a sense of humor can help anyone avoid any trouble.

Unlike the rather shady characters in the distance, this hero of the hour is up-front, front and center, and feeling good about life—energetic and positive, hopeful and strong.

It is time for the weapons to be removed so that the chance of any more conflict can be removed, too. This is a classic picture of the aftermath of World War II, when the United Nations was created and the big cleanup began in Europe.

There were questions about territory and staked claims. The tents represent temporary entitlement to some kind of space or position. Who owns what, who belongs where, or who has the right to be anywhere in life? These are pertinent questions. The issue here is what belongs to which person.

There is a definite risk here, however. The eyes of the leading character in this drama are closed, if you look carefully, and this person is going to tumble and perhaps suffer injury unless there is less joking around and smug satisfaction and a bit more awareness.

Time is of the essence, too. Leave it much longer and the huddled group, clearly carrying Swords (as this is a Swords card), could descend. Then, as now, the key to evading future conflict or escaping from potential battles is swift action. This card is telling you or somebody else to get a move on, but also not to drop the bundle. Move fast but take a bit more care, or something could go wrong here.

Seven Swords are too much to carry, so the amused peacemaker will have to do this in two trips. What is at stake? The tents suggest territory, ownership. It may actually be about a house, an apartment, a garden, a block of land, or perhaps other sorts of property, like intellectual property. Now that's an interesting question.

This rather sinister group of people disguised in silhouette plots and plans in the far left corner in the shadows. Black hearts under a gray cloud.

This is an uncannily prescient card, because Smith's illustration foreshadowed the late 1930s and future British prime minister Neville Chamberlain and the appeasement of Hitler and the Nazis. Anyone who beamed about "Peace in our time" was not properly paying attention. Chamberlain wriggled away with an agreement which allegedly avoided war, but Hitler lied. Chamberlain did not look before he leaped. The territory in question was Poland.

There is fantastic potential here for smart strategy—if one is smart. The issue of timing—how fast to move before the shady group descends?—has to be weighed against the effectiveness of the strategy. As with all Smith's cards, there is room to move. Props can be brought in or new characters. What or who are inside the tents? The running figure with the Swords is headed in one direction, but there are other options. The idea of "burying the hatchet" is very strong here. Also the word *disarming* and the idea of disarming the enemy.

Pamela Colman Smith & Seven of Swords

Smith was close to Shakespearean actors and strongly influenced by Ellen Terry, who was her host at Smallhythe where the deck was partly dreamed up in 1909. Thus, we see shades of *Macbeth* here or perhaps *Henry V*.

Smith created her cards at a time when the reality of quantum mechanics was dawning on science. Her images are all full of possibility for a parallel outcome.

Astrology & Seven of Swords

You invariably need to look for natal Mars under transit when this card shows up, or you are looking for transiting Mars aspecting an important planet, asteroid, point, or angle in the chart. There may be transits of the Fourth House, involving the zodiac sign Cancer, as the tents are a pointer to territory and turf. Equally, as tents go with camping, the great outdoors, and adventure holidays, you may be looking for the Ninth House and Sagittarius. It really depends on you and your personal situation.

EIGHT OF SWORDS
Quick Look

Another blindfolded woman is here, but this is a woman who cannot see or move—she is trapped by her own inability to act. In fact, a new future is waiting. She could easily travel to the promising accommodations in the distance if she were to remove her blindfold. This means loosening what restricts or confines her, and she needs to use the Swords (past attacks or threats) psychologically to do it.

Description

A blindfolded woman is surrounded by fallen Swords, which create a jail for her. She is also tied up. A castle is in the background but not too far away. She could cry for help, but that might take weeks. The damsel in distress is here, but the answer is not always a distress call. She would be much better off using her own initiative and sensing when she is out of danger—then taking a Sword to cut the fabric that binds her arms and hands.

This card usually turns up when a woman (sometimes literally with dark hair) is trapped emotionally, psychologically, and spiritually. Don't get too fixated on the hair color or the gender, but in my experience as a hands-on Tarot reader in my twenties and thirties, it is often a wife in a bad marriage or a career woman in a bad professional situation.

If you look closely at the card, you will notice the Swords are only just lodged in the sand and mud of the receding tide. If she waits long enough, the tide will come in and the Swords will be dislodged. That could be dangerous, though. If she cannot wriggle free, she risks drowning. So, even though these Swords representing the slings and arrows of outrageous fortune are wobbling, she can't afford to hang around.

This is real action hero stuff. Once her hands are free, this woman can take away her blindfold and see just how close the castle is, as well as other options not visible in the landscape of the card. The castle is a symbol of a new house, apartment, or workspace. Perhaps it's just a really good holiday—the kind that transports you. There is quite a distance to walk, climb, or journey, but it is not so far that she cannot sense it.

This card encourages you or someone else to use intuition and the sixth sense, because when one cannot see—symbolically blindfolded—there is only the inner, psychic sense to lean on.

Use who or what hurt you to break free. That is the message of this card.

There is no point calling out for help because there is no evidence at all that there is any figure in the castle on the cliffs—or even just out of sight beyond the margins of the card—to save her. Instead, this woman must set about the determined task of using who/what hurt her, threatened her, or encircled her to break free. If this were an episode of *Doctor Who* and we were looking at Sarah Jane Smith trapped by the antics of Daleks or Cybermen, we would be giving her stage directions, shouting instructions at the television.

If the woman in this card senses she is safe—and she should: we can see no further threats in the picture—it is time to wriggle over to the Swords and use them to chafe the ties that bind until they are broken. The blindfold can then be removed, and the woman will see just how secure she is; just how nonthreatening those Swords, thrown a long time ago, actually are; just how free she is to make her move, leave the scene, embark on the journey, and head for that new home or exhilarating holiday.

This card advises planning, strategy, some caution, some persistence, determination, and stamina. Yet there is absolutely no reason why a woman who has been trapped in a miserable situation psychologically should not be liberated from all the restrictions and given the gift of clear vision to make her way onward and upward.

Pamela Colman Smith & Eight of Swords

There surely are links here with the suffragettes Smith was part of. This card may be seen in the light of the women's suffrage movement of 1909 or Women's Liberation in the 1970s when her deck had its rebirth thanks to U.S. Games Systems. This is woman ("hear me roar," to quote Helen Reddy), but there is not much roaring going on yet. Women working to break free from male oppression and gain their own rights to vote take off the blindfold and untether from what had previously bound them.

Astrology & Eight of Swords

It is a symbol of Mars (action) but also Uranus (the process of liberation). So transiting Mars or Uranus may be involved, or there may be transits to your natal Mars or Uranus.

NINE OF SWORDS

Quick Look

This is insomnia or a nightmare. It may also be worrying in bed no matter what time of day or night it happens to be. This is all in the person's mind—figments of the imagination or memories interpreted in a negative way. The answer here is meditation, mindfulness, healing, cognitive therapy, relaxation techniques, and perhaps astrology. Look at the quilt.

Description

The person with insomnia or even illness is using the first position in Reiki. This Japanese healing discipline asks people to put their hands in a sequence of poses. This is the initial one.

This card is a very good example of Smith's intuitive grasp of quantum mechanics. There is no single objective reality. We find reality when we measure it. Every Sword is in this person's head. It is all a memory, construed in a particular way, or a fear of what is to come. Swords are painful, sharp, threatening. So can the imagination be, or a memory, but nothing is real. The whole point of Smith's cards, guided by Waite, was to empower people to take control.

The bed is comfortable, even luxurious. It's shabby chic. The pallet itself below the mattress shows past conflict or a complicated relationship. That is what underlies everything. So this is a case of "making one's bed and lying in it," and the figures in the decoration are at odds with each other. One has to face the past to get on with the present and the future. There is no point in "sleeping on it" if there is something troublesome in the past. It never really goes away, and here it is at the foundation of what keeps someone awake at night or gives them nightmares. Thus, this card suggests it might be useful to confront what one has "laid to rest" but is still very much there. Counseling can help or a good friend or family member. Sometimes it helps to just pick up the phone and call a suicide hotline.

The key to this card is that nothing is real; it is all in the person's mind. Turning gray with worry is not something anyone wants to do. This person has gray hair, and perhaps stress is responsible as stem cells can be affected by anxiety. The solution is Reiki, which uses the palms-on-face pose you see here—that is an amazing synchronicity, unless Smith drew it deliberately.

We might also talk about spiritual healing, hypnosis (Paul McKenna has generously given his talents free on YouTube), an appointment with the doctor, or a relaxation technique to make sleep better. There are more options, of course, and everyone has their own road to a good night's rest.

Without the floating imaginary Swords this person would actually enjoy a good night's sleep in what appears to be quite a cozy sanctuary. It is so important to remember that Smith's cards worked as a stage set to be directed by you, the reader. Remove the floating, imaginary weapons, bring a candle into the room, a cup of herbal tea, perhaps a friendly cat or dog—and this is the very picture of domestic harmony and a good night's sleep.

Pamela Colman Smith, Astrology & Nine of Swords

Look closely and you will see zodiac signs on the bedspread. Smith was required to learn astrology as part of her Golden Dawn training. You can see the glyph for the Sun, but also Aries, Leo, Sagittarius, Taurus, Libra, Gemini, and more. Astrology here is a comfort; that is the suggestion. This is what Americans call a comforter or generally a quilt. I find it interesting that the zodiac signs are so blatantly illustrated on what would normally be a piece of patchwork. How is astrology a comfort?

The greatest comfort of astrology is this: the cycles of time have an end point. Even if you are worried about your past, present, or possible future, the challenging cycles of Saturn, for example, can be timed with a clear end date. And it helps to have astrology's wisdom and ancient knowledge as a tool to handle life. Just knowing your chart, in the eyes of an astrologer, gives you protection and comfort—just like a good quilt.

TEN OF SWORDS

Quick Look

This is a picture of a group attack, and someone who is almost but not quite down for the count. A closer look will reveal that this person is a survivor who is going to get up and live to see another day. In fact, despite the difficulty of being the sole, vulnerable object of the negativity, threat, or actual damage of a whole number of people, this is a card showing the chance of a comeback.

Description

This is one of Smith's bleakest images. We might think of "the many against the one" with this picture. It can be a classic illustration of a peer group engaged in bullying at school or a political party which turns against its own leader and forces a challenge for the top position. This is also the soccer player whose team becomes critical en masse of their captain. It can be a symbol of mutiny. However, it can also be a picture of the odds being stacked against a person from a situation where the numbers are unfair.

Look at the new day dawning in the background. This person is not finished yet. The hands show crossed fingers—perhaps luck is with them—or the Buddhist vitarka mudra gesture, which means debate or discussion. Will this person rise again and walk away? It's up for debate.

Crucially, you need to consider the group of aggressors who stabbed, not from the front, but the back. This is betrayal. It is Caesar at the moment of his assassination, stabbed in the back by his so-called friend Marcus Junius Brutus, recognizing him as one of the pack.

The choice belongs to the figure on the ground. A new day will dawn. The Sun will rise again. The landscape will look brighter, lighter, and clearer, and there is a chance to get up and walk away, to begin a new life. There is also the sea—perhaps a boat can arrive and transport the survivor to a new existence. Are these the "flesh wounds" of *Monty Python & the Holy Grail* or is this not as bad as it looks?

So much depends on the person who is crossing their fingers or making a significant gesture. It's really about willpower and the capacity to heal oneself or request healing—the prone figure can always yell for help and hope someone comes.

It can also go the other way. Faced with such a mammoth task ahead, rather than revive, recover, and relaunch, the victim of this group effort may decide to just give up. This card holds a very clear choice.

Pamela Colman Smith & Ten of Swords

It is important to remember that Smith created this deck on Waite's instruction with perhaps posterity in mind. It was to be a deck for the ages. Thus, it has seen Tarot readers through two world wars. This may have been a picture of a lone soldier, pilot, or sailor, trying to survive a collective attack by the enemy.

The Golden Dawn is literally seen over the mountains. As a magical group it was notorious for its infighting and some of the people in Smith and Waite's circle did feel a sense of betrayal.

Astrology & Ten of Swords

Look to the Eleventh House of the astrological chart here. It rules the collective. Smith's life in the theater saw her moving in Shakespearean circles. The *Tragedy of Julius Caesar* by Shakespeare may be referenced here. *Et tu, Brute?* is a Latin phrase meaning "Even you, Brutus?" Caesar uttered when the collective turned against him.

PAGE OF SWORDS

Quick Look

A person younger than you has a mission. This is about an attack or perhaps a defense. The winds of change are blowing hard and action calls. This is a green light. What is odd about this illustration is that there is hesitation. The Page is not sure if he should charge full steam ahead or linger longer. This is a card of mixed signals, like a traffic light moving between green and yellow.

Description

Pages were young male servants in the theater of Smith's day. This is a younger male, with the red boots of Aries (its color is red) and the Sword of Mars, the ruler of Aries. Of course girls and young women can dress up as young men. Who is this person? Perhaps it is a youthful and energetic part of your own personality as much as a real individual?

We might associate this card with "Up and atom" or "Up and at 'em" depending on how you read it—energy. There is a certain amount of testosterone here, if the person in question is a young man or boy. The weather depicted by Smith in this card is significant. This is not a calm, quiet, sunny day. It is really a day of tremendous gusts of wind, blowing us around, in search of a new direction. West, east, north, or south? The Page is unsure.

The family tree to the left is being blown sideways. This may be significant, if relatives or close family members are switching direction or if there is some kind of disruption. Perhaps someone has come home to stay, or there is a departure. Maybe there is family politics, so the tree of one's ancestors is being shaken. This seems to be part of the story even though it is in the background. It may be a background issue, or belong to the past, thus influencing the drive, personality, and mixed feelings of this Page of Swords.

Note that yellow, the color of fear, is here, too. The colors in Smith's cards really matter. Saturn is a pale yellow and symbolizes delays. Stay or go? Thrust and parry or head back? The winds of change are urging the Page east, but one foot is still turning west. This idea of turning on one's heel is really important if you are looking at the astrological chart, because we may be seeing a retrograde planet somewhere: likely Mars, but possibly Saturn (yellow) or even Mercury. There is a feeling of "Should I Stay or Should I Go?" here like the Clash anthem. If he goes there will be trouble, but if he stays it will be double . . .

Pamela Colman Smith & Page of Swords

The group of birds, symbolizing the Eleventh House, is scattering. In Smith's cards, read every detail. She knew groups very well, having been in the Golden Dawn, which indeed scattered its membership, and also involved in the women's suffrage movement of early last century. She was quite sensitive to the hive or group mind, and it shows up in quite a few of her cards. Here we see it as a flock, disrupted by the winds of change. This is another background feature, so it may belong to the past or be an element of the situation approaching from the future.

Astrology & Page of Swords

Perhaps look to Mars in your chart, natally or by transit. Mars Retrograde or Mars in square or opposition to other chart factors can result in this kind of green light/yellow light mixed signal.

KNIGHT OF SWORDS
Quick Look

A Knight in shining armor on the attack or defense can be a welcome sight. It really depends if this Knight of Swords is for or against you. There is great haste here and blood pumping in male veins. Testosterone. This card has to be read in context. Pure impulse, aggression, and drive can be all that powers a savior or hero—the firefighter with the axe ready to break down a door. If this is a conflict of another kind, the Knight of Swords can cause damage. This is Mars in astrology.

Description

The Knight of Swords is a younger man, who drives fast on his motorcycle or in his car, in his speedboat or on his Jet Ski. In ancient Rome he would have been galloping on his horse, of course. He lives for the moment and responds in the heat of the moment, too.

He is a symbol of Mars and Aries in astrology: an energetic, fierce, fast, and furious man wearing red—the Aries/Mars color—hurtling at breakneck speed toward some kind of attack, or defense. I mentioned circumstances and context. You have to fill in the rest of the picture here. Is he part of a United Nations Peacekeeping force? Is he the enemy as far as you are concerned?

Very occasionally this card can be you. You will know immediately if this is the case. You will recognize your fast and furious intention and the impact that adrenaline is having on you. There is not a great deal of thought or contemplation here—just pure heat.

The trees on the left-hand side of the card are being bent backward. This may be a comment on a family in the picture (family tree). Perhaps that is part of the issue. The Knight of Swords is charging in to defend a family member or perhaps attack one. There may be strife in the clan. You can see *Braveheart* in the Knight of Swords.

The family tree may not be a directly connected part of the story here; it may be pure background or history. Perhaps the Knight of Swords comes from a troubled background where male aggression was the norm. This is really for you to interpret. Maybe he has ancestors who fought in one of the world wars. That legacy stays with him.

The horse cannot see; flying blind, all it can do is try to keep up. Who or what is the vehicle for the Knight's energy? Perhaps he has attached himself to a cause. It may be a "blind" cause, and so those involved may lack awareness or insight. They cannot see what you can see. That happens, too, in war and in peace.

There is a healthy warning here about driving too fast or driving oneself or other people too hard. Accidents can happen, as Elvis Costello noted. What we really get from this card is a sense of rushing, not thinking—not seeing or understanding much beyond the core mission or just the immediate reaction. That can lead to speeding fines or worse.

The rider is also rather blind. Look at the eyes and you will find the Knight of Swords is in an altered state. You might call it a frenzy, the heat of the moment. We talk about "seeing red" when we are angry.

Are there other ways to fight the good fight or seize the day than this? And what is the motivation here? What on earth is at stake? This is the Charge of the Light Brigade, but also the Vietnam War, which was going on when Smith and Waite's cards were popularly revived in the early seventies by Stuart R. Kaplan.

The idea of harnessing energy and controlling feelings is very close to this card. Even if you are racing into an emergency, there must be time—even if only a few minutes—to plot and plan, to pause and strategize. Not everything has to be done in a single streak of raw energy. There is a saying: "He who hesitates is lost," but in this case, I am sure you can see that even a modest amount of hesitation could help this Knight achieve what he wants in a more successful way. There is something so reckless about this flight of his.

The rest of this card really has to be interpreted by you, as it is so personal. Some of the seventies readers of this card—popular among the hippies of California—would have been in the peace movement and strongly disapproved of Vietnam. Others may have had quite different feelings about the war and found the Knight of Swords to be a valiant force for good worth encouraging.

Pamela Colman Smith & Knight of Swords

Smith created this image a few years before World War I but accurately portrayed the rush to the front, which of course involved horses as well as riders and claimed the lives of so many young men of her generation. This card was dreamed up in 1909 under the guidance of Waite, Smith's mentor and employer, from the Golden Dawn.

Astrology & Knight of Swords

You can see the Aries glyph on the reins. Aries is of course ruled by Mars, which Smith would have known. Aries is a really good way into this card. Aries the Ram is a symbol of male aggression where there is territory at stake or the need to compete, fight, and win. Aries the Ram is also linked to the idea of a battering ram—an ancient weapon.

QUEEN OF SWORDS
Quick Look

This is a strong woman with a powerful sense of boundaries. She seems to be saying "This far and no further" to the invisible person, or people, facing her just outside the margin of the card. In myth Psyche is shown by butterflies and reveals what lives forever. The butterfly of Psyche is on this Queen's crown and throne. She, or something about her, is immortal.

Description

Is this you or someone else? If it is you, you will have instant recognition; you are clearly a tough cookie or currently forced to be on guard, keeping people or situations at bay. This is a formidable woman who is immediately recognizable in history as well as modern politics. The card denotes strong boundaries, an intimidating presence. The coloring is red/orange, so here we have someone who has the zodiac fire signs of Aries, Leo, and/or Sagittarius emphasized in their horoscope.

What is really interesting about the Queen of Swords is that she is also spiritual. Are those rosary beads on her wrist or a traditional Buddhist mala? And how can you be tough but spiritual or religious at the same time? This is the interesting conundrum about this particular Queen. She is open, inviting the world in, but also defensive, keeping people at arm's length.

As mentioned earlier, the butterflies of Psyche, the Roman goddess of immortality, are hidden on the Queen's throne and in her crown. This asteroid (Psyche) in your astrological chart is a symbol of what or who lasts forever, despite tests and trials. In mythology, Psyche was put to tests and trials by Venus, her jealous mother-in-law. Psyche passed them all and was rewarded with immortality by the gods.

If we take Queen Elizabeth I or Queen Elizabeth II as the archetype for the Queen of Swords, we can see some of this enduring power. Good Queen Bess goes on in art, in history, in literature, in film, in television. Like her modern namesake, she was a religious woman. The late Queen Elizabeth II will go on forever, if only because her features are on the currency of Commonwealth nations—not to mention the legacy she will leave.

This, then, is no ordinary woman. No matter what happens to her, the beat goes on. She is also a survivor. Psyche put up with all kinds of torments from Venus, who resented her great beauty. You get the impression that the Queen of Swords has made it through various conflicts or battles, feuds or spats. No wonder she is so determined to maintain her defenses with her mighty Sword. She has been tested. Now, she puts others to the test. She decides who comes into her space.

On the left, the family tree is blowing sideways—indicating the winds of change. This has happened and is still affecting her or is taking place now. Relatives may be displaced, for example, or there could be separations, departures, arrivals within the clan. Differences or difficult episodes may be ahead, bringing some kind of turmoil.

It's very much in the background, but it adds to the picture and expands the information about this woman. Again, we are reminded of both Queen Elizabeth I and her sister Mary and the recently departed monarch and her family dramas.

Our Queen of Swords wears either a Roman Catholic rosary, a Buddhist mala, or perhaps a red string bracelet, which is a sacred Hindu piece of jewelry to ward off evil. The idea of being protected is strong with this card. Here is a woman who cares deeply about feeling safe and being safe, too, on the spiritual plane as well as the earthly one. So, with this card, you really have to look at her tactics, tools, and strategy.

The Queen of Swords can be adjusted. Her props can change. Others can come onto the stage set by the card. Her furniture can be altered. Everything about this picture suggests there are many, many ways to feel protected and be defended. Perhaps that big, heavy weapon is a burden, and there are other possibilities? And who or what is unseen beyond the margins of the card, ready to confront this woman so that her entire being is devoted to filtering who can come in and who must stay away?

Pamela Colman Smith & Queen of Swords

Smith's quantum clouds are on the Queen's robes and in the sky, and a single bird flies over her head. The clouds may also be smoke, a symbol for the planet Neptune. This card, thus, lends itself to stage direction, conscious creation, and deliberate choice. All of Smith's cards are examples of quantum uncertainty and the reality of parallel universes.

Astrology & Queen of Swords

The baby's face hidden in the stonework reminds us of the zodiac sign Leo (the Queen to a younger court) and the Fifth House of pregnancy, babies, and childhood. She may have transits in Leo, horoscope factors in Leo, or cycles which were/are important in the Fifth House. A great deal of who this woman is rests on the babies and infants from her past—or the pregnancies. Perhaps this is the godchildren or stepchildren, the small nieces or nephews as well as her own offspring. We can also see the ghost of lost pregnancies hidden in the throne. It really depends on who this person is or who you are, but it all forms the foundation this woman rests on, even if she is entirely unconscious of it.

The Sword is pure Mars. This is a posture of defense. You can approach her majesty but only so far. She will smite you if she wants to. She will put the Sword down, but only if she wishes. There is a strong message here about turf and territory.

KING OF SWORDS

Quick Look

Rigid, uncompromising, tough, and unyielding. It takes a great deal for the King of Swords to become another sort of King. It even takes quite a lot for him to merely open up, to accommodate you or others, to soften long enough for a deal to be struck or an alternative to be found. This is old-fashioned masculinity of the sort Smith knew very well back in 1909. Here is a future general in World War I.

Description

This man can axe people or make budget cuts. That is what his Sword is for. He is powerful, intimidating, and confronting. There are quite a few cards in Smith's deck suggesting Mars in astrology, and this is one of them. There is cold and controlled anger here. This man is a coiled spring. He is the kind of human being who populated the war that arrived in Smith's lifetime, but also World War II. We talk about "bloodless anger," and the pallor of the King's face suggests that this is someone who has felt all the emotion but tightly marshaled it. What we are left with is someone who is potentially lethal.

Of course, in civilized modern life the King is more likely to be the tough former husband, the difficult partner, the intimidating boss, the hard taskmaster father. It is unusual to find the armed services here, although it can happen. The brutal businessman is a good example of the King of Swords today—maybe the property developer who does not care who or what he destroys.

Perhaps it is the strongest and most formidable people who leave behind the longest legacies. This is certainly true if you think about military figures past. The Duke of Wellington sculpted in stone and lending his name to a New Zealand city as well as a famous kind of boot! The Queen and King of Swords, both with their butterflies, remind us that what is carved out endures. Like his female counterpart, the King of Swords hacks out a reputation or cuts his legacy.

We turn to the story of Cupid and Psyche being told on his throne, and perhaps the asteroid Cupido in astrology is also part of his past. To the Romans, Cupid was the lover of Psyche, the woman put to tests and trials by his mother Venus and rewarded with immortality. This intensely romantic story has been captured in sculpture, and it's there in the King's iconography. Part of his backstory involves a love that never died or never dies. The King of Swords is not conscious of it—no, not at all—but it is there, forming part of his background.

You can see another couple to the right of him in a pair of lovebirds. It's interesting that someone so apparently cut off from human emotions should be surrounded by so many symbols of past or potential future romance. Perhaps that is what has made him the way he is.

The King of Swords may be divorced and angry deep down. He may have been disappointed in love or just married and entered into family life but lost the passion that began it all. Thus, the feelings have gone to be replaced by this classically old-school masculine pose of control and strength.

The family trees of both his mother and father are shown to his left and right. This is interesting, if you know the story of either family, as it suggests that there is an explanation from either or both sides as to his character and life to date. The family trees are there for a reason, even if the King is not fully aware of them. Perhaps he is descended from the Army, Air Force, or Navy on one or both sides.

Note the clenched fist and furious, yet restrained, expression. This is a good man to have on your side when things are difficult and you need a champion or hero, but a terrifying one to have against you unless you can persuade him to negotiate peacefully.

Pamela Colman Smith & King of Swords

This, like all of Smith's cards, is there to be worked with although it is rather more difficult to get into than some of her other Tarot stage sets. How do you change this character? You can't. But you can introduce people or new props, which make it less important for this intimidating King to hang on quite so tightly to that enormous lethal weapon. You get the impression this King would have to be dragged kicking and screaming to the therapist's couch, and yet any psychologist would have a field day with his psyche. This brings us back to Psyche (capital *P*) and the question about who or what lives forever and endures about the King of Swords or his life.

Astrology & King of Swords

As well as Mars in this card, the butterflies on the King's throne suggest Psyche, a horoscope symbol of what lasts forever. Psyche's butterfly can also be found on the Queen of Swords card, as we've noted.

The Suit of Pentacles

Pentacles or Coins have to do with the material world, finance, career, and our outer surroundings. This suit is linked with the element of earth, and thus represents the signs of Taurus, Virgo, and Capricorn in the tradition of the Tarot cards.

ACE OF PENTACLES

Quick Look

If you believe that you want, need, and deserve a large amount of money and are prepared to reach for it, then you can have it. This substantial piece of cash flow or lump sum of money can be used to travel with, relocate, or improve your current residence or premises. Those are just three options, though, and you may want to donate it to a good cause. Your attitude toward money really matters when you interpret this card personally.

Description

A huge amount of money is on offer if you bring it down to earth and make it real. This is money saved or money made. Much depends on the question, but if this card is a general snapshot of the present, you are potentially in line for a bonus, an inheritance, a pay raise, an advance, a commission, a generous bank loan.

This card just came up recently when a friend of mine generously waived her usual fee for a charity project—she will potentially save us several thousand dollars. It can translate into money saved as well as gained. As with so many of Smith's cards, this shows a cloud of possibility: it exists, but only if you make it real.

Money can present us with all sorts of mixed feelings, despite what you might think. Perhaps it should be obvious that a lot of money is a good thing, a welcome thing. This is surprisingly not the case for many people, and the way that you talk about money is revealing. Do you see reaching for savings or profits as grasping or grabbing, for example? Do you associate greed with money?

This point of view or mindset is important. Developing a healthy relationship with abundance is the start. It is quite true that some corporations and individuals give a lot of money a bad name. However, if you think about responsible business, ethical investment, generous philanthropy, and so on, you can remove any mental obstacles to trusting and accepting what is possible. If you go back into your family's experiences with money, wealth, poverty, business, recessions and depressions, boom and bust—and right through the family history on either parent's side—you can often uncover where general attitudes toward finance come from. This card alone can prompt you to do that.

This card is usually about a bonus, tax refund, legacy, pay raise, or profit as I've mentioned. It can be used to improve your home or fund a trip away. It can be nice to daydream—but then to actually set goals. If you have asked about the outcome of a particular professional plan, this card gives it to you straight. It could potentially deliver a great deal to you financially.

The trick is believing in it, knowing you deserve it, and doing the work to make it happen. Until then it remains a tantalizing unpopped quantum possibility. You have ended up in a universe where you could gain—and not just a little, but a lot. This universe is as real as any of them, and the next step is pulling down the lump sum to save or make from the cloud of hypothetical reward. Yet why shouldn't you do that? Why couldn't you do that? Money is, after all, the road to freedom. In this card it makes all things possible, no matter if you want to explore the world or stay put and use it at home.

Pamela Colman Smith & Ace of Pentacles

Smith's famous clouds play a part here, as does the idea of different universes. See the possibility, which is surely what Smith intended as she placed the clouds in this card.

Astrology & Ace of Pentacles

The Ace of Pentacles (sometimes called Coins) shows up as Taurus and/or Scorpio in astrology. Taurus rules the Second House of personal finance and Scorpio rules the Eighth House of joint finance.

TWO OF PENTACLES

Quick Look

This card is exactly what it looks like: Someone juggling incomings and outgoings. Trying to balance profit and loss, expenditure and income. In the background you can see ships being tossed around on the ocean—all at sea. This is a metaphor for your local, national, or even the global economy, which is volatile and unpredictable. Yet there is a way out of this. It depends on tactics and strategy for the juggler here.

Description

The money going out and coming in keeps the juggler off-balance. The ships in the background show you Neptune. The economy is all at sea, tossing and turning, in his city, country, or perhaps between nations. Rather than jig around, expending enormous amounts of energy trying to shuffle money from one hand to another, this person needs to breathe, pause, and take control. He needs to stop reacting to uncertainty and insecurity in the moment and actually make a plan.

Maybe we think the hat looks rather like a condom. Is someone being a dick-head? A fine Australian word, but also represented in American slang as LOMBARD (lots of money but a real dickhead). You get the impression from this illustration that Smith knew one or two such men. The fact is, adopting this stance, where money is never really controlled but always in motion, tends to make it the center of one's existence. There is nothing else to do but think about it, talk about it, and focus on it—but perhaps not in the right way.

As with all of Smith's cards, there is tremendous scope for personal interpretation. I will give you an example. The Möbius strip shape or figure eight also resembles Elton John's glasses at a distance. Who or what is being blind about money here? John's relationship with money, shopping, and charity is well-known. Perhaps you are seeing something completely different, though. As with all the cards, you can step back from the computer screen, telephone, or actual object and see it from a slight distance. Reading things into the card is exactly what you are meant to do with it.

Smith's cards are also very much about active imagination. She worked as a theater set designer, so you can direct this image as you please. Stage directions might instruct this figure (is it you?) to stop trying to just make ends meet and instead trust the situation long enough to put the money down, sit, and draw up a budget. You are being told that there certainly needs to be time and space for other things in life than making the money go round.

The tossing ships in the background can be representative of world economic trade. Have a look at that when you interpret this card, too. Storms do not last forever. The ships will perhaps be wrecked here, but there is also a chance the weather will settle and the journeys will continue. This card raises so many questions for you about what is possible, what will happen, what you can see happening, what you can make happen. The two gold Coins or Pentacles might show two sources of profit even but a temporary inability to manage the same or taxes to be paid, which is a very common scenario. Does a professional need to be brought into this picture?

Pamela Colman Smith & Two of Pentacles

Some years ago I went to Bude in Cornwall, where Smith spent her last years. I visited the pub she lived upstairs of and saw a stunning painting of a famous shipwreck which is part of the history of the town. This was an astonishing piece of synchronicity as Smith frequently painted ships in her work, both inside and outside her Tarot deck. Her own life was occasionally financially stormy or insecure.

Astrology & Two of Pentacles

This is Scorpio and/or Taurus in astrology and the Eighth House of other people's money, but also the Second House of personal budgets. This man as a symbol of yourself or someone you know needs to focus, center, and ground themself.

THREE OF PENTACLES

Quick Look

This is the quest for the Holy Grail financially. Is the payoff actually there, or is this a wild goose chase? There are no guarantees with this card. The Three of Pentacles or Coins is also very much about three people or three organizations—a collaboration. Life is a gamble. It is a treasure hunt. It may be a complete waste of time or vindicate all the effort. Look at the three people, though. This is crucial. What/who is represented?

Description

Missing money, assets, or wealth, in the form of cash, property, or precious objects, is indicated. Where is it? Perhaps it's not even there. These people are in the dark. I would look at eclipses when this card turns up. Eclipses in astrology conceal; they never reveal. They obscure what and who is there. The darkness in this card, the shady depths, the blackout are really important. You can carry a torch, but how can that expose and reveal every nook and cranny? You also have to wonder at the tools being used for the search. You can almost hear one of the three explorers here saying, "It might be there. Then again it might not be . . ."

This is a treasure map, but what a map—it looks more like a cartoon. The man holding one corner looks like a jester, a joker. The other person, a monk. The third person is rather short. I find this interesting as an astrologer because dwarf planets like Ceres and Pluto are associated with searching, questing, exploring, seeking. Ceres spent an age looking for her daughter, who was hidden in the depths with Pluto. Pluto himself is associated with all that is buried, so coal (fossil fool fuel) but also diamonds and gold. A lot of people spend a lot of time and money searching for gold in Australia, long after the famous gold rush of the nineteenth century was over. It can be fruitless. It depends.

Yet what depends? Well, look at the three people and see if you think they are up to the task. Would you trust them to work together? Perhaps not. They seem like an odd trio. Maybe these are bands looking for a hit gold record. It might be the Jam or the Police in the 1970s and a great deal depends on the band staying together. (Neither did, though they did find their gold.)

The saying "Two's company, three's a crowd" might apply here as the way Smith has drawn the three characters suggests huge contrasts. The short man with the apron is a worker, is he not? The court jester is a clown, comedian, theatrical type. The monk is just that: a simple monk. A great deal depends on how you read the symbols or themes and apply them to your question and situation. What does it mean to you?

For some readers this card has suggested the Jimi Hendrix song "All Along the Watchtower": the joker and the thief looking for a way out. Reading the card personally is the solution as the situation may trigger all kinds of aha moments of recognition and realization once you go into the message. For one reader on my website, for example, this Hendrix song was reminiscent of the film *Withnail and I*, where it appears on the soundtrack. That film was famously about seeking funding, at the time, and the central theme is the acting life—poverty—and the search for paid work in a guessing-game profession!

There may be theft here or perhaps the "soft" theft of an organization or department not giving a refund when it should. We think about greedy banks and their insurance schemes deliberately drawing out the process of claims. We might also think about airlines making the process of refunds deliberately complicated so that customers will be put off their claims. Money can make some corporations or government departments pursue a strategy of quite conscious consumer confusion. The mystery here may be part of a corporate structure designed to stop the public from ever attempting to gain a payout or their money back.

The role of the comedian in looking for missing money is questionable. Of course, entertainers are forever on a quest for the hit show or number one box office smash that will make them rich. It only takes one success, then the royalties roll in forever, or that's the idea. Maybe the person with the jester's outfit is not a professional comedian, but in personality terms a bit of a fool or not someone who takes themself all that seriously. I find it interesting that the search for a stock market hit in 2020 led by pharmaceutical companies who all claimed the best vaccines for COVID-19 was led in part by entertainers either funding it or backing the jab.

Shares go down as well as up, don't they?! The search for a silver bullet for COVID-19—a simple solution to a complicated problem—is a really good example of how a real situation can be applied to an illustration that was created over a century ago. As I said, this card is personal to you and a great deal depends on how you apply the symbolic nature of the three explorers to your own situation.

When is buried or hidden treasure not? When it is tied to the stock market and what was valued very highly crashes because the product is found wanting. If ever there was a symbol for Wall Street and the Motley Fool, this card is it—but how could Smith possibly have known?

The third person has the torch and is a hardworking member of the middle or working class (the apron) but is rather short. Perhaps this person falls short for the task at hand.

There is a tremendous need here for the right people and the right strategy—not the wrong plan, the flawed mission, and entirely unsuitable people in charge of the search. Really look at that piece of paper the aproned figure holds. What do you see there? It's at the very least a rough sketch. What is important about this card is the lack of delivery or reward. There are so many Pentacle cards which actually show solid gold in the hand or at least at the fingertips. This is not one of them. Buyer beware.

Pamela Colman Smith & Three of Pentacles

The monk has surely taken vows of poverty, but the Catholic Church in Smith's day was hugely wealthy. She herself became the host of a holiday home for the Catholic Church. You may find a message in the monk. The Vatican and its views may be the story here. Perhaps the monk is just symbolic of nonattachment to money. Why is a penniless spiritual man even involved in a quest for three Coins, though?

Astrology & Three of Pentacles

The Second and Eighth Houses of finance, business, and property, or Taurus and Scorpio are suggested here. And look at the eclipses—is something being hidden?

FOUR OF PENTACLES

Quick Look

Wealth and security. There is not just one gold Coin or Pentacle here, but two to ground the person—and perhaps pay for designer shoes—and two more in hand. Yet the property market behind is a reminder that if houses, apartments, land, or other premises are the background story with the money, it is worth knowing the ever-changing property market very well.

Description

Sitting pretty or looking greedy? It really depends on your point of view. The Cancer symbol is hidden in this man's encircled arms. He is hugging the money, standing on the money, and it even adorns his crown. As with all Smith's illustrations, this man could be you, even if you are a woman. Here we have a picture of the Trump family, don't we? Those must be Trump's towers in the distance, and the clinging to cash is characteristic. Perhaps you see quite a different symbolic message. This card is for personal interpretation on the deepest level. Is this Scrooge? Perhaps it is you, with four sources of income, wondering who to pay or where to donate profits.

Behind this character is abundant property. The fact is, if you don't let go and invest or spend, you can find that the cash value of what you have and hold is irrelevant compared to the rising value of houses or apartments—or business towers. That is one message about this card. Bitcoin is all very well, but what about the skyrocketing value of particular towns or nations or specific listed buildings?

This man is grounded, yet also not grounded: he is floating in the air if you look carefully. He's "Eight Miles High," to quote the Byrds, or "Ten Feet Tall," to quote XTC. A great deal of money can be a high point: it makes us high; we hit the heights of success; we gain from investing in a high-rise (spreadsheets in the sky). This could be any of the four Beatles at the height of their wealth. As Ringo Starr observed, friends provided a crucial little help.

Money can make us grasping, of course. The metaphor in this card is "to have and to hold, for richer, for poorer." (He is holding on tightly, isn't he?) We think about clutching our money or hanging on to our values, perhaps. Safeguarding, protecting, but also grabbing are suggested here. We talk about "moneygrubbing," and maybe that is also here!

Happiness is here, though, too. This wealthy man seems satisfied, full, secure, abundant. You would have to say it's a rich symbol of someone who is really well set up.

The trick with this card is to ask yourself how money can best be managed. Hanging on and holding on is one strategy, but the buildings behind hint at the possibility of an investment in property or premises. You also have to wonder at what holding on to money so tightly does to a person's life and character.

The two big features in this card to interpret are the tightly folded arms and the feet on the ground/not on the ground. What are you being shown here, and where can you take the card, in terms of directing the action or adding props, characters, and backdrops?

Pamela Colman Smith & Four of Pentacles

Somewhere in that far-off city behind him is poverty. In Smith's day, especially in the thirties, which she lived through, the towns were full of the poor. Perhaps this person is on the verge of transforming his attitude toward money and will give one of his four Coins or 25 percent away—or maybe all of it.

Astrology & Four of Pentacles

The grounding comes from the feet on the Coins/Pentacles and the astrological association with Taurus, an earth sign, and money. Capricorn, another earth sign, is associated with high-rise apartments and the penthouse suite or top floor. (It is the mountain goat who climbs to the top peaks.) This is a mixed message. One is grounded in money like any good, materialistic, practical earth sign—Taurus is typical. Yet we also have someone whose feet do not touch the ground.

This card is also a symbol of the Fourth House ruled by Cancer (property), the Second House ruled by Taurus (cash flow), and the Eighth House ruled by Scorpio (assets), too. You can see the zodiac sign Cancer hidden in the curled arms. They resemble the Cancer the Crab glyph.

FIVE OF PENTACLES

Quick Look

A card showing illness or injury, depression, and hard times. Now is the winter of our discontent. (Smith was very close to Shakespearean actors like Ellen Terry.) The great hope, which the two people here are blind to, is the stained glass windows of the local church or cathedral, representing wealth. Religious organizations, then as now, offered charity and funded the poor and sick. There is an answer here, but you must interpret what the windows show you.

Description

Two people in a very bad way are out in the freezing cold—one on crutches with a head wound and the other depressed with a downcast head. We think about feeling down with depression, be it mild or severe: downcast, being down in the dumps, and so on. The other person has been crippled by something or someone. It is very important to interpret the two people in terms of your own situation or that of a person you are concerned about. Are they codependent? Perhaps they are strangers thrown together by their situation. They may be two homeless people who have met on the road. Yet this card can also show a long-married couple whose partnership rests on one being ill or having chronic conditions and the other being burdened with mental health problems—anxiety, for example. They go together because they feed or supply each other with the necessary attitude, mindset, and psychological loop.

Both are desperately poor, because in freezing conditions, surely you should have a car to travel in or at least be indoors? And yet and yet . . . there are five glowing, brilliant gold Pentacles or Coins in the stained glass window of the church beside them, which they cannot see or will not see. Then as now, the Roman Catholic

Church was a huge source of wealth, abundance, and also charity. No matter if the source of potential donations, handouts, or benefits is a religious institution or a bank—which also has its high priests and following—there is shelter here at least. Beyond shelter or sanctuary, there may also be money.

This is about a blind spot as these two people are walking straight past the obvious: the church with its collection plate for the poor and its central creed, which is the care of Jesus Christ for the impoverished and the Good Samaritan ethos.

The solution is for these two poor souls to step inside the church and ask for the charity it is there to provide. To get there, they will have to come up with a different strategy.

The depressed person is the prime mover here. You might think about the crutch you see in the card. Is someone acting as a crutch to lean on?

This card turns up when two people are in a codependent relationship with both believing suffering is a way of life and there is no way out. One person is able to walk, at least, without physical complaint—but there is depression or anxiety. The other person depends upon them just to keep going. You would assume the person on crutches has been helped along here, but is now trying to go it alone. Both are so embedded in their drama that they are putting one foot in front of the other, not very successfully, and completely ignoring—or perhaps just not seeing—the obvious and glittering source of warmth and potential financial support under their very noses.

The truth is, both could help each other. The person on crutches is a symbol of a human being who "needs a crutch," which may be alcohol, drugs, or their companion. Some marriages can function like this. The chronic invalid married to the person with depression. There is loyalty here, self-sacrifice, and love, which is priceless—you cannot put a monetary value on compassion and allegiance—and we are reminded of the marriage vows: Until death do us part. For richer, for poorer. In sickness and in health. For better, for worse. Perhaps the church is a reminder of the wedding ceremony of the past, when these two were joined in the eyes of God. Now, the stained glass windows are here with a reminder.

The person with hunched posture is in a better position to act on the option of sanctuary, assistance, financial support, comfort—perhaps immediate accommodation or emergency help—although their mental state will need to be tackled first.

The brilliant, beautiful Pentacles in the stained glass window symbolize a building, home, or organization not just rich, secure, and constructed with a spiritual purpose but also wondrous to behold. There is glory here and "the light" as well. Smith was a Roman Catholic later in life, and in her day, as now, nuns were the backbone of the church, giving all they had to support those in need. This may or may not be a message about, say, the work of St. Vincent de Paul or Buddhist monasteries which feed the poor, but whatever institution, organization, or person is represented by the church or cathedral windows emits a soothing glow. "Amazing Grace" is a hymn that springs to mind here—what was lost and now found.

The stained glass windows could also symbolize a government department or benevolent family. If you think about windows of opportunity, that may help with your interpretation.

The message with this card is change your attitude; look up and you will see an answer to your financial prayers so get moving and make help happen. On a purely practical note, you'd have to say the key is the lead figure, literally forging the way, and their mental health. If that can be tackled, then all else is possible.

I sometimes have readers drawing this card who have no money, no job, and no hope. They are living with a dependent family member who can't afford proper health care and have drawn a blank. I suggest free YouTube healing and hypnosis sessions from generous professionals like Paul McKenna, because although there are no guarantees that every expert will work for every reader, there is hope that one might.

This is very much a card about hope and also about generosity of spirit. People can and do seek meditation, distant healing, hypnotherapy, or counseling to help with depression and anxiety or even get rid of it. Thanks to the internet, a great deal of it is free of charge and might just be the key that turns the lock in the door, that lets these two into a dazzling and promising sanctuary, but you need to stop ignoring the problem and look for the hope.

Pamela Colman Smith & Five of Pentacles

In the Britain of 1909, when Smith created her card, there was no modern welfare state. Winter is also a metaphor for being out in the cold, being left cold, finding cold comfort, being frozen out by society—or other people.

I visited Bude, where Smith spent the last years of her life, and found the church where she may have been laid to rest. On a chilly autumn night when all around was dark and cold, the church doors were open and inside, candles were lit. The wooden pews were warm, and there were messages of hope.

Astrology & Five of Pentacles

This is about a blind spot, so an eclipse may be involved. Eclipses are very common when something or someone is hidden in plain sight. Neptune also distorts vision, if you are looking at astrological charts. Money is Taurus and/or Scorpio and the Second House and Eighth House of the chart. We may be looking at Virgo and the Sixth House, too, which rules illness, injury, and chronic conditions but also depression and anxiety. Virgo governs the remedy and cure for all this, too.

SIX OF PENTACLES

Quick Look

This is a fat cat giving generously to the poor. Someone who is rich enough to eat well, or just overeat, and buy the finest designer clothes. Those with nothing hold their hands out and gratefully receive. This may be a symbol of the prime minister in charge of unemployment benefits or a billionaire donor. If you are asking about your own financial prospects, you need to figure out if you are the donor or recipient!

Description

When you give money away, you create a power-based relationship. When you beg for money, you also create chemistry based on powerful feelings. Beyond the simple truth that money will be given away here—or perhaps loaned; this could arguably be a banker—there is a big question about what money does to the soul.

There is a principle at stake with this card: justice or fairness (the scales) and perhaps a legal ruling.

The gap between rich and poor shown is extreme. What will the beggars do when they have their cash? Is begging a lifelong pattern? Would the rich man let go of his wealth if it meant the extreme gap between rich/poor would be less severe?

I have seen this card turn up when someone is in the wonderful position of being able to pay others in a less fortunate position or even donate to them or lend them money. It also turns up when people are down on their luck and are about to enjoy the relief and release of someone helping them out with a handout. The only issue is the motivation of the giver. There are also the commonsense questions: When people get back on their feet, as you hope they will, how can they sensibly repay the original benefactor? Will there ever be a repayment?

Here you have a neat picture of capitalism. The rich—who are excessively rich because they are at the sharp, top, pointy end of the system—and the huddled masses down at the bottom who have almost nothing. These are small amounts being handed out, not notes. And the poor are not being covered in riches, they are receiving just a few coins. Given that the millionaire, multimillionaire, or billionaire—perhaps even multibillionaire—in question has so much one has to wonder why those in rags are being offered just a little.

There are more questions here to ask. Perhaps if those with nothing get too much—too much "something for nothing"—they will never know the value of money.

As with all the Coins/Pentacles cards, we are led back to Taurus, the sign which rules values. Your moral, ethical, and philosophical value system is intensely personal and bound to be triggered by this card. Not everyone likes taking charity. Look at the expressions on the faces of the recipients. Then again, there are people who live on benefits and quite deliberately play the system, according to some.

Look at the face of the donor. Look at the attitude and body language. There is a tremendous message in this card behind the mere fact of giving or lending. As with all Smith's cards, you also need to see if you can add stage directions. How could you direct this scene, add or remove actors or props? How could you turn it to your satisfaction, if indeed you have issues with what is being shown? This is Live Aid and Band Aid, isn't it? As always with this card, you also have to wonder: What happens next?

Astrology & Six of Pentacles

This is a symbol of Taurus and the Second House and/or Scorpio and the Eighth House. It is also very much a symbol of Libra with the scales in the rich man's hand. It's Robin Hood, isn't it? Or MacKenzie Scott, the former wife of Amazon's Jeff Bezos, donating to people suffering in the 2020 pandemic.

Smith quite deliberately put those meticulously balanced scales into the image. Libra rules the Seventh House of astrology, which describes former, current, and potential partners. The partnerships can be personal (marriage) or professional (business). Who are the two recipients of this generosity? Is there a partnership here and what does it count for?

Beyond Libra and the association with former, current, and potential partners, we find Venus, the ruler of Libra, and thus the scales, in the picture. Venus is about the cost of marriage and the price of adultery. It is also about the value of beauty and the reckoning up or settlement that comes with issues about justice: fair play, sometimes legal rulings.

SEVEN OF PENTACLES

Quick Look

Money grows on trees with this card. It is about "life gardening" in terms of asset management and the slow and steady cultivation of resources. This can literally be about growing fruit, vegetables, or herbs to sell at a local market. More commonly, it is about nursing a number of projects to recycle small profits into something more ambitious and perhaps hugely rewarding. It's a spread of investments. It's a host of nice little earners. The trick is in the approach!

Description

This is about money growing—if you do the work. Nothing in Smith's work is accidental or randomly placed. The gardening tools are just that: tools in a kit for productive hard work. You reap what you sow. You rake in profits—with a rake. You dig for buried treasure and for victory, too. (Smith's cards carried many Tarot readers through the last world war.)

So this is not easy money, but it is certainly money. Yet there is also a detail at the base of the card worth paying attention to: the Coin or Pentacle outside the gardener's sight line. There is something valuable right at this person's feet, but he is so dazed from the work or daydreaming so much about future wealth, he is missing the point. He cannot see the forest for the trees, perhaps.

There is also a warning—Neptune is in this card too, perhaps, as Neptune rules blindness and distorted vision. Eclipses also rule blind spots or things hidden in plain sight. The person here doesn't notice the money at his feet and so he is missing the point and missing profits. He is too busy dreaming about what might grow for him, as we've seen, or perhaps he is too busy working to stop and assess what is really there for him. There is a useful message in this card to look twice, three times, and look again—until you or someone else realizes what potential abundance or value is being missed.

Should this character just grab up the lot? Take the money and run? Common sense says, if the conditions are right (the climate), it is far better to put in some work, reap the rewards, and reinvest.

It is harvesttime or time to put back into the company, for example, and not time to grab and go or, even less productively, fantasize. Doing, not dreaming, is required here. Cultivating assets is tiring, and farmers do it, but you cannot lean on your spade forever and escape from the real world. Sooner or later, if you want to protect your assets or do a lot with a little, you have to get back to the hard work. This raises an important question about the value of financial reward versus the cost of effort and labor. What is the point of making money if you spend all your time making it and none enjoying it?

This is a card that reminds us that money does not grow on trees, but it does flourish over a longer period of time. So much depends on that alchemy between the right economic or business climate, the right professional setting, and the effort applied.

This card can appear when someone has worked hard and is waiting for the projects or tasks to pay off. It is very important that the Pentacle underfoot is recognized and put to good use.

I have seen this turn up when people have forgotten, or do not realize, that a best-selling book could be repurposed as an audiobook and made to earn more money. It has also turned up, oddly enough, when a client has been asking about how to lose weight. As only vegetables, nuts, and fruit grow on bushes, the answer was to lose meat, fish, and dairy! (The jury was out on sugar, which is also plant-based.)

Pamela Colman Smith & Seven of Pentacles

You can personalize this card to suit yourself, just as much as Smith's other cards lend themselves to highly individual interpretations. Analogies involving farmers ("Selling the farm") and gardening (rather like the song about pardons and rose gardens) and fruit ("The fruits of your labor") are all useful with this Tarot illustration. You can also add people, props, and other elements to this stage set using the technique of active imagination as surely Smith intended.

Astrology & Seven of Pentacles

This is a Taurus and Second House card because of the waiting game. Taurus the Bull moves slowly—his field is in the background. It's about what you plant, nurture, and cultivate that turns into financial reward. The potential here is vast, but it's really about being clever, aware, and careful. It's about thinking in the long term. This card is a challenge to anyone who is financially or business-minded but also raises questions about now or later as little can be accessed immediately or perhaps the whole lot—but at what cost to the glittering hypothetical wealth of "later"?

EIGHT OF PENTACLES

Quick Look

Working hard for the money—churning out gold records for EMI or Wedgwood china, a hit BBC series on DVD or a range of meat-free burgers. This is a card which might describe the creation of this Tarot deck itself, as Smith famously wrote in a letter to a friend that she was doing a big job for a small amount of money. Money does not grow on trees, but you can work for it and plan for the future, too. Note: there is a house or holiday home in the background.

Description

This is a symbol of Virgo (hard work) but also Taurus (working hard for the money). Money has to be earned by churning out products, goods, services, or projects. They are all the same, but there is pride in good craftsmanship here. This is the card of an artisan or craftsperson. Perhaps it is someone on a production line, but there is great beauty and value in each gold Pentacle.

The property in the background may be a fine hotel or a desirable home, but it is within reach—it can be purchased or leased—if the money is there. There is an old-fashioned message here about the Protestant work ethic and "no gain without pain" although there is not much that is genuinely painful on display—perhaps back problems, though, if time for regular breaks or exercise is not allocated. Smith's cards work together in stories as well as single-card readings, and there is a direct link between this card and the potential spinal problems you see in other illustrations. This is surely someone who needs a standing desk or at least a balanced lifestyle.

The tights are passionate red, the color of the sacral or sexual chakra. There is also a question here about the body and its needs, as opposed to "human as machine."

The major question here about money is about the value of the money being paid in terms of the property in the background—whatever that may be. So this is a card about price tags and assessments as well. It's not just about the health and fitness of the hardworking, industrious figure bent over the products or projects; it is also about weighing the value of pay-per-hour or payment-per-job against that of free time. One also needs to look at the cost of owning or renting a house, perhaps an apartment or premises, clearly shown in the distance. This may be geographical distance or the distant future.

Pamela Colman Smith & Eight of Pentacles

Smith was a freelance artist who lived and worked in a period of history when her illustrations were very much in demand. However, she was also obliged to almost become a one-woman production line to get them all done on budget and on deadline. She did, in fact, become a "machine" as a freelance illustrator, managing to create all seventy-eight Tarot cards, one of which you are looking at now. There is always something of her life and times in every card.

Astrology & Eight of Pentacles

This card reveals the natural trine between planets in Virgo in the Sixth House of workload and work-life balance and Taurus in the Second House of money earned. It is a down-to-earth picture showing the earth sign mentality—grounded in practical common sense and sheer grit.

Virgo and the Sixth House are associated with the body. Poor posture, which this figure has, leads to back problems, as I've mentioned, but perhaps you can see other issues with this very physical depiction of a hardworking hunched figure.

NINE OF PENTACLES
Quick Look

This is Lady Bountiful from *The Beaux' Stratagem* or MacKenzie Scott, one of the wealthiest woman in the world. There is abundance here, but also the need to find the right timing, as the snail suggests someone or something moving extremely slowly. The reverie is observable, but there is also a reminder to stay in touch with reality and remain grounded, alert, and practical. You need to be mindful when there is all of this at stake.

Description

This woman is abundant, with a rich vineyard, Coins at her fingertips, and a lush property in the background. Who or what is the falcon on her hand? This may have personal meaning for you.

As I've mentioned, pace and timing really matter in this situation. Just look again at the slow-moving snail Smith has popped into the foreground. This can be a slow market or slow-growth investment. The snail tells us so much. It may represent a person or organization you know. Patience is associated with the snail. Is there sloth or laziness there or just "slow and steady wins the race"? There may be snail mail or a snail's pace. The point is, the lucky lady can't see the snail or is ignoring it, yet God is in the details. This matters.

Everything in this woman's garden is lovely, but until she stops her reverie and comes back down to earth, nothing will grow. This is a symbol of the urgent need for investment, reinvestment, and thoughtful expansion and management. Without immediate care and attention, the grapes are going to wither on the vine. What a waste of a vintage year that could be. Grapes refer to Bacchus, the asteroid, in the astrology chart, too. Bacchus is a symbol of pure pleasure.

Here we have a falcon as well, in his hood, which can be interpreted as the eagle of Jupiter, as this is a bird that sees the big picture. There is a suggestion here that the lucky woman needs to rise above her current good fortune to also see the bigger picture, to expand and explore beyond her own immediate domestic or business bliss. If she were to view her garden from a higher perspective, she might gain a different vision of its potential. As the astrologer Patric Walker used to write, "Let distance lend enchantment to the view." There may be a person or organization playing the eagle or falcon here—a messenger, observer, or middle person or an agent or go-between. Perhaps technology is symbolized by the falcon, which could provide the broad scope of research and enquiry required to sweep the worldwide web for possibilities. Yet much depends on the lady.

This card turns up when someone enquires about the financial potential of a project and is told, "This is going to make a large amount of money." This card also reminds us that you have to grow grapes to make wine, but you also have to sell wine to make money—then keep replanting the grapes. It is not finite; you have to reinvest.

This card lends itself to active imagination. Perhaps a gardener or two could be brought in. The snail clearly needs a safe sanctuary among the leaves so there is no risk of being stepped on or swept up. Sometimes, over the years, I have seen chocolate in this card. I did in fact turn it up in a reading for a woman who had made her fortune from the chocolate industry.

You can imagine a financial advisor could be brought into the card, but there is also a great deal of monetary value placed on freedom, escapism, relaxation, bliss—nothing to do with bean counting—by this woman. She clearly finds escaping from the number crunching to be far more important than the calculator and profit margins.

There is also deep joy in her surroundings here, so this is literally "everything in the garden is lovely." It may be a symbol for rainforests or wilderness preserved from logging and deforestation, and that is quite priceless. Snails are obviously a delicacy in French restaurants, but it really depends on how you interpret the card; the meaning is much more likely to be slowness/delay/timing as an overlooked but important detail of the greater whole. A snail is part of a wider ecosystem, and its presence shows the larger health—and thus great value—of a thriving property or farm.

Astrology & Nine of Pentacles

The bird could be interpreted as an eagle, the bird of Jupiter. In astrology, Jupiter is associated with opportunities, growth, optimism, expansion, generosity, blessings, and largesse. There may be aspects to natal Jupiter when this card appears or transiting Jupiter may be making aspects, too. You might look to the Second House ruled by Taurus or the Eighth House, ruled by Scorpio. The grapes suggest Bacchus as a horoscope symbol—and Bacchus was the son of Jupiter.

TEN OF PENTACLES

Quick Look

It looks like family or friends' wealth—the merry-go-round of money. Three generations are shown here along with finance—perhaps actual cash value in a savings account or cash flow from a business—and abundant property. The old man, the couple, the dogs, and the child suggests a family, but a matriarch is missing.

Perhaps she is temporarily absent. The money obscures everything. There is an odd disconnect between these people. Yet there is money to be saved or made in abundance here.

Description

Family money—there is a legacy here. Property and money are there to be shared between three generations and two dogs. Like all Smith's illustrations of floating money, the cash to be saved or made is hypothetical. It is all potential until the moment comes or the people in the card notice what is there, reach for it, and claim it.

It may be useful to take each person in the card as a separate entity and read the face and body language, the attitude and mindset, individually. The child is grasping the dog. Is this a symbol of a greedy child, teenager, or millennial in the dynasty? Perhaps this youngest family member wants to make sure the family pets or livestock is included in the financial sharing-out—so, not grasping, but trying to be inclusive. It really depends on the family, assorted household, or group of family and friends you are dealing with. Think about the personalities and the issues.

The old man may be "my old man" or a symbol for Saturn, who is the bearded, white-haired god shown with a scythe or sickle. Saturn is associated with old age, defenses, protection, vulnerability, caution, and the realities of life beyond a certain age. We do not live forever. Wills and legacies must be made. Saturn by transit or transits to natal Saturn may be an issue for you or a key person in this reading.

The family members in this card are oblivious to the money—the couple in particular seems to be ignoring it or quite blind to it—but it is abundant: £10,000, £100,000, or more, in Smith's day. The digit 10 may be significant to you as part of an overall sum.

Is that a sales graph or a yacht repeated twice on the left-hand column? This is one of those highly detailed cards that speaks volumes once you peer into all the fine pen-and-ink work and personalize the message for yourself. The buildings in the card may speak to you.

The money goes around in this Tarot card as I noted earlier, even though the people concerned cannot see it. They could in fact reach for it and make it real at any time. Perhaps this is a legacy, and nobody wants to face it or deal with the reality of older family members eventually passing. I have seen this card turn up when the grandfather in a family has passed but his widow remains. She is "out of sight, out of mind" in a care home, but he remains as a spiritual presence, concerned about her while his son and daughter-in-law only have eyes for each other and the children are too busy playing with the dog.

This is a card symbolizing the old-age pension or retirement benefits, but also the last will and testament, as we have seen, or even dowry.

This card can (and should be) read in a personal way, unique to you, as it will reflect what is truthful for you or the people around you and nobody else. The situations I have outlined may not be the case at all for you—perhaps we are talking about a couple who are highly engaged together, because they have literally just become engaged, and the grandfather is part of a branch of an extended stepfamily.

Note, there is a fundamental emotional disconnect between the generations who seem set apart from each other. That could be changed. The relationships could become closer and literally richer, but it may take an understanding of the financial story here to make it happen. The finances are obscuring the family. That is quite deliberate. They need to be organized. The individuals in this household or clan should and could be closer.

There is another explanation for this card, and that is, the spirit world has "many mansions." It is possible for some of the characters in this card to have passed away already. That may explain why there are so many bubbles here. Nobody can see or hear anybody else. There is a huge amount in this card which is important because it pulls in three generations and two species.

Astrology & Ten of Pentacles

This is the Eighth House of Scorpio and/or Fourth House of Cancer card.

The dogs may be a symbol of Diana, the asteroid goddess who raises issues about marriage and children—and the rejection of the same in favor of freedom. There are many astrological associations, including Diana by transit or transits to natal Diana. Her dog was indeed the greyhound. Diana never married or had children so her money had to be left to . . . who or what? This card turned up once when I read for a dear friend who had not made a will, nor ever did. She had no dog, but liked them, and was certainly a Diana type. She had nieces and nephews but no offspring of her own, and the boyfriend she lived with departed.

PAGE OF PENTACLES
Quick Look

Ah, the lure of Coin, the Page appears besotted by it. "Money Changes Everything," like the song says, and also nodding to The Beatles, the birds and bees can have the free things. Isn't it amazing how even a little financial flush can entrance people? Or the dream of even a small profit? From something small, though, much larger results can grow.

Description

There is great reverence for money here, as if it held religious or spiritual meaning for the young man in the picture. I'm sure you've known men like this, who are enraptured at the thought of saving or making money. They may work in a bank, business, or charity. It may just be a phase a particular man is going through. It is important to note that a Page can be a girl, too. Or perhaps this is an aspect of your life and personality. The cash sings, though. From the Beatles to the Flying Lizards to Pink Floyd, money has always been music to our ears.

The question is, what is to be done with the cash? It could be used to tend to the field in the foreground, which surely holds good crops and possible future harvests. This is the Jupiter side of the card, and it may turn up when natal Jupiter is under transit or transiting Jupiter is aspecting the natal chart. From little acorns, mighty oaks do grow, eventually. And oak is a rich substance. Some priceless, listed buildings are made of the stuff. It is amazing to think it all began with a small acorn.

This field is a symbol of career or business building, or literally gardening. The family trees on the left are healthy and look quite inviting. Perhaps a relative can help. This is a solid grove. Not all the trees illustrated by Smith were this sturdy, but here have a family that has survived and thrived. It has weathered all sorts of storms and stands, firm and true, in the background. This may be the Page's clan or the relatives of someone important in the story—a family firm, perhaps.

The mountain as a symbol for Capricorn, the ambitious mountain goat, is also in the picture. Money can help the greatest journey to the top begin with a single step. Decisions, decisions! The foot turned left suggests an unconscious or unexpressed leaning toward the relatives or one's roots—the origins of the family tree on one or both sides. This suggests the Fourth House and Cancer just as the mountain suggests Capricorn.

Money is lovely, but it is not a religion and it is here to be used. This Coin, in such young or inexperienced hands—a Page is always a younger or less mature person!—should still be used in a sensible way, if it is to really go a long way. This is the young Richard Branson making cash from his student magazine, lost in daydreams—but he could so easily use it to start Virgin! In fact, that is what he did. You might also say it is the young Michael Eavis at Worthy Farm in 1970. Glastonbury Festival must surely have appeared in thousands of Tarot readings in that beautiful town over the years.

Astrology & Page of Pentacles

This is a classic Jupiter card, which appears when natal Jupiter is under transit or transiting Jupiter comes along. The actual Coin is of course Taurus or Scorpio—thus the Second House or Eighth House. This is one of those Tarot cards instantly mirroring the chart. This can really help with timing, as in "When should I invest?" or "When should I negotiate the deal?"

KNIGHT OF PENTACLES

Quick Look

There is business to be done, a negotiation to complete, money to be paid, or bills to be settled. An account book is among the Knight's possessions; you can see it on his saddle. Perhaps it's just a MacBook Air with accounting software. He's a closed shop, quite inaccessible—heavily armored—and a little intimidating. A mobile fortress of money-minded manhood. He could ride on. Yet there is so much potential around him in terms of cultivating, growing, planting, and reaping future dividends, profits, or rewards. You may be the Knight here or know someone who is playing that role.

Description

It is amazing what money or business can do to people. Perhaps because this man has been burned before, he has become quite defensive about what he has earned or all that he owns. This is a man on a tight budget—take it or leave it perhaps. It may also be a debt collector or rent collector, so he cannot afford to be nice.

This man is on a mission to pay or do a deal. You will have to negotiate. He is guarded, defended, perhaps hidden. He is probably not up to the task—he is too short for his horse. This may also be a brilliant symbol of the dwarf planet Pluto, ruler of Scorpio and thus the Eighth House of insurance, pensions, and retirement benefits, legacies and wills, banks and stock markets. The sense of tight control, a power-packed person, and lack of height are true of Pluto, too, who was a controlling god. Pluto literally rode a black horse. A dark horse is also something we might attach to this man and his character. He's a dark horse, alright. He doesn't give much away.

In the twenty-first century you would be looking at this man's car, as well as a horse, which may be too big or powerful for him. He's all about his exterior which conceals his interior.

He may be young or inexperienced. Yet you have to strike a bargain. Look at the fields which need maintenance. That costs money. What needs to be nurtured with cash? I mentioned the vast potential all around and doing a lot, eventually, with just a little. You can see this man sizing up the odds: calculating the costs and price, but also the possible rewards.

Money can make some people uptight or too heavily guarded, and that's a fact of life. Yet everybody needs to make a deal, and you do too. Is this card telling you to look at that aspect in yourself?

If this card turns up in connection with a relationship or marriage, it is very clear that man involved is not feeling remotely romantic. His priority is his side of the mortgage or rent and likely your own. A deal must be done—or not. This man could ride off into the sunset and not look back if terms are not sufficient. This card classically turns up when a man has a set price in his head but gives nothing away, hoping to get a bargain from you. A good literary agent or film and television agent will behave like this, of course. Bluffing is very much part of this man's process. A poker expression here (a poker face) also suggests an old-school gambler.

Astrology & Knight of Pentacles

In astrology, look to the zodiac signs Taurus and Scorpio and the Second House and Eighth House, as with all the Coins/Pentacles cards.

QUEEN OF PENTACLES

Quick Look

A woman in the most beautiful and abundant garden is sitting in a position of great contentment and happiness as she nurses a decent amount of money. This is one of Smith's rich women cards, and although there is none of the huge abundance of some other illustrations, there is more than enough here to make this Queen happy.

Description

Note the rabbit in the corner. Beatrix Potter was forty-three years old when Smith, also a gifted illustrator and artist, created her famous Tarot cards: what would later become known as the Smith-Waite. *The Tale of Peter Rabbit* had come out in 1902, and even today, thanks to the film, it makes money for the Potter estate.

The rabbit is also a reminder that you can have money, but perhaps you also need sex. (Rabbits can produce a litter a month, though, so be careful.) Playboy Bunnies, so sex again, are associated with rabbits. Being "at it like rabbits" is about frequent sex, and we can also link this creature with vegans as rabbit food is a nickname for a classic vegan diet. It really depends on where you locate the rabbit or bunny in your consciousness. It can be quite literal. I have known more than one well-off woman with a rabbit!

Sometimes this Queen turns up if there is a wealthy single woman enjoying her garden or the local wilderness, parkland, or woods—but sex won't go away. In fact, sex keeps nagging at her until she does something about it. The issue with "just sex" though (rabbit impulses) is that it's not really about making a good marriage or finding a soulmate and all the rest. It's just about the physical side of life. She may have to pay attention to that sooner or later—unless the rabbit hops away, of course. Yet what if it jumps into her lap? That rabbit holds a key to this entire card.

Some women I have read for identify with the rabbit as a sign of divorce, because they gain a settlement and the sex goes away down the rabbit hole. *Alice in Wonderland* sometimes holds meaning for people reading this card because of the White Rabbit and his pocket watch. Being late for a very important date can be another hint that one can be well-off financially—everything in the garden is literally lovely here—but also miss out on dating. For some people, the rabbit/bunny is "a bun in the oven" or pregnancy, and single women with enough money to have a child by themselves can pull this card. In fact, the bun in the oven is the next step after she has counted her pennies.

This is a contented woman gazing at her wealth, to be sure.

A baby's face peers out from the stone. Again, this is a hint about sex, in the background, in one's history (a pregnancy that did or did not happen) and nods to the rabbit. There are a curious amount of cherubic heads in the stonework in Smith's illustrations. In astrology this can be the asteroid Cupido, or Cupid, but over the years I have found women relate to the idea of historic pregnancies, abortions, or miscarriages. They are always unseen by the Queens in these cards—forgotten, suppressed, ignored. Adult children and their babyhood sometimes show up in this Queen's past. She's moved on, and she's interested in the money instead.

Romantic roses surround her, and she has, unusually, a bright green cloak: the color of conservation and the environment. What is this woman going to do with her money, why, and when? You will find more tiny details and clues personal to you here. She may work for Greenpeace. She may want to donate to the Wilderness Society. Nature is very close here, and she is at home in it.

Yet this money needs to be invested or put to good use. Something has to be done with it; one cannot sit gazing at it forever. And of course you cannot handle the cash and the rabbit at the same time. You will have to put the money in a safe place, spend it, or donate it, so you can be liberated enough to catch the rabbit before it hops away. Time is very much of the essence in the card if this woman does want to start a sexual relationship or even have a one-night stand.

Pamela Colman Smith & Queen of Pentacles

The Queen of Pentacles is one of many figures in Smith and Waite's Tarot who is pondering money, lost in daydreams, basking in the moment, which is financially secure.

Astrology & Queen of Pentacles

This is a Taurus and the Second House and/or Scorpio and the Eighth House card. Capricorn the Goat is hidden on her throne, so have a look at that. Perhaps her career (Capricorn) has made her secure.

KING OF PENTACLES

Quick Look

Very rich, quite inaccessible, and rather complicated, both in terms of his personality and his surroundings. You can see a man who is enamored of money but also trapped by it. In fact, he is encased in tangled investments, is he not? Or does the overgrowth all around him conceal something darker? This card may be an aspect of you, but more commonly, it is the very picture of a businessman, treasurer, or banker. Perhaps it is your ex-husband who you must go to for child support.

Description

Investments, shares, property, or cash has given this man a certain position. He is hard to get to, rather intimidating, and also surrounded by all that he has. It looks as if it has entombed him alive. There is not much freedom or space in this card.

Taurus is a fixed, earthy, stubborn sign which finds it hard to budge. This man—older than you or your age, if you are older!—is also stuck. The grapevines are keeping him trapped, and although Bacchus the asteroid of self-indulgence is suggested here (he rules grapes) and there is pleasure on his face at all that he possesses, the King is trapped by his wealth to the point where problems may begin. There is a fine property in the background, but he cannot see it. He is either ignoring it or has become quite blind to what is there. For this reason you might also look to an eclipse, which always delivers a blind spot, or Neptune.

He holds a gold spoon, magnifying glass, or mirror—depending on your point of view. Maybe, to reference The Who, a plastic spoon was there at birth. For some people this is a Welsh spoon. For others it is a cocaine spoon. For some, it is not a spoon at all, but a magnifying glass, and this man collects valuable stamps. What is this card telling you?

His garden needs weeding, and he needs to start moving.

This card must have turned up over and over again, between 1909 and the Wall Street Crash of 1929 as a warning to a particular sort of man to get a life, have a life, and start living—by spending, not hoarding. He needs to get rid of who/what has grown up all around him to the point where he is only living half a life because of it. There are tremendous questions here about self-worth tied to monetary worth but also the true value of lucrative shares if the market crashes and the apparently precious product or substance is worth less.

This man is ripe and ready to negotiate with the right person at the right time. He actually needs to, or he will become choked by those vines and slowly lose all power to move. This is where the card becomes most interesting because it is about power. It can be empowering to part with money over the right deal with the right person or organization.

With a little imagination you can see a rich businessman like this hiring Marie Kondo to "spark joy" in his life by getting rid of the clutter. The key to this card is to direct it like a stage set. Create a script, in particular. What needs to be said here? Communication is terribly important. Being heard, read, understood, and paid attention to—and swaying, persuading, and converting another—is central to its potential. Why on earth should this man give you some or all of his money? What is it about you and your life that is somehow shown by this King?

Pamela Colman Smith & King of Pentacles

We can see the Second House, Eighth House, and/or Fourth House of property and land here, which often turn up in Smith's Tarot cards, as so many people in the troubled twentieth century had questions about finance, security, and property. She created this picture in 1909, and twenty years later, the markets crashed.

Astrology & King of Pentacles

This is an established Taurus type, and the card is a symbol for this sign of the zodiac. (You can see the bulls hidden on the throne.) Look to Taurus and the Second House in this card. Neptune might also be a clue in the chart, natally or by transit, as it distorts vision. You can't see what is in front of your face in certain Neptune situations.

The Suit of Wands

The suit of Wands or Staves or Rods represents ideas, energy of movement, creativity, entrepreneurial spirit. What makes you tick both internally and externally. The element of Wands is fire, and thus represents the signs of Aries, Leo, and Sagittarius in the tradition of the Tarot cards.

ACE OF WANDS

Quick Look

This card depicts the arrival of a huge idea, brain wave, or flash of inspiration. There is so much potential here. It could be great on paper or online or in the media. It has to be brought down to earth and planted somewhere it can thrive. This could be the start of something big. However, its success is hypothetical. You have to make it happen. The white house or building in the distance may be the White House or just a symbol of the premises or home this idea requires.

Description

A big, bold, brilliant idea. It might be Obamacare or perhaps it is this Very British Tarot deck itself, created by Smith and Waite in 1909. Wands, Rods, or Staves are symbols of paper and the pulp from trees used to make books and newspapers, journals and posters over a century ago. In the Tarot they show possible websites or podcasts as much as they do likely song lyrics or computer programs. Also, they could be formulas for scientific breakthroughs.

However, unless this massive concept is brought down to earth and made real, it will remain forever a dream or fantasy. Yes, this could happen. It is *close* to becoming real, but unless you and/or others act and secure this somewhere it can grow, it may vanish with the next weather pattern. Live Aid and Band Aid had to be moved from the pub to the meeting room and then to the world via Wembley Stadium. This massive, groundbreaking charity enterprise began with Paula Yates and a message on her fridge door. Some things never happen at all without practical, down-to-earth thinking. She was a Taurus who inspired her then-partner, a Libra.

Time is of the essence here, because leaves are already falling from the branch. This thing has to be planted at the right time in the right place—and soon. It also has to be planted in the correct environment so now is the time for research, homework, and maybe asking around. Auditions for a secure future, you might call it.

Everything is in the uncertainty field of reality until you make a choice and make it real. Once you measure what is there, it becomes that. So measure your chances of transporting this from the realms of imagination or conjecture into a solid place for success. Like all branches, this can become a tree—perhaps literally the branch of a franchise—and then a mighty forest or acres of woodland in the years ahead.

You'd have to guess that the building in the background is the right place to park this. What is it and who inside can help here? In Smith's day this would have been the Rider publishing company which brought Waite's vision into being. Their deck found another home in the United States in the 1970s with U.S. Games Systems—not exactly the White House but "the right house" for the dream of a modern reproduction of Smith and Waite's old deck.

Pamela Colman Smith & Ace of Wands

Like all Smith's cloudy illustrations, this idea and its success are in the realm of a parallel possible universe. As we've seen, this Ace is also part of a typical quantum cloud, seen often in Smith's deck. She did not know it at the time, but she was channeling the new world of quantum uncertainty, proven by science in the double-slit experiment.

Astrology & Ace of Wands

The Ace of Wands in astrology can show up as Mercury, the planet of communication, as it is associated with big ideas on a computer or in a notebook.

TWO OF WANDS

Quick Look

Here we have one or two bright ideas—and they have to be exported or relocated to work. One or two budding concepts or plans are ready to be enacted. Perhaps these are qualifications. The person in the card is yearning or daydreaming for new pastures. This may be you or someone important to you. Yet speculating is not enough. There has to be action.

Description

Here we have Mercury the Messenger with only one leg to stand on. The first thing to say about this card is that it's not enough to have budding brain waves or concepts with potential or qualifications to show. You need to come back down to earth, ground and center yourself, and settle down before you can begin the quest. Where is the second leg here? Exactly. It's missing.

The time has come to take a big idea or qualification around the world. What is remarkable is the total lack of awareness of the second option, which is being ignored. It's all about "the one" idea and not both together or even both separately. This, along with the missing leg, brings out a couple of useful reminders. One is to ground oneself and the project or plan. The other is to wake up and see that this is a duet or double act, a pair. One is not more important than the other. This could even be two versions or two drafts of the same idea.

This is a big leap forward if it comes off. The roses on the left suggest the four compass points: east and west are red, and north and south are white. The one to two concepts could be planted much closer to home, if research and homework reveal other regions or countries are unsuitable. There is only one way to find out. The time has come to check and check again, to ask, to read widely and really size up one's chances.

Just look at the lush pasture in the foreground! Does this idea really have to travel all the way across the planet? It's time to think locally as well as globally. But don't take too long. Things wither and die unless they are planted on fertile ground, nurtured, and nourished. This will not last forever without a great deal of rapid work and practical hands-on knowledge-gathering.

A useful thing to do now is a yoga pose that centers your base chakra on the floor or ground. Walking barefoot on the grass can also work. So can any meditation which balances your base chakra. This card can show someone who is living from their throat, third eye, and crown chakras with no connection to the lower chakras, which pull us back down to Mother Earth.

So, along with the research about location, location, location, you also need to make sure you have that other leg to stand on. This also means support, credentials, qualifications, backup. You need a firm base if you are going to convince and persuade others to support you. Otherwise all you really have is the idea. This is rather like angel investors wanting to know who you are as well as what the big idea is.

Astrology & Two of Wands

This transit in your chart is likely of the Third and/or Ninth House, or there may be aspects to natal Mercury from the slow-moving outer planets or the Nodes. We have a clear symbol of Mercury Retrograde, perhaps, or Retroshadow/Retroshade. Maybe it is just Mercury blocked by other planets. This is not inevitably the case with this card, but it is very common. We also find Mercury under transit in your natal chart as he is the planet of ideas, messages, the worldwide web, export, relocation, travel, brain waves, and so on.

THREE OF WANDS

Quick Look

The potential here is vast, and the concepts, projects, ideas and/or qualifications are promising. Clearly all of this—and perhaps you—belongs in a different and more suitable location indicating overseas opportunities. It's like a great song: it is a hit in its home country but might do better as a sports anthem in a foreign city. Pace and timing make the difference as there is a real need to sort out paralysis versus haste.

Research, homework, knowledge-gathering, and thoughtful questioning can be the key. One cannot hang around forever, though. This will not last as it should or thrive as it could without proper action.

Description

There is a strange mixture of haste and paralysis here, as the person with the three ideas, plans, projects, or qualifications suggested by the three Wands is stuck fast on the cliff, looking out to sea, but has racing car checks on their cloak. Perhaps it is through lack of experience—the shawl is green.

I have often seen this card in readings on my website when the person concerned has a ton of good ideas, a lot of nervous energy, some trepidation about losing an opportunity, but also anxiety about going out there and making something happen. You often get a red light, yellow light, green light rapid rotation with this card. It is fixed by active imagination. Perhaps other people need to come into the scene. Maybe the position needs to be adjusted—the stance and attitude of the key person. What can be done with the actual three Wands, which are symbols of something on paper or on the computer?

With three we can get three drafts of the same script, three competing ideas, or a trio of compatible products. Or we can get two versions of the same concept and a third outlying idea. All should be taken as one, as the whole. It's all part of a mixed bag, but don't forget or neglect one or two to mono-task. Try to get the whole lot in front of you for assessment.

This card is about mixed feelings regarding the export of ideas and the distant shores of the worldwide web. That's the Grand Prix checks you can see (faster, faster, break the record), but note the rather stuck, planted, rooted nature of the pose. They want to go but don't not want to go!

Nothing can grow in the current location. There may be much better odds somewhere else. There may even be a race on or some kind of gold rush as the three ships in the foreground are speeding to a distant location. This may be about the need to compete and catch up but also having a fear of losing or coming last. You see this card when there is a competition for, say, cryptocurrency or an attempt at a vaccine for a virus.

There are any number of reasons for not joining the race or getting your feet wet: fear of failure, fear of success. A bit of analysis goes a long way with this card. Nobody doubts the potential of the idea or product, but the issue is the location, the timing, the competition, the personality of you/the key person.

But note, if the person in question does not make up their mind, things may never grow.

Astrology & Three of Wands

The short trip is Gemini; the longer journey is Sagittarius. The Third House is the hop to another city or region; the Ninth House is the foreign expedition. These can show up in the chart. You may also get Saturn by transit or transits to natal Saturn as this is a symbol of delay, fear, and sometimes self-sabotage in the chart.

FOUR OF WANDS

Quick Look

Here we see a celebration involving family, friends, or an important circle of people, and the gateway is a pair of sturdy plans or two really good ideas. A film director and producer can show up in this card as the entrance to an Oscar celebration. It can also be a long-distance relationship between two frequent correspondents or Zoom lovers whose story ends with a wedding. Wands show what is on a computer or on paper. There may be four people or plans as the "gate."

Description

This card is possibly about the Fourth House (family and shared households), and the Fourth House also rules housewarmings, homecomings, and house parties. The Wands/Staves/Rods in Tarot are generally about the Third House and Ninth House, too: so brain waves and courses. The key is the fact that one cannot enter the celebrations without going through the paperwork, the agreement, the plan, the notion, the degree, and so on.

This is about two sides of the same family or two branches of the same social circle coming together. This is likely a party, wedding, or other celebration, and as I've said, it can be the nuptials after a long-distance relationship conducted on Zoom and by email.

Abundance is here, and there is lots to share and enjoy. If you were a soulless creature, you would say this is a good opportunity for networking but far more likely it's the kind of occasion across one day, or maybe an entire week or two if it's a holiday, when people who are coming from the same or similar positions—shared ideas, thoughts, plans, projects—help each other out.

The dance in the background could be the Hokey Cokey or Nutbush City Limits, but the welcome mat is out. You occasionally see this card for political party conferences or corporate bonding weekends. This can be the dual efforts of two branches of one company involving two to four people which results in a gathering at the end. The Wands look like telegraph poles connecting cables, and so there is a sense here of a strong telephone presence and frequent, good communication.

The garlands of flowers suggest abundance, a happy atmosphere, and all that thrives and takes off. This is a lovely image of strong prospects, good feelings, and something to enjoy at the end. A transition is indicated. You pass through and across to get to the other side. The property or premises in the background may also be significant here. You can see why this card shows up when a house is being purchased by two parties and their agents, with the housewarming party once it's all settled.

Astrology & Four of Wands

The Fourth House (housewarmings, homecomings, and parties) is associated with Cancer. Of course, it may also be about the Tenth House and its ruler Capricorn, because the Wands are likely plans, concepts, or qualifications, which will be the gateway to achievement and good times.

FIVE OF WANDS

Quick Look

This appears to be a group in conflict. Who is in charge here? Nobody. This is the Amish raising a barn on a bad day or a group of builders arguing over which way is north. However, the potential is there for something sturdy, strong, and impressive which would reflect the different personalities and their tastes and preferences in a satisfying whole. Unfortunately nobody is doing anything productive while everyone is at cross-purposes. The solution is for people to pair off and cooperate and then at least two of the pairs to meet in the middle. Person number five or interested party number five is then the challenge, but it can all be overcome.

Description

This is the band about to split because of creative differences. It reminds one of every fractured rock group in history, from the Beatles to Fleetwood Mac. It is any group, actually, because all groups have to deal with the central problem of who will be the leader/the star (look at the shouty person on the left) and who is so wildly different from everybody else that they are on the outer rim (the person in the blue patterned tunic).

If you read the history of the Beatles, you find creativity and brilliance born from individual eccentricity and difference. The fifth Beatle was George Martin. At other times the fifth Beatle was Yoko Ono or a passing presence like Magic Alex. It is only when the four or five found common ground that they were able to raise an album. And those albums reflect what was going on at the time: productive tension.

"You Never Give Me Your Money," "Nowhere Man," and "The Two of Us" all tell the story of the Fab Four, but within a group of four plus one, you can get pairs and solo acts. It's all rather hard to manage.

This is why bands *have* managers, and it is amazing how often this card comes up with musicians and their tour or business manager. Or, in Spinal Tap style, you may find yourself with the odd creative girlfriend or dodgy A&R man to deal with. There is something funny about this card.

The ideas, theories, concepts, or plans are all similar. That's the giddy joke of this card. The actual notions or brain waves are virtually the same. The Wands look so much alike. Everyone wants to be a musician. Everyone wants to be a politician. Everyone wants to make a film. The individual personalities are really different, but what they are talking about or putting on paper or online is very similar and so the potential is there for unity.

Nothing can be built until people set their differences aside along with their narcissism or anger and cooperate.

Together these people will raise a barn or make a great album. Like they are now, they are a shambles, and those ideas are not going to last long. They need to be planted. The potential is vast here, but the problems are real. Without a secure place for what is on paper or online, nothing will ever grow and the whole thing will fall over sideways. This is the Troggs in the studio on a famous bootleg tape or the state of Australian politics for quite a few years, with leadership spills disrupting both the main parties. A great deal comes down to communication of the tactful but truthful sort. Someone here looks like they want to be loudest, up-front, and central. Is that really the case, though? Understanding the group dynamic can help.

Pamela Colman Smith & Five of Wands

Looking at the card, you can't help but think that perhaps Smith saw the humor in the frankly bonkers behavior of some members of the Golden Dawn, the magical secret society she belonged to with Waite, her cocreator in the Smith-Waite Tarot.

Astrology & Five of Wands

We have someone rather angry or overheated in red in the center. There is real potential for a split here. This is Mars the red planet if you are looking to the astrological chart, and of course the group itself is the Eleventh House ruled by Aquarius. Some or all of this may show up in the transits, so at least you can tell when the end point is and the potential for resolution. Look to Mercury in the chart, too, as Mercury rules communication, listening skills, and hearing as well as talking or shouting. Negotiation is key!

SIX OF WANDS

Quick Look

This is the card which has people punching the air and yelling "yes!" when they are asking about an election, a job interview, a book auction, and any other situation where success is not assured. The winner or leader has the right attitude—perhaps confidence is the secret to success. The faces in the crowd are important. This is quite clearly a group effort or one has a large following, but as always with a big win, there is gossip, questioning, envy, and sometimes outright criticism.

Description

Victory, success, and a big win on the board—this card delivers exactly what it shows. The Romans used to weave wreaths for triumphant leaders. Here we have a winning idea—actually, a winning project, plan, or argument which is composed of many similar ideas, many voices on the same hymn sheet. You can see two people in the army or team on the left who must have been involved or who have either backed the plan or perhaps not—I will leave it to you to judge the expressions. There is certainly a star here, as there always is when one wins the war or an election. Yet nothing happens because of a single person. And the crowd or the masses must be considered.

The leader or hero is front and center. The horse looks rather smug and coy, and this may represent a person or vehicle for the victor. This is the procession or inauguration, the ticker-tape parade or the grand celebration. Now what? All those ideas, projects, concepts, plans, and voices can now be put to good use. Great leaders or victors are not above the others. They may be "higher than" and in an elevated position for a time, riding high and all the rest, but sooner or later they have to realize that every single face in the crowd matters.

Don't rest on your laurels is the message here. The acorn shapes on the horse's bridle also suggest the saying, "From little acorns come mighty oaks." This is very much a card to look for if there is a Jupiter transit coming up, or transits to natal Jupiter, as it shows where and when the big finish might come from. Jupiter is forever associated with the grand finale and quite often with the massive relief and release that comes after a long period of not knowing. It is really important to identify who the figure on horseback is, though. Look for clues.

Pamela Colman Smith & Six of Wands

Jupiter also rules Sagittarius the Archer, and of course here we have a man on horseback, looking rather Sagittarian. Or it may be a woman; Smith worked with Shakespearean actors and their friends and colleagues, where gender was fluid to say the least.

Astrology & Six of Wands

Jupiter is in this picture because he rules oak leaves and oaks. This is an opportunity waiting to happen, which Jupiter is also associated with. Natally or by transit Jupiter may now be central to the chart. This card feels big. Jupiter rules whatever is huge, like a really thundering landslide, such as the one garnered by President Joe Biden and Vice President Kamala Harris in 2020.

SEVEN OF WANDS

Quick Look

If you are going to go in to bat for your ideas, opinions, plans, or cause, then you need to be grounded. Unless you are soundly on terra firma, you are not in a particularly strong or stable position when it comes to defending yourself against others or their concepts or thoughts. There is one against the many here. The irony is the actual views are rather similar, or the projects or concepts are almost identical. You have to wonder why people are at odds with each other. The solution is for the ungrounded person (yourself?) to stabilize, center, focus, find a solid position, and perhaps move physically so that some kind of unity can be achieved. And there is potential for unity here.

Description

This person is not grounded and practically being pulled apart, with one foot pointing east and the other west. There's nothing settled about this position: it's quite precarious and geographically split or intellectually/emotionally divided.

This card can appear if someone does not know where they stand or there is no fixed address or there are two business or work centers on opposite sides of the country or town or world. It's divisive. And, without a center to work from, how can any opinion, plan, or concept ever hope to get off the ground, much less hold its own against the ideas of the wider group? The irony is that the words or ideas are all pretty much the same, as already mentioned.

You can see the remedy here. The person doing battle with others' points of view needs to come back down to earth, stop reacting or imagining, and actually put faces to names and names to faces—to opinions. This is a classic internet fight card. You have a face on your X feed, but "the many" are anonymous, call themselves numbers, and use cartoon heads!

This situation is untenable, and depending on the state of mind of the person being pulled in two, it can be quite difficult and even risky. My issue with this card is the land under their feet. What happens if there is an earthquake? Not literally, perhaps, but symbolically? A leadership dispute can split the ground beneath your feet, so if you don't have a leg to stand on and do not have your feet firmly on the ground, you can fall into the abyss or over the edge. You can slip between the cracks.

This card sometimes turns up when a person has become distracted by the debate—which can be on social media as well as in the real world—and forgotten it is just about words. This card is literally about what is on paper, in the newspapers (particularly the disgraceful, unethical kind), or online. And the internet, as we know, can be a real quagmire. There is nothing physically going on here. And sticks and stones can impact bones, but words can never hurt you—unless you let them.

This person at the center of this war of words or intellectual opposition does not realize that the lack of stability or agreement stems partly from their own position, which is temporary, unstable, and divided between two places or two camps. The answer often lies in fixing oneself and one's situation. From there, negotiation and agreement are possible.

This can be a man coming back into the fold, as David Beckham did in soccer, despite being persona non grata for a time. This card tells us that rifts can close, balance can be achieved, unity can be found, harmony can be restored. It takes a lot of work on both sides, but mostly on the part of the person who is so divided and also quite divisive.

Pamela Colman Smith & Seven of Wands

The Golden Dawn, Smith's magical society, was similarly split down the middle, so it must often have felt like "one against the many" even though all the ideas were similarly based around astrology, the Tarot, and so on.

Astrology & Seven of Wands

There may be a lack of earth signs in the chart (Taurus, Virgo, and/or Capricorn). This is what happens when someone is living in their head without good grounding. (Air signs Gemini, Libra, and Aquarius live in a world of theories and ideas.) Look for those signs being prominent in your chart or that of the person who is at the heart of this conflict.

EIGHT OF WANDS

Quick Look

This is touch-and-go. Split-second timing is required to stop this group falling in a heap or to divert it so that it lands pretty much in unison in a good place with the potential for new construction. Move fast. The group, club, team, or circle may be purely social (X) or it may have a purpose (the Olympics). Are you an optimist about these people—of which you may be one—or a pessimist? Is everyone falling upward, ready to land together and make a start, or falling down, headed for the end or something near the end?

Description

Will everything fall in a heap or are we looking at this card the wrong way? Perhaps these Wands are floating upward and will be caught by their creators or other innovators and inventors to be built into something practical. No barn was ever raised, nor holiday log cabin built, without construction. Bits and pieces are not useful, and neither is a scattering or randomness about direction. The phrase *picking up the pieces* after a messy descent by a group, household, band, political party, and so on can refer to the situation suggested by this card.

Ideas, theories, and thoughts are of the air and in the air until they are brought down to earth. There is a lot of space between these Wands. They are not particularly close or intimate. This card suggests the element of air in astrology, and in particular Aquarius and groups and communities. A light, bright, breezy, cool, and easy space defines air sign connections. Yet this lot are too disparate—so apart, so gappy, that nothing and nobody is united.

Unless something is done to plant and nurture these Wands, nothing can grow or progress. At some point everything must be brought together in a united way. If you are one of the idea-makers, plan-makers, or opinion-makers in this group, you need to talk swiftly and get at least one person on your side so the two of you can pull the rest together. I don't think you can do it alone—or at least it would take a Herculean effort. Find one or two allies then do it together.

There is an urgency to the Eight of Wands. One has to act swiftly, securing agreement between all those people with all their opinions or projects so that instead of falling to pieces, they "fall up together" and unite in flight to explore the possibilities of a new environment to ground their notions and nurture their plans. Someone needs to research the lay of the land rapidly. Where is it safe to descend? This is so much like the last world war and the RAF who depended heavily on their navigators on the ground. Communication was absolutely essential, and thus radio operators, too. Today we would talk about the internet or phones. The web in particular is so rapid that it surely has to be your first resource in finding the right place to land and also in getting everyone together on a common plan and navigation.

This card often turns up when a group project is in danger of going nowhere fast, which would be a shame, as like all Wands, these budding new trees are for the future. Trees can be used for anything at all, from a sailing ship to fine woodworking. They are a symbol of potential growth for the ideas on paper or online.

There can be something mighty built here with a bit of luck and effort. What is most impressive of all, though, should success come, is the testament to your staying power and willpower and that of others involved.

Astrology & Eight of Wands

This is an Eleventh House or Aquarius card as it shows a group of ideas, a community of plans, a collection of concepts. Look to transits of the Eleventh House or transiting Uranus, which rules Aquarius, or just a fleeting stellium in Aquarius, the sign of the water bearer. An aquarius in Rome was the worker who supplied the Roman baths with water. They gave the community or group what it needed. This sign inevitably shows up with this card. Other signs to look at would be Libra and Gemini which share the correspondence to air.

NINE OF WANDS

Quick Look

An aggrieved person who has a headache from the stress of group opinion outside or against them is separated, alone, and on the fringe. There is healing to be done here. There may even be real injury. This is Winston Churchill during the Wilderness Years. There is potential for everyone to come back together again or for cooperation and recovery, but it will take hard work, communication, and time passing.

Description

A wounded, suspicious, and annoyed (perhaps angry) man holds his Wand (a symbol of communication) tightly to himself. Rods, Wands, or Staves show what is on paper or online—words, sometimes images. This is a card of rejection, because he has rejected them or they have rejected him.

I think we can all relate to this man with the headache. Haven't we all been there with a group of people? This can be peer pressure or mob rule. It can also be the disenfranchised position of someone with former friends or allies, who finds themself in disagreement with the others. This card turned up repeatedly during the Brexit civil war 2016 to 2020, and in the same period, the Trump resistance. You can see why my readers frequently saw it: these were times when people really did feel as if they were on the outside and everybody else was against them.

This man has been hurt. He looks hurt. His head hurts—and the head is where the ideas begin and opinions are formed.

Ironically the others in the group, or community, have remarkably similar thoughts to him. All these Wands around him are rather similar. Wands are tree branches, symbols of paper mills, which in Smith's day produced newspapers, posters and journals, books and scripts. What is interesting about this card, compared to others in the same suit, is that it shows physical outcomes of cerebral differences. In so many other cards nothing really affects people in a material way; it is all just ideas or words or views. Here, we have someone who is bandaged.

This brings to mind phrases like *injured feelings, head not heart, losing my mind*, and the rest. I am sure something will come to mind for you—and that in itself is a phrase you might use with this card: *mind over matter*. Everything depends on this person putting strong emotions and wounds to one side and focusing on the ideas. Collectively those ideas could unite everybody and together, these people could build something good.

As already mentioned, there is a tremendous need for healing and recovery time here. You can see the pain and also the frustration on the main character's face. This may be you or another you recognize immediately. Resentment grows and festers. People quit the scene or split completely, or they can hang around for years, feeling worse as time goes on.

Someone has to speak up and speak out—and reach out—from the group. Then at least some kind of negotiation or peace agreement can be reached, maybe even a reconciliation. This card speaks of Winston Churchill at odds with those in power in Great Britain or James Dean in *Rebel Without a Cause*. The bruised outsider, cruising for an intellectual bruising, is an archetype seen here quite clearly. Yet imagine what an impact there would be should this person go back into the fold. And imagine how much more productive each individual (represented by an idea) would be, if they were to learn from this other person.

What is interesting is that this card is so redolent of the internet itself. You have a face, or the protagonist has a face, but everyone else is faceless. These are just words. These are just a row of laptop computers filed sideways or a stack of pamphlets.

Astrology & Nine of Wands

Polarized situations are often shown by polar opposites, so in astrology this is any opposition by transit or natal opposition under transit. A Full Moon, with the Sun opposite the Moon, can often bring push to shove in such a situation. Look for Mercury-Mars patterns with this card, too. Mars-Mercury translates as a "war of words." The planet Uranus is a symbol of rejection so you might look for him natally or by transit. Aries rules the head, brain, and in fact the ram's charge: head down, horns forward. You might look to Aries and perhaps Mars, which rules Aries, and the First House of appearances and reputation as another option.

TEN OF WANDS

Quick Look

Something has to give. Instead of just stumbling forward with an overload of emails, books, projects, ideas, Zoom meetings, telephone messages, exams, blogs, articles, and the rest, stop and off-load. Get rid, perhaps. Delegate, if you can. Reschedule the timing, if possible. The goal here is obviously the house, apartment, or holiday home in the distance—paying the rent, saving up for renovations, or funding a vacation. What is the point, though, if getting there is so punishing for mind, body, and spirit? Pause and plan.

Description

This is one of Smith's easiest cards to understand and interpret. It's full-on overload! Stop and delegate, reschedule, or jettison what is there, or there will be a physical toll, as the human body is not a machine, robot, or computer. There may even be back issues. Too many projects, ideas, emails, websites, social media messages, too much to carry—the person here is stumbling blindly forward toward what they assume is the goal.

This may be a house or apartment to be purchased or paid off one day or to be renovated. Perhaps it's a hotel or holiday home. You have to wonder what the point is, though, when the journey is so difficult. Ask yourself: *Is the destination worth the struggle?*

This card is about the need to delegate or ditch and quite urgently so. How on earth did things even get this far? Talk about ignoring your better instincts or even your body. Nothing is going to work if the person just ends up stopping halfway or dropping everything. It's time to pause and look for a strategy, to ask for help, perhaps, or off-load. This clearly is someone overworking and risking their physical health. This is backbreaking burden, and of course the back is always the first to suffer when somebody is overloaded. Apart from anything else, if you sit hunched in a chair over a computer all day, your spine will not thank you. The solution here, as we have seen, is to stop, rest up, review, rethink, ditch, delegate, and strategize.

When the internet was first launched, this card would turn up a lot for clients shouldering the new burden of too many emails and not enough hours in the day. You also see it when a person is psychologically and emotionally overloaded with too many mental or spiritual burdens. This is the prime minister with a new baby, a new term, and one or more crises to load on their back. It is also the student who has taken on a part-time job, a relationship, exams, and God knows what else.

You tend to find people with difficult aspects or transits in their Sixth House drawing this card. Maybe you are one of them, but you know the solution. There are some big decisions to be made here about weighing the value of the house, holiday home, or apartment against the price tag you need to fix on actually having a life before you reach your goal.

Pamela Colman Smith & Ten of Wands

This card can be stage-managed like all Smith's cards. What does it tell you to do? Bring in people to help. Perhaps set up a camper or tent so this person can take a break for the weekend. Does one really need to throw so much mud at a wall in order to get some of it to stick? Maybe that approach is quite wrong, and now is the time to revise it.

Astrology & Ten of Wands

This is a Sixth House and Virgo card (life-work balance), but also a Tenth House and Capricorn card (ambition). It is also a Fourth House card of Cancer (the house or apartment, or premises, up ahead).

PAGE OF WANDS

Quick Look

The idea, concept, creation, qualification, or plan has wonderful, budding potential. Nothing will happen to help it thrive, or even just survive, unless it is planted in the right place at the right time and nurtured to fruition, though. Timing is everything, and a bit of research and homework is required, along with perhaps an approach to some helping hands. Why is everything held up here? What is inside this person's mind, that they are stalling, stuck, or operating at a snail's pace? Fear of success or fear of failure? Distracted narcissism? Is the Page so enamored by his idea that he's forgetting to act?

Description

This younger man is lost in his own self-admiration, or perhaps it's just the beauty of a good idea—not a great idea; a good idea—which entrances him. If it were great, then it would be flowering, blossoming, and blooming; it's just good. It has potential greatness in it, but only time will tell. It's rather like planting a gum tree in Australia. You just never know, and it really depends where it goes, when it goes in, and how you manage it.

If he doesn't get a move on and plant this concept, theory, or project on fertile ground, it will die. He is in the wrong place for it to grow; that's for sure. He stands on sandy ground, and nothing will thrive, flourish, and prosper until he stops daydreaming and starts moving in the direction of the right town, city, region, or country. He needs to research and find out rather than just imagine, or even worse, get distracted by his simply marvelous on-screen plan to the point that he forgets the real world exists as well.

He has a feather in his cap. What is it for? We talk about this when there is some achievement, qualification, or award to wear proudly.

This fellow may be you or someone else you know. It may be a younger student, for example, or a student of life who is below you in years. If so, you may be the one to lead the way—to show why it's not enough to be in love with an idea or a talent. It has to be planted somewhere it can actually succeed.

It is really clear that this Wand—shown as a branch with a few sprigs of growth—will not thrive unless something is done quickly in terms of bringing other people into the card, and thus the situation. It may dry up and fade to nothing in that arid environment unless you work the card with your active imagination and bring in allies, friends, colleagues, helpers.

Movement is required most of all because those are not hospitable conditions. Something or someone around the situation is dry. A dry personality, perhaps? Or is it just barren, arid conditions and a hostile environment for anything to grow? This Page needs to take this somewhere else fast.

Astrology & Page of Wands

Pyramids suggest trines (a trine is in the birth chart or emerging), and that will help. Sometimes trines involving Neptune can result in too much ease or flow, though. One goes with the flow so much that nothing at all gets done. There is no action, no effort.

KNIGHT OF WANDS

Quick Look

This Knight has a blazing, brilliant idea. It's hot: this project, concept, brain wave, or qualification. It has heat, as they say in Hollywood. Unfortunately he cannot see where he is going. Look at his eyes, and you will notice he is unfocused. He is also on a horse with a lack of focused vision. Thus, his vehicle is not what it could be. Quite clearly, the notion, the plan, or the letters after his name need to be taken somewhere hospitable and accommodating. The environment of the moment is quite wrong. A strategy is needed.

Description

This is all about preparation, focus, clarity, vision, and direction. Navigation and thought are required. This man on a mission cannot see properly—look at the eyes and you will find they are a little milky. God knows there is a lot to admire here, with all the heat and blazing brilliance. Yet, he could still fall off. What he is carrying could be dropped or get lost on the way. His vehicle may not carry him.

For example, a Hollywood film may be the vehicle for a song, but if the songwriter is on drugs and does not know what he is doing, the project could go sideways. That is extreme, but it has happened with this card.

Perhaps contact lenses or glasses need to be found, or this may be a metaphor for someone who is not seeing straight. I have worked in magazine and book publishing long enough to meet a few characters like this, who are impressive, passionate, on their way, and all the rest, but on closer inspection you realize they have really confused vision. And crucially, what/who they are "riding on" to take them "somewhere" (they don't know where) is equally unfocused. So this can be a publisher who is lacking direction, for example, with an author who has also not taken the time to have a good long self-talk in the mirror.

This is actually part of the solution. Both what/who this idea is riding on and the person in question need to talk to themselves or write things down honestly in a journal or have a cracking meditation session. Quite honestly, sitting down with the Tarot and a notebook to really analyze the project, concept, qualification, plan, or brain wave—and oneself—could save a great deal of time and trouble and even rescue a film, book, website, invention, or application.

The big idea, message, or campaign is firmly in hand. But it still must be planted in the right place (the desert sands of Egypt are not useful), or it will wither on the vine, like so many of Smith's Wands showing budding leaves. Phrases like *branching out* and *flowering, bursting open*, and *seeding* and *seed money* are appropriate with this card.

So many of the Wands cards are about "from little acorns, mighty oaks do grow." And here we have an acorn which has turned into what might become an oak tree one day, if only it could be planted, nurtured, and carefully tended. Acorns and oaks are ruled by Jupiter, and of course Sagittarius (the marksman on the horse) is ruled by Jupiter, too. The luck is with this person, as the image is impressive, the energy and drive are there, and the possible success really is hypothetically possible. It's all down to approach.

You have to admire the sheer chutzpah of the person on the mission, but it's not enough to be bold, daring, energetic, and charismatic. You have to do the work. You do see this card when Jupiter is around as everything is really big picture and wow factor, but Jupiter by transit and natally can also be a big fizzer. Big start and small finish are not what this rather magnificent human being deserves. And it may be you.

Astrology & Knight of Wands

The horse is a symbol of Sagittarius, and the Knight may be a symbol for Chiron. Sagittarius also suits the idea of exploring foreign lands. Chiron was of course a music teacher, and the Knight is holding a baton. The fire signs Aries and Leo are hinted at here along with Sagittarius, thanks to the flaming orange and gold coloring. There's a fair bit of Sagittarius/Jupiter about this card—the acorns and the horse as described above. Also look for Neptune by transit or transits to natal Neptune.

QUEEN OF WANDS

Quick Look

Here is a leader, teacher, mother, aunt, grandmother, godmother, mentor, captain, head prefect, CEO, professor, and so on. The younger generation, the heirs to her intellectual throne, are not pictured, but their presence is suggested in this card. The idea, concept, plan, or qualification is there, but it must be planted and nurtured. Then wonders prevail.

Description

This is a Leo card and so we can use Chanel as our model for this Queen, as she was a Leo. Here we have a woman who has never had children herself, but who leads with her designs and business concepts held firmly in her hand like a magic wand to pass on to one young generation after another. You could say Karl Lagerfeld was the heir to Chanel's throne.

You could look for Sun transits and transits to the Sun with this card but also the Fifth House, as Leo women are Queens to a younger court, no matter if you're talking the Duchess of Sussex, the Queen Mother, or Princess Margaret. This is really Meghan with her hair up, isn't it, with her son (the sunflower/son flower) blooming in her world and the latest charity mission or Netflix project grasped in her fingers.

There is pride here in the face. Leo is a sign associated with pride, because lions also move in a pride. The attitude is regal, confident, expectant, entitled.

The Wand is the online media or paper idea, the project, plan, or qualification. Our Queen has already done very well with one: that is the sturdy sunflower in her right hand. She'll need a collaborator (a right-hand man?) or assistant, colleague, or staff to create the next success. Queens need staff. They need courtiers and allies. Using active imagination, bring into the card the extra people the Queen needs to make this next implantation a success for everybody.

Note the tiny ginger cat brooch that holds the cloak together. Leo, of course, rules all kinds of felines and this is another of Smith's tiny hints. The black cat itself will be an intensely personal symbol for you. Make it your own or find out what it means to you.

Pamela Colman Smith & Queen of Wands

This was very likely one of Smith's friends, Edie, in the summer of 1909 at Smallhythe, in Kent. The black cat was probably in the household, too.

Smith was instructed to illustrate leopards here, for this card, following old occult ideas about the Queen of Staves but instead rather cheekily came up with a black cat—Snuffles, according to some authors—who lived at Smallhythe, where she created her cards in the stunning Kent countryside, in 1909.

This card is a good example of just how much of Smith there was in the cards and just how little there sometimes was of Waite, wonderful though he was. After all, without him this Very British Tarot would never have seen the light of day.

Astrology & Queen of Wands

This is a Leo card, with lions flanking the throne and appearing on the backdrop. Sunflowers ruled by the Sun are also Leo's blooms, as this sign is also solar-ruled, and there is a lot of solar power in this card symbolically speaking. The ramrod posture of Leo so often described by astrologers is here. The Queen holds her head high. Dignity is in the posture and body language. Noblesse oblige. The bob is something Chanel sported, and she was a Leo with lions on her tombstone. I doubt very much Smith knew about Gabrielle in the summer of 1909 but this card is also her, to the life. Maybe Chanel, who used the Lenormand Oracle cards, knew this deck too and was inspired by it.

This is a strong, clever woman with Leo in her chart, or going through a Leo transit.

KING OF WANDS

Quick Look

He has an idea, project, website, concept, qualification, or brain wave. As a King, he is already top at his game, his own boss, or a leading figure—head of the family or CEO in a company. The issue is what to do with what is so vast in potential. It needs to be planted and nurtured, or it will wither on the vine or just fall apart. Time is of the essence. He either has to get moving and DIY or delegate to a person who can help him. His Queen? Where is she, because she's not in the picture? His courtiers or allies? Again we can't see them. His staff? This is a card that requires action.

Description

All the Wands are tree branches or trunks. Pulp for paper mills in Smith and Waite's day, they symbolize paperwork, newspapers, books, magazines, scripts, and speeches.

This King is stuck or suspended. The branch needs to be planted in order to grow, but if he does not get moving, it will wither and die. His own paralysis is thwarting him and may endanger the success of the project. He can't just sit there and look hypothetically successful; he has to get on with it. That means leaving the throne unoccupied—a problem! Some schedule, some scheme, some plan, and certainly some allies or supporters must be found.

The idea or message will not work until someone helps him ground the project or message somewhere useful. Or he must get up from his throne and get a move on—entrusting the royal seat and presumably its power to an heir or his partner. This is really interesting because he may abdicate to pursue his plan, to chase his concept or qualification to its logical ending.

More commonly, kings leave someone else in charge, don't they, when they go to Windsor at Christmas, or are they just rulers in absentia?

Look at that lizard again, because details always matter in Smith's cards. What does this lizard mean to you? Perhaps it's the place: the Lizard. Maybe it's a band named after a lizard. We might also see a newt from the salamander family here in this card. It all depends on your point of view. Lizards are territorial—males fight other males—and use bright colors to attract mates. So these lizards are all rather like this King: colorful, never dull, and possibly on the lookout for his Queen of Wands or wondering where she is. (In another story in his life, no doubt. Another reading may reveal her.)

The crucial thing is that the King not waste this idea. That would, you sense, be a real problem for him emotionally or psychologically. Kings are born to succeed, not to fail.

Pamela Colman Smith & King of Wands

Smith and Waite were surrounded by journals, poetry, theater notes, and the like—advertising for Horlick's (Waite worked there) or stage notes at the Abbey Theatre (Smith worked there too, alongside W. B. Yeats who inducted her into the Golden Dawn). So here we have a figure Smith likely knew. It could easily have been Yeats or Waite. Bram Stoker is another male writer she worked with, and she also knew J. M. Barrie. This man seems almost alive, with his tense, expectant body language and his anticipatory expression.

Astrology & King of Wands

The message is the thing here, so look to Mercury in the chart and Mercury by transit. Mercury is the ruler of all communication, the messenger of the gods.

There may also be transits in the Third House and/or Ninth House of media and publishing.

There are lions (Leo) on the throne and a prominent lizard. Salamanders regenerate lost limbs. In myth, they were believed to be born from fire. There is a fiery hint in the red hair and orange robes of this King—so Leo, Sagittarius, and Aries are baked into the illustration and may be factors in the horoscope to consider. Aries is fast and wants action. Leo wants to rule. Sagittarius wants to travel and explore.

SOURCES AND BIBLIOGRAPHY

Adams, Jessica. *2020 Vision*. Viking, 2008.

Adams, Jessica. *Essential Astrology for Women: The Complete Astrology Guide to 2025*. HarperCollins, 2006.

Adams, Jessica. https://www.jessicaadams.com.

Astro Gold. Astrology app and software available for iOS, Android, and macOS. https://www.astrogold.io/.

Cheiro. *Cheiro's Book of Numbers*. Herbert Jenkins, 1935.

Cornelius, Geoffrey. *The Moment of Astrology: Origins in Divination*. The Wessex Astrologer, 2003.

Hone, Margaret E. *The Modern Text Book of Astrology*. L. N. Fowler, 1971.

Kaplan, Stuart R., Mary K. Greer, Elizabeth Foley O'Connor, and Melinda Boyd Parsons. *Pamela Colman Smith: The Untold Story*. U.S. Games Systems, 2018.

Oxford Research Encyclopedias. Oxford University Press, 2024. https://oxfordre.com/.

Sasportas, Howard. *The Gods of Change: Pain, Crisis and the Transits of Uranus, Neptune and Pluto*. Penguin, 1990.